MILESTONE DOCUMENTS IN AFRICAN AMERICAN HISTORY

Exploring the Essential Primary Sources

MILESTONE DOCUMENTS IN AFRICAN AMERICAN HISTORY

Exploring the Essential Primary Sources

Volume 1
1619 – 1852

Paul Finkelman, Editor in Chief

Schlager Group

Dallas, Texas

CONTENTS

VOLUME 1: 1619–1852

VOLUME 2: 1853–1900

EDITORIAL AND PRODUCTION STAFF

Copy Editors, Fact Checkers, Proofreaders

Jonathan Aretakis, Barbara Bigelow, John Fitzpatrick,
Gretchen Gordon, Carol Holmes, Michael Allen Holmes,
Michael J. O'Neal, Karen Schader, Matthew Van Atta

Indexer

Michael J. O'Neal

Imaging and Design

Patricia Moritz

Page Layout

Marco Di Vita

Schlager Group Editorial Staff

Rebecca Begley, R. Lynn Naughton, Benjamin Painter

Project Manager

Marcia Merryman-Means

Publisher

Neil Schlager

Contributors

ANGELA ALEXANDER
York Technical College

BARRY ALFONSO
Independent Scholar, Pittsburgh, Pennsylvania

OMAR H. ALI
Towson University

RAY ARSENAULT
University of South Florida St. Petersburg

H. ROBERT BAKER
Georgia State University

L. DIANE BARNES
Youngstown State University

BRADLEY BOND
Northern Illinois University

W. LEWIS BURKE
University of South Carolina

WILLIAM M. CARTER, JR.
Temple University Beasley School of Law

HENRY L. CHAMBERS, JR.
University of Richmond School of Law

GARNA L. CHRISTIAN
University of Houston-Downtown

CHARLES ORSON COOK
The Honors College, University of Houston

KIMBERLY RAVENSCROFT COOK
Winthrop University

ROBERT J. COTTROL
George Washington University

ALLAN L. DAMON
Horace Greeley High School (Ret.)

DONNA M. DeBLASIO
Youngstown State University

MARK ELLIOTT
University of North Carolina at Greensboro

CAROLE EMBERTON
State University of New York at Buffalo

KRISTEN EPPS
University of Kansas

PAUL FINKELMAN
Albany Law School

SHARON GLASS
Winthrop University

SALLY GREENE
Center for the Study of the American South at the University of
North Carolina at Chapel Hill

SIMON HALL
University of Leeds

SHELDON HALPERN
Albany Law School

CLAUDRENA N. HAROLD
University of Virginia

VERONICA C. HENDRICK
John Jay College of Criminal Justice

KATIE JOHNSON
National Underground Railroad Freedom Center

MATT KARLSEN
Educational Service District 112, Vancouver, Washington

KAREN LINKLETTER
California State University, Fullerton

M. PHILIP LUCAS
Cornell College

DANIEL R. MANDELL
Truman State University

DAVID McBRIDE
Pennsylvania State University

SCOTT MERRIMAN
Troy University

J. TODD MOYE
University of Texas at Austin

PAUL T. MURRAY
Siena College

RICHARD NEWMAN
Rochester Institute of Technology

MICHAEL J. O'NEAL
Independent Scholar, Moscow, Idaho

COLLEEN OSTIGUY
Albany Law School

CHESTER PACH
Ohio University

MARTHA PALLANTE
Youngstown State University

WILLIAM PETTIT
Independent Scholar, Stone Mountain, Georgia

CARL ROLLYSON
Baruch College, City University of New York

PEGGY RUSSO
Pennsylvania State University, Mont Alto

MATTHEW SALAFIA
North Dakota State University

PHILIP SCHWARZ
Virginia Commonwealth University (Emeritus)

KEITH EDWARDS SEALING
Widener University School of Law

BROOKS D. SIMPSON
Arizona State University

JOHN DAVID SMITH
University of North Carolina at Charlotte

MICHAEL T. SMITH
McNeese State University

MITCHELL SNAY
Denison University

WENDY THOWDIS
Gilder Lehrman Institute of American History

KEVERN VERNEY
Edge Hill University

JOHN R. VILE
Middle Tennessee State University

STEVE I. VLADECK
American University Washington College of Law

ANDERS WALKER
St. Louis University School of Law

PETER WALLENSTEIN
Virginia Polytechnic Institute and State University

MARYLOU WALSH
College of Saint Rose

JASON MORGAN WARD
Mississippi State University

LELAND WARE
University of Delaware

R. OWEN WILLIAMS
Yale University

ZACHERY WILLIAMS
University of Akron

CARY D. WINTZ
Texas Southern University

CHARLES L. ZELDEN
Nova Southeastern University

ACKNOWLEDGMENTS

Schlager Group gratefully acknowledges the permission granted to reproduce the copyright material in this book. Every effort has been made to trace copyright holders and to obtain their permission for the use of copyright material. The publisher apologizes for any errors or omissions in the list below and would be grateful if notified of any corrections that should be incorporated in future reprints or editions of this set.

Colin Powell's Commencement Address at Howard University: Reprinted courtesy of General Colin L. Powell, USA (Ret.).

Henry McNeal Turner's Speech on His Expulsion from the Georgia Legislature: From *Lift Every Voice and Sing: African American Oratory, 1787–1900*, ed. Philip S. Foner and Robert James Branham. Tuscaloosa: University of Alabama Press, 1998. Reprinted courtesy of the University of Alabama Press.

Jesse Owen's *Blackthink: My Life as Black Man and White Man*: From *Blackthink* by Jesse Owens and Paul G. Neimark. Copyright © 1972 by Jesse Owens and Paul G. Neimark. Reprinted by permission of HarperCollins Publishers.

John Edward Bruce's "Organized Resistance Is Our Best Remedy": From *Lift Every Voice and Sing: African American Oratory, 1787–1900*, ed. Philip S. Foner and Robert James Branham. Tuscaloosa: University of Alabama Press, 1998. Reprinted courtesy of the University of Alabama Press.

Marian Anderson's *My Lord, What a Morning*: "Easter Sunday," copyright (c) 1956, renewed 1984 by Marian Anderson, from *My Lord, What a Morning* by Marian Anderson. Used by permission of Viking Penguin, a division of Penguin Group (USA) Inc.

Martin Luther King, Jr.: Reprinted by arrangement with The Heirs to the Estate of Martin Luther King Jr., c/o Writers House as agent for the proprietor New York, NY.

- "Letter from Birmingham Jail": Copyright 1963 Dr. Martin Luther King Jr; copyright renewed 1991 Coretta Scott King

- "I Have a Dream": Copyright 1963 Dr. Martin Luther King Jr; copyright renewed 1991 Coretta Scott King

- "Beyond Vietnam: A Time to Break Silence": Copyright 1967 Dr. Martin Luther King Jr; copyright renewed 1991 Coretta Scott King

Malcolm X: "After the Bombing": Reprinted courtesy of the family of Malcolm X. Malcolm X™ is a trademark of the Family of Malcolm X / www.CMGWorldwide.com.

Overview

Milestone Documents in African American History represents a unique and innovative approach to history reference. Combining full-text primary sources with in-depth expert analysis, the 125 entries in the set cover nearly four hundred years of African American history. The set includes primary sources from the time of the arrival of blacks in America in 1619 to the Senate apology for slavery in 2009. Documents range from letters and personal narratives to laws and legal cases, from proclamations and petitions to political speeches. The documents are reprinted as they originally appeared and many contain grammatical oddities and unusual spellings peculiar to the time of their writing.

Organization

The set is organized chronologically in four volumes:

- Volume 1: 1619–1852
- Volume 2: 1853–1900
- Volume 3: 1901–1964
- Volume 4: 1965–2009

Within each volume, entries likewise are arranged chronologically by year.

Entry Format

Each entry in *Milestone Documents in African American History* follows the same structure using the same standardized headings. The entries are divided into two main sections: analysis and document text. Following is the full list of entry headings:

- **Overview** gives a brief summary of the primary source document and its importance in history.

- **Context** places the document in its historical framework.

- **Time Line** chronicles key events surrounding the writing of the document.

- **About the Author** presents a brief biographical profile of the person or persons who wrote the document.

- **Explanation and Analysis of the Document** consists of a detailed examination of the document text, generally in section-by-section or paragraph-by-paragraph format.

- **Audience** discusses the intended audience of the document's author.

- **Impact** examines the historical influence of the document.

- **Questions for Further Study** proposes study questions for students.

- **Further Reading** lists articles, books, and Web sites for further research.

- **Essential Quotes** offers a selection of key quotes from the document.

- **Document Text** gives the actual text of the primary document.

- **Glossary** defines important, difficult, or unusual terms in the document text.

Each entry features the byline of the scholar who wrote the analysis. Readers should note that in most entries the Document Text section includes the full text of the primary source document. In the case of lengthy documents, key portions have been excerpted for analysis.

Features

In addition to the text of the 125 entries, the set includes 233 photographs and illustrations. The front matter of Volume 1 includes an "Introduction" to the set, written by Editor in Chief Paul Finkelman; a "Contributors" list; and an "Acknowledgments" section. The back matter of Volume 4 has a section of interest to educators: "Teachers' Activity Guides." The latter comprises nine distinct guides, all of which are tied to the National History Standards and make use of the documents covered in this set. Following the Activity Guides, readers will find an "Index of Documents by Category" and a cumulative "Subject Index."

Questions

We welcome questions and comments about the set. Readers may address all such comments to the following address:

The Editor
Milestone Documents in African American History
Schlager Group Inc.
2501 Oak Lawn Avenue, Suite 440
Dallas, Texas 75219

Each February most schools and colleges recognize what is now called Black History Month. It began as Negro History Week, in February, to coincide with the birthdays of Frederick Douglass and Abraham Lincoln and was later expanded to a month-long focus on the history of African Americans. When it began in the 1920s, African Americans were virtually absent from American history books and the narrative of American history. Negro History Week (and then Black History Month) was an attempt to remind the nation—black and white—of the significant contributions of blacks to American history. Today it would be hard to imagine a history of America that would not include blacks. This history is no longer merely about the "contributions" of African Americans, but rather about the way issues of race and discrimination affected the entire development of the United States.

Milestone Documents in African American History offers a significant collection of primary sources on our nation's racial history. The collection begins with the first documentation of blacks coming to the English colonies, the arrival in 1619 of some twenty Africans in the Virginia colony a year before the Pilgrims reached Plymouth. At the time there was no slavery in the English colonies, and these blacks were treated as indentured servants, bound to serve their masters for a term of years. Some of these first Africans eventually became free residents of the colony and at least one of them, Anthony Johnson, later became a property owner in the colony. However, within forty years Virginia and most of the other colonies had adopted a system of slavery that was based entirely on race. On the eve of the American Revolution black slaves could be found in every one of the thirteen colonies. There were few slaves in New England, though many merchants in Boston, Providence, and New Haven owned some, often using them as household servants. Most middle-class families in New York and many in Philadelphia also owned household slaves. A few residents of the middle colonies owned significant numbers of slaves who worked on farms. Further south slavery was more common. Forty percent of all the residents of Virginia and about half the people in South Carolina were slaves.

Mennonites in Pennsylvania were the first to issue a protest against slaveholding on religious grounds, in "A Minute against Slavery, Addressed to Germantown Monthly Meeting" (1688). In the years leading up to the Revolution members of certain faiths—especially Quakers, Mennonites, Methodists, and some Baptists—argued that slavery was morally wrong and began to manumit their own slaves. During the Revolution many other northerners, and some southerners, concluded that slavery was incompatible with the Declaration of Independence. Thus, between 1780 and 1804 all of the states north of Maryland either ended slavery outright or passed gradual emancipation laws, which ended slavery over a generation—as Pennsylvania did with An Act for the Gradual Abolition of Slavery (1780). In the South numerous masters voluntarily freed their slaves, including George Washington, who did so at his death in 1799. Meanwhile, during the Revolution, Lord Dunmore, the royal governor of Virginia, offered freedom to slaves who would join his army (1775).

Despite the assertion that "all men are created equal," the Declaration of Independence did not end slavery, and the Constitution (1787) protected slavery in many ways. Thomas Jefferson, the author of the Declaration of Independence, defended the enslavement of blacks on racist and "scientific" grounds in his *Notes on the State of Virginia* (1784), though he later disingenuously tried to back away from this views when complimenting a black man, Benjamin Banneker, on his intellectual accomplishments. The number of free blacks grew substantially in the Revolutionary era, and in many places these blacks began to build their own institutions, including churches and Masonic lodges. However, at the same time, racism and slavery became embedded in American law, as in the Fugitive Slave Act of 1793 and the Black Codes of states such as Ohio (1803–1807).

During and after the Revolution, African Americans protested racism and slavery again and again, in documents ranging from the Petition of Prince Hall and Other African Americans to the Massachusetts General Court (1777) to David Walker's *Appeal to the Coloured Citizens of the World* (1829). Starting in the 1830s black opponents of slavery were joined by a growing number of white abolitionists, among them William Lloyd Garrison, and northern states governments that sought to protect black freedom. During this period, slaves, freeborn blacks, and fugitive slaves persisted in fighting bondage. Narratives of slave rebels, such as *The Confessions of Nat Turner* (1831); fugitive slaves, such as *Narrative of the Life of Henry Box Brown, Written by Himself* (1854); and other blacks caught up in slavery, like Solomon Northup's *Twelve Years a Slave* (1853), illustrated the many ways in which blacks protested slavery and fought against it. Some whites argued that blacks were well suited for slavery, but others, such as Judge Thomas Ruffin of North Carolina, in his opinion in *State v. Mann* (1830), admitted and understood that slavery was ultimately based on power, force, and violence. By mid-century it was clear to a majority of the Supreme Court, Congress, and the presidents that served in the 1850s that federal power had to supplement that of states and masters in enforcing slavery. This position is made clear in the Fugitive Slave Act of 1850 and such Court opinions as *Dred Scott v. Sandford* (1857).

The documents in the first third of this collection thus show how southern whites and the federal government maintained slavery and how blacks and their white allies fought it. They give us the voices of slaves, free blacks, white abolitionists, southern supporters of slavery, and northerners who supported racism and those who opposed it. They allow us understand the complexity of slavery and racism in America.

Slavery in the end tore the Union apart. In 1860–1861, eleven states left the Union because they feared that the incoming administration of President Abraham Lincoln threatened the "peculiar institution." Shortly before the Civil War, Confederate Vice President Alexander H. Stephens declared that slavery was the "cornerstone" of the Confederacy. No one, north or south, would have disagreed. The seceding states, one after another, declared they were leaving the Union to protect slavery. Ironically, it would be secession and the Civil War that allowed for emancipation. When he entered office, Lincoln had no constitutional power to end slavery, but under his powers as commander in chief, he issued the Emancipation Proclamation (it took effect in 1863), authorized the enlistment of black troops, and turned the war into a great crusade for human liberty. In the aftermath of the war, southerners attempted to re-impose racial controls on blacks, as evidenced, for example, by the Black Code of Mississippi (1865), but in the short run they were thwarted by the military, Congress, and such constitutional changes as the Thirteenth (1865), Fourteenth (1868), and Fifteenth (1870) Amendments—known as the Reconstruction Amendments.

Social change and equality were thwarted by southern white resistance, including lethal violence, and a Supreme Court that never seemed to understand that the Civil War had altered race relations and the power of the states to discriminate, as evidenced by *United States v. Cruikshank* (1873) and the Civil Rights Cases (1883). Blacks resisted this southern white counter-revolution. In 1874, for example, Congressman Richard Harvey Cain spoke in favor of the Civil Rights Act of 1875 in his speech "All That We Ask Is Equal Laws, Equal Legislation, and Equal Rights." John Edward Bruce took a more militant tone in his address "Organized Resistance Is Our Best Remedy" (1889). In the end, the push for civil rights was overwhelmed by white political and economic power, aggression and brutality, and a Supreme Court that cynically rejected the idea that the federal government should pass legislation to protect black equality and then, in *Plessy v. Ferguson* (1896), decided that the states were free to discriminate as they wished. By the end of the century black leaders could only hope to hold on to some power, rights, and dignity as, for example, Booker T. Washington counseled a slow and steady approach to winning a place for African Americans in his Atlanta Exposition Address (1895). In the face of growing discrimination imposed by law and extra-legal violence, retaining their rights proved impossible. At the turn of the century southern blacks—who still made up more than 90 percent

of all African Americans—were free and, in theory, equal, but they had lost almost all their political power and were struggling to resist lynching. Ida B. Wells-Barnett cast a light on this situation in "Lynch Law in America" (1900).

In the face of bloodshed and racist legislation in the South, the struggle for rights was once again centered in the North, as it had been during the antebellum period. Black intellectuals and activists struggled, with their white allies, to attack segregation in an organized fashion, as with the formation of the Niagara Movement in 1905, forerunner to the National Association for the Advancement of Colored People, which was founded in 1909 and signaled the beginning of a concerted effort in the North to fight racism. The struggle was thwarted not only by southerners but also by northerners, like President Theodore Roosevelt, who dealt harshly with black soldiers forced to defend their lives against white mobs in Texas (1906). Woodrow Wilson, the first southern-born president elected since 1848, authorized the segregation of federal facilities and prevented the nation's highest-ranking black officer from serving in World War I. In segregated units blacks served heroically in that war—the war that was meant to make the world safe for democracy—only to encounter continued brutality and increased segregation at home. The ongoing state of unrest is evidenced in Walter F. White's "The Eruption of Tulsa" (1921). A rare victory in the Supreme Court, in *Guinn v. United States* (1915), made it slightly more difficult for the South to prevent blacks from voting but did not stop the practice. Indeed, blacks would be effectively disfranchised in eighteen southern states until the 1960s.

The documents from the Civil War to the end of World War I illustrate the variety of black responses to the final push for freedom and the seemingly endless losing battle to give meaning to that freedom. This long and dismal period led to a new birth of black activism and cultural self-expression. The Back to Africa movement propounded by Marcus Garvey and other black nationalist organizations focused white attention on the deep disaffection of blacks, not just in the South but also in the North, while at the same time giving self-expression to black aspirations in such documents as Cyril Briggs's *Summary of the Program and Aims of the African Blood Brotherhood* (1920) and Garvey's "Principles of the Universal Negro Improvement Association" (1922).

In the 1920s the flowering of intellectual life known as the Harlem Renaissance, described in Alain Locke's "Enter the New Negro" (1925) and James Weldon Johnson's "Harlem: The Culture Capital" (1925) , brought new attention to African Americans. For the first time in American history significant numbers of whites became aware of black music, art, theater, poetry, and literature. In the North, blacks participated in politics and fought for equal opportunity in education and jobs. During the presidency of Franklin D. Roosevelt, they demanded (and won) attention from the federal government. John P. Davis indicted the efforts of Roosevelt to repair the country's economic woes during the Great Depression in "A Black Inventory of the New Deal" (1935), while Robert Clifton Weaver defended them in "The New Deal and the Negro: A Look at the Facts."

In 1931 the Scottsboro incident, in which a group of black teenagers were jailed (and nearly lynched) for a crime they had not committed, focused international attention on the pervasive racism in the South. The fact that the "Scottsboro boys" were neither lynched nor executed illustrates the power of national pressure. Almost two decades later, one of the defendants, Haywood Patterson, told his side of the story in *Scottsboro Boy* (1950). In another scandal from this era, the Tuskegee Syphilis Study was initiated in 1932 by physician-researchers at the U.S. Public Health Service to investigate the affects of untreated syphilis in black males. The research proceeded for forty years, with the infected men left deliberately untreated during these decades The experiment, which did not fully come to public light until the *Final Report of the Tuskegee Syphilis Study Ad Hoc Advisory Panel* was published (1973), illustrated the second-class (at best) medical care available to blacks in the 1930s.

By the eve of World War II significant numbers of blacks were no longer willing to accept second-class citizenship. Meanwhile, growing numbers of black migrants to the North had begun to affect national politics. The very threat of a black protest march on Washington—an idea put forth in A. Philip Randolph's "Call to Negro America to March on Washington" (1941)—led the Roosevelt administration to issue orders mandating equality in government contracts. After World War II, important changes in society began to be made. In 1946 the Brooklyn Dodgers signed Jackie Robinson, thus beginning the integration of American baseball and significantly altering the cultural landscape. Meanwhile, President Harry Truman, a midwesterner who hated segregation, moved against the institution where he could—as with Executive Order 9981 (1948), establishing equality of treatment in the armed forces. Drafted by Truman's Committee on Civil Rights, *To Secure These Rights* (1947) identified remarkable disparities in racial treatment in both the North and the South and called for a series of measures to improve race relations in the United States. Meanwhile, in *Sweatt v. Painter* (1950) and *Brown v. Board of Education* (1954), the Supreme Court took the lead in dismantling segregation. While southerners complained that such decisions were unconstitutional, this was both appropriate and ironic. The Court had eviscerated the three Reconstruction Amendments to the Constitution in the nineteenth century, so in the mid-twentieth century the Court brought the amendments back to life.

The civil rights movement was the result of many factors: black veterans returning from World War II who would no longer tolerate discrimination, changes in northern white attitudes, the political power of black voters in the North, and the pressures of cold war politics. But the three key factors were the effectiveness of the National Association for the Advancement of Colored People in bringing legal challenges to segregation and in organizing black protest, decisions by the Supreme Court that almost always favored civil rights, and a mass movement in the South, symbolized by Martin Luther King, Jr., in his speeches and marches, that drove home the relentlessness of tens of thousands of black southerners, willing to risk beatings and jailing to destroy segregation. The assassination of President John F. Kennedy altered the civil rights landscape in two ways. As he voiced in his Civil Rights Address (1963), Kennedy had been moving toward a stronger civil rights position in response to southern violence and resistance to court-ordered desegregation on the part of such segregation stalwarts as Alabama's governor, George Wallace (as he made plain that same year in his Inaugural Address). Kennedy's successor, Lyndon B. Johnson, was a southerner who, like Truman, knew segregation and hated it. He pushed Congress to pass the far-reaching Civil Rights Act of 1964 and then a voting rights act a year later. By the end of Johnson's term in 1969, segregation was no longer legal anywhere in the United States. Documents from this era teach us about the many faces of the civil rights movement and explore the contours of the civil rights revolution.

But the successes of the 1960s were mixed. Blacks in the North did not face legal segregation, but they were nevertheless segregated by housing patterns, economic discrimination, and institutional racism. Many were denied equal educational opportunities as suburban schools flourished and inner city schools crumbled. These conditions spawned more militant black organizations, such as the Black Panther Party, and calls for a take-charge approach, as outlined in the 1966 speech of Stokely Carmichael on "Black Power" at the University of California, Berkeley, and Eldridge Cleaver's essay "Education and Revolution" (1969). For the first time, significant numbers of blacks abandoned Christianity, joining the Nation of Islam—a group that in its present form holds a place on the Southern Poverty Law Center's list of active hate groups in the United States.

These issues were complicated by the Vietnam War—the first American war in which blacks fought in fully integrated units. But economics, draft laws, and social policy led to a new kind of discrimination as blacks were more likely than whites to be drafted, sent into combat, and die. Moreover, black activists like Martin Luther King, Jr., and the boxer Muhammad Ali realized that the war was sapping America's energy for racial equality and economic fairness. In "Beyond Vietnam: A Time to Break Silence" (1967), King denounced the war for deepening the problems of African Americans and poor people. That same year, Muhammad Ali was convicted for refusing induction into the armed services, a conviction that was reversed by the 1971 Supreme Court decision in *Clay v. United States*.

The half-century following Johnson's presidency witnessed new struggles and complexities in the history of African Americans. Politically, African Americans were more important than ever. In 1964 blacks from Mississippi could not be seated at the Democratic National Convention, a ban that Fannie Lou Hamer protested in her Testimony at the Democratic National Convention. Twenty years later Jesse Jackson made a major speech at the convention, as he sought and failed to win the presidential nomination (1984). By this time blacks held positions in Congress (Shirley Chisholm) and on the Supreme Court (Thurgood Marshall). By the end of the century African Americans such as Anita Hill, A. Leon Higginbotham, Colin Powell, and Clarence Thomas would be serving at the highest levels of civilian government and in the military as well as on the judiciary. President Bill Clinton appointed a commission to study race relations, chaired by the nation's most distinguished black scholar, the historian John Hope Franklin. In 1999 the commission issued *One America in the 21st Century: The Report of President Clinton's Commission on Race*. Exactly a decade later America would inaugurate its first black president, Barack Obama, and the U.S. Senate would pass the Resolution Apologizing for the Enslavement and Racial Segregation of African Americans.

The primary sources in *Milestone Documents in African American History* take us from the record of the arrival in the early seventeenth century of the first blacks in America—almost all of them anonymous and the circumstances of their lives unknown—through to the speeches of our nation's first black president, allowing us to read the words of those who shaped not just African American history but the entire history of the United States.

Paul Finkelman
President William McKinley Professor
Albany Law School

MILESTONE DOCUMENTS IN AFRICAN AMERICAN HISTORY

Exploring the Essential Primary Sources

Black Africans landing at Jamestown (Library of Congress)

JOHN ROLFE'S LETTER TO SIR EDWIN SANDYS

"He brought not anything but 20 and odd Negroes."

Overview

When John Rolfe related in a letter to Sir Edwin Sandys that "20 and odd Negroes" had been off-loaded by a Dutch ship at Point Comfort in 1619, he had no notion of the lasting importance of his account. The seemingly casual comment recorded the first documented case of Africans sold into servitude to British North America. Purchased as indenture servants in the labor-starved Virginia colony, these twenty-some souls disappeared into the anonymous pool of workers transported to the colony during its first decades. The origins of the Africans and their ultimate fates have long been debated by historians and others studying the account. Rolfe provided little detail and made no further mention of the group.

Rolfe's statement was part of a much longer missive written from the Virginia colony to one of his benefactors back in England. Rolfe hoped to endear himself by relating the recent events of the colony to the new treasurer of the Virginia Company of London, Sir Edwin Sandys. Under Sandys's leadership, the Virginia enterprise had entered a new phase in its existence and had recently undergone reorganization. Part of that process involved the establishment of the headright system (a system of land grants to settlers), which, in part, was responsible for the growing labor shortage of 1619 and 1620 as well as the rapid increase in the demand for unfree workers obtained through contracts of indenture.

Context

Virginia in 1619 was very much in a state of flux. Established in 1607 by the Virginia Company of London, a joint-stock enterprise, the settlement had endured great hardship, a constant turnover in leadership, and various financial crises. The recently introduced cash crop, tobacco, had for the first time made the prospect of profits from Virginia a realistic but as yet unrealized possibility. It was, however, labor- and land intensive. Another factor creating some upheaval was the death of the leader of the Powhatan

Confederacy, known as Powhatan, and his replacement by a chief much less friendly toward the English, Opechancanough, or Mangopeesomon ("Opachankano" in the document). The company was also in the process of making the transition from a merchant enterprise to a colonial property.

A power struggle within the Virginia Company of London had resulted in the ouster of its earlier leader, Sir Thomas Smith, and the recall of Samuel Argall, the settlement's governor, by Sir Edwin Sandys, the company's new treasurer, and his supporters. By mid-1619 the new governor, Francis Yeardley, had taken up residence in Virginia and initiated the reforms crafted by his colleagues. Among the most significant changes was the establishment of a framework for local governance—the Virginia Assembly and a governor's council—which would collectively be referred to as the Virginia House of Burgesses. Also included in the plan were attempts at economic diversification meant to encourage movement away from a single cash-crop economy based on tobacco cultivation and the creation of the headright system. Sandys's goal was to convert the Virginia venture from a place inhabited largely by transient laborers who sought at least modest fortunes in North America and then planned to return to England into a colony populated by individuals who would become permanent residents.

Sandys's plan produced an unprecedented demand for labor. The headright system was aimed at creating a sense of ownership in the colony by making landowners of the settlers. The plan distributed one hundred acres of land to all of the "Ancient Planters," or inhabitants of Virginia before 1618. All new arrivals became entitled to headrights, fifty acres of land, upon reaching the colony, as long as they met a few basic requirements: being male, adult, and free of indenture. Those who met the guidelines could also collect headrights on behalf of the others for whom they were responsible, including wives, children, and bound servants. This liberal dispersal of land and the profitability and labor-intensive nature of tobacco were largely responsible for the shortage of field hands. No one in possession of his own land worked on the land of another planter, and to be profitable even fifty acres of land needed many hands.

At this point in their development, Virginia's residents were particularly confused about the uses and nature of unfree labor. Their knowledge base drew upon the experi-

Time Line

1606

■ **April**
The Virginia Company of London receives its charter for land in North America.

■ **December 20**
Captain Christopher Newport departs from London with three ships and the Virginia enterprise's first employees.

1607

■ **May 13**
Captain Newport arrives at Chesapeake, and the site for the Virginia Company settlement is selected on the James River. The company employees surviving the voyage, 104 of them, establish the first permanent British outpost in the Americas.

1612

■ John Rolfe grows the first commercially salable tobacco crop in Virginia.

1613

■ **June 4**
Samuel Argall tricks Pocahontas, takes her hostage, and transports her to Jamestown.

1614

■ **April 5**
John Rolfe and Pocahontas, now known as Rebecca, marry at Jamestown.

1616

■ **June 3**
John and Rebecca Rolfe arrive in London with their native retinue.

■ The headright system is established by the Virginia Company; "Ancient Planters" are rewarded with one hundred acres of land.

1617

■ **March 17**
Rebecca Rolfe dies at Gravesend, England, and Rolfe returns to Virginia, leaving their young son, Thomas, behind to be raised by family.

---

ences and precedents established by their neighbors in the Caribbean: the Spanish and the Portuguese. They knew of the existence and use of slavery as a mainstay of the sugar economy of the Caribbean and South America but were unfamiliar with the specifics of the institution. Their own experiences in Great Britain had offered them no firsthand contact with slavery. English common law also had no provisions for slavery as a codified institution. Virginians were not opposed to slavery; they simply had no legal framework for its utilization. Instead, they relied on a different sort of legal framework, that for indenture. In England, this institution supplied a contractual agreement under which the servant bound himself for a period of years, usually five to seven, to a master, giving up his personal liberties in exchange for the basics necessary for survival: food, shelter, and clothing. At the end of service, the servant regained his freedom and a small payment usually referred to as freedom fees. In Virginia, this system was quickly distorted as the value of labor in the fields increased exponentially. Terms governing the length of service were extended for any violation of the contract, and bound laborers found themselves subject to much harsher conditions than they might have expected in England.

The first record of African laborers in the Virginia colony appears in the census of 1619. This document lists thirty-two Africans, fifteen men and seventeen women, in the employ of several planters as early as March 1619. Their origins are unclear; however, many scholars agree that a majority of the first Africans in the colony came not as resettlements or as natives from the West Indies but rather straight from western and central Africa. The appearance of Africans in early Virginia must also be considered in the larger context of the Atlantic world, where a brisk trade in unfree labor deposited African captives to be sold for their labor from New England southward to the Portuguese colony of Brazil. The dominant factor in this commercial venture was the Portuguese, who were acting under the Spanish *asiento*, or trade monopoly. Others who engaged in this trade, particularly the English and the Dutch, often acquired their cargoes by acting as freebooters or privateers.

About the Author

John Rolfe, born in Norfolk, England, probably in 1585, was not among the first of the Virginia venturers, but he was certainly among the Virginia Company's earliest recruits. He and his first wife left Plymouth, England, in June 1609 on the *Sea Venture*, the flagship of a flotilla dispatched to Virginia by the new governor, Thomas West, 12th Baron De La Warre, and under the command of his lieutenant governor, Sir Thomas Gates. All went well until they were shipwrecked along the coast of Bermuda after an encounter with a hurricane on July 23. In May of the following year, the survivors risked a voyage to Jamestown, completing their journey. Rolfe's wife, unnamed in the records of the time, died shortly after reaching Virginia.

In 1612 Rolfe produced his and the Virginia enterprise's first crop of salable tobacco. The natives of Virginia grew tobacco prior to the arrival of Englishmen, but that product was deemed too harsh. Europeans in general and the English in particular favored the mellower, sweeter tobacco varieties produced in the West Indies. Exactly where Rolfe procured his seed remains unclear—whether picked up during his sojourn on Bermuda or secured at considerable cost while he was still in England or after he arrived in Virginia. In any case, his 1612 experiment marked a turning point in the course of Virginia venturers' lives. By 1616 Virginia had its first major cash crop. It was this success that allowed Rolfe to frequent the company of Jamestown's controlling elite.

Those connections served him well, for by 1614 two significant events altered his status in Virginia. Sometime during that year Rolfe began to serve as the secretary and recorder for the colony, and on April 5 he married a young native woman commonly known as Pocahontas. The daughter of a powerful local chief named Powhatan, Pocahontas—or, as she called herself, Matoaka—was perceived by the English as akin to royalty. Taken hostage a year earlier as part of plan to exchange captives, Pocahontas had received considerable instruction in English and the precepts of the Christian faith and had submitted to baptism days before her wedding. The marriage, approved by the governor, Sir Thomas Dale, was perceived as a mechanism for civilizing the local tribes. This union is also generally credited with the temporary peace between the Jamestown inhabitants and members of the Powhatan Confederacy, who had recently been at war.

After the ceremony the couple returned to the property granted to Rolfe by the Virginia Company on Hog Island near Jamestown. There, Rolfe continued to refine his tobacco experimentations. Probably with the help and guidance of his wife, his crops flourished, and he solved some of the problems surrounding the curing and drying of tobacco (or the "weed," as many referred to it) that plagued his counterparts. In 1615 Pocahontas, by this time known as Rebecca Rolfe, bore the couple a son, Thomas. The following year John, Rebecca, and Thomas Rolfe, at the company's suggestion, traveled to England with Governor Dale on the *Treasure*, captained by Samuel Argall, a part owner of the vessel. The Rolfes and their native companions quickly became celebrities in London and received an introduction to Court. It was also during this period that Rolfe made the acquaintance of Sir Edwin Sandys, the person soon to be the controlling factor of the Virginia Company of London.

While the journey was a social and political success for the company, it was a personal disaster for the Rolfes. Rebecca Rolfe and her native companions did not fare well physically. By the end of 1616 all were affected by infectious diseases that proved much more virulent among Native Americans. In March 1617 the couple and their company made plans to return to Virginia with Argall, who had become the governor of the outpost. Shortly after leaving London, Rolfe requested that the captain dock at Gravesend because his wife had grown too ill, probably with

Time Line

1618

■ **May**
Powhatan dies, marking a sharp increase in tensions between colonists and natives, as Opechancanough begins to assume a leadership role.

■ **July 30**
Virginia House of Burgesses and the General Assembly meet for the first time.

1619

■ **May**
The Virginia census notes that thirty-two Africans were among the settlement inhabitants.

■ **August**
The Dutch ship, the *White Lion*, makes landfall at Point Comfort, where Captain John Colyn Jope sells twenty African captives to Governor George Yeardley and the merchant Abraham Piersey for food. Four days later the *Treasure*, an English privateer sailing in consort with Jope, arrives but is not welcomed.

■ Rolfe marries again, this time to Joan Pierce, his neighbor and fellow planter William Pierce's daughter.

1619–1620

■ Rolfe sends a letter to Sir Edwin Sandys citing the arrival in Virginia of "20 and odd Negroes." (Confusion with the date results from England's continued use of the Julian calendar, which recognized April 1 as the start of the new year.)

1621

■ John Rolfe is appointed to the Governor's Council in the Virginia House of Burgesses.

1622

■ **March 10**
Mortally ill, Rolfe makes his last will and testament.

■ **March 22**
The Powhatan uprising results in the deaths of 347 settlers and starts a war between the Native Americans and the British colonists in Virginia.

■ **March**
Rolfe dies.

1624

■ The Virginia Company, nearly bankrupt, loses its charter, and settlement reverts to royal possession.

1625

■ The Virginia colony becomes a royal colony with a charter from the king.

pneumonia, to travel. Rebecca died and was buried in the churchyard there shortly afterward. At this point, Rolfe also made the difficult decision to leave his son, Thomas, who was also affected by the contagion, behind with family in England.

Back in Virginia tobacco flourished, but all else foundered. The illness that had felled Rebecca spread rapidly among the local tribes. Powhatan, her father and longtime peacekeeper, also died in 1618, leaving the much more militant and anti-English Opechancanough in charge. Among the English community, Governor Argall faced continuing high death rates, shortages of food and other supplies, and growing frustration with the company's quasi-military rule. From England he received conflicting orders, bad advice, and complaints about the lack of profits. Rolfe, acting pragmatically, continued to curry favor with Argall and the soon-to-be secretary of the company, Sir Edwin Sandys. Shortly after Sandys's takeover and the arrival of his new governor, George Yeardley, Rolfe wrote an extensive missive to Sandys exhibiting his allegiance and intimate knowledge of Virginia and citing the presence of indentured African servants. He reminded Sandys of his connection to the Indians through his marriage to Pocahontas (Rebecca) but failed to reveal his recent marriage to Joan Pierce, the daughter of his friend and neighbor William Pierce.

Rolfe's plan evidently worked, for in 1621 he received an appointment to a newly reorganized council aimed at colonial restructuring. The officers of the Virginia Company, most particularly Sandys, knew enough of Rolfe's name and reputation to name him to the elite governor's council in the fledgling House of Burgesses. His tenure, however, was short-lived. Just before the Powhatan uprising of March 22, 1622, Rolfe contracted an illness from which he would not recover. He dictated his will on March 10, making provisions for his son, Thomas; his third wife, Joan; and his new daughter, Elizabeth. At the age of thirty-seven he died during yet another war with his second wife's people. This conflict had lasting repercussions for the Virginia settlements; in 1624 the financial problems that had plagued the colony from its beginning, combined with the effects of the war and yet another wave of pandemic disease, led to its bankruptcy. Within a year it would be reorganized as a royal colony under the new king, Charles I.

Explanation and Analysis of the Document

John Rolfe's statement in his 1619 letter to Sir Edwin Sandys concerning the arrival of "20 and odd Negroes" at Point Comfort, Virginia, represents the first documented arrival of Africans in the Virginia colony. The related sections of the letter constitute two short paragraphs about one-third of the way into a much larger missive. The reference to "negroes" appears almost casual in its tone and is certainly not the focus of Rolfe's interest or his purpose in writing the letter to Sandys.

By late 1619 Rolfe's personal political position in the colony, similar to that of Virginia itself, was in a state of flux. His earlier allegiances to the former governors Thomas Dale and Samuel Argall had become liabilities rather than advantages, and he had to quickly realign himself and find new patrons. The recent London upheaval within the controlling body of the Virginia Company and the ouster of its treasurer, Sir Thomas Smith, and his replacement by Sir Edwin Sandys called for action on Rolfe's part if he was to maintain his status in the colony. Although, in the letter, he continues to defend the deposed governor, he also begins to distance himself from Argall's actions and policies. He promptly reminds Sandys that he, Rolfe, has value in his connections through his late wife, Pocahontas, and their son, Thomas, to the leadership of the Powhatan Confederacy.

Rolfe's letter is interesting in the way in which he positions himself in reference to the colony's new governor, George Yeardley, and Yeardley's secretary, John Pory. While Rolfe clearly defers to their authority and their responsibility to report officially on the state of the colony, he points out that his ties and insider knowledge of the colony's personalities and inner workings might prove invaluable. In this vein, Rolfe pens his long and detailed letter to Sandys, recounting the happenings in the colony from the spring of 1619 through the winter of that year and thus illustrating his insight and his value to the new regime.

◆ Paragraphs 1–7

In the opening paragraph of his letter to Sandys, Rolfe gently reminds the new treasurer of the Virginia Company of his identity and offers his service "as a token of my grateful remembrance for your many favors and constant love shown me." In the next several paragraphs Rolfe relates the developments in the colony since the arrival of Yeardley, the new governor. These developments include the calling of the House of Burgesses, two trials held "according to the laudable Laws of England," and the dispatch and successful return of a ship under the command of a Captain Ward and another, the *George*, to the northern colony, probably New England, and to Newfoundland, respectively, to trade for fish to feed the hungry colonists. He also reports that the cattle that had arrived on board the *Trial* fared well during the voyage and that the horses and the mares should be easy to sell, as the population continued to grow through constant immigration to Virginia.

Wedding of Pocahontas to John Rolfe (Library of Congress)

♦ **Paragraph 9**

Rolfe then recounts events of August 1619, stating, "About the latter end of August, a Dutch man-of-war of the burden of a 160 tons arrived at Point Comfort, the Commander's name Captain Jope, his Pilot for the West Indies one Mr. Marmaduke, an Englishman." The ship, which was unnamed in Rolfe's letter, was the *White Lion*, which John Pory, the secretary of the colony, names as a "man of warre of Flushing," a privateer sailing from Vlissingen, a Dutch seaport noted as a haven for corsairs, or pirates. Rolfe describes this ship as capable of carrying a burden of 160 tons. In the seventeenth century that term referred to a measure of volume, usually wine or beer, in a cask rather than to a measure of weight. Point Comfort refers to the location of the ship's landing in Virginia and rests at the juncture of the James and York rivers as they empty into the Chesapeake Bay. The officers of the Virginia Company in London constantly recommended the maintenance of a "fort" at this location despite the fact that this point of land was largely swamp land and unhealthy in its aspect. Rolfe lists the ship's general officers rather incompletely as a Captain Jope and a Mr. Marmaduke. The *White Lion's* captain was, in reality, John Colyn Jope, an Englishman hailing from Cornwall. The gentleman named Marmaduke is identified by Pory as Marmaduke Rayner.

Rolfe continues by establishing the credentials of the Dutch ship and its relationship to its consort ship, the *Trea-*

sure: "They met with the *Treasure* in the West Indies and determined to hold consort ship hitherward, but in their passage lost one the other." For Rolfe's contemporaries reading the letter, this statement was among the most important. The *Treasure*—among whose stockholders were Robert Rich, the Earl of Warwick, and Samuel Argall, the deposed governor of Virginia—was captained by Daniel Elfrith and sailed under the English flag with a license from Victor Amadeus, the Duke of Savoy, to seize Spanish shipping. These two vessels met in the West Indies, and their captains agreed to sail in cooperation in search of Spanish plunder. Successful in their attempts, they boarded the *São Juan Batista*, a Portuguese slaver sailing out of Loanda, Angola, under a Spanish *asiento* (contract), and removed a number of the Africans held captive on board. On their way toward friendlier territory, the two ships lost sight of each other; the *White Lion* made port in Virginia in late August 1619.

Rolfe's next statement—"He brought not anything but 20 and odd Negroes"—represents the first recorded instance of Africans in captivity brought to Virginia and traded or sold in the colony. Although census data suggest that there were others brought to Virginia earlier, there is no extant record of their arrival or their disposition. According to Rolfe, Jope exchanged his Africans for food and other supplies needed to refit his ship. The governor, George Yeardley, and Abraham Piersey, the cape merchant for the

> *"He brought not anything but 20 and odd Negroes, which the Governor and Cape Merchant bought for victuals (whereof he was in great need as he pretended) at the best and easiest rate they could."*
>
> (Paragraph 9)

Virginia Company, purchased the lot, with seven of the Africans going with Yeardley back to Jamestown and the remainder in the possession of Piersey.

Rolfe spends the rest of this paragraph detailing Jope's credentials as a privateer, stating, "He had a large and ample Commission from his Excellency to range and to take purchase in the West Indies." The commission to which he refers came from Maurice, the Count of Nassau, and gave him license to raid Spanish shipping in the Caribbean and its surrounding water. This was significant, because Jope's actions—the raid on a Spanish ship—could, therefore, be seen by officials back in England as instigated by the English, who had recently signed a treaty with Spain.

♦ **Paragraph 10**

The next paragraph, while not directly commenting on Jope's sale or the fate of his twenty-some Africans, does illuminate Rolfe's position in the colony. Rolfe reports that the *Treasure* made landfall not far from Point Comfort, three or four days after the *White Lion*. Captain Daniel Elfrith, thinking that Argall was still in command, "sent word presently to the Governor to know his pleasure." Elfrith's presence in Virginia seriously disconcerted the newly arrived Governor Yeardley on several fronts: The *Treasure* was at least partially owned by members of the regime that he and Sandys had replaced; Argall was not only part owner of the vessel but also the former governor chased from the colony under clouds of suspicion; and, finally, the *Treasure* sailed and raided under an English flag, threatening James I's fragile new peace with the Spanish. Elfrith, taking heed of his hostile reception—"the unfriendly dealing of the Inhabitants of Keqnoughton"—quickly abandoned Virginia for Bermuda, where he found a friendlier welcome and a market for his cargo of captive Angolans.

♦ **Paragraphs 11–23**

In the remainder of the letter Rolfe describes the events occurring in the colony over the rest of the year. The most important of his accounts focus on a warning from Elfrith that a Spanish attack might come in the spring as well as on the deteriorating relationships with the local tribes, the establishment of new plantations and the division of land under Sandys's new system, and arrivals and departures from the colony. He closes with a pledge of his loyalty and a plea for Argall, his former patron.

Audience

The audience named by John Rolfe in his salutation consisted of a party of one, Sir Edwin Sandys. It is clear that much of what Rolfe says was intended specifically for Sandys. This is particularly true of the first and last paragraphs of the text. Rolfe was interested in cultivating a relationship with the man he perceived, quite correctly, as holding the keys to his and his family's future. His tone is deferential, and his language throughout the letter is almost penitent. However, in Rolfe's seventeenth-century world, both would be normal in a communication between an official and a subordinate and clearly define the relationship between the two men.

While Rolfe specifically addresses Sandys in the letter, he must also have intended for his work to be read by others. Given the common practice in early-modern England of reading aloud letters from distant places, it is reasonable that Rolfe expected Sandys to share at least selected passages from his text with others, most specifically those shareholders in the Virginia Company. Sandys's position in the company as secretary also suggests that he served as a conduit for information to and from the officers and holdings.

Impact

It is quite clear that Rolfe's mention of the sale of those twenty-some Africans in August of 1619 bears much more historical relevance in the eyes of twenty-first century Americans than it did in the eyes of seventeenth-century Englishmen or Virginians. Sandys, or perhaps his secretary, recorded at the end of the letter the items of importance discussed by Rolfe. That list contains no mention of the *White Lion* or the twenty or so Africans sold at Point Comfort in August of 1619. That sale is significant only in retrospect. Those doing the selling and the buying did not comprehend that their actions were the first steps toward a massive forced migration of Africans to British North America and the codification of the institution of slavery.

We know something of what became of two of the Africans who arrived in Virginia on that August day in 1619. According to Tim Hashaw, these two Africans, captives from the Angolan Kingdom of Ndongo, are found in a later Jamestown census under the names "John" Gowan and "Margaret" Cornish. John was taken as a servant by the planter William Evans ("Ewens" in the document), and Margaret became the slave of the planter Robert Shepphard. Although they lived apart, John and Margaret had a son. Many Africans in Jamestown were initially held as indentured servants, to be freed after a period of up to seven years. John soon gained his freedom and went on to start his own farm, but Margaret remained a slave.

Their story was not unique in early colonial times. It was typical for black men to be indentured but for black women to be held as slaves, creating an imbalance in possible marriage partners for these indentured black men when they gained their freedom. The freed black men went on to marry Indians and even white women and became planters with their own servants, some of them white. Within a generation such mixed marriages were banned, and the rights of free blacks were curtailed as the slave trade burgeoned and Virginians began to fear slave uprisings.

See also Virginia's Act XII: "Negro Women's Children to Serve according to the Conditions of the Mother" (1662); Virginia's Act III: Baptism Does Not Exempt Slaves from Bondage (1667).

Further Reading

■ Articles

Sluiter, Engel. "New Light on the '20. and Odd Negroes' Arriving in Virginia, August 1619." *William and Mary Quarterly*, Third Series 54, no. 2 (April 1997): 395–398.

Thorndale, William. "The Virginia Census of 1619." *Magazine of Virginia Genealogy* 33 (1995): 155–170.

Thornton, John. "The African Experience of the '20. and Odd Negroes' Arriving in Virginia in 1619." *William and Mary Quarterly*, Third Series 55, no. 3 (July 1998): 421–434.

Walsh, Lorena S. "The Transatlantic Slave Trade and Colonial Chesapeake Slavery." *OAH Magazine of History* 17, no. 3 (April 2003): 11–15.

■ Books

Blackburn, Robin. *The Making of New World Slavery: From the Baroque to the Modern, 1492–1800*. London: Verso, 1997.

Hashaw, Tim. *Children of Perdition: Melungeons and the Struggle of Mixed America*. Macon, Ga.: Mercer University Press, 2006.

Questions for Further Study

1. Describe the economic and agricultural circumstances that gave rise to slavery in what would become the United States.

2. Imagine that John Rolfe's first tobacco crop had failed. How might the history of the colonies and of the United States have been different?

3. What political intrigues in the Virginia colony and England contributed to the development of the institution of slavery?

4. How did the institution of slavery affect the Virginia settlers' relationships with Native Americans?

5. In 1619 the Spanish and the Portuguese had long had a foothold in the Americas and were using slave labor. How did the history of Spanish and Portuguese slavery affect the development of slavery in the North American colonies?

Hatfield, April Lee. *Atlantic Virginia: Intercolonial Relations in the Seventeenth Century*. Philadelphia: University of Pennsylvania Press, 2004.

Heywood, Linda M., and John K. Thornton. *Central Africans, Atlantic Creoles, and the Foundation of the Americas, 1585–1660*. New York: Cambridge University Press, 2007.

Horn, James. *Adapting to the New World: English Society in the Seventeenth Century Chesapeake*. Chapel Hill: University of North Carolina Press, 1994.

———. *A Land As God Made It: Jamestown and the Birth of America*. New York: Basic Books, 2005.

Kupperman, Karen Ordahl. *The Jamestown Project*. Cambridge, Mass.: Harvard University Press, 2007.

Mancall, Peter, ed. *The Atlantic World and Virginia, 1550-1624*. Chapel Hill: University of North Carolina Press, 2007.

Townsend, Camilla. *Pocahontas and the Powhatan Dilemma*. New York: Hill and Wang, 2004.

■ Web Sites

"John Rolfe." U.S. Department of the Interior National Park Service "Historic Jamestowne" Web site.
      www.nps.gov/jame/historyculture/john-rolfe.htm.

Pory, John. "Letter of John Pory, 1619." Wisconsin Historical Society Digital Library and Archives "American Journeys Collection."
      http://www.americanjourneys.org/pdf/AJ-081.pdf.

—Martha Pallante

John Rolfe's Letter to Sir Edwin Sandys

January 1619/20

Honored Sir:

Studying with myself what service I might do you, as a token of my grateful remembrance for your many favors and constant love shown me, as well in my absence as when I was present with you I could not at this time devise a better than to give you notice of some particulars both of our present estate and what happened since the departure of the *Diana*. And though I am well assured, you will be satisfied herein more fully by our Governor, yet I desire your kind acceptance of this my poor endeavor.

Presently, after the *Diana* had her dispatch, Sir George Yeardley (according to a Commission directed unto him and to the Council of State) caused Burgesses to be chosen in all place who met at James City, where all matters therein contained were debated by several Committees and approved and likewise such other laws enacted as were held expedient & requisite for the welfare and peaceable government of this Commonwealth. Captain Martin's Burgesses for his Plantation were not admitted to this Assembly; the reasons I am assured you shall receive from our Governor, who sends home a report of all those proceedings.

These principal men being at James City, Captain William Epps (who commands Smythe's Hundred Company) was arraigned (as near as might be) according to the laudable Laws of England, for killing one Captain Edward Roecroft alias Stallenge. He came hither from the North Colony in a ship of Sir Ferdinando Gorges (as he said) for some necessaries which he wanted and to coast along the shore to find and discover what Harbors and rivers he could. But through neglect of the Master of the ship and others, she was forced aground in a storm near Newport News and there sprang so great a leak that he could not carry her back again. This mischance happened through uncivil and unmanly words urged by Stallenge (there being no precedent malice) with which Captain Epps being much moved did strike him on the head with a sword in the scabbard such an unfortunate blow that within 2 days he died. The Jury…, hearing the Evidence, found him guilty of Manslaughter by Chance medley. The Governor finding him (though young) yet a proper civil gent and of good hopes, not long after restored him to his Command.

Captain Henry Spelman, being accused by Robert Poole (one of the interpreters of the Indian language) of many crimes which might be prejudicial to the State in general and to every man's safety in particular, received Censure at this general Assembly. But the Governor hoping he might redeem his fault, proceeding much of Childish ignorance, pardoned the punishment upon hope of amendment. In trial whereof he was employed as interpreter to Patawamack to trade for Corn.

Captain Ward in his ship went to Monahigon in the North Colony in May and returned the latter end of July, with fish which he caught there. He brought but a small quantity, by reason he had but little salt. There were some Plymouth ships where he harbored, who made great store of fish, which is far larger then Newfoundland fish.

The *George* was sent by the Cape Merchant (with the Governor's consent) to Newfoundland to trade and buy fish for the better relief of the Colony and to make trial of that passage. One other reason (as I take it) was, for that the Magazine was well stored with goods, it was somewhat doubtful, whether a ship would be sent to carry home the crop so soon as the *George* might upon her return back. She departed hence about the 9th of July and arrived here again about the 10th of September. She made her passage to Newfoundland in less than 3 weeks and was at the bank amongst the French fishermen in 14 days. She came back hither again in 3 weeks, with bare wind and brought so much fish as will make a saving voyage, which, beside the great relief, gives much content to the whole Colony.

The *Sturgeon* ship and the *Trial* departed hence together [in] July. Mr. Pountys has taken great pains in fishing, and toward Michaelmas (the weather being somewhat temperate) made some good sturgeon. He hopes by the spring to be better fitted, with Cellars and houses, and to do some good therein.

The Cattle in the *Trial* came exceeding well, and gave the Colony much joy and great encouragement. Both the horses and Mares will be very vendible here a long time, the Colony increasing with people as of late.

About the latter end of August, a Dutch man-of-war of the burden of a 160 tons arrived at Point Comfort, the Commander's name Captain Jope, his Pilot for the West Indies one Mr. Marmaduke, an Englishman. They met with the *Treasure* in the West Indies and determined to hold consort ship hitherward, but in their passage lost one the other. He brought not anything but 20 and odd Negroes, which the Governor and Cape Merchant bought for victuals (whereof he was in great need as he pretended) at the best and easiest rate they could. He had a large and ample Commission from his Excellency to range and to take purchase in the West Indies.

Three or 4 days after the *Treasure* arrived. At his arrival he sent word presently to the Governor to know his pleasure, who wrote to him, and did request myself, Lieutenant Peace, and Mr. Ewens to go down to him, to desire him to come up to James City. But before we got down, he had set sail and was gone out of the Bay. The occasion hereof happened by the unfriendly dealing of the Inhabitants of Keqnoughton, for he was in great want of victuals, wherewith they would not relieve him or his Company upon any terms. He reported (whilst he stayed at Keqnoughton) that if we got not some Ordinance planted at Point Comfort, the Colony would be quite undone—and that ere long—for that undoubtedly the Spaniard would be here the next spring which he gathered (as was said) from some Spaniard in the West Indies. This being spread abroad does much dishearten the people in general for we have no place of strength to retreat unto, no shipping of certainty (which would be to us as the wooden walls of England) no sound and experienced soldiers to undertake, no Engineers and earthmen to erect works, few Ordinance, not a serviceable carriage to mount them on; not Ammunition of powder, shot and lead, to fight 2 whole days, no, not one gunner belonging to the Plantation, so our sovereign's dignity, your honors or poor reputations, lives, and labors thus long spent lies too open to a sudden and to an inevitable hazard, if a foreign enemy oppose against us. Of this I cannot better do, to give you full satisfaction, than to refer you to the judgment and opinion of Captain Argall, who has often spoken hereof during his government and knows (none better) these defects.

About the beginning of September, Japazaws (the King of the Patawamack's brother) came to James City to the Governor. Among other frivolous messages, he requested, that 2 ships might be speedily to Patawamack, where they should trade for great stores of corn. Hereupon (according to his desire) the Governor sent an Englishman with him by land, and in the beginning of October, Captain Ward's ship and Somer-Island frigate departed James City hitherward.

Robert Poole, being wholly employed by the Governor of message to the great King, persuaded Sir George that if he would send Pledge, he would come to visit him. Our Corn and Tobacco being in great abundance in our ground (for a more plentiful year than this it hath not pleased God to send us since the beginning of this Plantation, yet very contagious for sickness, whereof many, both old and new men, died) the Governor sent two men unto him, who were returned with frivolous answers, saying he never had any intent to come unto him. The Governor being jealous of them (… because we had many straggling Plantations, much weakened by the great mortality, Poole likewise proving very dishonest) requested Captain William Powell and myself … to go in a shallop unto Pomonkey river, which we did. Going up that river within 5 miles of his house, we sent Captain Spelman and Thomas Hobson unto him with the Governor's message. The ship and frigate (being not far out of their way to Patawamack) went in the night about 12 miles into the river, and we hasting up with our shallop, the messengers were with Opachankano, before or as soon as any news came to him either of the ships or our arrival, which much daunted them and put them in great fear. Their entertainment at the first was harsh (Poole being even turned heathen), but after their message was delivered, it was kindly taken, they sent away lovingly, and Poole accused and Condemned by them, as an instrument that sought all the means he could to break or league. They seemed also to be very weary of him. Opachankano much wondered I would not go to him, but (as I wished the messengers) they said I was sick of an ague, wherewith they were satisfied. We had no order to bring Poole away, or to make any show of discontent to him, for fear he should persuade them to some mischief in our corn fields, hoping to get him away by fair means. So we returned in great love and amity to the great content of the Colony, which before lived in daily hazard, all message being untruly delivered by Poole on both sides.…

All the Ancient Planters being set free have chosen place for their dividend according to the Commission. Which giveth all great content, for now knowing their own land, they strive and are prepared to build houses & to clear their ground ready to plant, which gives the great encouragement and the greatest hope to make the Colony flourish that ever yet happened to them.

Upon the 4th of November the *Bona Nova* arrived at James City. All the passengers came lusty and in good health. They came by the West Indies, which passage at that season doth much refresh the people.

The proportion of Victuals brought for those 100 men fell so short that Captain Welden and Mr. Whitaker were forced (notwithstanding our plenty) to put out 50 or thereabout for a year by the Governor's and Council's advise, for whom they are to receive the next years 3 barrels of corn and 55 n of tobacco for a man; which their sickness considered (for seldom any escapes little or much) is more than they of themselves could get. By this means the next year, they will be instructed to proceed in their own business and be well instructed to teach newcomers. With the remainder (being about 25 apiece, the one is seated with one Captain Mathews 3 miles beyond Henrico for his own security, and to his great content. And Mr. Whitaker within 4 miles of James City on the Company's land.

Upon Saturday the 20th of November at night Mr. Ormerod died at James City, after a long and tedious sickness, the chief occasion the flux, which of late hath much reigned among us. His death is generally much lamented, the Colony receiving hereby a great loss, being a man of so good life, learning & carriage as his fellow here he left not behind him.

One Mr. Darmer, agent sent out by the Plymouth Company, arrived here about the end of September in a small bottom of 7 or 8 tons; he had coasted … to our Plantation, and found an Inland sea…, the depth whereof he could not search for want of means, and winter coming on. He is fitting his small vessel and purposes this spring to make a new trial.

Captain Lawne, at his arrival, seated himself in Warraskoyack Bay with his Company, but by his own sickness and his people's (wherein there was improvidence) he quitted his Plantation, went up to Charles City, and about November died. So his piece is likely (unless better followed and well seconded) to come to nothing.

Smythe's Hundred people are seated at Dauncing Point, the most convenient place within their limit. There has been much sickness among them: so yet this year no matter of gain or of great industry can be expected from them.

Martyne's Hundred men seated at Argall Towne with good & convenient houses have done best of all Newcomers. Many who were industrious having reaped good crops, but most not of equal spirit and industrious have less, yet exceeded other Newcomers. Many of these have also died by sickness, but not comparable to other places.

About the beginning of December Captain Ward with his ship and the frigate came from Patawamack. Japazaws had dealt falsely with them, for they could get little trade, so that they brought not about 800 bushels, the most part whereof they took by force from Japazaws' Country who deceived them, and a small quantity they traded for. But in conclusion being very peaceable with all the other Indians, at their departure they also made a firm peace again with Japazaws.

At this time also came Captain Woodiff in a small ship of Bristow, who brought his people very well, and made his passage in ten weeks.

Thus far as part of my duty (ever ready at your service) have I briefly made known unto you, some particulars of our estate and withal in conclusion cannot chose but reveal unto you the sorrow I conceive, to hear of the many accusations heaped upon Captain Argall, with whom my reputation has been unjustly joined, but I am persuaded he will answer well for himself. Here have also been divers depositions taken and sent home by the *Diana*; I will tax no man therein. But when it shall come to farther trial, I assure you that you shall find many dishonest and faithless men to Captain Argall, who have received much kindness at his hand & to his face will contradict, and be ashamed of much, which in his absence they have intimated against him. Lastly, I speak on my own experience for these 11 years, I never among so few, have seen so many falsehearted, envious, and malicious people (yea among some who march in the better rank), nor shall you ever hear of any the justest Governor here, who shall live free, from their scandal and shameless exclamations, if way be given to their report. And so desiring your kind acceptance hereof, being unwilling to conceal anything from yourself (who now, to mine and many others' comfort, stands at the helm to guide us and bring us to the Port of our best happiness, which of late we say principally by your goodness we now enjoy) either which you may be desirous to understand or which may further you for the advancement of this Christian Plantation I take my leave and will ever rest

At your service and command in all faithful duties. Jo: Rolf.

[Indorsed by Sir Edwin Sandys:] Mr. John Rolfe from Virginia Jan. 1619.

By the George.

Narration of the Late proceedings in Virginia.
Cape Cod fish larger than that of Newfoundland.
The fishing voyage of the *George*.
The *Treasure*'s return: Extreme fear of the Spaniards: Want of all things.
Ships sent to the King of Patawamack.
Voyage to Opachankano. Poole's villainy.
The 4 Burrough & public land set out.
Joy and good success of dividing the Lands.

The Voyage of the *Bona Nova*. Vide C. Welden's seat. Vide Death & praise of Mr Ormerod.
Mr. Darmer of Plymouth's discoveries.
Captain Ward's Voyage for Corn.
In favor of C. Argall. That people ill-conditioned to Sir Edwin Sandys.
[Addressed by self:] To the Honored and my much respected friend Sir Edwyn Sandys Kt, Treasurer for the Virginia Company these.

ague	fever
bottom	cargo ship
burgesses	representatives to an assembly
chance medley	from the Anglo-French *chance-medlee* ("mixed chance"), a term from English law used to describe a homicide arising from a quarrel or fight; akin to manslaughter as a killing without malice aforethought
earthmen	sappers, military specialists in field fortification
flux	dysentery, or another disease causing loss of bodily fluid
magazine	warehouse, storage building
Michaelmas	September 29, celebrated as the feast of Saint Michael the Archangel
ordinance	weapons
shallop	a large, heavy boat
wooden walls	warships

VIRGINIA'S ACT XII: NEGRO WOMEN'S CHILDREN TO SERVE ACCORDING TO THE CONDITION OF THE MOTHER

"All children borne in this country shall be held bond or free only according to the condition of the mother."

Overview

In December 1662 the Virginia House of Burgesses met for the second time that year and approved a set of twenty-three statutes that focused on various facets of colonial life. The most infamous of these laws, Act XII, made the civil status of African and African American slave women inheritable by their offspring. The burgesses, convened by the governor, Sir William Berkeley, and presided over by the speaker, Captain Robert Wynne, acted in response to their perceptions of the colonists' needs and interests. Other legislation passed during that session included the commission for a new city to be built at Jamestown, various attempts at regulating trade, several taxes and tax reforms, a law aimed at controlling brabbling (squabbling) or gossiping women, and six statutes governing the behavior and status of indentured servants.

The status of Virginia's unfree laborers, as illustrated by the number of laws passed regarding them, was prominent among the burgesses' concerns. These workers fell into two major categories, indentured servants and slaves. Together, these groups formed the majority of the laborers in the colony's burgeoning tobacco economy. Indentured servants were bound under contracts that negotiated away their right to profit from their labor in exchange for food and lodging as well as protection from the colony's enemies. These individuals hailed primarily from British Isles. Slaves, on the other hand, were of African descent and served for life.

Context

Virginians in 1662 lived in a world that for several decades had been fraught with change. The colony had grown from a ragtag frontier outpost established in 1607 to a cornerstone of England's imperial holdings. Virginia was established and initially owned by the Virginia Company of London, also known as the London Company, but reverted to royal ownership after the company's bankruptcy in 1624. From 1641 to 1660, the inhabitants of the British Empire endured considerable political turmoil and civil unrest. A civil war erupted in England, resulting in the deposal of

Charles I and his beheading in 1649 as well as the establishment of the Puritan-led Commonwealth under Oliver Cromwell. To fill the vacuum of power brought on by Cromwell's death in 1658, Parliament invited Charles II to take the throne in 1660; the monarchy was thus reinstated, and the period known as the Restoration began. For settlers in Virginia and other English colonies, that meant an adjustment to the return of imperial oversight after nearly two decades of neglect.

Some of the changes Virginia settlers experienced in the mid-seventeenth century were for the better. After five decades of high mortality rates among new immigrants, Virginia's population had finally stabilized. This occurred for a variety of reasons, including better and more plentiful food, the relocation of settlements farther away from malaria-ridden riverfronts and high-water tables, and better timing of the arrival of new settlers. In the eighteen-year period between 1644 and 1662, the population more than tripled, from approximately eight thousand to twenty-five thousand six hundred. While most of this increase resulted from immigration, greater longevity and increasing birth rates also contributed to the colony's growth.

Politically, the governmental structures and laws of Virginia loosely resembled those of the mother country. The House of Burgesses, established in 1619, was based on the British parliament. It was a bicameral body comprising the lower house, the Assembly, elected at the county level by members of the county court, and the Governor's Council, constituted of members of the elite. The county courts functioned much like the English quarter sessions, which were similar to common pleas courts presided over by the local justice of the peace and meeting four times a year. The difference lay in the percentage of the people who had the right to participate in the court; land ownership was common among free adult white males in Virginia, whereas in England land ownership was concentrated in the hands of a relative few. English common law had been the starting point for Virginia's lawmakers. In some respects, however, Virginia's laws strayed considerably from the English model. This was particularly true during the Commonwealth period, when direction from across the Atlantic was limited. As a consequence, Virginians created their own rules to fit their unique situation. The statutes concerning local

1606

■ **April**
King James I of England issues a charter to the Virginia Company of London (also known as the London Company) to colonize the eastern shore of North America between the latitudes of 34 and 41 degrees north.

■ **December 20**
Under the command of Admiral Christopher Newport, the three ships of the Virginia Company of London—the *Godspeed*, *Discovery*, and *Susan Constant*—leave for the New World.

1607

■ **March**
The Virginia Company's ships reach the coast of Virginia and explore the Chesapeake Bay vicinity through early May.

■ **May 13**
The 104 male settlers who survive the voyage, led by Captain John Smith and Bartholomew Gosnold, arrive at a site along the James River that becomes Jamestown; they begin construction of a fort the next day, thus establishing the first permanent British outpost in the Americas.

1612

■ John Rolfe grows the first commercially salable tobacco crop in Virginia.

1619

■ Upon gaining control of the Virginia Company of London, Sir Edwin Sandys reorganizes the venture as a colony with a representative government. On July 30, the first session of the Virginia House of Burgesses is convened.

■ **May**
The Virginia census counts thirty-two Africans among the colony's inhabitants.

■ **August**
The Dutch privateer *White Lion* makes landfall at the tip of the Virginia peninsula in Mobjack Bay. In exchange for food, its captain, John Colyn Jope, sells to Governor George Yeardley and the merchant Abraham Piersey some twenty African captives seized from a Portuguese ship.

defense and the use of unfree labor deviated the most from English common law because Virginians dealt with conditions that did not exist in England.

In economic terms, tobacco was the king of Virginia crops. Introduced in the 1610s by John Rolfe, the English husband of the Indian Pocahontas, tobacco provided Virginia with a viable cash crop that was grown nearly to the exclusion of anything else. The harvest of 1663 yielded seven million pounds shipped to London alone. This had a negative effect, however, for as supply increased, prices declined. Broad attempts at crop diversification continued to fail, though Virginians had begun to grow some of their own food. For most planters, large and small, the only way to increase their profits was to put more land into cultivation, which in turn required more labor. Since free males in Virginia usually owned property, labor by definition had to be performed by those who could not hold property in their own right: women, children, and the unfree.

During most of the first half century of the colony's existence, unfree labor had been integral to its economy. Throughout the 1610s, traditional indentured servants met that need. In August 1619 the colonists' regular source of bound labor from the British Isles was supplemented by the arrival of captive Africans aboard a Dutch privateer (warship) commanded by an English captain. John Rolfe identified this event in a letter to Sir Edwin Sandys in 1619/1620. This was the first documented sale of African slaves in Virginia; however, a census taken in May 1619 had already identified thirty-two Virginians of African origin.

Through the 1620s, the labor demands of the colony accelerated because of the expansion of the cash crop, tobacco. The demand far exceeded the supply of indentured labor from the British Isles. To alleviate that stress, the House of Burgesses began to regulate more closely the laws controlling the behavior and contract terms of indentured servants. In addition to using indentured labor, Virginians also looked at the possibilities of exploiting people from cultures unlike their own, namely, Native Americans and Africans. Models of servitude developed by the Spanish and Portuguese in the West Indies and South America had introduced Virginians to such possibilities as well as to the institution of perpetual slavery. By the 1640s, some colonists had experimented with the enslavement of individuals not of their own race. In the case of the local indigenous peoples, that had proved to be unfeasible because of their familiarity with the countryside and the hostilities generated with their native tribes. To forestall additional trouble, the House of Burgesses passed legislation prohibiting the enslavement of local Native Americans, with a loophole that permitted the enslavement of those who had already been brought into the colony. Imported Africans proved easier to entrap into permanent servitude. They lacked local defenders and were markedly different in their physical characteristics and religious orientations. Additionally, English colonists could draw upon examples of African slavery from the Caribbean.

Throughout the Commonwealth period, when parliamentary oversight was limited, Virginians began to craft laws that altered the systems of servitude employed in the colony. They gradually lengthened terms of service for all unfree laborers and made provisions for the perpetual enslavement of Africans. In the era after 1660, conditions provided further impetus to continue down that path. The supply of English indentured servants stagnated and then declined as political and economic conditions in England stabilized with the restoration of Charles II. As mortality rates among new arrivals dropped, the financial advantages of holding a laborer for life began to outweigh the higher cost of a slave in comparison with an indentured servant, whose labor was bound for an average of five to seven years. This was also a period when English merchants seriously investigated the possibilities of engaging in the slave trade themselves.

About the Author

Identifying a specific author for Act XII: Negro Women's Children to Serve according to the Condition of the Mother, is an extremely difficult, if not impossible, task. The records of the burgesses' proceedings do not contain the names of the individuals who wrote specific laws. Other than specifying two persons, Sir William Berkeley and Captain Robert Wynne, the record leaves other possible legislative authors anonymous.

We can identify, however, what the burgesses were or represented, rather than exactly who produced the statute. In 1619 the House of Burgesses was established during a reorganization of the Virginia Company of London led by Sir Edwin Sandys, who had served earlier as the company's joint manager and treasurer. The House of Burgesses represents one facet of a larger scheme to transform the Virginia settlement from a commercial enterprise staffed by company employees into a colony of the British Empire. Officials of the Virginia Company hoped to encourage a sense of permanence and stability by granting land to the residents and providing them with at least the semblance of local governance.

The plan for the Virginia House of Burgesses called for a bicameral body that had the power to create and adjudicate local law. The burgesses could not, however, make laws that affected intercolonial trade, dispute aspects of English common law, or set themselves up in opposition to the monarchy or Parliament. The original body consisted of the Assembly and the Governor's Council. Members of the Assembly were elected by each county's court. The Assembly comprised two representatives per county, who usually were those individuals with the greatest social prestige and the most acreage. The county court consisted of adult male landowners. The members of the Governor's Council were selected in London by the stockholders of the Virginia Company. The councilors made up an elite body of individuals who wielded considerable clout on both sides of the Atlantic. Collectively, the two chambers represented the colony's powerful elite. By the 1660s, the burgesses met annually in two sessions; one took place in the spring of each year, and a second convened in the late fall.

Time Line

1619/ 1620
- John Rolfe writes a letter to Sir Edwin Sandys, noting the arrival in Virginia of "20 and odd Negroes" aboard a Dutch warship the previous August.

1624
- The Virginia Company of London, now nearly bankrupt and beset by litigation, loses its charter, and the Virginia colony reverts to direct royal control.

1625
- After the accession of Charles I to the throne of England, the Virginia colony is granted a royal charter.

1641
- Sir William Berkeley is named governor of Virginia.

1642
- The English Civil War begins.

1647
- **June** After several decisive military victories, the Roundheads, Puritan rebels led by Oliver Cromwell, take Charles I prisoner.

1649
- Charles I is beheaded; the Commonwealth Parliament is established, and Oliver Cromwell becomes Lord Protector.

1652
- Governor Berkeley is removed from office.

1660
- **May 29** The English monarchy is reinstated with the accession of Charles II to the throne, ushering in the Restoration.

1662
- Berkeley becomes governor of Virginia again.
- **December** The House of Burgesses passes twenty-three statutes, one of which, Act XII, is subtitled "Negro Women's Children to Serve according to the Condition of the Mother."

Time Line

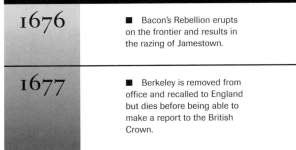

1676
- Bacon's Rebellion erupts on the frontier and results in the razing of Jamestown.

1677
- Berkeley is removed from office and recalled to England but dies before being able to make a report to the British Crown.

Sir William Berkeley is the better known of the two individuals explicitly associated with Act XII. Like most of Virginia's colonial governors, Berkeley had been born in England. He received his initial appointment to the governorship of Virginia in 1641 and took up residence in the colony in 1642. Commissioned by King Charles I, Berkeley was a firm royalist who supported the monarchy during the English Civil War. He went so far as to offer supporters of the monarchy sanctuary in Virginia. Removed from office in 1652 under threat of imprisonment for treason, he negotiated a compromise that kept him in Virginia and in possession of his estates. After the Restoration began in 1660, he was recommended as governor and served again until his recall in 1677 in the aftermath of Bacon's Rebellion, an uprising of colonists on the frontier against both Native Americans and the ruling white political elite.

Less is known of Captain Robert Wynne. A roster of burgesses present for the sessions of 1661–1663 lists him as the speaker and suggests that he held property in Charles City County, which is located on the north side of the James River roughly equidistant from Jamestown and Henrico. Many of Virginia's earliest settlers resided in this vicinity. His title, captain, was most likely in recognition of his status in the local militias and not an indicator of military rank. His selection as speaker was a mark of respect among his colleagues and gave him some power over the phrasing of the presentation of materials to the body.

Explanation and Analysis of the Document

The House of Burgesses session of December 1662, which produced the statute known as Negro Women's Children to Serve according to the Condition of the Mother, deliberated and acted on a variety of issues. Their discussions included matters concerning the construction of a new "James Citty," or Jamestown, (Act XVI) and laws to deal with debtors in default (Act I). Among their most pressing concerns were those involving bound laborers. During that session alone, the burgesses approved six acts concerning the status of bound laborers.

Act XII, the sixth statute concerning bound servants passed by this body, made an African American child's civil status—whether slave or free—inheritable from his or her mother. As with the other laws dealing with slaves and servants, it is altogether possible that this legislation, rather than being proactive, was passed in response to existing circumstances. As the wording of the act suggests, there had already arisen questions and at least one legal case concerning the status of children born to slaves. In January 1655 Elizabeth Key, a woman born in 1630 to an unnamed African servant and an English father, Thomas Key, filed suit for her freedom on the ground that her father had been a free man. (He had also been a burgess.) The Northumberland County Court ruled in her favor in July 1656.

Act XII is divided into two segments. The first portion deals with the status of children born to African and African American women in the Virginia colony. The second section addresses the issue of sexual intercourse between Africans and Anglo-Americans. The opening clause of the act states: "Whereas some doubts have arisen whether children got by any Englishman upon a negro woman should be slave or free." This suggests that the burgesses were aware that miscegenation, or sexual intercourse between individuals of different races, had occurred in the Virginia colony and that laws concerning the civil status of the offspring of such unions were insufficient. Seventeenth-century English common law clearly delineated children as the recipient of their father's civil status and further noted children as the responsibility of their sires. By the 1660s, Virginians had begun to question those precepts and their corresponding obligations when the female parent was of African descent.

Captain John Smith (Library of Congress)

"Some doubts have arisen whether children got by any Englishman upon a negro woman should be slave or free."

"All children borne in this country shall be held bond or free only according to the condition of the mother."

The middle section of the statute begins with a formulaic statement: "*Be it therefore enacted and declared by this present grand assembly.*" Virtually every statute passed by the House of Burgesses in this period contained similar, if not identical, phrasing. However, it is the latter part of this section that puts forth the central premise of the act: "All children borne in this country shall be held bond or free only according to the condition of the mother." It placed the offspring of "negro" mothers outside the normal boundaries of English law and made them special cases. It also absolved the fathers of those children of all responsibilities for them or claims to them. A father might have retained some claim over his child only in situations where the mother was free or he was the master of a mother who was his female bound servant. Otherwise, the paternal rights normally jealously guarded by English common law were to be negated when the mother was of African descent by designating the child as the property of the mother's master. No person could claim responsibility for another's chattels.

The last clause of the law calls attention to the perceived problem of sexual intercourse between persons of English and African descent: "*And* that if any christian shall commit fornication with a negro man or woman, he or she so offending shall pay double the fines imposed by the former act." While Virginians of this era disapproved of any form of sexual intercourse outside traditional marriage, miscegenation was considered particularly repugnant, and this portion of the act is an explicit warning against such activity. Justices of the peace levied fines against those found guilty of acts of extramarital sex according to local customs that varied from county to county. Justices often required public penance by the offenders in church as well. In most cases the guilty couple shared responsibility for payment of the fine, or the male assumed the entire debt. In cases of miscegenation, however, the expectation was that the "christian," a euphemism for an Anglo-American in the statute, would bear the full cost, regardless of his or her gender. Furthermore, it is implicit in the clause's wording that the burgesses did not consider blacks to be Christians but rather heathens.

Audience

There are, in a sense, three separate audiences for this document: the Virginians who created and implemented the statutes, the residents and officials of the larger British Empire who would later model similar legislation on it, and those persons whose actions directly affected female African slaves and their progeny. All three audiences had vested interests in the act's implementation and perceived it differently. Anglo-Virginians perceived the legislation largely as expedient. For large landowners, the inheritability of slaves' status provided a captive labor force that would increase over time. It also clearly defined distinct racial lines between Anglo-Americans and their African slaves. Officials in different areas of the British Empire had similar motives for accepting and adapting the legislation. In England, primarily the members of Parliament and merchants responded to the statute, albeit at a distance. Neither slavery nor its inheritability affected their daily lives. In other British colonies, Anglo-Americans recognized slavery as part of an emerging network of trade and law that governed their access to labor. Africans and African Americans found themselves in the unenviable position of being subject to the law without having had any voice in its passage or implementation.

Impact

For Anglo-Virginians, the statute represented economic pragmatism and implicit racism. In Virginia, tobacco was quite literally money, and larger crops represented larger incomes. In a period when prices had stagnated and then dropped, the only way to increase profits was to cultivate more of the cash crop. The leveling of tobacco prices coincided with a decline in the utility and availability of white indentured servants. Simultaneously, Virginians recognized that the declining mortality rates among new arrivals to the colony made holding servants bound for life more viable than purchasing an indentured servant who would serve for a limited period of years. Africans were the most vulnerable to being bound for life because they had no voice in the system that created the laws and because of their subservient role in extant Spanish and Portuguese models of labor exploitation. Once slavery for life became a reality, making it a legally inheritable status was the logical conclusion.

People in England had only a limited perception of what African slavery meant or entailed. Those who recognized it at all saw it as an exotic institution and perhaps as a necessary evil. The residents of other British colonies, particularly those in the West Indies, already engaged in similar practices, and their laws existed in a symbiotic relationship with those of Virginia.

For African Americans, whether enslaved or free, the passage of this statute represented the closure of one of the last loopholes that had permitted them and their offspring to escape the institution of slavery. The statute contained elements that would characterize Anglo-American slavery for the next two hundred years. It explicitly acknowledged slavery as an institution in Virginia, limited it to Africans and African Americans, and made it an inheritable condition.

See also John Rolfe's Letter to Sir Edwin Sandys (1619/1620); Virginia's Act III: Baptism Does Not Exempt Slaves from Bondage (1667); Virginia Slave Code (1860).

Further Reading

■ Articles

Billings, Warren M. "The Cases of Fernando and Elizabeth Key: A Note on the Status of Blacks in Seventeenth-Century Virginia." *William and Mary Quarterly*, 3rd series, 30, no. 3 (July 1973): 467–474.

Mumford, Kevin. "After Hugh: Statutory Race Segregation in Colonial America, 1630–1725." *American Journal of Legal History* 43, no. 3 (July 1999): 280–305.

Zackodnik, Teresa. "Fixing the Color Line: The Mulatto, Southern Courts, and Racial Identity," *American Quarterly*, 53, no. 3 (September 2001): 420–451.

■ Books

Berkin, Carol, and Leslie Horowitz, eds. *Women's Voices, Women's Lives: Documents in Early American History*. Boston: Northeastern University Press, 1998.

Blackburn, Robin. *The Making of New World Slavery: From the Baroque to the Modern, 1492–1800*. London: Verso/New Left Books, 1997.

Questions for Further Study

1. In colonial Virginia, the need for labor was persistently more pressing than the need for land. Discuss this proposition.

2. Using this document in conjunction with John Rolfe's Letter to Sir Edwin Sandys and Virginia's Act III: Baptism Does Not Exempt Slaves from Bondage, prepare a time line of the most significant events in Virginia's colonial history, particularly as they affected slaves.

3.This document was one of the earliest in Virginia establishing the position of slaves. Among the last was the Virginia Slave Code of 1860. Comparing the two documents and their historical contexts, explain what, if anything, changed in Virginia over the course of two-plus centuries.

4. What specific circumstances led to the passage of Virginia's Act XII?

5. Given that Virginia was a colony of Great Britain and thus subject to Britain's laws, why do you believe Britain tolerated, or ignored, the codification of slavery in its colony?

Hatfield, April Lee. *Atlantic Virginia: Intercolonial Relations in the Seventeenth Century*. Philadelphia: University of Pennsylvania Press, 2004.

Horn, James. *Adapting to the New World: English Society in the Seventeenth-Century Chesapeake*. Chapel Hill: University of North Carolina Press, 1994.

Jordon Winthrop D. *White over Black: American Attitudes toward the Negro, 1550–1812*. Chapel Hill: University of North Carolina Press, 1968.

Mancall, Peter C., ed. *The Atlantic World and Virginia, 1550–1624*. Chapel Hill: University of North Carolina Press, 2007.

Morgan, Edmund. *American Slavery, American Freedom: The Ordeal of Colonial Virginia*. New York: W. W. Norton, 1975.

Morgan, Kenneth. *Slavery and Servitude in Colonial North America: A Short History*. New York: New York University Press, 2001.

Parent, Anthony S., Jr. *Foul Means: The Formation of a Slave Society in Virginia, 1660–1740*. Chapel Hill: University of North Carolina Press, 2003.

■ Web Sites

Billings, Warren M. "Sir William Berkeley." Virtual Jamestown "Jamestown Interpretive Essays" Web site.
http://www.virtualjamestown.org/essays/billings_essay.html.

Hening, William Waller. "Hening's Statutes at Large." VaGenWeb Web site.
http://www.vagenweb.org/hening/index.htm.

—Martha Pallante

Virginia's Act XII: Negro Women's Children to Serve according to the Condition of the Mother

Whereas some doubts have arisen whether children got by any Englishman upon a negro woman should be slave or free, *Be it therefore enacted and declared by this present grand assembly*, that all children borne in this country shall be held bond or free only according to the condition of the mother, *And* that if any christian shall commit fornication with a negro man or woman, he or she so offending shall pay double the fines imposed by the former act.

Virginia's Act III: Baptism Does Not Exempt Slaves from Bondage

"Baptism doth not alter the condition of the person as to his bondage or freedom."

Overview

In 1667 in Jamestown, Virginia, the House of Burgesses approved a statute, Act III of September 1667, that answered the following query: Does the conferring of the Christian sacrament of baptism in any way change the legal status of a slave? The legislators ruled that baptism did not alter a slave's legal status, with the act thus titled "An act declaring that baptism of slaves doth not exempt them from bondage." Their decision, when added to certain previous rulings made concerning the colony's enslaved blacks, revealed a distinct pattern of behavior. Virginia's House of Burgesses slowly, over a period of years, crafted a legal system that identified enslaved blacks and their descendants as a permanent source of cheap labor. Through that process, British colonials sowed the seeds of institutionalized slavery based on race, a system that survived in the Chesapeake region for more than two centuries.

Context

Englishmen made their first attempts to settle the Chesapeake region of North America in the late sixteenth century, a time when Europeans tested one another's limits through fierce competition for dominance over lucrative transatlantic trade routes and the colonization of the Western Hemisphere. British nobles, ill prepared to confront the harsh realities of life in Virginia, were responsible for the failures of the colony's earliest settlements. In 1606, Britain's King James I granted a land charter to investors of the Virginia Company of London, hoping the entrepreneurs would shape the overseas colony into a profitable asset. The company's shareholders placed their money and their faith in the hands of merchants who pledged large profits and proclaimed their intent to Christianize the region's indigenous people.

During this stage of European exploration, the British were not alone in identifying religious conversion as a primary goal of colonization. Most seventeenth-century Christians considered non-Christians uncivilized pagans in desperate need of Christian salvation and a subsequent imposition of European cultural norms. Their beliefs were rooted in the religiously inspired Crusades between western Christendom and Muslims that began in the eleventh century, with the aim of reclaiming the Holy Land. Generally, Europeans viewed the process of colonization as beneficial to all participants involved. The majority of the British colonizers who settled Jamestown belonged to the Anglican Church of England. They understood that proselytizing and profit making were tandem goals of British colonization. However, in practice, Virginia's early Christians spent more of their energy and efforts struggling to survive than preaching for conversion. In 1624 King James I, frustrated with the Virginia Company's mismanagement of the colony, proclaimed Virginia a royal colony and replaced company officials with men of his own choosing. In addition, the king recognized the Anglican Church of England as the colony's prominent religious institution and mandated that all settlers support the church with taxes. Thereafter, Anglican authorities expected their colonial ministers and Virginia's ruling planter class to promote Christianity among their indentured servants and slaves.

Prior to the king's intervention, the Virginia Company of London planned to strategically manage the colony's economic growth. The intent was to export settlers trained in assorted occupations, who would then build and sustain a diverse economy capable of producing stable dividends for investors. However, Virginia was an ocean away in a time of limited means of communication, and the colony's large landholders had their own ideas regarding growth and economics. Virginia planters rejected a diverse economy and instead focused their efforts on the production of a single crop, tobacco. In the seventeenth century tobacco was a popular commodity in Europe. Within a decade of the founding of Jamestown, the tobacco produced by Virginia planters was selling in British and European markets. By the 1620s tobacco planters, motivated by strong sales of the product in European markets, focused their efforts on increased production. Initially, tobacco sales returned good profits for planters. That changed when England insisted the colonies restrict their trade to English markets alone. Britain's restrictive trade policies and an overabundance of tobacco created a glut in the market. By 1660 the price of

Time Line

1606

- King James I of England grants the Virginia Company of London a land charter in North America.

1607

- **May 13**
  Jamestown, Virginia, is settled by English traders.

1619

- **August**
  A Dutch trading vessel arrives in Jamestown, and twenty Africans are sold into slavery.

- **July 30**
  The House of Burgesses convenes in Jamestown.

1624

- The Virginia Company loses its charter, and Virginia is proclaimed a royal colony.

- **March 24**
  The Anglican Church of England is recognized as the colony's dominant denomination.

1640

- **January**
  The House of Burgesses decrees that blacks cannot carry arms.

1641

- Massachusetts legalizes slavery.

1642

- In Virginia, harboring and assisting an escaped slave are ruled criminal acts.

- **March**
  The House of Burgesses passes a tax on black female slaves at a rate comparable to that for male servants thus giving their owners an economic incentive to send them into the tobacco fields to maximize their own gains.

1660

- Virginia legalizes slavery.

1662

- **December**
  Virginia's House of Burgesses makes slavery hereditary according to the mother's status.

---

tobacco would decline to such low levels that most tobacco planters would spend more years coping with debts than being economically solvent. This turnabout in market prices and reduced profits would leave tobacco planters committed to maintaining a cheap source of labor.

The fact that tobacco is an agricultural product grown in rural environments hindered the development of urban centers in the Virginia colony. The colony's large landholders established independent communities on their tobacco plantations and relied on indentured servants and slaves to fashion the necessities of everyday life. Although the Virginia Company of London set out to build a colony sustained by a stable and diverse economy, many of the early colonial tradesmen and artisans encouraged to settle in Jamestown returned to Britain complaining that they could not find work in their chosen fields. Virginia's economic identity developed into a plantation system of production, and the tobacco planters shared a common goal, to obtain and keep a large labor force at minimum cost in order to secure profits. To meet that goal they looked to three possible sources of labor: They enslaved Native Americans, appealed to the Virginia Company for more indentured servants, and copied the method used by British planters in the Caribbean colonies of Jamaica and Barbados, the increased importation of enslaved West Africans.

British colonials discovered that sustaining a large labor force from enslaved Native Americans was difficult and deadly. Foremost, Native Americans died in staggering numbers from exposure to devastating European diseases. Second, enslaved Native Americans, familiar with the region's natural resources and geographical terrain, proved to be successful runaways who were rarely recaptured. Finally, since their earliest encounters, British colonials considered the indigenous people of the Chesapeake region to be savage and inferior beings. Misunderstandings related to cultural differences and language barriers often ended in acts of violent aggression by both parties. In 1622 a confederation of Native Americans came together and attacked Jamestown, leaving more than three hundred inhabitants dead. Although the attack did not drive the British out of Virginia, it did teach the lesson that Native Americans, if united, were powerful enough to challenge the colony's survival. Colonial tobacco planters turned to their second source for labor and urged company officials in England to supply the great numbers of laborers necessary for successful tobacco production.

The Virginia Company distributed pamphlets and posters advertising Virginia as a land of opportunity. The timing proved advantageous, as Britain's population had increased disproportionate to its economy in the sixteenth century. This uneven growth continued until the middle of the seventeenth century and left in its wake a large class of unemployed and poverty-stricken British citizens. In exchange for their passage, shelter, and food, many of them signed labor contracts and arrived in Virginia as indentured servants bound to a master for a specific number of years. The British government also sanctioned the shipping of convicted criminals and political prisoners to its British colonies for the purpose of serving out their sentences. With this large influx of laborers, Virginia's planter class could now meet their labor demands.

Throughout the first half of the seventeenth century, the majority of colonial laborers were white indentured servants. Gradually, the steady stream of indentured servants arriving from England slowed in relationship to its economic prosperity and political stability. Over the years, merchants and sailors carried stories of the colony's famines, sicknesses, and deadly conflicts with Native Americans back to England. Their tales refuted the lure of opportunity and discouraged laborers from signing indentures. Britain's colonial holdings were successfully supplying resources and creating markets for English goods. As a result, English laborers could now find jobs in England instead of seeking opportunities in distant colonies. The diminished supply of white indentured servants persuaded tobacco planters to use their third possible source for labor, enslaved West Africans.

Initially, black slaves appeared randomly in small numbers during Virginia's early years. Most of them were transported to the colony either because they were considered unfit for sugar production in the Caribbean or to fulfill a specific request for slaves of a certain age or gender. Often pirates smuggled slaves into the colony, hoping to turn a quick profit. After they were sold, enslaved West Africans worked shoulder to shoulder with whites and small numbers of Native Americans. When the day's work was done, social contact among this diverse labor force spilled over into their private lives and, by extension, into the lives of their communities.

At this time the social order in Virginia was divided by class, not race. Economic assets and royal pedigrees determined a person's status in the community. Under this system Virginia's most marginalized class was the landless working class of indentured servants and slaves. Away from work, in their private worlds, this mix of people created friendships, engaged in recreational activities, maintained intimate relations, married, and had children. While struggling to survive colonial hardships, they found common bonds they could share. As time went on, former servants and some slaves who acquired their freedom through various means carved out new lives for themselves in the colonial wilderness. Although class boundaries were apparent in the first half of the seventeenth century, white legislators had not yet cemented racial boundaries into legal statutes. A small number of blacks managed to take advantage of the fluidity and became small landholding farmers of the yeoman class with servants and slaves of their own. Their successes demonstrated to enslaved blacks that opportunities existed if they could find a way out of slavery.

West Africans of various ethnicities understood slavery through their own life experiences. While slavery in any form is rarely a desirable state of existence, West African norms permitted slaves, over time, to assimilate into their enslaver's extended family unit either through marriage or by proving themselves to be extremely valuable assets. That is not to say that all slaves in West African societies had such opportunities; it is just an acknowledgment that the

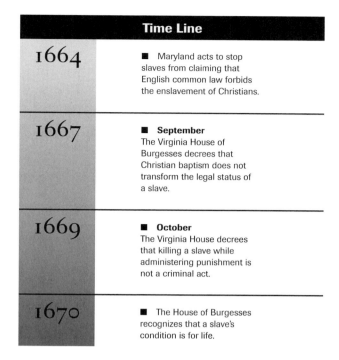

slaves of early colonial Virginia came from a world where to be enslaved was not necessarily a life sentence. Enslaved blacks surely found the conditions of servitude in Virginia harsh and at times unbearable, as evidenced by their regular efforts to resist their enslavement. One means of resistance repeatedly documented was to challenge the legality of captivity by petitioning the colony's courts for freedom. In the first half of the seventeenth century, the possibility of successfully maneuvering through and out of the permeable boundaries of slavery still existed. Choosing to convert to Christianity was one of the paths black slaves hoped would lead to freedom.

White Anglican ministers were generally unsuccessful at persuading blacks to abandon their chosen faith and embrace Christian ideals. Most enslaved West Africans arrived in the Western Hemisphere practicing Islam or one of the many indigenous faiths of their homelands. They demonstrated little interest in adopting the faith of the white planter class that held them in bondage and governed the colony. Still, small numbers of black slaves did accept the sacrament of baptism and converted to Christianity. Their reasons for doing so are explained by colonial court records that detail petitions filed by blacks who challenged their legal status as slaves, arguing it was unlawful, under English common law, to enslave a fellow Christian. For those slaves, adopting the religion of one's master was simply a means to an end and little different from wearing European dress or learning to speak English. Freedom was their ultimate goal, and, drawing on their West African understanding of slavery, assimilation was their means.

As fellow Christians, enslaved blacks believed they shared a common bond with their owners, a bond that they could use as a path to freedom. Baptism was a documented event, written into church ledgers and sometimes baptismal

Cultivation of tobacco in colonial Virginia (AP/Wide World Photos)

certificates. The ceremony's rituals and subsequent recording lent an air of validation to the act; it also presented the possibility of entering into something more than the state of enslavement. The process of conversion was a public invitation into a community of believers who shared ceremonial and spiritual bonds. As communal members, enslaved blacks felt justified in challenging their legal status. The colonial courts and legislators were faced with a dilemma. Some slaves had already won their freedom by proving they were Christians. If that trend continued, it was likely that slaves throughout Virginia might join the Anglican Church in record numbers. In addition, awarding freedom for conversion acknowledged equality, at least in the sphere of religion. That could set a precedent for equality in colonial political and economic institutions.

Virginia's white legislators were not alone in their struggle to define a legal relationship between conversion and bondage. Maryland's legislators ruled on the issue in 1664. In many British colonies, legislators were dealing with judicial challenges from enslaved blacks who were seeking legal loopholes for gaining their freedom. Virginia's legisla-

tors ruled in 1667 that converting to Christianity through the sacrament of baptism did not change the legal status of a slave. Their decision echoed the choice made by legislators in Maryland. Through that ruling, Virginia's lawmakers created two distinct categories of Christians, free and enslaved. That black slaves living in the colony understood the path to freedom through conversion was closed is evident in the low numbers of slaves who converted to Christianity over the next five decades. The majority of black slaves generally avoided Christianity until the middle of the eighteenth century, when evangelical Protestants interjected some semblance of equality into the religious practices of the First Great Awakening.

About the Author

The white men who voted to legalize the 1667 Virginia statute regarding slavery and Christian conversion were members of the House of Burgesses. The governing body was the first representative political assembly established in

"It is enacted and declared by this grand assembly, and the authority thereof, that the conferring of baptism doth not alter the condition of the person as to his bondage or freedom."

a British colony. In 1619 the General Assembly convened for its initial session in Jamestown, Virginia. The political body consisted of a governor and several appointed council members selected by the officials of the Virginia Company of London. In addition, individual settlements in the colony were permitted to send two elected representatives called burgesses to Jamestown. Only landholding freemen were allowed to vote for the burgesses. For most of its existence, the men who served in the colonial assembly shared common bonds of wealth and race. In 1624 the colony's representative government was placed under royal control, and the governor and council members were chosen by the king. Although certain historical events in England influenced the development of the colonial governing body, the impact was minimal owing to the geographical distance. In general, the House of Burgesses independently shaped the colony's legal, economic, and social foundations. The representative assembly was also responsible for drafting membership requirements and regulating the colony's tax system. In 1776, during the American Revolution, the House of Burgesses evolved into the Virginia House of Delegates.

Explanation and Analysis of the Document

When the British crossed the Atlantic Ocean and claimed what they considered a new world, they arrived with their cultural norms intact. The negative relationships they constructed with coastal Native Americans exposed their long-held views of English superiority. Furthermore, that sense of entitlement or ethnocentrism also tainted their dealings with free and enslaved colonial blacks. An examination of Virginia's earliest records reveals that before legislators recognized slavery as a legal institution, whites had various ways of marking blacks as a different class of people. The clerks who wrote in the census books identified blacks by name and race. There were no racial identities given for white settlers, only names. In several court cases where black and white individuals were convicted of committing the same crime, white judges sentenced blacks to harsher physical punishments. Gradually, blacks were identified in legal records using only their first names, as if their surnames were somehow irrelevant and unnecessary.

Masters marked black female slaves as being different from white female servants by assigning only black females to work in the tobacco fields. In small increments whites labeled blacks as second-rate and unusual in a negative way. As time passed, the social contact and sexual intimacy that was so ordinary between black and white laborers in the colony's early years ended. Instead, sexual relationships between the races drew condemnation and social ostracism for whites and physical punishments for blacks. British ethnocentrism reached its legal pinnacle in Virginia in 1669 when the House of Burgesses declared no criminal charges would be filed against a master who killed a slave while administering punishment. Clearly, whites had decided that blacks were disposable commodities. All of the actions mentioned—certainly not a complete list—leave little doubt that most white colonials considered West Africans to be inferior creatures and structured the social norms of Virginia society to ensure white racial supremacy.

Thus, in the first half of the seventeenth century, whites consolidated their control over the lives of free and enslaved blacks. Blacks responded with determined will and crafted overt and covert means of resistance. Too often the success of their challenges was curbed by their limited access to political and economic power. Repeatedly, the steps taken by the colony's legislators demonstrate their actions were responses to enslaved blacks who persisted in pressing for liberty. In 1656 Elizabeth Key petitioned the courts for her liberty on the ground that she had inherited the free status of her father. Key also let it be known that she was a Christian. Traditionally, English common law validated paternal hereditary claims and supported the enslavement of non-Christians who were identified as infidels. Elizabeth Key was not the only slave in the colony who thought being Christian offered an opportunity for freedom.

Conversion to Christianity was an open door to freedom that legislators decidedly closed and, in that process, continued their pattern of legally ensuring a sizable supply of inexpensive labor for tobacco production. Simultaneously, the act encouraged slaveholders to Christianize slaves while reaffirming the Crown's intent to build Christian colonies. With the passage of the 1667 statute, Virginia's burgesses reminded the colony's slaveholding taxpayers that they were expected to contribute to more than just the fiscal support of the colonial Anglican Church, something they had done through taxes since 1624. The law regarding the baptism of slaves called for the "propagation" of new members. The act identified slaveholders as additional sources to share the responsibility for the religious training and conversion of black slaves. Slaveholders were expected to seed the growing colony with Christian laborers obedient to their masters.

Audience

The statutes passed by the House of Burgesses were legal measures designed to regulate and control the various groups of people living in the colony. The statute on baptism passed by the colonial assembly in 1667 was directed at slaveholders and constructed judiciary restraints designed to legally clarify that religious rites of passage carried no legitimate secular weight. Since newspapers did not appear in the Virginia colony until the eighteenth century, the majority of its inhabitants would have learned of the 1667 statute through verbal means. Although some colonists corresponded through letters, most colonists shared their news by discussing various topics in taverns, shops, and churches. News from the colonial legislature was also carried from farm to farm by merchants, family, and friends.

Impact

Prior to 1667, masters hesitated to convert their slaves, owing to the uncertainty concerning whether baptism altered a slave's legal status. The ruling of the General Assembly finally cleared the ambiguity surrounding conversion. During the second half of the seventeenth century and forward, Anglican ministers continued to encourage masters to convert slaves, arguing that Christianity would make a slave humble, obedient, and less likely to dispute enslavement. The Church of England, like most Christian institutions at that time, found no contradiction between slavery and Christian principles. Once slave owners understood that conversion was not a threat and, at its best, might be a tool to strengthen their control over slaves, they encouraged slaves to convert. In addition, the ruling offered greater financial security to tobacco planters, in that it protected their investments. Every time colonial legislators passed a law that benefited a slave owner, they were encouraging the expansion of Virginia's slave population.

For enslaved blacks the 1667 statute regarding conversion was yet one more obstacle Virginia legislators designed and implemented to preserve the colony's supply of cheap labor. By the second half of the seventeenth century it was apparent to colonial blacks, both free and enslaved, that the political power in Virginia rested with the large landholders, who were also the lawmakers. The choices made by planters in the colony's founding years to reject a diverse economy in favor of quick returns from the lone crop of tobacco set the stage for the birth of institutionalized slavery in Virginia. Through the remainder of the century the House of Burgesses continued to pass restrictive laws that marginalized West Africans and their African American descendants. Such laws must have been discouraging to enslaved blacks, but the laws failed to stop them from pursuing alternate avenues to freedom. Throughout Britain's North American colonies, enslaved blacks continued to petition courts for their liberty while simultaneously resisting and refusing to assimilate into the inferior identities that were crafted for them by colonial whites. British ethnocentrism defined the roles that the historical actors would play in a drama full of human suffering and freedom struggles that did not end until the American Civil War.

See also John Rolfe's Letter to Sir Edwin Sandys (1619/1620); Virginia's Act XII: Negro Women's Children to Serve according to the Condition of the Mother (1662).

Questions for Further Study

1. In what specific ways did agriculture in the Virginia colony contribute to the development of the slave system and the social system that supported it?

2. In its early years, the Virginia colony was marked by dissension, mismanagement, and other assorted ills. Using this document in conjunction with John Rolfe's Letter to Sir Edwin Sandys, outline the problems Virginia faced and how the authorities tried to solve them.

3. What social circumstances involving indentured servants, Indians, and slaves in early Virginia led to Virginia's Act III: Baptism Does Not Exempt Slaves from Bondage?

4. What factors entered into the Virginia House of Burgesses' deliberations about the relationship between bondage and conversion to Christianity?

Further Reading

■ Books

Adams, Francis D., and Barry Sanders. *Alienable Rights: The Exclusion of African Americans in a White Man's Land, 1619–2000*. New York: HarperCollins, 2003.

Higginbotham, A. Leon, Jr. *Shades of Freedom: Racial Politics and Presumptions of the American Legal Process*. New York: Oxford University Press, 1996.

Morgan, Edmund S. *American Slavery, American Freedom: The Ordeal of Colonial Virginia*. New York: W. W. Norton, 2003.

Woods, Betty. *The Origins of American Slavery: Freedom and Bondage in the English Colonies*. New York: Hill and Wang, 1997.

■ Web Sites

"Slavery and the Law in Virginia." Colonial Williamsburg Web site. http://www.history.org/History/teaching/slavelaw.cfm.

"The Terrible Transformation." PBS's "Africans in America" Web site. http://www.pbs.org/wgbh/aia/part1/title.html.

"The Virginia Company of London." National Park Service "Historic Jamestowne" Web site.
http://www.nps.gov/jame/historyculture/the-virginia-company-of-london.htm.

—Mary Lou Walsh

Virginia's Act III: Baptism Does Not Exempt Slaves from Bondage

Whereas some doubts have arisen whether children that are slaves by birth, and by the charity and piety of their owners made partakers of the blessed sacrament of baptism, should by virtue of their baptism be made free; It is enacted and declared by this grand assembly, and the authority thereof, that the conferring of baptism doth not alter the condition of the person as to his bondage or freedom; that diverse masters, freed from this doubt, may more carefully endeavor the propagation of Christianity by permitting children, though slaves, or those of greater growth if capable to be admitted to that sacrament.

Bas-relief of Francis Pastorius (Library of Congress)

"A Minute against Slavery, Addressed to Germantown Monthly Meeting"

"Is there any that would be ...

sold or made a slave for all the time of his life?"

Overview

On February 18, 1688, Quakers met in Germantown, Pennsylvania, located about five miles northwest of Philadelphia, and issued the first known statement in British North America proclaiming the evils of slavery and urging the abolition of the institution. The petition, titled "A Minute against Slavery, Addressed to Germantown Monthly Meeting," raised points that would become the basis for eighteenth-century arguments for the abolition of slavery: It violated the Golden Rule, to do unto others as you would have done to you; it was theft; it inspired the growth of vices such as adultery and caused family dissolution; it detracted from the humanity of the owner; and it presented the constant threat of insurrection and rebellion by those enslaved.

The members of the Germantown Monthly Meeting drafted the resolutions in accordance with their interpretations of the belief system governing Quakers throughout the colony. Part of the most radical faction of the Protestant Reformation, Quakers acknowledge the primacy of following the divine presence known as the Inner Light and, as a consequence, relegate man-made dogmas and rites to lesser significance. The group also adheres to the concept of the "brotherhood" of all individuals and the basic equality of all souls. Finally, they agree that individuals can and should work to remove all taint of sin from their souls and their lives while on earth. The significance of their beliefs and their desire to put into practice what they preach is evident in the Germantown Quakers' statements condemning slavery.

Context

The colony in which the Germantown protesters lived was unique in many ways. Pennsylvania, meaning "Penn's Woods," owed its existence to William Penn (1644–1718) and his plans for a "Holy Experiment." Penn, a member of the English elite and the son of Admiral Sir William Penn, became enamored of radical Protestant theology at the University of Oxford and converted to Quakerism at the age of twenty-three under the guidance of Thomas

Loe, an itinerant Quaker minister. The Religious Society of Friends, or Quakers, had organized in England during the Commonwealth period (when England was governed by Oliver Cromwell as Lord Protector rather than a king), around the spiritual teaching of George Fox, to emerge as an identifiable entity in 1652. Similar to other Anabaptist sects appearing in Europe at the same time, the Friends emphasized deep personal and spiritual connections to God, the brotherhood of all humans, pacifism, and the possibility that individuals could achieve grace and perfection of the soul while on earth. Quakers, Mennonites, Moravians, Dutch and German Reformists, and pietistic Lutherans, among others, reject Trinitarian doctrines (belief in the unity of three persons in one god), the validity of man-made dogmas and creeds, and an organized clergy. In most places, with the exception of the Netherlands, Anabaptists were deemed heretics and persecuted on that basis.

Penn, who was politically protected by his status and family connections, recognized the vulnerability of those less fortunate than he and sought to provide safe refuge for persecuted believers. In 1681 he used his ties to the British Crown to acquire a proprietary grant for the territory west of the Delaware River in exchange for a debt of £16,000 owed to his father, and on February 28, 1681, Charles II signed the Charter for the Province of Pennsylvania. Penn clearly understood the similarities and common plight of Quakers and other Anabaptist communities in mainland Europe, and he recruited heavily among them for immigrants to his "Holy Experiment." By 1685 nearly eight thousand religious dissenters had joined Penn's colonial venture. His plan called for broad-based religious toleration and the disestablishment of the church from the state. This made his colony particularly attractive to radical reformers in the Rhineland region, whence the settlers destined for Germantown originated. The disassociation of faith from the structures of governance—combined with the general lack of religious uniformity and the Quakers' and other Anabaptists' emphasis on the Inner Light and independent searching for answers and moral guidance—brought about a colonial system where community morality was adjudicated by civil rather than religious authorities, and individuals were charged with the responsibility of moving their communities toward moral and ethical ideals.

Time Line

1681

■ **February 28**
King Charles II signs the Charter for the Province of Pennsylvania, which William Penn intends to be a safe haven for those suffering religious persecution.

1683

■ **May–June** The Frankfort Land Company, organized by German Pietists with Francis Daniel Pastorius as their agent, purchases land from Penn.

■ **October**
A number of original immigrants, including Pastorius and the Opden Graff brothers, arrive in Germantown, Pennsylvania.

■ The Germantown Quaker meeting is organized and begins gathering in local homes.

1685

■ Gerhard Henderich immigrates with his family to Germantown.

1688

■ **February 18**
Antislavery resolutions, signed by Pastorius, Henderich, and Derick and Abram Opden Graff, are issued as "A Minute against Slavery, Addressed to the Germantown Monthly Meeting."

1692–1694

■ The Keithian schism splits the Quaker meetings of Pennsylvania and drives many adherents from the faith, including many of the Germantown cohort.

Despite the fact that the residents of Germantown were inhabitants of an Anglo-American colony established by royal charter, the members of their community and their meeting were not English but rather German and Dutch. The immigrants to the community consisted in large part of pietistic Germans recruited by the Frankfort Land Company, established in 1683, and of Germans and Dutch Quakers organized separately from the town of Krefeld, in the Rhineland region, along the border between the German principalities and the Netherlands. The groups' acknowledged leader, Francis Daniel Pastorius, a pietistic Lutheran, represented the Frankfort Land Company as its legal agent and was the only member of the company to venture to Pennsylvania. He organized and recruited many of the original settlers and collaborated heavily with the Krefeld contingent; he was thus in many ways the architect of the company's Germantown settlement. They had dual goals for their experiment: They sought both to establish a spiritual and physical haven for other radical religious reformers and to ensure the success of their financial investment.

Between 1683 and 1690 the stable core of the Germantown community consisted of the households of thirteen of the original Krefelders—twelve of whom were Quakers. Earlier scholarship suggested that the composition of this cohort was Mennonite, a version of German Anabaptists, in origin, but more recent evidence indicates that they were not Mennonite at this time; although several would abandon Quakerism for Mennonite ideals after the schism led by George Keith in 1692, during the 1680s they were professing Quakers. Shortly after their immigration to the colony and by the end of 1683, the leaders of the Germantown community organized their own Quaker meeting under the guidance of Pastorius. The group affiliated with the larger Philadelphia Monthly Meeting during 1684 and with the Abington Quarterly Meeting, located in New Jersey and the oldest and superior meeting of the region, by 1688.

When the Quaker meeting at Germantown issued "A Minute against Slavery, Addressed to Germantown Monthly Meeting" in 1688, the group operated within a societal framework that was for the seventeenth century remarkably flexible and heterogeneous. In Germantown alone, there resided individuals hailing from several distinct German and Dutch communities as well as English immigrants. Virtually all of the inhabitants practiced some form of radical Protestantism; there were German Lutheran Pietists, German Reformists, and Dutch and English Quakers.

About the Author

While the antislavery resolutions were intended as a general statement from the Quaker meeting at Germantown to the affiliate Dublin Monthly Meeting, it was signed by four specific members of the group: Gerhard (or as signed in the text, "Garret") Henderich, Derick Opden Graff ("up de Graeff"), Francis Daniel ("daniell") Pastorius, and Abram Opden Graff ("Abraham up Den graef"). Pastorius, perhaps the most famous of the quartet, represented the interests of the Frankfort Land Company. The two Opden Graffs were part of the original Krefeld contingent, while Henderich arrived in 1685.

Pastorius, the son of a burgher, was born in 1651 and grew up in an urban and commercial atmosphere. He attended four universities and was well traveled. By the 1680s he was practicing law in Frankfurt am Main. Pastorius was familiar with William Penn even before his arrival in Pennsylvania, having frequently served as the liaison between the residents of Germantown and the colony's bureaucratic structures. He also became well acquainted with the colony leaders David Lloyd and James Logan, and he shared their vision of Pennsylvania as a commercial and mercantile venture. Similarly, he recognized the value of Pennsylvania as a refuge for western Europe's most radical Protestant reformers, the Anabaptists. Pastorius encouraged the inhabitants of Germantown to adapt to their new environment. He suggested that his fellow immigrants learn and practice English, familiarize themselves with English laws and systems of governance, and intermingle with the larger English population of the colony. Pastorius played a leading role in the organization and recognition of the Germantown Monthly Meeting and actively encouraged its correspondence and affiliation with others throughout the region. He continued to serve as spokesperson and promoter for Germantown and the larger colony until his death in 1720.

Derick and Abram Opden Graff were two of three brothers who emigrated from Krefeld to Germantown in July 1683. According to the contract negotiated in Rotterdam between William Penn and Jacob Telner, Jan Streypers, and Dirck Sipman on March 10, 1683, the proprietor promised the signers five thousand acres of land each in exchange for a guarantee of settlement. The Opden Graff trio received two thousand acres of land from Telner, after the contract was signed. The third brother, Herman, agreed to act as agent for Sipman, another Krefeld landholder who never ventured to Pennsylvania. Later that summer, Derick, Abram, and Herman Opden Graff, along with thirty other Krefelders closely tied by blood and marriage, immigrated to Pennsylvania. The brothers were among the original membership of the Germantown Quaker meeting organized later that year and housed by 1686 in the Kirchlein, a log meetinghouse.

Gerhard Henderich is the member of the group about which the littlest is known. He arrived in Germantown in 1685 on either the *Francis* or the *Dorothy* along with a number of other German and Dutch immigrants. Henderich, accompanied by his wife, Mary, and daughter, Sarah, originated in Krisheim, a community near Krefeld on the Dutch side of the border. Claiming two hundred acres purchased from Sipman upon his arrival, he was by 1688 a substantial member of the Germantown community. As a Dutch Quaker, he, too, aligned himself with the heterogeneous Quaker meeting at Germantown. By 1692, Derick and Abram Opden Graff had parted ways as the consequence of a larger religious controversy, the Keithian schism, which debated the corruption of Quakers in Pennsylvania by secular concerns. Abram, aligning with the Keithians, left Germantown for Perkiomen, the Dutch township. In 1704 Abram Opden Graff, as the last surviving of the brothers, sold the remaining 828 acres of land in Germantown. Of Henderich there is little mention after 1693, when he was recorded on a Germantown tax list.

Explanation and Analysis of the Document

The Germantown Quakers' Monthly Meeting felt an obligation to protest against what they perceived as immo-

William Penn (Library of Congress)

rality surrounding them. The Rhinelanders, coming from a situation in Europe in which they were actively hounded and disenfranchised for their beliefs, were particularly sensitive to the plights of others they saw as mistreated simply on the basis of who they were. In creating "A Minute against Slavery" they acted in accord with their belief system, which requires Quakers to seek independent answers to pressing social issues, to strive for moral perfection, and to abjure violence.

The authors of the Germantown protest—Pastorius, the Opden Graffs, and Henderich—open their statement with the title "A Minute against Slavery, Addressed to Germantown Monthly Meeting." Here, *minute* refers to a formal record of matters of importance to the writers, often for a superior audience and especially in the context of a meeting. In this case, the authors drafted a statement of their arguments against slavery at the Germantown Monthly Meeting, for formal presentation at the regional Monthly Meeting held at Richard Worrell's house in Dublin Township, Bucks County. The authors proceed to voice their protests against slavery and to present evidence supporting their points. Their prefatory statement, "These are the reasons why we are against the traffick of men-body," clearly indicates their intent: They oppose the selling, buying, and use of human beings as slaves.

The first point raised by the Germantown protesters echoes the Golden Rule. They ask their audience, "Is there any that would be done or handled at this man-

"Is there any that would be done or handled at this manner? viz., to be sold or made a slave for all the time of his life?"

(Paragraph 1)

"Now, tho they are black, we can not conceive there is more liberty to have them slaves, as it is to have other white ones. There is a saying that we shall doe to all men like as we will be done ourselves; making no difference of what generation, descent or colour they are."

(Paragraph 1)

"In Europe there are many oppressed for conscience sake; and here there are those oppressed who are of a black colour."

(Paragraph 1)

"Pray, what thing in the world can be done worse towards us, than if men should rob or steal us away, and sell us for slaves to strange countries; separating husbands from their wives and children. Being now that this is not done in the manner we would be done at therefore we contradict and are against this traffic of men-body."

(Paragraph 1)

ner? viz., to be sold or made a slave for all the time of his life?" In other words, they ask their fellow colonists how many of them would appreciate being taken and sold into permanent bondage without their consent. They remind their readers of the fear inspired by the Turks and their practice of taking Christian captives in eastern Europe and around the Mediterranean basin, and they ask if Africans facing the same danger should feel less terror or believe themselves less wronged. A bit later in the document the authors will return to this theme, suggesting that the racial origin of slaves should not be a factor in determining the morality of enslaving others. Here they affirm,

Now, tho they are black, we can not conceive there is more liberty to have them slaves, as it is to have other white ones. There is a saying that we shall doe to all men like as we will be done ourselves; making no difference of what generation, descent or colour they are.

Thus the Germantowners explicitly invoke the Golden Rule and make reference to issues of race and equality, emphasizing the obligation to treat others, no matter how different, as they themselves would wish to be treated. They return to this point a final time in drawing a very specific comparison between the plight of those abused for the nature of their faiths—"for conscience sake"—in Europe and the plight of "those oppressed who are of a black colour" in America.

Next the protesters turn to two issues they perceive as threats to the morality of the enslavers: their participation in theft and the temptations of vice. Opening their argument on this point, they characterize those who take slaves as thieves and those who purchase the captives as accomplices, stating, "And those who steal or robb men, and those who buy or purchase them, are they not all alike?" The Germantowners suggest that in Pennsylvania there is "liberty of Conscience," or freedom of faith, as well as freedom of "body"; thus, to steal and sell the body of a person without consent is a sin that they, the members of the meeting at Germantown, must oppose. Later in the opening paragraph they return to this point and emphasize their obligation to stop such behavior, contending, "And we who profess that it is not lawful to steal, must, likewise, avoid to purchase such things as are stolen, but rather help to stop this robbing and stealing if possible." Here, their argument reaches its most radical and far-reaching point. They continue by suggesting, in accord with Christian obligation, not only that the trafficking of human beings should be stopped but also that the unlawfully enslaved "ought to be delivered out of ye hands of ye robbers, and set free" everywhere. This is a clear denunciation of the slave trade and of slavery in general; it is a call to abolition.

In the course of the first paragraph, the authors also worry about the exposure of their brethren to other vices, in particular those associated with the sanctity of marriage and the family. They argue that slavery presents the opportunity for adultery. They specifically cite the evils of "separating wives from their husbands and giving them to others." They also refer to the consequences of family dissolution imposed when the offspring of slaves are sold away from their parents. The petitioners warn their audience that Christians ought not do such things, not simply because they are sins but also because those actions damage the image of the colony and threaten the morality of the whole Pennsylvania enterprise.

The Germantown protesters proceed to question both the inhumanity of slavery and the appearance of their colony in the eyes of the larger world should they permit the institution to flourish within their boundaries. They challenge the morality of all who engage in the institution of slavery, condemning not only those who own slaves and profit from their unlawful labors but also those who join in the buying and selling of slaves. The petitioners then point out that Europeans pay attention to the residents of the colonies and judge their behaviors, and they ask what the nature of European opinions will be when "they hear of, that ye Quakers doe here handel men as they handel there ye cattle." The Germantowners then profess doubt regarding any possible defense against such judgments. In their eyes, slavery violates the most basic of Christian tenets—treat others as you wish to be treated—and they can find no way to "maintain this your cause, or pleid for it." They also imply that colonists who participate in slavery exceed the European evils of religious and political oppression through their sinful treatment of their fellow men. Drawing on their own experiences, they suggest to those Christians engaged in slavery, "You surpass Holland and Germany in this thing"—in the mistreatment of their fellow human beings. The protesters close the opening paragraph with clear opposition to the reduction of Africans to objects to be bought and sold and used as chattel. Referring to how morality is skewed by the presence of slavery in society, they state in closing, "Europeans are desirous to know in what manner ye Quakers doe rule in their province;—and most of them doe look upon us with an envious eye. But if this is done well, what shall we say is done evil?"

The second paragraph of the protest contains a warning of a different sort, one that is nearly prophetic in its content. It is a statement concerning the ongoing dangers of holding men in bondage against their wills. The Germantowners here assume the slaveholders' arguments and turn them against those who employ slaves. Owners, supporting permanent bondage of Africans, voice the notion that their slaves represent the basest of all human beings and need to be enslaved. The authors thus ask what would stop these "wicked and stubbern men" from aggressively seeking their liberty and thereupon using "their masters and mastrisses as they did handel them before." The authors go on to ask slaveholders if they would then rebel against the injustice of permanent servitude, wondering, "have these negers not as much right to fight for their freedom, as you have to keep them slaves?" These questions touch on the deepest fears of slave owners and foreshadow the slave rebellions brewing on the horizon. The Germantowners are furthermore expressing concerns over the bearing of arms in response to the threat of revolt. Ingrained in the Quaker belief system is a commitment to pacifism. The petitioners question the ability of slave-owning Quakers to resist the temptation of defending themselves, by taking "the sword at hand," in the case of an insurrection.

The argument closes in the third paragraph with a formal request to be informed of the regional meeting's findings concerning their protests. In good Quaker fashion, they state, "And in case you find it to be good to handle these blacks at that manner, we desire and require you hereby lovingly, that you may inform us herein." They do not demand that their counterparts, meeting at Richard Worrell's house in Dublin, support their cause but rather request that the members of the Dublin Meeting search their consciences and report their findings. They note that up to this point no religious authority had defined the Christian legitimacy of slavery; thus, they in Germantown needed guidance and answers to their questions. They also hoped to calm the fears of their brethren back in their "natif country"—that is, both Germany and Holland—"to whose it is a terror, or fairful thing, that men should be handeld so in Pennsylvania."

"A Minute against Slavery" concludes as it begins, by formally addressing the protests to the next regional Monthly Meeting at Worrell's house. The four signers of the document—Henderich, Pastorius, and the two Opden Graff brothers—follow in no particular order and with no reference to rank or status within Germantown. This presentation is very Quakerly, in that it privileges none of the participants and so emphasizes their equality. The four were, perhaps, more important for what they represented about their community. Although not indicated in the document, Pastorius's name carried considerable weight beyond Germantown, and any petition from the community without his support would have been treated with greater suspicion. The other signers represented the diversity of Germantown and its possible factions. The Opden Graffs were German in origin and among the first wave of colonists. Henderich represented the Dutch voices in the meeting and was a fairly recent arrival. Together the men embodied the larger population of their community.

Audience

The intended audiences of "A Minute against Slavery" were the Monthly, Quarterly, and Yearly Meetings of Pennsylvania and New Jersey with which the Germantown Quakers' meeting was affiliated. In the document itself, the Germantowners address themselves specifically to the "Monthly Meeting held at Richard Worrell's." This gathering at Dublin, in Bucks County farther north of Philadelphia, had been settled in the initial movement to the colony, and its residents came primarily from the British Isles. They reviewed the Germantown petition on February 30, 1688, and chose not to act on it but rather to forward it to the Quarterly Meeting with which they were affiliated. Their response, signed by P. Joseph Hart, states, "We find it so weighty that we think it not expedient for us to meddle with it here, but do rather commit it to ye consideration of ye Quarterly meeting." On April 4, 1688, that meeting, lodged in Philadelphia, agreed on the gravity of the questions raised and in turn referred the protest to the Yearly Meeting to be held in Burlington, New Jersey, on July 5, 1688. The reaction of the meeting at Burlington is ambiguous. They recognize "a Paper being here presented by some German Friends Concerning the Lawfulness and Unlawfulness of Buying and keeping Negroes" and consider it "not to be so proper for this Meeting to give a Positive Judgment in the case, It having so General a Relation to many other Parts." That is, given their connections, commercial and personal, with slaveholding regions and individuals, they indefinitely tabled the petition.

There also existed a secondary audience for the resolution: those who in the following decades would read or refer to it. While the Germantown Quakers' immediate readers and listeners in the affiliate meetings might have rejected their petition by refusing to act upon it, the ideas that they put forth could not be permanently ignored.

Impact

The immediate impact of "A Minute against Slavery" was negligible. Those meetings petitioned by the Germantown cohort refused to act on the resolutions, instead passing the petition on to the succeeding affiliate meeting or, in the case of the Burlington meeting, postponing action on the measure. The protest did, however, foreshadow the wider emergence of antislavery sentiments in Pennsylvania's Quaker communities. By 1750 there would be at least fifteen such Anglo-American statements against slavery, nearly all authored by Quakers. The earliest of these succeeding statements was issued at a 1696 Yearly Meeting wherein the membership strongly discouraged engagement in the slave trade; in 1715 that same Pennsylvania body made participation in slavery an offense subjecting the member to expulsion from the meeting. While such an action had no legal standing, a Friend's exclusion from Quaker circles in Pennsylvania would have been a serious matter in the colonial era.

What is particularly interesting about the Germantown protest is how accurately the members defined what would become the most politically significant arguments against slavery. They drew on their belief system to construct the condemnation of an institution they considered morally and spiritually repugnant. Germantown's Quakers asked their fellow worshippers to acknowledge their own beliefs in the brotherhood of all humanity, in the obligation to strive for moral perfection, and in the Golden Rule. They also warned their audiences of the consequences of failure to join them in renouncing the institution of slavery: slave owners and holders invited and would suffer the approbation of their European counterparts, the burdens and temptations of sin, and the threat of rebellion.

See also John Woolman's *Some Considerations on the Keeping of Negroes* (1754).

Questions for Further Study

1. Why—and how—did the Quakers become the leaders of the abolitionist movement in the seventeenth and eighteenth centuries?

2. In what way was the Pennsylvania colony ethnically distinct from the other American colonies? How and why did this occur? What impact did this difference have, if any, on the early abolition movement?

3. On what basis did the men who signed the minute oppose slavery?

4. Why do you believe the audience for "A Minute against Slavery" refused to act on it?

5. Compare this document with John Woolman's *Some Considerations on the Keeping of Negroes* (1754). What similar arguments are made? How do the documents differ?

Further Reading

■ Articles

Aptheker, Herbert. "The Quakers and Negro Slavery." *Journal of Negro History* 25, no. 3 (July 1940): 331–362.

Binder-Johnson, Hildegard. "The Germantown Protest of 1688 against Negro Slavery." *Pennsylvania Magazine of History and Biography* 65, no. 2 (April 1941): 145–156.

Cadbury, Henry J. "An Early Quaker Anti-Slavery Statement." *Journal of Negro History* 22, no. 4 (October 1937): 488–493.

Eichhoff, Jürgen. "The Three Hundredth Anniversary of the Germantown Protest against Slavery." *Monatshefte* 80, no. 3 (Fall 1988): 265–267.

Pennypacker, Samuel W. "The Settlement of Germantown, and the Causes Which Led to It." *Pennsylvania Magazine of History and Biography* 4, no. 1 (1880): 1–41.

■ Books

Jordan, Winthrop D. *White over Black: American Attitudes toward the Negro, 1550–1812.* New York: W. W. Norton, 1977.

Shuffelton, Frank, ed. *A Mixed Race: Ethnicity in Early America.* New York: Oxford University Press, 1993.

Tolles, Frederick. *Meeting House and Counting House: The Quaker Merchants of Colonial Philadelphia, 1682–1763.* New York: W. W. Norton, 1948.

Wolf, Stephanie Grauman. *Urban Village: Population, Community, and Family Structure in Germantown, Pennsylvania, 1683–1800.* Princeton, N.J.: Princeton University Press, 1976.

■ Web Sites

"1688 Protest against Slavery, by German Mennonites and Quakers in Germantown, Pennyslvania." Quaker Information Center Web site.
http://www.quakerinfo.org/history/slavery.html.

"Excerpts from Frame of Government of Pennsylvania, by William Penn, 1682." Constitution Society Web site.
http://www.constitution.org/bcp/frampenn.htm.

"Francis Daniel Pastorius: Leader of Germantown Settlement." ushistory.org "Historic Germantown" Web site.
http://www.ushistory.org/Germantown/people/pastorius.htm.

—Martha Pallante

"A Minute against Slavery, Addressed to Germantown Monthly Meeting"

This is to ye Monthly Meeting held at Richard Worrell's

These are the reasons why we are against the traffick of men-body, as foloweth. Is there any that would be done or handled at this manner? viz., to be sold or made a slave for all the time of his life? How fearful and faint-hearted are many on sea, when they see a strange vessel,—being afraid it should be a Turk, and they should be taken, and sold for slaves into Turkey. Now what is this better done, as Turks doe? Yea, rather it is worse for them, which say they are Christians; for we hear that ye most part of such negers are brought hither against their will and consent, and that many of them are stolen. Now, tho they are black, we can not conceive there is more liberty to have them slaves, as it is to have other white ones. There is a saying that we shall doe to all men like as we will be done ourselves; making no difference of what generation, descent or colour they are. And those who steal or robb men, and those who buy or purchase them, are they not all alike? Here is liberty of conscience wch is right and reasonable; here ought to be liberty of ye body, except of evil-doers, wch is an other case. But to bring men hither, or to rob and sell them against their will, we stand against. In Europe there are many oppressed for conscience sake; and here there are those oppressed who are of a black colour. And we who know that men must not comitt adultery,—some do commit adultery, in separating wives from their husbands and giving them to others; and some sell the children of these poor creatures to other men. Ah! doe consider will this thing, you who doe it, if you would be done at this manner? And if it is done according to Christianity? You surpass Holland and Germany in this thing. This makes an ill report in all those countries of Europe, where they hear of, that ye Quakers doe here handel men as they handel there ye cattle. And for that reason some have no mind or inclination to come hither. And who shall maintain this your cause, or pleid for it. Truly we can not do so, except you shall inform us better hereof, viz., that Christians have liberty to practise these things. Pray, what thing in the world can be done worse towards us, than if men should rob or steal us away, and sell us for slaves to strange countries; separating husbands from their wives and children. Being now that this is not done in the manner we would be done at therefore we contradict and are against this traffic of men-body. And we who profess that it is not lawful to steal, must, likewise, avoid to purchase such things as are stolen, but rather help to stop this robbing and stealing if possible. And such men ought to be delivered out of ye hands of ye robbers, and set free as well as in Europe. Then is Pennsylvania to have a good report, instead it hath now a bad one for this sake in other countries. Especially whereas ye Europeans are desirous to know in what manner ye Quakers doe rule in their province;—and most of them doe look upon us with an envious eye. But if this is done well, what shall we say is done evil?

If once these slaves (wch they say are so wicked and stubbern men) should join themselves,—fight for their freedom,—and handel their masters and mastrisses as they did handel them before; will these masters and mastrisses take the sword at hand and warr against these poor slaves, licke, we are able to believe, some will not refuse to doe; or have these negers not as much right to fight for their freedom, as you have to keep them slaves?

Now consider will this thing, if it is good or bad? And in case you find it to be good to handle these blacks at that manner, we desire and require you hereby lovingly, that you may inform us herein, which at this time never was done, viz., that Christians have such a liberty to do so. To the end we shall be be satisfied in this point, and satisfie likewise our good friends and acquaintances in our natif country, to whose it is a terror, or fairful thing, that men should be handeld so in Pennsylvania.

This is from our meeting at Germantown, held ye18 of the 2 month, 1688, to be delivered to the Monthly Meeting at Richard Worrell's.

Garret henderich
derick up de graeff
Francis daniell Pastorius
Abraham up Den graef.

Monthly Meeting Response

At our Monthly Meeting at Dublin, ye 30–2 mo., 1688, we have inspected ye matter, above mentioned, and considered of it, we find it so weighty that we think it not expedient for us to meddle with it here, but do rather commit it to ye consideration of ye Quarterly Meeting; ye tenor of it being nearly related to ye Truth. On behalf of ye Monthly Meeting,
    Signed, P. Jo. Hart.

Quarterly Meeting Response

This, above mentioned, was read in our Quarterly Meeting at Philadelphia, the 4 of ye 4th mo. '88, and was from thence recommended to the Yearly Meeting, and the above said Derick, and the other two mentioned therein, to present the same to ye above said meeting, it being a thing of too great a weight for this meeting to determine.
    Signed by order of ye meeting,
    Anthony Morris.

Yearly Meeting Response

At a Yearly Meeting held at Burlington the 5th day of the 7th month, 1688.
A Paper being here presented by some German Friends Concerning the Lawfulness and Unlawfulness of Buying and keeping Negroes, It was adjusted not to be so proper for this Meeting to give a Positive Judgment in the case, It having so General a Relation to many other Parts, and therefore at present they forbear It.

Glossary

mastrisses	mistresses
natif	native
negers	an antique (and not derogatory) form of "Negro," based on the Germanic word for "black."
pleid	plead
Turks	a reference to the Barbary pirates operating off the north coast of Africa
viz.	an abbreviation of the Latin *videlicet*, meaning "that is."
wch	which
ye	the

JOHN WOOLMAN'S *SOME CONSIDERATIONS ON THE KEEPING OF NEGROES*

"When a People dwell under the liberal Distribution of Favours from Heaven, it behoves them carefully to inspect their Ways."

Overview

Some Considerations on the Keeping of Negroes remains one of the earliest and most influential antislavery tracts written in North America. Composed by the Quaker John Woolman in 1753, it gained approval by the Society of Friends in 1754, marking the beginnings of committed Quaker opposition to slaveholding. Prior to that point, Quakers in the American colonies had been ambivalent about the moral status of slavery, many even owning slaves themselves.

Writing at a time when prevailing colonial attitudes toward Africans presumed their inferiority, Woolman made a remarkably forward-looking case for racial equality. Not only did Woolman argue that Africans belonged to the same human family as Europeans but he also even suggested that many of the perceived differences between blacks and whites were actually the product of patterns of discrimination over time—what modern scholars would call "socially constructed."

Countering arguments that slavery exercised a positive, Christianizing effect, Woolman stressed its negative spiritual implications for both slaves and their owners. Slaves, he maintained, developed a series of negative behaviors precisely because they were forced to labor against their will. Meanwhile, both owners and their children developed evil habits that distanced them from Christ, forgetting the importance of humility, antimaterialism, and self-sacrifice. Of particular concern to Woolman were children who grew up accustomed to seeing tyranny as a natural part of dealing with others.

A not insignificant number of Quaker slave owners were so moved by Woolman's thesis that they decided to manumit their human chattel. Over half a century later, Quakers inspired by Woolman's work helped to form the American Colonization Society in 1817, dedicated to returning slaves to Africa. More radical abolitionists also drew inspiration from Woolman's work, using it to fight for the complete eradication of slavery in the United States. Over two hundred years after its publication, proponents of civil rights in the 1960s cited Woolman's tract for its eloquent arguments against racial repression and in favor of racial equality.

Context

John Woolman lived during a time of rapid demographic growth and remarkable political ferment. At the time of his birth in 1720, only half a million people lived in the colonies, a number that would surge to over two million by the time of his death in 1772. Much of this population growth was due to immigration, a third of Pennsylvania's inhabitants being of (non-Quaker) German origin by 1800. As immigrants poured into the colonies, religious groups like the Quakers found themselves rapidly becoming a minority even in their own strongholds, places like Pennsylvania and western New Jersey. Yet, precisely because they arrived first, Quakers remained a financial and political elite into the nineteenth century.

To preserve their power, Quakers required the labor of others. This presented a problem, given that many immigrants proved more interested in procuring their own land on Pennsylvania's western frontier than in the traditional indentured servitude. The resulting labor shortage encouraged wealthy Quakers to purchase slaves. First shipped to Philadelphia in the 1680s, slaves became a relatively common sight in the northern colonies during the eighteenth century. Although they were never as numerous as in the South, they made up roughly 10 percent of the populations of Philadelphia, New York, and New Jersey by 1770. Newport, Rhode Island, became a hub of slave trading in the eighteenth century, boasting a slave population upward of 20 percent by 1800.

While Quaker elites proved willing to accommodate slave owning, dissenting voices emerged within the Society of Friends. Long before John Woolman, for example, John Hepburn decried the ownership of slaves in his 1715 tract *The American Defense of the Golden Rule*. Eighteen years later, Elihu Coleman penned another diatribe against slavery titled *A Testimony against That Anti-Christian Practice of Making Slaves of Men*. Yet neither Coleman nor Hepburn won the support of a majority of the Society of Friends, making Woolman's *Considerations* an important turning point in Quaker attitudes toward slavery generally in colonies.

Just as slavery engendered tensions within the Quaker community, so too did relations with Native Americans

1664
- The colony of New Jersey is founded when an English fleet arrives, taking the colony from the Dutch.

1673
- John Berkeley, 1st Baron Berkeley of Stratton, sells his share of New Jersey to the Quakers.

1681
- King Charles II grants territory west of the Delaware River to William Penn.

1682
- Penn drafts the Frame of Government of Pennsylvania, guaranteeing religious freedom.

1689
- **May 24**
  The English Parliament passes the Act of Toleration, granting limited freedom to Quakers.

1704
- Penn approves the creation of Delaware.

1720
- **October 19**
  John Woolman is born in Northampton, New Jersey.

1739
- George Whitefield tours the colonies, sparking the First Great Awakening.

1740
- French-allied Indians attack on the Pennsylvania frontier, presaging King George's War (1744–1748).

1746
- The (Presbyterian) College of New Jersey is founded at Princeton.

1753
- Woolman writes *Some Considerations on the Keeping of Negroes, Part I*, which was distributed the following year following approval by the Quaker Meeting.

complicate Quaker colonial politics. For most of the seventeenth and eighteenth centuries, Quakers advocated a peaceful approach to Indian-colonial relations. William Penn insisted on negotiating settlement rights with Native Americans, generally purchasing their land before allowing white settlers to move onto it. Perhaps the most memorable negotiations that Penn engaged in involved the Delaware chief Tammany, from whom Penn negotiated land purchases in 1682 and 1683. Penn's reputation for fair dealing became so well known that Indians often settled in Pennsylvania after being displaced from other colonies.

Despite Quaker efforts, two factors converged to complicate colonial Indian relations. One was the unending influx of European immigrants to the colonies, pushing the western frontier ever farther onto Indian lands. The other was the growing tension and ultimately intermittent war between France and Britain, both of whom used Indian allies to advance their imperial interests. Such tensions began in 1689, when English forces and their Iroquois allies attacked French-controlled Montreal, only to be repulsed and counterattacked by French-Algonquin forces in New York, New Hampshire, and Maine. Although overt hostilities ended by treaty in 1697, they resurfaced in 1704, when French forces and their Algonquin allies again attacked English settlements, this time kidnapping women and children from frontier outposts in Massachusetts. Enraged, English military leaders ordered a counterstrike against a strategic French fortress at Port Royal in Acadia (modern-day Nova Scotia), eventually leading to British control over Newfoundland, Hudson's Bay, and Acadia. France challenged this control in 1740, leading to a protracted eight-year war along the frontier until British forces seized another strategic French fortress at Louisbourg on Cape Breton Island in 1745. Afraid that they might lose their foothold in the Ohio River valley, the French sent an armed force down the Ohio River, recruiting Indian allies to kill and expel a significant number of English-speaking settlers from the valley in 1752.

Violence on the Pennsylvania frontier led white settlers to challenge the traditional Quaker insistence on pacifism. Quaker faith in pacifism, such critics argued, was preventing colonial authorities in Philadelphia from raising the necessary military force to counter the Indian threat. Such critiques gained force in 1755, when Native Americans launched a devastating offensive against frontier communities on Pennsylvania's western border. Popular outrage over the death of white women and children at the hands of Indians confounded Pennsylvania Quakers, who had long pursued a strategy of accommodation with Native Americans, struggling to convert them to Christianity in a peaceful manner. Although such strategies enjoyed some success, the ensuing French and Indian War incited non-Quakers—by then a majority in Pennsylvania—to call for swift retribution. Quakers themselves split over the question of whether to accommodate violent reprisals or denounce them and effectively withdrew from colonial politics. Quaker pacifism was also challenged by the need to protect Quaker ships' crewmen from impressment by British naval vessels.

The resulting rift marked a decline in Quaker hegemony in Pennsylvania, even as it proved to be the handmaiden of more radical Quaker politics, of which Woolman would become a prominent leader.

Yet Quakers as a whole proved reluctant to come out against slavery. Part of this was due to a larger colonial acceptance of legal restrictions on liberty; indentured servitude was common in Quaker colonies, for example, and Quakers resented British attempts to forgive indentures in exchange for joining the British army. Another factor was Quaker slave owning, a practice common not simply in southern colonies but among elites in Pennsylvania, New Jersey, and Rhode Island as well.

John Woolman was not alone among eighteenth-century Protestant leaders in calling for a return to fundamental principles. In fact, one might say that his decision to oppose slavery fell firmly within a religious resurgence that historians have since termed the First Great Awakening. Although it was transdenominational, the Awakening was sparked by the arrival from England of an evangelical Anglican named George Whitefield in 1738. Much as Woolman would later do, Whitefield toured different colonies, preaching fiery sermons designed to kindle spirituality in increasingly materialist hearts. In Pennsylvania, William and George Tennent, a father-and-son team, established a special Presbyterian school to train evangelical ministers, later inspiring the establishment of the College of New Jersey, or what would become Princeton University, in 1746. At the center of the Tennents' preaching was a conviction that congregants should scrutinize the faith of their clergy. This eventually led to a schism within the Presbyterian Church between young reformers, or New Lights, who believed that the church should reaffirm basic Calvinist principles, and Old Lights, who had come to accept a less impassioned, arguably more compromised faith.

Almost every Protestant denomination underwent an awakening from the 1730s to the 1770s, as dynamic itinerant preachers traveled the colonies electrifying audiences. While most of the beneficiaries of this Awakening were already members of congregations, some colonies witnessed dramatic rises in church membership, particularly Methodists and Baptists in the American South. The most fervent proponents of religious reform tended to be the young and dispossessed, the very people who had not benefited from material gain during the first half of the eighteenth century. Frustration at the types of religious compromise endorsed by older, more established religious elites helped describe many Great Awakeners, John Woolman included.

About the Author

Born to a prominent Quaker family in Northampton, New Jersey, in 1720, John Woolman began life as a farmer, shopkeeper, and tailor. Hardworking and frugal, Woolman succeeded financially at a young age, only to struggle with the inevitable interrelationship between commerce and force. Over a decade before the sharp decline of Quaker

Time Line	
1754	■ Hostilities break out between the French and English on Pennsylvania's western frontier, leading to the French and Indian War (called the Seven Years' War in Europe).
1755	■ Quaker insistence on pacifism leads frontier people to vote them out of power in the colony of Pennsylvania.
1760s	■ The First Great Awakening reaches its apex in the American South.
1762	■ Woolman issues *Some Considerations on the Keeping of Negroes, Part II*.
1774	■ Quakers make the selling of slaves ground for excommunication.
1780	■ Pennsylvania passes An Act for the Gradual Abolition of Slavery.
1790	■ The Society of Friends petitions Congress to abolish slavery.
1817	■ Quakers inspired by Woolman found the American Colonization Society.

power at the hands of internal disagreements between pacifism and wealth, John Woolman recognized that war and commerce were inextricably linked, and he minimized his business activity to pursue the life of a traveling minister. Quaker ministers did most of their work outside the church, or meeting house, and spent much of their time conducting family visits or traveling between distant congregations aiding in intrafaith correspondence.

Woolman's travels brought him into direct contact with the institution of slavery and with Quaker slave owners. This was true even of his first journey, which led him to slave markets in Perth Amboy, New Jersey, in 1843. In 1846, Woolman traveled directly into the South, visiting Virginia and North Carolina. He later recalled, in his *Journal* feeling "uneasy" about fellow Quakers living "in ease on the hard labour of their slaves" In particular, Woolman lamented the "vices and corruptions" that slavery encouraged

The evangelical Anglican preacher George Whitefield
(Library of Congress)

among whites. That Woolman was bothered by slavery was perhaps not surprising for a Quaker who had already mitigated his commitment to commerce in order to remain true to his inner light. The doctrine of the inner light predisposed many Quakers to notions of social equality, on the ground that it was absurd that God would shine more brightly in some than others.

Aware of the tacit approval that Quakers had developed toward human bondage, Woolman initially engaged only in quiet protest, refusing to draft the wills of Quakers who wanted to bequeath slaves, rather than manumit them. Then, in 1753, he set down his treatise on the subject, *Some Considerations on the Keeping of Negroes*, which he published the following year. By 1756, Woolman dared to oppose not only slavery but also the payment of a war tax to defend white settlers against Indian attacks on the frontier. As Quaker political power in Pennsylvania crumbled, Woolman emerged as the leader of a radical new reformist bloc, freed from involvement in politics.

Three years after completing his *Considerations*, Woolman ventured back to the South, finding conditions even more deplorable than he had before. Many of the slaves

he observed were excruciatingly thin, with barely enough clothes to cover their bodies. Others suffered severe punishments or witnessed their children being sold off. One of the most disturbing aspects of his visit, however, was the indolence of white slave owners who, though they were Quaker, evinced behavior not in accord with the enterprising, hardworking ethos of their faith. Woolman found similarly disturbing conditions in New England, particularly in the port of Providence, Rhode Island, a heavily Quaker town with an equally heavy involvement in the slave trade. Shocked at the dire impact of slavery on both North and South, Woolman composed a sequel to his original essay, also titled *Some Considerations on the Keeping of Negroes*, that went into greater depth regarding the negative impact that slavery had on Africans, particularly children, and whites.

Woolman's radicalism drove him to increasing solitude and arguably even eccentricity. In 1761 he stopped wearing dyed clothing because of slave involvement in dye making, leading many Quakers to wonder at his rejection of traditional garments. He also gave up the use of any other product tied to slavery, including molasses, rum, and sugar—all key products of the "triangular trade" between Africa, America, and Europe. Although peers deemed such actions unconventional, Woolman continued writing and traveling, producing texts against slavery, materialism, and greed. Noteworthy among these works was his memoir, which described the details of his life and thought. Published posthumously in 1744 as *The Journal of John Woolman*, it quickly became accepted as a classic of American literature. In 1772 he traveled to England, contracted smallpox, and died shortly thereafter, in York.

Explanation and Analysis of Document

Written in 1754, Woolman's short treatise against slavery raised objections that were both strategic and forward-looking. He appealed to the self-interest of slave owners by documenting the negative impact that bondage had on whites, and he prefigured more contemporary debates about the socially constructed nature of race.

♦ "The General Disadvantage Which These Poor *Africans* Lie Under"

Following a scriptural invocation, Woolman begins his original *Considerations* (1754) by acknowledging that the conditions under which slaves live depended in large part on the particular circumstances and attitudes of their masters. Thus, it might be completely possible that some slaves were treated well, better even than freed people who could not claim an owner as protector. Nevertheless, even good treatment belied a deeper problem with the institution itself, namely that it placed the souls of slave owners in jeopardy. Equating slave owners to "Men under high Favours" (such as the Chosen People of Israel—the Jews), Woolman warns that such individuals are "apt to err in their Opinions concerning others." Indeed, he says, they are like the first "Jewish Christians," who would not

Defeat of General Braddock in the French and Indian War (Library of Congress)

"so much as eat," with their Gentile Christian brethren. Equating slaves with the Gentiles of New Testament times (that is, the earliest non-Jewish Christian converts), Woolman notes that, like blacks, Gentiles could also be physically distinguished from Jews, their lack of circumcision being analogous to the difference in skin color. Implicit in such a comparison is the notion that skin color is a superficial quality, not an indicator of genuine dissimilarity. Just as Gentile converts, despite their superficial differences, were genuine Christians, so black slaves must be considered our brothers today.

♦ **"Favours … Peculiar to One Nation"**

Assuming something like the modern conception of race as a "socially constructed" category, Woolman claims that anyone who believes "Favours" are "peculiar to one Nation" suffers from a "Darkness in the Understanding." Inherent in that darkness is the misconception that blacks are congenitally inferior, when in fact societal circumstances could explain their plight. Examples of such circumstances included the fact that they had been forced into servitude, made to perform menial tasks, denied education, and robbed of any reward for their work. Such circumstances, in turn, quickly explained the develop-

ment of other "odious" habits, including laziness, which is actually the logical response for people forced into an occupation against their will. In a particularly eloquent passage, Woolman suggests that were Europeans treated like slaves, they too would come to adopt characteristics commonly attributed to Africans. "Suppose, then that our Ancestors and we had been exposed to constant Servitude … [and] had generally been treated as a contemptible, ignorant Part of Mankind: Should we, in that Case, be less abject than they now are?"

Just as Woolman recognizes that structural factors could contribute to the appearance of inferiority, so too he observes that structural changes might have the opposite effect. If "our Conduct towards [African Americans] be seasoned with his [Christ's] Love," for example, then "'sloth' and 'other Habits appearing odious to us' would disappear." Before that could happen, however, whites had to recognize that slavery falsely elevated Europeans above blacks, corrupting their perceptions of reality and truth.

♦ **"When *Self-love* Presides in Our Minds"**

Continuing with his emphasis on whites, Woolman equates slaveholding with pride, or "self-love," warning that its tendency was to lead the slave owner away from

"When a People dwell under the liberal Distribution of Favours from Heaven, it behoves them carefully to inspect their Ways, and consider the Purposes for which those Favours were bestowed."

("The General Disadvantage Which These Poor *Africans* Lie Under")

"To consider Mankind otherwise than Brethren, to think Favours are peculiar to one Nation, and exclude others, plainly supposes a Darkness in the Understanding."

("Favours ... Peculiar to One Nation")

"Suppose, then, that our Ancestors and we had been exposed to constant Servitude in the more servile and inferior Employments of Life ... that while others, in Ease, have plentifully heap'd up the Fruit of our Labour, we had receiv'd barely enough to relieve Nature, and being wholly at the Command of others, had generally been treated as a contemptible, ignorant Part of Mankind: Should we, in that Case, be less abject than they now are?"

("Favours ... Peculiar to One Nation")

Christ. Specifically, slavery precluded slave owners from honoring Christ's command to treat all men "as becometh Sons of one Father" as well as the command in Leviticus 14:33–34 to love the stranger as oneself. Conceding that owners might be concerned about their investments in slaves as well as the threat that freedpeople of color might pose to public safety, Woolman invokes the notion that whites possess a collective responsibility for blacks, which necessitates risking death and financial ruin. Indeed, financial ruin is not necessarily a bad thing in Woolman's eyes, for worldly wealth itself represented a "snare" that only tempted slave owners with "the getting of riches," driving a wedge between themselves and the Gospels of Christ.

Children, in particular, warns Woolman, are threatened by the corrupting influences of slavery. Whereas those children who are "prudently employed in the necessary Affairs of Life" tend to benefit from hard work, children of slave owners experience an "Ease and Idleness" that invariably lead to "evil habits." Exacerbating this is the fact that children of slave owners grow used to "lording it over their Fellow Creatures," making the attainment of true humility and grace virtually impossible.

♦ **"This Seems to Contradict the Design of Providence"**

Placing Christ's emphasis on humility, poverty, and selflessness at the heart of his considerations, Woolman concludes his somewhat rambling eighteen-page essay by making a compelling case that slavery is antithetical to "the Design of Providence." Slave owners should not recoil from this revelation, argues Woolman, but instead take it as an opportunity to free their slaves and bring upon themselves hardships that would win God's grace. They should draw inspiration from biblical figures such as Abraham, Jacob, Joseph, and David, all of whom suffered and, in their suffering, won God's favor.

Pitching his complaint against slavery as a desperate bid to save the souls of slave owners, Woolman emphasizes that all great figures in the Bible had suffered moments when they were "very low and dejected," only to find that material loss translated invariably into spiritual gain. Conversely, those who did not recognize God's will risked incurring God's wrath, another possible fate of the slave owner who failed to see how slavery alienated him from the teachings of Jesus. Those whose ownership of slaves only made them more "selfish, earthly, and sensual" would "wander in a Maze of dark Anxiety."

Audience

Woolman's audience was primarily Quaker. He presented his *Considerations* to the Philadelphia Yearly Meeting of Quaker leadership in the colonies in 1753. At the time, Quakers had accumulated considerable material wealth in northern colonies like Pennsylvania, New Jersey, and Delaware and in southern colonies like Virginia and North Carolina. Slaveholding contributed to such fortunes, as Quaker slave owners in the South used blacks to work their crops and Quaker businessmen in the North used slaves to work their farms and shops, meanwhile profiting from the triangle trade, shipbuilding, and slave auctions. Woolman hoped to break through to such Quakers, persuading them to manumit their slaves and, in so doing, come closer to God.

Woolman also hoped to make a larger argument, namely that Quakers in the colonies had strayed from their religious principles generally. This message came at an opportune time, just as Quaker elites found themselves voted out of office by war-hungry frontiersmen. Although such elites attempted to hold on to their power by compromise, Woolman provided a counterargument that Quaker values of humility and pacifism could not coexist with material gain and slaveholding. This made Woolman an important voice for the restoration of fundamental Quaker principles, precisely at a moment when such principals could provide a tonic for political defeat.

Impact

Evidence that Woolman succeeded emerged shortly after he presented his tract to the Philadelphia Yearly Meeting. Rather than reject him, as they had prior opponents of slavery, Quaker leaders authorized his work for general publication to Quaker communities both in the American colonies and England, declaring it the official position of the Virginia Yearly Meeting in 1754. This marked a significant departure from past accommodations on the question of slavery, ushering in a new era of Quaker leadership in what would become the abolition movement. It might be said that Woolman transformed the decline of Quaker hegemony in Pennsylvania politics into a spiritual opportunity, successfully reinvigorating the spiritual life of the Society of Friends.

Woolman's public denunciation of slavery came on the eve of catastrophe for Quaker America, providing a new vision for one of America's great faiths. One year after the completion of his *Considerations*, Native Americans and their French allies mounted a vicious offensive against white settlers on the Pennsylvania frontier, even killing the British colonial commander in chief, General Edward Braddock, on the Monongahela River. One year later, France and England entered the Seven Years' War, heightening tensions between the English colonists of Pennsylvania and their Indian foes, many of whom allied themselves with France in the hope that an English defeat might enable them to regain their lands. Convinced of the need for a strong military, colonists endorsed a war tax to fund efforts against the French and their Indian allies.

John Woolman spoke out against the war tax, and his religious attack on slavery alienated him from more secular Quakers even as it helped him cobble together a new vision for colonial Quaker society, one made all the more important by the crumbling of Quaker hegemony in Pennsylvania and western Jersey as Quaker political elites were voted out of office by colonists desperate for military reinforcements on the frontier. Indeed, Woolman emerged from the "crisis of 1755"—the collapse of Quaker political power in Pennsylvania—a spiritual leader with a new vi-

---

Questions for Further Study

1. Describe the economic conditions that expanded the slave system during Woolman's lifetime. Why did the ready availability of land make slavery an attractive option for many settlers?

2. Explain the relationship between Native Americans and the Quakers. What implications did this relationship have for the history of slavery during the eighteenth century?

3. What was the Great Awakening? What role did this movement have in creating conditions for opposition to slavery?

4. Why is Woolman's tract often considered forward looking in the attitudes it expresses?

5. Compare this document with Thomas Jefferson's *Notes on the State of Virginia*, written three decades later. Do the two documents share any views? How are they different?

sion for the church. Much like other religious leaders of the Great Awakening, Woolman drove home the message that congregants needed to recommit themselves to their faith, returning to first principles as a guide.

Woolman's *Considerations* became an immediate inspiration to Quakers in the American colonies, prompting many to manumit their slaves. In fact, his leadership transformed American Quakerism into a vanguard of antislavery activism in the United States. Two years after his death in 1772, Quaker leadership made the selling or transferring of slaves ground for excommunication, and in 1776 the leadership ordered all Quakers to free their human chattel. In 1780, Pennsylvania passed An Act for the Gradual Abolition of Slavery, and in 1790 the Society of Friends petitioned Congress requesting the abolition of slavery. By 1817 Quakers inspired by Woolman founded the American Colonization Society, calling for the manumission of slaves and their return to Africa. Later abolitionists borrowed from Woolman's arguments to lobby for the eradication of slavery in the United States. Leading public intellectuals like Ralph Waldo Emerson publicly praised Woolman's work for its eloquent prose and sweeping ideas. The poet John Greenleaf Whittier took inspiration from him. Almost two hundred years after his death, civil rights activists recovered Woolman's work in the 1960s, finding inspiration in his proclamations of racial equality and spiritual denunciations of racial injustice. A radical at the time that he wrote, Woolman's views of slavery made him a visionary model to later generations.

See also "A Minute against Slavery, Addressed to Germantown Monthly Meeting" (1688); Pennsylvania: An Act for the Gradual Abolition of Slavery (1780).

Further Reading

■ **Books**

Barbour, Hugh, and J. William Frost. *The Quakers*. New York: Greenwood Press, 1988.

Cady, Edwin H. *John Woolman: The Mind of the Quaker Saint.* New York: Washington Square Press, 1965.

Drake, Thomas E. *Quakers and Slavery in America*. New Haven, Conn.: Yale University Press, 1950.

Marietta, Jack D. *The Reformation of American Quakerism, 1748– 1783*. Philadelphia: University of Pennsylvania Press, 1984.

Olmsted, Sterling, and Mike Heller, eds. *John Woolman: A Nonviolence and Social Change Source Book*. Wilmington, Ohio: Wilmington College Peace Resource Center, 1997.

Shi, David E. *The Simple Life: Plain Living and High Thinking in American Culture*. New York: Oxford University Press, 1985.

Soderlund, Jean R. *Quakers and Slavery: A Divided Spirit*. Princeton, N.J.: Princeton University Press, 1985.

Whitney, Janet. *John Woolman: American Quaker*. Boston: Little, Brown, 1942.

Woolman, John. *The Journal and Major Essays of John Woolman*, ed. Phillips P. Moulton. Richmond, Ind.: Friends United Press, 1989.

—Anders Walker

John Woolman's *Some Considerations on the Keeping of Negroes*

Forasmuch as ye did it to the least of these my Brethren, ye did it unto me, Matt. xxv. 40.

As Many Times there are different Motives to the same Actions; and one does that from a generous Heart, which another does for selfish Ends:— The like may be said in this Case.

There are various Circumstances amongst them that keep *Negroes*, and different Ways by which they fall under their Care; and, I doubt not, there are many well disposed Persons amongst them who desire rather to manage wisely and justly in this difficult Matter, than to make Gain of it.

But the general Disadvantage which these poor *Africans* lie under in an enlight'ned Christian Country, having often fill'd me with real Sadness, and been like undigested Matter on my Mind, I now think it my Duty, through Divine Aid, to offer some Thoughts thereon to the Consideration of others.

When we remember that all Nations are of one Blood, *Gen.* iii. 20. that in this World we are but Sojourners, that we are subject to the like Afflictions and Infirmities of Body, the like Disorders and Frailties in Mind, the like Temptations, the same Death, and the same Judgment, and, that the Alwise Being is Judge and Lord over us all, it seems to raise an Idea of a general Brotherhood, and a Disposition easy to be touched with a Feeling of each others Afflictions: But when we forget those Things, and look chiefly at our outward Circumstances, in this and some Ages past, constantly retaining in our Minds the Distinction betwixt us and them, with respect to our Knowledge and Improvement in Things divine, natural and artificial, our Breasts being apt to be filled with fond Notions of Superiority, there is Danger of erring in our Conduct toward them.

We allow them to be of the same Species with ourselves, the Odds is, we are in a higher Station, and enjoy greater Favours than they: And when it is thus, that our heavenly Father endoweth some of his Children with distinguished Gifts, they are intended for good Ends; but if those thus gifted are thereby lifted up above their Brethren, not considering themselves as Debtors to the Weak, nor behaving themselves as faithful Stewards, none who judge impartially can suppose them free from Ingratitude.

When a People dwell under the liberal Distribution of Favours from Heaven, it behoves them carefully to inspect their Ways, and consider the Purposes for which those Favours were bestowed, lest, through Forgetfulness of God, and Misusing his Gifts, they incur his heavy Displeasure, whose Judgments are just and equal, who exalteth and humbleth to the Dust as he seeth meet.

It appears by Holy Record that Men under high Favours have been apt to err in their Opinions concerning others. Thus *Israel*, according to the Description of the Prophet, *Isai.* lxv. 5. when exceedingly corrupted and degenerated, yet remembered they were the chosen People of God and could say, *Stand by thyself, come not near me, for I am holier than thou.* That this was no chance Language, but their common Opinion of other People, more fully appears by considering the Circumstances which attended when God was beginning to fulfil his precious Promises concerning the Gathering of the *Gentiles*.

The Most High, in a Vision, undeceived *Peter*, first prepared his Heart to believe; and, at the House of Cornelius, shewed him of a Certainty that God was no Respector of Persons.

The Effusion of the Holy Ghost upon a People with whom they, the *Jewish* Christians, would not so much as eat, was strange to them: All they of the Circumcision were astonished to see it; and the Apostles and Brethren of *Judea* contended with *Peter* about it, till he, having rehearsed the whole Matter, and fully shewn that the Father's Love was unlimited, they are thereat struck with Admiration, and cry out; *Then hath God also to the* Gentiles *granted Repentance unto Life!*

The Opinion of peculiar Favours being confined to them, was deeply rooted, or else the above Instance had been less strange to them, for these Reasons: *First,* They were generally acquainted with the Writings of the Prophets, by whom this Time was repeatedly spoken of, and pointed at. *Secondly,* Our Blessed Lord shortly before expressly said, *I have other Sheep, not of this Fold, them also must I bring,* &c. *Lastly,* His Words to them after his Resurrection, at the very Time of his Ascension, *Ye shall be Witnesses to me, not only in* Jerusalem, Judea, *and* Samaria, *but to the uttermost Parts of the Earth.*

Those concurring Circumstances, one would think, might have raised a strong Expectation of seeing such a Time; yet, when it came, it proved Matter of Offence and Astonishment.

To consider Mankind otherwise than Brethren, to think Favours are peculiar to one Nation, and exclude others, plainly supposes a Darkness in the Understanding: For as God's Love is universal, so where the Mind is sufficiently influenced by it, it begets a Likeness of itself, and the Heart is enlarged towards all Men. Again, to conclude a People forward [*sic*], perverse, and worse by Nature than others (who ungratefully receive Favours, and apply them to bad Ends) this will excite a Behaviour toward them unbecoming the Excellence of true Religion.

To prevent such Error, let us calmly consider their Circumstance; and, the better to do it, make their Case ours. Suppose, then, that our Ancestors and we had been exposed to constant Servitude in the more servile and inferior Employments of Life; that we had been destitute of the Help of Reading and good Company; that amongst ourselves we had had few wise and pious Instructors; that the Religious amongst our Superiors seldom took Notice of us; that while others, in Ease, have plentifully heap'd up the Fruit of our Labour, we had receiv'd barely enough to relieve Nature, and being wholly at the Command of others, had generally been treated as a contemptible, ignorant Part of Mankind: Should we, in that Case, be less abject than they now are? Again, If Oppression be so hard to bear, that a wise Man is made mad by it, *Eccl.* vii. 7. then a Series of those Things altering the Behaviour and Manners of a People, is what may reasonably be expected.

When our Property is taken contrary to our Mind, by Means appearing to us unjust, it is only through divine Influence, and the Enlargement of Heart from thence proceeding, that we can love our reputed Oppressors: If the *Negroes* fall short in this, an uneasy, if not a disconsolate Disposition, will be awak'ned, and remain like Seeds in their Minds, producing Sloth and many other Habits appearing odious to us, with which being free Men, they, perhaps, had not been chargeable. These, and other Circumstances, rightly considered, will lessen that too great Disparity, which some make between us and them.

Integrity of Heart hath appeared in some of them; so that if we continue in the Word of Christ [previous to Discipleship, *John* viii. 31.] and our Conduct towards them be seasoned with his Love, we may hope to see the good Effect of it: The which, in a good Degree, is the Case with some into whose Hands they have fallen: But that too many treat them otherwise, not seeming concious of any Neglect, is, alas! too evident.

When *Self-love* presides in our Minds, our Opinions are bias'd in our own Favour; in this Condition, being concerned with a People so situated, that they have no Voice to plead their own Cause, there's Danger of using ourselves to an undisturbed Partiality, till, by long Custom, the Mind becomes reconciled with it, and the Judgment itself infected.

To humbly apply to God for Wisdom, that we may thereby be enabled to see Things as they are, and ought to be, is very needful; hereby the hidden Things of Darkness may be brought to light, and the Judgment made clear: We shall then consider Mankind as Brethren: Though different Degrees and a Variety of Qualifications and Abilities, one dependant on another, be admitted, yet high Thoughts will be laid aside, and all Men treated as becometh the Sons of one Father, agreeable to the Doctrine of Christ Jesus.

He hath laid down the best Criterion, by which Mankind ought to judge of their own Conduct, and others judge for them of theirs, one towards another, *viz. Whatsoever ye would that Men should do unto you, do ye even so to them.* I take it, that all Men by Nature, are equally entitled to the Equity of this Rule, and under the indispensable Obligations of it. One Man ought not to look upon another Man, or Society of Men, as so far beneath him, but that he should put himself in their Place, in all his Actions towards them, and bring all to this Test, *viz.* How should I approve of this Conduct, were I in their Circumstance and they in mine?

A. Arscot's Considerations, Part III. Fol. 107.

This Doctrine being of a moral unchangeable Nature, hath been likewise inculcated in the former Dispensation; *If a Stranger sojourn with thee in your Land, ye shall not vex him; but the Stranger that dwelleth with you, shall be as One born amongst you, and thou shalt love him as thyself.* Lev. xix. 33, 34. Had these People come voluntarily and dwelt amongst us, to have called them Strangers would be proper; and their being brought by Force, with Regret, and a languishing Mind, may well raise Compassion in a Heart rightly disposed: But there is Nothing in such Treatment, which upon a wise and judicious Consideration, will any Ways lessen their Right of being treated as Strangers. If the Treatment which many of them meet with, be rightly examined and compared with those Precepts, *Thou shalt not vex him nor oppress him; he shall be as one born amongst you, and thou shalt love him as thyself,* Lev. xix. 33. Deut. xxvii. 19. there will appear an important Difference betwixt them.

It may be objected there is Cost of Purchase, and Risque of their Lives to them who possess 'em, and therefore needful that they make the best Use of their Time: In a Practice just and reasonable, such Objections may have Weight; but if the Work be wrong from the Beginning, there's little or no Force in them. If I purchase a Man who hath never forfeited his Liberty, the natural Right of Freedom is in him; and shall I keep him and his Posterity in Servitude and Ignorance? "How should I approve of this Conduct, were I in his Circumstances, and he in mine?" It may be thought, that to treat them as we would willingly be treated, our Gain by them would be inconsiderable: And it were, in divers Respects, better that there were none in our Country.

We may further consider, that they are now amongst us, and those of our Nation the Cause of their being here; that whatsoever Difficulty accrues thereon, we are justly chargeable with, and to bear all Inconveniences attending it, with a serious and weighty Concern of Mind to do our Duty by them, is the best we can do. To seek a Remedy by continuing the Oppression, because we have Power to do it, and see others do it, will, I apprehend, not be doing as we would be done by.

How deeply soever Men are involved in the most exquisite Difficulties, Sincerity of Heart, and upright Walking before God, freely submitting to his Providence, is the most sure Remedy: He only is able to relieve, not only Persons, but Nations, in their greatest Calamities.

David, in a great Strait, when the Sense of his past Error, and the full Expectation of an impending Calamity, as the Reward of it, were united to the agravating of his Distress, after some Deliberation, saith, *Let me fall now into the Hands of the Lord, for very great are his Mercies; let me not fall into the Hand of Man*, 1 Chron. xxi. 13.

To act continually with Integrity of Heart, above all narrow or selfish Motives, is a sure Token of our being Partakers of that Salvation which *God hath appointed for Walls and Bulwarks*, Isa. v. 26. Rom. xv. 8. and is, beyond all Contradiction, a more happy Situation than can ever be promised by the utmost Reach of Art and Power united, not proceeding from heavenly Wisdom.

A Supply to Nature's lawful Wants, joined with a peaceful, humble Mind, is the truest Happiness in this Life; and if here we arrive to this, and remain to walk in the Path of the Just, our Case will be truly happy: And though herein we may part with, or miss of some glaring Shews of Riches, and leave our Children little else but wise Instructions, a good Example, and the Knowledge of some honest Em-

ployment, these, with the Blessing of Providence, are sufficient for their Happiness, and are more likely to prove so, than laying up Treasures for them, which are often rather a Snare, than any real Benefit; especially to them, who, instead of being exampled to Temperance, are in all Things taught to prefer the getting of Riches, and to eye the temporal Distinctions they give, as the principal Business of this Life. These readily overlook the true Happiness of Man, as it results from the Enjoyment of all Things in the Fear of God, and, miserably substituting an inferior Good, dangerous in the Acquiring, and uncertain in the Fruition, they are subject to many Disappointments, and every Sweet carries its Sting.

It is the Conclusion of our blessed Lord and his Apostles, as appears by their Lives and Doctrines, that the highest Delights of Sense, or most pleasing Objects visible, ought ever to be accounted infinitely inferior to that real intellectual Happiness suited to Man in his primitive Innocence, and now to be found in true Renovation of Mind; and that the Comforts of our present Life, the Things most grateful to us, ought always to be receiv'd with Temperance, and never made the chief Objects of our Desire, Hope, or Love: But that our whole Heart and Affections be principally looking to that *City which hath Foundations, whose Maker and Builder is God.* Did we so improve the Gifts bestowed on us, that our Children might have an Education suited to these Doctrines, and our Example to confirm it, we might rejoice in Hopes of their being Heirs of an Inheritance incorruptible.

This Inheritance, as Christians, we esteem the most valuable; and how then can we fail to desire it for our Children? O that we were consistent with ourselves, in pursuing Means necessary to obtain it!

It appears, by Experience, that where Children are educated in Fulness, Ease and Idleness, evil Habits are more prevalent, than in common amongst such who are prudently employed in the necessary Affairs of Life: And if Children are not only educated in the Way of so great Temptation, but have also the Opportunity of lording it over their Fellow Creatures, and being Masters of Men in their Childhood, how can we hope otherwise than that their tender Minds will be possessed with Thoughts too high for them? Which, by Continuance, gaining Strength, will prove, like a slow Current, gradually separating them from [or keeping from Acquaintance with] that Humility and Meekness in which alone lasting Happiness can be enjoyed.

Man is born to labour, and Experience abundantly sheweth, that it is for our Good: But where the Powerful lay the Burthen on the Inferior, without affording a Christian Education, and suitable Opportunity of improving the Mind, and a Treatment which we, in their Case, should approve, that themselves may live at Ease, and fare sumptuously, and lay up Riches for their Posterity, this seems to contradict the Design of Providence, and, I doubt, is sometimes the Effect of a perverted Mind: For while the Life of one is made grievous by the Rigour of another, it entails Misery on both.

Amongst the manifold Works of Providence, displayed in the different Ages of the World, these which follow [with many others] may afford Instruction.

Abraham was called of God to leave his Country and Kindred, to sojourn amongst Strangers: Through Famine, and Danger of Death, he was forced to flee from one Kingdom to another: He, at length, not only had Assurance of being the Father of many Nations, but became a mighty Prince, *Gen.* xxiii. 6.

Remarkable was the Dealings of God with *Jacob* in a low Estate, the just Sense he retained of them after his Advancement, appears by his Words; *I am not worthy of the Least of all thy Mercies*, Gen. xxxii. 10. xlviii. 15.

The numerous Afflictions of *Joseph*, are very singular; the particular Providence of God therein, no less manifest: He, at length, became Governor of *Egypt*, and famous for Wisdom and Virtue.

The Series of Troubles *David* passed through, few amongst us are ignorant of; and yet he afterwards became as one of the great Men of the Earth.

Some Evidences of the Divine Wisdom appears in those Things, in that such who are intended for high Stations, have first been very low and dejected, that Truth might be sealed on their Hearts, and that the Characters there imprinted by Bitterness and Adversity, might in after Years remain, suggesting compassionate Ideas, and, in their Prosperity, quicken their Regard to those in the like Condition: Which yet further appears in the Case of *Israel*: They were well acquainted with grievous Sufferings, a long and rigorous Servitude, then, through many notable Events, were made Chief amongst the Nations: To them we find a Repetition of Precepts to the Purpose abovesaid: Though, for Ends agreeable to infinite Wisdom, they were chose as a peculiar People for a Time; yet the Most High acquaints them, that his Love is not confined, but extends to the Stranger;

Abraham	in the Christian Old Testament, the founding patriarch of the Israelites
Alwise	all wise
Apple of his Eye	an image used in various biblical books, including Deuteronomy, Psalms, Proverbs, Lamentations, and Zechariah
Ascension	the doctrine that after his death Christ rose to heaven
Chron.	the Christian Old Testament books of Chronicles
City which hath Foundations …	quotation from the biblical book of Hebrews, chapter 11, verse 10
Cornelius	a non-Jew whose house Peter and his companions entered to dine, the first time Peter had ever eaten with a Gentile
David	a king of Israel in biblical times
Deut.	the Christian Old Testament book of Deuteronomy
divers	divers
Eccl.	the Christian Old Testament book of Ecclesiastes
Exod.	the Christian Old Testament book of Exodus
Gen.	the Christian Old Testament book of Genesis
Gentiles	non-Jews
Holy Record	the Bible

and, to excite their Compassion, reminds them of Times past, *Ye were Strangers in the Land of* Egypt, Deut. x. 19. Again, *Thou shalt not oppress a Stranger, for ye know the Heart of a Stranger, seeing ye were Strangers in the Land of* Egypt, Exod. xxiii. 9.

If we call to Mind our Beginning, some of us may find a Time, wherein our Fathers were under Afflictions, Reproaches, and manifold Sufferings.

Respecting our Progress in this Land, the Time is short since our Beginning was small and Number few, compared with the native Inhabitants. He that sleeps not by Day nor Night, hath watched over us, and kept us as the Apple of his Eye. His Almighty Arm hath been round about us, and saved us from Dangers.

The Wilderness and solitary Desarts in which our Fathers passed the Days of their Pilgrimage, are now turned into pleasant Fields; the Natives are gone from before us, and we established peaceably in the Possession of the Land, enjoying our civil and religious Liberties; and, while many Parts of the World have groaned under the heavy Calamities of War, our Habitation remains quiet, and our Land fruitful.

When we trace back the Steps we have trodden, and see how the Lord hath opened a Way in the Wilderness for us, to the Wise it will easily appear, that all this was not done to be buried in Oblivion; but to prepare a People for more fruitful Returns, and the Remembrance thereof, ought to humble us in Prosperity, and excite in us a Christian Benevolence towards our Inferiors.

If we do not consider these Things aright, but, through a stupid Indolence, conceive Views of Inter-

Glossary

Holy Writ	the Bible
I have other Sheep …	quotation from the book of John, chapter 10, verse 16
Isai.	the Christian Old Testament book of Isaiah
Jacob	in the Christian Old Testament, the third patriarch of the Israelites
Jer.	the Christian Old Testament book of Jeremiah
Judea	in biblical times the southern part of Israel
Judg.	the Christian Old Testament book of Judges
Lev.	the Christian Old Testament book of Leviticus
Matt.	the Christian New Testament Gospel of Matthew
meet	fitting, appropriate
Peter	one of Christ's apostles
Risque	risk
Rom.	the Christian New Testament Epistle of Paul to the Romans
Shews	shows
Then hath God also to the *Gentiles* …	quotation from Acts of the Apostles, chapter 11, verse 18
they of the Circumcision	Jews, traditionally known for circumcising male infants
Whatsoever ye would that Men …	the Golden Rule, from the Gospel of Matthew, chapter 7, verse 12
Ye shall be Witnesses to me …	quotation from Acts of the Apostles, chapter 1, verse 8

est, separate from the general Good of the great Brotherhood, and, in Pursuance thereof, treat our Inferiors with Rigour, to increase our Wealth, and gain Riches for our Children, what then shall we do, when God riseth up, and when he visiteth, what shall we Answer him? Did not he that made Us, make Them, and *Did not one Fashion us in the Womb?* Job. xxxi. 14, 15.

To our great Master we stand or fall, to judge or condemn is most suitable to his Wisdom and Authority; my Inclination is to persuade, and intreat, and simply give Hints of my Way of Thinking.

If the Christian Religion be considered, both respecting its Doctrines, and the happy Influence which it hath on the Minds and Manners of all real Christians, it looks reasonable to think, that the miraculous Manifestation thereof to the World, is a Kindness beyond Expression.

Are we the People thus favoured? Are we they whose Minds are opened, influenced, and govern'd by the Spirit of Christ, and thereby made Sons of God? Is it not a fair Conclusion, that we, like our heavenly Father, ought, in our Degree, to be active in the same great Cause, of the Eternal Happiness of, at least, our whole Families, and more, if thereto capacitated?

If we, by the Operation of the Spirit of Christ, become Heirs with him in the Kingdom of his Father, and are redeemed from the alluring counterfeit Joys of this World, and the Joy of Christ remain in us, to suppose that One remaining in this happy Condition, can for the Sake of earthly Riches, not only deprive his Fellow Creatures of the Sweetness of Freedom [which, rightly used, is one of the greatest temporal Blessings] but therewith neglect using proper Means, for their Acquaintance with the Holy Scriptures, and the Advantage of true Religion, seems, at least, a Contradiction to Reason.

Whoever rightly advocates the Cause of some, thereby promotes the Good of all. The State of Mankind was harmonious in the Beginning, and tho' Sin hath introduced Discord, yet, through the wonderful Love of God, in Christ Jesus our Lord, the Way is open for our Redemption, and Means appointed to restore us to primitive Harmony. That if one suffer, by the Unfaithfulness of another, the Mind, the most noble Part of him that occasions the Discord, is thereby alienated from its true and real Happiness.

Our Duty and Interest is inseparably united, and when we neglect or misuse our Talents, we necessarily depart from the heavenly Fellowship, and are in the Way to the greatest of Evils.

Therefore, to examine and prove ourselves, to find what Harmony the Power presiding in us bears with the Divine Nature, is a Duty not more incumbent and necessary, than it would be beneficial.

In Holy Writ the Divine Being saith of himself, *I am the Lord, which exercise Loving Kindness, Judgment and Righteousness in the Earth; for in these Things I delight, saith the Lord*, Jer. ix. 24. Again, speaking in the Way of Man, to shew his Compassion to *Israel*, whose Wickedness had occasioned a Calamity, and then being humbled under it, it is said, *His Soul was grieved for their Miseries*, Judg. x. 16. If we consider the Life of our Blessed Saviour when on Earth, as it is recorded by his Followers, we shall find, that one uniform Desire for the eternal, and temporal Good of Mankind, discovered itself in all his Actions.

If we observe Men, both Apostles and others, in many different Ages, who have really come to the Unity of the Spirit, and the Fellowship of the Saints, there still appears the like Disposition, and in them the Desire of the real Happiness of Mankind, has out-ballanced the Desire of Ease, Liberty, and, many Times, Life itself.

If upon a true Search, we find that our Natures are so far renewed, that to exercise Righteousness and Loving Kindness [according to our Ability] towards all Men, without Respect of Persons, is easy to us, or is our Delight; if our Love be so orderly, and regular, that he who doth the Will of our Father, who is in Heaven, appears in our View, to be our nearest Relation, our Brother, and Sister, and Mother; if this be our Case, there is a good Foundation to hope, that the Blessing of God will sweeten our Treasures during our Stay in this Life, and our Memory be savory, when we are entered into Rest.

To conclude, 'Tis a Truth most certain, that a Life guided by Wisdom from above, agreeable with Justice, Equity, and Mercy, is throughout consistent and amiable, and truly beneficial to Society; the Serenity and Calmness of Mind in it, affords an unparallel'd Comfort in this Life, and the End of it is blessed.

And, no less true, that they, who in the Midst of high Favours, remain ungrateful, and under all the Advantages that a Christian can desire, are selfish, earthly, and sensual, do miss the true Fountain of Happiness, and wander in a Maze of dark Anxiety, where all their Treasures are insufficient to quiet their Minds: Hence, from an insatiable Craving, they neglect doing Good with what they have acquired, and too often add Oppression to Vanity, that they may compass more.

O that they were wise, that they understood this, that they would consider their latter End! Deut. xxxii, 29.

LORD DUNMORE'S PROCLAMATION

"I do hereby further declare all ... Negroes ... free that are able and willing to bear Arms."

Overview

On November 7, 1775, John Murray, 4th Earl of Dunmore, who had been royal governor of the colony of Virginia since 1771, drafted a document. This Proclamation, published on November 14, named the Patriot rebels of Virginia as traitors to the Crown, declared martial law in Virginia, and—the part that elicited the greatest response and had the widest impact—declared as free any slaves or indentured servants who would join Dunmore's forces against the rebels. Many slaves ran away from their masters to join the British because of their offer of freedom, and the Virginians did whatever they could to prevent it.

The results of this Proclamation were not as dramatic as Dunmore had hoped, as harassment, disease, and a decisive defeat all worked against him and his vision for an army supplemented heavily with African American troops. However, the Proclamation deserves to be remembered as the first mass emancipation of slaves in America. The number of slaves escaping their masters during the American Revolution, in large part because of this Proclamation, would also be the greatest number to escape slavery until the Civil War.

Context

Africans who arrived in the colony, starting in 1619, were not originally slaves. Most of them worked as servants, with the same rights, duties, and treatment as indentured servants. Like indentured servants, these Africans worked for a master a certain number of years, after which they could be released and were free to buy land. Black men could even have white servants and testify in court against white people.

Before long, however, white Virginians began to draw a more distinct line—in life and in law—between themselves and black Africans. By 1662, Virginia had introduced Act XII: Negro Women's Children to Serve according to the Condition of the Mother, implementing the possibility of life servitude—slavery—for blacks, with the conferral of slave status through the mother, thus guaranteeing that the children of unions between white masters and female slaves would be born into slavery. In 1667, Act III declared that the legal status of slaves would not change as a result of baptism. In 1670, Virginia law specified that free blacks could no longer have Christian servants, thus ruling out all whites and even some fellow blacks. A year earlier Virginia had ruled that if a black slave should die while being punished, the master would not be charged with a crime.

In the 1680s the laws regulating slavery and the separation of whites and blacks became even more rigid. The laws about trials for blacks grew much stricter, and slaves were punished more severely. The conferral of permanent slave status on all imported black servants was solidified at this time. Punishments for runaways worsened. At the end of this decade, in 1691, any white person who married a black or a mulatto was subject to banishment from the colony, and systematic procedures for the capture of runaway slaves had been approved. In 1705 Virginia declared that all black, mulatto, and Indian slaves were to be treated as "real estate." This same year, the punishment of disorderly slaves by dismemberment was made legal. Gone were the days—less than a century previous—when blacks could testify in court against whites or when black servants would be given freedom and allowed to buy land or keep servants of their own after their term of service. For almost one hundred years—since a law enacted in 1691—the manumission of slaves was not allowed in Virginia. It was not until 1782 that Virginia passed a law permitting slaveholders to free their slaves if they wished. Clearly, in Dunmore's time, it can be imagined that anyone who tried to emancipate any slaves—whether their own or someone else's—would be seen as the worst of villains.

In 1775, however, Lord Dunmore, royal governor of Virginia, found himself in an increasingly desperate position. The Patriots in Virginia were numerous and powerful, and they threatened British government of the colony. Tension had been rising since before Dunmore was assigned the governorship in 1771, and he did little to alleviate it, disbanding the Virginia House of Burgesses as soon as he arrived. By April 1775, the atmosphere had become so heavy that, as a preventive measure, Dunmore decided to remove the gunpowder stored in the public magazine. This move further angered the colonials, to the point that Dunmore

Time Line

1770

- Lord Dunmore is appointed royal governor of New York.

1771

- **September 25**
Dunmore becomes royal governor of Virginia; he subsequently dismisses the Virginia House of Burgesses.

1772

- **April**
Dunmore writes to Lord Dartmouth, the British secretary of state for the colonies, suggesting that slaves could be encouraged to fight for the British in large numbers.

1774

- Dunmore negotiates a treaty with the Shawnees after their defeat at the Battle of Point Pleasant.

1775

- **March 20**
At the Virginia Convention, Patrick Henry's speech (in which he famously says, "Give me liberty or give me death") proposes arming the Virginia militia.

- **April 18**
The battles of Lexington and Concord in Massachusetts initiate the Revolutionary War.

- **May**
Dunmore writes again to Lord Dartmouth, telling him that if he could arm the slaves and Indians, then he would use them.

- **June 8**
Dunmore flees Williamsburg for Yorktown, taking refuge on the man-of-war *Fowey*.

- **November 7**
Dunmore drafts his Proclamation.

- **November 12**
Dunmore's force, with the help of African American privates, routs the colonial militia at Kemp's Landing on the Elizabeth River.

- **November 14**
Dunmore enters Kemp's Landing as the victor and orders that the Proclamation be published.

---

fled the capital of Williamsburg on June 8, bound for the man-of-war *Fowey* near Yorktown. His forces had been diminished both by harassment from rebels and by desertion to approximately three hundred troops.

In April, a group of slaves had visited Dunmore at the governor's mansion, sensing that things were about to change. They volunteered their services, despite the punishment they risked in running away from their masters. The time was not right for a public rift with the Patriots, however, so Dunmore had the slaves sent away. Dunmore had contemplated enlisting African Americans held in bondage as early as 1772 and said as much in a May 1775 letter to William Legge, 2nd Earl of Dartmouth, who was British secretary of state for the colonies. Slaves and Native Americans, if armed, could supplement the dwindling numbers of British troops. Dunmore also knew that if the British did not arm the slaves, the rebels might; as he says in his letter to Dartmouth, "Whoever promises freedom to the slaves shall have all of them at his disposal."

After fleeing Williamsburg in June for the *Fowey*, Dunmore started, unofficially, to act on his scheme, reinforcing his ranks with raids and inviting anyone not against them to join them. This led to the practice of enlisting African Americans of "uncertain origins" (that is, free or slave), with no questions asked. To increase the yield of potential troops, Dunmore decided that he would issue an official proclamation promising freedom to slaves in return for service. He drafted this Proclamation on November 7, 1775, but he knew he needed to wait for the right moment to issue it.

The moment came a week later with the defeat of the rebel forces at a skirmish at Kemp's Landing along the Elizabeth River. Dunmore had learned that a group of about 150 militiamen were on their way to join Colonel William Woodford. Taking about 350 British—regulars, Loyalists, and runaway slaves—he left from Norfolk, a port town along the southeast coast of Chesapeake Bay and the home of Loyalist Scottish merchants, to intercept them. On November 14, the colonial militia was routed, and two commanding colonels were captured—one of them by African American privates who had joined Dunmore's forces. This success encouraged Dunmore to trust his decision to use African American soldiers. When he entered Kemp's Landing on November 15, he ordered the Proclamation to be published.

About the Author

John Murray, the future Lord Dunmore, was born in England in 1732, a direct, albeit distant, descendant of royalty. He later inherited his title, making him the 4th Earl of Dunmore. Dunmore served briefly in the House of Lords in Parliament, until, in 1770, he was appointed the royal governor of the New York Colony. Approximately a year later he left to be the royal governor of Virginia.

The first thing Dunmore did as governor was to eliminate the Virginia House of Burgesses, which was controlled by Patriots like Thomas Jefferson. In 1774, problems with the Shawnee Indians, who were in bitter conflict with the settlers in western Virginia, caused Dunmore to gather troops and hasten to the field of battle. At Point Pleasant, on the Virginia (later West Virginia) side of the Ohio River, one part of Dunmore's troops, led by General Andrew Lewis, was attacked by great numbers of the Shawnees. In a daylong battle, the Virginians came out victorious, though at great cost in numbers of men. Dunmore then negotiated a treaty with the Shawnees, which stated that the tribe would not hunt south of the Ohio River. This successfully cleared the way for English settlement in Kentucky.

Despite this victory, problems with the Patriots worsened. In June 1775, after an unsuccessful attempt at emptying the public magazine of gunpowder, Dunmore fled Williamsburg for the ship *Fowey*. From shipboard he considered his next move and gathered troops. After issuing his Proclamation in November 1775, Dunmore was derisively nicknamed "African Hero" by Richard Henry Lee, one of the Virginia delegates to the Continental Congress. In the summer of 1776, Dunmore disbanded his fleet and returned to England. However, in early 1782, Dunmore, with no official assignment, tried to advance a plan in Charleston, South Carolina, to recruit slaves into the British army again on a large scale. Nearly ten thousand men would be placed under the command of provincial officers. Although he was encouraged by other officers to accept the plan, commander in chief Henry Clinton refused to do so. In 1787, Dunmore was appointed royal governor of the Bahamas in the British West Indies. There he was responsible for building most of the forts in and around Nassau. One of the forts was dubbed "Dunmore's Folly" for being built at great cost in an area of the Bahamas where attack was highly improbable. He died in England in 1809.

Explanation and Analysis of the Document

The Proclamation begins with Lord Dunmore's own name and credentials: "His Majesty's Lieutenant and Governor General of the Colony and Dominion of Virginia, and Vice Admiral of the same." ("Lieutenant" here signifies not a junior officer but rather invokes the literal meaning of one who "holds the place of" the king.) These credentials entitled Dunmore to make the following Proclamation. Although Dunmore says he had sought an "Accommodation" (a reconciliation) between the unhappy rebels and the British, matters had reached a point where something had to be done to force the rebels to recognize the authority of the Crown. Rebel colonists were forming an army and firing on British troops and "well-disposed subjects of this Colony"—those loyal to Britain—alike. These people were committing treason as well as disrupting the peace, order, and justice of the colony; this state of affairs could not be allowed to continue, and the Proclamation aimed to put a stop to it.

Civil laws did not seem to be working toward this end anymore, however. Thus, Dunmore declares that martial law had to be instituted in the rebellious colony. He points out that the power to institute martial law lay with him, a

Time Line

1775

■ **November 24**
A letter is published in the *Virginia Gazette* warning slaves that they should not "ruin themselves" by running to Lord Dunmore, himself a slaveholder.

■ **December 2**
The Continental Congress orders ships to capture or destroy Dunmore's fleet.

■ **December 4**
The Continental Congress tells the Virginia Convention to do whatever it can to oppose Dunmore.

■ **December 8**
The Virginia Convention assembles to answer the Proclamation.

■ **December 9**
The Patriots defeat Dunmore's force, half of them African American, at Great Bridge.

■ **December 13**
The Virginia Convention replies to Dunmore's Proclamation with their own Virginia Declaration, which repudiates Dunmore's offer of freedom to slaves.

1776

■ **July**
Dunmore's fleet disbands after taking refuge at Saint George's Island in the Potomac River, with some African American soldiers heading north for further service.

1782

■ **Early**
Dunmore's large-scale plan to recruit African American soldiers into the British army is rejected in Charleston by commander in chief Henry Clinton.

1787

■ Dunmore is appointed governor of the Bahamas.

1809

■ **February 25**
Dunmore dies in England.

Sir Henry Clinton (Library of Congress)

power given to him by the king and one he would use to restore the peace. Furthermore, so that this restoration of peace and order could be more swiftly executed, Dunmore summoned every man capable of bearing arms to report to "His Majesty's Standard." To summon men to report to the king's standard was tantamount to saying "Rally around the flag" or, more literally, "Come and join our side in the fighting." Those who did not join the British against the rebels were to be regarded as traitors, such treason being punishable by confiscation of land or even loss of life.

What follows is the part of the Proclamation that elicited the strongest response. Dunmore declares free all "indented [indentured] Servants, Negroes, or others"—black or white—belonging to "Rebels" who are "able and willing to bear Arms" in the company of the British troops to fight against the traitors. Note that the offer applied only to able-bodied men—a point that would later be seized upon by colonial rebels. Dunmore took this action for "speedily reducing this Colony to a proper Sense of their Duty"—putting them in their proper place, as it were. This measure was not altruistic; it did not come from any sense that slavery was inherently wrong. Dunmore himself owned slaves and by most accounts was a harsh master. And, as colonial gov-

ernor, he had refused to sign a bill stopping the slave trade into Virginia. The Virginia House of Burgesses wanted to pass this bill to hurt the British economy, since international slave trade was controlled by Britain. In this context, it is no wonder that Dunmore withheld his signature.

Emancipating the slaves of his enemy was an act of war. There were a number of reasons for Dunmore to take this step. It would increase the numbers of his army, diminished through desertion and harassment by the Patriots. He hoped that as slaves left their masters, those masters would decide to stay home to care for their property and their families. The fear of a mass slave insurrection would also turn the attention of planters from the British. Dunmore also realized that if he did not get some of these people on his side, he would eventually be compelled to fight them.

The last part of the Proclamation orders all people to "retain their Quit-rents, or any other Taxes due or that may become due, in their own Custody, till such a time as Peace may be again restored to this at present most unhappy Country." Quit-rents were a type of rent or property tax due to the royal treasury and were used to cover the expenses of royal colonial government. Most officers who collected these taxes were British or Loyalists, and sending these men to collect these taxes during the insurrection put them in grave danger.

Dunmore closes conventionally by stating where and when he was issuing the Proclamation: "the 7th day of November in the Sixteenth Year of His Majesty's Reign," on board the *William*. He ends with "GOD save the KING," the common declaration appended to documents and toasts, a sign of loyalty for subjects and officers of the monarch.

Audience

Lord Dunmore meant his Proclamation to be read by as wide an audience as possible. This was certainly achieved, as many newspapers reprinted it, often in its entirety. The rebels were to know that their actions had consequences. The loyal subjects of Britain were to be reassured that they would be protected and that attacks on them were also attacks on Britain. And the free African Americans and slaves were to know that their freedom could be secured if they were willing and able to get to the British lines and help them fight.

Impact

The impact of Lord Dunmore's Proclamation was instantaneous and far reaching. Almost immediately, area newspapers reprinted the entire Proclamation, both as information and as a warning. Restrictions on slave meetings were tightened, patrols doubled, and roads carefully watched. Anyone owning a small boat was warned to be particularly alert to the possibility of theft by runaways. Maryland also ordered a stricter alert for military forces to watch for runaways in Saint Mary's County. Many colonials—Patriot and Loyalist alike—feared a major slave rebellion because of

"To defeat such treasonable Purposes, and that all such Traitors, and their Abettors, may be brought to Justice, and that the Peace, and good Order of this Colony may be again restored … I have thought fit to issue this my Proclamation."

"I do in Virtue of the Power and Authority to Me given, by His Majesty, determine to execute Martial Law, and cause the same to be executed throughout this Colony."

"I do require every Person capable of bearing Arms, to resort to His Majesty's Standard, or be looked upon as Traitors to His Majesty's Crown and Government."

"And I do hereby further declare all indented Servants, Negroes, or others, (appertaining to Rebels,) free that are able and willing to bear Arms, they joining His Majesty's Troops as soon as may be, for the more speedily reducing this Colony to a proper Sense of their Duty, to his Majesty's Crown and Dignity."

the Proclamation. The growing distrust between slaves and masters was made worse.

Rumors began to spread that slaves were "stampeding" to the British lines. That there were actually enough slaves running to join the British to constitute a "stampede" is doubtful. However, because British propaganda promised good treatment from the governor—and, of course, freedom from slavery—about two hundred men joined the British within a few days, and within a week of the Proclamation's publication, there were about three hundred. Within the month, approximately eight hundred had enlisted. Undoubtedly there were many more who attempted to run away but did not succeed. The number of recruits might have been higher had the governor not been in exile aboard the *William* at the time.

The African Americans who reached the British lines were usually in good health and capable of being put to a great many uses. Indeed, Dunmore did put them to di-

verse service. Mainly, he envisioned them as soldiers. By December 1, 1775, approximately three hundred of his black troops were given military garb with the inscription "Liberty to Slaves" upon it. These troops were called Lord Dunmore's Ethiopian Regiment.

Dunmore also used his African American troops in maritime service, often as pilots, since they knew the area better than the British. They were also used for foraging and messenger service on land. Being on the ground in Virginia was more dangerous at this time for British soldiers than it was even for runaway slaves. Dunmore was accused, too, of using the African American troops for biological warfare, by inoculating a few with smallpox and sending them onto land to infect the rebels. This was most likely propaganda rather than truth, but it made the rebels angry all the same. This propaganda also held a shred of truth, since many African American troops were indeed infected with smallpox. The cramped space on the ships where they were based and the lack of proper clothing made for horrible conditions, and the majority of the black men who fled to Dunmore ultimately died of disease.

The Patriots did their best to prevent slaves from running to enemy lines. The newspapers, besides printing the Proclamation in its entirety, also engaged in a type of psychological warfare. They published letters urging slaves not to join Dunmore, including several printed in the *Virginia Gazette*, pointing out that Dunmore was cruel to his own slaves and that the British were much harsher masters all around. If the Patriots lost, these black troops would be sold to the West Indies by the British. The *Gazette* also pointed out that Dunmore would free only those slaves who could bear arms, leaving women, children, the aged, and the infirm still in bondage and subject to the wrath of their masters. The slaves' best bet was to place their hopes not on the British but "on a better condition in the next world," according to one letter.

On December 2, 1775, the Continental Congress in Philadelphia responded to the Proclamation by ordering ships to capture or destroy the governor's fleet. Two days later, the Congress also told the Virginia Convention that they should do everything they could to oppose Dunmore. On December 8, the Virginia Convention met to appoint a committee to prepare an answer to the Proclamation. Five days later, the committee reported back and was authorized to draw up a declaration stating that runaways to the British would be pardoned if they put down their arms and returned within ten days. If they did not, then they would be punished. This Virginia Declaration also reminded the runaways that the usual punishment for slave insurrection was death without the benefit of clergy. The Declaration was published as a broadside in order to reach the widest audience possible.

Despite this warning, the death penalty was in fact used sparingly. In general, slaves caught running to Dunmore were simply returned to their masters. Those captured "in arms" were sold to the West Indies, and the money from the sale, minus expenses, was given to the slaves' masters. Slaves of British sympathizers who were caught were sent to work in the lead mines.

The only real military action seen by those African Americans joining Dunmore after the Proclamation was the Battle at Great Bridge on the Elizabeth River on December 9, 1775. Because of the victory at Kemp's Landing the month before and the fresh influx of black troops, Dunmore became overconfident and took the offensive at Great Bridge. His defeat was decisive, with at least one hundred casualties, half of them African American troops. After this failure, Dunmore was forced to operate exclusively from shipboard and never regained a foothold on the Virginia mainland.

As noted, many of the African Americans who ran away to join Dunmore died from disease. Otherwise, he might have had as many as two thousand African American troops. In the event, smallpox and harassment by the Virginia and Maryland militias forced Dunmore to move his fleet northward in May 1776. By June, fewer than one hundred and fifty African American soldiers were fit for duty. On August 6 Dunmore ordered his fleet to be broken apart (some dispersed and others destroyed), and the ablest of the African Americans were sent north for further military service with the British.

Had things gone better for Dunmore, his plan might have succeeded. However, one consequence of the Proclamation would have been unavoidable. The Proclamation helped secure to the Patriots those white colonists who had previously been moderate or undecided about the British. Many of them saw this Proclamation as the last straw: It

Questions for Further Study

1. Describe the legislative history of slavery in the Virginia colony. How did slave-owning Virginians react to Lord Dunmore's Proclamation?

2. What military circumstances provoked Dunmore to issue the Proclamation? Why did he issue it when he did?

3. Why do you think the Proclamation failed to create a "stampede" of Virginia slaves and free blacks going over to the British side in the Revolutionary War?

4. Other than to recruit troops for the British army, what other motivations did Dunmore have in issuing the Proclamation?

5. In some respects, the promise of freedom offered by Lord Dunmore's Proclamation made matters worse for Virginia's slaves. How so?

was an attack on private property and on their way of life and their peace, since it threatened to create a slave insurrection. These things reminded moderates that their ideals were the same as those of the more radical Patriots and that these ideals were worth fighting for.

See also Virginia's Act XII: Negro Women's Children to Serve according to the Condition of the Mother (1662); Virginia's Act III: Baptism Does Not Exempt Slaves from Bondage (1667); Thomas Jefferson's *Notes on the State of Virginia* (1784).

Further Reading

■ Books

Egerton, Douglas R. *Death or Liberty: African Americans and Revolutionary America*. New York: Oxford University Press, 2009.

Frey, Sylvia R. *Water from the Rock: Black Resistance in a Revolutionary Age*. Princeton, N.J.: Princeton University Press, 1991.

Nash, Gary B. *The Forgotten Fifth: African Americans in the Age of Revolution*. Cambridge, Mass.: Harvard University Press, 2006.

Quarles, Benjamin. *The Negro in the American Revolution*. New York: W. W. Norton, 1973.

————. *Black Mosaic: Essays in Afro-American History and Historiography*. Amherst, Mass.: University of Massachusetts Press, 1988.

■ Web Sites

"Dunmore's Proclamation: A Time to Choose." Colonial Williamsburg Web site.
http://www.history.org/almanack/people/african/aadunpro.cfm.

—Angela M. Alexander

LORD DUNMORE'S PROCLAMATION

By His Excellency the Right Honorable John Earl of Dunmore, His Majesty's Lieutenant and Governor General of the Colony and Dominion of Virginia, and Vice Admiral of the same.

A PROCLAMATION

As I have ever entertained Hopes, that an Accommodation might have taken Place between Great Britain and this Colony, without being compelled by my Duty to this most disagreeable but now absolutely necessary Step, rendered so by a Body of armed Men unlawfully assembled, firing upon His Majesty's Tenders, and the formation of an Army, and that Army now on their March to attack his Majesty's Troops and destroy the well-disposed subjects of this Colony. To defeat such treasonable Purposes, and that all such Traitors, and their Abettors, may be brought to Justice, and that the Peace and good Order of this Colony may be again restored, which the ordinary Course of the Civil Law is unable to effect; I have thought fit to issue this my Proclamation, hereby declaring, that until the aforesaid good Purpose can be obtained, I do in Virtue of the Power and Authority to Me given, by His Majesty, determine to execute Martial Law, and cause the same to be executed throughout this Colony: And to the end that Peace and good Order may the sooner be restored, I do require every Person capable of bearing Arms, to resort to His Majesty's Standard, or be looked upon as Traitors to His Majesty's Crown and Government, and thereby become liable to the Penalty the Law inflicts upon such Offenses; such as forfeiture of Life, confiscation of Lands, &c. &c. And I do hereby further declare all indented Servants, Negroes, or others, (appertaining to Rebels,) free that are able and willing to bear Arms, they joining His Majesty's Troops as soon as may be, for the more speedily reducing this Colony to a proper Sense of their Duty, to His Majesty's Crown and Dignity. I do further order, and require, all His Majesty's Liege Subjects, to retain their Quit-rents, or any other Taxes due or that may become due, in their own Custody, till such a Time as Peace may be again restored to this at present most unhappy Country, or demanded of them for their former salutary Purposes, by Officers properly authorized to receive the same.

Given under my Hand on board the Ship WILLIAM by Norfolk, the 7th Day of November in the Sixteenth Year of His Majesty's Reign.

DUNMORE

(GOD save the KING.)

Glossary

indented servants	indentured servants, that is, servants bound to their master for a term of years, after which they are released
Liege	bound by obligation; faithful, loyal
Lieutenant	literally, "one who holds the place of," in this instance, of the king of England; the king's representative
Quit-rents	a land tax imposed on owned or leased land by the landowning authority, usually the government
Sixteenth year of His Majesty's reign	1775, the sixteenth year of the reign of George III of England, who assumed the throne in 1760
Tenders	generally, small ships or boats used to attend other ships and supply them with provisions

137

To the Honorable Council & House of Representatives for the State of Massachusetts-Bay, in General Court assembled January 13th 1777 —

The Petition of a great number of Negroes who are detained in a state of Slavery, in the Bowels of a free & Christian Country Humbly shewing —

That your Petitioners apprehend that they have, in common with all other Men, a natural & unalienable right to that freedom, which the great Parent of the Universe hath bestowed equally on all Mankind, & which they have never forfeited by any compact or agreement whatever — But they were unjustly dragged, by the cruel hand of Power, from their dearest friends & some of them were torn from the Embraces of their tender Parents — From a populous, pleasant & plentiful Country — & in Violation of the Laws of Nature & of Nations & in defiance of all the tender feelings of humanity, brought hither to be sold like Beasts of Burthen, & like them condemned to slavery for Life — Among a People professing the mild Religion of Jesus A People not insensible of the sweets of rational freedom — Nor without Spirit to resent the unjust endeavours of others, to reduce them to a State of Bondage & Subjection — Your Honors need not to be informed that a Life of Slavery, like that of your Petitioners, deprived of every social priviledge, of every thing requisite to render Life even tolerable is far worse than Nonexistence — In imitation of the laudable example of the good People of these States, your Petitioners have long & patiently waited the event of Petition after Petition, by them presented to the Legislative Body of this State, & can not but with grief reflect that their success has been but too similar — They can not but express their astonishment that it has never been considered, that every principle

The 1777 petition to the Massachusetts General Court (Courtesy Massachusetts Archives)

PETITION OF PRINCE HALL AND OTHER AFRICAN AMERICANS TO THE MASSACHUSETTS GENERAL COURT

"They were ... torn from the embraces of their tender Parents from a ... pleasant and plentiful Country."

Overview

On January 13, 1777, Prince Hall and seven other African American men—most of them probably free—submitted a petition to the Massachusetts General Court, which at that time consisted of the Massachusetts Revolutionary Council and the House of Representatives. This petition sought freedom for "a great number of Negroes who are detained ... in the Bowels of a free & Christian Country." The petition was one of several that African Americans in New England submitted during the late eighteenth century. This one was particularly noteworthy because it challenged the Commonwealth of Massachusetts's government to live up to the human rights principles that had been set forth less than a year earlier in the Declaration of Independence. Little is known of Prince Hall before 1780, and there are conflicting stories of his origins, but what we do know of Hall's life points to him as the leader of this effort.

The Massachusetts legislature failed to pass any laws in response to this petition; however, the *Quock Walker v. Jennison* case, in which an African American filed a claim of unjust enslavement, soon resulted in a jury decision in 1781 and an upper-court ruling in 1783 that spelled the end of slavery in Massachusetts. In the coming years, other northern states passed laws that ended slavery gradually and thus avoided what many whites viewed as the socioeconomic chaos that could have been brought on by immediate abolition. While these governmental actions are usually credited with having ended slavery above the Mason-Dixon Line, the petition of January 1777 and similar formal appeals played critical foundational roles in the process. These petitions also to some extent represent the starting point for the establishment of organized African American communities in New England and elsewhere in the North.

Context

The number of Africans and their descendants in southern New England had risen from about one thousand in 1700 to around eleven thousand by the middle of the eigh-

teenth century, largely because prominent merchants in the region had become deeply involved in the slave trade. These merchants sold most of their slaves to owners in the West Indies, but they processed and routed slaves through Boston as well as Newport, Rhode Island, and other New England ports. Also, some slaves were sold within New England to meet the demand for domestic servants and skilled laborers. Most slaves probably had come directly from Africa, but some were from the West Indies or the southern American colonies. The percentage of American-born blacks grew throughout the eighteenth century, and the demographic balance between men and women began to even out. Nevertheless, in 1765 most of the twenty-seven hundred adult African Americans living in Massachusetts were men. About a third lived in Boston, the region's center of commerce and government.

Although most blacks in colonial New England were slaves, a significant number were free. The situation of blacks in New England, regardless of their status, was markedly different from that of blacks in other colonies. Most lived in port towns and worked in semiskilled or unskilled jobs for which Anglo-American labor was scarce. The few who resided in rural villages were probably slaves and served as status symbols for their masters. Rural slaves also provided a pool of menial labor for the local elites, particularly ministers. Of those African Americans who already were free, a very few became successful. For example, a slave named "Emmanuel," after having gained freedom from his master, Gabriel Bernon, in 1736, opened a popular oyster house in Providence, Rhode Island, and when he died in 1796 left an estate worth £569.

Like indentured white servants and apprentices, all slaves and nearly all free blacks in colonial New England lived as dependents in the homes of Anglo-Americans and were considered members of extended households. As dependents, they lacked individual autonomy and were expected to adapt quickly to the dominant culture and community. But even under these circumstances there were opportunities for betterment. Slaves were usually taught to read so that they could understand the Bible. Many slaves were able to hire themselves out to work for other employers and potentially could even buy their freedom. Those living in port towns worked alongside free, apprenticed,

1772

■ **June 22**
The Chief Justice of the King's Bench issues the Somerset decision, which stated that slavery could not exist in England or British colonies unless written law had already established it.

1773

■ **January 6**
Felix Holbrook petitions the Massachusetts colonial government for "relief" from slavery.

■ **April 20**
Five African Americans from Boston, including Holbrook, petition the Massachusetts colonial government for their freedom.

1774

■ **May 25**
African Americans submit a petition asking for freedom to the British military governor Thomas Gage and the Massachusetts House of Representatives, the first of two petitions.

1775

■ **March 6**
Fifteen Boston blacks join the Masonic lodge attached to the British Army in Boston.

1777

■ **January 13**
Eight Boston blacks, including Prince Hall, petition for freedom for "a great number of Negroes."

1781

■ In *Brom & Bett v. Ashley*, a jury decides in favor of Elizabeth Freeman, a slave who sued her owner for her freedom on the basis on the first article of the Massachusetts state constitution of 1780.

■ Chief Justice William Cushing of the Massachusetts Supreme Judicial Court hands down the Quock Walker ruling.

■ **November**
Prince Hall offers to recruit African American men to help put down Shays's Rebellion in western Massachusetts.

and indentured laborers and often caroused with them in pubs after work. In Massachusetts, even slaves had many civil rights, including trial by jury as well as the right to enter into contracts, to sue for abuse or fraud, and to sue if they considered themselves unjustly enslaved. However, blacks and indentured whites were subject to special laws designed to exert an extra measure of control over potentially dangerous minorities. Blacks could not marry whites, and in many towns slaves and indentured whites had to carry passes from their masters if they were moving about after dark. Townspeople were often on edge about the potential for disorder. In Boston in 1753, groups of blacks and poor whites were accused of parading through streets, building bonfires, and abusing pedestrians. In response, the Massachusetts assembly passed laws that barred three or more men from parading in the streets, and blacks who disobeyed this law were to be punished with ten stripes.

There was one yearly event when blacks were allowed to take collective action: the so-called Negro election festivals, which had begun in the mid-eighteenth century and continued until after slavery ended in Massachusetts. These festivals served several purposes. Blacks in a given locale would elect a man who would serve as their representative with Anglo-American community leaders and might be called upon to judge disputes between slaves. Those elected were often from noble African families. These events were also carnival-like events where the social restrictions were set aside, providing a release from repressive social norms but paradoxically also reaffirming them. Whites and Native Americans also partook in these festivals.

While servitude and racism were facts of life in eighteenth-century New England, as elsewhere in colonial America, the region's culture also nurtured a nascent opposition to the slave trade. This opposition was rooted in the Puritan view that permitted the enslaving of war captives but frowned on "man stealing." In 1700 Massachusetts chief justice Samuel Sewall published *The Selling of Joseph: A Memorial*, which began, "It is most certain that all Men, as they are the Sons of *Adam*, are Coheirs; and have equal Right unto Liberty, and all other outward Comforts of Life." It is therefore perhaps not surprising that slaves, with the support of sympathetic whites, began in 1765 to file a series of lawsuits challenging their status. Juries became more sympathetic to the cause of slaves as popular opposition to Britain's measures intensified in the colonies. Many colonists began to contemplate the apparent contradiction between democratic ideals and the existence slavery in their midst. The Boston attorney James Otis, in his famed pamphlet *The Rights of British Colonies* (1764), wrote: "The Colonists are by the law of nature free born, as indeed all men are, white or black.... Does it follow that 'tis right to enslave a man because he is black?" Slavery, Otis noted, "is the most shocking violation of the law of nature, has a direct tendency to diminish the idea of the inestimable value of liberty, and makes every dealer in it a tyrant.... Those who every day barter away other men's liberty will soon care little for their own."

Not surprisingly, African Americans became involved the cause for freedom from British rule. One of the more famous examples occurred on March 2, 1770, when the mixed-race sailor Crispus Attucks was the first man killed in the Boston Massacre, a violent skirmish between dockworkers and British military forces. Along with the others slain, Attucks was honored as a martyr. Phillis Wheatley, born in West Africa in 1753 or 1754 and sold to John Wheatley in Boston at the age of seven, gained fame in the late 1760s as a teenage poet prodigy. Although some of her most famous works gave thanks for being brought to a Christian America, her public view shifted in the Revolutionary environment. In 1772 Phillis wrote a long work that linked her love of the emerging concept of American freedom to her "cruel fate" of being "snatch'd from Afric's fancy'd happy seat." But the most important embrace by blacks of Revolutionary goals came in a series of petitions that began in 1773.

The first petition was sent to the colonial Massachusetts governor Thomas Hutchinson, the Governor's Council, and the House of Representatives, on January 6, 1773. The petitioner was a black man named Felix (probably Felix Holbrook, who also signed subsequent petitions), who made his application on behalf of "many Slaves" in Boston and elsewhere in Massachusetts. He began with an appeal to Christianity and then referred in an oblique way to the Somerset court decision by invoking God, who "hath lately put it into the Hearts of Multitudes on both Sides of the Water, to bear our Burthens, some of whom are Men of great Note and Influence; who have pleaded our Cause." In the Somerset case, the chief justice of the King's Bench had ruled in June 1772 that slavery could not exist in England or its colonies unless it was explicitly established by written law. In his petition Felix conceded that "some of the Negroes are vicious," but he insisted that most slaves would be industrious if they were freed. He also pointedly observed that although male slaves were deprived of everything considered proper for men (wives, property, and children), they would obey their masters as long as they remained slaves. According to Felix, they wanted only "such Relief" that would cause the "least Wrong or Injury to our Masters." Felix clearly advocated freedom for slaves yet did not mention the word. While he was the only signatory, on the same day an individual known as Hume wrote a letter in support of Felix's petition to the governor and the House of Representatives. That letter, published in the *Massachusetts Spy* on January 28, brought up the Somerset ruling, moral arguments against slavery, and broader movements in the colony for the recognition of human rights.

Three and a half months later, on April 20, there came a very different petition from Felix Holbrook, Peter Bestes (or Bess), Sambo Freeman, and Chester Joe. Addressed to delegates in the House of Representatives, it was printed so that it could be distributed widely. The petition began by noting with considerable irony that the House's recent efforts "to free themselves from slavery"—that is, the colony's opposition to the Sugar Act, Stamp Act, and Townshend Revenue Act—"gave us, who are in that deplorable state,

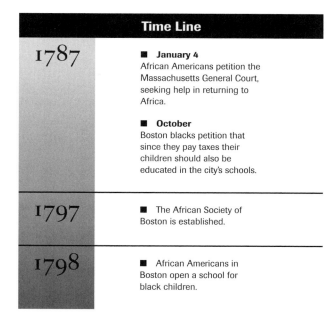

Time Line

1787
- **January 4**
African Americans petition the Massachusetts General Court, seeking help in returning to Africa.

- **October**
Boston blacks petition that since they pay taxes their children should also be educated in the city's schools.

1797
- The African Society of Boston is established.

1798
- African Americans in Boston open a school for black children.

a high degree of satisfaction" and then added: "We expect great things from men who have made such a noble stand against the designs of their *fellow-men* to enslave them." As in Felix's earlier petition, the signatories assured their readers that they were not demanding all that was due to them by "right," because that would harm their masters. Nor did they want to "dictate" policy to the House of Representatives, but they expected that the delegates, motivated by "principles of equity and justice," would take their "deplorable case" into consideration. This time, the petitioners asked for their "natural right" to "freedom" and offered to submit to whatever laws and regulations were imposed until they could earn enough money to return to the coast of Africa—a goal not mentioned in the petition of January 1773.

Approximately a year later, on May 25 and again in June, two more petitions from African Americans were submitted, this time to the British governor Thomas Gage and the military government that had just been imposed in Massachusetts in response to popular unrest. There is no surviving record of signatories for either petition. The May petition referenced the Somerset decision and asserted that blacks were held in slavery "by divine permission," which implied that the laws of Massachusetts had not permitted their enslavement. This petition stated that "the laws of the Land … doth not justify but condemns Slavery" and that those held in bondage had "a natural right" to freedom. It also included an extended discussion of how slaves had been prevented from acting as husbands, wives, or even parents. The petitioners concluded with requests to be "liberated and made free men" and to be given land for farms. The petition of June 1777 pointed to the Somerset decision and noted that no laws or contracts had made blacks slaves; it also put more emphasis on religion and even hinted at a connection between the forced servitude of African Americans and that of the Israelites in Egypt. This petition asked for recognition of the "Natural rights or freedoms" of slaves

Thomas Gage (Library of Congress)

and for their children to be freed at age twenty-one, but it made no request for land and did not mention Africa, apart from the reference to the Israelites' bondage.

As the politics of the region spun toward revolution and war, African Americans took sides with both the colonists and the British. Perhaps this was because many slaves were seeking the best opportunity for freedom. On September 22, 1774, Abigail Adams wrote to her husband, the future president John Adams, that she had heard in Boston of "a conspiracy of the negroes," who had offered Governor Gage their military service if he armed and freed them. Perhaps this rumor was connected to the May and June petitions, but the colonists would have been particularly fearful, given Parliament's imposition of the Intolerable Acts (also known as the Coercive Acts) in punishment for the Boston Tea Party. Those measures blockaded Boston, required the colonists to house British soldiers, and exempted British officials from local courts, and also repealed the Massachusetts charter and put the province under martial law directed by Gage. On March 6, 1775, as angry colonists moved to resist these measures, fifteen free black men, including Peter Best and Prince Hall, became members of the Masonic lodge that was affiliated with a British army regiment quartered in Boston. About three weeks later, African Americans in Bristol and Worcester counties asked the Revolutionary committees of correspondence in Worcester County to help them gain freedom. On April 19 came the outbreak of war at Lexington and Concord. Free and enslaved African Americans fought with town militias at those engagements and were among the forces of colonists at Charlestown that besieged Boston and tried to hold the line on June 17 at the Battle of Bunker Hill. By that time, General Gage was indeed considering enlisting African Americans, if only to entice them away from helping the American forces.

Congress appointed George Washington commander of American forces on June 15, 1775. When he arrived in Massachusetts in July, with British troops still besieged in Boston, he and his staff were scandalized to find blacks in the ranks. On October 8, his council tried to eject slaves and free blacks from the Continental army. But the protests of militia officers and shortfalls in recruiting—plus the willingness of the British to enlist blacks—forced Washington to change course. He first tolerated and then encouraged free blacks to enlist and finally asked Congress to allow slaves to enlist with their owners' permission. While a few black units were formed, most African American soldiers served in integrated units. It would not be until the Korean War during the early 1950s, over one hundred seventy years later, that African Americans would again serve their country in integrated units. On March 17, 1776, the British Army evacuated Boston; before they left, black members of the Masonic lodge were granted limited dispensation to maintain their group. On July 4, 1776, Congress declared independence. Five months later, on January 13, 1777, Prince Hall and seven other African Americans submitted a petition to the Massachusetts General Court on behalf of "a great number of Negroes" that called for an end to slavery.

About the Author

Eight men put their names on the petition of January 13, 1777: Lancaster Hill, Peter Bess (probably Best), Prince Hall, Jack Purpont, Brister Slenser, Nero Suneto, Newport Symner, and Job Lark. Four were literate enough to sign instead of simply making a mark next to their names: Hill, Hall, Slenser, and Lark. Hall, Best, and Slenser were three of the fifteen black members of the Masonic lodge and had obviously chosen not to leave with the British but rather to remain in Boston. Bess also had signed the petition of April 20, 1773. There is, however, extensive information about only one signatory, Prince Hall, largely because of his leadership of the African American Masonic lodge and other black community organizations in Boston after the Revolutionary War. Hall's subsequent speeches and petitions were written in a style similar to that of this petition, which indicates that he may have also been its author.

Little has been documented of Hall's life before the American Revolution. The Masonic tradition holds that he was born a free man in Barbados on September 12, 1748, and sailed to Boston in March 1765. By the age of twenty-five he owned a soap-making business, had purchased a home, and was qualified to vote in the city. A non-Masonic biographer has provided a different biography. According to this version, Hall was born in 1735, birthplace unknown, and first appeared in Boston in the 1740s as a slave belonging to William Hall. In support of this version, Hall himself testified just before his death in 1807 that he was about seventy years old. In 1756 he fathered a son named Primus, whose mother was Delia, a servant in another household. In 1770 Hall was given freedom by his master one month after the Boston Massacre. It is unknown whether Hall fought during the American Revolution. Besides this petition, the only documents about Hall that date from the war years are records that he owned property and paid taxes. There is also a bill that he submitted on April 24, 1777, for five drumheads, which shows that his trade was leather dressing.

Hall became the leader of the Boston African American community—the largest in New England—as it became a coherent entity and developed social, religious, and educational institutions. He began with the African American Masonic lodge and tried without success to receive official recognition of it from the American branch of the Masons. In March 1784 he asked the leaders of the fraternal order of Free and Accepted Masons in London for a charter that would give the African American lodge in Boston the same powers as other lodges, including the ability to initiate new Masons. That charter was granted in the spring of 1787, officially recognizing African Lodge No. 1 with Prince Hall as Master. The lodge provided services to black Bostonians: free firewood, periodic food drives for those in need, weekly "sick dues," and loans for members and their families. It later became known as the Prince Hall Lodge; today there are forty-seven Prince Hall Lodges that have grown out of the original Boston lodge.

Hall sought to strengthen political bonds between African Americans and Massachusetts political leaders. In late November 1786 Hall offered Governor James Bowdoin seven hundred African American men to help put down Shays's Rebellion. Farmers and gentry in the poorer, rural, western part of the state, angered at their inability to pay high state taxes imposed to meet Revolutionary War debts, held mostly by wealthy Bostonians, had taken up weapons and forced the county courts to close in order to stop foreclosures. Boston merchants helped pay for an army assembled in the east, since more local militia seemed untrustworthy; that force confronted and dispersed the "rebels" and arrested many. But the governor turned down Hall's offer, probably because he and other Boston elites feared placing weapons in the hands of so many African American men. One month later, perhaps in part because of the governor's rebuff, Hall submitted a petition from the African Lodge to the General Court that complained about society's poor treatment of blacks and the lack of opportunity for them; the petition also sought assistance in returning blacks to Africa. In October 1787 Hall submitted a petition with many signatories that charged that since African Americans paid district taxes their children had the right to be educated in the city's schools. A few months later, he organized a petition signed by twenty-two Masons for the return of three free Boston African Americans who had been kidnapped and subsequently sold as slaves. On March 26, 1788, the General Court responded with an act that banned the slave trade

Portrait of James Otis on the cover of the Boston Almanack
(Library of Congress)

and gained relief for blacks kidnapped from Massachusetts and resold into slavery. The return of the three men in July 1788 was celebrated at the African lodge.

During the 1790s Hall was instrumental in the creation of organizations to meet the needs of Boston's African American community. In June 1792 he delivered a speech in Charlestown, "A Charge Delivered to the Brethren of the African Lodge," in which he criticized Massachusetts districts (towns) for taxing African Americans while refusing to allow their children to attend local schools. The speech was published that year. Four years afterward, he brought up this same issue with the Boston selectmen but again failed to gain admittance of black children to area schools. Hall then established an independent black school at the Boston African Meeting House, with his son, Primus, as teacher. In 1797 Hall helped found the African Society of Boston, which provided various forms of assistance to Boston-area blacks who were not Masons. Society members were required to live according to an upright moral code and emulate middle-class social values, even though the majority of blacks were of very limited means and un-

"They have, in common with all other Men, a natural & unalienable right to that freedom, which the great Parent of the Universe hath bestowed equally on all mankind, & which they have never forfeited by any compact or agreement whatever."

"They were unjustly dragged ... from their dearest friends, & some of them even torn from the embraces of their tender Parents from a populous, pleasant and plentiful Country—& in Violation of the Laws of Nature & of Nation."

"They can not but express their astonishment, that it has never been considered, that every principle from which America has acted in the course of their unhappy difficulties with Great-Britain, pleads stronger than a thousand arguments in favor of your Petitioners."

able to attain a middle-class living standard. The last public record of Hall's thought was an address to the African Masonic Lodge on June 24, 1797, in which he celebrated the success of the Haitian slave revolt of 1791 and urged his brothers to exercise patience despite their regular abuse in Boston. He died ten years later.

Explanation and Analysis of the Document

The petition of January 1777 begins by stating that it was an appeal on behalf of not only the signatories but also "a great number of Negroes," many then living in a "state of Slavery." The three previous petitions for freedom submitted between January 1773 and May 1774 had begun similarly. But the 1777 petition was the first effort by African Americans to improve their situation after the country had declared itself free of British rule. The petition relied heavily on concepts that had emerged with the European Enlightenment in the late seventeenth century, particularly the notion first expressed by the English political philosopher John Locke in 1690 that all humans were born with the "natural" rights of life, liberty, and property. Locke and later Enlightenment thinkers also held that government was not something imposed by God on sinful humans but

a contract created by people long ago in order to protect their natural rights from greed or passion; if a government violated those rights, the people had the right to change the government. These concepts would become foundations of the American Revolution and were carefully chosen by Thomas Jefferson to open the Declaration of Independence—published just six months before the eight Boston blacks presented their petition for freedom. The petition also critiques the hypocrisy of calling for freedom while allowing slavery to continue. This argument was quite different from that advanced in the other four petitions, all of which made only passing nods at Enlightenment thought and instead emphasized Christian morality, the "unmanly" situations of the petitioners, and the Somerset court decision.

Although the document is not divided into sections, it may be considered in three parts. In the first part, the petitioners call forth concepts cherished by political leaders in the state (and country) and condemn the international slave trade as a violation of those values. They declare that blacks have "a natural & unalienable right" to the freedom granted to all humankind, "which they have never forfeited by any compact or agreement." This phrasing is significant not only because of the reference to natural rights but also because the giver of freedom is described not as Christ or God but as the "great Parent of the Universe"—a phrase in tune with Enlightenment notions of the universe as a machine that God created with predictable rules understandable by human beings. The opening perhaps also retains the hint of a reference to the Somerset decision. The next clause invokes the emerging Euro-American notion of sentimentalism, that citizens in a republic needed to develop the virtuous and benevolent moral feelings that could be fostered only within a loving family and by the manly bonds of friendship. Thus the petitioners decry the "cruel hand" of the slave traders, who "unjustly dragged" blacks "from their dearest friends," some "even torn from the embraces of their tender Parents." These practices are condemned as being in violation of the "Laws of Nature & of Nation"—a reference to Locke and the Somerset ruling—as well as "in defiance of all the tender feelings of humanity." In perhaps the most unexpected clause, the petitioners associate their lost happiness with "a populous, pleasant and plentiful Country," rather than an African continent more usually depicted (even by Phillis Wheatley in her popular poems) as barbaric, savage, and dark.

The next part first offers flowery praise, then bitter criticism. Here, the petition extols New Englanders for "professing the mild Religion of Jesus" (the tone of the word *professing* being perhaps mildly scolding) and being "not insensible of the sweets of rational freedom." By commending the "spirit" by which the American colonists had resisted "the unjust endeavors of others to reduce them to a State of Bondage & Subjection," this section makes the connection between the ideals of the American Revolution and freedom from slavery. The petitioners then pointedly note that the leaders of the state did not have to be "informed" that a life of slavery without any rights was "far worse than Non-Existence"—that is, even harsher than life under British military rule and Parliament's authority. The petitioners voice their bewilderment and "grief" at how, "in imitation of the laudable example" of American democratic practices, they had submitted "Petition after Petition" to the state legislature. Yet their efforts had been to no avail, much as the efforts of colonial American leaders had failed to gain a sympathetic ear in Parliament. There is no indication that this rebuke was meant to threaten a potential uprising by Massachusetts slaves, but it was a veiled hint at the level of their collective frustration. The petitioners then express "their astonishment" that their fellow Americans had not yet conceded that the principles upon which the Revolution was grounded pleaded "stronger than a thousand arguments" in support of freedom for slaves.

The third part of the petition is its most substantive section. It calls on the legislature to pass a measure ending slavery, though the petitioners are willing for their children born in America to remain slaves until the age of twenty-one. They observe that ending slavery would not be giving slaves new rights but restoring them "to the enjoyment of that freedom which is the natural right of all Men." Again, the petitioners call attention to the principle of natural rights. Unlike previous requests, this petition does not propose that any consideration should be given to slave owners. Likewise, it does not ask for land on which for-

mer slaves could start farms, nor is there any suggestion that blacks would return to Africa. If the legislature were to grant the petition's request, Prince Hall and the other signatories note, it would free the people of Massachusetts from "the inconsistency of acting, themselves, the part which they condemn & oppose in others." The people of Massachusetts would therefore certainly "be prospered in their present glorious struggles for Liberty."

Audience

This petition was addressed to the Massachusetts legislature, consisting of the House of Representatives and the Revolutionary Council, which functioned as the upper legislative house before the state constitution of 1780 took effect. Clearly, the petition was also directed at various community leaders (ministers, merchants, and lawyers), the general public, and African Americans throughout New England. The petitioners knew that their request would be reported and circulated widely.

Impact

The first response to the petition came from the Massachusetts legislature, which drafted and considered a bill that would have outlawed slavery, declaring it "unjustifiable in a civil government at a time when [the former colonies] are asserting their natural freedom." It also would have given freedmen "all the Freedom, Rights, privileges & immunities" of white adult males living in the state, which would have included the right to vote and hold office for those who also met the property-ownership requirement. The bill would have barred any agreements that conveyed or transferred ownership of any person aged twenty-one or older. It also would have tried to avoid adding to the tax burden of towns by "allowing" slaves who were "incapable of earning their living by reason of age or infirmities" to remain in service to their owners (and be supported by said owners) if they "voluntarily declare the same before two justices of the County." The bill also would have allowed ship owners to import indentured servants who were not from Africa or from the United States. The measure did not become law, however, apparently because the state assembly was reluctant to be the first in the union to take such an action. Instead, the question of emancipation was referred to the Continental Congress, which did nothing.

In a less direct fashion, the petition may have influenced the wording of the Massachusetts constitution and the outcome of two pivotal legal cases in which slaves had brought suit against their owners. Several Massachusetts towns rejected the draft of the state constitution of 1778 partly because it contained no explicit condemnation of slavery. Although the state constitution of 1780 also lacked a ban on slavery, its first article declared that "all men are born free and equal"—a statement that indeed led to the end of slavery in Massachusetts. In 1781 Elizabeth Freeman, a slave owned by John Ashley of Sheffield, cited the first article of the state constitution in her lawsuit asking for her freedom. A local jury decided in her favor. That same year, Quock Walker sued his owner, Nathaniel Jennison; during this trial Chief Justice William Cushing instructed the court that the first article had effectively banned slavery in the state. While there is no direct connection between the petition of January 1777 and these developments, certainly this petition and others like it helped lay the ideological groundwork for the abolition of slavery. Petitions submitted by African Americans to the Connecticut and New Hampshire legislatures may have similarly influenced the passage of the gradual emancipation laws in those states.

A third significant impact of the petitions of Prince Hall and others was the emergence of African American leadership and institutions in Boston as well as in other cities and states. Prince Hall's exceptional efforts as a community leader highlight that development, but he was clearly not alone. Because African Americans lived scattered around the city and mostly within white-headed households until the 1820s, the petitions submitted before, during, and after the American Revolution were not simply requests or demands for legislative action; just as importantly, they served to unify and organize the African American community.

See also *Prince Hall: A Charge Delivered to the African Lodge* (1797).

Further Reading

■ Articles

Mandell, Daniel. "Shifting Boundaries of Race and Ethnicity: Indian-Black Intermarriage in Southern New England, 1760–1880." *Journal of American History* 85, no. 2 (September 1998): 466–501.

■ Books

Butterfield, L. H., et al. eds. *Adams Family Correspondence*. Vol.1: *December 1761–May 1776*. Cambridge: Belknap Press of Harvard University Press, 1963.

Cottrol, Robert J. *The Afro-Yankees: Providence's Black Community in the Antebellum Era*. Westport, Conn.: Greenwood Press, 1982.

Holton, Woody, ed. *Black Americans in the Revolutionary Era: A Brief History with Documents*. New York: Bedford/St. Martin's, 2009.

Horton, James Oliver, and Lois E. Horton. *Black Bostonians: Family Life and Community Struggle in the Antebellum North*. New York: Holmes & Meier Publishers, 1979.

———. *In Hope of Liberty: Culture, Community, and Protest among Northern Free Blacks, 1700–1860*. New York: Oxford University Press, 1997.

Kaplan, Sidney, and Emma Nogrady Kaplan. *The Black Presence in the Era of the American Revolution*. Rev. ed. Amherst: University of Massachusetts Press, 1989.

Nash, Gary B. *Race and Revolution*. Lanham, Md.: Rowan and Littlefield, 2001.

Moore, George H. *Notes on the History of Slavery in Massachusetts*. New York: D. Appleton, 1866.

Questions for Further Study

1. How did Prince Hall's petition lay the foundation for abolition in Massachusetts and, ultimately, throughout the northern United States?

2. How did the status and circumstances of slaves in New England differ from those of slaves in the rural South? What factors contributed to these differences?

3. What role did religion play in the formation of early abolitionist sentiments in Massachusetts and throughout New England?

4. What events preceding and during the American Revolution contributed to the reasoning of Massachusetts petitioners in their quest for freedom? How did the authorities respond?

5. Compare this document with the court's decision in the legal case *Quock Walker v. Jennison*. To what extent do the two documents express similar views and rationales?

Otis, James. *The Rights of British Colonies Asserted and Proved.* Boston: Edes and Gill, 1764.

Piersen, William D. *Black Yankees: The Development of an Afro-American Subculture in Eighteenth-Century New England.* Amherst: University of Massachusetts Press, 1988.

Sewall, Samuel. *The Selling of Joseph: A Memorial.* Boston: Green and Allen, 1700.

Shields, John, ed. *The Collected Works of Phillis Wheatley.* New York: Oxford University Press, 1988.

—Daniel R. Mandell

PETITION OF PRINCE HALL AND OTHER AFRICAN AMERICANS TO THE MASSACHUSETTS GENERAL COURT

To the Honorable Council & House of Representatives for the State of Massachusetts Bay in General Court assembled January 13, 1777.

The Petition of a great number of Negroes who are detained in a state of Slavery in the Bowels of a free & Christian Country Humbly Shewing.

That your Petitioners apprehend that they have, in common with all other Men, a natural & unalienable right to that freedom, which the great Parent of the Universe hath bestowed equally on all mankind, & which they have never forfeited by any compact or agreement whatever. That they were unjustly dragged by the cruel hand of Power, from their dearest friends, & some of them even torn from the embraces of their tender Parents from a populous, pleasant and plentiful Country—& in Violation of the Laws of Nature & of Nation & in defiance of all the tender feelings of humanity, brought hither to be sold like Beasts of Burden, & like them condemned to slavery for Life. Among a People professing the mild Religion of Jesus—A People not insensible of the sweets of rational freedom—Nor without spirit to resent the unjust endeavors of others to reduce them to a State of Bondage & Subjection—Your donors need not to be informed that a Life of Slavery, like that of your petitioners, deprived of every social privilege, of every thing requisite to render Life even tolerable, is far worse than Non-Existence. In imitation of the laudable example of the People of these States, your Petitioners have long & patiently waited the event of Petition after Petition by them presented to the legislative Body of this State, & can not but with grief reflect that their success has been but too similar. They can not but express their astonishment, that it has never been considered, that every principle from which America has acted in the course of their unhappy difficulties with Great-Britain, pleads stronger than a thousand arguments in favor of your Petitioners. They therefore humbly beseech your Honors to give this Petition its due weight & consideration, & cause an Act of the Legislature to be passed whereby they may be restored to the enjoyment of that freedom which is the natural right of all Men—& their Children (who were born in this Land of Liberty) may not be held as Slaves after they arrive at the age of twenty one years. So may the Inhabitants of this State (no longer chargeable with the inconsistency of acting, themselves, the part which they condemn & oppose in others) be prospered in their present glorious struggles for Liberty: & have those blessings secured to them by Heaven of which benevolent minds can not wish to deprive their fellow Men.

And your Petitioners as in Duty Bound shall ever pray

Lancaster Hill
Peter Bess
Brister Slenser
Prince Hall
Jack Purpont [mark]
Nero Suneto [mark]
Newport Symner [mark]
Job Lark

𝔄𝔫 𝔄𝔠𝔱 for the gradual Aboli-tion of Slavery.

WHEN we contemplate our Abhorrence of that Condition to which the Arms and Tyranny of Great Britain were exerted to reduce us; when we look back on the Variety of Dangers to which we have been exposed, and how miraculously our Wants in many Instances have been supplied and our Deliverances wrought, when even Hope and human fortitude have become unequal to the Conflict; we are unavoidably led to a serious and grateful Sense of the manifold Blessings which we have undeservedly received _ from the hand of that Being from whom every good and perfect Gift cometh Impressed with these Ideas we conceive that it is our duty, and we rejoice that it is in our Power, to extend a Portion of that freedom to others, which hath been extended to us; and a Release from that State of Thraldom, to which we ourselves were tyrannically doomed, and from which we have now every Prospect of being delivered. It is not for us to enquire, why, in the Creation of Mankind, the Inhabitants of the several parts of the Earth, were distinguished

The Pennsylvania Gradual Abolition Act (The Pennsylvania State Archives)

PENNSYLVANIA: AN ACT FOR THE GRADUAL ABOLITION OF SLAVERY

"It is sufficient to know that all are the work of an Almighty Hand."

Overview

On March 1, 1780, with the Revolution still raging and its outcome in doubt, the Pennsylvania legislature became the first legislature in history to take steps to abolish slavery. Pennsylvania's Act for the Gradual Abolition of Slavery is both idealistic and practical. It tries to balance the idea of liberty, which was at the heart of the Revolution, with the founding generation's deep respect for private property. The law also recognizes the significance of race in both the creation of slavery and the perpetuation of discrimination against former slaves. Eventually four other states and a Canadian province—Connecticut (1784), Rhode Island (1784), New York (1799), New Jersey (1804), and Upper Canada (present-day Ontario; 1794)—adopted similar laws to end slavery. Thus the Pennsylvania law became a model for how places with slavery ended the institution. These places accomplished what no other societies before them had: the peaceful eradication of slavery.

Unlike the ending of slavery in the rest of the United States, the Pennsylvania law took into account the need to provide some equality and protection for former slaves. It also recognized that masters had a property interest in their slaves. While the American Revolutionaries used the rhetoric of liberty throughout their struggle, they also persistently acknowledged and argued for the right of property. Thomas Jefferson's famous language from the Declaration of Independence—that all people are entitled to "life, liberty, and the pursuit of happiness"—is a paraphrase of John Locke's trinity of "life, liberty, and property" from his *Two Treatises of Government* (1690), and almost all white Americans accepted that property was essential to liberty.

Context

When the American Revolution began in 1775, slavery was legal in all of the thirteen colonies. In New England, where the war started, some masters allowed their male slaves to enlist to fight for both their liberty and the liberty of the new nation. In the first battles in Massa-chusetts—at Lexington and Concord and then at Bunker Hill—a few blacks, such as Salem Poor and Peter Salem, distinguished themselves in battle. When the slaveholding George Washington took command of the Revolutionary Army based outside Boston, he was shocked to see armed and uniformed blacks in the ranks of the militias from New England. Initially Washington demanded that these black soldiers be mustered out of the army; within a few months, impressed by their skill and courage and desperate for any soldiers, Washington changed his mind and welcomed black soldiers. By the end of the war one of his favorite units was the First Rhode Island Infantry, even though about half the soldiers in that unit had been slaves when the war began. Washington quickly came to admire the dedication of those black soldiers who fought for their own liberty—and that of their families—as well as for the independence of the new nation.

Eventually thousands of slaves gained freedom for themselves and their families through military service, but these individual emancipations did not solve the great problem of slavery in the new nation. At the time of the Revolution, slavery presented the first great—and for a long time the most enduring—contradiction in American history. The Declaration of Independence asserts, "All men are created equal" and have a right to "life, liberty, and the pursuit of happiness." This language seems to condemn slavery. But the man who wrote these words, Thomas Jefferson, owned about 150 slaves at the time, and by the end of his life he owned more than two hundred slaves. The English literary figure Samuel Johnson pointedly asked during the Revolution, "How is it that we hear the loudest yelps for liberty among the drivers of negroes?"

In the South most Americans tried to ignore the issue of slavery, although hundreds if not thousands of individual southerners privately freed their slaves during and after the Revolution. Most famously, Washington provided for the freedom of all of his slaves when he died in 1799. The less famous, but still significant South Carolina Revolutionary Henry Laurens freed his slaves during his lifetime. Indeed, during and after the Revolution as many as fifty thousand southern slaves were freed by their owners, but this hardly made a dent in the overall southern slave population, which numbered more than one million when the Revolution ended.

1688

■ **February**
Germantown Quakers issue first protest against slavery in the New World.

1737

■ Benjamin Lay publishes *All Slave-Keepers That Keep the Innocent in Bondage, Apostates Pretending to Lay Claim to the Pure and Holy Christian Religion.*

1754

■ John Woolman publishes *Some Considerations on the Keeping of Negroes.*

1758

■ Philadelphia Yearly Meeting of the Society of Friends (Quakers) officially urges all Quakers to emancipate their slaves.

1762

■ Anthony Benezet publishes *A Short Account of That Part of Africa Inhabited by the Negroes.*

1772

■ Benezet publishes *Some Historical Account of Guinea.*

1773

■ Benjamin Rush publishes *An Address to the Inhabitants of the British Settlements in America, upon Slave-Keeping.*

1775

■ **April**
First antislavery society in America is organized in Philadelphia, calling itself the Society for the Relief of Free Negroes Unlawfully Held in Bondage.

■ **April 19**
Battles of Lexington and Concord in Massachusetts ignite the American Revolution.

1776

■ **July 4**
Continental Congress meeting in Philadelphia issues the Declaration of Independence.

In the North, social and economic factors led to greater opposition to slavery. The religious background of many northerners—Quakers, Congregationalists, Methodists, and Baptists—led to significant opposition to slavery in Pennsylvania and New England. This contrasted with the dominance of Anglican/Episcopalian leadership in the South. Antislavery sentiment was particular strong in Pennsylvania, where Quakers and other pietists had long opposed slavery, as did freethinkers like Benjamin Franklin and Benjamin Rush. Opposition to slavery in Pennsylvania was rooted, to a great extent, in the state's religious heritage. Pennsylvania took the lead in ending slavery in part because Quakers, Mennonites, and other members of pietistic faiths were among the earliest opponents of slavery in America. In February 1688, Quakers in Germantown, Pennsylvania, issued a resolution that sets out "the reasons why we are against the traffic of men-body." The resolution notes the revulsion Europeans had for the thought of being enslaved by Turks and then argues, "Now, though they are black, we cannot conceive there is more liberty to have them slaves" than it is for the Turks to enslave white Europeans. The resolution also argues that slavery violates the fundamental tenets of Christianity: "There is a saying, that we should do to all men like as we will be done ourselves; making no difference of what generation, descent, or colour they are." Finally, the Germantown Quakers argue that slavery in effect violates the commandment against adultery, because "separating wives from their husbands, and giving them to others," as slave traders did, was the equivalent of sanctioning adultery. The resolution specifically singles out fellow Quakers in Pennsylvania who "here handel men as they handel there the cattle." This seemed particularly wrong because the Quakers had been persecuted for their beliefs in Europe and some were now persecuting men for their color.

The Germantown resolution set the tone for religious antislavery protests in Pennsylvania. Soon Quakers throughout the colony were asserting that blacks were equal to whites and thus could not be enslaved. Other Quakers, however, argued that slavery was sanctioned by the Bible and that the only obligation of Christians was to treat slaves humanely and to teach them the Gospel. This issue divided many Quaker meetings. By the mid-1700s, however, almost all Quakers accepted the idea that slavery was wrong. In 1737 Benjamin Lay published *All Slave-Keepers That Keep the Innocent in Bondage, Apostates Pretending to Lay Claim to the Pure and Holy Christian Religion.* The book was printed by Benjamin Franklin; it is likely that in setting the type for this book (and, in fact, helping Lay organize his notes), Franklin began to understand the deep problem that slavery presented for a just society. Eventually Franklin became a vigorous opponent of slavery and the president of the Pennsylvania Society for the Abolition of Slavery. With its pretentious title and aggressive attacks on slaveholding, Lay's book antagonized many people. But it also stimulated opposition to slavery and led to the emergence of John Woolman as the first significant antislavery activist in Pennsylvania. He was soon joined by his fellow Quaker Anthony

Benezet in a vigorous and mostly successful campaign to convince Quakers that slavery was wrong.

By the eve of the Revolution, a significant percentage of the people in Pennsylvania believed that slavery was morally wrong. This understanding extended beyond Quakers. In 1773 the respected physician and soon-to-be patriot leader Benjamin Rush (who had been influenced by Benezet) published *An Address to the Inhabitants of the British Settlements in America, upon Slave-Keeping*. Rush argued for racial equality on medical grounds and against slavery. Three years later Rush, along with Franklin, signed the Declaration of Independence. In 1775 Thomas Paine, a recent migrant to Philadelphia, published an essay attacking slavery. He soon became the most famous pamphleteer of the Revolution, writing the classic *Common Sense* (1776) and *The American Crisis* (1776–1783). Paine's essay against slavery appeared in a Philadelphia newspaper on the very eve of the Revolution. Paine asked "with what consistency or decency" would the Americans complain that the British king was trying to enslave them, "while they hold so many hundred thousands in slavery." In April 1775, less than a week before the first battles of the Revolution, ten men in Philadelphia organized the Society for the Relief of Free Negroes Unlawfully Held in Bondage. This was the first antislavery organization in the Americas or in England, and its establishment confirmed Philadelphia's status as the center of antislavery thought and action. Quakers led the movement, but Presbyterians like Rush and deists like Franklin and Paine were also vitally concerned about the problem of slavery and slaveholding.

Ironically, while the Revolution brought opponents of slavery like Rush, Paine, and Franklin into the political mainstream, it undermined the political significance of the Quakers, who were the most active antislavery group in the new state. Many Quakers sympathized with the British, and those who did not sympathize refused to take up arms because they were pacifists. Thus, during the Revolution, Quakers saw their political power erode. However, by this time, opposition to slavery was not confined to the Quakers. In 1779 George Bryan, a Presbyterian member of the new state legislature, proposed legislation to end slavery in Pennsylvania. His bill received an enthusiastic reception, although some opposition came from those who feared free blacks and those who owned slaves. In January 1780 more than 60 percent of the state legislators voted to pass Bryan's bill. The law came into effect on March 1, 1780.

About the Author

The 1780 act was proposed by George Bryan, a member of the Pennsylvania legislature. Like most pieces of legislation, it has no single author. Legislators altered and amended the act as it went through committees and was read on the floor of the legislature. Bryan is considered the father of the law. Born in Dublin, Ireland, Bryan came to Philadelphia when he was about twenty years old. He practiced law, became a Patriot leader, and was a devout Presbyterian

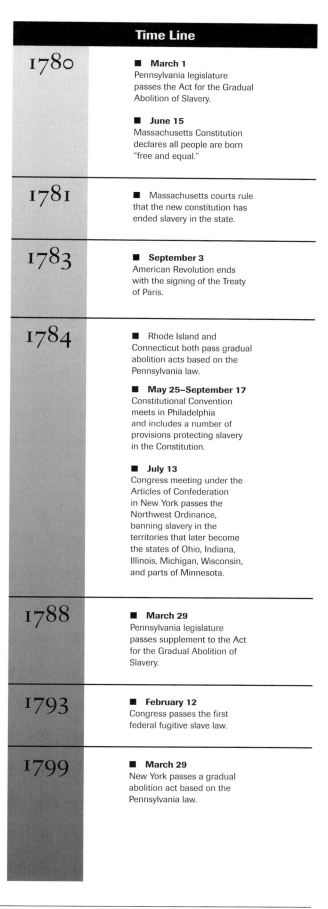

Time Line

1780

■ **March 1**
Pennsylvania legislature passes the Act for the Gradual Abolition of Slavery.

■ **June 15**
Massachusetts Constitution declares all people are born "free and equal."

1781

■ Massachusetts courts rule that the new constitution has ended slavery in the state.

1783

■ **September 3**
American Revolution ends with the signing of the Treaty of Paris.

1784

■ Rhode Island and Connecticut both pass gradual abolition acts based on the Pennsylvania law.

■ **May 25–September 17**
Constitutional Convention meets in Philadelphia and includes a number of provisions protecting slavery in the Constitution.

■ **July 13**
Congress meeting under the Articles of Confederation in New York passes the Northwest Ordinance, banning slavery in the territories that later become the states of Ohio, Indiana, Illinois, Michigan, Wisconsin, and parts of Minnesota.

1788

■ **March 29**
Pennsylvania legislature passes supplement to the Act for the Gradual Abolition of Slavery.

1793

■ **February 12**
Congress passes the first federal fugitive slave law.

1799

■ **March 29**
New York passes a gradual abolition act based on the Pennsylvania law.

1804

- **February 15**
  New Jersey passes a gradual abolition act based on the Pennsylvania law.

1808

- **January 1**
  Congress officially bans the African slave trade.

1820

- **Missouri Compromise** allows slavery in Missouri but bans it north and west of Missouri.

- **July 4**
  New York frees all remaining slaves in the state.

whose religious values influenced his opposition to slavery. Before the Revolution, Bryan was a delegate to the Stamp Act Congress (October 1765), and from 1777 to 1779 he served on the Supreme Executive Council of the state, usually as the council's vice president but for a time as the president, which was the equivalent of being the governor of the state. In 1779 he was elected to the state assembly, where he immediately proposed the Act for the Gradual Abolition of Slavery. Shortly after passage of the act he became a judge.

Explanation and Analysis of the Document

The 1780 Act for the Gradual Abolition of Slavery was part of the social and political revolution associated with the rebellion that led to American independence. Emancipation dovetailed with the stated claims of the American Revolutionaries, and structurally the 1780 act resembles the Declaration of Independence. Each has a two-paragraph preamble, which sets out the document's purpose. The Declaration is not a statute but rather a series of statements justifying independence. The 1780 act, as a statute, becomes less dramatic after the preamble, because it must explain how emancipation is to work.

In addition to this structural resemblance to the Declaration of Independence, the statute can be seen as a legislative implementation of the Declaration. That document asserts, "We hold these truths to be self-evident, that all men are created equal, that they are endowed by their Creator with certain unalienable rights, that among these are life, liberty, and the pursuit of happiness." Clearly, slavery was incompatible with these ideals.

♦ **Preamble and Section 2**

The Pennsylvania legislature surely understood the relationship of slavery to the Declaration. Thus, in Section 2 (a

second preamble) the statute notes that bondage "deprived" slaves "of the common blessings that they were by nature entitled to." Beyond this, the statute's initial sections ignore the general assertions of liberty in the Declaration, and it instead focuses on the specific harms of slavery and the relationship of slavery to the Revolution. Equally intriguing is the deistic approach to this issue.

The preamble begins by noting the difficulties of the Revolution. In comparison with subsequent wars—especially the U.S. Civil War and the massive conflicts of the twentieth century—the approximately 4,500 military deaths in the Revolution seem relatively small in number. But for the emerging American states these were painful losses that affected communities across the new nation. The Revolution was costly in treasure and blood, and the people of Pennsylvania understood that. By 1780 they also knew that even though the war was not over, it was likely that sooner or later they would gain independence. For five years they had held off the greatest military power in the world. The horrible and bloody struggle for independence leads to another parallel with the Declaration.

In the Declaration, Thomas Jefferson avoided any reference to a particular faith or even to the generally shared notions of what today might be called a Judeo-Christian tradition or shared views of the Bible. Thus, Jefferson used phrases like "their creator" and "nature's God" when making claims to liberty based on natural law. Similarly, the authors of the 1780 act marveled at the accomplishment of independence and, while not specifying any particular faith or religion, ascribed their success to Divine Providence. The opening sentence of the preamble to the statute reflects the secular religiosity of the age. The Pennsylvania legislators came from a variety of religious backgrounds and had no interest in asserting allegiance to a particular faith or sect. At the same time, they understood a sense of Divine Providence. Thus, the statute's preamble later refers to the "Almighty Hand" in explaining the differences among the races. Faith, but not denomination, church, or sect, is important to the legislators, but only as it reflects and supports their larger social goal.

This goal, of course, is ending slavery. The statute's authors assert they have no more right to own slaves than England has a right to rule them. This is surely the logic of the Revolution and a logic that had been discussed in Pennsylvania and elsewhere since the early 1770s. Just as the Americans in 1776 (in the Declaration of Independence) felt they had to explain to the world why they were rebelling against England, so too did the Pennsylvania legislators have to explain why they were taking the radical step of ending slavery. The natural law arguments in the preamble of the Declaration ("We hold these truths to be self-evident ...") were not sufficient to convince the world or even a significant number of Americans that a rebellion was necessary. Thus the Congress, in 1776, asserted in the Declaration that "a decent respect to the opinions of mankind requires that they should declare the causes which impel them to the separation." This led to a long list of reasons for the rebellion that constituted the bulk of the Declaration of Independence.

While not explicitly stating it the way the Declaration does, the Pennsylvania statute follows the same logic. Having stated the moral argument for emancipation, the legislators turned to defusing arguments against it while elaborating the reasons for the law. First, the 1780 preamble explains that there is a moral obligation to bring freedom to slaves, just as the colonists are being delivered from English rule. However, many Americans doubted that blacks were like white people and even deserved freedom. The Pennsylvania legislature dismissed this, using an argument that appealed to both religion and science: "It is not for us to enquire why, in the creation of mankind, the inhabitants of the several parts of the earth were distinguished by a difference in feature or complexion. It is sufficient to know that all are the work of an Almighty Hand."

The legislature simply refused to be drawn into a debate over race. All men were created by the "Almighty Hand" and thus no person had a right to question the reasons why some had a different skin color. Indeed, because the "Almighty Hand" had delivered Pennsylvania from British tyranny, the legislature felt an obligation to help deliver others from bondage.

Having dealt with the race issue, the legislators remind readers about the horrors of slavery. Section 2 of the act, which is a second preamble, sets out what became one of the most powerful arguments against slavery: It leads to "an unnatural separation and sale of husband and wife from each other and from their children; an injury, the greatness of which can only be conceived by supposing that we were in the same unhappy case." Few people in Pennsylvania, at least, could argue against the idea that separating families was deeply immoral. The last part of this sentence is also a blow against racial thinking. By suggesting that white Pennsylvanians could understand the suffering of slaves only by "supposing that we were in the same unhappy case," the legislators in effect asked whites to imagine they were black slaves.

Having asserted why the act was proper, the legislature then turned to the far more difficult task of setting out how slavery in the state should be terminated. This was not easy. Even as they condemned slaveholding, the legislators knew they could not simply take property away from those who owned it. If the Revolution was about liberty, it was also about property. Indeed, the key slogan of the period before the Revolution, "Taxation without representation is tyranny," underscored the extent to which this was a revolution of middle-class property owners who believed that liberty and property went hand in hand.

♦ Section 3

There was no perfect answer to the problem of how to give freedom to one person without taking property away from someone else. In the end, the Pennsylvania legislature solved the problem by not, in fact, freeing anyone while still ensuring a relatively speedy end to all slavery in the state. The legislature provided that all slaves living in the state would remain slaves for the rest of their lives or for as long as their masters chose to keep them in bondage. For

all the rhetoric of liberty in the preamble, *no one* actually gained his or her freedom under the law. Therefore no one in the state could complain that he or she had lost property under the law.

What, then, did the law accomplish? The key provision is Section 3 of the act, which states that every child born in Pennsylvania after the passage of the act, even if the child of a slave woman, would be born free. Since the status of slavery passed through the mother, the ultimate result was obvious. As the existing slaves died off, there would be no new slaves to replace them. Quite literally, slavery would soon die out in Pennsylvania. This provision is reinforced by Section 10 of the law, which prohibits anyone from bringing slaves into the state except on temporary visits.

♦ Section 5

Section 5 of the law requires that all slaveholders register each slave with a local court, giving the slave's name, age, and gender. Each registration would be accompanied by a two-dollar fee—not a large sum, but enough money to make some master try to avoid paying it. Any blacks not registered under this provision by November 1, 1780, were considered free people. The Pennsylvania courts interpreted these rules strictly. In *Wilson v. Belinda* (1817) the Pennsylvania Supreme Court ruled that the slave woman Belinda, then about forty years old, was free because in 1780 her master had neglected to list her gender on the registration form. The master clearly believed the name *Belinda* could indicate only a female, but the court disagreed.

The registration had to be accurate to prevent fraud, and a strict interpretation of the law favored freedom. In *Respublica v. Blackmore* (1797) the court ruled that slaves owned by citizens of Pennsylvania could not be registered if they were not living in Pennsylvania at the time the act went into effect. In this case Blackmore lost her slaves because she and her husband had not brought them into the state before the law went into effect; merely owning them in Maryland was not sufficient.

The registration process, the generally hostile climate toward slavery in the state, and the dislocations of the Revolution clearly had an effect on slaveholding. In 1765, a decade before the Revolution began, there were about 1,400 slaves in Philadelphia and 100 free blacks out of a total population of 2,400. By 1790 Philadelphia had about 28,500 people, but fewer than 400 of them were slaves, and about 2,000 were free blacks. In the rest of the state the process of emancipation was slower but still significant. Before the Revolution almost all of the blacks in Pennsylvania were slaves. By 1790 there were more than 6,500 free blacks in the state and just 3,700 slaves. A decade later there were just 1,700 slaves and more than 1,400 free blacks in the state. By 1820 there were only about 200 slaves in the state but more than 30,000 free blacks. In forty years slavery in Pennsylvania had all but disappeared.

♦ Section 4 and Sections 6 to 14

The ending of slavery was not, however, a simple factor of letting slavery die out. The legislators understood that

"When we look back on the variety of dangers to which we have been exposed, and how miraculously our wants in many instances have been supplied, ... when even hope and human fortitude have become unequal to the conflict; we are unavoidably led to a serious and grateful sence of the manifold blessings which we have undeservedly received from the hand of that Being from whom every good and perfect gift cometh."

(Section 1)

"It is not for us to enquire why, in the creation of mankind, the inhabitants of the several parts of the earth were distinguished by a difference in feature or complexion. It is sufficient to know that all are the work of an Almighty Hand."

(Section 1)

"We find in the distribution of the human species, that the most fertile as well as the most barren parts of the earth are inhabited by men of complexions different from ours, and from each other; from whence we may reasonably, as well as religiously, infer, that He who placed them in their various situations, hath extended equally his care and protection to all, and that it becometh not us to counteract his mercies."

(Section 1)

slavery was a complex institution, with many human issues in what was a very inhumane system. The status of the children of slaves posed a serious problem for the gradual abolition process. Under slavery, masters had a huge financial interest in the children of their slave women. Every child born to a slave woman was a financial asset. The child of a slave woman born under a gradual abolition scheme became a financial liability. The child would be born free, and the master, as the owner of the mother, would have to pay to raise the child. Furthermore, general society would face a growing population of children of former slaves who would have few skills and might become burdens on the entire society.

The legislators understood that if the children of slaves were not trained and educated for freedom they would not succeed in a free society. To solve this problem, the legislature used two tactics. First the law declares that the children of slave women, while born free, would be subject to an indenture until age twenty-eight. This would enable the

master to recover the full cost of raising such children and actually give the masters a decent profit on each child. Modern economists have estimated that masters were handsomely compensated for raising the children of slaves if they kept them as servants until age twenty-eight. During this indenture period, masters were required to educate their black servants and prepare them for freedom. There was a strong incentive for doing so, because, under Section 6 of the law, masters were financially responsible for any blacks who could not take care of themselves. However, if masters freed their servants before age twenty-eight, they were not responsible for them. This incentive, combined with the growing public hostility toward slavery, probably accounts for the steep decline of slavery and bondage in Philadelphia. However, in the rural areas of the state, especially along the Maryland and Virginia border, slaveholding lingered into the first two decades of the nineteenth century.

The act also allows free blacks, including those indentured until age twenty-eight, to testify against their masters or any other white person. This was an enormously important step in guaranteeing equal justice for blacks in the state. As indentured servants, the children of slave women had a number of legal rights and protections, and this provision of the law allowed them to vindicate those rights. This provision also served as a warning to masters not to abuse or mistreat the children of their female slaves, who would one day be free.

When Pennsylvania passed its abolition act, slavery was legal in all of the thirteen new states. Pennsylvania's goal was not to make war with its neighbors. Thus the 1780 act contains a number of provisions to protect the interests of out-of-state slaveholders, such as allowing visitors to bring slaves into the state for up to six months. This provision led to controversies, as opponents of slavery tried to manipulate the law to free slaves who had not yet been in the state for six months. Just as the courts were strict on the registration procedures, so too were they strict on this provision. The courts rejected the argument that the six months could be cumulative, asserting that it had to be one continuous six-month period, unless there was a fraudulent attempt to evade the law by moving a slave back and forth across the border on a regular basis. Similarly, when abolitionists claimed that six lunar months would satisfy the law, the court summarily rejected the freedom suit. In another attempt to ensure sectional harmony, the 1780 act allows masters to recover runaway slaves who escaped into Pennsylvania. Seven years before the Constitutional Convention provided for the return of fugitive slaves, Pennsylvania did so.

The act also allows members of Congress and other government officials, as well as foreign ambassadors, to keep slaves indefinitely in the state. At the time, Philadelphia was the nation's capital, and this rule was absolutely necessary for national harmony. Even after the capital had moved to Washington, the courts held that congressmen could move slaves into the state for indefinite periods of time. During the War of 1812, Langdon Cheves, a congressman from South Carolina, stayed in Philadelphia with his slaves for more than six months, and the state supreme court upheld his right to do so. However, when Pierce Butler, another southerner, stayed in the state after his term expired, he lost his slaves.

Audience

This act was aimed at the people of Pennsylvania. Slave owners needed to understand that if they wanted to hold on to their slaves, they had to fulfill all of the requirements of the new statute. Judges and lawyers needed to understand just what those requirements were. In addition, like the Declaration of Independence, this act was aimed at a larger public opinion. The preamble, in particular, was an appeal to "a decent respect to the opinions of mankind" and was designed to convince Americans as well as Europeans that slavery was wrong and that the people of Pennsylvania took seriously the ideology of the American Revolution. In a sense, the first two paragraphs of the law provide an answer to Samuel Johnson's query: "How is it that we hear the loudest yelps for liberty among the drivers of negroes?" In Pennsylvania, the demands for liberty were now coming from people who would no longer tolerate slavery.

Impact

The Pennsylvania Gradual Abolition Act of 1780 was the first of its kind in the modern world. Never before had a slaveholding jurisdiction taken steps to end human bondage. Never before had slave owners acquiesced in the end of slavery. The law was not passed unanimously, and after it was passed, there was a backlash led by slave owners, who campaigned against those legislators who had supported abolition. In 1781 a new legislature considered a bill to repeal or modify the law. The bill failed, in part because of petitions and protests by blacks, who actively worked to keep their recently acquired freedom. The rapid decline of slaveholding, especially in Philadelphia, guaranteed that the 1780 law would not be undone. On the contrary, in 1788 the legislature passed an elaborate act to close some loopholes in the law and further protect free blacks, indentured blacks, and slaves.

The twenty-eight-year indenture was far too long, and masters profited too much from it, while the children of slave women were forced to give a substantial number of their productive years to their mothers' owners. Otherwise the act was a valiant and mostly successful pioneering effort to dismantle slavery. In 1784 Rhode Island and Connecticut passed similar laws, as did New York in 1799 and New Jersey in 1804. In 1794 Upper Canada also passed a similar law. All of these statutes had shorter indentures for the children of slave women. On the other hand, some did not give blacks as many legal rights as the Pennsylvania law. In the end, these differences were not nearly as important as the general direction of all these laws. Without riots, rebellions, or great social upheaval, these places brought about an end to slavery and started on a path that led to a freed North. All of these states eventually sped up the abolition process by either freeing all slaves or at least (as in New Jersey) turning them into indentured servants with legal protections as rights. On July 4, 1827, New York, having previously passed a gradual abolition act, became the first state to fully end slavery. By 1850 there were no slaves in any of these states, although in New Jersey there were still a few hundred former slaves who had become indentured servants.

Blacks did not gain full legal equality in most of the North, and everywhere they faced social inequality. The Pennsylvania law did not anticipate segregation or the depth of white hostility to freed blacks. For all its flaws, the law was a remarkable first step on the road to fulfilling the promise of the Revolution and the Declaration of Independence, that America would become a nation where all people could exercise their "unalienable rights" to "life, liberty, and the pursuit of happiness."

See also Peter Williams, Jr.'s "Oration on the Abolition of the Slave Trade" (1808); William Lloyd Garrison's First *Liberator* Editorial (1831); Emancipation Proclamation (1863).

Further Reading

■ Articles

Fogel, Robert W., and Stanley L. Engerman. "Philanthropy at Bargain Prices: Notes on the Economics of Gradual Emancipation." *Journal of Legal Studies* 3, no. 2 (1974): 377–401.

■ Books

"An Act for the Gradual Abolition of Slavery." In *Laws of the State of New-York*, vol. 3. Albany, N.Y.: Charles R. and George Webster, 1800. Available online. http://www.courts.state.ny.us/history/pdf/lemmon/l1799%20ch62.pdf.

Finkelman, Paul. *An Imperfect Union: Slavery, Federalism, and Comity.* Chapel Hill: University of North Carolina Press, 1981.

Hall, Kermit, et al. *American Legal History: Cases and Materials.* 3rd ed. New York: Oxford University Press, 2000.

Murphy, Arthur. *The Works of Samuel Johnson, LL.D.* 2 vols. New York: Arthur V. Blake, 1838.

Nash, Gary B. *Forging Freedom: The Formation of Philadelphia's Black Community, 1720–1840.* Cambridge, Mass.: Harvard University Press, 1988.

Nash, Gary B., and Jean R. Soderlund. *Freedom by Degrees: Emancipation in Pennsylvania and Its Aftermath.* New York: Oxford University Press, 1991.

Zilversmit, Arthur. *The First Emancipation.* Chicago: University of Chicago Press, 1967.

■ Web Sites

An Act to Explain and Amend an Act Entitled "An Act for the Gradual Abolition of Slavery.". 13 Stat. Penn. 52 (1788). http://www.palrb.us/statutesatlarge/17001799/1788/0/act/1345.pdf.

—Paul Finkelman

Questions for Further Study

1. What reasons does the legislature give for ending slavery in the state?

2. What were the procedures that a master had to fulfill in order to keep slaves owned before March 1, 1780?

3. Can you think of any ways in which masters might have avoided the law in order to get the most value out of their slaves?

4. What other provisions would you have wanted in this law if you were a slave or the child of a slave?

PENNSYLVANIA: AN ACT FOR THE GRADUAL ABOLITION OF SLAVERY

◆ Preamble.

WHEN we contemplate our abhorrence of that condition to which the arms and tyranny of Great Britain were exerted to reduce us; when we look back on the variety of dangers to which we have been exposed, and how miraculously our wants in many instances have been supplied, and our deliverances wrought, when even hope and human fortitude have become unequal to the conflict; we are unavoidably led to a serious and grateful sence of the manifold blessings which we have undeservedly received from the hand of that Being from whom every good and perfect gift cometh. Impressed with there ideas, we conceive that it is our duty, and we rejoice that it is in our power to extend a portion of that freedom to others, which hath been extended to us; and a release from that state of thraldom to which we ourselves were tyrannically doomed, and from which we have now every prospect of being delivered. It is not for us to enquire why, in the creation of mankind, the inhabitants of the several parts of the earth were distinguished by a difference in feature or complexion. It is sufficient to know that all are the work of an Almighty Hand. We find in the distribution of the human species, that the most fertile as well as the most barren parts of the earth are inhabited by men of complexions different from ours, and from each other; from whence we may reasonably, as well as religiously, infer, that He who placed them in their various situations, hath extended equally his care and protection to all, and that it becometh not us to counteract his mercies. We esteem it a peculiar blessing granted to us, that we are enabled this day to add one more step to universal civilization, by removing as much as possible the sorrows of those who have lived in undeserved bondage, and from which, by the assumed authority of the kings of Great Britain, no effectual, legal relies could be obtained. Weaned by a long course of experience from those narrower prejudices and partialities we had imbibed, we find our hearts enlarged with kindness and benevolence towards men of all conditions and nations; and we conceive ourselves at this particular period extraordinarily called upon, by the blessings which we have received, to manifest the sincerity of our profession, and to give a Substantial proof of our gratitude.

◆ Section 2.

And whereas the condition of those persons who have heretofore been denominated Negro and Mulatto slaves, has been attended with circumstances which not only deprived them of the common blessings that they were by nature entitled to, but has cast them into the deepest afflictions, by an unnatural separation and sale of husband and wife from each other and from their children; an injury, the greatness of which can only be conceived by supposing that we were in the same unhappy case. In justice therefore to persons So unhappily circumstanced, and who, having no prospect before them whereon they may rest their sorrows and their hopes, have no reasonable inducement to render their service to society, which they otherwise might; and also in grateful commemoration of our own happy deliverance from that state of unconditional submission to which we were doomed by the tyranny of Britain.

◆ Section 3.

Be it enacted, and it is hereby enacted, by the representatives of the freeman of the commonwealth of Pennsylvania, in general assembly met, and by the authority of the same, That all persons, as well Negroes and Mulattoes as others, who shall be born within this state from and after the passing of this act, shall not be deemed and considered as servants for life, or slaves; and that all servitude for life, or slavery of children, in consequence of the slavery of their mothers, in the case of all children born within this state, from and after the passing of this act as aforesaid, shall be, and hereby is utterly taken away, extinguished and for ever abolished.

◆ Section 4.

Provided always, and be it further enacted by the authority aforesaid, That every Negro and Mulatto child born within this state after the passing of this act as aforesaid (who would, in case this act had not been made, have been born a servent for years, or life, or a slave) shall be deemed to be and shall be by virtue of this act the servant of such person or his or her assigns, who would in such case have been entitled to the service of such child, until such child shall attain unto the age of twenty eight years, in the manner and on the conditions whereon servants bound by indenture for four years are or may be retained and holder; and shall be liable to like correction and punishment, and entitled to like relies in case he or she be evilly treated by his or her master or mistress, and to like freedom dues and other privileges as servants bound by indenture for four years are or may be entitled, unless the person to whom the service of any such child shall belong shall abandon his or her claim to the same; in which case the overseers of the poor of the city, township or district respectively, where such child shall be So abandoned, shall by indenture bind out every child so abandoned, as an apprentice for a time not exceeding the age herein before limited for the service of such children.

◆ Section 5.

And be it further enacted by the authority aforesaid, That every person, who is or shall be the owner of any Negro or Mulatto slave or servant for life or till the age of thirty one years, now within this state, or his lawful attorney, shall on or before the said first day of November next deliver or calm to be delivered in writing to the clerk of the peace of the county, or to the clerk of the court of record of the city of Philadelphia, in which he or she shall respectively inhabit, the name and surname and occupation or profession of such owner, and the name of the county and township, district or ward wherein he or she resideth; and also the name and names of any such slave and slaves, and servant and servants for life or till the age of thirty one years, together with their ages and sexes severally and respectively set forth and annexed, by such person owned or statedly employed and then being within this state, in order to ascertain and distinguish the slaves and servants for life, and till the age of thirty one years, within this state, who shall be such on the said first day of November next, from all other persons; which particulars shall by said clerk of the sessions asked clerk of the said city court be entered in books to be provided for that purpose by the said clerks; and that no Negro or Mulatto, now within this state, shall from and after the said first day of November, be deemed a slave or servant for life, or till the age of thirty one years, unless his or her name shall be entered as aforesaid on such record, except such Negro and Mulatto slaves and servants as are herein after excepted; the said clerk to be entitled to a fee of two dollars for each slave or servant so entered as aforesaid from the treasurer of the county, to be allowed to him in his accounts.

◆ Section 6.

Provided always, That any person, in whom the ownership or right to the service of any Negro or Mulatto shall be vested at the passing of this act, other than such as are herein before excepted, his or her heirs, executors, administrators and assigns, and all and every of them severally shall be liable to the overseers of the poor of the city, township or district to which any such Negro or Mulatto shall become chargeable, for such necessary expence, with costs of suit thereon, as such overseers may be put to, through the neglect of the owner, master or mistress of such Negro or Mulatto; notwithstanding the name and other descriptions of such Negro or Mulatto shall not be entered and recorded as aforesaid; unless his or her master or owner shall before such slave or servant attain his or her twenty eighth year execute and record in the proper county a deed or instrument, securing to such slave or or servant his or her freedom.

◆ Section 7.

And be it further enacted by the authority aforesaid, That the offences and crimes of Negroes and Mulattoes, as well slaves and servants as freemen, shall be enquired of, adjudged, corrected and punished in like manner as the offences and crimes of the other inhabitants of this state are and shall be enquired of, adjudged, corrected and punished, and not otherwise; except that a slave shall not be admitted to bear witness against a freeman.

◆ Section 8.

And be it further enacted by the authority aforesaid, That in all cases wherein sentence of death shall be pronounced against a slave, the jury before whom he or she shall be tried, shall appraise and declare the value of such slave; and in case such sentence be executed, the court shall make an order on the state treasurer, payable to the owner for the same and for the costs of prosecution; but case of remission or mitigation, for the costs only.

◆ Section 9.

And be it further enacted by the authority aforesaid, That the reward for taking up runaway and absconding Negro and Mulatto slaves and servants, and the penalties for enticing away, dealing with, or harbouring, concealing or employing Negro and Mulatto slaves and servants, shall be the same, and shall be recovered in like manner as in case of servants bound for four years.

Section 10.

And be it further enacted by the authority aforesaid, That no man or woman of any nation or colour, except the Negroes or Mulattoes who shall be registered as aforesaid, shall at any time hereafter be deemed, adjudged, or holden within the territories of this commonwealth as slaves or servants for life, but as free men and free women; except the domestic slaves attending upon delegates in congress from the other American states, foreign ministers and consuls, and persons passing through or sojourning in this state, and not becoming resident therein; and seamen employed in ships not belonging to any inhabitant of this state, nor employed in any ship owned by any such inhabitant. Provided such domestic slaves be not aliened or sold to any inhabitants nor (except in the case of members of congress, foreign ministers and consuls) retained in this state longer than six months.

Section 11.

Provided always; And be it further enacted by the authority aforesaid, That this act or any thing in it contained shall not give any relies or shelter to any absconding or runaway Negro or Mulatto slave or servant, who has absented himself or shall absent himself from his or her owner, master or mistress residing in any other state or country, but such owner, master or mistress shall have like right and aid to demand, claim and take away his slave or servant, as he might have had in case this act had not been made: And that all Negro and Mulatto slaves now owned and heretofore resident in this state, who have absented themselves, or been clandestinely carried away, or who may be employed abroad as seamen and have not returned or been brought back to their owners, masters or mistresses, before the passing of this act, may within five years be registered as effectually as is ordered by this act concerning those who are now within the state, on producing such slave before any two justices of the peace, and satisfying the said justices by due proof of the former residence, absconding, taking away, or absence of such slaves as aforesaid; who thereupon shall direct and order the said slave to be entered on the record as aforesaid.

Section 12.

And whereas attempts maybe made to evade this act, by introducing into this state Negroes and Mulattoes bound by covenant to serve for long and unreasonable terms of years, if the same be not prevented.

Section 13.

Be it therefore enacted by the authority aforesaid, That no covenant of personal servitude or apprenticeship whatsoever shall be valid or binding on a Negro or Mulatto for a longer time than seven years, unless such servant or apprentice were at the commencement of such servitude or apprenticeship under the age of twenty one years; in which case such Negro or Mulatto may be holden as a servant or apprentice respectively, according to the covenant, as the case shall be, until he or she shall attain the age of twenty eight years, but no longer.

Section 14.

And be it further enacted by the authority aforesaid, That an act of assembly of the province of Pennsylvania, passed in the year one thousand Seven hundred and five, intitled, "an Act for the trial of Negroes;" and another act of assembly of the said province, passed in the year one thousand seven hundred and twenty five, intitled, "An Act for the better regulating of Negroes in this province;" and another act of assembly of the said province, passed in the year one thousand seven hundred and sixty one, intitled, ... "An Act for laying a duty on Negro and Mulatto slaves imported into this province;" and also another act of assembly of the said province, passed in the year one thousand seven hundred and seventy three, inititled, "An Act making perpetual an Act laying a duty on Negro and Mulatto slaves imported into this province, and for laying an additional duty said slaves," shall be and are hereby repealed, annulled and made void.

John Bayard, Speaker

Enabled into a law at Philadelphia, on Wednesday, the first day of March, A.D. 1780

Thomas Paine, clerk of the general assembly.

Glossary

covenant	contract or agreement between two or more people
indenture	contract under which a laborer (an indentured servant) agrees to work for someone (a master) for a specific term of years, after which time the master is usually required to give the former servant money or goods to start out in life as a free person

Thomas Jefferson (Library of Congress)

"I advance it therefore as a suspicion only, that the blacks ... are inferior to the whites in the endowments both of body and mind."

Overview

In 1781, while he was still governor of Virginia during the Revolutionary War, Thomas Jefferson was given a series of questions about his beloved state posed by a diplomat, François Barbé-Marbois, marquis de Barbé-Marbois, on behalf of the French government. Jefferson began writing on a series of twenty-three topics, supplementing his own knowledge with that of persons he considered more expert in fields such as the natural sciences. Jefferson's responses to Barbé-Marbois's questions were eventually published as the *Notes on the State of Virginia*.

The *Notes* are significant for a number of reasons. In addition to recording his and other experts' knowledge of Virginia's geography and natural resources, Jefferson also addresses social constructs such as manners and the organization of Virginia's laws. The book consists of twenty-three chapters called "Queries," which are, in effect, answers to the queries he received. Topics included such matters as rivers, seaports, climate, population, and commerce. In the section on manners (Query XVIII), Jefferson discusses his moral reservations about the existence of slavery in America. In the section regarding laws (Query XIV), Jefferson dedicates considerable attention to what he saw as the natural differences between slaves and whites. Jefferson believed that there were real, evolutionary differences among the different types of people—Indians, whites, and blacks—and that those differences extended deeper than surface appearance. He concluded that the two groups—blacks and whites—could not live together peaceably in America and that the only solution was to remove African Americans from the new nation.

Context

During the Revolutionary War, the Virginia General Assembly was working its way through the new state's laws in an effort to scrub out those regulations that existed only because Virginia had inherited laws from Great Britain. No longer obliged to preserve Britain's laws, Virginia placed the entirety of its legal code under review—including the ways in which slaves were passed from one member of the family to another through inheritance and how they were treated in the criminal code. There was even a proposal to provide for gradual emancipation. Few people at the time thought that an immediate or outright abolition of slavery was possible, but there were calls in several quarters for gradual emancipation.

This idea is one that Jefferson sought to address in the *Notes*, specifically in Query XIV. Originally written for a select audience of French and other European intellectuals and the close circle of Jefferson's friends, *Notes on the State of Virginia* was eventually published for public consumption first in France (1784) and later in the United States and England (1787). As Jefferson continued to edit and revise the *Notes*, a variety of local, national, and international events also required his attention. In 1783 the Treaty of Paris officially ended the Revolutionary War; the following year, Jefferson accepted an appointment as minister to France.

Among the issues that Jefferson struggled with while he was overseas was the state of government in the newly formed American nation. The various states had begun the process of developing their new constitutions as early as 1776, but it took until 1780 for the last state—Massachusetts—to approve a constitution. The situation was further complicated on the national level, as representatives from the various states attempted to reach some form of compromise regarding the composition of a new national government. The initial result of these efforts was the Articles of Confederation, which were ratified in 1781 and served as the nation's blueprint until they were replaced by the Constitution of the United States in 1787. Foreign ambassadors (such as Jefferson) and other prominent figures found the articles frustratingly insufficient, for they left the United States more a collection of states than a unified nation, making it difficult for foreign powers to maintain relations with the new nation. Jefferson's *Notes* represented an effort on his part to explain the state of Virginia and, by implication, the United States to his foreign audience and to refute the notion, common in Europe, that the New World was degenerated in comparison with the Old World.

Time Line

1743
- ■ **April 13**
  Thomas Jefferson is born in Albemarle County, Virginia.

1769
- ■ Jefferson, a new member of Virginia's House of Burgesses, submits a proposal to provide for the emancipation of Virginia's slaves.

1774
- ■ **July**
  Jefferson lists slavery as one of the wrongs inflicted upon the colonies by Great Britain in *A Summary View of the Rights of British America.*

1775
- ■ Jefferson is named to the Second Continental Congress in Philadelphia.

1776
- ■ **July 4**
  The Second Continental Congress adopts the Declaration of Independence, drafted by Jefferson.

1779
- ■ African Americans in New Hampshire use Jefferson's language from the Declaration of Independence when petitioning the state legislature to grant their freedom on the ground that freedom is a natural right of all humans.

1781
- ■ Jefferson begins to write *Notes on the State of Virginia.*

1782
- ■ Jefferson revises and expands his *Notes.*

1783
- ■ Virginia grants freedom to slaves who fought for the Patriot cause in the American Revolution.

1784
- ■ *Notes on the State of Virginia* is published in France.

1787
- ■ *Notes on the State of Virginia* is published in English in London.

About the Author

Thomas Jefferson was born in Albemarle County, Virginia, on April 13, 1743, the son of Peter Jefferson, a largely self-made plantation owner, and Jane Randolph, daughter of one of Virginia's most prosperous and powerful colonial families. Among Jefferson's earliest memories was being carried on a pillow by one of his father's slaves. Peter Jefferson died in 1757, when Thomas was only fourteen. Jefferson enrolled at Virginia's College of William and Mary in 1760 and graduated just two years later. By the time Jefferson married a fellow Virginian, Martha Wayles Skelton, in 1772, he was an established attorney, a plantation owner, and a slaveholder, with two and a half years of experience as a member of Virginia's colonial legislature, which at the time was called the House of Burgesses.

Jefferson's reputation as a talented writer grew in part because of his authorship of *A Summary View of the Rights of British America*, which he drafted in 1774 for the House of Burgesses in Williamsburg. In it Jefferson spelled out for King George III specific grievances that colonists believed had been inflicted upon them by the British Parliament and both chastised the king and appealed to him for assistance. Among the complaints listed in *A Summary View* was that the colonies had no representative in Parliament, where taxation policies were made, and that Britain had introduced slavery into the colonies.

Jefferson was named to Virginia's delegation to the Second Continental Congress in 1775. By the summer of 1776, Jefferson had established a reputation in Philadelphia as a better writer than a public speaker. Along with John Adams, Benjamin Franklin, Robert Livingston, and Roger Sherman, he was appointed to a committee that wrote the Declaration of Independence. Jefferson did the lion's share of the writing.

During the Revolutionary War (1775–1783), Jefferson spent two years as governor of Virginia (1779–1781). In 1781 he wrote *Notes on the State of Virginia*, which he would revise and rewrite over the course of the next several years. In 1782, when his wife, Martha, died, Jefferson sank into a deep depression, from which he took months to recover. Between 1784 and 1789 Jefferson served the newly formed United States of America as ambassador, primarily in France. It was during this period that *Notes on the State of Virginia* was first offered to the public in France and in the United States.

Jefferson returned to the United States in 1790 and urged, along with his friend and political protégé James Madison, the addition of the Bill of Rights to the Constitution. He also served as the first secretary of state under President George Washington, which helped bring him into frequent and vehement conflict with Alexander Hamilton, then secretary of the Treasury, over the new nation's economic and political course. Jefferson's conflicts with Hamilton became so severe that Jefferson resigned from Washington's cabinet at the end of 1793 and went home to Monticello. His retirement was short-lived, however, as he returned to the national stage just three years later when he was elected as John Adams's vice president. His long-standing friendship with Adams was damaged during the Adams administration as the two clashed over a number of political issues. Jefferson led the attack on the Alien and Sedition Acts passed by the Adams administration, which he judged to be unconstitutional and dangerous to free expression.

In 1800, Jefferson himself was elected to the presidency. In 1803 he engineered the Louisiana Purchase (the acquisition from the French of land that today encompasses all or part of fourteen U.S. states) and dispatched Meriwether Lewis and William Clark on their famous exploration of the American West. Jefferson was easily reelected in 1804, but his second term did not progress as smoothly as his first. Among the troubles Jefferson experienced was the death of his daughter Maria, one of only two legitimate Jefferson offspring to live to adulthood. Jefferson also began to struggle with health issues during his second term.

During his second term Jefferson was also plagued by a number of political problems. One was the continuing hostility between France and Great Britain. Jefferson, who never favored the presence of a large standing military force, had restricted the growth of the American naval forces. When the struggle for dominance between France and Britain grew to encompass the Atlantic Ocean, American trading vessels found themselves caught in the middle. Jefferson's answer to this maritime trouble was the Embargo Act of 1807, intended to seal off American ports from foreign shipping. The unintended effect of the Embargo Act was severe stress for the American economy from the closing of U.S. ports to foreign trade. The domestic front proved similarly troublesome for Jefferson when his former vice president, Aaron Burr, was accused of treason. Jefferson wanted Burr found guilty, but he suffered yet another political loss when Burr was acquitted.

Jefferson retired to Monticello in 1809 and began plans for what would become the University of Virginia at Charlottesville. He persuaded many of his long-time political and personal allies to join in his efforts, including James Madison. In addition to promoting higher education in Virginia, Jefferson and John Adams renewed via correspondence their old friendship. They maintained their correspondence for the remainder of their lives, both of them passing away on July 4, 1826.

Explanation and Analysis of the Document

Jefferson's enthusiasm for studying and learning are fully displayed in the *Notes*, which underwent a series of revisions as Jefferson sought to increase his knowledge about natural science and edit his work based on the information of more accomplished scientists. There was a theory, popularized by French naturalists, that animal life in the New World had degenerated from that in Europe, and Jefferson wanted to correct this notion; his response to this subject forms the largest section of the *Notes*. In addition to natural science, Jefferson answered queries about Virginia's manners, laws, population, institutions, religion, commerce, and other subjects. Although slaves are referred to in several sections of the *Notes*, Jefferson confines the

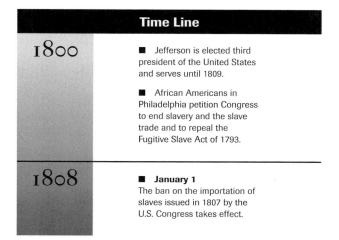

majority of his musings on African Americans and slavery to two sections: that on Virginia's laws (Query XIV) and that on Virginians' manners (Query XVIII).

◆ "Laws"

Jefferson had serious moral reservations about slavery and expressed them in the "Manners" section of the *Notes* (Query XVIII). Nevertheless, his discussion of African Americans in "Laws" strikes a different tone. Jefferson here describes a proposed amendment to Virginia's legal code that called for the emancipation of "all slaves born after passing the act." The amendment would have slave children remain with their parents and be trained at public expense "according to their geniuses" in various trades. When male slaves reached the age of twenty-one and females eighteen, they were to be sent away from America. Jefferson does not specify where he thought the young people should be sent, merely that they should be "colonized to such place as the circumstances of the time should render most proper."

In order to help the newly colonized young people, the amendment proposed that they be given supplies, the support of Virginia, and the protection of the United States until they had established themselves as an independent entity. The amendment further proposed that white Europeans be enticed to come to the United States to replace the labor of those who had been removed. In this way and over a period of years, African Americans would disappear from America as the older slaves stopped producing children and died off.

Jefferson anticipates a question from his audience when he writes, "Why not retain and incorporate the blacks into the state, and thus save the expense of supplying ... the vacancies they will leave?" The answer to this question, Jefferson believes, is that inherent evolutionary differences between African Americans and white Americans as well as the strain of slavery on both groups have made it impossible for them to live together harmoniously. Jefferson cites political, physical, and moral incompatibilities between the groups. "Deep rooted prejudices entertained by the whites," Jefferson claims, "ten thousand recollections, by the blacks, of the injuries they have sustained ... the real distinctions nature has made ... will divide us into parties, and produce convul-

Descendants of Thomas Jefferson and descendants of his slave Sally Hemings pose for a group shot at his plantation during the Monticello Association's Annual meeting on May 15, 1999. (AP/Wide World Photos)

sions which will probably never end but in the extermination of the one or the other race."

Jefferson devotes a considerable amount of space to a list of the real and perceived differences between African Americans and Caucasians. The first difference is color. Here Jefferson's tone clearly expresses his personal bias. "Are not the fine mixtures of red and white, the expressions of every passion by greater or less suffusions of colour of the one, preferable to that eternal monotony, ... that immoveable veil of black which covers all the emotions of the other race?" He goes on to cite slaves' "own judgment in favour of the whites, declared by their preference of them." Jefferson was referring to a popularly held belief that white beauty was superior to black beauty to the point that slaves themselves preferred white to black. He further poses this question: "The circumstance of superior beauty, is thought worthy of attention in the propagation of our horses, dogs, and other domestic animals; why not in that of man?" Clearly Jefferson believed it was.

In addition to a deficit of physical beauty compared with whites, African Americans, Jefferson believed, suffered from other deficiencies. Intellectual aptitude was extremely important to Jefferson the lifelong student, and it was his observation that African Americans lacked the intellect of Caucasians or Native Americans. As evidence to support his

assertions, Jefferson offers the following: "Those numberless afflictions, which render it doubtful whether heaven has given life to us in mercy or in wrath, are less felt [by African Americans], and sooner forgotten by them. In general, their existence appears to participate more of sensation than reflection." Jefferson carries his argument further, writing that "comparing them by their faculties of memory, reason, and imagination, it appears to me, that in memory they are equal to whites; in reason much inferior ... and that in imagination they are dull, tasteless, and anomalous."

It is at this point that Jefferson unfavorably compares African Americans with Native Americans. Jefferson believed that slaves, some of whom had "been liberally educated ... and lived in countries where the arts and sciences are cultivated to a considerable degree, and have had before their eyes samples of the best works from abroad" had not taken the full cultural advantage of their association with whites. The Indians, on the other hand, "with no advantages of this kind ... astonish you with strokes of the most sublime oratory; such as prove their reason and sentiment strong, their imagination glowing and elevated. But never yet could I find a black had uttered a thought above the level of plain narration."

Jefferson's interest in natural history reasserts itself after his lengthy recitation of the perceived deficiencies of African Americans. "To our reproach it must be said," he writes, "that though for a century and a half we have had under our eyes the races of black and of red men, they have never yet been viewed by us as subjects of natural history." He is willing to admit that the inferiority of African Americans might be suspicion rather than fact, but regardless, the "unfortunate difference of colour, and perhaps of faculty, is a powerful obstacle to the emancipation of these people."

In addition to comparing African American slaves with Native Americans on racial terms, Jefferson also compared African American slaves to Roman slaves based on their shared condition of servitude. Once again, Jefferson finds the comparison to disfavor African Americans. Jefferson notes that Roman slaves, who were typically white, "might mix with, without staining the blood of his master." African Americans, however, "when freed," must be "removed beyond the reach of mixture." He meant that blacks and whites were to be separated so that there would be no possibility that they would produce mixed-race offspring. Given Jefferson's belief that the mixing of the races would "[stain] the blood of the master" and the proposal to remove African Americans from America altogether by colonizing and gradual emancipation, it is perhaps logical that the penalty for slave criminals included in the Notes is that they be "transported to Africa, or elsewhere, as the circumstances of the time admit, there to be continued in slavery." Of course, later historians have found this belief highly ironic, for it is widely accepted (through DNA evidence) that Jefferson himself fathered children with one of his slaves, Sally Hemings, a woman believed to have been a half-sister of his wife, Martha.

♦ Manners

In "Manners," Jefferson begins by noting that it is difficult for a citizen of a country to comment on its manners, for such a person has been habituated to the surrounding society. Nevertheless, he uses discussion of American manners to lament the "unhappy influence on the manners of our people produced by the existence of slavery among us." Further, he laments that children, by observing the behavior of adults, can grow to treat slaves with cruelty, simply because they do not know any better and they have learned to do so from their elders. He recognizes the discordance between the institution of slavery and the nation's belief in a republican form of government in which all men are created equal. "With what execration," Jefferson asks rhetorically, "should the statesman be loaded, who permitting one half the citizens thus to trample on the rights of the other, transforms those into despots, and these into enemies, destroys the morals of the one part, and the amor patriae [patriotism] of the other." Here he adopts language that reflects the principles he espoused in the Declaration of Independence.

Jefferson expresses sympathy for the slave, recognizing that the slave labors for others who themselves do not perform labor, and he wonders why a slave would even want to live in the United States. He goes further when he suggests that slavery destroys the moral fiber of the nation, for the presence of slaves strips their owners of any desire to perform useful labor. Jefferson expresses fear of divine retribution for America's use of slaves: "Indeed I tremble for my country when [I] reflect that God is just: that his justice cannot sleep forever … the spirit of the master is abating, that of the slave rising from the dust." As a whole, the section reflects Jefferson's own ambivalence about slavery.

Audience

Barbé-Marbois, for whom Jefferson initially compiled what would become Notes on the State of Virginia, can be considered Jefferson's primary audience. Jefferson sought initially to answer queries about the various American colonies. Virginia was not the only new American state to whom Marbois's questions were addressed, but it was the Virginian Jefferson who gave the most extensive answers. Indeed, he was widely recognized as a careful, dedicated student who sought to accumulate knowledge throughout his life, and he corresponded widely with people on both sides of the Atlantic. He thus shared his Notes on Virginia with a variety of highly educated personages, Americans and Europeans alike, who formed a second audience. Jefferson suspected that some of his thoughts, particularly those in Query XIV ("Manners"), would incite controversy, and so he originally intended the Notes to remain private. The work was greeted with such enthusiasm by acquaintances on both sides of the Atlantic, however, that Jefferson was eventually persuaded to allow copies to be distributed publicly, including at his alma mater—the College of William and Mary. As word of Jefferson's work spread and more people requested copies, Jefferson eventually decided to publish, first in Europe and later in the United States. Given Jefferson's interest in the natural sciences, scientists, too, could be considered a separate audience, for Notes contains extensive observations on the flora, fauna, and geography of Virginia.

Impact

Assessing the impact of Jefferson's Notes is problematic, mainly in light of subsequent events and particularly those events having a bearing on slavery, emancipation, and race relations. On the one hand, Thomas Jefferson is an icon of American democracy, one of the most revered Founding Fathers. He was a man of widespread erudition and towering intellect, prompting President John F. Kennedy to remark to a gathering of forty-nine Nobel Prize winners in 1962, "I think this is the most extraordinary collection of talent and of human knowledge that has ever been gathered together at the White House—with the possible exception of when Thomas Jefferson dined alone." He wrote the stirring words of the Declaration of Independence, and he is regarded as the fountainhead of the separation of church and state, religious freedom, limited government, and defense of civil liberties.

Nevertheless, Jefferson owned slaves. He called for separation of the races, yet he fathered children by one of his

"Deep rooted prejudices entertained by the whites; ten thousand recollections, by the blacks, of the injuries they have sustained; new provocations; the real distinctions nature has made; and many other circumstances, will divide us into parties, and produce convulsions which will probably never end but in the extermination of one or the other race."

("Laws")

"The Indians ... astonish you with strokes of the most sublime oratory; such as prove their reason and sentiment strong, their imagination glowing and elevated. But never yet could I find that a black had uttered a thought above the level of plain narration."

("Laws")

"The improvement of the blacks in body and mind, in the first instance of their mixture with the whites, has been observed by every one, and proves that their inferiority is not the effect merely of their condition of life."

("Laws")

"I advance it therefore as a suspicion only, that the blacks, whether originally a distinct race, or made distinct by time and circumstances, are inferior to the whites in the endowments both of body and mind.... This unfortunate difference of colour, and perhaps of faculty, is a powerful obstacle to the emancipation of these people."

("Laws")

"The spirit of the master is abating, that of the slave rising from the dust, his condition mollifying, the way I hope preparing, under the auspices of heaven, for a total emancipation, and that this is disposed, in the order of events, to be with the consent of the masters, rather than by their extirpation."

("Manners")

slaves. And in *Notes* he expresses views about African Americans that were probably widely held at the time but that are considered repugnant today. In the minds of some Americans, Jefferson was guilty of enormous hypocrisy by stating, in the Declaration of Independence, that "all men are created equal" while being a slaveholder. Still, although Jefferson owned slaves, he long advocated their emancipation or at least the elimination of the slave trade; an early draft of the Declaration of Independence contained a clause condemning the British Crown for supporting the slave trade, but the clause was deleted during debates on the Declaration's wording. Jefferson clearly was often troubled by his conscience. On the one hand he recognized the evils of slavery, which he enumerates in "Manners," but on the other he had to contend with nearly lifelong extensive personal debt, and he recognized that the economic viability of much of the South depended on slave labor. He further believed that habit and custom would make it impossible for slaves to live as free men and women, but he later repudiated this belief. In sum, he hoped to see the eradication of the slave trade and, in future years, the abolition of the institution of slavery itself.

Jefferson's *Notes* became a popular work because of its detailed nature. Indeed, the *Notes* were greeted enthusiastically by certain liberal Europeans, such as the English philosopher and preacher Dr. Richard Price, a supporter of the American Revolution; an activist in republican, liberal, and even radical causes; and an advocate of Jefferson's vision of limited government. Thus, abolitionists such as Price would have welcomed Jefferson's proposal in Query XIV for gradual emancipation. The *Notes* have remained popular with scholars because they encapsulate the thoughts and opinions of one of America's most prominent Founding Fathers. Jefferson's biographer Dumas Malone wrote that "nobody had ever before given such a description of an American state … the most important scientific work that had yet been compiled in America." Malone went further when he described the *Notes* as Jefferson's "most memorable personal contribution in the name of his country to the enlightenment of Europe."

Prominent African Americans at the time responded to Jefferson's *Notes*. Among them was Benjamin Banneker, whose 1791 Letter to Thomas Jefferson included an almanac that Banneker prepared—with a view perhaps to countering Jefferson's view that African Americans were people of lesser intellect. In 1794 Richard Allen delivered his "Address to Those Who Keep Slaves and Uphold the Practice," refuting Jefferson's view that slavery was a necessary evil and urging slave owners to abandon the practice. In 1829 David Walker's *Appeal to the Coloured Citizens of the World* was in large part a response, again, to the view that African Americans were intellectually inferior to whites. Each of these writers took up strains from Jefferson's *Notes* and attempted to rebut them, suggesting the widespread impact that Jefferson's book had.

See also Benjamin Banneker's Letter to Thomas Jefferson (1791); Fugitive Slave Act of 1793; Peter Williams, Jr.'s "Oration on the Abolition of the Slave Trade" (1808); David Walker's *Appeal to the Coloured Citizens of the World* (1829).

Questions for Further Study

1. How would you explain Thomas Jefferson's attitude toward slavery, especially considering that he owned slaves?

2. If Jefferson supported the gradual emancipation of slaves, why did he propose sending them away rather than incorporating them into the social and economic system of the United States?

3. To what extent do you believe that Jefferson's attitude toward African Americans was a product, at least in part, of the time and place in which he lived?

4. Many people at the time opposed slavery as much for the effects it had on slave owners as for the effects it had on the slaves. How, in Jefferson's view, did slavery affect the white population?

5. Several African Americans responded to Jefferson's *Notes*, including Benjamin Banneker in his Letter to Thomas Jefferson (1791), Peter Williams in "An Oration on the Abolition of the Slave Trade" (1808), Richard Allen in his "Address to Those Who Keep Slaves and Uphold the Practice" (1794), and David Walker in *Appeal to the Coloured Citizens of the World* (1829). Compare this document with one of those listed. How did the later writer respond to Jefferson?

Further Reading

■ Books

Bonwick, Colin. *The American Revolution*. 2nd ed. New York: Palgrave Macmillan, 2005.

Cappon, Lester J., ed. *The Adams-Jefferson Letters: The Complete Correspondence between Thomas Jefferson and Abigail and John Adams*. Chapel Hill: University of North Carolina Press, 1988.

Cowan, Thomas Dale, and Jack Maguire. *Timelines of African-American History: 500 Years of Black Achievement*. New York: Berkley Publishing Group, 1994.

Ellis, Joseph J. *American Sphinx: The Character of Thomas Jefferson*. New York: Vintage Books, 1998.

Hellenbrand, Harold. *The Unfinished Revolution: Education and Politics in the Thought of Thomas Jefferson*. Newark: University of Delaware Press, 1990.

Malone, Dumas. *Jefferson and His Time*. Vol. 1: *Jefferson the Virginian*. Boston: Little, Brown, 1948. Vol. 2: *Jefferson and the Rights of Man*. Boston: Little, Brown, 1951.

Onuf, Peter S., ed. *Jeffersonian Legacies*. Charlottesville: University Press of Virginia, 1993.

Public Papers of the Presidents of the United States: John F. Kennedy. 3 vols. Washington, D.C.: Government Printing Office, 1964.

Wood, Gordon S. *Revolutionary Characters: What Made the Founders Different*. New York: Penguin, 2006.

■ Web Sites

"Jefferson, Thomas, 1743–1826. Notes on the State of Virginia." Electronic Text Center, University of Virginia Library.
http://etext.virginia.edu/toc/modeng/public/JefVirg.html.

—Sharon T. Glass

THOMAS JEFFERSON'S
NOTES ON THE STATE OF VIRGINIA

"Laws"

♦ *The administration of justice and description of the laws?...*

Slaves pass by descent and dower as lands do. Where the descent is from a parent, the heir is bound to pay an equal share of their value in money to each of his brothers and sisters.

Slaves, as well as lands, were entailable during the monarchy: but, by an act of the first republican assembly, all donees [sic] in tail, present and future, were vested with the absolute dominion of the entailed subject.

Bills of exchange, being protested, carry 10 per cent interest from their date.

No person is allowed, in any other case, to take more than five per cent per annum simple interest, for the loan of monies.

Gaming debts are made void, and monies actually paid to discharge such debts (if they exceeded 40 shillings) may be recovered by the payer within three months, or by any other person afterwards.

Tobacco, flour, beef, pork, tar, pitch, and turpentine, must be inspected by persons publicly appointed, before they can be exported.

The erecting of iron-works and mills is encouraged by many privileges; with necessary cautions however to prevent their dams from obstructing the navigation of the water-courses. The general assembly have on several occasions shewn a great desire to encourage the opening of the great falls of James and Patowmac rivers. As yet, however, neither of these have been effected.

The laws have also descended to the preservation and improvement of the races of useful animals, such as horses, cattle, deer; to the extirpation of those which are noxious, as wolves, squirrels, crows, blackbirds; and to the guarding of our citizens against infectious disorders, by obliging suspected vessels coming into the state, to perform quarantine, and by regulating the conduct of persons having such disorders within the state.

The mode of acquiring lands, in the earliest times of our settlement, was by petition to the general assembly. If the lands prayed for were already cleared of the Indian title, and the assembly thought the prayer reasonable, they passed the property by their vote to the petitioner. But if they had not yet been ceded by the Indians, it was necessary that the petitioner should previously purchase their right. This purchase the assembly verified, by enquiries of the Indian proprietors; and being satisfied of its reality and fairness, proceeded further to examine the reasonableness of the petition, and its consistence with policy; and, according to the result, either granted or rejected the petition. The company also sometimes, though very rarely, granted lands, independently of the general assembly. As the colony increased, and individual applications for land multiplied, it was found to give too much occupation to the general assembly to enquire into and execute the grant in every special case. They therefore thought it better to establish general rules, according to which all grants should be made, and to leave to the governor the execution of them, under these rules. This they did by what have been usually called the land laws, amending them from time to time, as their defects were developed. According to these laws, when an individual wished a portion of unappropriated land, he was to locate and survey it by a public officer, appointed for that purpose: its breadth was to bear a certain proportion to its length: the grant was to be executed by the governor: and the lands were to be improved in a certain manner, within a given time. From these regulations there resulted to the state a sole and exclusive power of taking conveyances of the Indian right of soil: since, according to them, an Indian conveyance alone could give no right to an individual, which the laws would acknowledge. The state, or the crown, thereafter, made general purchases of the Indians from time to time, and the governor parcelled them out by special grants, conformed to the rules before described, which it was not in his power, or in that of the crown, to dispense with. Grants, unaccompanied by their proper legal circumstances, were set aside regularly by *scire facias*, or by bill in Chancery. Since the establishment of our new government, this order of things is but little changed. An individual, wishing to appropriate to himself lands still unappropriated by any other, pays to the public treasurer a sum of money proportioned to the quantity he wants. He carries the treasurer's receipt to the auditors of public accompts [sic], who thereupon debit the treasurer with the sum, and order the register of the land-office to give the party a warrant for his land. With this warrant from the register, he goes to the surveyor of the county where the land lies on which he has cast his eye. The surveyor lays it off for him, gives him its exact description, in the form of a certificate, which certificate he returns to the land-office, where a grant is made out, and is signed by the governor. This vests in him a perfect dominion in his lands, transmissible to whom he pleases by deed or will, or by descent to his heirs if he die intestate.

Many of the laws which were in force during the monarchy being relative merely to that form of government, or inculcating principles inconsistent with republicanism, the first assembly which met after the establishment of the commonwealth appointed a committee to revise the whole code, to reduce it into proper form and volume, and report it to the assembly. This work has been executed by three gentlemen, and reported; but probably will not be taken up till a restoration of peace shall leave to the legislature leisure to go through such a work.

The plan of the revisal was this. The common law of England, by which is meant, that part of the English law which was anterior to the date of the oldest statutes extant, is made the basis of the work. It was thought dangerous to attempt to reduce it to a text: it was therefore left to be collected from the usual monuments of it. Necessary alterations in that, and so much of the whole body of the British statutes, and of acts of assembly, as were thought proper to be retained, were digested into 126 new acts, in which simplicity of stile was aimed at, as far as was safe. The following are the most remarkable alterations proposed:

To change the rules of descent, so as that the lands of any person dying intestate shall be divisible equally among all his children, or other representatives, in equal degree.

To make slaves distributable among the next of kin, as other moveables.

To have all public expenses, whether of the general treasury, or of a parish or county, (as for the maintenance of the poor, building bridges, court-houses, &c.) supplied by assessments on the citizens, in proportion to their property.

To hire undertakers for keeping the public roads in repair, and indemnify individuals through whose lands new roads shall be opened.

To define with precision the rules whereby aliens should become citizens, and citizens make themselves aliens.

To establish religious freedom on the broadest bottom.

To emancipate all slaves born after passing the act. The bill reported by the revisors does not itself contain this proposition; but an amendment containing it was prepared, to be offered to the legislature whenever the bill should be taken up, and further directing, that they should continue with their parents to a certain age, then be brought up, at the public expense, to tillage, arts or sciences, according to their geniuses, till the females should be eighteen, and the males twenty-one years of age, when they should be colonized to such place as the circumstances of the time should render most proper, sending them out with arms, implements of household and of the handicraft arts, feeds, pairs of the useful domestic animals, &c. to declare them a free and independent people, and extend to them our alliance and protection, till they shall have acquired strength; and to send vessels at the same time to other parts of the world for an equal number of white inhabitants; to induce whom to migrate hither, proper encouragements were to be proposed. It will probably be asked, Why not retain and incorporate the blacks into the state, and thus save the expense of supplying, by importation of white settlers, the vacancies they will leave? Deep rooted prejudices entertained by the whites; ten thousand recollections, by the blacks, of the injuries they have sustained; new provocations; the real distinctions which nature has made; and many other circumstances, will divide us into parties, and produce convulsions which will probably never end but in the extermination of the one or the other race.—To these objections, which are political, may be added others, which are physical and moral. The first difference which strikes us is that of colour. Whether the black of the negro resides in the reticular membrane between the skin and scarf-skin, or in the scarf-skin itself; whether it proceeds from the colour of the blood, the colour of the bile, or from that of some other secretion, the difference is fixed in nature, and is as real as if its seat and cause were better known to us. And is this difference of no importance? Is it not the foundation of a greater or less share of beauty in the two races? Are not the fine mixtures of red and white, the expressions of every passion by greater or less suffusions of colour in the one, preferable to that eternal monotony, which reigns in the countenances, that immoveable veil of black which covers all the emotions of the other race? Add to these, flowing hair, a more elegant symmetry of form, their own judgment in favour of the whites, declared by their preference of them, as uniformly as is the preference of the Oranootan [sic] for the black women over those of his own species.

The circumstance of superior beauty, is thought worthy of attention in the propagation of our horses, dogs, and other domestic animals; why not in that of man? Besides those of colour, figure, and hair, there are other physical distinctions proving a difference of race. They have less hair on the face and body. They secrete less by the kidneys, and more by the glands of the skin, which gives them a very strong and disagreeable odour. This greater degree of transpiration renders them more tolerant of heat, and less so of cold, than the whites. Perhaps too a difference of structure in the pulmonary apparatus, which a late ingenious experimentalist has discovered to be the principal regulator of animal heat, may have disabled them from extricating, in the act of inspiration, so much of that fluid from the outer air, or obliged them in expiration, to part with more of it. They seem to require less sleep. A black, after hard labour through the day, will be induced by the slightest amusements to sit up till midnight, or later, though knowing he must be out with the first dawn of the morning. They are at least as brave, and more adventuresome. But this may perhaps proceed from a want of forethought, which prevents their seeing a danger till it be present. When present, they do not go through it with more coolness or steadiness than the whites. They are more ardent after their female: but love seems with them to be more an eager desire, than a tender delicate mixture of sentiment and sensation. Their griefs are transient. Those numberless afflictions, which render it doubtful whether heaven has given life to us in mercy or in wrath, are less felt, and sooner forgotten with them. In general, their existence appears to participate more of sensation than reflection. To this must be ascribed their disposition to sleep when abstracted from their diversions, and unemployed in labour. An animal whose body is at rest, and who does not reflect, must be disposed to sleep of course. Comparing them by their faculties of memory, reason, and imagination, it appears to me, that in memory they are equal to the whites; in reason much inferior, as I think one could scarcely be found capable of tracing and comprehending the investigations of Euclid; and that in imagination they are dull, tasteless, and anomalous. It would be unfair to follow them to Africa for this investigation. We will consider them here, on the same stage with the whites, and where the facts are not apocryphal on which a judgment is to be formed. It will be right to make great allowances for the difference of condition, of education, of conversation, of the sphere in which they move. Many millions of them have been brought to, and born in America. Most of them indeed have been confined to tillage, to their own homes, and their own society: yet many have been so situated, that they might have availed themselves of the conversation of their masters; many have been brought up to the handicraft arts, and from that circumstance have always been associated with the whites. Some have been liberally educated, and all have lived in countries where the arts and sciences are cultivated to a considerable degree, and have had before their eyes samples of the best works from abroad. The Indians, with no advantages of this kind, will often carve figures on their pipes not destitute of design and merit. They will crayon out an animal, a plant, or a country, so as to prove the existence of a germ in their minds which only wants cultivation. They astonish you with strokes of the most sublime oratory; such as prove their reason and sentiment strong, their imagination glowing and elevated. But never yet could I find that a black had uttered a thought above the level of plain narration; never see even an elementary trait of painting or sculpture. In music they are more generally gifted than the whites with accurate ears for tune and time, and they have been found capable of imagining a small catch. Whether they will be equal to the composition of a more extensive run of melody, or of complicated harmony, is yet to be proved. Misery is often the parent of the most affecting touches in poetry.—Among the blacks is misery enough, God knows, but no poetry. Love is the peculiar estrum of the poet. Their love is ardent, but it kindles the senses only, not the imagination. Religion indeed has produced a Phyllis Whately [sic]; but it could not produce a poet. The compositions published under her name are below the dignity of criticism. The heroes of the Dunciad are to her, as Hercules to the author of that poem. Ignatius Sancho has approached nearer to merit in composition; yet his letters do more honour to the heart than the head. They breathe the purest effusions of friendship and general philanthropy, and shew how great a degree of the latter may be compounded with strong religious zeal. He is often happy in the turn of his compliments, and his style is easy and familiar, except when he affects a Shandean fabrication of words. But his imagination is wild and extravagant, escapes incessantly from every restraint of reason and taste, and, in the course of its vagaries leaves a tract of thought as incoherent and eccentric, as is the course of a meteor through the sky. His subjects should often have led him to a process of sober reasoning: yet we find him always substituting sentiment for demonstration. Upon the whole, though we admit him to the first place among those of his own colour who have presented themselves to the public judgment, yet when we compare him with the writers of the race among whom he lived, and particularly with the epistolary class, in which he has taken his own stand, we are compelled to enroll him at the bottom of the column. This criticism supposes the letters published under his name to be genuine, and to have received amendment from no other hand; points which would not be of easy investigation. The improvement of the blacks in body and mind, in the first instance of their mixture with the whites, has been observed by every one, and proves that their inferiority is not the effect merely of their condition of life. We know that among the Romans, about the Augustan age especially, the condition of their slaves was much more deplorable than that of the blacks on the continent of America. The two sexes were confined in separate apartments, because to raise a child cost the master more than to buy one. Cato, for a very restricted indulgence to his slaves in this particular, took from them a certain price. But in this country the slaves multiply as fast as the free inhabitants. Their situation and manners place the commerce between the two sexes almost without restraint.—The same Cato, on a principle of economy, always sold his sick and superannuated slaves. He gives it as a standing precept to a master visiting his farm, to sell his old oxen, old waggons, old tools, old and diseased servants, and every thing else become useless. "Vendat boves vetulos, plaustrum vetus, ferramenta vetera, servum senem, servum morbosum, & si quid aliud supersit vendat." Cato de re rustica. c. 2. The American slaves cannot enumerate this among the injuries and

accompts	accounts
Aesculapius	the Greek and Roman god of medicine
amor patriae	Latin for "love of country"
attainder	a bill passed by a legislature making something a crime, thus creating criminals without benefit of a trial
Augustan age	the period in Roman history when Caesar Augustus was the first emperor
bills of exchange	negotiable instruments acknowledging debts
catholic	here, universal
Cato	Marcus Porcius Cato, known as Cato the Elder, a Roman statesman, warrior, and writer, author of *De re rustica* (*On Agriculture*)
Chancery	a court that deals with such matters as real estate and inheritance (rather than criminal law)
corruption of blood	the incapacity to inherit because of a bill of attainder
descent and dower	legal terms referring to the inheritance of property, either by descent (property passes to natural heirs) or dower (property passes to a wife as part of a deceased husband's estate)
Dunciad	an eighteenth-century satirical poem by the British poet Alexander Pope
Emperor Claudius	Tiberius Claudius Caesar Augustus Germanicus, the fourth Roman emperor
entailable	able to be entailed; reference to property that passes to heirs "in tail," meaning that heirs use it and control it but cannot sell it, for it passes to subsequent heirs
Epictetus	a Stoic philosopher in ancient Greece
estrum	a state of sexual excitability
Euclid	an ancient Greek mathematician, the "Father of Geometry"

insults they receive. It was the common practice to expose in the island of Aesculapius, in the Tyber, diseased slaves, whose cure was like to become tedious. The Emperor Claudius, by an edict, gave freedom to such of them as should recover, and first declared, that if any person chose to kill rather than to expose them, it should be deemed homicide. The exposing them is a crime of which no instance has existed with us; and were it to be followed by death, it would be punished capitally. We are told of a certain Vedius Pollio, who, in the presence of Augustus, would have given a slave as food to his fish, for having broken a glass. With the Romans, the regular method of taking the evidence of their slaves was under torture. Here it has been thought better never to resort to their evidence. When a master was murdered, all his slaves, in the same

house, or within hearing, were condemned to death. Here punishment falls on the guilty only, and as precise proof is required against him as against a freeman. Yet notwithstanding these and other discouraging circumstances among the Romans, their slaves were often their rarest artists. They excelled too in science, insomuch as to be usually employed as tutors to their master's children. Epictetus, Terence, and Phaedrus, were slaves. But they were of the race of whites. It is not their condition then, but nature, which has produced the distinction.—Whether further observation will or will not verify the conjecture, that nature has been less bountiful to them in the endowments of the head, I believe that in those of the heart she will be found to have done them justice. That disposition to theft with which they have been branded, must be as-

Glossary

Ignatius Sancho	an eighteenth-century British composer, actor, and writer and the first known black to vote in a British election
Jove fix'd it certain …	from Alexander Pope's translation of Homer's *Odyssey*, book 17, lines 392–393
Oranootan	orangutan
Phaedrus	an ancient Roman writer of fables
Phyllis Whately	Phillis Wheatley, an eighteenth-century slave poet
reticular membrane	a thin layer of tissue that covers a surface, lines a cavity, or divides a space or organ
scarf-skin	the outermost layer of skin
scire facias	a Latin term referring to a court command to a borrower to show up at a hearing and show cause why a foreclosure should not be authorized
Shandean	a reference to Laurence Sterne's novel *Tristram Shandy* (1759–1769), famous for its extravagant language and stylistic peculiarities
shewn	an antique form of "shown"
stile	an antique form of "style"
Terence	Publius Terentius Afer, a playwright in the ancient Roman Republic
Tyber	the Tiber River, which runs through Rome; the Tiber Island is associated with healing and the god of medicine, Aesculapius
undertakers	people who have a statutory right to execute roadworks
Vedius Pollio	Publius Vedius Pollio, a Roman equestrian and friend of Augustus, known for his cruelty to slaves
"Vendat boves vetulos …"	The precise quote, from Cato's *De re rustica*, is "Vendat … boves vetulos, armenta delicula, oves deliculas, lanam, pelles, plostrum vetus, ferramenta vetera, servum senem, servum morbosum, et siquid aliut supersit, vendat" or, in English, "Sell worn-out oxen, blemished cattle, blemished sheep, wool, hides, an old wagon, old tools, an old slave, a sickly slave, and whatever else is not required."

cribed to their situation, and not to any depravity of the moral sense. The man, in whose favour no laws of property exist, probably feels himself less bound to respect those made in favour of others. When arguing for ourselves, we lay it down as a fundamental, that laws, to be just, must give a reciprocation of right: that, without this, they are mere arbitrary rules of conduct, founded in force, and not in conscience: and it is a problem which give to the master to solve, whether the religious precepts against the violation of property were not framed for him as well as his slave? And whether the slave may not as justifiably take a little from one, who has taken all from him, as he may slay one who would slay him? That a change in the relations in which a man is placed should change his ideas of moral right and wrong, is neither new, nor peculiar to the colour of the blacks. Homer tells us it was so 2600 years ago.

Jove fix'd it certain, that whatever day
Makes man a slave, takes half his worth away

But the slaves of which Homer speaks were whites. Notwithstanding these considerations which must weaken their respect for the laws of property, we find among them numerous instances of the most rigid integrity, and as many as among their better instructed masters, of benevolence, gratitude, and unshaken fidelity. —The opinion, that they are inferior in the faculties of reason and imagination, must be hazarded with great diffidence. To justify a general conclusion, requires many observations, even where the subject may be submitted to the Anatomical knife, to Optical glasses, to analysis by fire, or by solvents. How much more then where it is a faculty, not a substance, we are examining; where it eludes the research of all the senses; where the conditions of its existence are various and variously combined; where the effects of those which are present or absent bid defiance to calculation; let me add too, as a circumstance of great tenderness, where our conclusion would degrade a whole race of men from the rank in the scale of beings which their Creator may perhaps have given them. To our reproach it must be said, that though for a century and a half we have had under our eyes the races of black and of red men, they have never yet been viewed by us as subjects of natural history. I advance it therefore as a suspicion only, that the blacks, whether originally a distinct race, or made distinct by time and circumstances, are inferior to the whites in the endowments both of body and mind. It is not against experience to suppose, that different species of the same genus,

or varieties of the same species, may possess different qualifications. Will not a lover of natural history then, one who views the gradations in all the races of animals with the eye of philosophy, excuse an effort to keep those in the department of man as distinct as nature has formed them? This unfortunate difference of colour, and perhaps of faculty, is a powerful obstacle to the emancipation of these people. Many of their advocates, while they wish to vindicate the liberty of human nature, are anxious also to preserve its dignity and beauty. Some of these, embarrassed by the question "What further is to be done with them?" join themselves in opposition with those who are actuated by sordid avarice only. Among the Romans emancipation required but one effort. The slave, when made free, might mix with, without staining the blood of his master. But with us a second is necessary, unknown to history. When freed, he is to be removed beyond the reach of mixture.

The revised code further proposes to proportion crimes and punishments....

Pardon and privilege of clergy are proposed to be abolished; but if the verdict be against the defendant, the court in their discretion, may allow a new trial. No attainder to cause a corruption of blood, or forfeiture of dower. Slaves guilty of offences punishable in others by labour, to be transported to Africa, or elsewhere, as the circumstances of the time admit, there to be continued in slavery. A rigorous regimen proposed for those condemned to labour....

Lastly, it is proposed, by a bill in this revisal, to begin a public library and gallery, by laying out a certain sum annually in books, paintings, and statues....

"Manners"

♦ *The particular customs and manners that may happen to be received in that state?*

It is difficult to determine on the standard by which the manners of a nation may be tried, whether *catholic*, or *particular*. It is more difficult for a native to bring to that standard the manners of his own nation, familiarized to him by habit. There must doubtless be an unhappy influence on the manners of our people produced by the existence of slavery among us. The whole commerce between master and slave is a perpetual exercise of the most boisterous passions, the most unremitting despotism on the one part, and degrading submissions on the other. Our children see this, and learn to imitate it; for man is an imitative animal. This quality is the germ of all education in him. From his cradle to his grave he is learning to do what he sees others do. If a parent could find no motive either in his philanthropy or his self-love, for restraining the intemperance of passion towards his slave, it should always be a sufficient one that his child is present. But generally it is not sufficient. The parent storms, the child looks on, catches the lineaments of wrath, puts on the same airs in the circle of smaller slaves, gives a loose to his worst of passions, and thus nursed, educated, and daily exercised in tyranny, cannot but be stamped by it with odious peculiarities. The man must be a prodigy who can retain his manners and morals undepraved by such circumstances. And with what execration should the statesman be loaded, who permitting one half the citizens thus to trample on the rights of the other, transforms those into despots, and these into enemies, destroys the morals of the one part, and the amor patriae of the other. For if a slave can have a country in this world, it must be any other in preference to that in which he is born to live and labour for another: in which he must lock up the faculties of his nature, contribute as far as depends on his individual endeavours to the evanishment of the human race, or entail his own miserable condition on the endless generations proceeding from him. With the morals of the people, their industry also is destroyed. For in a warm climate, no man will labour for himself who can make another labour for him. This is so true, that of the proprietors of slaves a very small proportion indeed are ever seen to labour. And can the liberties of a nation be thought secure when we have removed their only firm basis, a conviction in the minds of the people that these liberties are of the gift of God? That they are not to be violated but with his wrath? Indeed I tremble for my country when I reflect that God is just: that his justice cannot sleep for ever: that considering numbers, nature and natural means only, a revolution of the wheel of fortune, an exchange of situation, is among possible events: that it may become probable by supernatural interference! The Almighty has no attribute which can take side with us in such a contest.—But it is impossible to be temperate and to pursue this subject through the various considerations of policy, of morals, of history natural and civil. We must be contented to hope they will force their way into every one's mind. I think a change already perceptible, since the origin of the present revolution. The spirit of the master is abating, that of the slave rising from the dust, his condition mollifying, the way I hope preparing, under the auspices of heaven, for a total emancipation, and that this is disposed, in the order of events, to be with the consent of the masters, rather than by their extirpation.

Gouverneur Morris (Library of Congress)

SLAVERY CLAUSES IN THE U.S. CONSTITUTION

"Representatives and direct Taxes shall be apportioned among the several States ... according to their respective Numbers."

Overview

The U.S. Constitution was written at a convention that met in Philadelphia from May 25 until September 17, 1787. At the time, slavery was legal and a vibrant economic institution in eight states, while two (Massachusetts and New Hampshire) had abolished it, and three others (Pennsylvania, Rhode Island, and Connecticut) had passed gradual abolition acts. There were about 700,000 slaves in the nation, with more than 600,000 in Virginia, South Carolina, North Carolina, and Maryland. Virginia's 300,000 slaves constituted just over 40 percent of the state, while South Carolina's 107,000 slaves made up 43 percent of the state. Slaves were property and enormously valuable. They were also central to the southern economy. Indeed, with the exception of real estate, slaves represented the single most valuable form of privately held property in the nation. And, as people, they comprised more than a third of the entire population of the South. Not surprisingly, this important economic interest and this peculiar social relationship led to significant debates at the Constitutional Convention.

The issues of slavery affected discussion about the Constitution from the very first day of debates until the end of the convention. The final document did not use the word *slave*, because northern delegates feared that the use of the term would make ratification in their states more difficult. But slavery was embedded into the Constitution in many places and shaped the Constitution in at least five important ways. First, the delegates had to determine how slaves would be counted for purposes of representation. Naturally, southerners wanted to count all of them when allocating seats in Congress. Most northerners believed that slavery was deeply immoral and had no place in the allocation of power in a free country. How the Convention dealt with this issue would determine how power would be shared within the new government. In the end, the Convention compromised by counting slaves on a three-fifths basis. This compromise gave the South significant power in Congress and in the Electoral College.

The second area of debate concerned the power of Congress over commerce and the African slave trade. The docu-

ment written in Philadelphia ultimately prevented Congress from interfering with the trade for at least twenty years. Third, the slaveholders at the convention—a majority of the delegates—insisted that the Constitution provide explicit federal protections for slavery. This was accomplished with clauses providing for the suppression of slave rebellions and a ban on export taxes, which southerners feared would be used to harm their slave-based agricultural economy. In addition to promises of federal protection, the slave owners at the convention insisted on guarantees that the states would also afford protection for their property. Thus, they prevailed upon the northern delegates to support a fugitive slave clause that would prohibit free states from emancipating fugitive slaves and instead guarantee that masters could capture their runaways. Finally, the Constitution created a government of limited powers that had no power over slavery in the states.

At no time did the Constitutional Convention consider giving the national government power to end slavery or even regulate it in the states where it existed. Numerous times during the convention the southern delegates made clear that they would not support the Constitution unless their slave property was protected from the general government. They gained this end through the overall structure of the Constitution. Thus, when he returned from the Convention, South Carolina's most important delegate, General Charles Cotesworth Pinckney, proudly told his state legislature: "We have a security that the general government can never emancipate them, for no such authority is granted and it is admitted, on all hands, that the general government has no powers but what are expressly granted by the Constitution, and that all rights not expressed were reserved by the several states."

Context

At the beginning of the American Revolution slavery was legal in every one of the thirteen colonies. As early as the 1680s Quakers and Mennonites had challenged the morality of slavery, but very few other white Americans questioned slavery. In 1700 the Puritan lawyer Samuel Sewall published *The Selling of Joseph*, which argued that slavery was inconsistent with Christian values. However, other Pu-

1688

■ The Quakers of Germantown, Pennsylvania, publish the first protest on slavery in America.

1700

■ Samuel Sewall publishes *The Selling of Joseph* in Boston.

1712

■ The slave population surpasses the free population of South Carolina. The colony will have a black majority until the Revolution.

1770

■ **March 5**
The Boston Massacre takes place; one of the five Americans killed is Crispus Attucks, a former slave.

1772

■ In *Somerset v. Stewart*, Lord Chief Justice Mansfield rules that a slave who is brought to England by his master or who escapes to England cannot be brought back to a slaveholding colony against his will.

1775

■ **April 18**
The American Revolution begins with the battles of Lexington and Concord; many free blacks serve in the Massachusetts militias.

1776

■ **July 4**
The Continental Congress formally approves the Declaration of Independence, which declares that "all men are created equal" and entitled to the rights of "life, liberty, and the pursuit of happiness," though it is unclear whether the delegates intended to apply these words to their many slaves. The primary author, Thomas Jefferson, owns about 150 slaves at this time.

1781

■ The Articles of Confederation go into effect, creating a weak national government with limited powers.

ritans and most other mainstream Christians did not accept this premise. By the eve of the Revolution, Baptists, Methodists, and some New England Congregationalists and Unitarians opposed slavery on religious grounds, but most white Americans found no inconsistency between Christianity and ownership of slaves.

The growing religious opposition to slavery—especially among Quakers, Methodists, and some Baptists—dovetailed with mounting political antislavery sentiment immediately before and during the Revolution. As white Americans challenged the justice of Great Britain's sovereignty over them, black Americans challenged the justice of slavery. Even before the Revolution, slaves in Massachusetts petitioned the colonial legislature to free them. The Revolution accelerated this growing opposition to slavery. The assertions of the Declaration of Independence—that we are all "created equal" and "endowed" with the "unalienable rights" of "life, liberty, and the pursuit of happiness"—led many Americans to question the morality and justice of slavery. In addition, from the moment the war began, slaves, especially in the North, moved to gain their own freedom. Throughout New England many masters manumitted their male slaves so that they could serve in the Revolutionary Army. In the South slaves ran away to armies on both sides. A few Patriot masters also freed their slaves.

During the war opposition to slavery took more concrete forms. In 1778 the people of Massachusetts rejected a proposed state constitution because it did not abolish human bondage. Two years late the people approved a constitution written largely by John Adams that began (in Article 1) with an assertion of universal liberty: "All men are born free and equal, and have certain natural, essential, and unalienable rights, among which may be reckoned the right of enjoying and defending their lives and liberties; that of acquiring, possessing, and protecting property; in fine, that of seeking and obtaining their safety and happiness." A year later the state's highest court confirmed, in *Commonwealth v. Jennison* (1781), that this clause had abolished slavery in the Bay State. Meanwhile, in Pennsylvania the state legislature passed a gradual abolition law, which did not lead to an immediate end to slavery but set the stage for the institution to gradually disappear. In 1783 New Hampshire followed the Massachusetts model, abolishing slavery in its new Constitution and in 1784 both Connecticut and Rhode Island passed gradual abolition laws. During this period, residents of Vermont, which would become the fourteenth state, wrote a constitution that explicitly banned slavery in the state. At this time slavery was made strong and economically important in New York and New Jersey, where slaves made up more than 6 percent of the population.

Thus, when the Constitutional Convention began, the nation was slowly moving along the road to becoming, in the words of Abraham Lincoln in his "House Divided" speech (1858), "half slave and half free." However, it was not yet "half free." Slavery was still legal in eleven of the thirteen states, and the gradual abolition acts in Pennsylvania, Connecticut, and Rhode Island were experiments that had not yet fully ended bondage. Nevertheless, the delegates from the five biggest slave states—Virginia, Maryland, North Carolina, South Carolina, and Georgia—feared that a stronger national government would threaten their most important economic and social and institution. Thus, from the beginning of the Constitutional Convention, they insisted on specific protections for slavery. They gained them, as noted, throughout the Constitution. In the end, slaves were counted for representation and for the election of the president, even though slaves could not vote. Congress was prohibited from ending the African slave trade before 1808 but was not required to do it then. The federal government promised to help suppress domestic insurrections, which for the South meant slave revolts. The structure of the Constitution made it extremely difficult to amend the document. The requirement that three-fourths of the states ratify an amendment gave the slave states what amounted to a perpetual veto over any constitutional amendment.

The two most important slavery-related issues at the convention were the counting of slaves for representation and the demands of the Deep South that the African slave trade be given special protection from the national legislature. Most delegates believed that if the new Congress had the power to regulate international commerce, it would ban the slave trade. The delegates debated these issues a number of times during the convention. What they said and how they voted reflected their own political inclinations. Virtually all of the southerners insisted on counting slaves for representation in Congress. Some demanded that slaves be counted fully, while others were willing to accept what became the three-fifths compromise. The African slave trade was more complicated. Delegates from the Deep South insisted on a clause to prevent the new Congress from closing the trade. Many of the delegates from the Chesapeake region opposed this on a variety of grounds. Some thought the trade was immoral (even though they were not ready to end slavery itself for this reason), and some thought it dangerous to bring new slaves from Africa to the nation. Equally important, by the end of the Revolution both Virginia and Maryland had a surplus of slaves and thus did not need the African trade; if the trade stopped, they could sell their extra slaves to the Deep South at higher prices.

Northern delegates were also split on the slavery issues, but in different directions. Some adamantly opposed counting slaves for purposes of representation not only on moral grounds but also because it would strengthen the South and thus weaken their own section in the Congress. Others were more willing to compromise on this issue. The same was true for the slave trade. New Englanders in the end were willing to join South Carolinians in protecting the slave trade because South Carolinians were willing to support their interest in allowing Congress to regulate all interstate and foreign commerce. Delegates from the Middle Colonies were less willing to compromise on what they considered a "nefarious" commerce.

Fifty-five delegates attended. Thirty-nine delegates remaining at the end of the convention signed the Constitution, and three refused to do so. More than half the delegates came from states that would maintain slavery until the Civil

Time Line

1783

■ The American Revolution ends, and the new United States is governed by Congress under the Articles of Confederation. There is no president and no national court system, and the states regulate almost everything, including personal status—whether someone is slave or free.

■ **August 29**
Shays's Rebellion, an uprising of farmers, closes the courts in western Massachusetts to prevent foreclosures on farms during an economic downturn.

■ **September 11**
A convention meets in Annapolis, Maryland, to discuss issues of interstate trade and commerce, but only twelve delegates from just five states—New York, Pennsylvania, New Jersey, Delaware, and Virginia—show up.

■ **September 14**
The Annapolis Convention ends in failure, but two of the delegates who attend—James Madison of Virginia and Alexander Hamilton of New York—work out a plan to hold a national convention (the Constitutional Convention) in Philadelphia the following spring, to revise the Articles of Confederation.

1787

■ **January**
Shays's Rebellion is suppressed by a privately hired army. The failure of the United States government to put down the rebellion underscores the weakness of the national government.

■ **May 25–September 17**
The Constitutional Convention meets in Philadelphia to write the Constitution. Issues of slavery are debated throughout the Convention; on the last day, two delegates refuse to sign the document, in part because of the provisions involving slavery.

1788

■ **June 21**
New Hampshire becomes the ninth state to ratify the Constitution, making it the new basis of government for the United States.

1789

■ **March 4**
A new Congress meets in New York City.

War, and more than half were also slave owners, including all of the delegates from Virginia and South Carolina and some from the North. The delegates differed substantially on slavery. Generally, the southern delegates were adamant in their desire to protect slavery, while the northerners were more willing to compromise to gain a stronger Union.

The debates over the Constitution reveal the way the Framers viewed slavery. Almost all the southerners, who made up more than half the delegates, were unanimous in support of counting slaves for representation and in other ways protecting slavery. The only issue they disagreed on was the African slave trade. The northerners were mostly opposed to slavery, but few were willing to risk confronting the South on this issue. Antislavery sentiment, such as it existed in the North, was confined to ending slavery in the northern states and to not interfering with slavery where it existed. Thus, at the insistence of slave owners, the delegates to the Constitutional Convention wrote slavery into the document.

When the Constitution was sent to the states for ratification, a number of opponents of the new form of government focused on the slavery provisions, especially those prohibiting Congress from ending the African slave trade. A New Yorker complained (in the *New York Journal* of January 22, 1788) that the Constitution condoned "drenching the bowels of Africa in gore, for the sake of enslaving its free-born innocent inhabitants." The anonymous "Countryman from Duchess County," another Antifederalist, sarcastically noted that the slave trade provision was an "excellent clause" for "an Algerian constitution: but not so well calculated (I hope) for the latitude of America." Three Antifederalists in Massachusetts, writing to the Northampton *Hampshire Gazette* (April 1788), warned that "this lust for slavery [was] portentous of much evil in America, for the cry of innocent blood, … hath undoubtedly reached to the Heavens, to which that cry is always directed, and will draw down upon them vengeance adequate to the enormity of the crime."

On the other side of the argument, southern supporters of the Constitution praised the document precisely because it protected slavery. In the Virginia ratifying convention, Edmund Randolph told the delegates they had nothing to fear from a stronger national government. He challenged opponents of the Constitution to show "*Where* is the part that has a tendency to the *abolition of* slavery?" He answered his own question in asserting, "Were it right here to mention what passed in [the Philadelphia] convention … I might tell you *that the Southern States, even South Carolina herself, conceived this property to be secure*" and that "there was not a member of the Virginia delegation who had *the smallest suspicion of the abolition of slavery.*" Similarly, Pinckney, who had been one of the ablest defenders of slavery at the Convention, proudly told the South Carolina House of Representatives: "In short, considering all circumstances, we have made the best terms for the security of this species of property it was in our power to make. We would have made better if we could; but on the whole, I do not think them bad."

About the Author

The Constitution was not written by any single individual. James Madison of Virginia is often called "the Father of the Constitution," because he worked tirelessly at the convention and kept notes of the debates. When the convention began, Edmund Randolph of Virginia, the governor of the state at the time, introduced the "Virginia Plan," which became the basis for debate. Madison most likely drafted the Virginia Plan (also sometimes called the "Randolph Plan"), but the final Constitution differed significantly from the Virginia Plan. It was, in the end, truly the work of the convention.

A few delegates strongly opposed slavery. Benjamin Franklin of Pennsylvania was the president of the Pennsylvania Society for the Abolition of Slavery, the most active and important antislavery society in the country. Although he had owned a few slaves during his life, using them as house servants, by this time he was adamantly opposed to human bondage. Alexander Hamilton of New York was a founding member of the New York Manumission Society, the main antislavery organization in his state. Hamilton had grown up on the Caribbean island of Nevis, where he had seen slavery throughout his childhood. He moved to New York as a teenager to attend school and was forever an opponent of slavery. Gouverneur Morris was the convention's most vocal opponent of slavery. Morris came from a very wealthy family with landholdings in New York and New Jersey but represented Pennsylvania at the convention. Morris's grandfather Lewis Morris had once been the largest slaveholder in the Middle Colonies, with more than sixty-five slaves. But Gouverneur Morris vigorously opposed the compromises over slavery, especially the slave-trade provisions. On the floor of the convention he tied counting slaves for representation to the clause protecting the African slave trade, noting

> When fairly explained [it] comes to this: that the inhabitant of Georgia and South Carolina who goes to the Coast of Africa, and in defiance of the most sacred laws of humanity tears away his fellow creatures from their dearest connections and damns them to the most cruel bondages, shall have more votes in a Government instituted for protection of the rights of mankind, than the Citizen of Pennsylvania or New Jersey who views with a laudable horror, so nefarious a practice.

Most of the other northern delegates were ambivalent about slavery. They understood that slavery was an important institution in the South, and they were prepared to compromise when southerners demanded special protection for the institution. A handful of the northern delegates owned a few slaves, as household servants. In the end most of the northern states voted to support the three-fifths clause; on the final vote over the slave trade provision, three New England states joined the South in preventing Congress from ending the trade before 1808. The strongest support on this issue came from Connecticut, where at least one of the delegates, John Dickinson of Delaware, argued that protecting the slave trade was "inadmissible on every principle of honor and safety." (He owned slaves but disliked his status as "master" and would eventually free them.) James Madison said this provision was "dishonorable to the National character" and would "produce all the mischief that can be apprehended from the liberty to import slaves." But New Englanders saw it differently, as they voted to support South Carolina's demand for protection for the trade. Oliver Ellsworth of Connecticut, who would later become chief justice of the United States, refused to debate the "morality or wisdom of slavery," simply asserting that "what enriches a part enriches the whole." When one southerner pointed out that the trade would produce immoral results, he replied that he "had never owned a slave" and thus declared that he "could not judge of the effects of slavery on character." Roger Sherman, also from Connecticut, backed the slave trade because he wanted South Carolina to support the new Constitution. He argued that "the public good did not require" an end to the trade and that "it was expedient to have as few objections as possible" to the new Constitution. Indeed, none of the northern delegates favored slavery, but most thought it expedient to support the demands of the South to protect it.

By 1787 George Washington had privately committed himself to freeing his own slaves when he died—an unusual act at the time. He also vowed never to buy or sell another slave. James Madison would never free any of his slaves, but he was deeply uncomfortable with the institution, as were George Wythe and James McClurg of Virginia. Still, almost all the southerners supported counting slaves for representation. The only real division among them was on the slave trade. A majority of the delegates from Virginia and Delaware opposed protecting the slave trade, while the Maryland delegation was split.

The delegates from the Deep South had no qualms about slavery or the slave trade. Charles Cotesworth Pinckney, the leader of the South Carolina delegation, owned huge numbers of slaves and was committed to preserving and protecting the institution. So, too, was his younger cousin, Charles Pinckney, and his fellow planter Pierce Butler, who would later become a U.S. senator. During the debate over the slave trade, Charles Pinckney defused moral arguments with historical references. Citing ancient Rome and Greece, Pinckney declared that slavery was "justified by the example of all the world." In demanding that slaves be counted equally with whites for

Oliver Ellsworth (Library of Congress)

purposes of representation, Butler argued that "the labour of a slave in South Carolina was as productive and valuable as that of a freeman in Massachusetts." Reflecting the nonegalitarian ideas of slave-owning South Carolina, Butler argued that since the national government "was instituted principally for the protection of property," slaves should be counted fully for representation.

Explanation and Analysis of the Document

The word *slavery* does not appear in the U.S. Constitution as written in Philadelphia in 1787. The first mention of slavery is in the Thirteenth Amendment, ratified in 1865, which ended slavery throughout the United States after the Civil War. Throughout the Constitutional Convention the delegates talked frankly about slaves and slavery, but in the final document they did not use the term. The reason is clear. Some delegates were embarrassed by it, while others, especially in the North, feared that the direct mention of slavery would harm chances for ratification, as some northerners would vote against a Constitution that directly endorsed the practice. The records of the convention make this clear. During the debate over the slave trade, Gouvernor Morris, who hated slavery, suggested that the clause declare that the importation of slaves into North Carolina, South Carolina, and Georgia not be prohibited before a certain date. Other delegates rejected this idea, both because

"Representatives and direct Taxes shall be apportioned among the several States ... according to their respective Numbers, which shall be determined by adding to the whole Number of free Persons ... three fifths of all other Persons."

(Article I, Section 2)

"No Person held to Service or Labour in one State, under the Laws thereof, escaping into another, shall in Consequence of any Law or Regulation therein, be discharged from such Service or Labour, but shall be delivered up on Claim of the Party to whom such Service or Labour may be due."

(Article IV, Section 2)

it would single out three states and because it would alert their constituents to the proslavery aspects of the Constitution. Connecticut's Roger Sherman, who voted with the Deep South to allow the trade, declared that he "liked a description better than the terms proposed," which had been declined by the old Congress and "were not pleasing to some people." George Clymer of Pennsylvania concurred with Sherman. In the North Carolina ratifying convention, James Iredell, who had been a delegate in Philadelphia, explained that the "word *slave* is not mentioned" because "the northern delegates, owing to their particular scruples on the subject of slavery, did not choose the word *slave* to be mentioned."

But even without the word's appearance in the Constitution, slavery is found in a number of places and is more indirectly connected to the Constitution in many other places. The delegates used descriptions of slaves, calling them "other persons," "such persons," and "persons owing service or labour." In other ways there were recognitions of slavery. Thus, in discussing apportionment in the three-fifths clause, the Constitution authorizes counting the "whole Number of free Persons," in each state and then added "three-fifths of all other Persons." The use of the term "free Persons" naturally implied that the "other Persons" were not free but were slaves. Thus, even as the framers avoided the word *slave*, they acknowledged the importance of slaves to the nation and the constitutional structure.

♦ **Preamble**

The Constitution begins with a preamble asserting that it had been formed by "We the People." The preamble states that the Constitution was written to "form a more perfect Union" and to "establish Justice, insure domestic Tranquility, provide for the common defense, promote the general Welfare, and secure the Blessings of Liberty" for the American people. Each of these issues raised questions about slavery and race.

"The people" who formed the more perfect Union were, of course, the "people" of the United States. Presumably that did not include slaves, since they were not allowed to participate in the political process. But it must have included free blacks in those states—Massachusetts, New Hampshire, New York, Pennsylvania, New Jersey, and North Carolina—where they could vote and even hold office. In *Dred Scott v. Sandford* (1857) the Supreme Court would declare that blacks could never be citizens of the United States, even if free. But this was surely problematic, since free blacks in at least six states participated in the ratification of the Constitution, just as blacks from a majority of the states had served in the Revolutionary armies that won independence from Great Britain.

The rest of the preamble spoke to other questions of slavery and liberty. The Constitution was designed to "establish Justice." Did this include justice for those born to slavery or just justice for their masters? The Constitution guaranteed that the national government would suppress insurrections, which would "insure domestic Tranquility." This in part meant suppressing slave rebellions, which the national government helped do on a handful of occasions before the Civil War. But when the master class revolted to set up a new nation—the Confederate States of America—based on slavery, the national government would suppress this insurrection as well. Meanwhile, "the common defense" was undermined, as many opponents of slavery pointed out, by the very presence of slaves, who might side with an enemy in time of war. The Deep South would discover the truth of this during the Civil War as more than two hundred thousand black men—the vast majority slaves before the war—fought to preserve the Union and end slavery. Did slavery help or hinder "the general Welfare" of the nation? Obviously slave owners thought bondage served their welfare. But how could slavery be protected by a Constitution designed to "secure the Blessing of Liberty"? The answer depended on how one viewed slavery. For the South, one of the "blessings" of the new nation was the liberty to own other people and hold them in perpetual servitude. Slaves, and those who opposed their bondage, believed that the Constitution and the government it created failed to live up to the goal of securing "liberty."

♦ **Representation**

Article I, Section 2 of the Constitution set out how seats would be allocated in the new House of Representatives. A census would count everyone in the nation, except Indians living outside American jurisdictions (called "Indians not taxed"). Slaves would be counted separately from whites. Sixty percent of the slave population would be added to the whole free population to determine the state's population, and representatives would be based on that number. This was the "three-fifths clause." It did not designate blacks to be three-fifths of a person, as many people incorrectly believe. On the contrary, free blacks were counted in the same way as whites. What the clause did was to add to the power of the southern states in Congress by giving them extra representation for their slaves.

The importance of this clause is made clear when we look at the slave populations in the South in the 1790 census. Slaves constituted more than a third of the population in the five states from Maryland to Georgia. South Carolina was 43 percent slave. Virginia was the largest state in the nation, with 692,000 people, but Virginia's free population of just over 400,000 was second to Pennsylvania's and not much bigger than that of Massachusetts. North Carolina, with about 394,000 people, was the third-largest state, but only 288,000 of those people were free. If slaves had not been counted for representation, Virginia would have had the second-largest delegation in Congress, and North Carolina would have fallen from third to fifth. Similarly, Maryland, the sixth-largest state, would fall behind Connecticut if its 103,000 slaves were not counted for representation. Most dramatically of all, South Carolina, with 249,000 people, was the seventh-largest state in the Union. But if 107,000 slaves were not counted, the state would fall to eleventh place, behind Connecticut, New Jersey, and New Hampshire. By counting slaves for representation, the southern states gained a number of seats in the Congress that they would not have had if only free people had been counted.

In the Constitutional Convention, William Paterson of New Jersey had complained bitterly about the injustice of counting slaves to determine representation in a government designed for free people. Paterson argued that slaves

were not "free agents, have no personal liberty, no faculty of acquiring property, but on the contrary are themselves property, and like other property entirely at the will of the Master." Paterson pointedly asked whether a man in Virginia had a number of votes in proportion to the number of his slaves. He noted that slaves were not counted in allocating representation in southern state legislatures and asked why they should be represented in the general government. Similarly, Elbridge Gerry of Massachusetts sarcastically asked if slaves were "property," in the South, why should their "representation be increased to the southward on account of the number of slaves, than horses or oxen to the north?" He wondered "Are we to enter into a Compact with Slaves?" In the end the Convention accepted the demand of the South that slaves be counted for representation, but on a three-fifths ratio.

In the long run this clause would give the South extra muscle in Congress, helping to provide the margin of victory for allowing slavery in Missouri, annexing Texas, and passing the Fugitive Slave Act of 1850. Because the Electoral College, which elects the president—set out in Article II—was based on representation in Congress, the three-fifths clause also helped elect slaveholding presidents. In 1800 the slaveholding Thomas Jefferson defeated the non-slaveholder John Adams because of electoral votes created by counting slaves for representation.

The clause also provided that if direct taxes were ever levied on the states, the states would pay according to a population including three-fifths of the slaves. Had the national government ever imposed direct taxes on the states—such as a tax on every person in the state—before the Civil War, this clause would have added to the tax burden of the slave states. But no one expected such taxes, and at the Convention a number of delegates said so. In fact, none was imposed. Thus, while it was *apparently* a compromise over taxation and representation, it was a clause that affected only representation and the election of the president.

♦ **The Slave Trade**

Article I, Section 9 of the Constitution provides that the "Migration or Importation of such Persons as any of the States now existing shall think proper to admit, shall not be prohibited by Congress" before 1808. This was awkwardly phrased, perhaps in the hope that opponents of the slave trade would miss the point. Under this provision Congress could not end the African slave trade before 1808, even though Congress had the power to regulate all other forms of international commerce. A divided convention adopted this clause after a touchy, three-day debate. The clause generated significant opposition to the Constitution throughout the North but also in Virginia. At the convention the South Carolina delegates said they could not support the Constitution without some protection for the African trade, but in 1787 none of the states was actually importing slaves. During the Revolution all the states voluntarily stopped the African trade because Great Britain dominated the trade and buying slaves from Africa would be a form of trading with the enemy. South Carolina did not reopen the African trade until 1803. In the next five years about seventy thousand new slaves would be brought into South Carolina and Georgia—the largest importations in any similar period in American history. On January 1, 1808, the United States would ban the trade. In the next half century there would be some smuggling—probably no more than ten thousand slaves were brought into the country illegally. In 1821 the United States would declare that slave trading was piracy, punishable by death, but no trader would be executed until the Lincoln administration.

♦ **The Fugitive Slave Clause**

Article IV, Section 2 provides that "persons held to Service or Labour" and escaping into another state be "delivered up on Claim of the Party to whom such Service or Labour may be due." There was almost debate over this clause at the convention, and there is little sense of how people expected the clause to operate. Pierce Butler, who introduced it, was a wealthy planter from South Carolina and probably assumed that runaway slaves would be stopped by local sheriffs and held until someone claimed them. This is how it worked in the South, where any black—even if free—was subject to investigation if he or she was found without a master or was unknown to local officials. In the North, where slavery was ending, blacks were not presumed to be slaves. In 1793 Congress passed a fugitive slave law to implement this clause. The Supreme Court would uphold this law in *Prigg v. Pennsvylvaia* in 1842. In 1850 Congress passed a stronger law. The clause never worked well and led to enormous hostility in the North and great frustration in the South. Rather than creating a "more perfect Union," the clause dramatically undermined the Union. Southern states cited failure to enforce the clause as a reason for secession; northerners viewed the clause as legalizing kidnapping and a symbol of southern oppression.

♦ **The Amendment Process**

The Constitution provided for a complicated and difficult amendment process. Two-thirds of each house of Congress had to approve an amendment, which then had to be ratified by three-fourths of the states. This gave the South what amounted to a perpetual veto over any amendments. In 1861 there were fifteen slave states. If all fifteen were still slave states in the modern era, it would still be impossible to amend the Constitution to end slavery. If fifteen slave states voted against an amendment it would take forty-five free states to outvote them, necessitating a sixty-state Union. Only secession allowed for the Civil War Amendments, which ended slavery, made all people born in the nation citizens without regard to race, and prohibited discrimination in voting on the basis of race.

♦ **Other Clauses Affecting Slavery**

In addition to the clauses specifically designed to protect slavery, others also affected the system. The two insurrection clauses (Article I, Section 8, and Article IV, Section 4) created a guarantee that the U.S. government would suppress slave rebellions, as it did on a number of occasions. The Electoral College folded the three-fifths clause into the Electoral College so that slaves would help elect the president. The delegates were very specific about this. At the convention James Madison said that "the people at large" were "the fittest" to choose the president. But "one difficulty ... of a serious nature" made election by the people impossible: "The Southern States ... could have no influence in the election on the score of the Negroes." In other words, slaves would not help elect presidents. More openly, Hugh Williamson of North Carolina observed that if there were a direct election of the president, Virginia would not be able to elect "her" leaders president because "her slaves will have no suffrage." The slave states also insisted—and obtained—prohibitions on export taxes (in Article I, Sections 9 and 10) so that the products of slave labor might not be indirectly taxed.

Other parts of the Constitution put the national government in the position of having to regulate slavery. Article I, Section 8 gave Congress power to create and govern a national capital—which became Washington, D.C. Eventually located between Maryland and Virginia, it would be a slaveholding city until Congress exercised its power to end slavery there in 1862. Similarly, the power to admit new states and regulate the territories (Article IV, Section 3) gave Congress the power to ban slavery in the territories. From 1791 until 1857 Congress regulated slavery in the territories and debated the admission of new states on the basis of slavery. This led to enormous political conflict and, in Kansas, a civil war known as Bleeding Kansas. In *Dred Scott v. Sandford* (1857), Supreme Court Chief Justice Roger Taney ruled that Congress could not ban slavery in the territories. This attempt to solve the problem backfired and helped elect Lincoln, which in turn led to secession by slave-state politicians who could not imagine a Union led by an actual opponent of slavery. In 1862 Congress ignored Taney's decision and banned slavery in the territories.

The ultimate protection of slavery in the Constitution was the creation of a limited government. Under the pre–Civil War Constitution neither the president nor Congress had the power to touch slavery in the states. Since slavery was an institution created by state law, this meant that Congress could never end slavery. In that sense, the Constitution created a slaveholders' republic that lacked the internal structure to change itself. At the ratifying Convention in South Carolina, Charles Cotesworth Pinckney proudly noted,

We have a security that the general government can never emancipate them, for no such authority is granted and it is admitted, on all hands, that the general government has no powers but what are expressly granted by the Constitution, and that all rights not expressed were reserved by the several states.

Only secession and the Civil War could change that.

Audience

The U.S. Constitution was designed to create "a more perfect Union." The audience was the voters of the America. The Framers wanted to gain support for the new Constitution and then set up a new, stronger, and more vibrant government. With regard to slavery, there were three audiences. First the Framers wanted to attract southern support for the Constitution by giving the states representation in Congress based on their slave populations, protecting the right of masters to recover fugitive slaves, and guaranteeing that the national government would never interfere with slavery in the states. Second, the Framers wanted to gain the support of the three most southern states—the Carolinas and Georgia—by guaranteeing their right to import slaves for *at least* twenty years. Finally, the Framers wanted to shape the proslavery provisions so that they would not offend northerners who opposed all slavery as well as Virginia and Maryland voters who opposed the African trade.

Impact

At first glance, the slavery provisions of the Constitution were enormously successful. Despite northern opposition to slavery—and some southern opposition to the slave trade provision—the people of the states ratified the Constitution. For the next seventy-two years the Constitution protected slavery and slaveholders. The slave population grew from 698,000 in 1790 to 3,954,000 in 1860. Slaveholders dominated the presidency, the Congress, and the Supreme Court. Even when slave owners were not in office, they were able to secure positions for northerners sympathetic to slavery. But while the slave population grew rapidly, the population of the free states grew even faster. So, too, did opposition to slavery, not only in the United States but also, indeed, throughout the world. In 1787 slavery was legal everywhere in the Atlantic world except Massachusetts, New Hampshire, the soon-to-be state of Vermont, England, and France. By 1860 slavery was legal only in the American South, a few Spanish islands in the Caribbean, and Brazil. For a majority of northerners, and for most of the Western World, slavery was a "relic of barbarism," as the Republican Party platform called it in 1856. Still, the Constitution may have protected slavery too well. There was no political or constitutional way to end bondage, even in the far-distant future. Southerners, meanwhile, saw the election of Abraham Lincoln as a direct threat to slavery, even though neither the president nor Congress had any power to touch slavery in the fifteen slave states. The eleven southern states seceded to protect slavery, which the Confederate Vice President Alexander Stephens called "the cornerstone of the Confederacy." When these states left the Union, they lost the ability to block constitutional changes. Thus, in 1865 the United States added the Thirteenth Amendment to the Constitution, ending slavery forever.

See also *Prigg v. Pennsylvania* (1850); Fugitive Slave Act of 1850; *Dred Scott v. Sandford* (1857); Thirteenth Amendment to the U.S. Constitution (1865); *Plessy v. Ferguson* (1896).

Questions for Further Study

1. In modern discussions it is often stated that the U.S. Constitution regarded slaves as "three-fifths" of a person. In what sense, though, is this misleading? Put differently, why would the northern states that opposed slavery have been more content if slaves had not been counted as persons at all?

2. The U.S. Constitution deferred the issue of abolishing the slave trade (but not slavery) for two decades. What was the outcome of this provision of the Constitution? For help, see "An Oration on the Abolition of the Slave Trade" by Peter Williams, Jr.

3. What historical factors made slavery an entrenched institution in the American South but less so in the North? Were there any circumstances in which this pattern might have been reversed?

4. The U.S. Constitution was a product of negotiation and compromise in a number of respects—between large states and small states; between agricultural states and those whose economies were based more on trade, manufacture, and finance; and, of course, between slave states and free states. What motivated the Framers of the Constitution to accede to these sorts of compromises?

5. Who were the Federalists and the Antifederalists in the debate over ratification of the U.S. Constitution? What were the positions of these incipient political parties on slavery and the slave trade?

Further Reading

■ Articles

Finkelman, Paul. "Regulating the African Slave Trade." *Civil War History* 54, no. 4 (2008): 379–405.

■ Books

Beeman, Richard. *Plain, Honest Men: The Making of the American Constitution.* New York: Random House, 2009.

Elliot, Jonathan. *The Debates in the Several State Conventions on the Adoption of the Federal Constitution.* 5 vols. 1888. Reprint. New York: Burt Franklin, 1987.

Farrand, Max, ed. *The Records of the Federal Convention of 1787.* 4 vols. New Haven, Conn.: Yale University Press, 1966.

Finkelman, Paul. *Slavery and the Founders: Race and Liberty in the Age of Jefferson.* Armonk, N.Y.: M. E. Sharpe, 2001.

Jensen, Merrill, et al., eds. *Documentary History of the Ratification of the Constitution.* Madison, Wis.: Wisconsin Historical Society, 1976–.

Stewart, David O. *The Summer of 1787: The Men Who Invented the Constitution.* New York: Simon and Schuster, 2007.

Storing, Herbert J., ed., *The Complete Anti-Federalist.* 7 vols. Chicago: University of Chicago Press, 1981.

Waldstreicher, David. *Slavery's Constitution: From Revolution to Ratification.* New York: Hill and Wang, 2009.

■ Web Sites

Elliot, Jonathan, comp. *The Debates in the Several State Conventions on the Adoption of the Federal Constitution.* Library of Congress "American Memory: Continental Congress and the Constitutional Convention" Web site.
    http://memory.loc.gov/ammem/amlaw/lwed.html.

Madison, James. *The Debates in the Federal Convention of 1787.* Constitution Society Web site.
    http://www.constitution.org/dfc/dfc_0000.htm.

"Notes on the Debates in the Federal Convention." Yale Law School's "Avalon Project" Web site.
    http://avalon.law.yale.edu/subject_menus/debcont.asp.

—Paul Finkelman

SLAVERY CLAUSES IN THE U.S. CONSTITUTION

Preamble

We the People of the United States, in Order to form a more perfect Union, establish Justice, insure domestic Tranquility, provide for the common defense, promote the general Welfare, and secure the Blessings of Liberty to ourselves and our Posterity, do ordain and establish this Constitution for the United States of America.

Article I

◆ Section 1

All legislative Powers herein granted shall be vested in a Congress of the United States, which shall consist of a Senate and House of Representatives.

◆ Section 2

The House of Representatives shall be composed of Members chosen every second Year by the People of the several States, and the Electors in each State shall have the Qualifications requisite for Electors of the most numerous Branch of the State Legislature.

No Person shall be a Representative who shall not have attained to the Age of twenty five Years, and been seven Years a Citizen of the United States, and who shall not, when elected, be an Inhabitant of that State in which he shall be chosen.

Representatives and direct Taxes shall be apportioned among the several States which may be included within this Union, according to their respective Numbers, which shall be determined by adding to the whole Number of free Persons, including those bound to Service for a Term of Years, and excluding Indians not taxed, three fifths of all other Persons. The actual Enumeration shall be made within three Years after the first Meeting of the Congress of the United States, and within every subsequent Term of ten Years, in such Manner as they shall by Law direct. The Number of Representatives shall not exceed one for every thirty Thousand, but each State shall have at Least one Representative; and until such enumeration shall be made, the State of New Hampshire shall be entitled to chuse three, Massachusetts eight, Rhode-Island and Providence Plantations one, Connecticut five, New-York six, New Jersey four, Penn-sylvania eight, Delaware one, Maryland six, Virginia ten, North Carolina five, South Carolina five, and Georgia three....

◆ Section 3

The Senate of the United States shall be composed of two Senators from each State, chosen by the Legislature thereof for six Years; and each Senator shall have one Vote....

◆ Section 5

Each House shall be the Judge of the Elections, Returns and Qualifications of its own Members, and a Majority of each shall constitute a Quorum to do Business; but a smaller Number may adjourn from day to day, and may be authorized to compel the Attendance of absent Members, in such Manner, and under such Penalties as each House may provide.

Each House may determine the Rules of its Proceedings, punish its Members for disorderly Behaviour, and, with the Concurrence of two thirds, expel a Member.

Each House shall keep a Journal of its Proceedings, and from time to time publish the same, excepting such Parts as may in their Judgment require Secrecy; and the Yeas and Nays of the Members of either House on any question shall, at the Desire of one fifth of those Present, be entered on the Journal....

◆ Section 6

The Senators and Representatives shall receive a Compensation for their Services, to be ascertained by Law, and paid out of the Treasury of the United States. They shall in all Cases, except Treason, Felony and Breach of the Peace, be privileged from Arrest during their Attendance at the Session of their respective Houses, and in going to and returning from the same; and for any Speech or Debate in either House, they shall not be questioned in any other Place....

◆ Section 7

All Bills for raising Revenue shall originate in the House of Representatives; but the Senate may propose or concur with Amendments as on other Bills.

Every Bill which shall have passed the House of Representatives and the Senate, shall, before it become a Law, be presented to the President of the United States: If he approve he shall sign it, but if not he shall return it, with his Objections to that House in which it shall have originated, who shall enter the Objections at large on their Journal, and proceed to reconsider it. If after such Reconsideration two thirds of that House shall agree to pass the Bill, it shall be sent, together with the Objections, to the other House, by which it shall likewise be reconsidered, and if approved by two thirds of that House, it shall become a Law. But in all such Cases the Votes of both Houses shall be determined by yeas and Nays, and the Names of the Persons voting for and against the Bill shall be entered on the Journal of each House respectively. If any Bill shall not be returned by the President within ten Days (Sundays excepted) after it shall have been presented to him, the Same shall be a Law, in like Manner as if he had signed it, unless the Congress by their Adjournment prevent its Return, in which Case it shall not be a Law....

♦ **Section 8**

The Congress shall have Power To lay and collect Taxes, Duties, Imposts and Excises, to pay the Debts and provide for the common Defence and general Welfare of the United States; but all Duties, Imposts and Excises shall be uniform throughout the United States;

To borrow Money on the credit of the United States;

To regulate Commerce with foreign Nations, and among the several States, and with the Indian Tribes;

To establish an uniform Rule of Naturalization, and uniform Laws on the subject of Bankruptcies throughout the United States;

To coin Money, regulate the Value thereof, and of foreign Coin, and fix the Standard of Weights and Measures;

To provide for the Punishment of counterfeiting the Securities and current Coin of the United States;

To establish Post Offices and post Roads;

To promote the Progress of Science and useful Arts, by securing for limited Times to Authors and Inventors the exclusive Right to their respective Writings and Discoveries;

To constitute Tribunals inferior to the supreme Court;

To define and punish Piracies and Felonies committed on the high Seas, and Offences against the Law of Nations;

To declare War, grant Letters of Marque and Reprisal, and make Rules concerning Captures on Land and Water;

To raise and support Armies, but no Appropriation of Money to that Use shall be for a longer Term than two Years;

To provide and maintain a Navy;

To make Rules for the Government and Regulation of the land and naval Forces;

To provide for calling forth the Militia to execute the Laws of the Union, suppress Insurrections and repel Invasions;

To provide for organizing, arming, and disciplining, the Militia, and for governing such Part of them as may be employed in the Service of the United States, reserving to the States respectively, the Appointment of the Officers, and the Authority of training the Militia according to the discipline prescribed by Congress;

To exercise exclusive Legislation in all Cases whatsoever, over such District (not exceeding ten Miles square) as may, by Cession of particular States, and the Acceptance of Congress, become the Seat of the Government of the United States, and to exercise like Authority over all Places purchased by the Consent of the Legislature of the State in which the Same shall be, for the Erection of Forts, Magazines, Arsenals, dock-Yards, and other needful Buildings;— And

To make all Laws which shall be necessary and proper for carrying into Execution the foregoing Powers, and all other Powers vested by this Constitution in the Government of the United States, or in any Department or Officer thereof.

♦ **Section 9**

The Migration or Importation of such Persons as any of the States now existing shall think proper to admit, shall not be prohibited by the Congress prior to the Year one thousand eight hundred and eight, but a Tax or duty may be imposed on such Importation, not exceeding ten dollars for each Person.

The Privilege of the Writ of Habeas Corpus shall not be suspended, unless when in Cases of Rebellion or Invasion the public Safety may require it.

No Bill of Attainder or ex post facto Law shall be passed.

No Capitation, or other direct, Tax shall be laid, unless in Proportion to the Census or enumeration herein before directed to be taken.

No Tax or Duty shall be laid on Articles exported from any State.

No Preference shall be given by any Regulation of Commerce or Revenue to the Ports of one State over those of another; nor shall Vessels bound to, or from, one State, be obliged to enter, clear, or pay Duties in another.

No Money shall be drawn from the Treasury, but in Consequence of Appropriations made by Law; and a regular Statement and Account of the Receipts and Expenditures of all public Money shall be published from time to time.

No Title of Nobility shall be granted by the United States: And no Person holding any Office of Profit or Trust under them, shall, without the Consent of the Congress, accept of any present, Emolument, Office, or Title, of any kind whatever, from any King, Prince, or foreign State.

◆ Section 10

No State shall enter into any Treaty, Alliance, or Confederation; grant Letters of Marque and Reprisal; coin Money; emit Bills of Credit; make any Thing but gold and silver Coin a Tender in Payment of Debts; pass any Bill of Attainder, ex post facto Law, or Law impairing the Obligation of Contracts, or grant any Title of Nobility.

No State shall, without the Consent of the Congress, lay any Imposts or Duties on Imports or Exports, except what may be absolutely necessary for executing its inspection Laws: and the net Produce of all Duties and Imposts, laid by any State on Imports or Exports, shall be for the Use of the Treasury of the United States; and all such Laws shall be subject to the Revision and Controul of the Congress.

No State shall, without the Consent of Congress, lay any Duty of Tonnage, keep Troops, or Ships of War in time of Peace, enter into any Agreement or Compact with another State, or with a foreign Power, or engage in War, unless actually invaded, or in such imminent Danger as will not admit of delay.

Article II

◆ Section 1

The executive Power shall be vested in a President of the United States of America. He shall hold his Office during the Term of four Years, and, together with the Vice President, chosen for the same Term, be elected, as follows:

Each State shall appoint, in such Manner as the Legislature thereof may direct, a Number of Electors, equal to the whole Number of Senators and Representatives to which the State may be entitled in the Congress: but no Senator or Representative, or Person holding an Office of Trust or Profit under the United States, shall be appointed an Elector.

The Electors shall meet in their respective States, and vote by Ballot for two Persons, of whom one at least shall not be an Inhabitant of the same State with themselves. And they shall make a List of all the Persons voted for, and of the Number of Votes for each; which List they shall sign and certify, and transmit sealed to the Seat of the Government of the United States, directed to the President of the Senate. The President of the Senate shall, in the Presence of the Senate and House of Representatives, open all the Certificates, and the Votes shall then be counted. The Person having the greatest Number of Votes shall be the President, if such Number be a Majority of the whole Number of Electors appointed; and if there be more than one who have such Majority, and have an equal Number of Votes, then the House of Representatives shall immediately chuse by Ballot one of them for President; and if no Person have a Majority, then from the five highest on the List the said House shall in like Manner chuse the President. But in chusing the President, the Votes shall be taken by States, the Representation from each State having one Vote; a quorum for this purpose shall consist of a Member or Members from two thirds of the States, and a Majority of all the States shall be necessary to a Choice. In every Case, after the Choice of the President, the Person having the greatest Number of Votes of the Electors shall be the Vice President. But if there should remain two or more who have equal Votes, the Senate shall chuse from them by Ballot the Vice President.

The Congress may determine the Time of chusing the Electors, and the Day on which they shall give their Votes; which Day shall be the same throughout the United States.

No Person except a natural born Citizen, or a Citizen of the United States, at the time of the Adoption of this Constitution, shall be eligible to the Office of President; neither shall any Person be eligible to that Office who shall not have attained to the Age of thirty five Years, and been fourteen Years a Resident within the United States.

In Case of the Removal of the President from Office, or of his Death, Resignation, or Inability to discharge the Powers and Duties of the said Office, the Same shall devolve on the Vice President, and the Congress may by Law provide for the Case of Removal, Death, Resignation or Inability, both of the President and Vice President, declaring what Officer shall then act as President, and such Officer shall act accordingly, until the Disability be removed, or a President shall be elected.

The President shall, at stated Times, receive for his Services, a Compensation, which shall neither be increased nor diminished during the Period for which he shall have been elected, and he shall not receive within that Period any other Emolument from the United States, or any of them.

Before he enter on the Execution of his Office, he shall take the following Oath or Affirmation:—"I do solemnly swear (or affirm) that I will faithfully execute the Office of President of the United States, and will to the best of my Ability, preserve, protect and defend the Constitution of the United States."

◆ Section 2

The President shall be Commander in Chief of the Army and Navy of the United States, and of the Militia of the several States, when called into the actual Service of the United States; he may require the Opinion, in writing, of the principal Officer in each of the executive Departments, upon any Subject relating to the Duties of their respective Offices, and he shall have Power to grant Reprieves and Pardons for Offences against the United States, except in Cases of Impeachment....

◆ Section 4

The President, Vice President and all civil Officers of the United States, shall be removed from Office on Impeachment for, and Conviction of, Treason, Bribery, or other high Crimes and Misdemeanors.

Article III

◆ Section 1

The judicial Power of the United States shall be vested in one supreme Court, and in such inferior Courts as the Congress may from time to time ordain and establish. The Judges, both of the supreme and inferior Courts, shall hold their Offices during good Behaviour, and shall, at stated Times, receive for their Services a Compensation, which shall not be diminished during their Continuance in Office.

◆ Section 2

The judicial Power shall extend to all Cases, in Law and Equity, arising under this Constitution, the Laws of the United States, and Treaties made, or which shall be made, under their Authority;—to all Cases affecting Ambassadors, other public Min-

isters and Consuls;—to all Cases of admiralty and maritime Jurisdiction;—to Controversies to which the United States shall be a Party;—to Controversies between two or more States;— between a State and Citizens of another State;—between Citizens of different States;—between Citizens of the same State claiming Lands under Grants of different States, and between a State, or the Citizens thereof, and foreign States, Citizens or Subjects.

In all Cases affecting Ambassadors, other public Ministers and Consuls, and those in which a State shall be Party, the supreme Court shall have original Jurisdiction. In all the other Cases before mentioned, the supreme Court shall have appellate Jurisdiction, both as to Law and Fact, with such Exceptions, and under such Regulations as the Congress shall make.

The Trial of all Crimes, except in Cases of Impeachment, shall be by Jury; and such Trial shall be held in the State where the said Crimes shall have been committed; but when not committed within any State, the Trial shall be at such Place or Places as the Congress may by Law have directed.

◆ Section 3

Treason against the United States, shall consist only in levying War against them, or in adhering to their Enemies, giving them Aid and Comfort. No Person shall be convicted of Treason unless on the Testimony of two Witnesses to the same overt Act, or on Confession in open Court.

The Congress shall have Power to declare the Punishment of Treason, but no Attainder of Treason shall work Corruption of Blood, or Forfeiture except during the Life of the Person attainted.

Article IV

◆ Section 1

Full Faith and Credit shall be given in each State to the public Acts, Records, and judicial Proceedings of every other State. And the Congress may by general Laws prescribe the Manner in which such Acts, Records and Proceedings shall be proved, and the Effect thereof.

◆ Section 2

The Citizens of each State shall be entitled to all Privileges and Immunities of Citizens in the several States.

A Person charged in any State with Treason, Felony, or other Crime, who shall flee from Justice, and be found in another State, shall on Demand of the executive Authority of the State from which he fled, be delivered up, to be removed to the State having Jurisdiction of the Crime. No Person held to Service or Labour in one State, under the Laws thereof, escaping into another, shall, in Consequence of any Law or Regulation therein, be discharged from such Service or Labour, but shall be delivered up on Claim of the Party to whom such Service or Labour may be due.

◆ Section 3

New States may be admitted by the Congress into this Union; but no new State shall be formed or erected within the Jurisdiction of any other State; nor any State be formed by the Junction of two or more States, or Parts of States, without the Consent of the Legislatures of the States concerned as well as of the Congress.

The Congress shall have Power to dispose of and make all needful Rules and Regulations respecting the Territory or other Property belonging to the United States; and nothing in this Constitution shall be so construed as to Prejudice any Claims of the United States, or of any particular State.

◆ Section 4

The United States shall guarantee to every State in this Union a Republican Form of Government, and shall protect each of them against Invasion; and on Application of the Legislature, or of the Executive (when the Legislature cannot be convened), against domestic Violence.

Article V

The Congress, whenever two thirds of both Houses shall deem it necessary, shall propose Amendments to this Constitution, or, on the Application of the Legislatures of two thirds of the several States, shall call a Convention for proposing Amendments, which, in either Case, shall be valid to all Intents and Purposes, as Part of this Constitution, when ratified by the Legislatures of three fourths of the several States, or by Conventions in three fourths thereof, as the one or the other Mode of Ratification may be proposed by the Congress; Provided that no Amendment which may be made prior to the Year One thousand eight hundred and eight shall in any Manner affect the first and fourth Clauses in the Ninth Section of the first Article; and that no State, without its Consent, shall be deprived of its equal Suffrage in the Senate.

Article VI

All Debts contracted and Engagements entered into, before the Adoption of this Constitution, shall be as valid against the United States under this Constitution, as under the Confederation.

This Constitution, and the Laws of the United States which shall be made in Pursuance thereof; and all Treaties made, or which shall be made, under the Authority of the United States, shall be the supreme Law of the Land; and the Judges in every State shall be bound thereby, any Thing in the Constitution or Laws of any State to the Contrary notwithstanding.

The Senators and Representatives before mentioned, and the Members of the several State Legislatures, and all executive and judicial Officers, both of the United States and of the several States, shall be bound by Oath or Affirmation, to support this Constitution; but no religious Test shall ever be required as a Qualification to any Office or public Trust under the United States.

Article VII

The Ratification of the Conventions of nine States, shall be sufficient for the Establishment of this Constitution between the States so ratifying the Same.

The Word, "the," being interlined between the seventh and eighth Lines of the first Page, the Word "Thirty" being partly written on an Erazure in the fifteenth Line of the first Page, The Words "is tried" being interlined between the thirty second and thirty third Lines of the first Page and the Word "the" being interlined between the forty third and forty fourth Lines of the second Page.

Attest William Jackson Secretary

Done in Convention by the Unanimous Consent of the States present the Seventeenth Day of September in the Year of our Lord one thousand seven hundred and Eighty seven and of the Independence of the United States of America the Twelfth In witness whereof We have hereunto subscribed our Names,

G. Washington
Presidt. and deputy from Virginia
New Jersey
Wil: Livingston
David Brearley
Wm. Paterson
Jona: Dayton

PENNSYLVANIA
B Franklin
Thomas Mifflin
Robt. Morris
Geo. Clymer
Thos. FitzSimons
Jared Ingersoll
James Wilson
Gouv Morris

NEW HAMPSHIRE
John Langdon
Nicholas Gilman

MASSACHUSETTS
Nathaniel Gorham
Rufus King

CONNECTICUT
Wm. Saml. Johnson
Roger Sherman

NEW YORK
Alexander Hamilton

DELAWARE
Geo: Read
Gunning Bedford jun
John Dickinson
Richard Bassett
Jaco: Broom

MARYLAND
James McHenry
Dan of St Thos. Jenifer
Danl. Carroll

VIRGINIA
John Blair
James Madison Jr.

NORTH CAROLINA
Wm. Blount
Richd. Dobbs Spaight
Hu Williamson

SOUTH CAROLINA
J. Rutledge
Charles Cotesworth Pinckney
Charles Pinckney
Pierce Butler

GEORGIA
William Few
Abr Baldwin

Portrait of Benjamin Banneker (AP/Wide World Photos)

BENJAMIN BANNEKER'S LETTER TO THOMAS JEFFERSON

"We have long been considered rather as brutish than human."

Overview

Benjamin Banneker's letter to Thomas Jefferson was written August 19, 1791, to accompany a copy of the almanac that Banneker was to have published in the next year. In the eighteenth and nineteenth centuries almanacs were not simply catalogs of information providing calendars, astronomical and seasonal predictions, weather forecasts, and agricultural ideas; they also included entertaining and educating stories, commentaries, and even poetry, therefore offering much more in the way of reading material at a time when such things were scarce. And since almanacs were common to most households, a wide variety of people were likely to have read Banneker's *Almanac*.

Banneker based his almanac predictions on his own table of the position of celestial bodies, called an ephemeris. Creating an accurate ephemeris was not an easy task; it took great mathematical and astronomical skill. Thomas Jefferson, as a farmer and someone with a keen interest in astronomy, would have recognized this fact and possibly marveled that a black man had put together an almanac, since he regarded those with African ancestry to be inferior to white people. Banneker sent the almanac, along with the letter, to Jefferson, who was then the U.S. secretary of state. On August 30, 1791, Jefferson wrote a response to Banneker, thanking him for the almanac and informing him that he was sending it on to the secretary of the Academy of Sciences in Paris, Nicolas de Condorcet. Both Banneker's letter and Jefferson's response were published in pamphlet form the following year and then in the 1793 edition of Banneker's almanac.

Context

On July 4, 1776, the Declaration of Independence was signed, stating that "all men are created equal" and entitled to "certain unalienable rights." Every colony had practiced slavery, and slavery was legal in all the colonies at the time the Declaration was signed. Americans fought a war for independence from Britain, ultimately winning and giving birth to a new nation. During the Revolutionary War many slave masters persuaded their slaves to fight in the American army against the British. Some were ordered to fight, while others were swayed by promises of freedom. When the fervor of republicanism and liberty for all died down after the war, however, few of these promises were actually kept.

In the midst of a country built on the virtues of freedom, liberty, and republicanism, there was the contradiction of slavery. The territory of Vermont banned slavery when it broke from New York in 1777 and maintained this ban in its constitution when it became the fourteenth state in 1791. Pennsylvania abolished slavery from the state in 1780, Massachusetts in 1781, New Hampshire in 1783, and Rhode Island and Connecticut in 1784. But despite these states' decisions to emancipate their slaves, whether immediately or gradually, and the budding social movement toward abolition, the second government of the United States under the Constitution, adopted in 1787, protected the rights of slave owners and, in consequence, the institution of slavery in America.

The American institution of slavery was based on race. The first slaves introduced into North America, after it was found that Native Americans were not a viable option as slave labor, were brought over from the western coast of Africa. The racial nature of American slavery gave rise to many arguments in defense of the institution that also were based on race. Many of the arguments in favor of slavery stressed much-debated theories about the mental and moral inferiority, heartier physical constitutions, and greater suitability for hard labor of African natives. Thus, slavery was said to provide a way for Africans to be cared for, since they lacked the mental abilities to care for themselves, to have their moral deficiencies checked, and to have their strength yoked for the economic good of the entire country—whether or not this country technically included the African slaves.

In his *Notes on the State of Virginia*, published in 1787, Thomas Jefferson wrote against the abolition of slavery, using much the same argument about the inherent inferiority of black Africans. It was well known in America at the time that Jefferson, a slave owner from Virginia, regarded slavery as a necessary evil; he believed that the practice was indispensable to ensuring the economic health of the southern states

Time Line

1776
- **July 4**
The Declaration of Independence is signed.

1787
- **Thomas Jefferson** publishes his *Notes on the State of Virginia*.
- **September 17**
The U.S. Constitution is adopted.

1788
- **Banneker predicts an eclipse** of the sun, almost completely accurately.

1791
- **Banneker assists Major Andrew Ellicott** in surveying land for the new national capital.
- **August 19**
Banneker writes a letter to Thomas Jefferson to accompany a copy of his almanac.
- **August 30**
Thomas Jefferson writes a reply to Benjamin Banneker.

1792
- **Banneker's first almanac** is published.

1792–1797
- **Twenty-eight editions** of six almanacs by Banneker are published.

1800
- **December 1**
The seat of government is moved from Philadelphia to Washington, D.C.

1806
- **October 25**
Benjamin Banneker dies.

---

and of the nation as a whole. However, in Jefferson's opinion, the evil had more to do with the effect of slavery upon the slaveholder himself, not upon the slave. The *Notes* provided a basis for quite a few proslavery arguments that would be developed more fully in the early nineteenth century.

In a world where the ability to read and write, much less to calculate an ephemeris for an almanac, were rare for African Americans, even freedmen, Benjamin Banneker's letter to Jefferson stands out. His prose is clear, and his arguments are coherent and logical. Many white Americans would not have been able to compose a letter half so well. Abolitionists in Banneker's time, as well as in the later antebellum period, used his achievements to demonstrate that the proslavery writers—who held that African Americans did not have the mental or moral capacity to take care of themselves—were wrong. Correspondingly, Jefferson's arguments in *Notes on the State of Virginia* could also be refuted by arguments based upon Banneker's achievements.

About the Author

Benjamin Banneker was born in Baltimore, Maryland, on November 9, 1731. Banneker's maternal grandmother, Molly Welsh, was an Englishwoman who had been falsely accused and convicted of theft. As punishment, she became an indentured servant to a Maryland tobacco farmer. After she finished her service, she farmed some rented land, which enabled her to buy two slaves; she freed both later. Molly married one of these former slaves, Banneky, in defiance of Maryland law. One of their daughters, Mary, also married a freed African slave, Robert, who took the name Banneker as his own family name. Benjamin Banneker was their first child.

Mary and Robert Banneker and their children lived with Mary's mother as they worked to earn enough money for their own farm. Molly taught Benjamin to read, and for a short time he attended a small interracial Quaker school. Growing up, he showed a great capacity for mathematics and mechanics, and he read while other children played. His talent led him to construct a striking clock at the age of twenty-two, made mostly of wood and based on his own designs and computations. Despite the fact that he had seen only one pocket watch at this point in his life, the clock he made not only worked but, indeed, continued to run until it was destroyed by a fire forty years later.

Banneker's talents were nurtured further by his friendship with the Ellicott brothers. The Ellicott family was a Quaker family who owned flour mills and had furthered the technology of flour production and wheat cultivation. The family was known for stressing the importance of education and for bringing in the best teachers for the instruction of all the children in the community. Like Banneker, George Ellicott was a mathematician with a keen interest in astronomy, and he had probably encouraged Banneker's own interests. In 1788, making use of books and tools of Ellicott's, Banneker predicted an eclipse of the sun almost exactly. (He would have timed it precisely, except that one of his sources contained an error.)

In 1791, Major Andrew Ellicott (a cousin of George's and his brother Elias Ellicott) brought Banneker with him to the banks of the Potomac River to participate in an engineering project. This project was the surveying and designing of the city that would be the new federal capital. The Georgetown *Weekly Ledger* mentioned that Ellicott was "attended by Benjamin Banneker, an Ethiopian, whose abilities, as a surveyor, and an astronomer, clearly prove that Mr. Jefferson's concluding that race of men were void of mental endowments, was without foundation." After the French architect of the project, Pierre Charles L'Enfant, quit in 1792, taking his plans with him, Banneker proved his capacities yet again. Duplicating L'Enfant's plans from memory, he enabled the group to finish laying out the capital city.

In 1792, Banneker published his first almanac, the same one he had sent to Jefferson with his letter in August of the previous year. Over the next six years, he published six almanacs in twenty-eight editions. Although he associated with the Quakers and even wore Quaker clothing, he never formally joined the Society of Friends. He never married, and he lived alone, renting and selling off his land, until his death in 1806. His house caught fire and burned down (including the still-working clock) on the day he was buried.

Explanation and Analysis of the Document

In the first paragraph of the letter, Banneker states that he is aware of the "liberty which seemed to me scarcely allowable" that he takes in sending a copy of his almanac and writing this letter to Jefferson, who was then in the "distinguished and dignified station" of secretary of state. Additionally, Banneker does not deny that it is an even further liberty since he is a black man and, as such, is generally looked down upon. However, he does write this missive to Jefferson, wherein he brings up issues of great significance. Taking a deferential tone for the entire letter, Banneker nonetheless makes sure the secretary of state knows where he stands.

After his humble acknowledgment of the freedom he takes in writing this letter, Banneker begins by reminding his reader of the well-recognized state of black people in America. They have been, for an extensive period of time, exploited, condemned, degraded, and regarded as incompetent in mental endeavors, considered more animal than human.

In contrast to the attitude that most white people have toward African Americans, both slave and free, Banneker reflects that he believes Jefferson to be a man "far less inflexible" and "measurably friendly." Historians speculate that Banneker had never read Jefferson's *Notes on the State of Virginia* or he may not have tried to approach Jefferson in a letter at all. Nevertheless, Banneker certainly thought that such a man as Jefferson might be more disposed than most to helping black people in America. If, too, Jefferson were so amiable, then naturally he would match his disposition to his actions and help ease and erase, whenever the opportunity arose, the "train of absurd and false ideas and opinions, which so generally prevails with respect to us."

Furthermore, says Banneker, if Jefferson believes that a "Father"—God—created all, he would also see that all, no matter what station, situation, or color, are human and thus capable of the same feelings and with the same capacity for intelligence. Because of this, all people are part of one family with that one Father, presumably a father who would not have any of his children exploited by the others.

Later in the antebellum era, proslavery apologists began to rely heavily on the claim that Africans were descended from the son of the biblical Noah, Ham, who had been cursed. The story is from Genesis 9:18–29, where Ham sees that his father has gotten drunk and fallen asleep, naked, in his tent. He goes to tell his brothers, Japheth and Shem, who immediately walk backward into the tent, putting a robe between them to cover their father. When Noah awakens and hears what happened, he curses Ham's son, Canaan, to serve his relatives. The descendents of Canaan were said by proslavery writers to be black-skinned, and, therefore, Africans were destined to be the slaves of the earth. At the time Banneker wrote to Jefferson, this argument had not gained the position it would later have.

In the next paragraph, the fourth, Banneker points out that if Jefferson agrees that there is one universal Father of all humankind, then he would also agree that it is his Christian—and human—duty to see to it that all forms of inhumane treatment to fellow human beings are stopped. Banneker can see that white people love their liberties, their rights, the laws that give them these rights, and themselves, and if they are really sincere about the value of all these things, then they should want no less for everyone else, particularly those who have been living in oppression and degradation.

Banneker writes that he is a black man and, by the grace of God, a free one, who does not have to experience the "inhuman captivity" of his brethren. As a free man, he has the privilege of partaking of many of the same liberties and rights that Jefferson has. He hopes that Jefferson realizes that his own freedom comes from the merciful hand of God, just as Banneker's has.

In paragraph 6, Banneker reminds Jefferson of the time, still fresh in memory, since it had been so few decades ago, "in which the arms and tyranny of the British crown were exerted, with every powerful effort, in order to reduce you to a state of servitude." He asks Jefferson to remember how the colonists felt, how they thought, and how they reacted to the tyranny of British rule. Did they not feel as if they were to be slaves to the British? Did they not see every move by Parliament as one step closer to that servitude, as one more trespass upon their rights as human beings? Did they not feel their own hopelessness to do anything and despair that things would be this way forever? Despite this, Banneker asserts, the colonists persevered, and they gained their freedom, with the "blessing of Heaven."

Continuing in this same line of thinking, Banneker writes that Americans at this time felt "the injustice of a state of slavery." Because they could not tolerate the present condition or the future possibility of living in such a state, Jefferson wrote these words in the Declaration of Independence: "We hold these truths to be self-evident, that all men are created equal, that they are endowed by their Creator with certain unalienable rights, and that among these are, life, liberty, and the pursuit of happiness." The American colonists regarded themselves highly enough to make sure they would not be slaves to anyone and that "the great violation of liberty" would go no further. And yet even

"We have long been considered rather as brutish than human, and scarcely capable of mental endowments."

(Paragraph 2)

"I apprehend you will embrace every opportunity, to eradicate that train of absurd and false ideas and opinions, which so generally prevails with respect to us."

(Paragraph 3)

"Sir, I have long been convinced, that if your love for yourselves, and for those inestimable laws, which preserved to you the rights of human nature, was founded on sincerity, you could not but be solicitous, that every individual, of whatever rank or distinction, might with you equally enjoy the blessings thereof."

(Paragraph 4)

"This, Sir, was a time [the Revolutionary War] when you clearly saw into the injustice of a state of slavery, and ... the horrors of its condition.... Your abhorrence thereof was so excited, that you publicly held forth this true and invaluable doctrine ... 'We hold these truths to be self-evident, that all men are created equal.'"

(Paragraph 7)

"Neither shall I presume to prescribe methods by which [my brethren] may be relieved, otherwise than by recommending to you and all others, to wean yourselves from those narrow prejudices which you have imbibed with respect to them, and ... 'put your soul in their souls' stead.'"

(Paragraph 8)

though there was a war fought over these words, over these ideas, these same colonies held enormous numbers of Africans in brutal and merciless bondage, using any means necessary to keep these men and women restrained. Banneker states that there is a contradiction demonstrated by people who rally around the statement "all men are created equal" but also publicly and vehemently deny an entire category of

people those same unalienable rights. Abraham Lincoln, a politician from Illinois, would also point out this inconsistency in many of his speeches of the mid-1800s.

Not presuming to tell Jefferson, who supposedly already knew well, the "situation of my brethren" or to propose specific solutions to the problem of slavery, in paragraph 8 Banneker simply says that he thinks that a person should, as the biblical Job urged his friends (Job 8), "put your soul in their souls' stead" and "wean yourselves from those narrow prejudices which you have imbibed with respect to them." One might think that Banneker here makes an indirect barb at Jefferson's notions (well-known even beyond his *Notes*) that black people were inferior to whites, particularly with regard to intellect. If, however, Jefferson and other whites could do as Job wisely told his friends to do, then perhaps they would feel some compassion toward those who were held in harsh servitude merely by reason of their skin color. And once they felt that compassion, no one would have to tell them how to act or how to progress regarding the question of slavery.

In closing the paragraph, Banneker explains that he had not intended to go into everything he had written about but that his caring for his fellow African Americans under bonds led him to do so at length. He hopes that Jefferson would forgive the digression and still accept the gift of an almanac, which had been the original reason for writing.

In telling Jefferson something about the almanac, Banneker observes that he is at an "advanced stage of life" and that he had "long had unbounded desires to become acquainted with the secrets of nature." This indicates that he had been doing this type of study for a long time, and, even if he had never published any of his findings before now, he had not come to the calculations without some knowledge and experience. He takes a collegial tone here, as he shares with Jefferson that he had had many "difficulties and disadvantages" in taking up astronomical studies on his own, "which I need not recount to you." Jefferson, as an amateur astronomer himself, would well know the complexities associated with the study and would recognize, too, the work that Banneker would have had to put in as a man who had had little formal schooling.

In the last full paragraph, he continues by commenting to Jefferson that the almanac had almost had to wait, since he had been spending so much time assisting Mr. Andrew Ellicott "at the Federal Territory." This is Banneker's allusion to his work on the plans of the capital city, which Jefferson would have realized, since he had recommended Banneker for the project. However, says Banneker, he had already told several printers in the area about his proposed almanac, so when he arrived home from the banks of the Potomac, he got to work on his calculations straight away.

Here, then, is the product, Banneker tells Jefferson, which he hopes will be accepted in the spirit it was intended. He has sent a manuscript, so that Jefferson not only could have an advance copy but also could see it in Banneker's own hand. This appears to be a subtle acknowledgment that Jefferson might not take the almanac for Banneker's own work unless he sees it written in the author's own hand. As it happens, years later Jefferson wrote a letter to his friend Joel Barlow saying that he did not think that Banneker had come up with his ephemeris by himself, that someone had helped him substantially in his calculations. He also refers to Banneker's letter, telling Barlow that he believed that it "shows him to have had a mind of very common stature indeed." Even so, Jefferson's letter in answer

to Banneker's does not appear to indicate this seemingly cynical view.

Banneker closes by acknowledging "the most profound respect" toward Jefferson. The respect Banneker speaks of rings throughout the letter, in the sincerity with which he writes, even as he criticizes the American custom of slaveholding and the contradiction it presents. The last part of the closing, "Your most obedient humble servant," by no means should be taken as a statement of subservience. One of the points of Banneker's letter was to dispel the assumption, to which Jefferson also seemed to subscribe, that African Americans were inferior to white Americans, and he suggests clearly that African Americans should not be subservient based on such a misconception. The phrase "your most obedient humble servant" was simply a common closing in formal letters at the time, and, in fact, Jefferson closes his own letter to Banneker using the same phrase.

Audience

Benjamin Banneker sent his letter to Thomas Jefferson, the widely acknowledged primary writer of the Declaration of Independence, who was also a slaveholder. Jefferson's ideas on the inferiority of African Americans had been published, even though he seemed to be, as Banneker writes, "measurably friendly and well disposed" toward them. In fact, however, *Notes on the State of Virginia* discloses that Jefferson's views on the questions of slavery and race tended to be conflicting.

Although Jefferson was the first and main audience for the letter, a much wider audience was included when a printer in Philadelphia, Daniel Lawrence, published the exchange between Banneker and Jefferson in a pamphlet within six months. In 1792 the periodical *Universal Asylum and Columbian Magazine* also printed the letters. Banneker included the correspondence in the 1793 edition of the almanac.

Impact

Thomas Jefferson answered Benjamin Banneker's letter within a few days, writing his reply on August 30, 1791. In this rather brief letter, Jefferson courteously thanks Banneker for his almanac and letter, adding,

No body wishes more than I do, to see such proofs as you exhibit, that nature has given to our black brethren talents equal to those of the other colors of men; and that the appearance of the want of them, is owing merely to the degraded condition of their existence, both in Africa and America.

He also writes that he would like to see their situation bettered, as far as it could be. The almanac, Jefferson tells Banneker, he has sent to Monsieur de Condorcet, secretary of the Academy of Sciences at Paris, "because I considered it as a document, to which your whole color had a right for their justification, against the doubts which have been entertained of them." Jefferson does not comment further on either the almanac or the significant concerns in Banneker's letter.

Both letters were subsequently published, in 1792 as a pamphlet and in the popular periodical the *Universal Asylum and Columbian Magazine*, and also included in Banneker's 1793 almanac. The pamphlets sold out in 1792 and were reprinted by Daniel Lawrence. Banneker's almanacs, which were produced by Goddard Angell and John Hayes in Baltimore and Joseph Crukshank in Philadelphia, were outselling the almanacs of established mathematicians like Major Andrew Ellicott. Another Philadelphia publisher, William Young, soon procured permission to print an edition of his own. The almanac and letters supplied many subjects of debate in many arenas, and the Pennsylvania Society for the Promotion of the Abolition of Slavery used the almanacs and pamphlets effectively as propaganda in its cause.

The letters also were used in another way. Jefferson's critics were quick to point out the contradictions between his ideas on the African American as expressed in *Notes on the State of Virginia* and as he expressed them in his reply to Banneker. Many opponents of Jefferson's, both for and against slavery, used his letter to Banneker as ammunition against him in the 1800 presidential election. Those for slavery thought he had gone too far in elevating the mental abilities of the African American, and those against slavery thought he had not gone far enough. Either way, because of his own letter and his own claims to genius in mathematics and astronomy, during this time Benjamin Banneker became a symbol of all those of color could be if they were not shackled by the oppressions of slavery.

See also Thomas Jefferson's *Notes on the State of Virginia* (1784); Slavery Clauses in the U.S. Constitution (1787).

Further Reading

■ Books

Bedini, Silvio A. *The Life of Benjamin Banneker*. New York: Charles Scribner's Sons, 1972.

Finkelman, Paul. *Defending Slavery: Proslavery Thought in the Old South*. Boston: Bedford/St. Martin's, 2003.

Zinn, Howard, and Arnold Arnove, eds. *Voices of a People's History of the United States*. New York: Seven Stories Press, 2004.

■ Web Sites

"Africans in America/Part 2/Benjamin Banneker." PBS Online Web site.
    http://www.pbs.org/wgbh/aia/part2/2p84.html.

"Today in History: November 9." Library of Congress "American Memory" Web site.
    http://memory.loc.gov/ammem/today/nov09.html.

—Angela M. Alexander

Questions for Further Study

1. Why would Banneker's almanac have been considered such an extraordinary achievement at the time?

2. Make the argument that Banneker was familiar with Jefferson's views as expressed in *Notes on the State of Virginia* and that he deliberately sent his almanac to Jefferson with the intention of countering those views. Do you think such an argument would be plausible? Why or why not?

3. Much has been made, both at the time and in the twenty-first century, of the fact that Thomas Jefferson, the principal writer of the Declaration of Independence, was also a slave owner. Do you believe that this fact undermines Jefferson's place in American history? Do you believe that, if he were alive today, Jefferson would accept the obvious view that slavery is wrong?

4. Compare and contrast Banneker's thinking about slavery with that expressed in the Petition of Prince Hall and Other African Americans to the Massachusetts General Court.

5. Members of the Quaker religion were at the forefront of the early abolitionist movement. To what extent did Quakerism play a role in Banneker's intellectual achievements?

BENJAMIN BANNEKER'S LETTER TO THOMAS JEFFERSON

Maryland, Baltimore County, August 19, 1791.

Sir,

I am fully sensible of the greatness of that freedom, which I take with you on the present occasion; a liberty which seemed to me scarcely allowable, when I reflected on that distinguished and dignified station in which you stand, and the almost general prejudice and prepossession, which is so prevalent in the world against those of my complexion.

I suppose it is a truth too well attested to you, to need a proof here, that we are a race of beings, who have long labored under the abuse and censure of the world; that we have long been looked upon with an eye of contempt; and that we have long been considered rather as brutish than human, and scarcely capable of mental endowments.

Sir, I hope I may safely admit, in consequence of that report which hath reached me, that you are a man far less inflexible in sentiments of this nature, than many others; that you are measurably friendly, and well disposed towards us; and that you are willing and ready to lend your aid and assistance to our relief, from those many distresses, and numerous calamities, to which we are reduced. Now Sir, if this is founded in truth, I apprehend you will embrace every opportunity, to eradicate that train of absurd and false ideas and opinions, which so generally prevails with respect to us; and that your sentiments are concurrent with mine, which are, that one universal Father hath given being to us all; and that he hath not only made us all of one flesh, but that he hath also, without partiality, afforded us all the same sensations and endowed us all with the same faculties; and that however variable we may be in our religion, however diversified in situation or color, we are all of the same family, and stand in the same relation to him.

Sir, if these are sentiments of which you are fully persuaded, I hope you cannot but acknowledge, that it is the indispensible duty of those, who maintain for themselves the rights of human nature, and who possess the obligations of Christianity, to extend their power and influence to the relief of every part of the human race, from whatever burden or oppression they may unjustly labor under; and this, I apprehend, a full conviction of the truth and obligation of these principles should lead all to. Sir, I have long been convinced, that if your love for yourselves, and for those inestimable laws, which preserved to you the rights of human nature, was founded on sincerity, you could not but be solicitous, that every individual, of whatever rank or distinction, might with you equally enjoy the blessings thereof; neither could you rest satisfied short of the most active effusion of your exertions, in order to their promotion from any state of degradation, to which the unjustifiable cruelty and barbarism of men may have reduced them.

Sir, I freely and cheerfully acknowledge, that I am of the African race, and in that color which is natural to them of the deepest dye; and it is under a sense of the most profound gratitude to the Supreme Ruler of the Universe, that I now confess to you, that I am not under that state of tyrannical thraldom, and inhuman captivity, to which too many of my brethren are doomed, but that I have abundantly tasted of the fruition of those blessings, which proceed from that free and unequalled liberty with which you are favored; and which, I hope, you will willingly allow you have mercifully received, from the immediate hand of that Being, from whom proceedeth every good and perfect Gift.

Sir, suffer me to recall to your mind that time, in which the arms and tyranny of the British crown were exerted, with every powerful effort, in order to reduce you to a state of servitude: look back, I entreat you, on the variety of dangers to which you were exposed; reflect on that time, in which every human aid appeared unavailable, and in which even hope and fortitude wore the aspect of inability to the conflict, and you cannot but be led to a serious and grateful sense of your miraculous and providential preservation; you cannot but acknowledge, that the present freedom and tranquility which you enjoy you have mercifully received, and that it is the peculiar blessing of Heaven.

This, Sir, was a time when you clearly saw into the injustice of a state of slavery, and in which you had just apprehensions of the horrors of its condition. It was now that your abhorrence thereof was so excited, that you publicly held forth this true and invaluable doctrine, which is worthy to be recorded and remembered in all succeeding ages: "We hold these truths to be self-evident, that all men are created equal; that they are endowed by their Creator with certain un-alienable rights, and that among these are, life, liberty, and the pursuit of happiness." Here was a time, in which your tender feelings for yourselves had engaged you thus to declare, you were then impressed with proper ideas of the great violation of liberty, and the free possession of those blessings, to which you were entitled by nature; but, Sir, how pitiable is it to reflect, that although you were so fully convinced of the benevolence of the Father of Mankind, and of his equal and impartial distribution of these rights and privileges, which he hath conferred upon them, that you should at the same time counteract his mercies, in detaining by fraud and violence so numerous a part of my brethren, under groaning captivity and cruel oppression, that you should at the same time be found guilty of that most criminal act, which you professedly detested in others, with respect to yourselves.

I suppose that your knowledge of the situation of my brethren is too extensive to need a recital here; neither shall I presume to prescribe methods by which they may be relieved, otherwise than by recommending to you and all others, to wean yourselves from those narrow prejudices which you have imbibed with respect to them, and as Job proposed to his friends, "put your soul in their souls' stead"; thus shall your hearts be enlarged with kindness and benevolence towards them; and thus shall you need neither the direction of myself or others, in what manner to proceed herein. And now, Sir, although my sympathy and affection for my brethren hath caused my enlargement thus far, I ardently hope, that your candor and generosity will plead with you

in my behalf, when I make known to you, that it was not originally my design; but having taken up my pen in order to direct to you, as a present, a copy of an Almanac, which I have calculated for the succeeding year, I was unexpectedly and unavoidably led thereto.

This calculation is the production of my arduous study, in this my advanced stage of life; for having long had unbounded desires to become acquainted with the secrets of nature, I have had to gratify my curiosity herein, through my own assiduous application to Astronomical Study, in which I need not recount to you the many difficulties and disadvantages, which I have had to encounter.

And although I had almost declined to make my calculation for the ensuing year, in consequence of that time which I had allotted therefor, being taken up at the Federal Territory, by the request of Mr. Andrew Ellicott, yet finding myself under several engagements to Printers of this state, to whom I had communicated my design, on my return to my place of residence, I industriously applied myself thereto, which I hope I have accomplished with correctness and accuracy; a copy of which I have taken the liberty to direct to you, and which I humbly request you will favorably receive; and although you may have the opportunity of perusing it after its publication, yet I choose to send it to you in manuscript previous thereto, that thereby you might not only have an earlier inspection, but that you might also view it in my own hand writing.

And now, Sir, I shall conclude, and subscribe myself, with the most profound respect,

Your most obedient humble servant,

Benjamin Banneker.

Roger Sherman of Connecticut, who served on the Senate committee that drafted the Fugitive Slave Act (Library of Congress)

FUGITIVE SLAVE ACT OF 1793

"Any person who ... shall harbor or conceal [a fugitive slave shall] forfeit and pay the sum of five hundred dollars."

Overview

In 1793, Congress passed "An Act respecting fugitives from justice, and persons escaping from the service of their masters." Although only half of the act dealt with fugitive slaves, the statute became known as the Fugitive Slave Act of 1793. It would remain on the books until it was substantially amended in 1850 and eventually repealed in 1864.

The Fugitive Slave Act was one of the most tangible manifestations of the U.S. Constitution's protection of slavery. It gave slaveholders legal authority to seize fugitives who had crossed state lines. The law was vague in spelling out rendition procedure, however, and this created the potential problem that kidnappers would seize free blacks, claiming them as fugitives and then selling them into slavery. States responded by passing "personal liberty laws" that protected the liberty of free blacks. While these laws often worked in tandem with the Fugitive Slave Act, they nonetheless created conflicts, especially as the abolition movement quickened in the 1830s. Eventually, these conflicts came before the U.S. Supreme Court in the 1842 case of *Prigg v. Pennsylvania*, where the Court upheld the constitutionality of the Fugitive Slave Act and struck down the states' personal liberty laws that interfered with slaveholders' rights.

Context

Slavery was unknown to the English common law, and so British colonists in North America generally borrowed from other sources to regulate slavery. At its heart, the relationship of master to slave was one of absolute dominion. Masters could do virtually what they wished with their slaves, subject to the regulations passed by colonial legislatures. Some customs were borrowed from the English law concerning master and servant, notably the common-law right of "recaption." If servants ran away, masters had the right to track them down, seize them, and return them to service. This right was embodied in the hierarchical relationship of the common law of persons and extended to husband and wife as well as to father and child.

Because the common-law right of recaption was universally recognized, it was not uncommon for masters or their agents to pursue fugitive servants and slaves into other colonies, recapture them, and return them to service. The gradual disappearance in the eighteenth century of white indentured servitude meant that the majority of fugitives would be slaves, although some white indentured servants did remain. In 1775, for instance, George Washington offered a reward for two British-born white servants who had fled their contractual obligations. But by the Revolutionary era, it was mainly black slaves who ran. In most instances, masters relied upon this common law of recaption to seize and forcibly return slaves to their plantations.

Recaption, however, had its limits. The beginnings of an international abolition movement in the eighteenth century challenged slavery on moral, ethical, and legal grounds. One such challenge involved James Somerset (also spelled "Somersett"), a free-born African who was kidnapped, reduced to slavery, and sold to Charles Stewart (also spelled "Steurt"), a Scot who made his fortune in the North American colonies. In 1769, Stewart set sail for the British Isles and brought Somerset with him. When they arrived in London, Somerset escaped. Stewart's agents arrested him, chained him, and put him aboard a ship destined for the West Indies. Abolitionists caught wind of the case and petitioned the King's Bench for a writ of habeas corpus. Habeas corpus was, by 1772, the standard remedy for testing wrongful detention. It required the jailer (in this case, the captain of the vessel where Somerset languished in chains) to specify by what authority he detained the prisoner. In Somerset's case (*R. v. Knowles, ex parte Somersett*), Charles Stewart argued that Somerset was a slave by the laws of Virginia, and as such the right of recaption allowed him to seize Somerset, detain him, and forcibly remove him from England.

William Murray, 1st Earl of Mansfield, who was chief justice of the King's Bench, disagreed. He released Somerset, declaring that slavery was "so odious, that nothing can be suffered to support it, but positive law." By "positive law," Lord Mansfield meant a legislative enactment specifically endorsing slavery. Virginia's colonial legislature might allow slavery, Lord Mansfield was saying, but those laws extended only so far as Virginia's borders. The law had no

1780

- **March 1**
Pennsylvania passes its Act for the Gradual Abolition of Slavery.

1783

- The slave John Davis gains free status under Pennsylvania's 1780 Act for the Gradual Abolition of Slavery, though his Virginia master continues to hold him in bondage.

1788

- John Davis escapes from Virginia.

- **May**
John Davis is kidnapped and taken to Virginia.

- **September 17**
The Constitution, including the fugitive slave clause in Article IV, Section 2, is transmitted from the Constitutional Convention to the Continental Congress.

1791

- **June 20**
Governor Beverly Randolph of Virginia refuses the extradition request of Governor Thomas Mifflin of Pennsylvania for the three men charged with kidnapping John Davis.

- **October 27**
President George Washington communicates the extradition request of Pennsylvania Governor Thomas Mifflin to the U.S. Congress.

1793

- **February 12**
President George Washington signs the Fugitive Slave Act of 1793.

1826

- **March 25**
Pennsylvania passes a personal liberty law protecting free blacks from kidnapping and providing procedures for fugitive slave rendition.

1842

- The U.S. Supreme Court upholds the Fugitive Slave Act of 1793 in *Prigg v. Pennsylvania*.

effect in England, and as such Somerset was not being held by any law. Accordingly, he had to be released. The common-law right of recaption, in other words, did not exist in the case of slavery, unless specifically allowed by statute.

The principle of Somerset's Case (as it came to be known) reverberated across the Atlantic. It was an age of liberty, and colonists from Georgia to Massachusetts were busy debating the precise nature of political freedom and self-government—a debate that, as they well understood in 1772, might lead to war. But slavery was entrenched in the colonies at this time, which created an obvious disjunction between reality and political rhetoric. Nonetheless, nascent abolitionism took hold in several northern colonies. In 1780, Pennsylvania became the first colony to pass a statute for gradual abolition, promising to end all slavery within several generations. Other states, including Virginia, also considered plans for gradual abolition.

The prospect of abolition in northern colonies, when combined with the principle of Somerset's Case, suddenly made the future of slavery in the United States seem precarious. Southern delegates to the Constitutional Convention of 1787—especially the state delegations from South Carolina and Georgia—were well aware of this danger and worked hard to make sure that their slave property was protected under the Constitution. Practically, the convention had to deal with three specific problems. The first was the question of whether slaves would be counted for the purpose of representation. The second was whether Congress would have the authority to regulate the international slave trade. The third was the problem of fugitive slaves. Of the three, the first two were the more serious and threatened more than once to stalemate the convention. Ultimately, the delegates settled with the three-fifths compromise, which counted three slaves for every five for the purposes of both taxation and representation. They also agreed that Congress could ban the slave trade, but not for twenty years.

There was comparatively little controversy over the question of fugitive slaves. When in August 1787, as the delegates were winding up their business, South Carolina delegates Pierce Butler and Charles C. Pinckney proposed adding a clause that required fugitives to be delivered up like criminals, the only protest it drew from northern delegates was that it would be costly because it would obligate state officers to spend time and resources locating, capturing, and extraditing fugitive slaves. Butler and Pinckney withdrew their motion and resubmitted one the next day that would become, with one small modification, the exact wording of Article IV, Section 2:

> No Person held to Service or Labour in one State, under the Laws thereof, escaping into another, shall, in Consequence of any Law or Regulation therein, be discharged from such Service or Labour, but shall be delivered up on Claim of the Party to whom such Service or Labour may be due.

The fact that the fugitive slave clause encountered no opposition at the Constitutional Convention indicates how deeply embedded was respect for property rights, even by abolitionists. Pennsylvania's 1780 Act for the Gradual Abolition of Slavery had a fugitive slave clause as well, thus guaranteeing slaveholders from other states that their fugitive slaves would not become free by Pennsylvania's laws. Likewise, the Northwest Ordinance (1787), which prohibited slavery in the Northwest Territory (today's upper Midwest) also contained a fugitive slave exception. The language of the Ordinance clause itself clearly embraced the fundamental principle of Somerset's Case: that slavery could be sustained only by explicit command. Yet the fugitive slave clause explicitly prohibited the states from freeing fugitive slaves, instead commanding that they "be delivered up." What was unclear was whether Congress or the states had the constitutional power to legislate with regard to fugitive slaves and precisely what the limits of that power were.

The Fugitive Slave Act was passed by the Second U.S. Congress in direct response to a situation that arose in western Pennsylvania. Confusion over the location of the Pennsylvania-Virginia border had led to the establishment of a joint commission between the two states to permanently fix its location. Consequently, some Virginians suddenly found that they were living in Pennsylvania. This had important consequences for slaves and slaveholders, because Pennsylvania's gradual abolition act specified that any and all slaves had to be registered and accounted for. Most slaveholders did register their slaves with the state, but a few did not. One slave, John Davis, was not properly registered and became legally free in 1783. His purported owner nonetheless rented him out to a Virginia planter. Davis escaped in 1788 and fled to Pennsylvania, but three Virginians pursued him, captured him, and forcibly removed him to Virginia.

This kidnapping of John Davis touched off a storm of legal activity. A Pennsylvania grand jury indicted the three Virginians for kidnapping. Pennsylvania Governor Thomas Mifflin officially requested the extradition of the men, but Virginia Governor Beverly Randolph declined to extradite him, on advice from his attorney general. The governor of Pennsylvania collected the official correspondence from the affair and sent it to President George Washington, asking him to submit it to Congress for resolution. Washington did so on October 27, 1791.

The issue at hand was not fugitive slaves but instead the extradition of fugitives from justice (namely, the three Virginian kidnappers). Perhaps because Article IV, Section 2, of the Constitution addresses these subjects together, the two subjects were joined when the House of Representatives appointed a committee to draft a law dealing with both fugitives from justice and fugitive slaves. Although the committee's work did not result in adoption of a law, the House of Representatives had established the precedent that the subjects of fugitives from justice and fugitive slaves would be joined.

The Senate first appointed a committee in March 1792 to consider the dual problem of fugitives from labor and fugitives from justice. Chaired by George Cabot of Massachusetts, the three-man committee had two northern senators (from Massachusetts and Connecticut) and one southerner

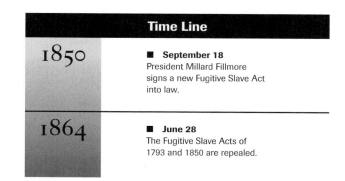

Time Line

1850

■ September 18
President Millard Fillmore signs a new Fugitive Slave Act into law.

1864

■ June 28
The Fugitive Slave Acts of 1793 and 1850 are repealed.

(from South Carolina). This committee, too, never reported a bill and was in essence dissolved when the Senate adjourned. At its next session, the Senate appointed a new committee to address the issue. George Cabot was named chair again, but now George Read of Delaware and Samuel Johnston of North Carolina—both from slave states—rounded out the committee. On December 20, Johnston reported out a bill that caused a heated debate in the Senate, likely because the bill encroached on state sovereignty by requiring state officers to execute federal law and spelled out substantial penalties for those who did not assist in capturing fugitives from justice. The Senate returned the bill to the committee and added to its membership Roger Sherman of Connecticut and John Taylor of Virginia.

Throughout the bill-drafting process, southerners proved ready to vote as a bloc when the issue was the protection of slave property. This did not mean that any measure supporting slavery would be passed—as Samuel Johnston's failed bill indicates—but it did mean that slaveholders could command much better terms than northern abolitionists, who had little presence in these early congresses. The newly reconstituted committee—still dominated by senators from slave states—produced a brand-new bill, which was reported back to the Senate floor on January 3, 1793. The bill was debated and amended considerably and was finally passed and sent to the House of Representatives on January 17. After a minor revision to the section dealing with fugitives from justice, the House passed the bill, and it was signed into law on February 12, 1793, by President Washington.

About the Author

Congressional bills rarely have a single author. They are usually drafted by committee and then amended numerous times on the legislative floor before being adopted. Such was the case with the Fugitive Slave Act of 1793. The five senators who served on the committee that drafted the bill that was ultimately passed were George Cabot (1752–1823), Massachusetts; George Read (1733–1798), Delaware; Samuel Johnston (1733–1816), North Carolina; Roger Sherman (1721–1793), Connecticut; and John Taylor (1753–1824), Virginia. At this early stage in congressional history, members were not identified by party affiliation.

William Murray, 1st Earl of Mansfield (Library of Congress)

Explanation and Analysis of the Document

The Fugitive Slave Act of 1793 engaged some of the most important issues in antebellum America, including proper constitutional interpretation and the relationship of the states to the federal government. Crucial to understanding the Fugitive Slave Act are its sources of law, which included not just the fugitive slave clause of the Constitution but also the law of master and slave and natural law theories of justice. In addition, the application of the Fugitive Slave Act changed during the six decades of its operation, in part because the circumstances under which it operated evolved considerably during that time.

Congress struggled with constitutional ambiguity when it considered the subject of fugitives from justice or labor, and it took several drafts before the final version of the Fugitive Slave Act of 1793 was enacted. Sections 1 and 2 of the statute dealt with the rendition of fugitives from justice. Article IV, Section 2, of the Constitution commanded that those charged with "Treason, Felony, or other Crime" who fled from one state to another "shall on Demand of the executive Authority of the State from which he fled, be

delivered up, to be removed to the State having Jurisdiction of the Crime." Section 1 required that the executive authority's demand for a fugitive be accompanied by a copy of an indictment or an affidavit sworn before a magistrate charging the fugitive with having committed treason, felony, or another crime. Once this legal requirement was met, it became the "the duty of the executive authority of the state or territory to which such person shall have fled, to cause him or her to be arrested." States were required to hold fugitives for at least six months before agents arrived to collect them, and expenses were to be borne by the state making the demand for the fugitive. Section 2 of the act gave state agents the right to transport fugitives across state lines back to the state or territory from which they had fled. This section also made forcible rescue of such fugitives a federal crime, punishable by a fine of up to $500 and one year in prison.

Sections 3 and 4 of the statute dealt with the rendition of fugitive slaves. The process differed significantly from the rendition of fugitives from justice. Section 3 authorized slaveholders or their agents to seize fugitive slaves without an arrest warrant and take them before any federal judge residing in the state or any state magistrate. The section further empowered state and federal judges to issue warrants for removal across state lines "upon proof to the satisfaction of such judge or magistrate, either by oral testimony or affidavit" that the man, woman, or child seized was in fact a fugitive slave. Section 4 gave relief to slaveholders who faced difficulties in retrieving their fugitive slaves. Any person "knowingly and willingly" obstructing or hindering a slaveholder from arresting a fugitive, or rescuing a fugitive in a slaveholder's custody, or harboring or concealing a fugitive slave after notice was given of the fugitive's status was liable to the slaveholder in an action of debt for $500.

This act, on the whole, represented a conservative interpretation of Article IV, Section 2, by Congress. Although the law spelled out the duties of state officers, it preserved the role of the states in rendering fugitives. The differences between the treatment of fugitives from justice and fugitive slaves, however, is instructive. In the case of fugitives from justice, rendition was public, conducted by the executive authority of the state. The governor was expected to deploy law enforcement officers, make an arrest, and hold a fugitive in the state's jails. There was to be no judicial hearing, nor did the statute provide any federal relief if a state governor refused to extradite a fugitive. This proved problematic, and somewhat ironic, when Governor Salmon P. Chase of Ohio refused in 1859 to extradite a free black man named Willis Lago to Kentucky to face an indictment for the crime of "helping a slave escape." The U.S. Supreme Court heard the case in *Kentucky v. Dennison* (1861) and ruled that the federal government lacked the constitutional authority to compel states to render fugitives from justice.

In contrast, the rendition of fugitive slaves was a private affair. Arresting the fugitive was up to the slaveholder, as was the transport of the slave back to the slaveholder's state. The state bore no responsibility for these processes. Likewise, the rescue of a fugitive from justice was treated as a crime, whereas the rescue of a fugitive slave would be remedied in civil court. The extension of federal jurisdiction to fugitive slave cases also meant that the slaveholders' private property right in a slave was, in essence, constitutionalized. Nonetheless, there were limits to this constitutional right. Given that the Fugitive Slave Act did not specify what constituted proof of fugitive status for either federal or state judges, state legislatures could and did define it. The Fugitive Slave Act did, however, specify that a judge alone could issue a certificate of removal without the aid of a jury. This was in potential conflict with the Fifth Amendment's requirement that no person be deprived of liberty without due process of law and the Sixth Amendment's promise of a jury trial in all criminal cases. Abolitionists would later raise this complaint in numerous cases, but they were continually rebuffed by state and federal judges.

Audience

The Fugitive Slave Act of 1793 would have been read by judges, state legislators, governors, and other public officers who were charged with enforcing the law. The law's passage would have immediately been broadcast, as the newspapers of the time regularly reported on the laws passed by Congress. Very few laypeople would have read the actual law, at least until the 1830s, when parts of its text became famous because of the multitude of court cases arising from it and the public discussion that followed.

Impact

The results of the Fugitive Slave Act of 1793 emerged over time. At first, the law's impact was minimal, although it did provide an example of how the early Congress understood federalism (that is, the relation of the national government to state governments). The law had not been passed to stem a tide of fugitive slaves and did not appear to have any immediate impact either on the number of slaves who fled or the number returned to slaveholding states.

Closely related to the fugitive slave problem was kidnapping—the act of seizing a free black and selling him or her into slavery. In April 1796, the House of Representatives asked its Committee of Commerce and Manufactures to consider the problem of kidnapping. After debate, the committee declined to report an antikidnapping bill. Another house committee appointed in 1799 concluded that the Fugitive Slave Act might be contributing to the problem of kidnapping. Because the statute authorized slaveholders to seize their slaves without a warrant, unscrupulous kidnappers could easily seize and carry off free blacks simply by claiming them as fugitive slaves. Despite evidence of these practices, Congress declined to act in the 1790s, leaving the problem and its resolution to the individual states.

Kidnapping became a more serious problem after 1800. The expanding Atlantic market created a cotton and sugar boom in the trans-Appalachian South. Planters moved westward to take advantage of the huge profits in these cash

crops and, in the process, created a huge demand for labor. Congress closed the international slave trade in 1808, leaving western planters without a ready supply of slave labor to fill plantations in the southern interior. The result was the creation of an internal slave trade. All told, more than one million slaves were carried across the Appalachians between 1810 and 1861, destined for plantations as far west as Texas and as far north as Missouri. This high demand created a ready market for unscrupulous kidnappers.

In response to this situation, states passed antikidnapping laws, commonly called "personal liberty laws." Some states, such as Pennsylvania, Massachusetts, and Virginia, already had antikidnapping laws on the books. Ohio passed an antikidnapping law in 1804, Vermont in 1806, and New York in 1808. By 1830, all free states (excepting New Hampshire and Rhode Island) had personal liberty laws. Slave states did as well. Virginia and Delaware had such laws as early as 1787. Mississippi passed an antikidnapping statute in 1820 and Georgia passed one in 1835. These laws were not mere window dressing. Delaware, a slave state, actively prosecuted kidnappers under its laws.

Personal liberty laws often specified procedures for fugitive slave rendition as well, giving magistrates guidelines as to what evidence would constitute proof of a fugitive's status. Many of these laws, such as Ohio's 1804 law, were favorable to slaveholders. Pennsylvania, where abolitionists became increasingly influential, passed stricter laws. In 1820 the state withdrew the use of its resources to aid in fugitive slave rendition and fixed a twenty-year prison sentence for kidnapping a free black. This made fugitive slave recaption difficult. Slaveholders could not rely on the skeletal federal court system to obtain legal cover for seizing fugitives and now faced almost certain indictment under Pennsylvania law if they failed to gain legal cover. After an official complaint from the Maryland legislature, Pennsylvania revised its law in 1826. The new personal liberty law outlawed private recaption by requiring slaveholders to obtain a warrant for the arrest of an alleged fugitive. After capture, an alleged fugitive had an opportunity to prove his or her freedom before a judge before a certificate of removal would be issued.

Although this law followed the basic dictates of the Fugitive Slave Act in that it prescribed a summary procedure for fugitive slave rendition and made the states' courts and peace officers available to slaveholders, it deviated significantly from the federal law by prohibiting private recaption. Nonetheless, the law was the product of cooperation on the part of Maryland and Pennsylvania and was meant to fulfill the state's requirements under the fugitive slave clause of the Constitution and to protect free blacks' liberty. New York and New Jersey passed similar laws in the 1820s.

Many abolitionists were not content with protecting free blacks from kidnapping, but wanted to strike a more general blow at slavery. One way to do so was to protect fugitives, whom abolitionists regarded as refugees from a morally reprehensible and illegal slave regime. Abolitionists had extended legal help to fugitives since the late eighteenth century but stepped up efforts in the 1810s.

"When a person held to labour in any of the United States, or in either of the territories on the northwest or south of the river Ohio, under the laws thereof, shall escape into any other of the said states or territory, the person to whom such labour or service may be due, his agent or attorney, is hereby empowered to seize or arrest such fugitive from labour."

(Section 3)

"Upon proof to the satisfaction of such judge or magistrate, either by oral testimony or affidavit ... that the person so seized or arrested, doth ... owe service or labour to the person claiming him or her, it shall be the duty of such judge or magistrate to give a certificate thereof to such claimant, ... which shall be sufficient warrant for removing the said fugitive from labour, to the state or territory from which he or she fled."

(Section 3)

"Any person who shall knowingly and willingly obstruct or hinder such claimant ... in so seizing or arresting such fugitive from labour, or shall rescue such fugitive from such claimant ... or shall harbor or conceal such person after notice that he or she was a fugitive from labor, as aforesaid, shall, for either of the said offences, forfeit and pay the sum of five hundred dollars."

(Section 4)

One abolitionist courtroom tactic was to argue that the Fugitive Slave Act of 1793 was unconstitutional on three grounds. First, abolitionists complained that the institution of a summary procedure violated the Sixth Amendment's guarantee of a jury trial in all cases where liberty was at stake. Second, they argued that the determination of someone's status was a matter of plenary state authority. Because the Tenth Amendment reserved all powers not expressly enumerated in the Constitution to the states, the determination of who was a fugitive belonged to the individual states. Third, abolitionists argued that Congress had no constitutional warrant to legislate with regard to fugitive slaves at all. Continuing with the argument that sovereignty was reserved to the states, it followed that the only powers held by the federal government were "express powers" (that is, those expressly enumerated in the Constitution), they argued that the fugitive slave clause lacked "enabling"

language and therefore did not empower Congress to act. Against those who said that the power to act should be implied, abolitionists pointed to specific enabling clauses in all the other sections of Article IV. Following the judicial rule of statutory construction that *expressio unius, exclusio alterius*—"the express mention of one thing excludes all others"—abolitionists concluded that the lack of an enabling clause in Article IV, Section 2, must have been intentional. In short, abolitionist lawyers made a strong states' rights argument against Congress's ability to enforce the fugitive slave clause.

These arguments did not fare well in the courtroom. Judges proved uniformly reluctant to declare the Fugitive Slave Act of 1793 unconstitutional and consistently refused to extend Sixth Amendment jury trials to alleged fugitives on the principle that slaves were not a party to the Constitution and thus were offered no protections under the Bill of Rights. Nonetheless, courts did extend some protection to alleged fugitive slaves. The Pennsylvania Supreme Court ruled in *Wright v. Deacon* (1819) that a state habeas corpus proceeding was allowed under the Fugitive Slave Act of 1793. The Massachusetts Supreme Court reached a similar decision in *Commonwealth v. Griffith* (1823). These decisions, it should be noted, both resulted in the return of fugitive slaves to slavery. Nonetheless, they reaffirmed the power of the states to protect their free black residents.

When the Fugitive Slave Act and personal liberty laws conflicted, courts often ruled in favor of federal law. Such was the case with *In re Susan* (1818), when the federal district court in Indiana ruled that the Fugitive Slave Act took precedence over the state's personal liberty law. The New York Supreme Court ruled similarly in *Jack v. Martin* (1834), hinting for the first time that personal liberty laws themselves might be unconstitutional. Although the case was upheld in the New York Court for the Correction of Errors in 1835, that court refused to suggest that personal liberty laws were unconstitutional. Not every court ruled that federal law had to take precedence. Chief Justice Joseph Hornblower of the New Jersey Superior Court ruled in 1836 that a writ of habeas corpus could interrupt a federal hearing for a certificate of removal.

The Supreme Court addressed the Fugitive Slave Act of 1793 in the landmark case of *Prigg v. Pennsylvania* (1842). The case stemmed from the capture of Margaret Morgan and her two children. Margaret was the child of slaves who had been freed after the War of 1812. She married a free man and moved from Maryland to Pennsylvania. In 1837 the widow of Margaret's former owner sent an agent, Edward Prigg, to reclaim Margaret as a fugitive slave. When Prigg could not find a Pennsylvania magistrate to issue him a certificate of removal, he took Margaret Morgan and her children to Maryland anyway and was indicted by a Pennsylvania grand jury for kidnapping under Pennsylvania's 1826 personal liberty law. Given that one of Morgan's children had been born in Pennsylvania and was thus free by Pennsylvania law, the state had a compelling kidnapping case. Maryland's governor refused to extradite Prigg, but after commissioners from the two states communicated, the Pennsylvania legislature created a pro forma case that went to the U.S. Supreme Court with the consent of all parties.

The Supreme Court's decision in *Prigg v. Pennsylvania* upheld the Fugitive Slave Act of 1793 as a constitutional exercise of congressional power. Additionally, the Court held that personal liberty laws that interfered with fugitive slave extradition were unconstitutional. This opinion benefited slaveholders immensely, freeing them from the threat of legal action and cumbersome legal procedures imposed by the states. But it also left slaveholders exposed. The Supreme Court had held that no constitutional authority could compel the states to enforce the fugitive slave clause of the Constitution. Subsequently, Pennsylvania, Massachusetts, and Rhode Island passed laws forbidding state officers to assist in fugitive slave rendition. In Iowa, Indiana, and Michigan, abolitionists continued to fight the Fugitive Slave Act utilizing state laws and were successful more than once. Although the ruling in *Prigg v. Pennsylvania* was upheld again by the Supreme Court in *Jones v. Van Zandt* (1847), the law was virtually useless at this point in returning escaped slaves to chains. By 1850 southern states complained that nearly a thousand slaves per year were escaping north to freedom.

On September 18, 1850, President Millard Fillmore signed a new Fugitive Slave Act into law that, in essence, replaced the first. The new law created an exclusive federal jurisdiction for fugitive slave rendition and forbade the states from interfering in any way with the process. It proved to be one of the most controversial laws passed by

Questions for Further Study

1. Compare the 1793 Fugitive Slave Act with the Fugitive Slave Act of 1850. What circumstances changed that made the later law supposedly necessary?

2. How was the Fugitive Slave Act an outgrowth of the U.S. Constitution's tolerance of slavery? What circumstances led to the passage of this act?

3. What impact did international events relative to slavery have on the passage of the Fugitive Slave Act?

4. What actions did some states, particularly in the North, take to circumvent the Fugitive Slave Act? How effective were those actions?

5. Compare this document with the 1842 Supreme Court case *Prigg v. Pennsylvania*. On what basis did the Court uphold the constitutionality of the Fugitive Slave Act?

the antebellum Congress and was repealed in 1864 by a Congress shorn of representatives from the slaveholding states, which had seceded before the Civil War.

See also Pennsylvania: An Act for the Gradual Abolition of Slavery (1780); *Prigg v. Pennsylvania* (1842); Fugitive Slave Act of 1850.

Further Reading

■ Books

Cover, Robert M. *Justice Accused: Antislavery and the Judicial Process*. New Haven, Conn.: Yale University Press, 1975.

Fehrenbacher, Don Edward. *The Slaveholding Republic: An Account of the United States Government's Relations to Slavery*. New York: Oxford University Press, 2001.

Finkelman, Paul. *Slavery and the Founders: Race and Liberty in the Age of Jefferson*. 2nd ed. Armonk, N.Y.: M. E. Sharpe, 2001.

Morris, Thomas D. *Free Men All: The Personal Liberty Laws of the North, 1780–1861*. Baltimore, Md.: Johns Hopkins University Press, 1974.

■ Web Sites

"A Century of Lawmaking for a New Nation: U.S. Congressional Documents and Debates, 1774–1875." Library of Congress "American Memory" Web site.
    http://memory.loc.gov/ammem/amlaw/lawhome.html.

"Samuel J. May Anti-Slavery Collection." Cornell University Library, Division of Rare and Manuscript Collections.
    http://dlxs.library.cornell.edu/m/mayantislavery/collection.html.

"Slaves and the Courts, 1740–1860." Library of Congress "American Memory" Web site.
    http://memory.loc.gov/ammem/sthtml/sthome.html.

—H. Robert Baker

FUGITIVE SLAVE ACT OF 1793

Chap. VII. &—*An Act respecting fugitives from justice, and persons escaping from the service of their masters. (a)*

SECTION 1. *Be it enacted by the Senate and House of Representatives of the United States of America in Congress assembled*, That whenever the executive authority of any state in the Union, or of either of the territories northwest or south of the river Ohio, shall demand any person as a fugitive from justice, of the executive authority of any such state or territory to which such person shall have fled, and shall moreover produce the copy of an indictment found, or an affidavit made before a magistrate of any state or territory as aforesaid, charging the person so demanded, with having committed treason, felony or other crime, certified as authentic by the governor or chief magistrate of the state or territory from whence the person so charged fled, it shall be the duty of the executive authority of the state or territory to which such person shall have fled, to cause him or her to be arrested and secured, and notice of the arrest to be given to the executive authority making such demand, or to the agent of such authority appointed to receive the fugitive, and to cause the fugitive to be delivered to such agent when he shall appear: But if no such agent shall appear within six months from the time of the arrest, the prisoner may be discharged. And all costs or expenses incurred in the apprehending, securing, and transmitting such fugitive to the state or territory making such demand, shall be paid by such state or territory.

SEC. 2. *And be it further enacted*, That any agent, appointed as aforesaid, who shall receive the fugitive into his custody, shall be empowered to transport him or her to the state or territory from which he or she shall have fled. And if any person or persons shall by force set at liberty, or rescue the fugitive from such agent while transporting, as aforesaid, the person or persons so offending shall, on conviction, be fined not exceeding five hundred dollars, and be imprisoned not exceeding one year.

SEC. 3. *And be it also enacted*, That when a person held to labour in any of the United States, or in either of the territories on the northwest or south of the river Ohio, under the laws thereof, shall escape into any other of the said states or territory, the person to whom such labour or service may be due, his agent or attorney, is hereby empowered to seize or arrest such fugitive from labour, *(b)* and to take him or her before any judge of the circuit or district courts of the United States, residing or being within the state, or before any magistrate of a county, city or town corporate, wherein such seizure or arrest shall be made, and upon proof to the satisfaction of such judge or magistrate, either by oral testimony or affidavit taken before and certified by a magistrate of any such state or territory, that the person so seized or arrested, doth, under the laws of the state or territory from which he or she fled, owe service or labour to the person claiming him or her, it shall be the duty of such judge or magistrate to give a certificate thereof to such claimant, his agent or attorney, which shall be sufficient warrant for removing the said fugitive from labour, to the state or territory from which he or she fled.

SEC. 4. *And be it further enacted*, That any person who shall knowingly and willingly obstruct or hinder such claimant, his agent or attorney in so seizing or arresting such fugitive from labour, or shall rescue such fugitive from such claimant, his agent or attorney when so arrested pursuant to the authority herein given or declared; or shall harbor or conceal such person after notice that he or she was a fugitive from labour, as aforesaid, shall, for either of the said offences, forfeit and pay the sum of five hundred dollars. Which penalty may be recovered by and for the benefit of such claimant, by action of debt, in any court proper to try the same; saving moreover to the person claiming such labour or service, his right of action for or on account of the said injuries or either of them.

Glossary

doth	does

RICHARD ALLEN: "AN ADDRESS TO THOSE WHO KEEP SLAVES, AND APPROVE THE PRACTICE"

1794

"Clear your hands from slaves, burthen not your children or your country with them."

Overview

The first abolitionist essay authored by the celebrated black activist and minister Richard Allen, "An Address to Those Who Keep Slaves, and Approve the Practice," was among the most important black abolitionist proclamations of the late eighteenth century. Originally published in 1794 as part of a longer document titled *A Narrative of the Proceedings of the Black People, during the Late Awful Calamity in Philadelphia, in the Year 1793*, which he coauthored with his fellow black churchman Absalom Jones, Allen's antislavery address challenged Americans to end both slavery and racial injustice. With his hometown of Philadelphia serving as the nation's temporary governing capital between 1790 and 1800, he believed that he had a unique opportunity to mold antislavery policy and compel American leaders to create a biracial republic that would shine in the eyes of both God and man.

Context

During the late eighteenth century, American abolitionism underwent a profound transformation. Up through the American Revolution, most racial reformers had limited success getting abolitionist laws passed in any slaveholding polity. In North America, the Society of Friends, commonly known as the Quakers, had produced a long tradition of antislavery testimony, including celebrated abolitionist treatises by such writers as Ralph Sandiford, Benjamin Lay, John Woolman, and Anthony Benezet. But Pennsylvania Quakers themselves did not adopt abolitionist rules until the mid-1700s. Moreover, even Quaker strictures against slaveholding, which were in full force by the 1770s, ruled only the Society of Friends.

The American Revolution's intense focus on human rights put new pressure on the institution of slavery. Between the 1770s and 1790s, a wave of secular antislavery writers picked up the dissident strains of Quaker abolitionism, creating the first sustained public attack on bondage. Enslaved people intensified antislavery discussions among both slaveholders and politicians by running away from their masters during the War of Independence. Tens of thousands of American slaves escaped between 1775, when Britain's John Murray, 4th Earl of Dunmore—known as Lord Dunmore—issued a proclamation offering freedom to runaway slaves loyal to the Crown, and 1783, when hostilities ceased. While many enslaved people departed with the British, others attained their liberty through service in Patriot forces. Nevertheless, slavery survived the American Revolution, with perhaps half a million bondmen then spread throughout the Union.

Revolutionary ideology, combined with the rise of evangelical Christianity, which envisioned widespread human brotherhood, prompted many statesmen to consider passing abolitionist laws. On March 1, 1780, Pennsylvania adopted An Act for the Gradual Abolition of Slavery, the nation's first such law, which would liberate any slave born after 1780 at the age of twenty-eight. With approximately seven thousand enslaved people in the state, Pennsylvania offered a model for ending bondage via state policy. Connecticut and Rhode Island soon passed similar laws. Below the Mason-Dixon Line, though, where the majority of enslaved people resided, many slaveholders feared such government-sanctioned liberation laws. But responding to black restiveness and white planters' expressions of guilt, southern states eased emancipation restrictions, which had formally required preapproval for private manumissions. Virginia's 1782 law allowing masters to manumit bondmen without legislative sanction prompted perhaps as many as six thousand manumissions over the next twenty-five years.

In addition to these antislavery trends at the political and social levels, abolitionism acquired a new institutional status during the late eighteenth century. The Pennsylvania Abolition Society, established in 1775 and then reorganized in 1784 as the Pennsylvania Society for Promoting the Abolition of Slavery and for the Relief of Free Negroes Unlawfully Held in Bondage, was the world's first abolition group. Similar groups were formed in New York City and Providence, Rhode Island, as well as in parts of both Maryland and Virginia. Adhering to a gradual abolitionist mind-set that recognized slaveholders' property rights, these early antislavery groups hoped to pressure state lawmakers to pass laws that would slowly curtail bondage and shut down both domestic and international slave trades. Early abolitionists also rendered legal aid to kidnapped free blacks and, on occasion, fugitive slaves.

Although the abolitionist future seemed bright, the movement stalled by the 1790s—a fact that Richard Allen recognized. Although the first federal census in 1790 counted over sixty thousand free people of color, it also found that there were seven hundred thousand enslaved people in the United States. In addition, many politicians avoided the slavery issue, which they deemed too sensitive a topic in the new Union. At the Constitutional Convention in 1787, for example, Benjamin Franklin declined to present an abolitionist memorial against the continuance of the slave trade, fearing that this would divide northern and southern delegates. At the state level, New York, with roughly twenty thousand slaves, failed to pass a gradual abolition law until 1799, though reform politicians had attempted to adopt one much earlier. Meanwhile, abolitionists in Virginia faced hostile slaveholders, who were allowed to join southern gradual abolition societies and thereby often militated against broad attacks on slavery. Finally, in the Deep South states of South Carolina and Georgia, slaveholding itself became identified with economic progress and white cultural uplift. In short, abolitionism in the 1790s was not a widely popular movement.

Further evidence of this fact came in 1793, when Congress passed the nation's first Fugitive Slave Act. Abolitionist complaints about the law paled next to slaveholders' belief that property rights in man had been sanctioned by the Constitution. Ironically, the impetus for the fugitive slave law may have come from Allen's own state of Pennsylvania, which served as an antislavery borderland. The Quaker State's gradual abolition law prompted enslaved people from Delaware, Maryland, and Virginia to head for the Pennsylvania line. Congressional slaveholders became especially concerned when traveling to Philadelphia while it was serving as the nation's capital. Although they had six months to comply with the gradual abolition statute, out-of-state masters still had to worry about runaways who might find refuge among the city's vibrant free black community, which numbered over two thousand by 1790, or gain legal support from the Pennsylvania Abolition Society. Pierce Butler, a South Carolina congressman, sued the Pennsylvania abolitionist Isaac Hopper for allegedly helping a slave escape.

International events also made abolitionism a divisive topic in American statecraft. In 1791 a massive slave rebellion in the prosperous French colony of Saint Domingue (later renamed Haiti) began; by 1794 rebel slaves had compelled the French government to issue an emancipation decree banning bondage throughout the French Empire. Before that law took effect that year, many French slaveholders fled the Caribbean, often bringing their slaves to American shores. In Philadelphia, escaping French masters arrived at the city's doorstep with hundreds of slaves in tow. Although Pennsylvania would not grant them immunity from gradual abolition, many francophone masters sought refuge in the state anyway. As a result, perhaps as many as nine hundred former slaves came to call the City of Brotherly Love home, telling tales of black revolution in the Caribbean. Some of these black émigrés attended Allen's Bethel Church.

Philadelphia's yellow fever epidemic of 1793 made race relations a hot topic in Allen's hometown. From August through November, perhaps as many as four to five thousand people died, including roughly four hundred people of color. So many white citizens fled the infected city that some officials worried about the future of the federal government there. African Americans, led by Allen, Absalom Jones, and many others, supported civic reform initiatives, in addition to serving as nurses, pallbearers, and gravediggers, which they were hired to do. Like Allen (who almost died from yellow fever), African Americans risked their lives to prove their fitness for equal citizenship. Yet some white citizens complained that African Americans were attempting to transcend their formerly servile status by asking for equal wages for rescue work. The celebrated white printer Mathew Carey turned such complaints into a broad stereotype about alleged black crime and insolence in his bestselling pamphlet history of the epidemic, *A Short Account of the Malignant Fever, Lately Prevalent in Philadelphia*, published at the close of 1793.

Carey's history infuriated Allen, who with Jones published a reply not long after. Their document, *A Narrative of the Proceedings of the Black People, during the Late Awful Calamity in Philadelphia, in the Year 1793: And a Refutation of Some Censures, Thrown upon Them in Some Late Publications*, attempted to set the record straight by describing blacks' heroism in the stricken city. After they published the work in January 1794, Allen took a copy to the federal clerk's office for the state of Pennsylvania and secured what became the first copyright for African American authors in the United States.

Believing that he would soon have the public spotlight, as returning congressmen would learn of black benevolence during the recent crisis, Allen inserted his antislavery address into the yellow fever narrative. He believed that through the skillful use of his pen, he could foment national racial reform. As he put it, the Lord has "from time to time raised up instruments" to spread righteousness throughout the world; as a black leader intent on eradicating slavery from federal politics and society, Allen viewed himself as just such an instrument.

About the Author

Richard Allen was born a slave on February 14, 1760, probably in Philadelphia. His first master, the jurist Benjamin Chew, owned property and slaves in both Pennsylvania and Delaware. He sold Allen's family to Stokely Sturgis, outside Dover, Delaware, in the late 1760s. After Sturgis sold Allen's mother in the late 1770s, the young enslaved man sought comfort in evangelical religion, converting to Methodism in his teens. In 1780 he struck a freedom agreement with Sturgis, which he paid off early, allowing him

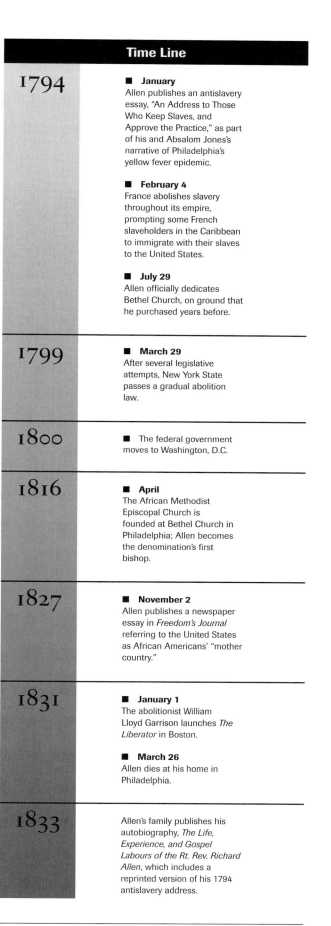

Time Line

1794

■ **January**
Allen publishes an antislavery essay, "An Address to Those Who Keep Slaves, and Approve the Practice," as part of his and Absalom Jones's narrative of Philadelphia's yellow fever epidemic.

■ **February 4**
France abolishes slavery throughout its empire, prompting some French slaveholders in the Caribbean to immigrate with their slaves to the United States.

■ **July 29**
Allen officially dedicates Bethel Church, on ground that he purchased years before.

1799

■ **March 29**
After several legislative attempts, New York State passes a gradual abolition law.

1800

■ The federal government moves to Washington, D.C.

1816

■ **April**
The African Methodist Episcopal Church is founded at Bethel Church in Philadelphia; Allen becomes the denomination's first bishop.

1827

■ **November 2**
Allen publishes a newspaper essay in *Freedom's Journal* referring to the United States as African Americans' "mother country."

1831

■ **January 1**
The abolitionist William Lloyd Garrison launches *The Liberator* in Boston.

■ **March 26**
Allen dies at his home in Philadelphia.

1833

Allen's family publishes his autobiography, *The Life, Experience, and Gospel Labours of the Rt. Rev. Richard Allen*, which includes a reprinted version of his 1794 antislavery address.

Portraits of Richard Allen and other A.M.E. bishops, surrounded by scenes including Wilberforce University, Payne Institute, missionaries in Haiti, and the A.M.E. church book depository in Philadelphia (Library of Congress)

to then gain fame on the mid-Atlantic revival circuit. He moved to Philadelphia in 1786 to preach at Saint George's Methodist Church, where he planned to bolster African American membership. Allen helped form the Free African Society, one of the first African American benevolent groups in the early Republic. Disputes with white preachers at Saint George's led to a famous walkout by black members, including Allen. By June 1794 he had officially formed Bethel Church, on ground that he had purchased years before. Bethel grew to well over a thousand members by the early nineteenth century, setting the stage for another breakaway: In 1816, after a Pennsylvania Supreme Court ruling declared that white Methodists did not own Allen's church, he and black Methodists from several mid-Atlantic states formed the African Methodist Episcopal denomination, with Allen's church renamed Mother Bethel African Methodist Episcopal Church. Allen became the denomination's first bishop and the only African American to ascend to such a position in the United States before the 1820s.

Allen was one of the leading black abolitionists in the early Republic. He published three antislavery essays during the 1790s, signed several abolitionist petitions to the federal government, and aided both kidnapped free blacks and fugitive slaves. Although he was fiercely in favor of black rights within the United States, Allen entered a period of profound doubt about the future of American race relations between 1815 and 1830. During these years he supported African, Haitian, and Canadian emigration movements, believing that people of color needed a safety-valve option to escape the withering racism of the urban North. Allen himself never left America, however, and in 1827 he wrote a famous essay in *Freedom's Journal* claiming the United States as African Americans' "mother country." In September 1830, he hosted the first convention of free black activists at Mother Bethel Church in Philadelphia. His autobiography, published in 1833 by his son, explains Allen's spiritual and political journey in American culture and was celebrated as the first memoir of the black founding generation.

"We believe if you would try the experiment of taking a few black children, and cultivate their minds with the same care, and let them have the same prospect in view as to living in the world, as you would wish for your own children, you would find upon the trial, they were not inferior in mental endowments."

(Paragraph 1)

"It is in our posterity enjoying the same privileges with your own, that you ought to look for better things."

(Paragraph 2)

"If you love your children, if you love your country, if you love the God of love, clear your hands from slaves, burthen not your children or your country with them."

(Paragraph 5)

Allen was married twice, the first time to a former enslaved woman named Flora (who died in 1801) and the second time to a former enslaved woman from Virginia named Sarah Bass. With his second wife, he had six children. Allen owned several rental properties and country property outside Philadelphia, making him one of the wealthiest black Philadelphians of the early Republic. When he died on March 26, 1831, Allen was hailed by African Americans throughout the country as a seminal black abolitionist. None other than the former slave Frederick Douglass considered Allen a heroic precursor to the more famous generation of black and white abolitionists to which he belonged.

Explanation and Analysis of the Document

Richard Allen's antislavery address remains striking for its brevity and focus on a few main ideas. Unlike many antebellum African American reformers (most notably Douglass, whose elaborate speech "What to the Slave Is the Fourth of July?" (delivered on July 5, 1852) arguably remains the epitome of nineteenth-century black political commentary), Allen did not train himself in the art of extended rhetorical analysis. As a preacher, he wanted to craft an essay that was direct and calculated to appeal to learned statesmen as well as average Americans. The cogency of his argument notwithstanding (the entire tract being less than a thousand words), Allen's antislavery address had broad relevance in early national reform circles.

◆ The Bible and the Declaration of Independence

Allen was convinced that both the Bible and the Declaration of Independence were antislavery documents. Indeed, his 1794 address offers several allusions to biblical antislavery. The story of Exodus, he believed, foretold the divine retribution that would accompany unrepentant slaveholding. For just as Egyptian masters faced eternal damnation, so too would recalcitrant American slaveholders invite harsh retribution by a just God. As Allen states, "I do not wish to make you angry, but excite attention to consider how hateful slavery is, in the sight of that God who hath destroyed kings and princes, for their oppression of the poor slaves." By comparing black bondage to the plight of ancient Israelites, Allen attempts to show that an almighty being would intervene in human affairs. Remember, he argues, "that God himself was the first pleader of the cause of slaves." Allen also focuses on the New Testament book of the Acts of the Apostles, which declares that God "hath made of one blood all nations of men for to dwell on all the face of the earth." Like other early black leaders, Allen believed that this proclamation sanctioned universal equality.

On the secular front, Allen criticizes American slaveholders who refused to concede the contradiction of slavery in a republic devoted to freedom. He observes, "Men must be wilfully blind, and extremely partial, that cannot see the contrary effects of liberty and slavery upon the mind of man." For a country born of revolutionary liberty, Allen concludes, slavery's maintenance is nothing short of hypocritical.

◆ **The Problem of Slave Vengeance**

Allen also critiques the psychology of American slaveholders. In particular, he tries to diminish masters' fears of slave vengeance. Many slaveholders, he realized, refused to consider abolitionism because they worried about black retribution. Thomas Jefferson had once asked (in *Notes on the State of Virginia*), "Why not retain and incorporate the blacks into the state?" Part of the answer was "deep-rooted prejudices entertained by the whites," but cited as equally dangerous were the "10,000 recollections by the blacks of the injuries they have sustained" in bondage. One issue framing Jefferson's fears was massive slave runaways from Virginia to British lines during the late 1770s. For the rest of his life, the Virginian conjured these (and other) images of black unrest when thinking about African American freedom. Allen refutes these fears by pointing out that enslaved people would be grateful for liberation. In addition, the increasing number of enslaved Christians in the United States would realize that they were forbidden to retaliate by the same Bible that condemned slaveholding as a sin. Referring again to Egypt's enslaved Israelites, Allen comments, "That God who knows the hearts of all men, and the propensity of a slave to hate his oppressor, hath strictly forbidden it to his chosen people"; Allen cites this admonition from Deuteronomy 23:7.

As for secular solutions, Allen asks slaveholders to treat enslaved people not as enemies to be controlled but as family members to be educated. He explains,

> We believe if you would try the experiment of taking a few black children, and cultivate their minds with the same care, and let them have the same prospect in view as to living in the world, as you would wish for your own children, you would find upon the trial, they were not inferior in mental endowments.

Put another way, Allen suggests that if slaveholders altered the conditions in which people of color lived, then African Americans would thrive as citizens of the United States. Here, then, Allen offers one of the first and most significant examples of the concept of nurture over nature in American racial sociology.

◆ **Thomas Jefferson**

In his address, Allen also takes on Jefferson himself, the slaveholding Revolutionary who hated slavery in theory but feared abolitionism even more. Allen declares, "If you love your children, if you love your country, if you love the God of love, clear your hands from slaves, burthen not your children or your country with them." This reference alludes to Jefferson's *Notes on the State of Virginia*, a survey of Virginia's political, social, and geographical makeup originally prepared for a foreign diplomat in the 1780s. Jefferson comments under Query XVIII, "I tremble for my country when I reflect that God is just." In that section he pensively observes, "The whole commerce between master and slave is a perpetual exercise of the most boisterous passions, the most unremitting despotism on the one part, and degrading submissions on the other. Our children see this, and learn to imitate it." Despite these worries, Jefferson would not support any government-backed abolition program throughout the 1790s.

The Virginia founder (who lived briefly in Philadelphia before the yellow fever epidemic of 1793) exemplified the slaveholder's dilemma: Although he recognized that slavery was wrong, he feared that universal emancipation might undermine American democracy by allowing former slaves with little education to claim equal citizenship. In subsequent years, Jefferson embraced the colonization of freed blacks as the only safe route to a liberated—and lily-white—America. The historian William Freehling calls this notion "conditional termination": slavery would go only when emancipated blacks themselves could be removed. Allen refused to let such logic go unchallenged, declaring abolition-without-colonization safe in southern as well as northern states.

Allen read Jefferson's views in *Benjamin Banneker's Pennsylvania, Delaware, Maryland and Virginia Almanack and Ephemeris*, produced by the free black Baltimorean Banneker. In 1792 Banneker printed Jefferson's thoughts on slavery, and that edition of the almanac was also reprinted in Philadelphia. Allen thus saw that Jefferson feared the wrath of the just God to whom he and other American Revolutionaries once appealed for freedom from the British. In 1794, Allen tried to use Jefferson's hatred of slavery in the abstract as an argument for national emancipation.

◆ **Legitimizing Emancipation and Black Protest**

In confronting Jeffersonian doubts about slave emancipation, Allen also attacks the intellectual foundations of bondage, especially those that saw African Americans as brute machines unprepared for liberty. He deconstructs such beliefs by arguing that slaveholders perpetuated black ignorance and therefore generated their own fears about abolitionism. "Will you," Allen wonders, "plead our incapacity for freedom, and our contented condition under oppression, as a sufficient cause for keeping us under the grievous yoke"? When blacks "plead with our masters" for liberty, it is "deemed insolence." Yet when blacks did not rebel en masse, whites believed they were "contented" simpletons. The matter need not be so complicated, Allen concludes. African Americans now offered ample evidence of their desire for freedom, providing sacred and secular justifications for emancipation. Slaveholders should stop delaying and get on with the business of emancipating their Christian brethren.

◆ **Black Abolitionism**

Allen's antislavery address exemplifies a hallmark of black abolitionism: the belief that racial equality must accompany emancipation. Envisioning the antislavery cause as patriotic and pious, Allen tries to show it to be compatible with American religious and political doctrine. Far from ruining the American Republic, abolitionism would save it by aligning black and white interests in freedom. He states, "It is in our posterity enjoying the same privileges with your own, that you ought to look for better things." White abolitionists, in fact, did not always agree that equality must follow emancipation. The well-respected Pennsylvania Abolition Society believed that former slaves needed the equivalent of a probationary period in freedom, including white guidance and oversight, before gaining access to full political rights. Moreover, the group did not admit black members until the 1840s.

Black abolitionism also diverged stylistically from the elite legal and political maneuvering that often characterized white abolitionism. Whereas members of the Pennsylvania Abolition Society had access to courts of law and political salons, black abolitionists like Allen had to craft printed appeals in the public realm. Like proto–civil rights pamphlets written by Prince Hall, James Forten, Daniel Coker, and others, Allen's antislavery address was polemical rather than autobiographical. Yet while ostensibly different from the slave narratives that dominated antebellum letters, black abolitionists' pamphlets of protest prefigured them by seeking to raise Americans' consciousness about the grievous wrongs of racial oppression. As would Douglass before the Civil War, Allen uses words that would alarm any Christian or patriotic citizen: Slavery was "oppression" and "dominion" of the worst sort, slaves longed for "freedom," and "the God of love" commanded American masters to abolish bondage and institute equality.

Audience

While he hoped to persuade as many Americans as possible to become abolitionists through his antislavery essay, Allen was particularly interested in reaching the nation's governing elite. To do this, he couched his address in statesmanlike language calculated to illustrate African Americans' reasoning ability. Though he directly challenged American masters, the black preacher also moderated his anger against whites in an attempt to prove that blacks were rational and intelligent beings. His opening sets the tone of the piece: "The judicious part of mankind will think it unreasonable that a superior good conduct is looked for from our race, by those who stigmatize us as men, whose baseness is incurable, and may therefore be held in a state of servitude, that a merciful man would not doom a beast to." Yet, he continues, "a black man, although reduced to the most abject state human nature is capable of, short of real madness, can think, reflect and feel injuries." By utilizing the polished discourse of Enlightenment-era statesmen, Allen showed that he and other blacks could produce an acceptable form of intellectual resistance. Indeed, in an age of heroic rhetoric, he hoped his carefully chosen words would reshape the oppressive world around him.

Impact

Despite its artful argumentation, Allen's antislavery address did not lead to federal abolitionist legislation in the 1790s. Although he likewise attempted to stir American consciences in subsequent antislavery addresses—most notably in his eulogy of George Washington of December 1799—Allen watched as slavery expanded during his lifetime. By 1830, the enslaved population had grown to roughly 1.5 million and remained an important part of the American economy.

When an aging Allen began dictating his autobiography, he instructed his son to include his antislavery address in the hope of reinvigorating abolitionism. Allen saw much promise in the vanguard of new antislavery leaders now on the scene, including the radical abolitionist printer William Lloyd Garrison, who launched *The Liberator* in Boston in 1831. But Allen also sought to ensure that racial equality remained a key part of present abolitionists' agenda. Allen's antislavery appeal of 1794 shows that black abolitionism dated to the founding era, demonstrating African Americans' coequal status within the radical antislavery struggle.

See also John Woolman's *Some Considerations on the Keeping of Negroes* (1754); Lord Dunmore's Proclamation (1775); Pennsylvania: An Act for the Gradual Abolition of Slavery (1780); Thomas Jefferson's *Notes on the State of Virginia* (1784); Slavery Clauses in the U.S. Constitution (1787); Fugitive Slave Act of 1793; William Lloyd Garrison's First *Liberator* Editorial (1831); Frederick Douglass's "What to the Slave Is the Fourth of July?" (1852).

Further Reading

■ Books

Egerton, Douglas. *Death or Liberty: African Americans and Revolutionary America*. New York: Oxford University Press, 2008.

Freehling, William W. *The Road to Disunion*. Vol. 1: *Secessionists at Bay, 1776–1854*. New York: Oxford University Press, 1990.

Gellman, David. *Emancipating New York: The Politics of Slavery and Freedom, 1777–1827*. Baton Rouge: Louisiana State University Press, 2006.

Nash, Gary B. *Forging Freedom: The Formation of Philadelphia's African American Community, 1720–1840*. Cambridge, Mass.: Harvard University Press, 1991.

Newman, Richard. *Freedom's Prophet: Bishop Richard Allen, the AME Church, and the Black Founding Fathers*. New York: New York University Press, 2008.

———, et al., eds. *Pamphlets of Protest: An Anthology of Early African-American Protest Literature, 1790–1860*. New York: Routledge, 2001.

Wolf, Eva Sheppard. *Race and Liberty in the New Nation: Emancipation in Virginia from the Revolution to Nat Turner's Rebellion.* Baton Rouge: Louisiana State University Press, 2006.

■ **Web Sites**

"Jefferson, Thomas, 1743–1826. Notes on the State of Virginia / From the Writings of Thomas Jefferson: Volume 2." Electronic Text Center, University of Virginia Library Web site.
http://etext.lib.virginia.edu/toc/modeng/public/JefBv021.html.

"Richard Allen, 1760–1831: The Life, Experience, and Gospel Labours of the Rt. Rev. Richard Allen." University Library, University of North Carolina at Chapel Hill "Documenting the American South" Web site.
http://docsouth.unc.edu/neh/allen/menu.html.

—Richard Newman

Questions for Further Study

1. Compare this document with John Woolman's *Some Considerations on the Keeping of Negroes* (1754). What similar arguments do the two documents make?

2. Compare this document with a later antislavery tract, such as Peter Williams, Jr.'s "Oration on the Abolition of the Slave Trade" (1808), David Walker's *Appeal to the Coloured Citizens of the World* (1829), or William Lloyd Garrison's First *Liberator* Editorial (1831). Do you see any changes taking place in the nature of the arguments used to oppose slavery that are brought about by changed historical circumstances? Explain.

3. What developments created momentum behind the abolitionist movement in the late eighteenth century? What developments slowed that momentum?

4. What role did international events have on the abolition movement at this time?

5. Compare this document with Thomas Jefferson's *Notes on the State of Virginia* written ten years earlier. In what specific ways did Allen respond to Jefferson?

RICHARD ALLEN: "AN ADDRESS TO THOSE WHO KEEP SLAVES, AND APPROVE THE PRACTICE"

The judicious part of mankind will think it unreasonable that a superior good conduct is looked for from our race, by those who stigmatize us as men, whose baseness is incurable, and may therefore be held in a state of servitude, that a merciful man would not doom a beast to; yet you try what you can, to prevent our rising from a state of barbarism you represent us to be in, but we can tell you from a degree of experience, that a black man, although reduced to the most abject state human nature is capable of, short of real madness, can think, reflect, and feel injuries, although it may not be with the same degree of keen resentment and revenge, that you who have been, and are our great oppressors would manifest, if reduced to the pitiable condition of a slave. We believe if you would try the experiment of taking a few black children, and cultivate their minds with the same care, and let them have the same prospect in view as to living in the world, as you would wish for your own children, you would find upon the trial, they were not inferior in mental endowments.

I do not wish to make you angry, but excite your attention to consider how hateful slavery is, in the sight of that God who hath destroyed kings and princes, for their oppression of the poor slaves. Pharaoh and his princes with the posterity of king Saul, were destroyed by the protector and avenger of slaves. Would you not suppose the Israelites to be utterly unfit for freedom, and that it was impossible for them, to obtain to any degree of excellence? Their history shews how slavery had debased their spirits. Men must be wilfully blind, and extremely partial, that cannot see the contrary effects of liberty and slavery upon the mind of man; I truly confess the vile habits often acquired in a state of servitude, are not easily thrown off; the example of the Israelites shews, who with all that Moses could do to reclaim them from it, still continued in their habits more or less; and why will you look for better from us, why will you look for grapes from thorns, or figs from thistles? It is in our posterity enjoying the same privileges with your own, that you ought to look for better things.

When you are pleaded with, do not you reply as Pharaoh did, "Wherefore do ye Moses and Aaron let the people from their work, behold the people of the land now are many, and you make them rest from their burthens." We wish you to consider, that God himself was the first pleader of the cause of slaves.

That God who knows the hearts of all men, and the propensity of a slave to hate his oppressor, hath strictly forbidden it to his chosen people, "Thou

Glossary

burthens	burdens
Deut.	the Christian Old Testament book of Deuteronomy
Israelites	the Jewish people whose history is chronicled in the Christian Old Testament
Moses	the Christian Old Testament leader, prophet, and lawgiver who led the Israelites out of bondage in Egypt
Pharaoh	the ruler of the Egyptians in biblical times
Saul	a king of the Israelites in biblical times
shew	show
"Wherefore do ye Moses ..."	loosely quoted from the Christian Old Testament book of Exodus, chapter 5, verses 4–5

shalt not abhor an Egyptian, because thou wast a stranger in his land." Deut. 23.7. The meek and humble Jesus, the great pattern of humanity, and every other virtue that can adorn and dignify men, hath commanded to love our enemies, to do good to them that hate and despitefully use us. I feel the obligations, I wish to impress them on the minds of our colored brethren, and that we may all forgive you, as we wish to be forgiven, we think it a great mercy to have all anger and bitterness removed from our minds; I appeal to your own feelings, if it is not very disquieting to feel yourselves under dominion of wrathful disposition.

If you love your children, if you love your country, if you love the God of love, clear your hands from slaves, burthen not your children or your country with them, my heart has been sorry for the bloodshed of the oppressors, as well as the oppressed, both appear guilty of each others' blood, in the sight of him who hath said, he that sheddeth man's blood, by man shall his blood be shed.

Will you, because you have reduced us to the unhappy condition our color is in, plead our incapacity for freedom, and our contented condition under oppression, as a sufficient cause for keeping us under the grievous yoke? I have shown the cause,—I will also shew why they appear contented; were we to attempt to plead with our masters, it would be deemed insolence, for which cause they appear as contented as they can in your sight, but the dreadful insurrections they have made when opportunity has offered, is enough to convince a reasonable man, that great uneasiness and not contentment, is the inhabitant of their hearts. God himself hath pleaded their cause, he hath from time to time raised up instruments for that purpose, sometimes mean and contemptible in your sight, at other times he hath used such as it hath pleased him, with whom you have not thought it beneath your dignity to contend. Many have been convinced of their error, condemned their former conduct, and become zealous advocates for the cause of those, whom you will not suffer to plead for themselves.

PRINCE HALL: *A CHARGE DELIVERED TO THE AFRICAN LODGE*

"What was the reason that our African kings ... plung'd millions of their fellow countrymen into slavery?"

Overview

On June 24, 1797, Prince Hall delivered a speech to the African American Masonic lodge at Menotomy (now Arlington), Massachusetts, the scene of a Revolutionary War battle on April 19, 1775, as British troops returned to Boston from the battles at nearby Lexington and Concord. The lodge had been formed by former members of a British-based lodge that had admitted African American members but had removed to England at the start of the Revolutionary War. Colonial Masonic lodges did not admit African Americans, prompting Hall and others who had developed an interest in Freemasonry to form an entirely African American lodge that received its official sanction from Great Britain. Hall, speaking to an audience that probably consisted of freed former slaves and indentured servants and many former Revolutionary soldiers, exhorted his free brethren to support those of African descent still held in slavery. He did so by reference primarily to scriptural passages and to the successful slave revolt that was taking place in Haiti. The speech was later printed and bound and issued as a "charge" to the lodge. A copy of the booklet is housed in the Library of Congress's Rare Book and Special Collections Division.

Context

Understanding the context of Prince Hall's speech requires at least a brief survey of the history of Freemasonry in general and Prince Hall Freemasonry in particular. The male-only fraternal organization began in the late sixteenth or early seventeenth century, possibly in Scotland. The organization requires that all members express a belief in a Supreme Being, though, interestingly, discussion of religion is forbidden in Masonic lodges, so that no one is forced to defend a particular set of beliefs. Most lodges keep on display a copy of what is called a "Volume of Sacred Law"; often, this volume is a Christian Bible (King James Version in the Anglophone world), but many lodges display various religious texts, and Muslims, Hindus, and adherents of other religions—as well as those who practice no formal

religion—are invited to become Masons. The Masons not only provide fraternal activities for their members, including informal philosophical discussion, but also engage in extensive charitable work.

The word *Masons* reflects the organization's extensive use of the symbolism of architecture and building, some of which Hall mentions in his address. The Supreme Being, for example, is referred to as the Architect of the Universe. Common symbols used in Masonic rituals are the carpenter's square and the drafting compass. The underlying concept is that members are to "square" their lives with a sense of morality and good conduct and to circumscribe their passions. An important feature of Freemasonry is that it is entirely without dogma. Each lodge, for example, is free to conduct its rituals as it sees fit. Members are encouraged to speculate on the philosophical meaning of the organization's symbols. No one person or text "speaks" for all Freemasons.

Freemasonry is organized into grand lodges and lower-ranked lodges. The first Grand Lodge of England was formed in 1717, but in 1751 a schism between the "Moderns" (who advocated modernization) and the traditionalist "Antients" (or Ancients) resulted in two competing grand lodges. Thus, there were two competing grand lodges when Freemasonry gained a foothold in the North American colonies in the 1730s. After the Revolutionary War, independent grand lodges were formed in each state, with no overall grand lodge in the United States, although one, to be presided over by George Washington, was proposed.

Throughout its history, Freemasonry has been ridiculed, opposed, and subjected to harsh criticism. The organization's reliance on codes, handshakes, and secret words has likely contributed to the belief that Freemasonry is somehow nefarious and has to be "exposed." The Roman Catholic Church has long opposed Freemasonry because of the sense that its vision of the Creator is opposed to church teachings. The organization has been accused of corruption, political conspiracies, and anti-Semitism and has been suppressed at various times and in various places. Yet the roster of Freemasons in history is extensive, including many U.S. presidents, senators, congressmen, and Supreme Court justices as well as classical musicians, entertainers, and others.

Time Line

1735/ 1738
- Prince Hall is born in Barbados, Massachusetts, or England.

1749
- Hall is known to have lived in the home of William Hall in Boston.

1770
- **April 9** Hall is given manumission papers.

1775
- **March 6** Hall and fourteen other free African Americans join a British Army Freemasons lodge.
- **April 19** Skirmishes at Lexington and Concord, Massachusetts, signal the start of the American Revolutionary War.
- **June 17** At the Battle of Bunker Hill, Hall may have fought for the colonials.
- **July 3** Hall forms African Lodge No. 1, the first recognized African American Masonic lodge.

1777
- **April 24** Hall sells leather drumheads to the Boston Regiment of Artillery of the Continental army.

1783
- **September 3** The Treaty of Paris is signed, ending the Revolutionary War.

1784
- **January 14** The United States ratifies the Treaty of Paris.

1791
- **August 22** A slave revolt begins in the French colony of Saint Domingue (now Haiti).

African American Freemasonry is often called Prince Hall Freemasonry. In 1775 Prince Hall and fourteen other free African Americans were initiated into the Irish Constitution Military Lodge No. 441, a British army lodge that was part of the Thirty-eighth Foot Regiment, then resident in Boston. (British lodges had a policy of admitting blacks and did so up to the time of the Revolution, when they left the colony, forcing blacks to start their own lodges.) The others, who were all born free, were Cyrus Johnston, Bueston Slinger, Prince Rees, John Canton, Peter Freeman, Benjamin Tiler, Duff Ruform, Thomas Santerson, Prince Rayden, Cato Speain, Boston Smith, Peter Best, Forten Horward, and Richard Titley. When the regiment moved from the area (the Revolutionary War was just three months away), the lodge was given permission to function independently as a Masonic lodge. On July 3, 1775, Hall formed the group into the African Lodge No. 1, the first recognized African American lodge. In 1784 the group was given a charter by the Grand Lodge of England and became African Lodge No. 459. After 1813 the African Lodge was separated from the Grand Lodge of England, hence giving rise to the appellation Prince Hall Freemasonry. In the modern era, however, U.S. lodges recognize Prince Hall Freemasonry as a legitimate branch of the organization.

In Prince Hall's time and until the late twentieth century, Masonic lodges were heavily segregated. This was in part because new members could be initiated only after a secret ballot, often using white and black balls and a ballot box. Just one racially motivated negative vote could "blackball" an applicant. In addition, one membership rule (not always followed) required that the applicant be born a free man (one possible explanation for the origin of the term *Freemason*), excluding former slaves from membership. Prince Hall had been denied membership in a white Massachusetts Masonic lodge prior to being admitted to the Irish lodge.

Black Freemasonry was part of a broader effort on the part of black Americans at the time of the Revolutionary War and beyond to provide cultural, educational, and economic aid to the black community through churches, schools, benevolent societies, and mutual-aid groups. During the middle part of the eighteenth century, the number of African slaves in the United States had increased dramatically. Many slaves and free blacks felt strong cultural affinities with the large number of people arriving from Africa. Many organizations included the words *Africa* or *African* in their names. As slaves were freed, particularly throughout New England and in such states as New York and New Jersey (often because these slaves had fought for the new nation in the Revolutionary War), black households were being formed, extended black kinship groups were being established, and a sense of a black community was developing—characteristics that could not have existed under slavery, where families were separated, parents were sold away from their children, blacks were almost universally illiterate, and slaves lived in relative isolation from one another. The Revolutionary War, with its ideals of equality, held out some hope, however slim, that the new nation would have a place for free African Americans, and in the years following the war, there was a spirit of hope and vigor in the free black communities of such cities as New York, Boston, Philadelphia, and others.

Prince Hall was a vital and energetic part of this community. In 1777, for example, he petitioned for the abolition of slavery in Massachusetts. He also petitioned the governor of New York to allow the military help of some seven hundred blacks in putting down Shays's Rebellion in 1786. He joined with seventy-three other blacks in petitioning the state government for financial help for blacks who wanted to immigrate to Africa. He also petitioned the state for free public education for taxpaying citizens, of which he was one. The African Lodge, then, with Prince Hall's charge for its members to support blacks who were still enslaved, was part of a broad effort to ameliorate the condition of African Americans in the post–Revolutionary War era.

About the Author

There is substantial dispute about the birth date and place of Prince Hall. He may have been born in Barbados, Massachusetts, or England. It is possible that he was born in Barbados but came to America by way of England rather than directly from Barbados, thus giving rise to conjecture as to the site of his birth. His date of birth is reported as either 1735 or 1738. Misinformation about Prince Hall's life is widespread, much of it deriving from William Grimshaw's *The Official History of Freemasonry among the Colored People of North America* (1903). At least his date of death is known with certainty: December 4, 1807.

It is also unclear whether Hall was ever a slave. In 1749 he began living in the home of William Hall of Boston and working for him. On April 9, 1770, he was given his manumission papers—documents, signed by the slave owner, that protected the freed slave from recapture and also released the owner from any obligation to take care of the slave. However, Hall's manumission papers stated that "he is no longer to be reckoned a slave, but has been always accounted as a freeman by us." This suggests—and some biographical materials state as a fact—that Hall was never a slave and that the papers were signed simply to prove that he was a free man. He certainly could have been a slave in Boston; slavery in Massachusetts Colony did not end until a 1783 court case interpreted the 1780 state constitution as being inconsistent with slavery. However, even the relevance of these papers is uncertain, since there were twenty-one individuals named Prince Hall who lived in Massachusetts during that time period.

Hall is reported to have been married three times, although, once again, sources are in dispute as to the details. One source states that his first marriage was to Flora Gibbs, and this union produced his only child, Prince Africanus, who was baptized November 4, 1784. Nothing else is known about his first wife or son. He married a woman named Sarah in 1763. Sarah died in 1769, and he married Sylvia Johnson on June 28, 1804. Another source states that had a son, Primus, with a servant named Delia

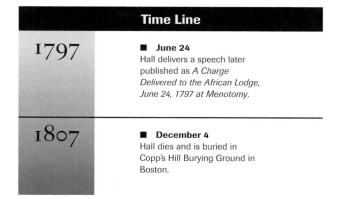

Time Line

1797

■ **June 24**
Hall delivers a speech later published as *A Charge Delivered to the African Lodge, June 24, 1797 at Menotomy.*

1807

■ **December 4**
Hall dies and is buried in Copp's Hill Burying Ground in Boston.

in 1756, married Sarah Ritchie some time after 1762 (on this marriage the two sources seem to agree), and married Flora Gibbs in 1780.

William Hall was a leather dresser, and Prince Hall learned this trade from his employer (or master) in the period 1749–1770 and became a leather dresser in Boston in his own right thereafter. He later became a caterer. As is typical of many facets of Prince Hall's biography, it is reported but not verified that Hall fought for independence in the American Revolution. Skirmishes at Lexington and Concord, Massachusetts, signaled the start of the American Revolutionary War on April 19, 1775. One source places Hall at the Battle of Bunker Hill on June 17, 1775, in which some twelve hundred colonial soldiers attempted to hold the hills surrounding besieged Boston against an attack by a superior British force. Although the colonial forces were ultimately driven back, the British suffered significant losses, and the colonial troops demonstrated their ability to withstand a sustained attack by regular army troops. Although it cannot be confirmed that Hall was at the battle, it is known that some three dozen freed former slaves were in the force, including Barzillai Lew, Salem Poor, and Peter Salem. It is known for certain that Prince Hall sold leather drumheads to the Boston Regiment of Artillery, as a bill of sale dated April 24, 1777, provides proof and the sale is consistent with Hall's known trade as a leather dresser. It does, however, seem unusual that Hall would engage in combat against the British army just three months after enrolling in a British Army Freemason lodge. He died in Boston.

Explanation and Analysis of the Document

Hall's speech was published as *A Charge Delivered to the African Lodge, June 24, 1797 at Menotomy*, but it is called by various names. The informal title of the text, "Thus Doth Ethiopia Stretch Forth Her Hand from Slavery, to Freedom and Equality" is taken from Psalm 68:31, which in the King James Version of the Bible says, "Princes shall come out of Egypt; Ethiopia shall soon stretch out her hands unto God." Various translations substitute "envoys" or "bronze" for "princes" and "Kush" or sometimes "Sudan" for "Ethio-

George Washington as a Freemason (Library of Congress)

pia." The Kush of the Christian Old Testament is sometimes considered to be part of modern-day Sudan, Egypt, or Ethiopia and may or may not correspond with the documented historical kingdom of Kush, which emerged from Egyptian control around 1000 BCE and began to decline in the second century CE. The biblical references spring from Cush the son of Ham (and grandson of Noah), traditionally considered the progenitor of the black race. Perhaps it is best to consider Ethiopia (or Kush) as the archetype of ancient black civilizations of northeastern Africa. From the time of the American Revolution, slaves equated Ethiopia with salvation for the black race.

After indicating that five years previously he had issued a "charge" to his fellow Masons (that is, a directive reminding Masons of their obligations to others), Hall calls upon his fellow Masons to show charity to all humankind regardless of race, but he also specifically exhorts them to consider "the numerous sons and daughters of distress," that is, those Africans still held in slavery. In making his point, he invokes the biblical character of Job, whose name is associated with the torments that he had to bear.

Hall makes a second biblical reference in connection with the slave trade. Revelation 18:11–13, in the King James Version, states:

And the merchants of the earth shall weep and mourn over her [Babylon]; for no man buyeth their merchan-

dise any more: The merchandise of gold, and silver, and precious stones, and of pearls, and fine linen, and purple, and silk, and scarlet, and all thyine wood [an evergreen, also called citron wood, burned in sacrifices because of its fragrance], and all manner vessels of ivory, and all manner vessels of most precious wood, and of brass, and iron, and marble, And cinnamon, and odours, and ointments, and frankincense, and wine, and oil, and fine flour, and wheat, and beasts, and sheep, and horses, and chariots, and slaves, and souls of men.

Babylon, in a variety of contexts from Revelation to Rastafarianism, has long been a metaphor for governments and institutions in rebellion against the rule of God, beginning with the Tower of Babel. Here, Hall uses the biblical metaphor in reference to the slave trade, though he also notes that there is cause for hope because events taking place in the West Indies will put an end to the "African traffick." At this point he makes reference to the "Ethiopeans," expressing hope that God will change their condition. He also mentions to the "bloody wars" taking place throughout the world and urges his listeners to "sympathize with them in their troubles" and to "weep with those that weep."

Hall describes what he calls a "chequered world," one in which bounty alternates with deprivation, festivity alternates with mourning, health and prosperity alternates with sickness and adversity. States and kingdoms experience similar ups and down, suggesting that "there is not an independent mortal on earth." All people, Hall says, are dependent on one another, in this way reinforcing the Masonic goal of mutual aid.

Hall makes further biblical allusions. He notes that in the book of Exodus, Moses, the lawgiver, received instruction from his father-in-law, an Ethiopian named Jethro. He narrates two stories from the Old Testament, one involving a captive servant who was able to cure her master of leprosy, despite his haughtiness and disdain for the direction of the biblical prophets. In contrast is the story of Obadiah from the first book of Kings, whose lesson is that "great and good men have, and always will have, a respect for ministers and servants of God." A similar story is told in the New Testament Acts of the Apostles, in which a white man is not afraid to accept the aid of a black man. Hall also cites the story of King Solomon of the Old Testament, who accepted the Queen of Sheba, the African queen who traveled to visit and bear gifts to Solomon because she had heard of his great wisdom.

Hall then describes the "daily insults" African Americans experience on the streets of Boston and calls upon his fellow Masons to pray to God for patience in the face of present troubles. This is a reference to antiblack riots in Boston led by "a mob or horde of shameless, low-lived, envious, spiteful persons." Reminding his listeners that "the darkest hour is just before the break of day," Hall turns to the events of "six years ago in the French West-Indies"—a slave rebellion on the island of Saint Domingue (Hispaniola) that began in 1791 and would eventually lead to the independent nation of Haiti. African Americans would have

Chart of Masonic emblems and history (Library of Congress)

followed the events in Haiti with keen interest, for it was the only successful slave rebellion in the Western Hemisphere. Saint Domingue was a leading supplier of sugar and France's most lucrative colony. White landowners developed enormous plantations, where they grew not only sugarcane but also coffee, indigo, and other export crops, all labor-intensive industries that depended on slaves imported from Africa. The plantation owners were vastly outnumbered, so they lived in fear of slave rebellions. Accordingly, they passed repressive laws that created, in effect, a caste system. Although Hall did not make this explicit connection, the situation could be seen as an analogy to the plight of free blacks in Massachusetts, who were relegated to second-class status despite being technically free. Throughout the middle and late 1700s, whites and blacks engaged in a series of violent clashes. Escaped slaves, called maroons, formed gangs that lived in the forests and repeatedly attacked French plantations.

Complicating matters was competition for the colony among the French, Spanish, and British and the French Revolution, which began in 1789. Free people of color were

emboldened by the revolutionary government's 1789 Declaration of the Rights of Man and of the Citizen and consequently were often called Black Jacobins, a reference to political radicals in revolutionary France. Free blacks agitated for civil rights, particularly the right to vote. In May 1791 the French revolutionary government granted French citizenship and civil rights to free blacks. White colonists refused to recognize the government's decision (which was later revoked). The result was a high state of tension between Haiti's former slaves and whites. The Haitian Revolution erupted on August 22, 1791, under the leadership of François-Dominique Toussaint-Louverture By the time hostilities were suspended in 1794, about one hundred thousand blacks and twenty-four thousand whites had lost their lives. That year, the French National Convention abolished slavery and granted full civil and political rights to all blacks in Haiti.

This was the state of affairs in Haiti at the time Hall gave his address. Blacks, particularly free blacks, in the United States would have followed the ongoing events in Haiti with keen interest and would have seen that nation's successful

"And this is not to be confined to parties or colours; not to towns or states; not to a kingdom, but to the kingdoms of the whole earth, over whom Christ the king is head and grand master."

(Paragraph 3)

"Among these numerous sons and daughters of distress, I shall begin with our friends and brethren; and first, let us see them dragg'd from their native country, by the iron hand of tyranny and oppression, from their dear friends and connections, with weeping eyes and aching hearts, to a strange land and strange people."

(Paragraph 4)

"Patience I say, for were we not possess'd of a great measure of it you could not bear up under the daily insults you meet with in the streets of Boston... how are you shamefully abus'd, and that at such a degree that you may truly be said to carry your lives in your hands; and the arrows of death are flying about your heads."

(Paragraph 13)

"Thus doth Ethiopia begin to stretch forth her hand, from the sink of slavery to freedom and equality."

(Paragraph 14)

"What was the reason that our African kings and princes have ... plung'd millions of their fellow countrymen into slavery and cruel bondage?"

(Paragraph 16)

"Give the right hand of affection and fellowship to whom it justly belongs let their colour or complexion be what it will: let their nation be what it may, for they are your brethren, and it is your indispensible duty so to do."

(Paragraph 19)

efforts to end slavery as a beacon of hope. On an optimistic note, Hall says, "Thus doth Ethiopia stretch forth her hand from slavery, to freedom and equality," suggesting that those ideals (again with Ethiopia used as the archetype of ancient black civilizations) would eventually be realized by all victims of the African diaspora. He urges his listeners to avoid the "slavish fear of man," alluding then to African kingdoms, where "the fear of the report of a great gun or the glittering of arms and swords" induces fear, panic and disorder and leads African kings and princes to sell their countrymen into bondage. Hall cautions his listeners against fear, urging them to respect others but to worship none. The duty of Christians and Masons is to worship God.

Having discussed the biblical and historical backdrop for his remarks, Hall then issues the core of his charge to his listeners. He calls on them to "have a fellow feeling for our distress'd brethren of the human race." He cites examples of neighbors coming to the relief of a person whose house has burned or rescuers of a person who has been shipwrecked. He makes reference to the "captives among the Algerines," possibly an allusion to *The Algerine Captive; or, The Life and Adventures of Doctor Updike Underhill: Six Years a Prisoner among the Algerines*, a fictitious memoir published the same year by Royall Tyler and one that reflected Americans' interest in events in and around the Mediterranean Sea. Alternatively, he could be referring more generally to the ransoming of captives held by the Barbary Coast pirates (a region that included Algiers). Again, Hall's theme is that the hand of God can and will deliver people from distress.

Hall concludes by calling on his fellows to "live and act as Masons" by extending the hand of friendship to all people "let their colour or complexion be what it will." He sees the people of the United States as the Mason's "brethren," and states that it is the duty of all Masons to do the same.

Audience

The speech was printed as a booklet in 1797 and sold in Prince Hall's shop in Boston. Hall was speaking to a closed audience of his fellow African American Masons in Boston. The African American population living in the area at that time would have consisted of escaped slaves, freed slaves, former indentured servants, and former residents of various Caribbean colonies.

Impact

While it is difficult to trace the precise impact that a speech delivered behind closed doors would have had, in a general sense it can be said that black Freemasonry and the "charges" of Prince Hall helped sustain and create broader efforts to improve the condition of the nation's post-Revolutionary black community. As such, the African Lodge was one of numerous benevolent societies and other organizations that were formed to help blacks, both free blacks and slaves. Boston, for example, was the home of the African Society. The African Marine Fund for the Relief of the Distressed Orphans, and Poor Members of This Fund was an early example of a black relief agency. The Brotherly Union Society was instituted in Philadelphia, a city that in the 1790s was home to an estimated two thousand free blacks and would have over fourteen thousand within a generation. The African Church of Saint Thomas and the Free African Society were also formed in Philadelphia. In Rhode Island, the Free African Benevolent Society provided mutual aid to Newport's large black community.

Although Hall's speech would have been scarcely noted, if at all, outside the confines of African Lodge No. 459, the

Questions for Further Study

1. What political and social circumstances made Freemasonry and other benevolent organizations attractive to many African Americans in the late eighteenth century?

2. What impact did the events in Haiti have on African Americans? Why were these events considered important?

3. Compare this document to the Petition of Prince Hall and Other African Americans to the Massachusetts General Court. Do the two documents make similar arguments? What picture do the two documents, taken together, give you of African American life in the North in the late eighteenth century?

4. Why do you think Prince Hall made so many biblical references in his charge? What do these biblical references add to his argument?

5. To this day, black Freemasonry is often called Prince Hall Freemasonry. Does it trouble you that there appears to be a separate organization for blacks?

fact that a line of African Masonic lodges continues to this day is ample demonstration of the success of Hall's early efforts at continuing African American Masonic activities after the Revolutionary War ended. The roster of Prince Hall Freemasons since then has included William Wells Brown, W. E. B. Du Bois, Martin R. Delany, T. Thomas Fortune, Jesse Jackson, Sr., Thurgood Marshall, A. Philip Randolph, Booker T. Washington, and numerous other African American leaders. Hall's heartfelt call for sympathy toward and unity with those still in slavery must have had a significant impact on his listeners.

See also Petition of Prince Hall and Other African Americans to the Massachusetts General Court (1777).

Further Reading

■ Books

Asante, Molefi Kete. *100 Greatest African Americans: A Biographical Encyclopedia*. Amherst, N.Y.: Prometheus Books, 2002.

Gray, David L. *Inside Prince Hall*. Lancaster, Va.: Anchor Communications, 2004.

Grimshaw, William H. *The Official History of Freemasonry among the Colored People of North America*. 1903. Reprint. Whitefish, Mont.: Kessinger Publishing, 1994.

Kaplan, Sidney, and Emma Nogrady Kaplan. *The Black Presence in the Era of the American Revolution*. Rev. ed. Amherst: University of Massachusetts Press, 1989.

Muraskin, William Alan. *Middle-Class Blacks in a White Society: Prince Hall Freemasonry in America*. Berkeley: University of California Press, 1975.

Palmer, Colin A., ed. *Encyclopedia of African-American Culture and History*. 2nd ed. Detroit, Mich.: Macmillan Reference USA, 2006.

Roundtree, Alton G., and Paul M. Bessel. *Out of the Shadows: Prince Hall Freemasonry in America, 200 Years of Endurance*. Forestville, Md.: KLR Publishing, 2006.

Walkes, Joseph A., Jr. *Black Square and Compass: 200 Years of Prince Hall Freemasonry*. Richmond, Va.: Macoy Publishing, 1994.

■ Web Sites

"Prince Hall." Africa Within Web site.
http://www.africawithin.com/bios/prince_hall.htm.

"Prince Hall." PBS "Africans in America" Web site.
http://www.pbs.org/wgbh/aia/part2/2p37.html.

"Prince Hall." Pride of the Hilltop, F. & A. M. No. 110 Web site.
http://www.hilltop110.org/prince_hall.htm.

"Who was Prince Hall?" The Prince Hall Memorial Project Web site.
http://www.princehallmemorial.org/ph/index.php?option=com_content&view=article&id=47&Itemid=2

—Keith E. Sealing

PRINCE HALL: *A CHARGE DELIVERED TO THE AFRICAN LODGE*

'Tis now five years since I deliver'd a Charge to you on some parts and points of Masonry. As one branch or superstructure on the foundation; when I endeavoured to shew you the duty of a Mason to a Mason, and charity or love to all mankind, as the mark and image of the great God, and the Father of the human race.

I shall now attempt to shew you, that it is our duty to sympathise with our fellow men under their troubles: the families of our brethren who are gone: we hope to the Grand Lodge above, here to return no more. But the cheerfulness that you have ever had to relieve them, and ease their burdens, under their sorrows, will never be forgotten by them; and in this manner you will never be weary in doing good.

But my brethren, although we are to begin here, we must not end here; for only look around you and you will see and hear of numbers of our fellow men crying out with holy Job, Have pity on me, O my friends, for the hand of the Lord hath touched me. And this is not to be confined to parties or colours; not to towns or states; not to a kingdom, but to the kingdoms of the whole earth, over whom Christ the king is head and grand master.

Among these numerous sons and daughters of distress, I shall begin with our friends and brethren; and first, let us see them dragg'd from their native country, by the iron hand of tyranny and oppression, from their dear friends and connections, with weeping eyes and aching hearts, to a strange land and strange people, whose tender mercies are cruel; and there to bear the iron yoke of slavery & cruelty till death as a friend shall relieve them. And must not the unhappy condition of these our fellow men draw forth our hearty prayer and wishes for their deliverance from these merchants and traders, whose characters you have in the xviii chap. of Revelations, 11, 12, & 13 verses, and who knows but these same sort of traders may in a short time, in the like manner, bewail the loss of the African traffick, to their shame and confusion: and if I mistake not, it now begins to dawn in some of the West-India islands; which puts me in mind of a nation (that I have somewhere read of) called Ethiopeans, that cannot change their skin: But God can and will change their conditions, and their hearts too; and let Boston and the world know, that He hath no respect of persons; and that that bulwark of envy, pride, scorn and contempt; which is so visible to be seen in some and felt, shall fall, to rise no more.

When we hear of the bloody wars which are now in the world, and thousands of our fellow men slain; fathers and mothers bewailing the loss of their sons; wives for the loss of their husbands; towns and cities burnt and destroy'd; what must be the heart-felt sorrow and distress of these poor and unhappy people! Though we cannot help them, the distance begin too great, yet we may sympathize with them in their troubles, and mingle a tear of sorrow with them, and do as we are exhorted to—weep with those that weep.

Thus my brethren we see what a chequered world we live in. Sometimes happy in having our wives and children like olive-branches about our tables; receiving the bounties of our great Benefactor. The next year, or month, or week, we may be deprived of some of them, and we go mourning about the streets: so in societies; we are this day to celebrate this Feast of St. John's, and the next week we might be called upon to attend a funeral of some one here, as we have experienced since our last in this Lodge. So in the common affairs of life, we sometimes enjoy health and prosperity; at another time sickness and adversity, crosses and disappointments.

So in states and kingdoms; sometimes in tranquility; then wars and tumults; rich today and poor tomorrow; which shews that there is not an independent mortal on earth; but dependent one upon the other, from the king to the beggar.

The great law-giver, Moses, who instructed by his father-in-law, Jethro, an Ethiopean, how to regulate his courts of just, and what sort of men to choose for the different offices; hear now my words, said he, I will give you counsel, and God shall be with you; be thou for the people to Godward, that thou mayest bring the causes unto God, and thou shall teach them ordinances and laws, and shall shew the way wherein the must walk; and the work that they must do: moreover thou shall provide out of all the people, able men, such as fear God, men of truth, hating covetousness, and place such over them, to be rulers of the thousands, and hundreds and of tens.

So Moses hearkened to the voice of his father-in-law, and did all that he said.—Exodus xviii, 22–24.

This is the first and grandest lecture that Moses ever received from the mouth of man; for Jethro understood geometry as well as laws, *that* a Mason may plainly see: so a little captive servant maid by whose advice Nomen, the great general of Syria's army was healed of his leprosy.... The feelings of this little captive, for this great man, her captor, was so great, that she forgot her state of captivity, and felt for the distress of her enemy. Would to God (said she to her mistress) my lord were with the prophets in Samaria, he should be healed of his leprosy: So after he went to the prophet, his proud host was so haughty that he not only disdain'd the prophets' direction, but derided the good old prophet.; and had it not been for his servant, he would have gone to his grave....

How unlike was this great general's behaviour to that of as grand a character, and as well beloved by his prince as he was; I mean Obadiah, to a like prophet. See for this 1st Kings, xviii. from 7 to the 16th.

And as Obadiah was in the way, behold Elijah met him, and he knew him, and fell on his face, and said, Art not thou, my Lord, Elijah, and he told him, Yea, go and tell thy Lord, behold Elijah is here....Thus we see, that great and good men have, and always will have, a respect for ministers and servants of God. Another instance of this is in Acts viii. 27 to 31, of the European Eunich, a man of great authority, to Philip, the apostle: here is mutual love and friendship between them. This minister of Jesus Christ did not think himself too good to receive the hand, and ride in a chariot with a black man in the face of day.... So our Grand Master, Solomon, was not asham'd to take the Queen of Sheba by the hand, and lead her into his court, at the hour of high twelve, and there converse with her on points of masonry (for if ever there was a female mason in the world she was one) and other curious matters; and gratified her, by shewing her all his riches and curious pieces of architecture in the temple, and in his house....

Now my brethren, as we see and experience, that all things here are frail and changeable and nothing here to be depended upon: Let us seek those things which are above ... and at the same time let us pray to almighty God, while we remain in the tabernacle, that he would give us the grace of patience and strength to bear up under all our troubles, which at this day God knows we have our share. Patience I say, for were we not possess'd of a great measure of it you could not bear up under the daily insults you meet with in the streets of Boston ... how are you shamefully abus'd, and that at such a degree that you may truly be said to carry your lives in your hands; and the arrows of death are flying about your heads; helpless old women have

their clothes torn off their backs, even to the exposing of their nakedness; and by whom are these disgraceful and abusive actions committed, not by the men born and bred in Boston, for they are better bred; but by a mob or horde of shameless, low-lived , envious, spiteful persons, some of them not long since servants in gentlemen's kitchings [*sic*], scouring knives, tending horses, and driving chaise. 'Twas said by a gentleman who saw that filthy behaviour in the common, that in all the places he had been in, he never saw so cruel behaviour in all his life, and that a slave in the West-Indies, on Sunday or holidays enjoys himself and friends without molestation. Not only this man, but many in town ... have wonder'd at the patience of the Blacks: 'tis not for want of courage in you, for they know that they dare not face you man for man, but in a mob, which we despise, and had rather suffer wrong than to do wrong, to the disturbance of the community and the disgrace of our reputation: for every good citizen doth honor to the laws of the State where resides.

My brethren, let us not be cast down under these and many other abuses we at present labour under: for the darkest is before the break of day: My brethren, let us remember what a dark day it was with our African brethren six years ago, in the French West-Indies. Nothing but the snap of the whip was heard from morning to evening: hanging, broken on the wheel, burning, and all manner of tortures inflicted on those unhappy people, for nothing else but to gratify their masters pride, wantonness and cruelty: but blessed be God, the scene is changed; they now confess that God hath no respect of persons, and therefore receive them as their friends, and treat them as brothers. Thus doth Ethiopia begin to stretch forth her hand, from the sink of slavery to freedom and equality....

Another thing I would warn you against, is the slavish fear of man, which bringest a snare, saith Solomon. This passion of fear, like pride and envy, hath slain its thousands ....

What was the reason that our African kings and princes have plunged themselves and their peaceable kingdoms into bloody wars, to the destroying of towns and kingdoms, but the fear of the report of a great gun or the glittering of arms and swords, which struck these kings near the seaports with such a panic of fear, as not only to destroy the peace and happiness of their inland brethren, but plung'd millions of their fellow countrymen into slavery and cruel bondage....

Thus we see my brethren, what a miserable condition it is to be under the slavish fear of men; it is of such a destructive nature to mankind, that the scriptures every where from Genesis to the Revelations warns us against it; and even our blessed Saviour himself forbids us from this slavish fear of man, in his sermon on the mount.... My brethren let us pay all due respect to all whom God hath put in places of honor over us: do justly and be faithful to them that hire you, and treat them with that respect they may deserve; but worship no man. Worship God, this much is your duty as Christians and as masons.

We see then how becoming and necessary it is to have a fellow feeling for our distress'd brethren of the human race, in their troubles, both spiritual and temporal....How doth it cheer up the heart of a man when his house is on fire, to see a number of friends coming to his relief.... So a man wreck'd at sea, how must it revive his drooping heart to see a ship bearing down for his relief....Where is the man that has the least spark of humanity, that will not rejoice … and bless a righteous God who knows how and when to relieve the oppressed, as we see he did in the deliverance of the captives among the Algerines; how sud-

den were they delivered by the sympathising members of the Congress of the United States, who now enjoy the free air of peace and liberty, to their great joy and surprise.... Here we see the hand of God in various ways, bringing about his own glory for the good of mankind, by the mutual help of their fellow men; which ought to teach us in all our straits, be they what they may, to put our trust in Him, firmly believing that he is able and will deliver us....

Live and act as Masons, that you may die as Masons.... If they will let us we shall call ourselves a charter'd lodge, of just and lawful Masons.... Give the right hand of affection and fellowship to whom it justly belongs let their colour or complexion be what it will: let their nation be what it may, for they are your brethren, and it is your indispensible duty so to do; let them as Masons deny this, and we & the world know what to think of them be they ever so grand: for we know this was Solomon's creed.... It is the decree of the Almighty, and all Masons have learnt it: plain market language and plain and true facts need no apologies.

Glossary

Algerines	Algerians
Ethiopians	a name commonly used at the time for Africans
Feast of St. John's	the feast of Saint John the Baptist, celebrated typically on June 24
French West-Indies	islands in the Caribbean under French control, at the time primarily Hispaniola, which comprised the nations of Haiti and Saint-Domingue
Moses	the Christian Old Testament lawgiver who led the Israelites out of bondage in Egypt
Nomen	usually spelled Naamen, a Syrian general
Queen of Sheba	an African queen who visited Solomon
Samaria	a portion of biblical Israel corresponding roughly to today's West Bank
shew	an antique spelling of "show"
Solomon	the Christian Old Testament king of the Israelites, legendary for his wisdom

OHIO BLACK CODE

"No black or mulatto person, shall be permitted to ... reside in this state, unless he [produces a] certificate ... of his or her actual freedom."

Overview

Immediately after Ohio achieved statehood in 1802, the Ohio legislature tried to define the meaning and limitations of freedom for African Americans in the new state. Between 1803 and 1807 the legislature passed and subsequently amended a series of laws known as the Black Code. With these laws, white Ohioans legislated the second-class status of African Americans in the state. The laws foremost required immigrating African Americans to register their freedom with the county courts. In addition, the laws dictated that as residents of the state, African Americans could not vote, bear arms, testify in court, or attend public schools.

Ohio's Black Code demonstrates the ways in which white Americans sought to limit the freedom of blacks in antebellum America. In other northern states as well, the gradual emancipation of African Americans was coupled with restrictions on black rights. While chattel slavery was never legal in Ohio, the Black Code in this nominally free state highlights the pervasiveness of racism throughout the country. Many historians point to economic factors as contributory to the antiblack sentiment that grew among white Ohioans: Jobs in early nineteenth-century Ohio were scarce, and whites opposed the prospect of competing with blacks for the limited employment opportunities available in the state. In addition, as the first state carved out of the federally governed Northwest Territory, Ohio set the precedent for other midwestern states. Indiana and Illinois similarly passed Black Codes upon moving to statehood. Over time, however, black Ohioans organized resistance to the Black Codes; the ultimate repeal of these restrictive laws highlights the power of black protest in pre–Civil War America.

Context

In 1787 the American nation was in its infancy. The land west of the Appalachian Mountains was a territory largely unsettled by white Americans. On July 13, 1787, just two months before the signing of the U.S. Constitution, the American Confederation passed the Northwest Ordinance, which arranged for the orderly settlement of the territory north of the Ohio River.

The Northwest Territory would eventually become the states of Ohio, Indiana, Illinois, Michigan, and Wisconsin. Article 6 of the ordinance banned slavery and involuntary servitude in the territory. This was significant because slavery was legal south of the Ohio River in Kentucky and Virginia. The Ohio River itself is the confluence of two rivers, the Allegheny and Monongahela rivers in western Pennsylvania. Along its thousand-mile course to the Mississippi River, the river borders West Virginia, Ohio, Kentucky, Indiana, and Illinois. The Ohio River, therefore, served as the divide between slave and free territory. In the summer of 1795 Native Americans ceded the southern two-thirds of what would become Ohio to the United States in the Treaty of Greenville. Once the treaty opened the region to settlement, white Americans streamed into the new territory. As they entered the future state, white and black Americans tried to define the meaning of the border between slavery and freedom.

When Ohioans wrote their state constitution in 1802, they affirmed Article 6 of the Northwest Ordinance and banned slavery and involuntary servitude in the new state. The Ohio River was not a very strict barrier between slave and free states, however. Although political leaders banned slavery in Ohio, they did not support racial equality. Many of the white residents of Ohio in the early 1800s came from states that allowed slavery, including nearby Virginia and Kentucky. In fact, early statehood leaders such as Edward Tiffin and Thomas Worthington brought freed slaves with them to Ohio and bound them as servants. Some southern Ohioans worshiped at the same churches as their southern neighbors, socialized with them at local taverns, and clearly shared racist beliefs with their neighbors in bordering slave states.

Indeed, it could be said that white Ohioans feared the immigration of African Americans. In the early 1800s Americans throughout the country feared the notion of dependency. Wage labor was uncommon in the early republic. Instead, laborers worked for others, sometimes as tenants on farms or bound to skilled craftsmen as apprentices. Therefore, Americans believed that land ownership was the

1787

■ **July 13**
The Northwest Ordinance is passed, providing for settlement of the territory north of the Ohio River.

1788

■ **June 21**
The U.S. Constitution is officially ratified.

1792

■ Kentucky becomes the fifteenth American state.

1793

■ **February 12**
Congress passes the Fugitive Slave Act, meant to enforce the return of runaway slaves.

1795

■ **August 3**
The Treaty of Greenville opens Ohio to white settlement.

1799

■ Kentucky's government formally protects slavery within the state.

1802

■ Ohio becomes the seventeenth American state.

1803

■ The Ohio legislature passes a law forming a state militia, but it limits the militia to white men.

1804

■ The Ohio legislature passes a law in 1804 that strictly limits the rights of African Americans, especially former slaves, who migrate to the state.

1807

■ Further restrictions are placed on African Americans in Ohio when the state legislature passes a law in 1807 that serves as a deterrent to black migration to the state.

1808

■ The U.S. Congress officially bans transatlantic slave trade to America.

only way for a person to be truly independent. Otherwise, one would be dependent on another for his livelihood.

When Ohio became a state, the legislators formed the Overseers of the Poor to keep tabs on dependent residents. The specific responsibilities of the Overseers of the Poor included offering financial relief to those who needed it, paying residents for boarding homeless Ohioans, binding children and unemployed men and women to established residents, and expelling unruly paupers from the community. The overall purpose of the Overseers was to maintain the virtue of the community by keeping men and women from becoming charges of the county. Their primary means of accomplishing this goal was to keep everyone working. President Thomas Jefferson believed that the United States should be a country of independent farmers. Many white Ohioans believed that African Americans were racially inferior to whites and therefore predisposed to a life of dependency—a condition that threatened the social fabric of the republic. According to this theory, the influx of African Americans into the state would also be an influx of dependent citizens. These dependent citizens would then become liabilities—burdens on the state who could potentially break down the social order. Clearly, the racial ideas of the time were directly linked to the creation of the laws known collectively as the Black Code.

About the Author

The Ohio legislature wrote and approved the laws known as the Black Code. Many of the representatives in Ohio's first legislature were Jeffersonian Republicans originally from slaveholding states such as Virginia and Kentucky. Philemon Beecher authored the original bill proposal in 1803. James Dunlap served as chairman of the committee responsible for drafting the statute. Stephen Wood and James Smith also helped draft the statute, and William Gaffs advised the senate about the legislation.

Philemon Beecher was primarily responsible for the 1807 amendments. In 1806, Beecher authored the bill to revise the 1804 act. Beecher was born in Connecticut, where he was also educated as a lawyer. He moved to Lancaster, Ohio, in 1801 and continued to practice law; two years later he was elected to the first of two terms in the state house of representatives. Beecher identified with the Federalist Party, which stood for a strong central government and the growth of industry in the United States. He was elected to the U.S. House of Representatives as a Federalist in 1817, serving until 1821. During this time he participated in the debates over the admission of Missouri to the Union as a slave state. He voted for the Missouri Compromise, which brought Missouri into the Union as a slave state and Maine as a free state. Beecher was unseated in 1820 but won again in 1823 after running as a member of another political party. He served as an Ohio representative until 1829.

Explanation and Analysis of the Document

There were two primary goals of Ohio's Black Code: first, to discourage the migration of African Americans to the state and, second, to legislate the second-class citizenship of free African Americans. These two goals related directly to Ohio's position along the Ohio River. Ohio's proximity to Virginia and Kentucky, where tens of thousands of slaves resided, made the migration of African Americans to Ohio a logical move for freed blacks. The Ohio legislature made it difficult for African Americans to take up residency in Ohio by forcing them to register with county courts and find two property holders to vouch for their good behavior. Blacks in Ohio had to carry proof of their freedom at all times—a stipulation meant to discourage fugitive slaves from taking refuge in the nominally free state. In addition, by legislating the second-class citizenship of African Americans, the Ohio legislature defined the limits of American freedom along racial lines. African Americans in Ohio could not vote, bear arms, testify in court, or attend public schools.

◆ "An Act to Organize and Discipline the Militia"

The Ohio Black Code consisted of a series of laws meant to define African Americans as inferior to whites. In 1803 Ohioans passed what was termed an Act to Organize and Discipline the Militia. This law required all able-bodied "white male citizens" to enroll in the militia. In 1792 the U.S. Congress had barred blacks from military service. Ohio's militia law was thus consistent with federal militia policy.

In the early republic, Americans viewed militia service as both an obligation and a right. The Bill of Rights established the right to keep and bear arms as a fundamental privilege of American citizenship. Thus, the denial of blacks from the militia in Ohio was an explicit statement that African Americans did not share the same status as whites. In addition, in 1803 much of Ohio and the Northwest Territory remained unsettled by white Americans. Americans viewed guns as an essential tool of settlement, primarily for protection against the Native Americans who already occupied the area. Therefore, the right to bear arms and the obligation to serve in the militia were fundamental components of male citizenship on the early frontier. In denying African American men the honor of joining the militia, this law prevented them from fulfilling their social duty as male citizen protectors.

◆ "An Act to Regulate Black and Mulatto Persons"

Another of Ohio's black laws, an Act to Regulate Black and Mulatto Persons, was passed in January of 1804. This law more explicitly outlines the second-class citizenship of African Americans. The 1804 law addresses four issues: immigration, residency, fugitive reclamation, and kidnapping.

The law of 1804 required all blacks entering the state to provide proof of their freedom and to register with the county court. Only those certificates of freedom issued by a court and approved, signed, and sealed by the clerk of the court counted as viable proof of freedom. In order to

Time Line

1820	■ The admission of Missouri to the United States as a slave state precipitates sectional conflict over slavery in the halls of Congress.
1829	■ The first of three major race riots breaks out in Cincinnati, Ohio.
1836	■ Cincinnati is the site of an antiabolitionist riot.
1841	■ **August** Racial violence erupts again in Cincinnati when blacks refuse to turn over an alleged fugitive slave.
1849	■ The Ohio legislature repeals the laws of 1804 and 1807.
1850	■ **September 18** In an effort to strengthen the original law, this Fugitive Slave Act makes it a duty of federal marshals and other law-enforcement officials to arrest alleged runaway slaves.

establish residency, all blacks living in Ohio had to register with the county court and pay a registration fee of twelve and a half cents to the court clerk. African Americans living in Ohio prior to the passage of the 1804 code, as well as new immigrants, were required to register with the court. The law granted all blacks a two-year grace period to register their freedom. African Americans were expected to keep their court-issued certificates of residency with them at all times. The law also made court-issued certificates a requirement for free blacks to find employment. Whites faced a potential fine of fifty dollars for employing African Americans without a certificate or an alternative way to prove their freedom. In addition, if whites hired a fugitive slave, they could be fined fifty cents a day, payable to the owner, for every day of employment.

The immigration and residency requirements established in the 1804 law can be seen as white Ohioans' efforts to control immigration to the state. It is important to note that the law, while restricting immigration, did not completely prohibit blacks from entering Ohio. In the first decades of the nineteenth century the Ohio River was at best a fluid barrier: Whites and blacks regularly crossed this border as migrants and especially as laborers. Ohio's consti-

James Birney (Library of Congress)

tution banned slavery in the state, but early settlers continued to hire slaves from Kentucky to work on their farms in Ohio. In fact, historians estimate that Ohioans hired about two thousand slaves per year during the first decade of the nineteenth century. In response to this constant movement across the river, white Ohioans attempted to regulate the border between their free state and the slave states to the south. By forcing free African Americans entering the state to pay a fee, register their freedom, and provide their freedom papers when finding work, whites sought to ensure that all black immigrants were, in fact, free when they entered the state. This made it clear that Ohio was not a refuge for escaping slaves.

There are four reasons why the 1804 law should be seen as an attempt to restrict but not entirely prevent the immigration of African Americans. First, the registration fee was twelve and half cents, which provided only a small burden for immigrants. A higher fee would certainly have indicated an effort to prohibit immigration. Second, the law granted African Americans two years to register their freedom. This window allowed African Americans to obtain official manumission papers from former owners in slave states and gave them the chance to earn enough money to pay the registration fee. Third, the law offered no penalty for noncompliance, and county clerks only sporadically attempted to enforce registration. Finally, other states prohibited the immigration of African Americans outright. Many states in the South moved to this position in the antebellum period,

and Indiana, Ohio's western neighbor, prohibited black immigration in its 1851 constitution.

The law of 1804 also made Ohio's policy for the reclamation of fugitive slaves consistent with federal law. Early in 1793 the federal government passed the Fugitive Slave Act, which established the rights of owners to retrieve escaped slaves outside their state of residence. Ohio's law allowed masters or their agents to appeal to state judges or local justices of the peace for a certificate of removal to retrieve a runaway slave. Claimants provided some form of proof that the person was a runaway, and the judicial officer issued a warrant for the arrest of the alleged fugitive. Sheriffs were required to execute these orders. In addition, the law made people convicted of harboring or in any way hindering the retrieval of an alleged fugitive subject to a fine of ten to fifty dollars.

The final provision of the law dealt specifically with the kidnapping of free African Americans. The law dictated that a $1,000 fine be imposed on anyone who removed, attempted to remove, or assisted in the removal of a black person without following the legal process. Half of this fine went to the informer and the other half to the state. The fugitive reclamation and kidnapping provisions of the 1804 law deal directly with Ohio's long border with slaveholding states. The law confirmed the right of slaveholders to cross the border and retrieve escaped slaves. This was a clear statement that Ohio was not a refuge for fugitives. Therefore, while Ohio may have been a free state, white Ohioans placated their southern neighbors with their willingness to accommodate the peculiar needs of the so-called peculiar institution of slavery. However, the kidnapping provision also indicated that white Ohioans would not allow slaveholders complete liberty in their state. The law offered a stiff penalty for those attempting to kidnap and remove free African Americans. White Ohioans did, in fact, come to the aid of free blacks when Kentuckians came to carry them back across the border. This suggests that while many whites in Ohio may not have accepted African Americans as equals, at the very least many recognized African Americans as human beings who deserved the most basic level of liberty.

African Americans used the antikidnapping provision in combination with the registration requirement to protect themselves. While probably not the intention of legislators, the registration of their freedom in the courts provided free blacks in Ohio with documented proof of their freedom, which protected them from potential kidnapping.

♦ "An Act to Amend the Last Named Act 'An Act to Regulate Black and Mulatto Persons'"

In an effort led by Representative Beecher, the Ohio legislature amended the Act to Regulate Black and Mulatto Persons in January 1807. The 1807 amendments made a clearer statement about the second-class status of African Americans in Ohio. Under the new law, African Americans had to enter into a bond with two or more property holders "in the penal sum of five hundred dollars" within twenty days of immigrating to Ohio. This did not mean that African

Illustration of pioneers on the Ohio River settling the old Northwest Territory in the late 1700s (AP/Wide World Photos)

Americans had to pay five hundred dollars upon entry to the state; in fact, no money had to be posted by anyone. The bond required that the two property holders agree to pay five hundred dollars only if the migrating person of color failed to maintain "good behavior" and became a burden on the community. In addition, the law raised the fine for employing or harboring unregistered African Americans from fifty to one hundred dollars. Half of this fine was paid to the informant.

The 1804 law did not outline a penalty for African Americans who failed to register with the court. The amendment fixed this loophole and granted the Overseers of the Poor the authority to remove any noncompliant blacks from the township. The Overseers was a state agency charged with the responsibility of regulating paupers; essentially, this law extended the authority of the Overseers to include African Americans. The Overseers of the Poor had the authority to remove paupers, but the law did not require them to do so. In addition, paupers could avoid removal by posting a bond.

Whereas the 1804 laws were aimed primarily at controlling the immigration of African Americans, the 1807 amendments defined the place of African Americans within the state. Many white residents of Ohio had migrated from the slave states

of Kentucky and Virginia, where it was widely believed that slavery had made African Americans incapable of enjoying the privileges of freedom. Whites who held these beliefs feared that social anarchy would accompany any form of black emancipation. At the same time, they recognized the value of black labor—provided the terms of employment placed whites in a position of authority. Ohio's constitution allowed indentured servitude as long as both parties entered into the agreement in a perfect state of freedom. This demonstrates that while white Ohioans rejected chattel slavery in their state, they accepted, and perhaps even embraced, contractually bound black labor.

The 1807 amendment reflected this ambivalence. The 1804 law had failed to slow the tide of black migration, and Ohio legislators like Beecher feared that the state would be overrun by black migrants. The 1807 amendment made immigration more prohibitive by binding new migrants to established citizens. The law should be viewed as an attempt to apply the regulatory procedures of a slave system to Ohio's free society. Ohio's black laws put an agency and citizens, rather than slaveholders, directly in charge of regulating the African American population in order to ensure the "good behavior" of its members.

In reality, the immigration restrictions of the 1807 law were seldom enforced. In addition, the Overseers of the Poor received little support for the forceful eviction of unregistered African Americans from the state. The African American population in Ohio grew substantially throughout the pre–Civil War years. Between 1800 and 1830 the state's black population grew from roughly 340 to over 9,500, a fact that has led historians to conclude that the Black Code was much harsher on paper than in practice. Nonetheless, the code made it clear that African Americans were not welcome and, perhaps even more significant, not trusted in Ohio. The laws put the burden of proof of freedom on African Americans and were indicative of the precarious position of blacks in Ohio.

The final provisions of the 1807 amendment further restricted the rights of African Americans in Ohio: "No black or mulatto person or persons shall hereafter be permitted to be sworn or give evidence in any court of record, or elsewhere, in this state, in any cause depending, or matter of controversy, where either party to the same is a white person." A white person could testify in an Ohio court against a black person, but a black person could testify only in a case that involved another African American; thus, blacks could not offer testimony for or against white defendants. By denying them complete access to the justice system, this final provision further defined African Americans as second-class citizens in Ohio. African Americans were the only group specifically excluded from the courts. As a result of this law, whites were not prosecuted for crimes committed against African Americans. Free African Americans vehemently complained about this restriction in newspapers such as the *Colored American* and during the reformist convention movement of the 1840s—a movement to pressure local governments and the federal government to enfranchise black men and protect the civil rights of African Americans. Blacks believed that this law, perhaps more than any other, left them susceptible to persecution and even reenslavement.

Audience

Despite the fact that few Ohioans likely read the actual text of the laws, the Black Code addressed all Ohio residents and visitors. The laws also targeted two specific audiences: First, because they were meant to deter black migration to the state, the laws addressed free black residents and migrants to Ohio. Second, they addressed Ohio's neighbors to the south. The laws defined the procedures for African American movement across the border between slavery and freedom and thus were directed at white Kentuckians and Virginians.

Impact

Ohio's Black Code had little immediate impact on the movement of African Americans into the state. The immigration laws were seldom enforced, and African Americans continued to migrate to the state. The black population in

Ohio grew steadily throughout the antebellum period, with the city of Cincinnati developing a vibrant African American community. However, the laws did make clear that white Ohioans did not welcome African Americans into their state, and the statutes legislating the second-class status of African Americans, particularly their inability to testify in court in cases involving whites, had a stronger impact. African Americans were effectively unable to use the law to protect themselves from assaults by white Americans. Blacks repeatedly expressed their hatred of this law in newspapers such as the *Colored American*.

The Ohio Black Code gained symbolic importance throughout the antebellum period. White abolitionists such as James Birney and John Rankin joined free African Americans in attacking the injustice of the laws. Salmon P. Chase, an American lawyer who would later serve on the U.S. Supreme Court, made legal efforts to define Ohio's free soil and undermine the Black Code. The movement to repeal the laws gained steam in the 1830s, when free African Americans, led by the American educator and diplomat John Mercer Langston, launched the State Convention of Colored Men to formally protest the laws. At these conventions, black leaders targeted education, suffrage, and the right to testify in court in their petitions to the state government. The Ohio government repealed the black laws of 1804 and 1807 in 1849. While black and white antislavery leaders applied pressure on the government, ultimately the repeal was the result of a political deal between the Democratic Party and the Free Soil Party. Chase brought these parties together, bargaining for his own election as senator and the repeal of the Black Code in return for the election of two Democrats as Ohio's congressional representatives. Immediately on the heels of this repeal, however, the federal government enacted the Fugitive Slave Act of 1850, requiring law-enforcement officials to arrest alleged fugitive slaves and greatly undermining the security of black freedom throughout the country.

Historians have long understood Ohio's Black Code as symptomatic of the racist undertones that tainted northern claims of antislavery ideals. Most famously, Eugene Berwanger argues that white midwesterners were against slavery *because* they were antiblack. Essentially, Berwanger makes the argument that midwesterners' antislavery sentiment stemmed from their racial prejudice. Thus, they sought to keep slavery isolated to the South, with the hope of its eventual termination, because they believed that the end of slavery would also lead to the elimination of the African American population from the country. Specialists in the field of African American history have similarly used Ohio's Black Code to highlight the national scope of racism in early America and the limits on black freedom. More recently, experts have looked at the limitations and contradictions of these laws. Historians such as Stephen Middleton point to the ways in which African Americans challenged the legality of the Black Code and even used it to protect their freedom. Paul Finkelman highlights the relative weakness of the Ohio's Black Code in light of other laws dealing with race in northern states

"Each and every free, able-bodied, white male citizen of the state, who is or shall be of the age of eighteen and under the age of forty-five years, except as hereinafter excepted, shall severally and respectively be enrolled in the militia."

(An Act to Organize and Discipline the Militia)

"From and after the first day of June next [1804], no black or mulatto person, shall be permitted to settle or reside in this state, unless he or she shall first produce a fair certificate from some court with the United States, of his or her actual freedom, which certificate shall be attested by the clerk of said court."

(An Act to Regulate Black and Mulatto Persons)

"No person or persons' residents of this state, shall be permitted to hire, or in any way employ any black or mulatto person, unless such black or mulatto person shall have one of the certificates as aforesaid."

(An Act to Regulate Black and Mulatto Persons)

"In case any person or persons, his or their agents, claiming any black or mulatto person that now are, or hereafter may be in this state, may apply, upon making satisfactory proof that such black or mulatto person or persons is the property of him or her ... the associate judge or justice is thereby empowered ... to arrest such black or mulatto person or persons."

(An Act to Regulate Black and Mulatto Persons)

"No negro or mulatto person shall be permitted to ... settle within this state, unless such negro or mulatto person shall, within twenty days thereafter, enter into bond ... in the penal sum of five hundred dollars."

(An Act to Amend the Last Named Act "An Act to Regulate Black and Mulatto Persons")

"No black or mulatto person or persons shall hereafter be permitted to be sworn or give evidence in any court of record, or elsewhere, in this state, in any cause depending, or matter of controversy, where either party to the same is a white person."

(An Act to Amend the Last Named Act "An Act to Regulate Black and Mulatto Persons") and the lack of enforcement as evidence of white Ohioans' ambivalence about the presence of African Americans in the state. Still, much work remains to be done on the social and cultural impact of the Black Code outside of the legal system.

See also Fugitive Slave Act of 1793; Fugitive Slave Act of 1850; Black Code of Mississippi (1865).

Further Reading

■ Articles

Finkelman, Paul. "The Strange Career of Race Discrimination in Antebellum Ohio." *Case Western Reserve Law Review* 55, no. 2 (Winter 2004): 1–26.

■ Books

Berwanger, Eugene H. *Frontier against Slavery: Western Anti-Negro Prejudice and the Slavery Extension Controversy.* Urbana: University of Illinois Press, 1967.

Cayton, Andrew R. L., and Stuart D. Hobbs, eds. *The Center of a Great Empire: The Ohio Country in the Early Republic.* Athens: Ohio University Press, 2005.

Litwack, Leon F. *North of Slavery: The Negro in the Free States, 1790–1860.* Chicago: University of Chicago Press, 1961.

Middleton, Stephen. *The Black Laws: Race and the Legal Process in Early Ohio.* Athens: Ohio University Press, 2005.

Taylor, Nikki M. *Frontiers of Freedom: Cincinnati's Black Community, 1802–1868.* Athens: Ohio University Press, 2005.

■ Web Sites

"The African-American Experience in Ohio, 1850–1920." American Memory Collection, Library of Congress "American Memory Collection" Web site.
  http://memory.loc.gov/ammem/award97/ohshtml/aaeohome.html.

—Matthew Salafia

Questions for Further Study

1. Typically, the phrase *Black Code* is used to refer to the legal and social system that kept African Americans in subservient positions in the South after the Reconstruction period following the Civil War. Using this document in connection with the discussion surrounding the Ku Klux Klan Act, discuss the similarities and differences between the post-Reconstruction Black Codes and the Ohio Black Code.

2. In what way did the attitudes of the southern slave states makes themselves felt in Ohio, a nominally free state?

3. While the Ohio Black Code legislated the second-class status of African Americans, it at least afforded some measure of protection to African Americans and was not as severe as the laws in other states. Which provisions of the Ohio Black Code represented at least some measure of accommodation to African Americans? What steps were taken by individuals to lessen the severity of the Ohio Black Code?

4. Do you agree with Eugene Berwanger's thesis that midwesterners wanted to isolate slavery in the South because in that way African Americans would eventually disappear—thus suggesting that racism was as endemic in the North as it was in the South?

5. What effect did the Fugitive Slave Act of 1850 have in undermining the security of African Americans, despite the repeal of the Ohio Black Code in 1849?

OHIO BLACK CODE

♦ An Act to Organize and Discipline the Militia

Section 1. Be it enacted by the General Assembly of the State of Ohio, That each and every free, able-bodied, white male citizen of the state, who is or shall be of the age of eighteen and under the age of forty-five years, except as hereinafter excepted, shall severally and respectively be enrolled in the militia; by the captain or commanding officer of the company within whose bounds such citizens shall reside, within twenty days next after such residence.

♦ An Act to Regulate Black and Mulatto Persons

Section 1. Be it enacted by the General Assembly of the State of Ohio, that from and after the first day of June next, no black or mulatto person, shall be permitted to settle or reside in this state, unless he or she shall first produce a fair certificate from some court with the United States, of his or her actual freedom, which certificate shall be attested by the clerk of said court, and the seal thereof annexed thereto, by the said clerk.

Section 2. That every black or mulatto person residing within this state, on or before the first day of June, one thousand eight hundred and four, shall enter his or her name together with the name or names of his or her children, in the clerk's office in the county in which he, she, or they reside, which shall be entered on record by said clerk, and thereafter the clerk's certificate of such record shall pay to the clerk twelve and an half cents: Provided nevertheless, That nothing in this act contained shall bar the lawful claim to any black or mulatto person.

Section 3. That no person or persons' residents of this state, shall be permitted to hire, or in any way employ any black or mulatto person, unless such black or mulatto person shall have one of the certificates as aforesaid, under pain of forfeiting and paying any sum not less than ten nor more than fifty dollars, at the discretion of the court, for every such offense, one half thereof for the use of the informer, and the other half for the use of the state; and shall moreover pay to the owner, if any there be, of such black or mulatto person, the sum of fifty cents for every day he, she or they shall in otherwise employ, harbor or be recoverable before any court having cognizance thereof.

Section 4. That if any person or persons shall harbor or secret any black or mulatto person, the property of any person whatever, or shall in anywise hinder or prevent the lawful owner or owners from retaking and possessing his or her black or mulatto servant or servants, shall, upon conviction thereof, by indictment or information, be fined in any sum not less than ten nor more than fifty dollars, at the discretion of the court, one-half thereof for the use of the informer and the other half for the use of the state.

Section 5. That every black or mulatto person who shall come to reside in this state with such certificates as is required in the first section of this act, shall, within two years, have the same recorded in the clerk's office, in the county in which he or she means to reside, for which he or she shall pay to the clerk twelve and an half cents, and the clerk shall give him or her a certificate of such record.

Section 6. That in case any person or persons, his or their agent or agents, claiming any black or mulatto person that now are, or hereafter may be in this state, may apply, upon making satisfactory proof that such black or mulatto person or persons is the property of him or her who applies to any associate judge or justice of the pace within this state, the associate judge or justice is thereby empowered and required, by his precept, to direct the sheriff or constable to arrest such black or mulatto person or persons, and deliver the same in the county or township where such officers shall reside, to the claimant or claimants or his or their agents, for which service the sheriff or constable shall receive such compensation as they are entitled to receive in other cases for similar services.

Section 7. That any person or persons who shall attempt to remove or shall remove from this state, or who shall aid and assist in removing, contrary to the provisions of this act, any black or mulatto person or persons, without first proving as herein before directed, that he, she or they, is or are legally entitled so to do, shall on conviction thereof, before any court having cognizance of the same, forfeit and pay the sum of one thousand dollars, one-half to the use of the informer and the other half to the use of the state to be recovered by action of debt, *qui tam*, or indictment, and moreover be liable to the action of the party injured.

♦ An Act to Amend the Last Named Act "An Act to Regulate Black and Mulatto Persons"

Section 1. Be it enacted by the General Assembly of the State of Ohio, that no negro or mulatto person shall be permitted to emigrate into, and settle within this state, unless such negro or mulatto person shall, within twenty days thereafter, enter into bond with two or more freehold sureties, in the penal sum of five hundred dollars, before the clerk of the court of common pleas of the county in which such negro or mulatto person may wish to reside, (to be approved of by the clerk), conditioned for the good behavior of such negro or mulatto, and moreover to pay for the support of such person, in case he, she or they should thereafter be found within any township in this state, unable to support themselves. And if any negro or mulatto person shall migrate in this state, and not comply with the provisions of this act, it shall be the duty of the overseer of the poor of the township where such negro or mulatto person may be found to remove immediately such black or mulatto person, in the same manner as is required in the case of paupers.

Section 2. That it shall be the duty of the clerk, before whom such bond may be given as given as aforesaid, to file the same in his office, and give a certificate thereof to such negro or mulatto person; and the said clerk shall be entitled to receive the sum of one dollar for the bond and certificate aforesaid, on the delivery of the certificate.

Section 3. That if any person, being a resident of this state, shall employ, harbor or conceal any such negro or mulatto person aforesaid, contrary to the provisions of the first section of this act, any person offending shall forfeit and pay, for every such offence, any sum not exceeding one hundred dollars, the one half to the informer, and the other half for the use of the poor of the township in which such person may reside, to be recovered by action of debt, before any court having competent jurisdiction; and moreover be liable for the maintenance and support of such negro or mulatto, provided be, she or they shall become unable to support themselves.

Section 4. That no black or mulatto person or persons shall hereafter be permitted to be sworn or give evidence in any court of record, or elsewhere, in this state, in any cause depending, or matter of controversy, where either party to the same is a white person.

Section 5. That so much of the act, entitled "an act to regulate black and mulatto persons," as is contrary to this act, together with the sixth section thereof, be and the same is hereby repealed. This act shall take effect and be in force from and after the first day of April next.

Glossary

qui tam	a legal instrument whereby an individual who assists a prosecution can receive all or part of the monetary penalty imposed

PETER WILLIAMS, JR.'S "ORATION ON THE ABOLITION OF THE SLAVE TRADE"

"By [education], and similar methods, with divine assistance they assailed the dark dungeon of slavery."

Overview

On January 1, 1808, as part of the forenoon service at the African Church in New York City, Peter Williams, Jr., a young, free African American abolitionist, gave an address entitled "An Oration on the Abolition of the Slave Trade." The church was celebrating the implementation that day of a law passed the year before, banning the external slave trade in the United States. The day's events included two services with prayers, hymns, and orations as well as a reading of the 1807 act. Williams's oration tells some of the history of the African slave trade and the sorrows of slavery, but it also praises God for hearing the slaves' prayers and expresses gratitude to all the white abolitionists who had been striving for the end of the Atlantic slave trade and emancipation for African American slaves. After delivery of this oration, very little time was wasted before Williams was asked to put together a copy for publication. The result was one of the earliest publications on abolition by an African American.

Context

When the British colonies in North America declared their independence from the mother country in 1776, every colony except Rhode Island had, to some extent, a system of slave labor. During and shortly after the time of the Revolution, many northern states decided to adopt programs of gradual emancipation for their slaves. However, when the Constitutional Convention met in 1787, there was debate about whether the legislative branch of government, which would have power over trade, would be able to prohibit the importation of slaves into the country. The southern states would have none of this, and the northern states knew that if Congress were allowed to prohibit the slave trade right away, many of the slave states would not ratify the Constitution. Thus, a provision was made for keeping open the Atlantic slave trade until at least the year 1808 (Article I, Section 9). This served as a compromise between slaving interests and their opponents: The trade would be banned,

but not for twenty years—giving the slave states ample time to build up their labor supply from sources outside the country and to develop a self-sustaining system. Although it was not the best news for southern states, which still earned their economic livelihood through agriculture based upon slave labor, it was better than having the importation of slaves prohibited outright.

Many people opposed the Atlantic slave trade because of the manner in which it was conducted. Africans to be auctioned in the Americas were crowded into a ship so tightly packed that they could not turn over when they slept. The Middle Passage, as the trip across the Atlantic was called, was an ordeal in itself, as sickness was prevalent, conditions horrible, malnutrition rampant, and fresh air and exercise rare. Indeed, every so often one of these human cargo—for they were treated more like cargo than humans—would cast himself overboard rather than see what might lie at the trip's end.

Philanthropists and humanitarians found this trade abhorrent and worked to stop it. Northern states began to pass their own laws against the external slave trade, and New York itself, the home of Peter Williams, passed legislation ending the overseas importation of slaves into the state in 1788. The pressure of abolitionist groups upon President Thomas Jefferson caused him to recommend strongly in his 1806 year-end address that Congress adopt the bill that Senator Stephen Roe Bradley of Vermont had introduced the year before, designed to ensure the end of the Atlantic slave trade to the United States as soon as the Constitution would allow. On the second day of March in 1807, Congress passed the act that would prohibit the importation of slaves into the United States, effective January 1, 1808. On the very next day President Jefferson signed it into law.

This formal prohibition was hailed as a milestone in abolitionist and antislavery circles. It was tantamount to national recognition of the evils of the slave trade and perhaps slavery itself. The day it took effect in 1808, African Americans and white abolitionists alike celebrated all over the North; New York, with its great numbers of freed slaves and free blacks, was a particularly festive place to be. Nevertheless, an illicit international slave trade persisted in the United States wherever dealers could make a sale, and the legal buying and selling of slaves across state lines continued un-

Time Line

1787

- The Constitutional Convention at Philadelphia adopts a clause, in Article I, Section 9, that prohibits Congress from restricting the external slave trade until 1808.

1788

- New York State passes a law banning the importation of slaves into the state from outside the country.

1796

- Peter Williams, Sr., helps found, in New York City, the institution that would become the African Methodist Episcopal Zion Church.

1799

- New York adopts a policy of gradual emancipation for all the slaves in the state, to be complete by July 1827.

1805

- **December**
Senator Stephen Roe Bradley of Vermont introduces a bill in Congress to ban U.S. participation in the external slave trade, starting in 1808.

1806

- **December**
In his annual message, President Thomas Jefferson urges Congress to enact the ban.

1807

- **March**
Congress passes Bradley's bill, and President Jefferson signs it into law.

- **March 25**
The Abolition Act of Great Britain prohibits the slave trade on British ships throughout the empire.

1808

- **January 1**
The law banning the external slave trade in the United States goes into effect; Peter Williams, Jr., gives his "Oration on the Abolition of the Slave Trade" at the New York African Church, and publishes it later in the month

abated in the parts of the country where slavery still existed. Not until the formal end of slavery, with the passage of the Thirteenth Amendment in December 1865, would all slave trade, internal and external, legal or not, end.

About the Author

Peter Williams, Jr., was born around 1780, in Brunswick, New Jersey. His mother, Mary Durham, was an indentured servant from Saint Kitts, and his father, Peter Williams, Sr., was a slave who purchased his freedom in 1785. Williams, Sr., had fought on the side of the Patriots in the Revolutionary War and instilled in his son a love for the nation and its government. The family moved to New York, where a growing number of free blacks were living. There the elder Williams sold tobacco, while young Peter attended the African Free School and had private tutors. In 1796, Williams, Sr., helped found the first African Methodist Episcopal Zion Church in New York.

As an adult, Williams helped in the tobacco business and kept his father's books. He also began to participate in activism against slavery and joined the Episcopal Church. On the first day of the new year in 1808, the young man delivered "An Oration on the Abolition of the Slave Trade" at the African Church in New York, in order to celebrate the occasion of the official end of the legal Atlantic slave trade of Africans. Within a week, Williams was asked to provide a copy for publication.

In 1818, frustrated with the segregation in the Episcopal church he attended in New York (they could use the church only at certain times of the week), Williams established Saint Philip's African Church, which soon relocated to the village of Harlem in the north of Manhattan. He was consecrated as an Episcopal deacon and, in 1826, was ordained as the first black priest in the New York diocese (the second in the United States, after Absalom Jones). Although other Episcopal clergymen did not show Williams the customary respect and the congregation was not allowed into to the diocesan convention, Williams's church continued to grow and came to include several future notable abolitionists, like James McCune Smith and Alexander Crummell.

Williams was very active in different societies for abolition and for black education and relief, including the New York African Society for Mutual Relief and the American Anti-Slavery Society. The year after he was ordained a priest, Williams cofounded the *Freedom's Journal*, the first African American newspaper in the United States, to which some of the leading black writers and activists of the day submitted work. In 1830 he helped organize the Philadelphia National Negro Convention's first session. He founded the Phoenix Society in 1833 to further the education of African Americans. The society aided both children and adults, enrolling them in classes, programs, lectures, and apprenticeships as well as putting together libraries for their use, providing self-improvement groups, and supplying clothing to children who could not otherwise participate.

In July of 1834, as part of a series of area assaults on New York abolitionists, African Americans, and their organizations, Saint Philip's Church was attacked by a mob and damaged. Soon thereafter, Williams received a letter from his bishop advising him to resign from the Anti-Slavery Society for the good of the Episcopal Church and the community. This Williams did, in a public letter, humbly and respectfully. Throughout the rest of his life Williams supported and encouraged education for African Americans and the end of their oppression in all its forms across the nation. He died in New York City on October 17, 1840, a respected and beloved member of the community, remembered for his activism on behalf of African Americans and for his moral courage.

Explanation and Analysis of the Document

At the start of his oration, Williams exhorts his audience to be joyful that the day has come that the Atlantic slave trade—"this inhuman branch of commerce"—has ended and to be grateful to God and to all those who had worked to help it happen, along with those who would continue to work on behalf of black Americans. He also paints a picture of what Africans experienced when ripped from their homes and families and how societies within Africa had changed because of the slave trade. By juxtaposing the joyous news with the mournful and oppressive conditions of those who had been victims of the international slave trade, Williams highlights the gratitude and joy of those who can now celebrate its end.

In the first three paragraphs, Williams introduces the theme of happiness, which "must be extremely consonant to every philanthropic heart." He states that "to us, Africans, and descendants of Africans, this period is deeply interesting." "We are the ones," he goes on, "who have really borne the oppression of the slave trade on our backs; we have been the victims." For this, he notes, African Americans "owe a debt of gratitude to those who have steadily worked for the end of the Atlantic slave trade."

Next Williams describes the history of the slave trade, beginning with a depiction of the Africans before the intrusion of the Europeans on the western coast of Africa: simple, honest, hospitable, affectionate, happy, and close to nature, in a sort of paradise. This depiction may reflect a certain amount of naïveté; on the part of Williams, since Africans had practiced slavery in one form or another for centuries, namely, in the form of debt slavery and slavery as a consequence of war. Or the depiction may simply serve to provide a more dramatic contrast between the earlier West Africa, which practiced a relatively tame form of slavery, and the later West Africa, which seemed to cater to European desires upon its introduction of the economically driven overseas slave trade.

Starting with Christopher Columbus, he traces the history of "civilized man" in Europe and the way in which greed led people to cross the ocean and put the Native Americans to work for them in the mines. In this they "violated the

African captives leaping off a slave ship near the coast of Africa in the 1700s (AP/Wide World Photos)

sacred injunctions of the gospel." When these first settlers found the Native Americans unsuited for such heavy labor, they sought some other way to carry on the mining and other work. The means was found in the African slave trade.

Begun on a regular basis by the Genoese in 1517, according to Williams (following William Robertson's *History of America*, 1777), the slave trade "has increased to an astonishing, and almost incredible degree." The Africans to be sold were obtained at first by surprising and overwhelming coastal towns. Once the coastal towns realized what was happening, the people moved inland, joining with their fellows to defend their whole society. The intruders knew that if they could not separate the Africans, they could not capture any more slaves. So, feigning "a friendly countenance," they offered the people gifts and "gaudy trifles." By giving such gifts, they also gave them a spirit of avarice. Avarice, Williams laments in elaborate rhetoric, was the downfall of Greece, of Rome, and now of Africa.

Because of the spread of greed, the Africans started to turn on each other, make war on each other, and enforce stricter laws, since, according to the deal struck with the

"[The Slave Trade's] baneful footsteps are marked with blood; its infectious breath spreads war and desolation; and its train is composed of the complicated miseries, of cruel and unceasing bondage."

(Paragraph 4)

"A spectacle so truly distressing, is sufficient to blow into a blaze, the most latent spark of humanity: but, the adamantine heart of avarice, dead to every sensation of pity, regards not the voice of the sufferers, but hastily drives them to market for sale."

(Paragraph 16)

"[The African slaves'] lives, imbittered by reflection, anticipation, and present sorrows, they feel burthensome; and death, (whose dreary mansions appal the stoutest hearts) they view as their only shelter."

(Paragraph 17)

"By [education], and similar methods, with divine assistance they assailed the dark dungeon of slavery; shattered its rugged wall, and enlarging thousands of the captives, bestowed on them the blessings of civil society."

(Paragraph 29)

"Notwithstanding [our benefactors'] endeavours, they have yet remaining, from interest and prejudice, a number of opposers. These, carefully watching for every opportunity to injure the cause, will not fail to augment the smallest defects in our lives and conversation; and reproach our benefactors with them.... Let us, therefore, by a steady and upright deportment, by a strict obedience and respect to the laws of the land, form an invulnerable bulwark against the shafts of malice."

(Paragraph 31)

Europeans, they could keep getting their trifles in return for prisoners of war and convicts. As bad as this system already was—in that Africa had always had slaves as the result of debts and wars—it was made worse by the greed that encouraged the African people to engage in gratuitous wars with one another, to kidnap and sell one another to the slave traders.

Here Williams tells how the best rulers in Africa were made into tyrants, raiding the villages of their own allies in search of people to sell to the traders. Using rich imagery of the "shrieks of the women; the cries of the children," he conjures up an image of a town ravaged by war—a war started with a neighbor by a ruler who used to be a friend. He describes the different people affected by the battle, the fire that would settle upon the town in order to force them out. Whoever did not fall would go with the ally-turned-enemy as a captive to be sold to the slave traders. Aware that most people with any sort of heart would react with sympathy to the evocative emotional scenes he conjures up, Williams writes that he knows that those with the "adamantine heart of avarice, dead to every sensation of pity" would not be moved at all. Avarice made these scenes, and avarice would continue to harden and make cold the hearts of those who benefit.

Moving on to the trader's ship, he vividly describes what the people in the slave ships must have felt as they, "with aching hearts, bid adieu, to every prospect of joy and comfort." And here, on this journey, they know that "though defeated in the contest for liberty, their magnanimous souls scorn the gross indignity, and choose death in preference to slavery." They would rather die than become slaves. Williams turns to those in the audience who had come from Africa themselves, saying that they are even better qualified to describe the scenes of wretched parting than he. They know what it is like. But for those who are descendants of Africans, he begins to portray, so they can imagine, the picture of their misery on the slave ship and the forced parting of families once they had arrived at their destination: "See the parting tear, rolling down their fallen cheeks: hear the parting sigh, die on their quivering lips."

By ending the section on slavery with this image of the separation of families, Williams brings the audience back into the present. Although he does not say so specifically, the image is one that could be applied to arrival at port after bringing slaves to America or to the auction block in any town that deals in the internal slave trade. This type of separation would still happen as long as there was buying and selling of slaves in the United States. But this day, at least, they could celebrate one step in the right direction. With this image, Williams brings the audience back to the joyful occasion without letting them forget the work that was still ahead.

"Rejoice, Oh! Africans! ... Rejoice, Oh, ye descendants of Africans!" Williams proclaims. There no longer would be blood shed on African soil for the sake of the avarice of Americans. With eloquent repetition of the phrases "Rejoice!" and "No longer shall," Williams enumerates the atrocities committed by those engaged in the international slave trade—atrocities that would "no longer" happen on African soil. For that, Africans and anyone with "the smallest drop of African blood" should rejoice!

Since there is cause to rejoice, there is also cause to express gratitude. First, Williams prays in thanks to God for hearing the anguished voices of the Africans and for calling those forward who would help stop the slave trade. He thanks God for those who fought in the Revolutionary War and espoused the words of the Declaration of Independence (slightly misquoted) "that all men are created equal; that they are endowed by their Creator with certain unalienable rights; among which are life, liberty, and the pursuit of happiness." He thanks God for listening "when

the bleeding African, lifting his fetters, exclaimed, 'am I not a man and a brother[?]'" and sending help his way.

Here Williams starts to name some of the warriors against avarice—"they dared to despise the emoluments of ill gotten wealth, and to sacrifice much of their temporal interests at the shrine of benevolence"—and against slavery. The benefactors he names are John Woolman, Anthony Benezet, and William Wilberforce. John Woolman (1720–1772) was a Quaker abolitionist who traveled over America, exhorting "the denomination of friends" to give up slavery and to rally against it, which they eventually did. Anthony Benezet (1713–1774) believed that all people truly were equal, and because of this belief he founded the first school for African Americans in Philadelphia. A French-born Quaker, he was also an abolitionist as well as the founder of the first public girls' school in America. William Wilberforce (1759–1833), an abolitionist member of the British Parliament, helped put into effect the Abolition Act of Great Britain, which became law on March 25, 1807. This act, like the law passed in the United States earlier that same month, prohibited the carrying of slaves for trade on British ships, effectively limiting if not completely ending the Atlantic slave trade for the British and their colonies.

These are not the only benefactors of the African Americans, Williams asserts. "I have given but a few specimens of a countless number, and no more than the rude outlines of the beneficence of these." Here, the published version (accessible via the University of Nebraska Web site) appends a note naming also the Reverend Mr. Thomas Clarkson (1760–1846), an English abolitionist and Anglican deacon who was a great influence on Wilberforce. Williams begins to speak of the particular endeavors of the benefactors of the African American, both slave and free, basically stating that they had left no legal action untried or avenue untraveled. They had set up schools, worked to end slavery in several states, and helped former slaves make their way in the world with good virtues.

For all this, for the day "which we now celebrate," Williams points out that Africans and descendants of Africans owe these benefactors their utmost gratitude: They should "return to them from the altars of our hearts, the fragrant incense of incessant gratitude." This phrase recalls Psalm 141, verse 2—"let my prayer rise before you as incense"— used in the Episcopal liturgy, showing the influence of the church on Williams's oratory.

Williams closes with an exhortation to his fellow African Americans to learn as much as they can, to follow the laws of their country, and to "form an invulnerable bulwark against the shafts of malice" that others can use to hurt them. This is particularly important in order to keep their benefactors from criticism by their opponents. If anything African Americans do gives any fuel to the "opposers," it would be a poor thanks for all the help the benefactors have given them.

The printed version appends an explanation from Peter Williams that he understands there are some people who would not believe that a young African American had written this oration himself, so he would add here the certifications of four different white men, including Bishop Benjamin Moore, to vouch for his authorship. All four attest to the authenticity of the publication and to its author.

Audience

The audience gathered on January 1, 1808, in the African Church of New York likely consisted of church members as well as guests who had come to celebrate the ban on the external slave trade. Many of the people were African American, as Williams indicates in his speech—some even with the memory of being taken from Africa and brought to America to be slaves. No doubt the audience also included some of the white benefactors of whom Williams speaks, along with other abolitionists and sympathizers.

After its publication, the oration gained a wider audience. Abolitionist societies would have made sure of this. Many abolitionists held the opinion that the end of the external slave trade would lead to the emancipation of all slaves. The publication of this oration advanced the cause of abolitionists by demonstrating the intelligence of African Americans and by convincing skeptics that freed slaves, when educated properly—as Williams had been—would be an asset to society rather than a burden.

Impact

Not more than a week had passed before Peter Williams received a letter urging him to provide a copy of the oration, as "[The Committee of arrangements] apprehend a usefulness will arise from its publication." According to this letter, the reception of the oration was warm, and the audience was pleased. This committee hoped that the publication would be "a means of enlightening the minds of some, and of promoting the great work of emancipation, as it relates to the African race in general, who are still held in bondage in the United States, and in other parts of the world." As one of the first publications on abolition by an African American, the oration continues to hold a place of honor in African American history.

The prohibition of the slave trade had a positive, if not ideal, impact on the practice of slavery where it still existed. No longer did a slave master have a steady supply of slaves coming in from Africa and the West Indies. This limit to the supply chain forced slave masters to improve their treatment of slaves and their children—to treat them at least as well as they did their valued livestock—or else to pay higher prices for slaves traded internally. Cutting off the ready supply caused the price of slaves to increase, thus giving slaveholders an incentive to keep their slaves healthy, if not happy. It became more difficult to replace a slave who died or became incapacitated. Thus, slaveholders had to rethink their practices.

Of course, the end of the legal external slave trade was only a step. A large area of the country continued practicing slavery, even in the North (though Peter Williams's home state, New York, had adopted a policy of gradual emancipation in 1799, to be completed by July 4, 1827). Much

discrimination and prejudice against free African Americans also persisted in the North. The abolitionists simply kept going, trying to raise awareness—particularly among the increasingly oblivious northerners—about slavery and its evils. Unfortunately, in 1808 abolitionist societies were not quite ready to take on the proslavery arguments coming from the South. These societies had not come together yet to present a united front against the proslavery forces, with solid counterarguments, and so they did not have the power necessary to adequately fight these arguments. This would come about only over the next several decades. There were others in the wider antislavery movement who were not necessarily abolitionists but who were for eventual emancipation and against the spread of slavery to new areas of the country. When the country began to ponder whether territories added to United States would allow slavery, these other antislavery forces began to lend credence to some of the abolitionist arguments against slavery and its spread, as well as add new arguments. Thus, both abolitionist and antislavery forces were strengthened during this debate over the introduction of slavery into new territories (started in earnest because of Missouri's application for statehood and the resulting Missouri Compromise of 1820); it forced them to define themselves as a unified movement. Until this happened, however, abolitionist societies had limited power to persuade many in the North, much less the South, that slavery should be abolished in the entire nation.

In the early decades of the nineteenth century, abolitionist societies came together especially to educate freed slaves and poor African Americans and help them support themselves and their families. By educating African Americans, these societies sought to make them more acceptable in an overwhelmingly white North. This campaign succeeded, but only to a limited extent. Even Peter Williams himself, an educated, respected, and active abolitionist, was denied admittance to the 1806 Convention of Abolitionist Societies in Philadelphia because he was not white. There was still a great deal of work to be done.

See also John Woolman's "Some Considerations on the Keeping of Negroes" (1754); Slavery Clauses in the U.S. Constitution (1787); *Twelve Years a Slave: Narrative of Solomon Northup* (1853).

Further Reading

■ Books

Finkelman, Paul. *Slavery and the Founders: Race and Liberty in the Age of Jefferson*. 2nd ed. Armonk, N.Y.: M. E. Sharpe, 2001.

Foner, Philip S., and Robert James Branham. *Lift Every Voice: African American Oratory, 1787–1900*. Tuscaloosa: University of Alabama Press, 1998.

Horton, James O. *In Hope of Liberty: Culture, Community, and Protest Among Northern Free Blacks, 1700–1860*. New York: Oxford University Press, 1998.

■ **Web Sites**

"Peter Williams, Jr." *Slavery in New York: Life Stories—Profiles of Black New Yorkers during Slavery and Emancipation.* New-York Historical Society Web site.
    http://www.slaveryinnewyork.org/PDFs/Life_Stories.pdf.

Williams, Peter, Jr. "An Oration on the Abolition of the Slave Trade; Delivered in the African Church in the City of New-York, January 1, 1808." DigitalCommons@University of Nebraska—Lincoln Web site.
    http://digitalcommons.unl.edu/cgi/viewcontentcgi?article=101 5&context=etas.

—Angela M. Alexander

Questions for Further Study

1. Explain the difference between the abolition of slavery and the abolition of the slave trade.

2. How did the constitutional provisions for legally ending the slave trade represent a compromise between northern and southern interests? Why did the free states of the North acquiesce in part to southern demands to continue the slave trade?

3. Compare and contrast Williams's oration with David Walker's *Appeal to the Coloured Citizens of the World* (1829). Do the two documents have different emphases? Different tones? Explain.

4. According to Williams, what was the effect of the slave trade on Africa? How, for example, did it lead to the corruption of the people and their rulers?

5. The international slave trade was abolished, but that did not entirely eliminate the movement of people for the purposes of slavery. How did Americans respond to the abolition of the slave trade? How did an incident such as that discussed in the entry *United States v. Amistad* (1841) indicate that the horrors of the slave trade had not entirely ended?

PETER WILLIAMS, JR.'S "ORATION ON THE ABOLITION OF THE SLAVE TRADE"

Fathers, Brethren, and Fellow Citizens,

At this auspicious moment, I felicitate you, on the abolition of the Slave-Trade. This inhuman branch of commerce, which, for some centuries past, has been carried on to a considerable extent, is, by the singular interposition of Divine Providence, this day extinguished. An event so important, so pregnant with happy consequences, must be extremely consonant to every philanthropic heart.

But to us, Africans, and descendants of Africans, this period is deeply interesting. We have felt, sensibly felt, the sad effects of this abominable traffic. It has made, if not ourselves, our forefathers and kinsmen its unhappy victims; and pronounced on them, and their posterity, the sentence of perpetual slavery. But benevolent men, have voluntarily stepped forward, to obviate the consequences of this injustice and barbarity. They have striven, assiduously, to restore our natural rights; to guaranty them from fresh innovations; to furnish us with necessary information; and to stop the source from whence our evils have flowed.

The fruits of these laudable endeavors have long been visible; each moment they appear more conspicuous; and this day has produced an event which shall ever be memorable and glorious in the annals of history. We are now assembled to celebrate this momentous era; to recognize the beneficial influences of humane exertions; and by suitable demonstrations of joy, thanksgiving, and gratitude, to return to our heavenly Father, and to our earthly benefactors, our sincere acknowledgements.

Review, for a moment, my brethren, the history of the Slave Trade, engendered in the foul recesses of the sordid mind, the unnatural monster inflicted gross evils on the human race. Its baneful footsteps are marked with blood; its infectious breath spreads war and desolation; and its train is composed of the complicated miseries, of cruel and unceasing bondage.

Before the enterprising spirit of European genius explored the western coast of Africa, the state of our forefathers was a state of simplicity, innocence, and contentment. Unskilled in the arts of dissimulation, their bosoms were the seats of confidence; and their lips were the organs of truth. Strangers to the refinements of civilized society, they followed with implicit obedience, the (simple) dictates of nature. Peculiarly observant of hospitality, they offered a place of refreshment to the weary, and an asylum to the unfortunate. Ardent in their affections, their minds were susceptible of the warmest emotions of love, friendship, and gratitude.

Although unacquainted with the diversified luxuries and amusements of civilized nations, they enjoyed some singular advantages, from the bountiful hand of nature; and from their own innocent and amiable manners, which rendered them a happy people. But, alas! this delightful picture has long since vanished; the angel of bliss has deserted their dwelling; and the demon of indescribable misery, has rioted, uncontrolled, on the fair fields of our ancestors.

After Columbus unfolded to civilized man, the vast treasures of this western world, the desire of gain, which had chiefly induced the first colonists of America, to cross the waters of the Atlantic, surpassing the bounds of reasonable acquisition, violated the sacred injunctions of the gospel, frustrated the designs of the pious and humane; and enslaving the harmless aborigines, compelled them to drudge in the mines.

The severities of this employment was so insupportable to men who were unaccustomed to fatigue, that, according to Robertson's "History of America," upwards of nine hundred thousand, were destroyed in the space of fifteen years, on the island of Hispaniola. A consumption so rapid, must, in a short period, have deprived them of the instruments of labour; had not the same genius, which first produced it, found out another method to obtain them. This was no other than the importation of slaves, from the coast of Africa.

The Genoese made the first regular importation, in the year 1517, by virtue of a patent granted by Charles, of Austria, to a Flemish favorite; since which, this commerce has increased to an astonishing, and almost incredible degree.

After the manner of ancient piracy, descents were first made on the African coast; the towns bordering on the ocean were surprised, and a number of the inhabitants carried into slavery.

Alarmed at these depredations, the natives fled to the interior; and there united to secure themselves from the common foe. But the subtle invaders, were not easily deterred from their purpose. Their experience, corroborated by historical testimony, convinced them, that this spirit of unity, would baffle every violent attempt; and that the most powerful method to dissolve it, would be to diffuse in them, the same avaricious disposition which they themselves possessed; and to afford them the means of gratifying it, by ruining each other. Fatal engine: fatal thou hast proved to man in all ages: where the greatest violence has proved ineffectual, thy undermining principles have wrought destruction. By thy deadly power, the strong Grecian arm, which bid the world defiance, fell nerveless; by thy potent attacks, the solid pillars of Roman grandeur shook to their base; and, Oh! Africans! by this parent of the Slave Trade, this grandsire of misery, the mortal blow was struck, which crushed the peace and happiness of our country. Affairs now assumed a different aspect; the appearances of war were changed into the most amicable pretensions; presents apparently inestimable were made; and all the bewitching and alluring wiles of the seducer, were practised. The harmless African, taught to believe a friendly countenance, the sure token of a corresponding heart, soon disbanded his fears, and evinced a favourable disposition, towards his flattering enemies.

Thus the foe, obtaining an intercourse, by a dazzling display of European finery, bewildered their simple understandings, and corrupted their morals. Mutual agreements were then made; the Europeans were to supply the Africans, with those gaudy trifles which so strongly affected them; and the Africans in return, were to grant the Europeans, their prisoners of war, and convicts, as slaves. These stipulations naturally tending to delude the mind, answered the two-fold purpose of enlarging their criminal code, and of exciting incessant war, at the same time, that it furnished a specious pretext, for the prosecution of this inhuman traffic. Bad as this may appear, had it prescribed the bounds of injustice, millions of unhappy victims might have still been spared. But, extending widely beyond measure, and without control, large additions of slaves were made, by kidnapping, and the most unpalliated seizures.

Trace the past scenes of Africa, and you will manifestly perceive, these flagrant violations of human rights. The prince who once delighted in the happiness of his people; who felt himself bound by a sacred contract to defend their persons and property; was turned into their tyrant and scourge: he, who once strove to preserve peace, and good understanding with the different nations; who never unsheathed his sword, but in the cause of justice; at the signal of a slave ship, assembled his warriors, and rushed furiously upon his unsuspecting friends. What a scene does that town now present, which a few moments past was the abode of tranquillity. At the approach of the foe, alarm and confusion pervade every part; horror and dismay are depicted on every countenance; the aged chief starting from his couch, calls forth his men, to repulse the hostile invader: all ages obey the summons; feeble youth, and decrepit age, join the standard; while the foe, to effect his purpose, fires the town.

Now, with unimaginable terror the battle commences: hear now the shrieks of the women; the cries of the children; the shouts of the warriors; and the groans of the dying. See with what desperation the inhabitants fight in defence of their darling joys. But, alas! overpowered by a superior foe, their force is broken; their ablest warriors fall; and the wretched remnant are taken captives.

Where are now those pleasant dwellings, where peace and harmony reigned incessant? where those beautiful fields, whose smiling crops, and enchanting verdure, enlivened the heart of every beholder? Alas! those tenements are now enveloped in destructive flames; those fair fields are now bedewed with blood, and covered with mangled carcasses. Where are now those sounds of mirth and gladness, which loudly rang throughout the village? where those darling youth, those venerable aged, who mutually animated the festive throng? Alas! those exhilarating peals, are now changed into the dismal groans of inconceivable distress: the survivors of those happy people, are now carried into cruel captivity. Ah! driven from their native soil, they cast their languishing eyes behind, and with aching hearts, bid adieu, to every prospect of joy and comfort.

A spectacle so truly distressing, is sufficient to blow into a blaze, the most latent spark of humanity: but, the adamantine heart of avarice, dead to every sensation of pity, regards not the voice of the sufferers, but hastily drives them to market for sale.

Oh, Africa, Africa! to what horrid inhumanities have thy shores been witness; thy shores, which were once the garden of the world, the seat of almost paradisiacal joys, have been transformed into regions of woe: thy sons, who were once the happiest of mortals, are reduced to slavery, and bound in weighty shackles, now fill the trader's ship. But, though defeated in the contest for liberty, their magnanimous souls scorn the gross indignity, and choose death in preference to slavery. Painful; Ah! painful, must be that existence, which the rational mind can deliberately doom to self-destruction. Thus, the poor Africans, robbed of every joy, while they see not the most transient, glimmering, ray of hope, to cheer their saddened hearts, sink into the abyss of consummate misery. Their lives, imbittered by reflection, anticipation, and present sorrows, they feel burthensome; and death, (whose dreary mansions appal the stoutest hearts) they view as their only shelter.

You, my brethren, beloved Africans, who had passed the days of infancy, when you left your country; you best can tell the aggravated sufferings, of our unfortunate race: your memories can bring to view these scenes of bitter grief. What, my brethren, when dragged from your native land, on board the slave ship; what was the anguish which you saw, which you felt? what the pain, what the dreadful forebodings, which filled your throbbing bosoms?

But you, my brethren, descendants of African forefathers, I call upon you, to view a scene of unfathomable distress. Let your imagination carry you back to former days. Behold a vessel, bearing our forefathers and brethren, from the place of their nativity, to a distant and inhospitable clime: behold their dejected countenances; their streaming eyes; their fettered limbs: hear them, with piercing cries, and pitiful moans, deploring their wretched fate. After their arrival in port, see them separated without regard to the ties of blood or friendship: husband from wife; parent from child; brother from sister; friend from friend. See the parting tear, rolling down their fallen cheeks: hear the parting sigh, die on their quivering lips.

But, let us no longer pursue a theme of boundless affliction. An enchanting sound now demands your attention. Hail! hail! glorious day, whose resplendent rising, disperseth the clouds, which have hovered with destruction over the land of Africa; and illumines it, by the most brilliant rays of future prosperity. Rejoice, Oh! Africans! No longer shall tyranny, war, and injustice, with irresistible sway, desolate your native country: no longer shall torrents of human blood deluge its delightful plains: no longer shall it witness your countrymen, wielding among each other the instruments of death; nor the insidious kidnapper, darting from his midnight haunt, on the feeble and unprotected: no longer shall its shores resound, with the awful howlings of infatuated warriors, the death-like groans of vanquished innocents, nor the clanking fetters of woe-doomed captives. Rejoice, Oh, ye descendants of Africans! No longer shall the United States of America, nor the extensive colonies of Great-Britain, admit the degrading commerce, of the human species: no longer shall they

swell the tide of African misery, by the importation of slaves. Rejoice, my brethren, that the channels are obstructed through which slavery, and its direful concomitants, have been entailed on the African race. But, let incessant strains of gratitude be mingled with your expressions of joy. Through the infinite mercy of the great Jehovah, this day announces the abolition of the Slave-Trade. Let, therefore, the heart that is warmed by the smallest drop of African blood, glow in grateful transports; and cause the lofty arches of the sky to reverberate eternal praise to his boundless goodness.

Oh, God! we thank thee, that thou didst condescend to listen to the cries of Africa's wretched sons; and that thou didst interfere in their behalf At thy call humanity sprang forth, and espoused the cause of the oppressed: one hand she employed in drawing from their vitals the deadly arrows of injustice; and the other in holding a shield, to defend them from fresh assaults: and at that illustrious moment, when the sons of 76 pronounced these United States free and independent; when the spirit of patriotism, erected a temple sacred to liberty; when the inspired voice of Americans first uttered those noble sentiments, "we hold these truths to be self-evident, that all men are created equal; that they are endowed by their Creator with certain unalienable rights; among which are life, liberty, and the pursuit of happiness;" and when the bleeding African, lifting his fetters, exclaimed, "am I not a man and a brother;" then with redoubled efforts, the angel of humanity strove to restore to the African race, the inherent rights of man.

To the instruments of divine goodness, those benevolent men, who voluntarily obeyed the dictates of humanity, we owe much. Surrounded with innumerable difficulties, their undaunted spirits, dared to oppose a powerful host of interested men. Heedless to the voice of fame, their independent souls dared to oppose the strong gales of popular prejudice. Actuated by principles of genuine philanthropy, they dared to despise the emoluments of ill gotten wealth, and to sacrifice much of their temporal interests at the shrine of benevolence.

As an American, I glory in informing you, that Columbia boasts the first men, who distinguished themselves eminently, in the vindication of our rights, and the improvement of our state.

Conscious that slavery was unfavourable to the benign influences of christianity, the pious Woolman, loudly declaimed against it; and although destitute of fortune, he resolved to spare neither time nor pains to check its progress. With this view he travelled over several parts of North America on foot, and exhorted his brethren, of the denomination of friends, to abjure the iniquitous custom. These, convinced by the cogency of his arguments, denied the privileges of their society to the slave-holder; and zealously engaged in destroying the aggravated evil. Thus, through the beneficial labours of this pattern of piety and brotherly kindness, commenced a work which has since been promoted, by the humane of every denomination. His memory ought therefore to be deeply engraven on the tablets of our hearts; and ought ever to inspire us with the most ardent esteem.

Nor less to be prized are the useful exertions of Anthony Benezet. This inestimable person, sensible of the equality of mankind, rose superior to the illiberal opinions of the age; and, disallowing an inferiority in the African genius, established the first school to cultivate our understandings, and to better our condition.

Thus, by enlightening the mind, and implanting the seeds of virtue, he banished, in a degree, the mists of prejudice; and laid the foundations of our future happiness. Let, therefore, a due sense of his meritorious actions, ever create in us, a deep reverence of his beloved name. Justice to the occasion, as well as his merits, forbid me to pass in silence over the name of the honorable William Wilberforce. Possessing talents capable of adorning the greatest subjects, his comprehensive mind found none more worthy his constant attention, than the abolition of the Slave-Trade. For this he soared to the zenith of his towering eloquence, and for this he struggled with perpetual ardour. Thus, anxious in defence of our rights, he pledged himself never to desert the cause; and, by his repeated and strenuous exertions, he finally obtained the desirable end. His extensive services have, therefore, entitled him to a large share of our affections, and to a lasting tribute of our unfeigned thanks.

But think not, my brethren, that I pretend to enumerate the persons who have proved our strenuous advocates, or that I have pourtrayed the merits of those I have mentioned. No, I have given but a few specimens of a countless number, and no more than the rude outlines of the beneficence of these. Perhaps there never existed a human institution, which has displayed more intrinsic merit, than the societies for the abolition of slavery.

Reared on the pure basis of philanthropy, they extend to different quarters of the globe; and comprise a considerable number of humane and respectable men. These, greatly impressed with the importance of the work, entered into it with such disinterestedness, engagedness, and prudence, as does honour to their wisdom and virtue. To effect the purposes of these societies no legal means were left untried, which afforded the smallest prospects of success. Books were disseminated, and discourses delivered, wherein every argument was employed which the penetrating mind could adduce, from religion, justice or reason, to prove the turpitude of slavery, and numerous instances related, calculated to awaken sentiments of compassion. To further their charitable intentions, applications were constantly made, to different bodies of legislature, and every concession improved to our best possible advantage. Taught by preceding occurrences, that the waves of oppression are ever ready to overwhelm the defenceless, they became the vigilant guardians of all our reinstated joys. Sensible that the inexperienced mind, is greatly exposed to the allurements of vice, they cautioned us, by the most salutary precepts, and virtuous examples, against its fatal encroachments: and the better to establish us, in the paths of rectitude they instituted schools to instruct us in the knowledge of letters, and the principles of virtue.

By these, and similar methods, with divine assistance they assailed the dark dungeon of slavery; shattered its rugged wall, and enlarging thousands of the captives, bestowed on them the blessings of civil society. Yes, my brethren, through their efficiency, numbers of us now enjoy the invaluable gem of liberty; numbers have been secured from a relapse into bondage; and numbers have attained an useful education.

I need not, my brethren, take a farther view of our present circumstances, to convince you of the providential benefits which we have derived from our patrons; for if you take a retrospect of the past situation of Africans, and descendants of Africans, in this and other countries, to your observation our advancements must be obvious. From these considerations, added to the happy event, which we now celebrate, let us ever entertain the profoundest veneration for our munificent benefactors, and return to them from the altars of our hearts, the fragrant incense of incessant gratitude. But let not, my brethren, our demonstrations of gratitude, be confined to the mere expressions of our lips.

The active part which the friends of humanity have taken to ameliorate our sufferings, has rendered them in a measure, the pledges of our integrity. You must be well aware that notwithstanding their endeavours, they have yet remaining, from interest and prejudice, a number of opposers. These, carefully watching for every opportunity to injure the cause, will not fail to augment the smallest defects in our lives and conversation; and reproach our benefactors with them, as the fruits of their actions.

Let us, therefore, by a steady and upright deportment, by a strict obedience and respect to the laws of the land, form an invulnerable bulwark against the shafts of malice. Thus, evincing to the world that our garments are unpolluted by the stains of ingratitude, we shall reap increasing advantages from the favours conferred; the spirits of our departed ancestors shall smile with complacency on the change of our state; and posterity shall exult in the pleasing remembrance.

May the time speedily commence, when Ethiopia shall stretch forth her hands; when the sun of liberty shall beam resplendent on the whole African race; and its genial influences, promote the luxuriant growth of knowledge and virtue.

Glossary

"am I not a man and a brother"	the words on the seal of the Quaker-led Society for Effecting the Abolition of the Slave Trade, which met in London in 1787, when the seal was designed
Anthony Benezet	an eighteenth-century Quaker abolitionist
Columbia	America
Flemish favorite	Lorenzo de Gorrevod, who obtained a license to transport four thousand slaves
Hispaniola	the island consisting of present-day Haiti and the Dominican Republic
Jehovah	a name for God, commonly used in the Old Testament of the Bible
Robertson's "History of America"	a text by the Scottish historian William Robertson first published in 1777
sons of 76	the American colonists who proclaimed independence in 1776
tenements	dwelling places
William Wilberforce	a British member of Parliament who worked to abolish the slave trade in the late eighteenth and early nineteenth centuries
Woolman	John Woolman, an eighteenth-century Quaker abolitionist and itinerant preacher

Woodcut image of a supplicant male slave in chains, adopted as the seal of the Society for the Abolition of Slavery in England in the 1780s (Library of Congress)

"Useful knowledge of every kind, and everything that relates to Africa, shall find a ready admission into our columns."

Overview

On March 16, 1827, the first edition of the first African American newspaper in the United States, *Freedom's Journal*, was published. In this debut issue, the editors Samuel Cornish and John Russwurm set out their goals for the newspaper: to give a voice to African Americans, to help improve their minds and inform them of national and international events and issues in an impartial way, to encourage political and social activism among blacks, and to connect black Americans to a greater community of people beyond their own cities and regions. In the two years that it was in print, *Freedom's Journal* endeavored to do just that, publishing stories about lynchings and slavery; the latest national and international news, particularly about Haiti, Africa, and Sierra Leone; notices of school events and employment and housing opportunities; biographies of black men and women; essays, short stories, and poetry; and sermons, oratories, and announcements of deaths, births, and weddings.

Even after the paper ceased publication, *Freedom's Journal* left its mark by changing the environment of the times and opening up a whole new way for African Americans to be heard—through the printed word. Having access to a newspaper that voiced their opinions and views in print was a valuable and empowering tool for African Americans: It helped them forge a new path toward freedom from their oppressive environment. Black Americans realized that people who could write and get their writing out into the world could change things.

Context

Post–Revolutionary War America was a world of deep paradox. On the one hand, American colonists had issued a Declaration of Independence proclaiming that "all men are created equal." On the other hand, America was a land entrenched in slavery, where free blacks did not seem to have a place and therefore were subject to racism, segregation, discrimination, and prejudice. The citizens of the newly formed United States attempted in these early years

to find their identity as a nation and as a people. There were those in the country who wanted to define themselves without slavery, or at least to try to eradicate the system in the future. These individuals were mainly from the northern states, which started to abolish slavery as early as the 1770s; the southern states maintained their slave societies until after the Civil War.

Slavery was prohibited in the constitution of Vermont when it became an independent republic in 1777. Other northern states abolished slavery, some of them gradually, in the following decades, beginning with Pennsylvania in 1780. In the northern states, during and after abolition, racism was common. The new competition between whites and free African Americans for jobs, land, and political power translated into white hostility. Because of this hostility, African Americans faced challenges in educational, employment, and civil rights, along with threats to their personal safety. Some northern states adopted laws to keep African Americans out of their states completely, and so there were limits to where they could live and work. Blacks in the north were also more likely to be arrested, convicted, and imprisoned, and their prison sentences tended to be longer than those given to whites. Consequently, African Americans were grossly overrepresented in prisons, and this was often cited as proof of their degraded status.

In the midst of this hostility and discrimination, African American aid and antislavery societies started springing up among northern whites. In the late eighteenth century, these societies excluded black people from membership while inviting white slaveholders to join. Even members of these antislavery societies had grave reservations about what mass emancipation would mean for American society. It was in this atmosphere that African Americans sought to form their own perceptions of what was going on in America and how they might fit in. They believed in the rhetoric of the American Revolution and the Declaration of Independence and that this rhetoric could apply to them as Americans as well as it could to whites. Thus, the African Americans of the late eighteenth century started to build communities and political awareness and began to nurture true leaders, educate themselves, and endeavor to understand who they were and what they wanted. They began to petition for their rights, and, as they did, they developed a

Time Line

1804
- Haiti becomes an independent nation.

1808
- **January 1**
  The international slave trade in the United States is abolished.

1816
- The American Colonization Society (ACS) is founded.

1827
- Slavery is abolished in New York.
- **March 16**
  Freedom's Journal, based in New York City, publishes its first issue, with Cornish as the senior editor and Russwurm as the junior editor.
- **September**
  Cornish announces his resignation as editor of *Freedom's Journal,* leaving Russwurm as the sole editor.

1829
- **February**
  Russwurm announces in *Freedom's Journal* his support for the ACS's efforts to relocate free African Americans to Liberia.
- **March 28**
  The last edition of *Freedom's Journal* is published.

language to help claim those rights. They attempted to figure out how to address problems on their own terms while still working with those who were trying to help them. This was difficult because of the overwhelmingly paternalistic attitude of white benefactors, who assumed that they knew what was best for the African American population. The black community was left feeling that their destinies were still being decided by whites.

The early nineteenth century brought even more obstacles for free African Americans. Northern states became increasingly restrictive in legislation concerning black citizens. Even as restrictions on low-income whites were lifting, those states that did allow free African Americans to vote added more requirements to the voting process, such as proving a certain minimum value of land owned or possessing papers that had to be drawn up by lawyers at prohibitive fees.

However, two particular events gave African Americans hope. In 1804 the independent nation of Haiti was formed,

after more than ten years of rebellion against colonial oppressors. The rebels were people of color who lived in slavery on the island. The establishment of Haiti inspired African Americans to stand up for their rights in the United States. The second cause for hope was the 1808 abolition of the international slave trade to the United States. For many African Americans this signaled the beginning of the end of slavery altogether. Black orators and ministers gave speeches and sermons on the event, celebrating it annually, and they published them as pamphlets. Through these orations, they began to assert their rightful place as Americans while also honoring their African ties.

In 1816 the American Colonization Society (ACS), also known as the American Society for Colonizing the Free People of Color in the United States, was founded. This society, dominated by whites, aimed to help free African Americans relocate to the western coast of Africa, especially the colony of Liberia. Although some freedpeople joined this endeavor and even relocated, most African Americans were opposed to the idea. First, since the ACS was predominantly white, African Americans felt that they were having an identity forced upon them by outsiders. Second, the ACS eventually wanted to relocate all free blacks to Africa, whether they wanted to go or not. This appealed to some whites as a foolproof way to sidestep the problem of race in the United States. However, many African Americans strongly resented this attempt to get them out of the country, believing that it was a scheme on the part of proslavery forces to rid themselves of any blacks who might help other slaves run away or work for emancipation.

As African American opponents of colonization banded together, their sense of national consciousness and solidarity increased dramatically. Some opponents were not necessarily against colonization per se, they simply were against letting a white society dictate the terms of colonization; to them, the African American plan of immigration to Haiti was far more acceptable. It was their plan under their rules, and it also showed black pride in the success of the Haitian Revolution. Whether to go or not, too, was their own choice.

In the 1820s, in addition to community building organizations and mutual aid societies, free African Americans began founding literary societies, libraries, and reading rooms. They read to those who could not read, and they began to teach one another how to read and write. Literacy gave black Americans a sense of power and control over their destinies. In addition, it gave them another way to fight oppression. Early-nineteenth-century newspapers rarely showed African Americans in a favorable light. Coverage of the black community in white papers typically focused on criminal or illicit acts or racist parodies. Nevertheless, newspapers were enjoying wide circulation, and new periodicals were springing up, thanks to the fact that paper was inexpensive. Many marginalized groups were starting their own papers to make their own views and perspectives visible to a wider audience.

From this setting emerged the first African American newspaper, the New York–based *Freedom's Journal,* on March 16, 1827. The editors of the periodical intended

A view of Bass Cove, Liberia (Library of Congress)

to appeal to and reach a wide audience. The building of community institutions, the formation of literary societies, and the development of rhetoric in the struggle to gain basic civil and personal rights all came together to make possible the creation of this newspaper by and for African Americans. *Freedom's Journal* was not so much a reaction to racism as it was a forum for African Americans to communicate and learn. Realizing that writing was an instrument of freedom, black entrepreneurs decided it was time to use it in a bigger way.

About the Author

The first editorial in *Freedom's Journal* was penned by the senior and junior editors, Samuel E. Cornish and John B. Russwurm, respectively. They edited the paper together for six months, until Cornish decided to resign, leaving full editorship to Russwurm. The paper went on under Russwurm for another year and a half before it ceased publication, mainly for financial reasons.

Samuel Cornish was born a free African American in Delaware around 1795. In 1815 he moved to Philadelphia, where he taught in a Presbyterian school. He started his studies with ministers in the Philadelphia Presbytery in 1817 and had earned his license to preach by 1819. During the summer and fall of 1820, Cornish went to live on the Eastern Shore of Maryland as a missionary to slaves but found the hypocrisy of the so-called Christian slaveholders unspeakably horrible. Cornish later moved to New York City and founded the First Colored Presbyterian Church, the state's first African American Presbyterian church; in 1824 he was installed as its pastor.

Cornish participated actively in New York's African American community. For a time he was part of the Haytian Emigration Society, but after seeing so many black Americans return to the United States extremely disillusioned with life in Haiti, he came to oppose the idea of colonization altogether. Realizing that his church was having financial problems, Cornish asked to be released from his position. The New York Presbytery refused, telling him to try to raise more funds. At this point, in March 1827, Cornish became the senior editor of *Freedom's Journal*, but he stayed on as pastor at his church. In September of that same year, after only six months, Cornish resigned as editor of the paper, although he continued to support it by being an agent, and news of his ministry could be found on its pages.

"We wish to plead our own cause. Too long have others spoken for us. Too long has the public been deceived by misrepresentations, in things which concern us dearly."

(Paragraphs 3–4)

"It is surely time that we should awake from this lethargy of years, and make a concentrated effort for the education of our youth. We form a spoke in the human wheel, and it is necessary that we should understand our pendence on the different parts, and theirs on us, in order to perform our part with propriety."

(Paragraph 6)

"The world has grown too enlightened, to estimate any man's character by his personal appearance. Though all men acknowledge the excellency of [Benjamin] Franklin's maxims, yet comparatively few practice upon them."

(Paragraph 6)

"Useful knowledge of every kind, and everything that relates to Africa, shall find a ready admission into our columns; and as that vast continent becomes daily more known, we trust that many things will come to light, proving that the natives of it are neither so ignorant nor stupid as they have generally been supposed to be."

(Paragraph 12)

"Men whom we equally love and admire have not hesitated to represent us disadvantageously, without becoming personally acquainted with the true state of things, nor discerning between virtue and vice among us. The virtuous part of our people feel themselves sorely aggrieved under the existing state of things—they are not appreciated. Our vices and our degradation are ever arrayed against us, but our virtues are passed by unnoticed."

(Paragraphs 14–15)

Throughout the rest of the 1820s and all of the 1830s, Cornish worked variously as an editor, a writer, and an activist. In May of 1829 he started another paper, *Rights of All*, which lasted for just six months. In 1840, Cornish, along with eight other African American clergymen, created the American and Foreign Anti-Slavery Society. Throughout the 1840s and 1850s, Cornish kept on with ministerial work, helping to organize missionary associations. With Theodore Wright, a fellow minister and protégé, he wrote an important anticolonization pamphlet, *The Colonization Scheme Considered*. Cornish died in 1858.

John Russwurm was born a freeperson in Jamaica in 1799, the son of a black woman and a Virginia-born, English-educated white plantation owner. He was educated at a boarding school in Quebec from 1807 to 1812 and at private schools in Maine. In 1824 Russwurm became the first African American student admitted to Bowdoin College in Maine. Upon being invited, Russwurm joined the college's literary fraternity, the Athenian Society, whose president was the future short-story writer and novelist Nathaniel Hawthorne. The young Russwurm planned to study medicine in Boston and become a physician after graduation. His intention was to move to Haiti and open a practice there, but he ended up shifting his emigration focus from Haiti to Liberia and indicated interest in relocating there to teach or assist the colony's resident agent. However, when the ACS offered him a position in Liberia in late 1826, he declined for reasons he would not disclose. Instead, he moved New York and soon thereafter took the position as junior editor of *Freedom's Journal*.

After Cornish resigned in September 1827, Russwurm became the sole editor of the paper. Financial problems led to the paper's demise about a year and a half later. The last edition of *Freedom's Journal* was published on March 28, 1829. Shortly thereafter, Russwurm decided it was time to immigrate to Liberia. He left in September of that year, arrived in November, and became the superintendent of schools there. He also revived the *Liberia Herald* in March 1830. In 1833 he was married and also established a business partnership with a colonist from Virginia named Joseph Daily. Although he resolved to remain in Liberia, Russwurm was disappointed by the small role that African American colonists played in the Liberian government. In 1836 the board of the Maryland Colonization Society appointed Russwurm governor of Cape Palmas colony on the West African coast. Affairs in the new colony did not run exactly smoothly, largely because of conflict with neighboring African tribes. Russwurm persevered as well as he could, earning praise from the board for the way he handled the governance of the colony. He died in 1851.

Explanation and Analysis of the Document

When the first issue of *Freedom's Journal* appeared on March 16, 1827, Samuel Cornish and John Russwurm included an editorial headed "To Our Patrons," which served as an introduction to the newspaper's format and goals. The editors made it clear that their main concern was not reacting to white racism but instead concentrating on construction of an African American identity.

First, Cornish and Russwurm acknowledge both the audacity and the potential of what they are endeavoring to do. Since no newspaper for or by African Americans had ever existed, it was certainly a "new and untried business." Nevertheless, they had a real sense that it was time to try such a thing, since there were "so many schemes … in action concerning our people"—most likely a reference to colonization and the overall paternalistic attitude that whites had toward African Americans at that time. *Freedom's Journal*, they say, existed for the education, edification, and progress of people of color, so it had to be a good thing—something to which no decent human being could object.

A very important goal for *Freedom's Journal* was providing African Americans with a voice of their own. "Too long have others spoken for us," note Cornish and Russwurm in paragraph 3, referring to those who may have wanted to help promote black rights and so spoke on behalf of the black community in the United States. The editors go on to explain in paragraph 4 that these "others" did not truly understand or represent the needs and wants of African Americans. They then point out that the sins of one black person were far too often blown out of proportion by whites, casting doubt over the good character of African Americans collectively. Cornish and Russwurm acknowledge that "there are many instances of vice among us," but they suggest that such people had not been properly taught or educated in the ways outside a life of slavery.

Education was another important goal of *Freedom's Journal*, it "being an object of the highest importance to the welfare of society." The editors state in paragraph 5 that through the paper, they would support African Americans who were trying to teach their children good habits, encourage them in useful work, and give them the education they needed to become a constructive part of society.

Beginning with paragraph 7, the editors point out that people should not be judged by their outward appearance. In a reference to Benjamin Franklin's aphorisms (as put forward in *Poor Richard's Almanack*), they go on to say that "all men acknowledge the excellency of Franklin's maxims, yet comparatively few practice upon them." When "our brethren" did make the mistake of neglecting these truths, it would be the task of the editors to correct them. The paper would also do its best to make African Americans aware of their civil rights and civic responsibilities as participants in the U.S. government. Russwurm and Cornish go on to advise anyone who is qualified to vote to do so but pointed out that no one should be coerced into voting for a specific party. They should decide for themselves how they would cast their ballots.

In paragraphs 9 through 13, the editors stress the importance of reading, saying that young people should read works of substance. They intended to include useful and educational pieces in *Freedom's Journal* and express their wish to foster communication among people of color in different states in the nation. There were so many issues to debate and discuss, and here was a forum in which to do it. Here, according to Cornish and Russwurm, was a place where African Americans could exchange thoughts and present their own viewpoints, without the fear that those views would be sifted through the perspective of white society—even if it was an altruistic one. The editors would weigh in on the issues as well. Additionally, they planned to include coverage of any and all news available about Africa. As more became known of the continent, its people would be seen as "neither so ignorant nor stupid as they have generally been supposed to be." Cornish and Russwurm express confidence that an enlightened view of Africa and its people would translate into a more positive view of Africa's sons and daughters in the United States. Furthermore, those sons and daughters of Africa who remained in bondage in the South would not be forgotten by *Freedom's Journal*. They were brethren as well, and although the paper's subscribers could do little to ease their afflictions or change their situation, the newspaper would provide a forum for readers' "sympathies [to] be poured forth."

Paragraphs 14 and 15 revisit the themes of paragraphs 3 and 4—of African Americans finding and using their own voices and putting forward their perspectives on issues in which they had a vested interest. According to the editors, even well-meaning whites were sometimes unsuccessful in their attempts to represent the black cause accurately because they failed to listen to "the true state of things" before they spoke. Paragraph 15 opens with the line "Our vices and our degradation are ever arrayed against us, but our virtues are passed by unnoticed," indicating Cornish and Russwurm's disappointment with the snowballing effects of prejudice and discrimination. They lament the fact that the negative actions of a single member of the black community could poison the minds of whites against all blacks. They also express disappointment with those who claim to fight prejudice but seem to practice it. One of the goals of the newspaper would be to make the perceptions and wishes of African Americans known and dispel prejudice in the process. The editors acknowledge that even as they wished to upset no one, they most likely would; that could not stop them from putting forth their views and following their principles.

In paragraph 16, Cornish and Russwurm ask why black people alone have lived so long in "ignorance, poverty, and degradation," while other people learn and progress, making their own lives better. They proceed to answer the question, saying that the travels and tales of Dixon Denham and Hugh Clapperton, the first European explorers to make it across the Sahara and back alive, as well as the results of the Haitian Revolution and the progress of South America's people all point to the eventual end to the legacy of oppression foisted upon people of color. This newspaper could improve the lives of African Americans by helping to lift the veil of "ignorance, poverty, and degradation" to which they were not necessarily destined. The African American community needed a newspaper that would address its own set of needs.

The editors intended the newspaper to be impartial—not to divide but to bring the people together. Whatever would help or educate or might be of interest to anyone in the African American community was to be printed in the paper. Readers were encouraged to write, to subscribe, and to support *Freedom's Journal*, and in doing so they would help themselves. Cornish and Russwurm end the editorial by stating that if they were ever too fervent, readers should "attribute our zeal to the peculiarities of our situation; and our earnest engagedness in their well-being."

Audience

Freedom's Journal was published primarily for an African American audience, whether or not they were literate. The editors understood that those who could read would read it to those who could not. Certainly the support of white subscribers and readers was welcome, as one of the motives of the paper was to put forward the opinions, views, and voices of African Americans "to the publick." The newspaper was written principally for African American edification and enlightenment as well as to provide a forum for events and issues particular to their community.

This community, their audience, was envisioned as expanding well beyond New York. The paper employed fourteen to forty-four agents, who sold subscriptions for a fee of $3 per year; by the end of the paper's two-year stint, there were agents in eleven states—including the proslavery states of Virginia and North Carolina—along with the District of Columbia, Haiti, England, and Sierra Leone.

Approximately three hundred thousand African Americans lived in the northern states, and most would have had access to this paper. It is very possible that at least some issues of *Freedom's Journal* made their way into the South as well, touching the lives of both free and enslaved African Americans living there. Historians tie the probability of the paper's circulation in the South to the fact that one of the agents working for *Freedom's Journal* in Boston, David Walker, wrote the pamphlet *Appeal to the Coloured Citizens of the World*. This highly incendiary work found its way into the Deep South despite those states' banning its circulation.

Impact

Freedom's Journal gave a stronger, more authentic voice to African Americans. Since the periodical was written and edited by African Americans, their perspectives could be presented to a much wider audience with accuracy. Not only news pertinent to their communities and world but also essays, stories, sermons, and poetry, along with biographies of influential or inspiring African Americans, were presented in the paper. It was a place for African Americans to communicate—with one another and with any white readers—and to converse with one another on issues important to them. Although black writers and orators had published orations, sermons, and various pamphlets in the past, it was even more powerful to see a weekly newspaper for African Americans from the pens of African Americans. This weekly newspaper connected black people all over the country and even beyond it, building a greater community beyond city and region and giving voice to it. *Freedom's Journal* also shows that as early as 1827, African Americans were already organizing and endeavoring to improve their own lives and the lives of their brethren still in bondage well before white abolitionists started to make a concentrated effort in the 1830s with associations like the American Anti-Slavery Society.

Even though the paper itself did not continue beyond 1829, it led the way for the publication of future African American newspapers. *Freedom's Journal* proved that there was a true need in the United States for a wider African American forum for the encouragement of black activism and the fight for self-determination, civil rights, and freedom. It also allowed African Americans to debate issues among themselves and exchange views. Because of this need and the way in which an independent newspaper answered it, no fewer than twenty-four other black newspapers were started between the run of *Freedom's Journal* and the Civil War.

See also Pennsylvania: An Act for the Gradual Abolition of Slavery (1780); Peter Williams, Jr.'s "Oration on the Abolition of the Slave Trade" (1808); David Walker's *Appeal to the Coloured Citizens of the World* (1829); First Editorial of the *North Star* (1847).

Further Reading

■ Books

Bacon, Jacqueline. *Freedom's Journal: The First African-American Newspaper*. Lanham, Md.: Lexington Books, 2007.

Dann, Martin. *The Black Press, 1827–1890: The Quest for National Identity*. New York: G. P. Putnam Sons, 1971.

Hinks, Peter P. *To Awake My Afflicted Brethren: David Walker and the Problem of Antebellum Slave Resistance*. University Park: Pennsylvania State University Press, 1997.

Hutton, Frankie. *The Early Black Press in America, 1827 to 1860*. Westport, Conn.: Greenwood Press, 1993.

Vogel, Todd, ed. *The Black Press: New Literary and Historical Essays*. New Brunswick, N.J.: Rutgers University Press, 2001.

■ Web Sites

"African-American Newspapers and Periodicals: *Freedom's Journal*." Wisconsin Historical Society Web site.
    http://www.wisconsinhistory.org/libraryarchives/aanp/freedom/.

"*Freedom's Journal*." Mapping the African American Past Web site.
    http://maap.columbia.edu/place/29.

—Angela M. Alexander

Questions for Further Study

1. What contribution did *Freedom's Journal* make to African American life as the United States inched away from the slave system and toward abolition of slavery?

2. What was the American Colonization Society? Why did some, perhaps many, African Americans oppose the goals of the society?

3. What political events in the United States and abroad led to greater hope and aspirations for African Americans during this time period?

4. *Freedom's Journal* was one of a long line of newspapers and other publications that had as their audience black Americans. How do you think the goals of the journal were similar to or different from those of such contemporary publications as *Jet, Essence, Ebony,* or *The Washington Afro-American* newspaper?

5. Compare this document with a similar document, the First Editorial of the *North Star*, written by Frederick Douglass. Which do you think was more persuasive? More eloquent? Why has Douglass's name survived to be widely recognized in the twenty-first century while the names of Cornish and Russwurm are less well known?

SAMUEL CORNISH AND JOHN RUSSWURM'S FIRST *FREEDOM'S JOURNAL* EDITORIAL

To Our Patrons

In presenting our first number to our Patrons, we feel all the diffidence of persons entering upon a new and untried line of business. But a moment's reflections upon the noble objects, which we have in view by the publication of this Journal; the expediency of its appearance at this time, when so many schemes are in action concerning our people—encourage us to come boldly before an enlightened public. For we believe, that a paper devoted to the dissemination of useful knowledge among our brethren, and to their moral and religious improvement, must meet with the cordial approbation of every friend to humanity.

The peculiarities of this Journal, renders it important that we should advertise to the world our motives by which we are actuated, and the objects which we contemplate.

We wish to plead our own cause. Too long have others spoken for us.

Too long has the public been deceived by misrepresentations, in things which concern us dearly, though in the estimation of some mere trifles; for though there are many in society who exercise towards us benevolent feelings; still (with sorrow we confess it) there are others who make it their business to enlarge upon the least trifle, which tends to the discredit of any person of color; and pronounce anathemas and denounce our whole body for the misconduct of this guilty one. We are aware that there are many instances of vice among us, but we avow that it is because no one has taught its subjects to be virtuous; many instances of poverty, because no sufficient efforts accommodate to minds contracted by slavery, and deprived of early education have been made, to teach them how to husband their hard earnings, and to secure to themselves comfort.

Education being an object of the highest importance to the welfare of society, we shall endeavor to present just and adequate views of it, and to urge upon our brethren the necessity and expedience of training their children, while young, to habits of industry, and thus forming them for becoming useful members of society.

It is surely time that we should awake from this lethargy of years, and make a concentrated effort for the education of our youth. We form a spoke in the human wheel, and it is necessary that we should understand our pendence on the different parts, and theirs on us, in order to perform our part with propriety.

Though not desiring of dictating, we shall feel it our incumbent duty to dwell occasionally upon the general principles and rules of economy. The world has grown too enlightened, to estimate any man's character by his personal appearance. Though all men acknowledge the excellency of Franklin's maxims, yet comparatively few practice upon them. We may deplore when it is too late, the neglect of these self-evident truths, but it avails little to mourn. Ours will be the task of admonishing our brethren on these points.

The civil rights of a people being of the greatest value, it shall ever be our duty to vindicate our brethren, when oppressed; and to lay the case before the public. We shall also urge upon our brethren, (who are qualified by the laws of the different states) the expediency of using their elective franchise; and of making an independent use of the same. We wish them not to become the tools of party.

And as much time is frequently lost, and wrong principles instilled, by the perusal of works of trivial importance, we shall consider it a part of our duty to recommend to our young readers, such authors as will not only enlarge their stock of useful knowledge, but such as will also serve to stimulate them to higher attainments in science.

We trust also, that through the columns of the *Freedom's Journal*, many practical pieces, having for their bases, the improvements of our brethren, will be presented to them, from the pens of many of our respected friends, who have kindly promised their assistance.

It is our earnest wish to make our Journal a medium of intercourse between our brethren in the different states of this great confederacy: that through its columns an expression of our sentiments, on many interesting subjects which concern us, may be offered to the public: that plans which apparently are beneficial may be candidly discussed and properly weighted; if worth, receive our cordial approbation; if not, our marked disapprobation.

Useful knowledge of every kind, and everything that relates to Africa, shall find a ready admission into our columns; and as that vast continent becomes daily more known, we trust that many things will come to light, proving that the natives of it are neither so ignorant nor stupid as they have generally been supposed to be.

And while these important subjects shall occupy the columns of the *Freedom's Journal*, we would not be unmindful of our brethren who are still in the iron fetters of bondage. They are kindred by all the ties of nature; and though but little can be effected by us, still let our sympathies be poured forth, and our prayers in their behalf, ascend to Him who is able to succor them.

From the press and the pulpit we have suffered much by being incorrectly represented. Men whom we equally love and admire have not hesitated to represent us disadvantageously, without becoming personally acquainted with the true state of things, nor discerning between virtue and vice among us. The virtuous part of our people feel themselves sorely aggrieved under the existing state of things—they are not appreciated.

Our vices and our degradation are ever arrayed against us, but our virtues are passed by unnoticed. And what is still more lamentable, our friends, to whom we concede all the principles of humanity and religion, from these very causes seem to have fallen into the current of popular feelings and are imperceptibly floating on the stream—actually living in the practice of prejudice, while they abjure it in theory, and feel it not in their hearts. Is it not very desirable that such should know more of our actual condition; and of our efforts and feelings, that in forming or advocating plans for our amelioration, they may do it more understandingly? In the spirit of candor and humility we intend by a simple representation of facts to lay our case before the public, with a view to arrest the progress of prejudice, and

to shield ourselves against the consequent evils. We wish to conciliate all and to irritate none, yet we must be firm and unwavering in our principles, and persevering in our efforts.

If ignorance, poverty and degradation have hitherto been our unhappy lot; has the Eternal decree forth, that our race alone are to remain in this state, while knowledge and civilization are shedding their enlivening rays over the rest of the human family? The recent travels of Denham and Clapperton in the interior of Africa, and the interesting narrative which they have published; the establishment of the republic Hayti after years of sanguinary warfare; its subsequent progress in all the arts of civilization; and the advancement of liberal ideas in South America, where despotism has given place to free governments, and where many of our brethren now fill important civil and military stations, prove the contrary.

The interesting fact that there are five hundred thousand free persons of color, one half of whom might peruse, and the whole be benefitted by the publication of the Journal; that no publication, as yet, has been devoted exclusively to their improvement—that many selections from approved standard authors, which are within the reach of few, may occasionally be made—and more important still, that this large body of our citizens have no public channel—all serve to prove the real necessity, at present, for the appearance of the *Freedom's Journal*.

It shall ever be our desire so to conduct the editorial department of our paper as to give offence to none of our patrons; as nothing is farther from us than to make it the advocate of any partial views, either in politics or religion. What few days we can number, have been devoted to the improvement of our brethren; and it is our earnest wish that the remainder may be spent in the same delightful service.

Glossary

Denham and Clapperton	Dixon Denham and Hugh Clapperton, the first European explorers to cross the Sahara and return
elective franchise	the right to vote
Franklin's maxims	the aphorisms of Benjamin Franklin, one of the nation's founders, published notably in *Poor Richard's Almanack*
Hayti	the Caribbean nation of Haiti, the scene of a revolt against French colonial masters in the late eighteenth and early nineteenth centuries
pendence	dependence

In conclusion, whatever concerns us as a people, will ever find a ready admission into the *Freedom's Journal*, interwoven with all the principal news of the day.

And while every thing in our power shall be performed to support the character of our Journal, we would respectfully invite our numerous friends to assist by their communications, and our colored brethren to strengthen our hands by their subscriptions, as our labor is one of common cause, and worthy of their consideration and support. And we most earnestly solicit the latter, that if at any time we should seem to be zealous, or too pointed in the inculcation of any important lesson, they will remember, that they are equally interested in the cause in which we are engaged, and attribute our zeal to the peculiarities of our situation; and our earnest engagedness in their well-being.

DAVID WALKER'S *APPEAL TO THE COLOURED CITIZENS OF THE WORLD*

"They have no more right to hold us in slavery than we have to hold them."

Overview

David Walker, a free black man living in Boston, Massachusetts, published the first edition of his *Appeal to the Coloured Citizens of the World* in 1829, and the third and last revised edition of the pamphlet in June 1830. In this *Appeal* Walker encouraged his fellow African Americans in the United States, slave and free, to see themselves as human beings and to do something to elevate themselves from their "wretched state." In doing so, the arguments for slavery, racial slavery in particular, would be torn down, thus weakening the power of the slaveholders.

Because Walker was not beyond advocating the use of violence to help free slaves in America, his pamphlet was banned from several states in the South. Even some abolitionists were appalled by the suggestion that violence would be acceptable in the cause of emancipation. Called "incendiary" and "subversive" in the 1830s, the arguments put forth by Walker continued to provide a foundation upon which later generations of workers for abolition and civil rights in America would make their stand.

Context

Slave rebellion in the Americas is as old as slavery itself. Although rebellions were generally planned by word of mouth, by the Revolutionary War period slaves and freedmen even sometimes wrote secret notes to one another about potential revolts. Most revolts were thwarted before they could even get started, and some simply failed. Very few got off the ground, and fewer succeeded. Nonetheless, the ones that succeeded struck fear into the hearts of not only slaveholders but even whites who owned no slaves, all over the American South.

The revolt of the Haitian slaves against their French colonial masters was the most heart-stopping for southern slaveholders. This mass uprising of black and mulatto slaves in 1791 resulted in the burning of numerous cities and buildings and the massacre of a great portion of the white population. Over the next twelve years these former slaves became an effective army, known for its guerrilla tactics; they fought off not only the white planters and French colonial troops but also a British expeditionary force, a Spanish invasion, and even Napoléon Bonaparte's "invincible" army. After defeating the latter in 1803, Haiti declared its independence as a black republic.

For the planters of the American South, the horror of this event was threefold: There was the massacre of whites and burning of property in the beginning, the seeming invincibility of the Haitians, and the ominous transformation of a French colony controlled by slaveholding whites into a black republic. If it could happen in Haiti, it could happen in the American South. Most slaveholders in the South treated their slaves far better than the slaves in Haiti had been treated (where the trend was to work the slaves to death so that the planters would not have to care for them in old age), and so perhaps there would be less reason to revolt, particularly in such a violent manner. However, American slaves were generally more educated than those in Haiti, which meant they might get ideas from places outside the South. And, of course, the very example of the Haitians' success could not help but give the southern slaves something to think about.

Proving that the slaveholders' fears were not totally unfounded, a slave rebellion plot was uncovered in August 1800, in Richmond, Virginia. Gabriel Prosser, the ringleader, spent months gathering perhaps several thousand men and organizing them. The plan was to distract the whites with several fires and then take over the armory and government buildings of the city. Thus armed, the group would slaughter most of the whites and then make Virginia their kingdom, with Prosser as the king. Two slaves revealed the plot the day it was supposed to take place. Thus warned and aided by a fortuitous rainstorm that flooded the roads, making Prosser postpone the attack until the next day, the city armed itself. The rebels scattered. About thirty-five of them, including Prosser, were executed. Prosser, who could read, had been inspired by the Exodus of the Hebrew slaves in the Bible and by the revolution in Haiti.

Slaveholders invariably reacted to such rebellions by imposing harsher restrictions on their own slaves. Slaves would not be allowed to read or write, their religious services would be supervised, visitation of other farms or towns

CA. 1784

- David Walker is born in Wilmington, North Carolina. (Some sources say 1785, 1796, or 1797.)

1791

- **August 22**
A slave rebellion initiates the Haitian Revolution.

1800

- **August 30**
Gabriel Prosser's slave rebellion in Richmond, Virginia, is suppressed.

1804

- **January 1**
Haiti declares itself a free republic.

1820s

- **Early**
Walker moves to Charleston, South Carolina.

1822

- **May 30**
A slave betrays Denmark Vesey's plot to revolt, leading to the execution of Vesey and thirty-six of the conspirators in July.

1825

- Walker relocates to Boston, Massachusetts.

1827

- Walker becomes a contributor for the New York–based *Freedom's Journal*, the first black newspaper in the United States.

1829

- **September**
David Walker's Appeal. In Four Articles; Together with a Preamble to the Coloured Citizens of the World, but in Particular, and Very Expressly, to Those of the United States of America appears in pamphlet form.

would be curtailed, curfews would be strictly enforced, any type of slave gathering would be subject to suspicion and perhaps banned altogether, and freedmen would be watched more closely. While these restrictions tended to relax over time, each new upset would invite further harsh measures.

The next great upset, of which David Walker may have even been part, was Denmark Vesey's rebellion plot in Charleston, South Carolina, in 1822. Vesey, a former slave, was a relatively prosperous carpenter with some land. Hating slavery and slaveholding society, Vesey read all he could about antislavery arguments and agitated for freedom and equality for his fellow African Americans. He began to assemble a circle of leaders for a massive rebellion. By the time the plan was to go into effect, Vesey had enlisted about nine thousand free and slave blacks in and around Charleston. As with Prosser's rebellion, however, the scheme was betrayed by a participant, and Vesey was executed, along with thirty-six coconspirators. The reaction of whites was fierce enough to cause many free blacks to flee to the North.

Into this highly charged environment, Walker dropped his *Appeal* in 1829. Because of his own father's enslavement, Walker had seen firsthand the cruelty and barbarity involved in the American slave system. Once Walker left that environment for one where he could be educated and involved with antislavery efforts, he seemed to realize that his voice could count for something among his fellow African Americans. In the resulting pamphlet, he encouraged them to stop at nothing—including violence—to get free from slavery. Judging by the reaction of many white southerners, Walker might as well have plotted and implemented his own rebellion, rather than merely publishing a pamphlet. The *Appeal* evoked thoughts of Haiti, Prosser, and Vesey, and the fear of what could happen if the slave population—which was, in many southern states, the majority population—were to act on Walker's ideas. After Nat Turner's partially successful rebellion in 1831 (which resulted in a temporary escape and the death of some whites), many southern slaveholders felt their fears about Walker's pamphlet were confirmed.

About the Author

David Walker was born in Wilmington, North Carolina, to a free mother and a slave father. Because the status of the mother determined the status of the child, Walker was considered a free black. He was, however, fully familiar with slave life in his hometown, since his father was still in bondage. Sources conflict on the subject of his birth year; some sources give the year 1784 or 1785, and others maintain it was 1796 or 1797.

Early in the 1820s (when, by the later date of birth, he would have been in his twenties), Walker moved to Charleston, South Carolina. Historians speculate that he may have been involved in Denmark Vesey's plot to revolt against slaveholders in 1822. In any event, Walker moved again shortly after the execution of Vesey and his coconspirators—this time to the North, where many

African Americans were heading because of the trouble in Charleston.

In Boston, Massachusetts, Walker made a living for himself by running a used clothing store in the Fisherman's Wharf section of the city. It is there that he likely learned to read and write. In 1826 he married Eliza Butler, with whom he eventually had three children (including a daughter who died of consumption just days before her father's death). Very involved in the black community, Walker was a member of the May Street Methodist Church; the Prince Hall African (Masonic) Lodge No. 459; and the Massachusetts General Colored Association, Boston (later absorbed into the New England Anti-Slavery Society), of which he was a leader. Walker used his home and shop to provide shelter for fugitive slaves. He also began writing, and he submitted some of his work to the New York–based black newspaper *Freedom's Journal*.

In 1829, Walker published his *Appeal to the Coloured Citizens of the World*. He rewrote the pamphlet twice, publishing the third and final edition in June 1830. Many southern state governments put a price on Walker's head, offering $3,000 for his head and $10,000 to the one who could bring him to the South alive. His friends entreated him to go to Canada, but he refused. Instead, he used his secondhand clothes shop to help get banned copies of his *Appeal* into the South, sewing the pamphlets into the clothing so that sailors could take them to ports south.

Two months after the third edition of Walker's *Appeal* came out, the man mysteriously died. His death certificate states the cause as consumption (tuberculosis), of which his daughter had died a few days earlier. Historians have wondered whether he was poisoned by his enemies, but no reliable evidence has surfaced to support that hypothesis.

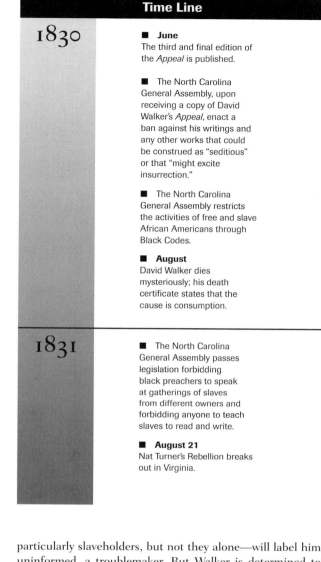

Time Line

1830

■ **June**
The third and final edition of the *Appeal* is published.

■ The North Carolina General Assembly, upon receiving a copy of David Walker's *Appeal*, enact a ban against his writings and any other works that could be construed as "seditious" or that "might excite insurrection."

■ The North Carolina General Assembly restricts the activities of free and slave African Americans through Black Codes.

■ **August**
David Walker dies mysteriously; his death certificate states that the cause is consumption.

1831

■ The North Carolina General Assembly passes legislation forbidding black preachers to speak at gatherings of slaves from different owners and forbidding anyone to teach slaves to read and write.

■ **August 21**
Nat Turner's Rebellion breaks out in Virginia.

Explanation and Analysis of the Document

The structure of David Walker's *Appeal* emulates, in part, the Constitution of the United States, having five parts—a preamble and four articles. In the preamble, Walker outlines his arguments in a very general way. The articles' titles reflect their content, each explicating a reason for the "wretchedness" of the slaves' lives and experiences: "Our Wretchedness in Consequence of Slavery," "Our Wretchedness in Consequence of Ignorance," "Our Wretchedness in Consequence of the Preachers of the Religion of Jesus Christ," and "Our Wretchedness in Consequence of the Colonizing Plan." The present volume reproduces only the Preamble, Article I, and a small part of Article IV.

♦ Preamble

In the preamble, Walker addresses what seems to him the greatest and most unbearable paradox of the United States: The misery of Walker's brethren comes at the hands of those who call themselves Christians. The causes of slavery are myriad, so much so that Walker states that he will not even try to lay them all out, but he will at least try to examine some of the worst of those causes. He knows that many people—

particularly slaveholders, but not they alone—will label him uninformed, a troublemaker. But Walker is determined to proceed with his appeal nonetheless.

Another contradiction in the United States is that of a slaveholding society existing within a *"Republican Land of Liberty."* Worse still is the resistance of slaves and free African Americans to change, because they believe that things can only get worse for them. Walker puts to them the question: "Can our condition be any worse?"

At this point in the preamble, he says that he will be breaking the pamphlet into separate sections, each illuminating a particular cause of their "wretchedness" for the reader. The first section will be on the subject of slavery itself, since it is the direct source of their misery. Their misery, however, will not go unchecked; likewise, the happiness of their masters and those participating in the slave culture will not continue forever. For, he says, God will appear on behalf of the oppressed, and he will make sure that the oppressors receive their rewards—whether from the hands of the oppressed or by other means: "Will he not cause the very children of the oppressors to rise up against them, and oftimes put them to death?"

Jean-Jacques Dessalines, a leader of the Haitian Revolution and the first ruler of an independent Haiti
(AP/Wide World Photos)

Next Walker refers to the biblical Exodus of the Hebrew slaves from Egypt and the plagues visited on the Egyptian slaveholders. He then touches on the history of ancient Sparta and of the Roman Empire and how those slaveholding empires, too, eventually met their downfall. He mentions the wars going on in Spain and Portugal—slaveholding empires—where people are slaughtering one another. In Walker's eyes, there can be no question as to the reason for these things: These societies were receiving "the judgments of God" for holding slaves and being oppressors.

In the closing paragraphs, Walker points out that anyone who is not blinded by the prejudices of the avaricious world can see that he and his brethren are *men* with feelings, just as white people have, and that God has them in his care too: "God Almighty is the *sole proprietor* or *master* of the WHOLE human family." And he hears their cries of misery: "Has He not the hearts of all men in His hand?"

♦ Article I: Our Wretchedness in Consequence of Slavery
Walker acknowledges that there have been slaves in many parts of the world at many times. His point, however, is that the slaves in the United States are the worst

off of them all, despite having an ostensibly "enlightened and Christian people" for masters. His goal with this article is to show any skeptic the truth of his claim through the use of history.

His first example is from the Bible, taken as a history of the Hebrew people and their time of slavery in Egypt as told in the books of Genesis and Exodus. Walker points out that even these heathen Egyptians—Africans—gave the Hebrews fertile land to live on. Unlike the American slaveholders, they never denied that the Hebrews were human beings. In contrast, even the admired Thomas Jefferson, in his *Notes on the State of Virginia*, said that those of African descent were inferior both mentally and physically to white people. The Egyptians did not seem to hold this view, much less voice it, for Pharaoh's daughter even adopted the Hebrew child Moses into the royal household, raising him as her own. He might even have attained the throne if he had not decided instead to cast his lot with his own people, groaning under bondage, to help them free themselves. Walker asks his own people at this point why they do not throw *their* lots in with their own, rather than snitching on their brethren behind their backs and helping keep one another in bondage.

Walker digresses from his examination of history, exhorting those in chains to pray and watch for the right time to free themselves. He tells them to watch but also to act: "Be not afraid or dismayed; for be you assured that Jesus Christ the King of heaven and of earth who is the God of justice and of armies, will surely go before you." This is by no means his most explicit call to action. In Article II, in fact, he presses black people to defend themselves when someone seeks to murder them, saying that they should kill or be killed. He next asks his audience if they wish they were white. He states they should not wish to be anything other than what God made them, even if white people suppose otherwise. And why should whites have any more right to hold black people in bondage than black people should to hold white people? Why could it not be the other way around? Additionally, the audience should not be afraid of their enemies, who happen to be greater in number and more educated. They may have the law on their side, but the wretched slaves of the nation have, if they are humble, God on theirs. Those who would not fight for their freedom should remain in chains.

Returning to history, Walker asks if there is anything that their African fathers had done to deserve being held in perpetual slavery along with their children. Their masters say that the Spartans held the Helots (a member of the Spartan class of serfs) in slavery and were cruel to them as well. Walker, demonstrating his impressive education, rejoins with the documented fact that the Helots had caused trouble in Sparta, even though they had been welcomed there. Thus, the Spartans sentenced them to slavery, along with their offspring. And even the pre-Christian Spartans never shackled their Helots or "dragged them from their wives and children."

Here Walker states that African American children should read books like Jefferson's *Notes*, so that they can

"But against all accusations which may or can be preferred against me, I appeal to Heaven for my motive in writing—who knows that my object is, if possible, to awaken in the breasts of my afflicted, degraded and slumbering brethren, a spirit of inquiry and investigation respecting our miseries and wretchedness in this Republican Land of Liberty!!!!!!"

(Preamble)

"We are men, *notwithstanding our* improminent noses *and* woolly heads, *and believe that we feel for our fathers, mothers, wives and children, as well as the whites do for theirs."*

(Preamble)

"They have no more right to hold us in slavery than we have to hold them, we have just as much right, in the sight of God, to hold them and their children in slavery and wretchedness, as they have to hold us, and no more."

(Article I)

"And those enemies who have for hundreds of years stolen our rights, and kept us ignorant of Him and His divine worship, he will remove. Millions of whom, are this day, so ignorant and avaricious, that they cannot conceive how God can have an attribute of justice, and show mercy to us because it pleased Him to make us black—which colour, Mr. Jefferson calls unfortunate !!!!!!"

(Article I)

"I have been for years troubling the pages of historians, to find out what our fathers have done to the white Christians of America, *to merit such condign punishment as they have inflicted on them.... But I must aver, that my researches have hitherto been to no effect. I have therefore, come to the immoveable conclusion, that they (Americans) have, and do continue to punish us for nothing else, but for enriching them and their country."*

(Article I)

be the ones to refute such arguments; he asks each brother to "buy a copy of Mr. Jefferson's 'Notes on Virginia,'" and put it in the hand of his son." Although it can be beneficial to have white friends refute Jefferson's arguments, these friends are not black and therefore cannot argue as well as African Americans can: "We, and the world, wish to see the charges of Mr. Jefferson refuted by the blacks *themselves*." Looking again at Jefferson's book, Walker points out Jefferson's example that Greek slaves under Roman rule made great strides in science, despite their condition, and this was because they were *whites*. At least the Romans, Walker asserts, let slaves buy their freedom, and once they were free, treated them like equals, even letting them take places in the government. Not only can slaves not buy their freedom in many states (or are stopped by extremely prohibitive laws) but also, if they did, they would not be allowed in the government.

Why are black men treated as brutes? They will meet the same maker when they die, and they are under the same supreme master as white men: "Have we any other Master but Jesus Christ alone? Is he not their Master as well as ours?" Somehow, Walker states, under Christianity white men have become much more brutal and cruel than they ever were before. The barbarians of Europe—Gaul, Britain, Spain—grew worse after becoming Christians. His theory is that heathens who are educated and enlightened learn new ways of being cruel and greedy. If this is true, then if God "were to give [white Christians] more sense, what would they do?" Walker thinks they would rebel against God himself: "Would they not *dethrone* Jehovah and seat themselves upon his throne?" African-American people, on the other hand, tend to become better people under Christianity, not worse.

♦ **Article IV: Our Wretchedness in Consequence of the Colonizing Plan**

Walker's *Appeal* also includes, at the end of Article IV, a portion on the Declaration of Independence. Here he speaks to "Americans," meaning the white population of the United States. He tells them they should take a look at their own Declaration of Independence, which states that "all men are created equal" and are "endowed with unalienable rights." How can white Americans reconcile these words with their actions toward black people? If these white Americans found British rule too much for them, how much worse must African Americans find American slavery in its brutality and oppression? And if it is any surprise to white Americans that African Americans might rise up "to throw off such government, and to provide new guards for their future security," then it must be the devil deceiving them. Walker tells these Americans that if he must be humble, so should they, since both answer to the same God. White Americans cannot hide from God, no matter how cautious they might be.

Audience

For David Walker, the title of his pamphlet announced his intended audience: *David Walker's Appeal. In Four Ar-*

ticles; Together with a Preamble to the Coloured Citizens of the World, but in Particular, and Very Expressly, to Those of the United States of America. He directly addressed the men and women held in bondage in the South. It can be surmised that he wrote so that the *Appeal* could be read aloud to the many illiterate slaves by those few who could read. In order to put the pamphlet in the hands of his intended audience, Walker relied on a few contacts in the South as well as the sailors who bought used clothing in his shop. Even after southern state and local governments banned his writings, he concealed pamphlets in the linings of the clothing he sold to sailors bound for southern ports.

Besides the intended audience, Walker's *Appeal* engaged—or, in the case of southern whites, repelled—a much wider range of readers. Both northerners and southerners read the pamphlet, with a wide range of reactions, from abhorrence to admiration. Walker's message certainly reached more than the enslaved people of the South.

Impact

Not long after the initial publication of the *Appeal*, the police of Savannah, Georgia, declared that they had confiscated sixty copies of the document. The governor asked the state legislature to prohibit the distribution of the *Appeal* and all other "incendiary publications." Lawmakers in North Carolina, South Carolina, Virginia, and Louisiana followed suit. A $3,000 reward would be issued for Walker's head and $10,000 for his entire person transported to the South alive.

Walker's publication frightened slaveholders to a new extreme. Already terrified of a bloody slave rebellion like the one in Haiti, they began restricting the few freedoms some had permitted their slaves. Slaves would no longer be taught to read or write, and unsupervised black religious services were banned in some areas, for fear that the ministers would spread Walker's arguments to their congregants. It was even rumored that southern planters plotted to kill Walker—which has led some historians to question the death certificate's statement that his death was by natural causes.

Many slaveholders also thought that Nat Turner's 1831 rebellion in Virginia was influenced by Walker's *Appeal*. At least fifty-five white people died in that revolt. Several years after Turner had a vision that revealed to him that he was to kill his enemies, Turner and six men started at the home of Turner's owner, killing all the whites in the household while they slept and then moved on from house to house in the same way. By the next day this force of seven had grown to about forty, most on horseback. A group of militia men then confronted them, causing the group to scatter. Eventually Turner and many of the rebels were captured and executed. Most historians doubt that Turner was directly influenced by Walker's *Appeal*. Nevertheless, the ideas in Walker's pamphlet were undoubtedly discussed in Virginia, as was the Haitian Revolution so feared by the southern planter culture.

The North reacted somewhat less vehemently than the South. Although abolitionist movements began to coalesce at this time, presenting a much stronger front, these groups tended to favor nonviolent ways of destroying the institution of slavery. One of the most prominent advocates for abolition, William Lloyd Garrison, wrote an editorial in his newspaper, *The Liberator*, in January 1831, saying that while he understood and sympathized with Walker's reasoning, he could not condone the author's encouragement of violent behavior from his brethren or his heated prose. Garrison did not want Walker's *Appeal* to be associated with the wider northern abolition movement precisely because its encouragement of hostility and rebellion only hardened slaveholders' hearts against the abolitionist message.

See also *The Confessions of Nat Turner* (1831).

Further Reading

■ Articles

Thomson, Jim. "The Haitian Revolution and the Forging of America." *History Teacher* 34, no. 1 (November 2000): 76–94. Available online.
http://www.historycooperative.org/journals/ht/34.1/thomson.html.

■ Books

Andrews, William L., ed. *The North Carolina Roots of African American Literature: An Anthology*. Chapel Hill: University of North Carolina Press, 2006.

Hinks, Peter P. *To Awaken My Afflicted Brethren: David Walker and the Problem of Antebellum Slave Resistance*. University Park: Pennsylvania State University Press, 1997.

Newman, Richard, et al., eds. *Pamphlets of Protest: An Anthology of Early African-American Protest Literature, 1790–1860*. New York: Routledge, 2001.

Pinn, Anthony B., ed. *Moral Evil and Redemptive Suffering: A History of Theodicy in African-American Religious Thought*. Gainesville: University Press of Florida, 2002.

■ Web Sites

"People and Events: David Walker, 1786–1830." PBS's "Africans in America" Web site.
http://www.pbs.org/wgbh/aia/part4/4p2930.html.

—Angela M. Alexander

Questions for Further Study

1. In what ways are the views expressed in David Walker's *Appeal to the Coloured Citizens of the World* similar to and different from those expressed in Malcolm X's "After the Bombing" speech in 1965?

2. Compare this document with the third chapter of W. E. B. Du Bois's *The Souls of Black Folk*—"Of Mr. Booker T. Washington and Others"—or Alain Locke's "Enter the New Negro." To what extent can Walker's speech be regarded as a precursor to the views expressed by Du Bois or Locke?

3. In what ways did the rebellion led by Nat Turner, discussed in *The Confessions of Nat Turner*, confirm the fears that Walker's speech evoked?

4. In what ways did Walker use the Judeo-Christian Bible to illustrate and buttress his points? Why do you think he included so many biblical references?

5. What was the reaction of northern abolitionists to Walker's appeal? Why do you believe they reacted in this way?

DAVID WALKER'S *APPEAL TO THE COLOURED CITIZENS OF THE WORLD*

My dearly beloved Brethren and Fellow Citizens.

Preamble

Having travelled over a considerable portion of these United States, and having, in the course of my travels, taken the most accurate observations of things as they exist—the result of my observations has warranted the full and unshaken conviction, that we, (coloured people of these United States,) are the most degraded, wretched, and abject set of beings that ever lived since the world began; and I pray God that none like us ever may live again until time shall be no more. They tell us of the Israelites in Egypt, the Helots in Sparta, and of the Roman Slaves, which last were made up from almost every nation under heaven, whose sufferings under those ancient and heathen nations, were, in comparison with ours, under this enlightened and Christian nation, no more than a cipher—or, in other words, those heathen nations of antiquity, had but little more among them than the name and form of slavery; while wretchedness and endless miseries were reserved, apparently in a phial, to be poured out upon our fathers, ourselves and our children, by *Christian* Americans!

These positions I shall endeavour, by the help of the Lord, to demonstrate in the course of this *Appeal*, to the satisfaction of the most incredulous mind—and may God Almighty, who is the Father of our Lord Jesus Christ, open your hearts to understand and believe the truth.

The *causes*, my brethren, which produce our wretchedness and miseries, are so very numerous and aggravating, that I believe the pen only of a Josephus or a Plutarch, can well enumerate and explain them. Upon subjects, then, of such incomprehensible magnitude, so impenetrable, and so notorious, I shall be obliged to omit a large class of, and content myself with giving you an exposition of a few of those, which do indeed rage to such an alarming pitch, that they cannot but be a perpetual source of terror and dismay to every reflecting mind.

I am fully aware, in making this appeal to my much afflicted and suffering brethren, that I shall not only be assailed by those whose greatest earthly desires are, to keep us in abject ignorance and wretchedness, and who are of the firm conviction that Heaven has designed us and our children to be slaves and *beasts of burden* to them and their children. I say, I do not only expect to be held up to the public as an ignorant, impudent and restless disturber of the public peace, by such avaricious creatures, as well as a mover of insubordination—and perhaps put in prison or to death, for giving a superficial exposition of our miseries, and exposing tyrants. But I am persuaded, that many of my brethren, particularly those who are ignorantly in league with slave-holders or tyrants, who acquire their daily bread by the blood and sweat of their more ignorant brethren—and not a few of those too, who are too ignorant to see an inch beyond their noses, will rise up and call me cursed—Yea, the jealous ones among us will perhaps use more abject subtlety, by affirming that this work is not worth perusing, that we are well situated, and there is no use in trying to better our condition, for we cannot. I will ask one question here.—Can our condition be any worse?—Can it be more mean and abject? If there are any changes, will they not be for the better, though they may appear for the worst at first? Can they get us any lower? Where can they get us? They are afraid to treat us worse, for they know well, the day they do it they are gone. But against all accusations which may or can be preferred against me, I appeal to Heaven for my motive in writing—who knows that my object is, if possible, to awaken in the breasts of my afflicted, degraded and slumbering brethren, a spirit of inquiry and investigation respecting our miseries and wretchedness in this *Republican Land of Liberty!!!!!!*

The sources from which our miseries are derived, and on which I shall comment, I shall not combine in one, but shall put them under distinct heads and expose them in their turn; in doing which, keeping truth on my side, and not departing from the strictest rules of morality, I shall endeavour to penetrate, search out, and lay them open for your inspection. If you cannot or will not profit by them, I shall have done *my* duty to you, my country and my God.

And as the inhuman system of *slavery*, is the *source* from which most of our miseries proceed, I shall begin with that *curse to nations*, which has spread terror and devastation through so many nations of antiquity, and which is raging to such a pitch at the present day in Spain and in Portugal. It had one tug in England, in France, and in the United States of America; yet the inhabitants thereof, do not learn wisdom, and erase it entirely from their dwellings and from all with whom they have to do. The fact is, the labour of slaves comes so cheap to the avaricious usurpers, and is (as they think) of such great utility to the country where it exists, that those who are actuated by sordid avarice only, overlook the evils, which will as sure as the Lord lives, follow after the good. In fact, they are so happy to keep in ignorance and degradation, and to receive the homage and the labour of the slaves, they forget that God rules in the armies of heaven and among the inhabitants of the earth, having his ears continually open to the cries, tears and groans of his oppressed people; and being a just and holy Being will at one day appear fully in behalf of the oppressed, and arrest the progress of the avaricious oppressors; for although the destruction of the oppressors God may not effect by the oppressed, yet the Lord our God will bring other destructions upon them—for not unfrequently will he cause them to rise up one against another, to be split and divided, and to oppress each other, and sometimes to open hostilities with sword in hand. Some may ask, what is the matter with this united and happy people?—Some say it is the cause of political usurpers, tyrants, oppressors, &c. But has not the Lord an oppressed and suffering people among them? Does the Lord condescend to hear their cries and see their tears in consequence of oppression? Will he let the oppressors rest comfortably and happy always? Will he not cause the very children of the oppressors to rise up against them, and oftimes put them to death? "God works in many ways his wonders to perform."

I will not here speak of the destructions which the Lord brought upon Egypt, in consequence of the oppression and consequent groans of the oppressed—of the hundreds and thousands of Egyptians whom God hurled into the Red Sea for afflicting his people in their land—of the Lord's suffering people in Sparta or Lacaedemon, the land of the truly famous Lycurgus—nor have I time to comment upon the cause which produced the fierceness with which Sylla usurped the title, and absolutely acted as dictator of the Roman people—the conspiracy of Cataline—the conspiracy against, and murder of Caesar in the Senate house—the spirit with which Marc Antony made himself master of the commonwealth—his associating Octavius and Lipidus with himself in power—their dividing the provinces of Rome among themselves—their attack and defeat, on the plains of Philippi, of the last defenders of their liberty, (Brutus and Cassius)—the tyranny of Tiberius, and from him to the final overthrow of Constantinople by the Turkish Sultan, Mahomed II, AD 1453. I say, I shall not take up time to speak of the *causes* which produced so much wretchedness and massacre among those heathen nations, for I am aware that you know too well, that God is just, as well as merciful!—I shall call your attention a few moments to that *Christian* nation, the Spaniards—while I shall leave almost unnoticed, that avaricious and cruel people, the Portuguese, among whom all true hearted Christians and lovers of Jesus Christ, must evidently see the judgments of God displayed. To show the judgments of God upon the Spaniards, I shall occupy but a little time, leaving a plenty of room for the candid and unprejudiced to reflect.

All persons who are acquainted with history, and particularly the Bible, who are not blinded by the God of this world, and are not actuated solely by avarice—who are able to lay aside prejudice long enough to view candidly and impartially, things as they were, are, and probably will be—who are willing to admit that God made man to serve Him *alone*, and that man should have no other Lord or Lords but Himself—that God Almighty is the *sole proprietor* or *master* of the Whole human family, and will not on any consideration admit of a colleague, being unwilling to divide his glory with another—and who can dispense with prejudice long enough to admit that we are men, notwithstanding our *improminent noses* and *woolly heads*, and believe that we feel for our fathers, mothers, wives and children, as well as the whites do for theirs.—I say, all who are permitted to see and believe these things, can easily recognize the judgments of God among the Spaniards. Though others may lay the cause of the fierceness with which they cut each other's throats, to some other circumstance, yet they who believe that God is a God of justice, will believe that Slavery *is the principal cause.*

While the Spaniards are running about upon the field of battle cutting each other's throats, has not the Lord an afflicted and suffering people in the midst of them, whose cries and groans in consequence of oppression are continually pouring into the ears of the God of justice? Would they not cease to cut each other's throats, if they could? But how can they? The very support which they draw from government to aid them in perpetrating such enormities, does it not arise in a great degree from the wretched victims of oppression among them? And yet they are calling for

Peace!—Peace!! Will any peace be given unto them? Their destruction may indeed be procrastinated awhile, but can it continue long, while they are oppressing the Lord's people? Has He not the hearts of all men in His hand? Will he suffer one part of his creatures to go on oppressing another like brutes always, with impunity? And yet, those avaricious wretches are calling for *Peace!!!!* I declare, it does appear to me, as though some nations think God is asleep, or that he made the Africans for nothing else but to dig their mines and work their farms, or they cannot believe history, sacred or profane. I ask every man who has a heart, and is blessed with the privilege of believing—Is not God a God of justice to *all* his creatures? Do you say he is? Then if he gives peace and tranquillity to tyrants, and permits them to keep our fathers, our mothers, ourselves and our children in eternal ignorance and wretchedness, to support them and their families, would he be to us a God of *justice?* I ask, O ye *Christians!!!* who hold us and our children in the most abject ignorance and degradation, that ever a people were afflicted with since the world began—I say, if God gives you peace and tranquillity, and suffers you thus to go on afflicting us, and our children, who have never given you the least provocation—would he be to us *a God of justice?* If you will allow that we are Men, who feel for each other, does not the blood of our fathers and of us their children, cry aloud to the Lord of Sabaoth against you, for the cruelties and murders with which you have, and do continue to afflict us. But it is time for me to close my remarks on the suburbs, just to enter more fully into the interior of this system of cruelty and oppression.

Article I. Our Wretchedness in Consequence of Slavery

My beloved brethren:—The Indians of North and of South America—the Greeks—the Irish, subjected under the king of Great Britain—the Jews, that ancient people of the Lord—the inhabitants of the islands of the sea—in fine, all the inhabitants of the earth, (except however, the sons of Africa) are called *men*, and of course are, and ought to be free. But we, (coloured people) and our children are *brutes!!* and of course are, and *ought to be* Slaves to the American people and their children forever!! to dig their mines and work their farms; and thus go on enriching them, from one generation to another with our *blood* and our *tears!!!!*

I promised in a preceding page to demonstrate to the satisfaction of the most incredulous, that we, (coloured people of these United States of America) are the *most wretched, degraded* and *abject* set of beings that *ever lived* since the world began, and that the white Americans having reduced us to the wretched state of *slavery*, treat us in that condition *more cruel* (they being an enlightened and Christian people), than any heathen nation did any people whom it had reduced to our condition. These affirmations are so well confirmed in the minds of all unprejudiced men, who have taken the trouble to read histories, that they need no elucidation from me. But to put them beyond all doubt, I refer you in the first place to the children of Jacob, or of Israel in Egypt, under Pharaoh and his people. Some of my brethren do not know who Pharaoh and the Egyptians were—I know it to be a fact, that some of them take the Egyptians to have been a gang of *devils*, not knowing any better, and that they (Egyptians) having got possession of the Lord's people, treated them *nearly* as cruel as *Christian Americans* do us, at the present day. For the information of such, I would only mention that the Egyptians, were Africans or coloured people, such as we are—some of them yellow and others dark—a mixture of Ethiopians and the natives of Egypt—about the same as you see the coloured people of the United States at the present day.—I say, I call your attention then, to the children of Jacob, while I point out particularly to you his son Joseph, among the rest, in Egypt.

"And Pharaoh said unto Joseph, thou shalt be over my house, and according unto thy word shall all my people be ruled: only in the throne will I be greater than thou."

"And Pharaoh said unto Joseph, see, I have set thee over all the land of Egypt."

"And Pharaoh said unto Joseph, I am Pharaoh, and without thee shall no man lift up his hand or foot in all the land of Egypt."

Now I appeal to heaven and to earth, and particularly to the American people themselves, who cease not to declare that our condition is not *hard*, and that we are comparatively satisfied to rest in wretchedness and misery, under them and their children. Not, indeed, to show me a coloured President, a Governor, a Legislator, a Senator, a Mayor, or an Attorney at the Bar.—But to show me a man of colour, who holds the low office of a Constable, or one who sits in a Juror Box, even on a case of one of his wretched brethren, throughout this great Republic!!—But let us pass Joseph the son of Israel a little farther in review, as he existed with that heathen nation.

"And Pharaoh called Joseph's name Zaphnath-paaneah; and he gave him to wife Asenath the daughter of Potipherah priest of On. And Joseph went out over all the land of Egypt."

Compare the above, with the American institutions. Do they not institute laws to prohibit us from marrying among the whites? I would wish, candidly, however, before the Lord, to be understood, that I would not give a *pinch of snuff* to be married to any white person I ever saw in all the days of my life. And I do say it, that the black man, or man of colour, who will leave his own colour (provided he can get one, who is good for any thing) and marry a white woman, to be a double slave to her, just because she is *white*, ought to be treated by her as he surely will be, viz: as a Niger!!!! It is not, indeed, what I care about inter-marriages with the whites, which induced me to pass this subject in review; for the Lord knows, that there is a day coming when they will be glad enough to get into the company of the blacks, notwithstanding, we are, in this generation, levelled by them, almost on a level with the brute creation: and some of us they treat even worse than they do the brutes that perish. I only made this extract to show how much lower we are held, and how much more cruel we are treated by the Americans, than were the children of Jacob, by the Egyptians.—We will notice the sufferings of Israel some further, under *heathen Pharaoh*, compared with ours under the *enlightened Christians of America.*

"And Pharaoh spake unto Joseph, saying, thy father and thy brethren are come unto thee:"

"The land of Egypt is before thee: in the best of the land make thy father and brethren to dwell; in the land of Goshen let them dwell: and if thou knowest any men of activity among them, then make them rulers over my cattle."

I ask those people who treat us so *well*, Oh! I ask them, where is the most barren spot of land which they have given unto us? Israel had the most fertile land in all Egypt. Need I mention the very notorious fact, that I have known a poor man of colour, who laboured night and day, to acquire a little money, and having acquired it, he vested it in a small piece of land, and got him a house erected thereon, and having paid for the whole, he moved his family into it, where he was suffered to remain but nine months, when he was cheated out of his property by a white man, and driven out of door! And is not this the case generally? Can a man of colour buy a piece of land

and keep it peaceably? Will not some white man try to get it from him, even if it is in a *mud hole*? I need not comment any farther on a subject, which all, both black and white, will readily admit. But I must, really, observe that in this very city, when a man of colour dies, if he owned any real estate it most generally falls into the hands of some white person. The wife and children of the deceased may weep and lament if they please, but the estate will be kept snug enough by its white possessor.

But to prove farther that the condition of the Israelites was better under the Egyptians than ours is under the whites. I call upon the professing philanthropist, I call upon the very tyrant himself, to show me a page of history, either sacred or profane, on which a verse can be found, which maintains, that the Egyptians heaped the *insupportable insult* upon the children of Israel, by telling them that they were not of the *human family.* Can the whites deny this charge? Have they not, after having reduced us to the deplorable condition of slaves under their feet, held us up as descending originally from the tribes of *Monkeys* or *Orang-Outangs?* O! my God! I appeal to every man of feeling—is not this insupportable? Is it not heaping the most gross insult upon our miseries, because they have got us under their feet and we cannot help ourselves? Oh! pity us we pray thee, Lord Jesus, Master.—Has Mr. Jefferson declared to the world, that we are inferior to the whites, both in the endowments of our bodies and of minds? It is indeed surprising, that a man of such great learning, combined with such excellent natural parts, should speak so of a set of men in chains. I do not know what to compare it to, unless, like putting one wild deer in an iron cage, where it will be secured, and hold another by the side of the same, then let it go, and expect the one in the cage to run as fast as the one at liberty. So far, my brethren, were the Egyptians from heaping these insults upon their slaves, that Pharaoh's daughter took Moses, a son of Israel for her own, as will appear by the following.

"And Pharaoh's daughter said unto her, [Moses' mother] take this child away, and nurse it for me, and I will pay thee thy wages. And the woman took the child [Moses] and nursed it."

"And the child grew, and she brought him unto Pharaoh's daughter and he became her son. And she called his name Moses: and she said because I drew him out of the water."

In all probability, Moses would have become Prince Regent to the throne, and no doubt, in process of time but he would have been seated on the throne of Egypt. But he had rather suffer shame, with the people of God, than to enjoy pleasures with that wicked people for a season. O! that the coloured people were long since of Moses' excellent disposition, instead of courting favour with, and telling news and lies to our *natural enemies*, against each other—aiding them to keep their hellish chains of slavery upon us. Would we not long before this time, have been respectable men, instead of such wretched victims of oppression as we are? Would they be able to drag our mothers, our fathers, our wives, our children and ourselves, around the world in chains and hand-cuffs as they do, to dig up gold and silver for them and theirs? This question, my brethren, I leave for you to digest; and may God Almighty force it home to your hearts. Remember that unless you are united, keeping your tongues within your teeth, you will be afraid to trust your secrets to each other, and thus perpetuate our miseries under the *Christians!!!!!* Addition.—

Remember, also to lay humble at the feet of our Lord and Master Jesus Christ, with prayers and fastings. Let our enemies go on with their butcheries, and at once fill up their cup. Never make an attempt to gain our freedom of *natural right*, from under our cruel oppressors and murderers, until you see your way clear*

[*It is not to be understood here, that I mean for us to wait until God shall take us by the hair of our heads and drag us out of abject wretchedness and slavery, nor do I mean to convey the idea for us to wait until our enemies shall make preparations, and call us to seize those preparations, take it away from them, and put every thing before us to death, in order to gain our freedom which God has given us. For you must remember that we are men as well as they. God has been pleased to give us two eyes, two hands, two feet, and some sense in our heads as well as they. They have no more right to hold us in slavery than we have to hold them, we have just as much right, in the sight of God, to hold them and their children in slavery and wretchedness, as they have to hold us, and no more.]

—when that hour arrives and you move, be not afraid or dismayed; for be you assured that Jesus Christ the King of heaven and of earth who is the God of justice and of armies, will surely go before you. And those enemies who have for hundreds of years stolen our *rights*, and kept us ignorant of Him and His divine worship, he will remove. Millions of whom, are this day, so ignorant and avaricious, that they cannot conceive how God can have an attribute of justice, and show mercy to us because it pleased Him to make

us black—which colour, Mr. Jefferson calls unfortunate!!!!!! As though we are not as thankful to our God, for having made us as it pleased himself, as they, (the whites,) are for having made them white. They think because they hold us in their infernal chains of slavery, that we wish to be white, or of their color—but they are dreadfully deceived—we wish to be just as it pleased our Creator to have made us, and no avaricious and unmerciful wretches, have any business to make slaves of, or hold us in slavery. How would they like for us to make slaves of, and hold them in cruel slavery, and murder them as they do us?—

But is Mr. Jefferson's assertions true? viz. "that it is unfortunate for us that our Creator has been pleased to make us black." We will not take his say so, for the fact. The world will have an opportunity to see whether it is unfortunate for us, that our Creator *has made us* darker than the *whites*.

Fear not the number and education of our *enemies*, against whom we shall have to contend for our lawful right; guaranteed to us by our Maker; for why should we be afraid, when God is, and will continue, (if we continue humble) to be on our side?

The man who would not fight under our Lord and Master Jesus Christ, in the glorious and heavenly cause of freedom and of God—to be delivered from the most wretched, abject and servile slavery, that ever a people was afflicted with since the foundation of the world, to the present day—ought to be kept with all of his children or family, in slavery, or in chains, to be butchered by his *cruel enemies*.

I saw a paragraph, a few years since, in a South Carolina paper, which, speaking of the barbarity of the Turks, it said: "The Turks are the most barbarous people in the world—they treat the Greeks more like brutes than human beings." And in the same paper was an advertisement, which said: "Eight well built Virginia and Maryland Negro fellows and four wenches will positively be sold this day, *to the highest bidder!*" And what astonished me still more was, to see in this same *humane* paper!! the cuts of three men, with clubs and budgets on their backs, and an advertisement offering a considerable sum of money for their apprehension and delivery. I declare, it is really so amusing to hear the Southerners and Westerners of this country talk about *barbarity*, that it is positively, enough to make a man *smile*.

The sufferings of the Helots among the Spartans, were somewhat severe, it is true, but to say that theirs, were as severe as ours among the Americans, I do most strenuously deny—for instance, can any man show me an article on a page of ancient history which specifies, that, the Spartans chained, and hand-cuffed the Helots, and dragged them from their wives and children, children from their parents, mothers from their suckling babes, wives from their husbands, driving them from one end of the country to the other? Notice the Spartans were heathens, who lived long before our Divine Master made his appearance in the flesh. Can Christian Americans deny these barbarous cruelties? Have you not, Americans, having subjected us under you, added to these miseries, by insulting us in telling us to our face, because we are helpless, that we are not of the human family? I ask you, O! Americans, I ask you, in the name of the Lord, can you deny these charges? Some perhaps may deny, by saying, that they never thought or said that we were not men. But do not actions speak louder than words?—have they not made provisions for the Greeks, and Irish? Nations who have never done the least thing for them, while *we*, who have enriched their country with our blood and tears—have dug up gold and silver for them and their children, from generation to generation, and are in more miseries than any other people under heaven, are not seen, but by comparatively, a handful of the American people? There are indeed, more ways to kill a dog, besides choking it to death with butter. Further—The Spartans or Lacedaemonians, had some frivolous pretext, for enslaving the Helots, for they (Helots) while being free inhabitants of Sparta, stirred up an intestine commotion, and were, by the Spartans subdued, and made prisoners of war. Consequently they and their children were condemned to perpetual slavery.

I have been for years troubling the pages of historians, to find out what our fathers have done to the *white Christians of America*, to merit such condign punishment as they have inflicted on them, and do continue to inflict on us their children. But I must aver, that my researches have hitherto been to no effect. I have therefore, come to the immoveable conclusion, that they (Americans) have, and do continue to punish us for nothing else, but for enriching them and their country. For I cannot conceive of any thing else. Nor will I ever believe otherwise, until the Lord shall convince me.

The world knows, that slavery as it existed among the Romans, (which was the primary cause of their destruction) was, comparatively speaking, no more than a *cypher*, when compared with ours under the Americans. Indeed I should not have noticed the Roman slaves, had not the very learned and penetrating Mr. Jefferson said, "when a master was murdered, all his slaves in the same house, or within hearing, were condemned to death."

—Here let me ask Mr. Jefferson, (but he is gone to answer at the bar of God, for the deeds done in his body while living,) I therefore ask the whole American people, had I not rather die, or be put to death, than to be a slave to any tyrant, who takes not only my own, but my wife and children's lives by the inches? Yea, would I meet death with avidity far! far!! in preference to such servile submission to the murderous hands of tyrants. Mr. Jefferson's very severe remarks on us have been so extensively argued upon by men whose attainments in literature, I shall never be able to reach, that I would not have meddled with it, were it not to solicit each of my brethren, who has the spirit of a man, to buy a copy of Mr. Jefferson's "Notes on Virginia," and put it in the hand of his son. For let no one of us suppose that the refutations which have been written by our white friends are enough—they are *whites*—we are *blacks*. We, and the world, wish to see the charges of Mr. Jefferson refuted by the blacks *themselves*, according to their chance; for we must remember that what the whites have written respecting this subject, is other men's labours, and did not emanate from the blacks. I know well, that there are some talents and learning among the coloured people of this country, which we have not a chance to develop, in consequence of oppression; but our oppression ought not to hinder us from acquiring all we can. For we will have a chance to develop them by and by. God will not suffer us, always to be oppressed. Our sufferings will come to an *end*, in spite of all the Americans this side of *eternity*. Then we will want all the learning and talents among ourselves, and perhaps more, to govern ourselves.— "Every dog must have its day," the American's is coming to an end.

But let us review Mr. Jefferson's remarks respecting us some further. Comparing our miserable fathers, with the learned philosophers of Greece, he says: "Yet notwithstanding these and other discouraging circumstances among the Romans, their slaves were often their rarest artists. They excelled too, in science, insomuch as to be usually employed as tutors to their master's children; Epictetus, Terence and Phaedrus, were slaves,—but they were of the race of whites. It is not their *condition* then, but *nature*, which has produced the distinction."

See this, my brethren!! Do you believe that this assertion is swallowed by millions of the whites? Do you know that Mr. Jefferson was one of as great character as ever lived among the whites? See his writings for the world, and public labours for the United States of America. Do you believe that the assertions of such a man, will pass away into oblivion unobserved by this people and the world? If you do you are much mistaken—See how the American people treat us—have we souls in our bodies? Are we men who have any spirits at all? I know that there are many *swell-bellied* fellows among us, whose greatest object is to fill their stomachs. Such I do not mean—I am after those who know and feel, that we are Men, as well as other people; to them, I say, that unless we try to refute Mr. Jefferson's arguments respecting us, we will only establish them.

But the slaves among the Romans. Every body who has read history, knows, that as soon as a slave among the Romans obtained his freedom, he could rise to the greatest eminence in the State, and there was no law instituted to hinder a slave from buying his freedom. Have not the Americans instituted laws to hinder us from obtaining our freedom? Do any deny this charge? Read the laws of Virginia, North Carolina, &c. Further: have not the Americans instituted laws to prohibit a man of colour from obtaining and holding any office whatever, under the government of the United States of America? Now, Mr. Jefferson tells us, that our condition is not so hard, as the slaves were under the Romans!!!!!!

It is time for me to bring this article to a close. But before I close it, I must observe to my brethren that at the close of the first Revolution in this country, with Great Britain, there were but thirteen States in the Union, now there are twenty-four, most of which are slave-holding States, and the whites are dragging us around in chains and in handcuffs, to their new States and Territories to work their mines and farms, to enrich them and their children—and millions of them believing firmly that we being a little darker than they, were made by our Creator to be an inheritance to them and their children for ever—the same as a parcel of *brutes*.

Are we Men!!—I ask you, O my brethren! are we Men? Did our Creator make us to be slaves to dust and ashes like ourselves? Are they not dying worms as well as we? Have they not to make their appearance before the tribunal of Heaven, to answer for the deeds done in the body, as well as we? Have we any other Master but Jesus Christ alone? Is he not their Master as well as ours?—What right then, have we to obey and call any other Master, but Himself? How we could be so *submissive* to a gang of men, whom we cannot tell whether they are *as good* as ourselves or not, I never could conceive. However, this is shut up with the Lord, and we cannot precisely tell—but I declare, we judge men by their works.

The whites have always been an unjust, jealous, unmerciful, avaricious and blood-thirsty set of beings, always seeking after power and authority.—We view them all over the confederacy of Greece, where they were first known to be any thing, (in consequence of education)

Glossary

"And Pharaoh said unto Joseph …"	quotations from the biblical book of Genesis, chapter 41
"And Pharaoh's daughter said unto her …"	quotations from the biblical book of Exodus, chapter 2
"And Pharaoh spake unto Joseph …"	quotation from the biblical book of Genesis, chapter 47
Caesar	Julius Caesar, Roman statesman and general of the first century BCE
Cataline	Lucius Sergius Catilina, a Roman who conspired to overthrow the Roman Republic
Epictetus	an ancient Stoic philosopher who was probably born a slave
Ethiopians	a term commonly used to refer to non-Egyptian Africans
"God works in many ways …"	loose quotation from William Cowper's 1774 hymn
Helots	the slave class in ancient Sparta
Jacob	the third patriarch of the Jewish people in the biblical Old Testament

we see them there, cutting each other's throats—trying to subject each other to wretchedness and misery—to effect which, they used all kinds of deceitful, unfair, and unmerciful means. We view them next in Rome, where the spirit of tyranny and deceit raged still higher. We view them in Gaul, Spain, and in Britain.—In fine, we view them all over Europe, together with what were scattered about in Asia and Africa, as heathens, and we see them acting more like devils than accountable men. But some may ask, did not the blacks of Africa, and the mulattoes of Asia, go on in the same way as did the whites of Europe. I answer, no—they never were half so avaricious, deceitful and unmerciful as the whites, according to their knowledge.

But we will leave the whites or Europeans as heathens, and take a view of them as Christians, in which capacity we see them as cruel, if not more so than ever. In fact, take them as a body, they are ten times more cruel, avaricious and unmerciful than ever they were; for while they were heathens, they were bad enough it is true, but it is positively a fact that they were not quite so audacious as to go and take vessel loads of men, women and children, and in cold blood, and through devilishness, throw them into the sea, and murder them in all kind of ways. While they were heathens, they were too ignorant for such barbarity. But being Christians, enlightened and sensible, they are completely prepared for such hellish cruelties. Now suppose God were to give them more sense, what would they do? If it were possible, would they not *dethrone* Jehovah and seat themselves upon his throne? I therefore, in the name and fear of the Lord God of Heaven and of earth, divested of prejudice either on the side of my colour or that of the whites, advance my suspicion of them, whether they are *as good by nature* as we are or not. Their actions, since they were known as a people, have been the reverse, I do indeed suspect them, but this, as I before observed, is shut up with the Lord, we cannot exactly tell, it will be proved in succeeding generations.—The whites have had the essence of the gospel as it was preached by my master and his apostles—the Ethiopians have not, who are to have it in its meridian splendor—the Lord will give it to them to their satisfaction. I hope and pray my God, that they will make good use of it, that it may be well with them.

It is my solemn belief, that if ever the world becomes Christianized, (which must certainly take place before

Joseph	one of Jacob's sons, sold into slavery in Egypt
Josephus	a Jewish historian of the first century
Lacedaemon	the name the ancient Greeks gave to Sparta
Lord of Sabaoth	God, literally the "Lord of Hosts," or armies
Lycurgus	a legendary law giver of ancient Sparta
Marc Antony	often spelled "Mark Anthony," a Roman politician and general who formed the Second Triumvirate with Octavian ("Octavius" in the document) and Marcus Lepidus
Mr. Jefferson	Thomas Jefferson, third U.S. president and author of *Notes on Virginia*.
Phaedrus	a writer of ancient Roman fables
plains of Philippi	the site of a battle in northern ancient Greece between Mark Anthony and the Second Triumvirate and Caesar's assassins, Marcus Junius Brutus and Gaius Cassius Longinus
Plutarch	a Greek philosopher of the first and second centuries CE
Sparta	a city-state in ancient Greece
Sylla	Lucius Sylla (more often spelled "Lucius Sulla"), a dictator of ancient Rome
Terence	a playwright in the ancient Roman Republic (whose Roman name was Publius Terentius Afer)
Tiberius	Tiberius Julius Caesar Augustus, a first-century Roman emperor

long) it will be through the means, under God of the Blacks, who are now held in wretchedness, and degradation, by the white Christians of the world, who before they learn to do justice to us before our Maker—and be reconciled to us, and reconcile us to them, and by that means have clear consciences before God and man.—Send out Missionaries to convert the Heathens, many of whom after they cease to worship gods, which neither see nor hear, become ten times more the children of Hell, then ever they were, why what is the reason? Why the reason is obvious, they must learn to do justice at home, before they go into distant lands, to display their charity, Christianity, and benevolence; when they learn to do justice, God will accept their offering, (no man may think that I am against Missionaries for I am not, my object is to see justice done at home, before we go to convert the Heathens)....

Article IV. Our Wretchedness in Consequence of the Colonizing Plan....

A declaration made July 4, 1776.
It says,
"When in the course of human events, it becomes necessary for one people to dissolve the political bands which have connected them with another, and to assume among the Powers of the earth, the separate and equal station to which the laws of nature and of nature's God entitle them. A decent respect for the opinions of mankind requires, that they should declare the causes which impel them to the separation.—We hold these truths to be self evident—that all men are created equal, that they are endowed by their Creator with certain unalienable rights: that among these, are life, liberty, and the pursuit of happiness that, to secure these rights, governments are instituted among men, deriving their just powers from the consent of the governed; that whenever any form of government becomes destructive of these ends, it is the right of the people to alter or to abolish it, and to institute a new government laying its foundation on such principles, and organizing its powers in such form, as to them shall seem most likely to effect their safety and happiness. Prudence, indeed, will dictate, that governments long established should not be changed for light and transient causes; and accordingly all experience hath shewn, that mankind are more disposed to suffer, while evils are sufferable, than to right themselves by abolishing the forms to which they are accustomed. But when a long train of abuses and usurpations, pursuing invariably the same object, evinces a design to reduce them under absolute despo-

tism, it is their right, it is their duty to throw off such government, and to provide new guards for their future security." See your Declaration Americans!!! Do you understand your own language? Hear your language, proclaimed to the world, July 4th, 1776—"We hold these truths to be self evident—that All Men Are Created Equal!! that they *are endowed by their Creator with certain unalienable rights*; that among these are life, *liberty*, and the pursuit of happiness!!" Compare your own language above, extracted from your Declaration of Independence, with your cruelties and murders inflicted by your cruel and unmerciful fathers and yourselves on our fathers and on us—men who have never given your fathers or you the least provocation!!!!!!

Hear your language further! "But when a long train of abuses and usurpations, pursuing invariably the same object, evinces a design to reduce them under absolute despotism, it is their *right*, it is their *duty*, to throw off such government, and to provide new guards for their future security."

Now, Americans! I ask you candidly, was your sufferings under Great Britain, one hundredth part as cruel and tyrannical as you have rendered ours under you? Some of you, no doubt, believe that we will never throw off your murderous government and "provide new guards for our future security." If Satan has made you believe it, will he not deceive you? ...

Do the whites say, I being a black man, ought to be humble, which I readily admit? I ask them, ought they not to be as humble as I? or do they think that they can measure arms with Jehovah? Will not the Lord yet humble them? or will not these very coloured people whom they now treat worse than brutes, yet under God, humble them low down enough? Some of the whites are ignorant enough to tell us, that we ought to be submissive to them, that they may keep their feet on our throats. And if we do not submit to be beaten to death by them, we are bad creatures and of course must be damned, &c. If any man wishes to hear this doctrine openly preached to us by the American preachers, let him go into the Southern and Western sections of this country—I do not speak from hear say—what I have written, is what I have seen and heard myself. No man may think that my book is made up of conjecture—I have travelled and observed nearly the whole of those things myself, and what little I did not get by my own observation, I received from those among the whites and blacks, in whom the greatest confidence may be placed.

The Americans may be as vigilant as they please, but they cannot be vigilant enough for the Lord, neither can they hide themselves, where he will not find and bring them out.

"The power of the master must be absolute to render the submission of the slave perfect."

Overview

State v. Mann has endured as perhaps the most important case in the entire body of American jurisprudence involving slavery. Of all the cases dealing with slaves and their masters, it is unrivaled for the stark, brutal coldness with which the master's authority is articulated. Writing for the North Carolina Supreme Court, Judge Thomas Ruffin gave masters (including those who merely hired the slaves of others) virtually unbridled physical dominion over their slaves. Ironically, the opinion's widest circulation emerged among abolitionists, who pointed to its rhetoric as confirmation of slavery's basic immorality. A body of criticism that reached a high note with Harriet Beecher Stowe in the 1850s was embraced, more than a century later, by revisionist legal historians for whom *State v. Mann* became emblematic of all that was wrong with the antebellum South.

The case arose from an incident that occurred in Edenton, North Carolina, on March 1, 1829. John Mann, a poor white, had in his possession a female slave who was actually owned by an underage orphan girl. Frustrated with the slave's resistance to his "chastisement" over what the trial court concluded was "a small offense," Mann shot her as she fled. The extent of her wounds is unknown. Mann was indicted for assault and battery. The trial took place in the fall in the Chowan County Superior Court. Upon an instruction that Mann, as one in possession of a slave owned by someone else, had only a "special property" in the slave, the jury found him guilty. Although the appeal to the North Carolina Supreme Court was filed during the fall 1829 term (hence its publication in a volume dated 1829), it was not heard until February 15, 1830. At that time, Ruffin had been serving on the court for little more than a month.

Context

State v. Mann arose against a backdrop of rising concerns about the security of the slave labor system. By 1829, North Carolina and Virginia were the only two states that continued to base voting rights on substantial property

ownership. Pressure to broaden access to the vote created alarm among the conservative slaveholding elite, who dominated the eastern parts of both states. They feared that expansion of the franchise to all white male citizens would open the door to increased rights for the enslaved. The political unrest that ultimately led to new constitutions in both states was reflected in incidents and threats of slave revolt. Well before Nat Turner's failed uprising of 1831, such revolts had become a constant threat. Both of these developments are important to understanding the context of *State v. Mann*.

The debate over voting rights came to a head first in Virginia. The Virginia Constitution of 1776, in effect, gave legislative control to the eastern region and its established plantation owners. As the population of small farmers in the western part of the state grew, however, the issue of the power imbalance demanded a resolution: Two-thirds of the state's white males were disenfranchised under this constitution. Arguing for reform, western Virginians appealed to the same abstract notions of the universal "rights of man" that had inspired the American Revolution.

In later years, Virginia's landed elite understood this appeal to fundamental human rights as an implicit challenge to the institution of slavery: "Were not slaves men?" one of them was prompted to ask. For these eastern plantation owners, the appeal to abstract "rights" that had driven the American Revolution was no longer compelling or convenient. Rather, they cited the disastrous outcome of such "rights" discourse in the French Revolution of 1789–1799 as well as the bloody slave revolt in Haiti (1791). For this argument, Edmund Burke's *Reflections on the Revolution in France* (1790) proved especially useful. Burke, an Anglo-Irish political philosopher, registered deep suspicions about appeals to idealized "rights": such notions, he concluded, were too easily abused. He argued for a politics of moderation and restraint that would tolerate certain inequities, with the understanding that no system was perfect.

Following Burke and other conservative thinkers, the slave owners of eastern Virginia counseled a kind of resignation that effectively justified the status quo. They privileged a social ethos in which individual will was subordinated to the good of the larger community, favoring the stability of tradition. After a protracted debate, in January 1830 a new

1787

- **November 17**
Thomas Ruffin is born at Newington, in the Tidewater region of Virginia.

1808

- Ruffin is admitted to the North Carolina bar.

1813

- Ruffin serves in the North Carolina House of Commons (to 1816).

1816

- Ruffin is elected as a judge of the North Carolina Superior Court, serving to 1818 (and also 1825–1828).

1822

- **June**
Denmark Vesey, inspired by the 1791 revolution in Saint Domingue (Haiti), is arrested in Charleston, S.C., charged with plotting insurrection.

1828

- Ruffin assumes the presidency of the State Bank of North Carolina, rescuing it from bankruptcy.

1829

- **Fall**
John Mann is found guilty in Chowan County (North Carolina) Superior Court of assault and battery upon a hired slave.

1830

- **January**
Ruffin joins the North Carolina Supreme Court.

- **January**
Virginia approves a new constitution that preserves the political dominance of eastern slave-owning conservatives.

- **February**
The appeal of John Mann's conviction is heard in the Supreme Court; subsequently Ruffin's opinion is published.

- **March**
David Walker's *Appeal to the Coloured Citizens of the World*, published in 1829, becomes widely known in North Carolina.

constitution was approved reflecting only minimal changes; the conservative majority had held its own.

Thomas Ruffin, a son of the eastern Virginia elite, would have been aware of Virginia's constitutional debates as well as the one closer to his North Carolina home. A similar demand for reform was heard in North Carolina beginning around 1820, though the eastern slaveholding establishment managed to hold off constitutional changes until 1835. Ruffin would also have known about the threats of slave insurrection that were troubling the region. Denmark Vesey's conspiracy in South Carolina, discovered in 1822, provoked widespread alarm. In North Carolina, one planned revolt was discovered in Onslow County in 1821 and another in Tarboro in 1825; from other counties into 1829 and early 1830 came anxious reports of the mobilization of runaway slaves. Surrounding Edenton (where the shooting had occurred) lived several thousand fugitive slaves, from the Albemarle Sound to the Great Dismal Swamp. They posed a constant threat.

Other signs of a restless political climate were the increased restrictions that North Carolina lawmakers placed on slaves and free blacks beginning in the 1820s. In 1827, for example, the legislature passed a law prohibiting the migration of any free blacks into the state, as well as an antivagrancy law requiring all able-bodied free blacks to be put to work.

David Walker's *Appeal to the Coloured Citizens of the World*, published in 1829 but not widely known in North Carolina until at least March 1830, is a text to which Ruffin may have been reacting. Walker, a free black born in North Carolina, was a lay evangelist closely associated with the African Methodist Episcopal minister Richard Allen. He combined revolutionary with biblical rhetoric to urge the enslaved to take freedom into their own hands, by force if necessary. Whether or not Ruffin knew about this incendiary publication before he wrote his opinion in *State v. Mann*, the greater circumstances place him squarely within the class of conservative planters who by the late 1820s held grave anxieties about the future of slavery.

State v. Mann can be read as part of a pattern reflected in the writings of an increasingly defensive slaveholding elite. The opinion can be situated along a continuum of proslavery polemics, between the positions taken by the conservative Virginians in 1829–1830, who sought at least to contain slavery as part of their successful campaign against efforts to dilute their power, and the full-throttle defense of slavery mounted by the educator and writer Thomas Dew in the aftermath of the Virginia slavery debates of 1831–1832.

About the Author

Thomas Carter Ruffin was born in 1787 in King and Queen County, Virginia, to a family with strong ties to the Virginia planter establishment. He graduated with honors in 1805 from Princeton University and studied law in Petersburg, Virginia, from 1806 to 1807, when he followed his family to Rockingham County, North Carolina. Admitted to the North Carolina bar in 1808, he moved the following year to Hillsborough. In December 1809 he married Anne Kirkland, daughter of a wealthy Scottish merchant. He joined the Episcopal Church, over time becoming one of the leading Episcopalians of the state. His daughter Anne married Paul Carrington Cameron, who reputedly became the wealthiest man in the state.

Ruffin quickly forged relationships with the lawyers, planters, and businessmen who were seeking to modernize the state's railroads and banking interests. In 1813 he was elected to the North Carolina House of Commons, becoming Speaker of the House in 1816. After two years' service on the superior court bench (1817–1818), he resigned to pursue private practice. In 1825 he returned to the superior court, and in 1828 he accepted a call to leave the bench to take charge of the failing State Bank of North Carolina, a task at which he succeeded handily.

The legal historian Eric Muller has investigated Ruffin's participation in the slave trade. Ruffin partnered with one Benjamin Chambers, who traded in slaves, selling them for profit in the Lower South. Ruffin provided the equity for this speculative venture but sought to avoid notice: The business was to be carried out in Chambers's name only. Muller has also expanded the scholarship documenting Ruffin's own abuse of certain slaves in his own household.

Meanwhile, Ruffin's public reputation remained strong. In December 1829 he was elected by the legislature to the Supreme Court of North Carolina. The court had been criticized throughout the 1820s by populist legislators who sought the popular election of judges and a variety of other anticourt measures. All of these proposals were defeated. Historians of the court have contended that the legal talent and personal integrity of Thomas Ruffin, combined with similar qualities possessed by his colleague William Gaston, were integral to the survival of the court during this challenging period.

Ruffin presided as chief justice of North Carolina from 1833 to 1852. Notably, he used the tools of the common law to hasten economic progress. Particularly notable was his decision in *Raleigh and Gaston Railroad Company v. Davis* (1837), a seminal case establishing the use of eminent domain for the taking of private land on behalf of a railroad. The twentieth-century legal historian Roscoe Pound named Ruffin one of the ten greatest judges of American history.

Off the bench, in an address before the Agricultural Society of North Carolina in 1855, Ruffin shared his thoughts about slavery. He acknowledged the existence of "cruel and devilish masters" but claimed that their numbers were kept in check by the power of public opinion, combined with the master's economic self-interest. Reflecting an evolution of thought that he shared with his fellow planters, in this address he went so far as to argue for slavery's positive good: "I appeal to everyone, if our experience [with slavery] is not in accordance with the divine statute."

During the secession crisis Ruffin proclaimed loyalty to the Union (and to the institution of slavery), lending his voice to the call for compromise. He served as delegate to a peace conference convened by Senator John J. Crittenden

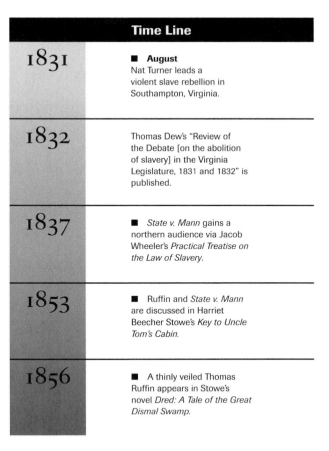

Time Line

1831	■ **August** Nat Turner leads a violent slave rebellion in Southampton, Virginia.
1832	Thomas Dew's "Review of the Debate [on the abolition of slavery] in the Virginia Legislature, 1831 and 1832" is published.
1837	■ *State v. Mann* gains a northern audience via Jacob Wheeler's *Practical Treatise on the Law of Slavery*.
1853	■ Ruffin and *State v. Mann* are discussed in Harriet Beecher Stowe's *Key to Uncle Tom's Cabin*.
1856	■ A thinly veiled Thomas Ruffin appears in Stowe's novel *Dred: A Tale of the Great Dismal Swamp*.

of Kentucky in February 1861. But the failure to achieve a workable middle ground disillusioned him. As the war broke out, he sided with the North Carolina secessionists.

After the war, Ruffin successfully sought a pardon from President Andrew Johnson, but on one important point he remained unreconciled: the drafting of North Carolina's postwar constitution. In 1866 Ruffin vigorously opposed the new method of apportioning representation, which was on the basis of the white population only, no longer including three-fifths of the enslaved population under the old federal formula. The new formula threatened a dramatic power shift. Ruffin challenged the very legitimacy of this constitution, holding fast to his commitment to the antebellum political structure. His Haw River plantation having been ravaged by Union occupation, he retired to Hillsborough, where he died in 1870.

Explanation and Analysis of the Document

State v. Mann overturned a Chowan County jury's conviction of a slave hirer, John Mann, for assault and battery upon a slave named Lydia, who belonged to Elizabeth Jones, a minor. (The hiring out of an orphan's enslaved property was part of a guardian's duties to maintain the value of the orphan's estate.) The record does not disclose why a criminal charge rather than a civil claim for damages was pursued, but Mann's poverty may have been a factor.

Frontispiece to Reflections on the French Revolution, *showing Edmund Burke on bended knee before Marie Antoinette*
(Library of Congress)

A jury of twelve men, most if not all of them slave owners, convicted him upon an instruction requiring them to assume that the assault had been "cruel and unreasonable" and, further, to recognize that as a hirer, he had only a "special property," or limited license, in the slave. Mann took an immediate appeal to the North Carolina Supreme Court, where he prevailed.

The four numbered statements that precede the opinion proper represent standard legal format of the time and are self-explanatory. In the first paragraph of the opinion proper, Ruffin purports to be deeply troubled by the decision that he is about to announce, emphasizing that "the duty of the magistrate" is to take responsibility for imposing the law of the state. Yet a careful analysis reveals that the law of North Carolina on this particular question was not at all clear: Ruffin could have upheld Mann's conviction through the application of settled common-law principles.

The key move that Ruffin makes in setting up the terms of his reversal is to declare the distinction between a hirer and an owner of a slave irrelevant: The hirer "is, for the time being, the owner." No precedent dictated this conclusion.

Nonetheless, having restated the issue as the extent to which any slave master might be answerable for criminal assault, Ruffin asserts, again without citing a legal authority, that the courts were powerless to limit a master's authority. "The power of the master must be absolute," Ruffin writes, "to render the submission of the slave perfect." Although he claims "a sense of harshness" over the severity of the decision, he seals the master's behavior from judicial interference.

The arguments that Ruffin employs echo those that conservative Virginia planters were making to defend the status quo—arguments that incorporated deeply held fears that expansion of the right to vote was a slippery slope that could result in a persuasive argument for the enfranchisement of slaves. The first justification presented for the master's "absolute" power is an appeal not to precedent but to the judgment of "the established habits and uniform practice of the country." Ruffin contrasts the abstract "principle of moral right" with "the actual condition of things," which dictates that "it must be so." That community standards must take precedence over slippery notions of abstract justice is reiterated in the penultimate paragraph of the opinion: Ruffin disdains "any rash expositions of abstract truths by a judiciary tainted with a false and fanatical philanthropy, seeking to redress an acknowledged evil by means still more wicked and appalling than that evil." His judgment thus accords with the conservative constitutionalist political philosophy of Edmund Burke.

This important distinction between the actual and the abstract was clearly expressed in the Virginia debate. Following Burke, conservatives argued that "truth" was a function of community norms established through actual, time-honored experience. Correspondingly, Ruffin declines to engage in the kind of case-by-case reasoning that would have allowed guilt to be decided by a jury: "We are forbidden to enter upon a train of general reasoning on the subject. We cannot allow the right of the master to be brought into discussion in the courts of justice."

Ruffin is not saying that a case in which a master has abused his authority might never arise—only that the question cannot be subjected to the uncertainties of a jury trial. Similarly in Virginia in 1828, although the eastern conservatives recognized that the westerners had a point as a matter of principle, as one eastern gentleman wrote to another, the argument for reform was not compelling enough to overcome "the actual condition of things."

The prosecution's argument that the master's authority should be subject to the same limits as that of a parent over a child, a tutor over a student, or a master over an apprentice is judged not persuasive: According to Ruffin, "There is no likeness between the cases." The difference is that in the master-slave relationship, the objective is "the profit of the master." The slave's obedience, he continues, "is a consequence only of uncontrolled authority over the body."

Within this assertion lies one of the most startling aspects of the opinion: the way in which Ruffin punctures the romantic fiction of the happy slaveholding "family." Although he appeals to the moral responsibility of the master to treat his slaves with restraint, he does not rest his argu-

"The established habits and uniform practice of the country in this respect is the best evidence of the portion of power deemed by the whole community requisite to the preservation of the master's dominion."

"The end [of slavery] is the profit of the master, his security and the public safety; the subject, one doomed in his own person and his posterity, to live without knowledge and without the capacity to make anything his own, and to toil that another may reap the fruits."

"The power of the master must be absolute to render the submission of the slave perfect."

"The slave, to remain a slave, must be made sensible that there is no appeal from his master; that his power is in no instance usurped; but is conferred by the laws of man at least, if not by the law of God."

ment on any notions of paternalism. Recognizing that the slave's loyalty is coerced, he acknowledges that the system of slavery is inherently unstable. Slavery had to be protected from external threats—and a legal constraint on the master's authority would have been seen as such a threat.

The trial court's conviction of John Mann for callously taking aim against a hired slave would seem an unlikely threat to the integrity of the entire slave system. Mann, an old seaman mired in debt, was a dubious torchbearer for the "absolute" rights of the master. But his conviction, while it vindicated the rights of Lydia's owner, also sent a message of sympathy—perhaps even reward—regarding a slave who had been shot while fleeing a white man's control. If Ruffin was indeed troubled by fears of political unrest and slave revolt, *State v. Mann* provided him with a ready platform: The case afforded an opportunity to consolidate the authority of white men, without regard to social rank. The reversal of Mann's conviction may be seen as a dramatic, preemptive expansion of the numbers of white men with an unqualified right of discipline over slaves.

Ruffin's elision of the difference between a slave owner and a slave hirer was a crucial strategic and rhetorical move

that enabled him to avoid nuance, to expound upon the issue of the master's authority in broad, firm strokes. The sense of inevitability that pervades the decision is another characteristic that aligns the opinion with the hardening positions of Ruffin's contemporaries in response to perceived threats to the institution of slavery. Such a sense is conveyed from the opinion's very opening lines: "It is impossible that the reasons on which [such cases] go can be appreciated, but where institutions similar to our own exist and are thoroughly understood…. It is useless, however, to complain of things inherent in our political state." In the passage citing physical force as the ultimate foundation for slavery, we find, again, a tone of somber resignation: "I most freely confess my sense of the harshness of this proposition; I feel it as deeply as any man can," Ruffin writes, but "this discipline belongs to the state of slavery."

The consequence of such fatalistic rhetoric is to preclude real debate—not simply to declare that one party is right (as a legal opinion must) but, indeed, to present the argument as closed from the beginning. Ruffin's opinion rejects the notion that any claim of assault brought on behalf of a slave against any "person having command of the slave" could prevail against the combined interest of "the property of the master, his security and the public safety." It avoids an analysis of conflicting principles. It is not seriously engaged in a balancing of competing interests (although the opportunity to weigh the interest of the hirer against that of the owner was certainly available). Within the conventions of a judicial opinion, it is a discourse upon the rules of behavior "while slavery exists among us in its present state," written with a wary eye toward those who would challenge its very existence.

Ruffin concludes by returning to his initial claim of regret for the necessity of addressing such a troubling issue. He asserts (again without citation to legal authority) that a limit to a slave master's physical power of correction could be established only by an act of the state legislature.

Audience

The immediate audience for the opinion would have been the defendant, John Mann, and the citizens of Chowan County. But the sweeping nature of Ruffin's rhetoric suggests that he intended a much broader audience. Ruffin's Virginia background, his position as a prominent North Carolina lawyer and planter, and evidence from the text itself all suggest that he was responding to an emerging resistance to pressures upon the planter elite to become a more inclusive polity (raising the theoretical possibility of voting rights for slaves), pressures accompanied by continuing threats of slave revolt. Certain passages explicitly suggest that he was addressing northern abolitionists. For example, his assertion at the beginning that a case such as this one cannot be fully "appreciated" except "where institutions similar to our own exist" can be seen as an appeal for the understanding of readers who lived beyond the regions in which slavery was practiced. (As noted, the opinion did reach abolitionists, but for the most part their interpretation was at odds with his intention. They took serious issue with the claim that the law required the reversal of Mann's conviction.) Within this uneasy context he also appears to have been speaking broadly to fellow southerners, strengthening the basis for their defense of slavery by explaining its foundation in "the actual condition of things."

Impact

As legal precedent, the impact of *State v. Mann* is unclear. Unquestionably, the opinion sanctioned the harsh, even reckless treatment of slaves. But subsequent opinions of the North Carolina Supreme Court chipped away at the master's "absolute" power. In *State v. Will* (1834), for example, the court recognized a slave's right of self-defense against a master's aggression.

The opinion owes its lasting fame, ironically, to northern abolitionists. Citing the text as reproduced in

Jacob Wheeler's *Practical Treatise on the Law of Slavery* (1837), they turned Ruffin's opinion on its head. What the abolitionists found interesting in *State v. Mann* was not so much its defense of the inviolability of the master-slave relationship as its tacit admission of slavery's inherent immorality. Ruffin had removed the veneer of "big house" gentility—the notion that slaves, presumably incapable of higher pursuits, lived happily under the benevolent, paternal rule of plantation owners. His concession that the basis for slavery lay ultimately in a brutal power relationship became, for the abolitionists, a testament to the evil at the root of the system. The opinion came to be cited by the likes of William Lloyd Garrison and Theodore Weld in what might today be called sound bites—isolated quotations selected for their extraordinary rhetorical force. (The particulars of the case were of little interest to these writers.) The assertion that the purpose of slavery was "the profit of the master" was considered especially revealing. Within the growing body of abolitionist literature, *State v. Mann* stood for quite the opposite of what its author intended. It came to be cited so often that allusions could be made to it without naming the judge or the case.

In her *Key to Uncle Tom's Cabin* (1853), Harriet Beecher Stowe quoted from *State v. Mann* at length as she built her own argument on the immorality of slavery. In her ideological interpretation, Ruffin was a moral man trapped within an immoral system. She believed him when he wrote of "the struggle ... in the Judge's own breast between the feelings of the man and the duty of the magistrate." Influencing generations of readers, Stowe took Ruffin at his word that something larger than his own moral code, something vast and immovable called "the law," compelled him to overturn Mann's conviction.

Stowe's novel *Dred: A Tale of the Great Dismal Swamp* (1865) inscribes the very text of *State v. Mann* within its plot. The case in the novel comes to be decided by Judge Clayton, a character who does genuinely engage in a moral struggle in which his heart is finally overcome by fidelity to an unbending law. His own son, an attorney who prosecuted the case in his father's court, responds by fleeing with his slaves to Canada. Thus recast as a morality tale demonstrating the failure of the laws of men, Ruffin's words reached an even broader audience than before.

The body of criticism initiated by the early abolitionists and amplified by Stowe was embraced and expanded in the twentieth century by academic legal historians. Speaking in 1996 about the first conference on the American law of slavery, held in 1971, the historian Stanley N. Katz noted, "It was as though a group of people who had never seen one another before discovered that they had all been raised in the same little village.... It was named *State v. Mann*."

See also David Walker's *Appeal to the Coloured Citizens of the World* (1829); *The Confessions of Nat Turner* (1831).

Further Reading

■ Articles

Greene, Sally. "*State v. Mann* Exhumed." *North Carolina Law Review* 87, no. 3 (2009): 701–755.

Korobkin, Laura H. "Appropriating Law in Harriet Beecher Stowe's *Dred*." *Nineteenth-Century Literature* 62, no. 3 (2007): 380–406.

Muller, Eric. "Judging Thomas Ruffin and the Hindsight Defense." *North Carolina Law Review* 87, no. 3 (2009): 757–798.

Wynn, James A., Jr. "*State v. Mann*: Judicial Choice or Judicial Duty?" *North Carolina Law Review* 87, no. 3 (2009): 991–1002.

■ Books

Anderson, Jean Bradley. *The Kirklands of Ayr Mount*. Chapel Hill: University of North Carolina Press, 1991.

Censer, Jane Turner. *North Carolina Planters and Their Children, 1800–1860*. Baton Rouge: Louisiana State University Press, 1984.

Dunn, Susan. *Dominion of Memories: Jefferson, Madison, and the Decline of Virginia*. New York: Basic Books, 2007.

Franklin, John Hope. *The Free Negro in North Carolina, 1790–1860*. Chapel Hill: University of North Carolina Press, 1943.

Hamilton, J. G. de Roulhac, ed. *The Papers of Thomas Ruffin*. Vol. 4. Raleigh, N.C.: Edwards and Broughton Printing, 1920.

Huebner, Timothy S. *The Southern Judicial Tradition: State Judges and Sectional Distinctiveness, 1790–1890*. Athens: University of Georgia Press, 1999.

Tushnet, Mark V. *Slave Law in the American South: State v. Mann in History and Literature*. Lawrence: University Press of Kansas, 2003.

—Sally Greene

Questions for Further Study

1. Describe the political issues that formed the backdrop for Ruffin's opinion in *State v. Mann*.

2. What events and documents dating back to the eighteenth century gave rise to the climate in which *State v. Mann* arose? How did these events and documents influence attitudes toward slavery in Virginia and North Carolina in the 1820s and 1830s?

3. Compare this document to David Walker's *Appeal to the Coloured Citizens of the World* (1829). Explain the extent to which Ruffin's opinion may have been a response to Walker.

4. Explain the distinction between "community standards" and "abstract justice" and how the distinction affected the outcome of *State v. Mann*.

5. In what way did the opinion in *State v. Mann* actually serve the interests of abolitionists in the antebellum North?

STATE V. MANN

1. The master is not liable to an indictment for a battery committed upon his slave.

2. One who has a right to the labor of a slave has also a right to all the means of controlling his conduct which the owner has.

3. Hence one who has hired a slave is not liable to an indictment for a battery on him, committed during the hiring.

4. But this rule does not interfere with the owner's right to damages for an injury affecting the value of a slave, which is regulated by the law of bailment.

The defendant was indicted for an assault and battery upon Lydia, the slave of one Elizabeth Jones.

On the trial it appeared that the defendant had hired the slave for a year; that during the term the slave had committed some small offense, for which the defendant undertook to chastise her; that while in the act of so doing the slave ran off, whereupon the defendant called upon her to stop, which being refused, he shot and wounded her.

His Honor, Judge Daniel, charged the jury that if they believed the punishment inflicted by the defendant was cruel and unwarrantable, and disproportionate to the offense committed by the slave, that in law the defendant was guilty, as he had only a special property in the slave.

A verdict was returned for the State, and the defendant appealed.

No counsel for the defendant.

The *Attorney-General*, for the State.

Ruffin, J. A Judge cannot but lament when such cases as the present are brought into judgment. It is impossible that the reasons on which they go can be appreciated, but where institutions similar to our own exist and are thoroughly understood. The struggle, too, in the Judge's own breast between the feelings of the man and the duty of the magistrate is a severe one, presenting strong temptation to put aside such questions, if it be possible. It is useless, however, to complain of things inherent in our political state. And it is criminal in a Court to avoid any responsibility which the laws impose. With whatever reluctance, therefore, it is done, the Court is compelled to express an opinion upon the extent of the dominion of the master over the slave in North Carolina.

The indictment charges a battery on Lydia, a slave of Elizabeth Jones. Upon the face of the indictment, the case is the same as *S. v. Hall [Hale]*.… No fault is found with the rule then adopted; nor would be, if it were now open. But it is not open; for the question, as it relates to a battery on a slave by a stranger, is considered as settled by that case. But the evidence makes this a different case. Here the slave had been hired by the defendant, and was in his possession; and the battery was committed during the period of hiring. With the liabilities of the hirer to the general owner for an injury permanently impairing the value of the slave no rule now laid down is intended to interfere. That is left upon the general doctrine of bailment. The inquiry here is whether a cruel and unreasonable battery on a slave by the hirer is indictable. The Judge below instructed the Jury that it is.

He seems to have put it on the ground that the defendant had but a special property. Our laws uniformly treat the master or other person having the possession and command of the slave as entitled to the same extent of authority. The object is the same—the services of the slave; and the same powers must be confided. In a criminal proceeding, and indeed in reference to all other persons but the general owner, the hirer and possessor of a slave, in relation to both rights and duties, is, for the time being, the owner. This opinion would, perhaps, dispose of this particular case; because the indictment, which charges a battery upon the slave of Elizabeth Jones, is not supported by proof of a battery upon defendant's own slave; since different justifications may be applicable to the two cases. But upon the general question whether the owner is answerable *criminaliter* for a battery upon his own slave, or other exercise of authority or force not forbidden by statute, the Court entertains but little doubt. That he is so liable has never yet been decided; nor, as far as is known, been hitherto contended. There have been no prosecutions of the sort. The established habits and uniform practice of the country in this respect is the best evidence of the portion of power deemed by the whole community requisite to the preservation of the master's dominion. If we thought differently we could not set our notions in array against the judgment of every body else, and say that this or that authority may be safely lopped off. This has indeed been assimilated at the bar to the other domestic relations; and arguments drawn from the well-established principles which confer and restrain the authority of the parent over the child, the tutor over the pupil, the master over the apprentice, have been pressed on us. The Court does not recognize their application. There is no likeness between the cases. They are in opposition to each other, and there is an impassable gulf between them. The difference is that which exists between freedom and slavery—and a greater cannot be imagined. In the one, the end in view is the happiness of the youth, born to equal rights with that governor, on whom the duty devolves of training the young to usefulness in a station which he is afterwards to assume among freemen. To such an end, and with such a subject, moral and intellectual instruction seem the natural means; and for the most part they are found to suffice. Moderate force is superadded, only to make the others effectual. If that fail it is better to leave the party to his own headstrong passions, and the ultimate correction of the law than to allow it to be immoderately inflicted by a private person. With slavery it is far otherwise. The end is the profit of the master, his security and the public safety; the subject, one doomed in his own person and his posterity, to live without knowledge and without the capacity to make anything his own, and to toil that another may reap the fruits. What moral considerations shall be addressed to such a being, to convince him what it is impossible but that the most stupid must feel and know can never be true—that he is thus to labor upon a principle of natural duty, or for the sake of his own personal happiness, such services can only be expected from one who has no will of his own; who surrenders his will in implicit obedience to that of another. Such obedience is the consequence only of uncontrolled authority over the body. There is nothing else which can operate to produce the effect. The power of the master must be absolute to render the submission of the slave perfect. I most freely confess my sense of the harshness of this proposition; I feel it as deeply as any man can; and as a principle of moral right every person in his retirement must repudiate it. But in the actual condition of things it must be so. There is no remedy. This discipline belongs to the state of slavery. They cannot be disunited without abrogating at once the rights of the master and absolving the slave from his subjection. It constitutes the curse of slavery to both the bond and free portion of our population. But it is inherent in the relation of master and slave.

That there may be particular instances of cruelty and deliberate barbarity where, in conscience, the law might properly interfere, is most probable. The difficulty is to determine where a Court may properly begin. Merely in the abstract it may well be asked, which power of the master accords with right? The answer will probably sweep away all of them. But we cannot look at the matter in that light. The truth is that we are forbidden to enter upon a train of general reasoning on the subject. We cannot allow the right of the master to be brought into discussion in the courts of justice. The slave, to remain a slave, must be made sensible, that there is no appeal from his master; that his power is in no instance usurped; but is conferred by the laws of man at least, if not by the law of God. The danger would be great, indeed, if the tribunals of justice should be called on to graduate the punishment appropriate to every temper and every dereliction of menial duty. No man can anticipate the many and aggravated provocations of the master which the slave would be constantly stimulated by his own passions or the instigation of others to give; or the consequent wrath of the master, prompting him to bloody vengeance upon the turbulent traitor—a vengeance generally practiced with impunity by reason of its privacy. The Court, therefore, disclaims the power of changing the relation in which these parts of our people stand to each other.

We are happy to see that there is daily less and less occasion for the interposition of the Courts. The protection already afforded by several statutes, that all-powerful motive, the private interest of the owner, the benevolences towards each other, seated in the hearts of those who have been born and bred together, the frowns and deep execrations of the community upon the barbarian who is guilty of excessive and brutal cruelty to his unprotected slave, all combined, have produced a mildness of treatment and attention to the comforts of the unfortunate class of slaves, greatly mitigating the rigors of servitude and ameliorating the condition of the slaves. The same causes are operating and will continue to operate with increased action until the disparity in numbers between the whites and blacks shall have rendered the latter in no degree dangerous to the former, when the police now existing may be further relaxed. This result, greatly to be desired, may be much more rationally expected from the events above alluded to, and now in progress, than from any rash expositions of abstract truths by a judiciary tainted with a false and fanatical philanthropy, seeking to redress an acknowledged evil by means still more wicked and appalling than even that evil.

I repeat that I would gladly have avoided this ungrateful question. But being brought to it the Court is compelled to declare that while slavery exists amongst us in its present state, or until it shall seem fit to the Legislature to interpose express enactments to the contrary, it will be the imperative duty of the Judges to recognize the full dominion of the owner over the slave, except where the exercise of it is forbidden by statute. And this we do upon the ground that this dominion is essential to the value of slaves as property, to the security of the master, and the public tranquility, greatly dependent upon their subordination; and, in fine, as most effectually securing the general protection and comfort of the slaves themselves.

Per Curiam. Reversed and judgment entered for the defendant.

Glossary

bailment	delivery of property by the owner to someone else, who holds the property for special purposes and then returns it to the owner
criminaliter	criminally, as opposed to civilly
per curiam	Latin for "by the court," referring to an opinion rendered by the entire appellate court (or a majority) rather than by justices individually
special property	property that a temporary holder has a limited right to use

William Lloyd Garrison (Library of Congress)

WILLIAM LLOYD GARRISON'S FIRST *LIBERATOR* EDITORIAL

1831

"Let all the enemies of the persecuted blacks tremble."

Overview

On January 1, 1831, a twenty-five-year-old editor named William Lloyd Garrison leaped to prominence as an advocate of immediate slave emancipation with the first publication of the *Liberator*. Garrison's new weekly journal was only four pages in size and boasted few initial subscribers, but it sent shock waves through the nation by virtue of its relentless attacks upon slavery and its unwillingness to make peace with more moderate slavery opponents. The *Liberator*'s inaugural editorial spelled out Garrison's essential beliefs, ones he adhered to during the thirty-five years of his publication's existence. Provocative, accusatory, and steeped in religious fervor, the editorial's words served as the opening shot in a campaign of ideas that would cease only with the emancipation of America's slaves.

Slavery did not rank high among the controversies that troubled America's political life during the 1830s. A desire to keep peace within the Union, a preoccupation with such issues as the tariff and westward expansion, and a pervasive racism in both the North and South kept slavery largely out of the public debate. Until the publication of the *Liberator*, the antislavery sentiment that existed was largely channeled into supporting the colonization of freed slaves overseas, with only a few dedicated souls actively working to free the millions of African Americans in bondage.

Context

In 1776 the newly approved Declaration of Independence asserted "that all men are created equal, that they are endowed by their Creator with certain unalienable rights." By the time the U.S. Constitution was officially declared in effect in 1789, however, it was clear that this statement of equality did not include the millions of slaves held in both the northern and southern states. Thomas Jefferson, Patrick Henry, and other Revolutionary leaders of southern birth considered slavery a moral evil and wished—in theory—to see it eradicated. While antislavery sentiment existed in Virginia and other southern states in the early

nineteenth century, the growing profitability of the slave-based plantation system helped keep the South wedded to the institution. The northern states gradually freed their own slaves, but they showed no real inclination to interfere with slavery south of the Mason-Dixon Line. Few organized bodies of private citizens cared to oppose slavery publicly. Among the established religious denominations, only the Quakers sought to convince others that slavery was wrong. The nation's unease over the idea of human servitude was reflected in the federal suppression of the African slave trade in 1808 (with a supplementary act in 1819) and in the controversy over slavery's extension leading up to the Missouri Compromise of 1820. For the most part, though, the subject was not a matter of wide concern among America's free white citizens. Abolitionists—those dedicated to abolishing slavery—were looked upon as impractical dreamers or dangerous fanatics.

Still, there were signs of a slowly growing antislavery sentiment scattered around the country. The mildest form was represented by the American Colonization Society, an organization established in 1816 to encourage the resettlement of freed slaves in overseas colonies. Those who favored more vigorous efforts to end slavery took encouragement from the work of Benjamin Lundy, a Quaker abolitionist who began publishing his newspaper the *Genius of Universal Emancipation* in 1821. Although he advocated gradual rather than immediate emancipation, Lundy won a small band of converts for his courage in attacking slavery at all. This group included a young William Lloyd Garrison, who became the coeditor of the *Genius* in 1829. That same year, David Walker, a free black man living in Boston, asserted the right of slaves to rebel against their masters in his pamphlet *Walker's Appeal ... to the Coloured Citizens of the World*. This angry document—which even Garrison condemned—marked the early stirrings of a new militancy among antislavery forces.

By 1830 a number of social, political, and religious trends in America increased sympathy for antislavery views. Such evangelical Protestant preachers as Charles G. Finney advocated the doctrine of perfectionism, which stressed personal responsibility for one's own salvation and encouraged involvement in humanitarian causes. Finney's teachings were widely embraced in the North during the 1820s

1775

■ **April 14**
The first U.S. antislavery society formed in Philadelphia, with Benjamin Franklin as the president.

1808

■ **January 1**
Importation of slaves into the United States is prohibited.

1816

■ **December**
First meeting of American Colonization Society is held.

1820

■ **March 3**
Missouri Compromise is passed by Congress, banning slavery west of the Mississippi River north of the 36°30' latitude line.

1829

■ **July 4**
William Lloyd Garrison delivers an important antislavery address at Park Street Church in Boston.

1831

■ **January 1**
First issue of the *Liberator* is published.

■ **November 11**
Nat Turner is hanged for leading a slave rebellion in Virginia.

1833

■ **December 4**
The American Anti-Slavery Society is organized in Philadelphia.

1835

■ **October 21**
Garrison is attacked by a mob at the Female Anti-Slavery Society meeting in Boston.

1848

■ **March 10**
U.S. Senate ratifies the Treaty of Guadalupe Hidalgo, ending the Mexican-American War and potentially opening new territories to slavery.

and helped spread abolitionist beliefs to newly founded communities in the Midwest. In New England, writers like Ralph Waldo Emerson and Margaret Fuller spearheaded an emerging transcendentalist movement during the mid-1830s that stressed the natural rights and individual worth of every man and woman—ideas with obvious antislavery implications. These stirrings began to affect American politics as well. The right of citizens to have antislavery petitions received by the U.S. Congress was vigorously debated in 1835, which in turn led to a larger debate over the rights of free speech, press, and assembly for abolitionists. The launching of Garrison's *Liberator* in January 1831 both benefited from these trends and helped advance them further.

About the Author

William Lloyd Garrison was born on December 10, 1805, in Newburyport, Massachusetts. His early years were disrupted when his father, the sailor Abijah Garrison, deserted his wife, Fanny, and their three children and disappeared into Canada. Childhood poverty shaped Garrison's youth and contributed to his later resentment of New England's ruling elite. His deeply religious mother instilled in her son an intense Christian faith, one that guided his life and work as an adult. After an unsuccessful apprenticeship to a Baltimore shoemaker, Garrison came home to Newburyport in 1818 and learned to set type at a local newspaper office. He quickly advanced to writing for and occasionally editing the publication. He went on to edit a series of periodicals before establishing the *Journal of the Times* in Bennington, Vermont, in 1828. He made his deepening antislavery views known in the *Journal* and began to lecture on the topic as well. His talk on slavery at Boston's Park Street Church on July 4, 1829, was particularly well received. His eloquence attracted the notice of the abolitionist Benjamin Lundy, who later that year asked Garrison to relocate to Baltimore and edit his *Genius of Universal Emancipation*, a small but influential antislavery paper.

As the editor of the *Genius*, Garrison grew increasingly hostile both toward slave owners and toward those who aided them. His condemnation of a Newburyport ship owner who carried slaves to the South led to a libel suit, resulting in Garrison's serving a forty-nine-day jail sentence. Lundy felt that Garrison's legal troubles had harmed his paper, and the two parted ways in July 1830. Garrison returned to Massachusetts in 1830 and began to attract followers through a series of antislavery lectures in Boston. By that time, he had become an advocate of immediate emancipation, rejecting Lundy's gradualist views. His tone of uncompromising righteousness (as well as his humble beginnings) earned him the opposition of many upper-class Bostonians, who considered his provocation of the South dangerous both to the Union and to their own financial interests. After considering a move to Washington, D.C., Garrison remained in Boston and, together with his business partner, Isaac Knapp, launched a new publication on January 1, 1831. Far more ambitious and militant than the

Genius, the *Liberator* set out to attack slavery within the broader context of universal human rights. The publication's masthead declared, "Our Country Is the World—Our Countrymen Are Mankind." This motto—so much at variance with the pervasive American nationalism of the time—served notice that the *Liberator*'s scope would be as wide as it would be controversial.

From the start, Garrison risked legal action and physical harm by publishing the *Liberator*. Rather than hide behind his editor's chair, he traveled and spoke widely during the 1830s to promote his causes. After meeting with antislavery leaders in England during the summer of 1833, he was determined to help found an effective abolitionist group in America. In December 1833, he played a key role in organizing the American Anti-Slavery Society at its first convention in Philadelphia. By the end of the decade, though, Garrison was embroiled in a series of controversies with fellow abolitionists over a range of issues. His advocacy of full equality for blacks and women and his attacks upon organized Christianity for its tolerance of slavery made him enemies within the antislavery movement. At an 1838 peace conference, he helped write a statement rejecting allegiance to all governments and calling for the abolition of all military forces—views that added to his reputation as an extremist. He also disagreed with those who sought to organize an abolitionist political party, believing that it was impossible to deal with a moral issue through electoral politics. To his detractors, Garrison was unrealistic, arrogant, and domineering; to his supporters, he was selfless, inspired, and heroic. The latter image was reinforced by his near escape from a violent Boston mob after an antislavery meeting in October 1835.

By most accounts, Garrison was personally warm and mild mannered. His marriage to Helen Benson in 1834 and the birth of his seven children allowed him to take refuge in a peaceful and satisfying family life. As an advocate for what he believed in, however, he only grew more confrontational as he aged. At a meeting of the Massachusetts Anti-Slavery Society in the spring of 1843, he offered a resolution advocating separation between the North and South, declaring the U.S. Constitution "a covenant with death and an agreement with Hell." His refusal to take part directly in political events of his era placed him on the sidelines as Americans debated the annexation of Texas, the Compromise of 1850, and the Kansas-Nebraska Act. As tempers rose in the North and South, he reiterated his disunionist stance, going so far as to publicly burn a copy of the Constitution in 1854.

Reactions to the U.S. Supreme Court's 1857 decision in the *Dred Scott* case and John Brown's 1859 raid on Harpers Ferry drove the North and South further apart and made Garrison's views seem less extreme. When the Civil War broke out in 1861, he gave qualified support to the Union cause as the best hope of abolishing slavery. When President Lincoln issued his preliminary Emancipation Proclamation in September 1862, Garrison offered guarded approval of this limited measure. By the close of the war, however, he took satisfaction in seeing slavery abolished at last. The final issue of the *Liberator* was published

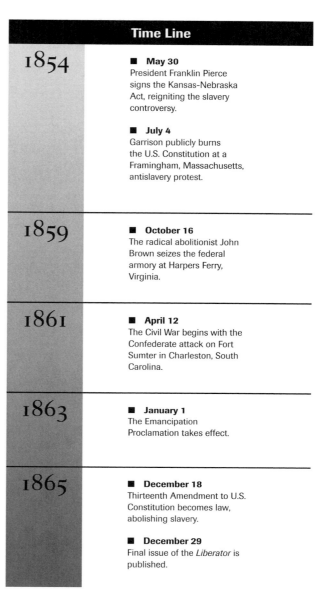

Time Line

1854
- **May 30**
President Franklin Pierce signs the Kansas-Nebraska Act, reigniting the slavery controversy.
- **July 4**
Garrison publicly burns the U.S. Constitution at a Framingham, Massachusetts, antislavery protest.

1859
- **October 16**
The radical abolitionist John Brown seizes the federal armory at Harpers Ferry, Virginia.

1861
- **April 12**
The Civil War begins with the Confederate attack on Fort Sumter in Charleston, South Carolina.

1863
- **January 1**
The Emancipation Proclamation takes effect.

1865
- **December 18**
Thirteenth Amendment to U.S. Constitution becomes law, abolishing slavery.
- **December 29**
Final issue of the *Liberator* is published.

on December 29, 1865, shortly after the ratification of the Thirteenth Amendment ended slavery. Believing that his work was largely done, Garrison resigned the presidency of the Massachusetts Anti-Slavery Society in January 1866. He continued to write and travel into the 1870s; financial gifts by admirers helped ensure a comfortable old age. Garrison died on May 24, 1879, in New York and is buried in Boston. At the funeral, his fellow antislavery crusader Wendell Phillips addressed Garrison: "Your heart, as it ceased to beat, felt certain, *certain*, that whether one flag or two shall rule this continent in time to come, one thing is settled—it never henceforth can be trodden by a slave!"

Explanation and Analysis of the Document

Garrison opens his editorial by noting that his initial attempt to launch the *Liberator* in Washington, D.C., was

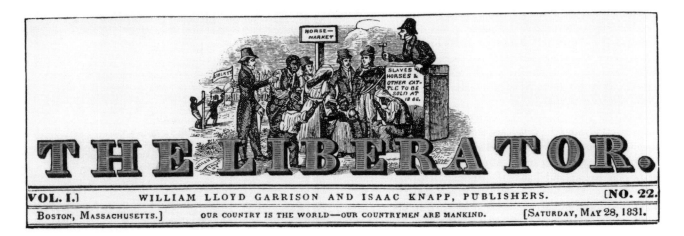

Masthead of the Liberator, 1831 (Library of Congress)

thwarted by "public indifference." In August 1830 he had circulated a proposal for a periodical to be called the *Public Liberator, and Journal of the Times,* to be published in the nation's capital. Although he raised modest funds, the American Colonization Society blocked him by buying out the printing establishment Garrison had hoped to purchase. This action—as well as the relocation of the *Genius of Universal Emancipation* to Washington—helped motivate him to try Boston as a base of operations.

However, Garrison found New England far from hospitable to his views. In the second paragraph, he states that opposition to the antislavery cause is greater in the North than in the South. This statement seems based upon his recent experience of denouncing (and being successfully sued by) a New Englander who profited from the interstate slave trade as well as the efforts of conservative civic leaders to stop him from speaking in Boston and Newburyport. Despite the "detraction" and "apathy" he faced, Garrison stated, he intended to preach his message in the shadow of Bunker Hill, the birthplace of America's struggle for freedom. (His statement was literally true; the famous battlefield was within sight of his office.) In the paragraph's final two sentences, Garrison adopts the tone that readers of the *Liberator* came to know well: militant, righteous, unyielding. He uses the language of a crusader, stating emphatically that his fight will continue until slavery is ended. It is indicative of Garrison's unshakable moral certainty that he—a poor and obscure advocate of an unpopular cause—demands that his foes "tremble" before him.

In paragraph 3, Garrison reaffirms the goals mentioned in his August 1830 proposal, which include "the abolition of slavery" and the "elevation of our colored population." To these aims he adds his intention to avoid partisan politics. This stance eventually placed him in opposition to other abolitionists, particularly the founders of the Liberty Party, who nominated James G. Birney for president on an antislavery platform in 1840 and 1844. From Garrison's perspective, participation in the political system established under the U.S. Constitution (a document which, in his view, upheld the legality of slavery) compromised an abolitionist's moral authority. Supporting a candidate with personal ambitions would degrade the integrity of the antislavery cause. Instead, Garrison takes an expansive view and seeks to influence individuals no matter what their religious or political affiliations might be.

In contrast to the fatally flawed Constitution, the Declaration of Independence offered confirmation that Garrison's antislavery position aligned with American ideals. In paragraph 4, Garrison quotes the declaration's preamble to bolster his advocacy of the immediate enfranchisement (a stronger word than mere *emancipation*) of slaves. In homing in on this theme, he makes it clear that his abolitionist views have changed over the past two years. He specifically renounces the position he advocated in his landmark address on July 4, 1829, at Park Street Church in Boston. While his remarks that day vigorously condemned slavery and the hypocrisy of supposedly Christian Americans in tolerating it, Garrison stopped short of advocating immediate emancipation. Further reading and consideration convinced him that gradual methods only represented a compromise with evil. By the time he had moved to Baltimore in August 1829, he had come to consider his earlier position one of "timidity, injustice and absurdity." By publicly asking forgiveness from God, his country, and "my brethren the poor slaves," he makes it plain that his dedication to the abolitionist cause is both a personal spiritual commitment and a larger humanitarian obligation.

The fifth paragraph contains the most frequently quoted lines of the editorial. Garrison acknowledges that his way of speaking is severe, but he immediately goes on to say that the times call for nothing less. With the fervor of a biblical prophet, he pledges to embody the principles of Truth and Justice. The direct, forceful words that follow have the cadence and visual impact of poetry. They pointedly ridicule the idea of attacking the evil of slavery with "moderation," drawing upon intensely emotional images (a burning house, a rape victim, a threatened child) to make his case. The tone of the language here is reminiscent of the Old Testament's book of Jeremiah in its denunciations of sin and moral blindness. As Garrison builds to a crescendo and declares, "I WILL BE HEARD," the defiance in his editorial voice is palpable. The reason for his wrathful tone is the public indifference toward evil; the apathy around him is wicked enough to hasten Judgment Day upon the world.

Garrison dismisses the idea that his intemperate language and uncompromising stance will do the abolitionist cause more harm than good. In paragraph 6, he asserts that his efforts will yield positive results in the short term and will be judged favorably by history in the long term. He quotes Proverbs 29:25 from the Old Testament in reaffirming his refusal to cower before public opinion. Finally, he closes his editorial with the poem "To Oppression," from the 1828 collection *Ephemerides; or, Occasional Poems* by Thomas Pringle. Well known in abolitionist circles, Pringle had championed the rights of native Africans as a British colonist in South Africa before serving as the secretary for the Anti-Slavery Society in London.

Audience

Garrison had no illusions about the willingness of the American people to consider the possibility of abolishing slavery in 1831. He considered the vast majority of his countrymen—especially his fellow New Englanders—to be selfish materialists who practiced a smug, lazy form of Christianity. In earlier years, his antislavery efforts had been condemned by respectable clergymen and hampered by government authorities. Even antislavery groups like the American Colonization Society had proved timid and hypocritical. It was not to institutions that Garrison spoke. Instead, the first editorial of the *Liberator* was aimed most broadly at the consciences of individuals wherever he could find them. By utilizing language explicitly and implicitly drawn from the Bible, he reached across class and racial lines to stir the most basic shared values of decency and justice. Fundamentally, Garrison desired to touch the common chord of humanity that would link the slaveholder and the slave.

More narrowly, Garrison spoke to the relatively small numbers of Americans who supported emancipation. His work with Lundy had already earned him a measure of notice among reform-minded northern citizens. Despite his complaints of "public indifference" in the editorial, he had already developed a reputation as an energetic (if controversial) opponent of slavery. Garrison knew that his heated advocacy of immediate emancipation would lead to divisions among abolitionists. He also knew that he would receive a sympathetic hearing from free African Americans in Boston, Philadelphia, and other northern cities. They would take heart from his words, even if white Americans turned away.

In a real sense, Garrison's target audience also included God and Garrison himself. His editorial was an act of individual confession and spiritual affirmation as well as a message to the public. The idea of personal responsibility was an essential part of his religious faith; to place himself in the forefront of the antislavery battle without fear of the consequences was vital to his own salvation. Much of the editorial (particularly paragraphs 4–6) is a statement of personal belief as much as an attempt to persuade others. In writing and publishing its words, Garrison was pledging before God to stand firm.

Impact

According to Garrison, the first issue of the *Liberator* was met with "suspicion and apathy." The exception was the free African American community of the Northeast, which gave the publication significant support. Garrison visited Philadelphia, New Haven, Hartford, and other cities to drum up interest; by the end of 1831, he counted more than five hundred free blacks among his subscribers. Although the *Liberator*'s paid circulation remained small for some years, its impact was far greater than the number of copies sold indicated. Its attacks upon the American Colonization Society stirred up debate within abolitionist circles across the North. Newspaper editors across the South reprinted its editorials as examples of northern antislavery extremism, increasing Garrison's influence and importance in the process. (Garrison, in turn, happily reprinted the denunciations of his fellow editors.) Even though it had no subscribers in the South, the *Liberator* was accused of inciting violence among slaves, especially after Nat Turner's slave rebellion in August 1831. A number of southern states and towns took steps to prosecute anyone caught circulating the paper. Garrison received death threats and was targeted for arrest (with a five-thousand-dollar reward offered) by the Georgia state legislature.

As time went on, the *Liberator* helped Garrison build a small but intensely loyal following among antislavery activists. Such notable figures as Wendell Phillips, Samuel J. May, Parker Pillsbury, Lydia Maria Child, and Maria Weston Chapman were among those he inspired to fight for immediate emancipation. He desired to attract allies who were as fervent and unyielding as he was. It has often been said that Garrison's editorials repelled far more than they persuaded. He was well aware of this effect and even reveled in the fact. "My language," he told May, "is exactly such as suits me; it will displease many, I know—to displease them is my intention."

While Garrison's militancy was straightforward, its effect had roundabout consequences that ultimately aided his cause. In 1836 four southern state legislatures sent formal requests to ten northern states asking them to make the publication and distribution of inflammatory antislavery material a penal offense—a move clearly aimed at publications like the *Liberator*. In the North, these actions raised freedom of speech issues and aroused a measure of

"Let Southern oppressors tremble—let their secret abettors tremble—let their Northern apologists tremble—let all the enemies of the persecuted blacks tremble."

(Paragraph 2)

"I shall not array myself as the political partisan of any man. In defending the great cause of human rights, I wish to derive the assistance of all religions and of all parties."

(Paragraph 3)

"I will be as harsh as truth, and as uncompromising as justice."

(Paragraph 5)

"I am in earnest—I will not equivocate—I will not excuse—I will not retreat a single inch—AND I WILL BE HEARD."

(Paragraph 5)

"I desire to thank God, that he enables me to disregard 'the fear of man which bringeth a snare,' and to speak his truth in its simplicity and power."

(Paragraph 6)

sympathy for Garrison. The refusal to suppress the *Liberator* increased the level of mistrust and resentment between North and South, a situation exacerbated by the acquisition of potential slave territory following the Mexican-American War (1846–1848) and the enforcement of the Compromise of 1850's Fugitive Slave Act provision. The *Liberator* never spoke for the more moderate (and more numerous) elements within the abolitionist community during the controversies of the 1840s and 1850s. Its advocacy of racial equality, women's rights, pacifism, and other causes—as well as its bitter attacks upon organized Christianity and the U.S. Constitution—likewise found little favor. However, it did manage to put many northerners in the position of defending its freedom to publish in the face of southern opposition, which in turn increased doubts among northern public opinion about the South's commitment to basic political and human rights.

The *Liberator* could never claim more than twenty-five hundred subscribers at any point in its thirty-five-year his-

tory. Garrison often had to appeal to his followers for financial support to keep his publication going. Yet its impact was pervasive in direct and indirect ways. Its use of highly charged moral language paved the way for such respectable politicians as William H. Seward, a senator from New York, to speak of a higher law than the U.S. Constitution in considering the evils of slavery. Garrison quoted the biblical admonition "A house divided against itself cannot stand" (Matthew 12:25) in his editorials decades before Abraham Lincoln began using the phrase. While the future president did not agree with most of Garrison's views, it is worth noting that Lincoln's law partner, William H. Herndon, was a *Liberator* reader who traveled to Boston to meet its editor in 1858. The Civil War and the Emancipation Proclamation were seen by many as vindications of the publication's views. While visiting Petersburg, Virginia, on April 6, 1865, Lincoln remarked that he was not chiefly responsible for freeing the slaves. "I have been only the instrument," he said. "The logic and moral power of Garrison, and the Anti-slavery people of the country, and the army have done all."

1. The angry, aggressive thrust of the *Liberator*'s inaugural editorial is unmistakable, yet Garrison always claimed he favored nonviolent approaches to ending slavery. Critics charged that despite his public commitment to pacifism, his writings at least indirectly encouraged slaves to revolt. By denouncing moderation in the face of absolute evil, Garrison could be seen as inspiring such militant abolitionists as John Brown to take direct action. How responsible was Garrison for increasing the likelihood of violence over the slavery issue? Were his stated pacifist beliefs in conflict with the content and tone of the first editorial in the *Liberator*?

2. Many southerners (and some northerners) called for the suppression of the *Liberator*. Attempts to stop Garrison from publishing won him defenders, even among those who disagreed with his views. Did the *Liberator* in fact threaten the peace and safety of southern society? If so, were southerners justified in attempting to suppress it? Are there issues involving freedom of the press and speech from Garrison's era that are relevant to America today?

3. Garrison favored ending slavery by appealing to the Christian morality of individuals, rather than by direct political or military action. As it happened, the Civil War ultimately brought about emancipation. Is there any historical evidence that Garrison's nonviolent, conscience-oriented approach could have been successful? In your discussion, contrast America's struggles over ending slavery with those in other countries (including Great Britain and Brazil).

4. As his first *Liberator* editorial makes clear, Garrison was unwilling to compromise over the issue of immediate emancipation. This inflexible stance earned him much criticism, particularly from other abolitionists. Was Garrison ultimately right in rejecting the gradual emancipation of slaves and denouncing those who disagreed with him? Could he have done more good—and possibly helped avert the Civil War—by being more moderate?

5. From its start, the *Liberator* drew heavily from both the Old and New Testaments to define its moral position and fashion its literary style. Garrison's form of Christianity—which led him into opposition with most established churches—stressed individual responsibility and advocated defiance of man-made law when it conflicted with biblical teachings. Southern supporters of slavery also drew upon the Bible to support their positions. What does the debate over slavery say about the role of religion in American politics? How have the religious implications of the antislavery debate been echoed in recent debates over abortion, gay rights, preemptive war, and other issues?

6. Compare the public careers of William Lloyd Garrison and Abraham Lincoln with respect to the slavery issue. Both considered slavery wrong, yet they radically diverged over how to bring about its end. Contrast their words and actions dealing with the subject, particularly during the 1850s as the country headed toward civil war. In retrospect, did Garrison or Lincoln uphold a higher moral standard? Which one had the most rational approach to abolishing slavery?

See also *David Walker's Appeal to the Coloured Citizens of the World* (1829); *The Confessions of Nat Turner* (1831); First Editorial of the *North Star* (1847); Emancipation Proclamation (1863).

Further Reading

■ Books

Barnes, Gilbert H. *The Antislavery Impulse, 1830–1844*. New York: American Historical Association, 1933.

Barzun, Jacques, ed. *The Selected Writings of John Jay Chapman*. New York: Farrar, Straus, and Cudahy, 1957.

Cain, William E., ed. *William Lloyd Garrison and the Fight against Slavery: Selections from "The Liberator."* Boston: Bedford Books of St. Martin's Press, 1995.

Duberman, Martin, ed. *The Antislavery Vanguard: New Essays on the Abolitionists*. Princeton, N.J.: Princeton University Press, 1965.

Garrison, Wendell Phillips, and Francis Jackson. *William Lloyd Garrison, 1805–1879: The Story of His Life, Told by His Children*. 4 vols. 1885. Reprint. New York: Negro Universities Press, 1969.

Jacoby, Susan. *Freethinkers: A History of American Secularism*. New York: Metropolitan Books, 2004.

Korngold, Ralph. *Two Friends of Man: The Story of William Lloyd Garrison and Wendell Phillips and Their Relationship with Abraham Lincoln*. Boston: Little, Brown, 1950.

Mayer, Henry. *All on Fire: William Lloyd Garrison and the Abolition of Slavery*. New York: St. Martin's Press, 1998.

Merrill, Walter M. *Against Wind and Tide: A Biography of William Lloyd Garrison*. Cambridge: Harvard University Press, 1963.

———, ed. *The Letters of William Lloyd Garrison*. 6 vols. Cambridge: Belknap Press of Harvard University Press, 1971–1981.

Nye, Russel B. *William Lloyd Garrison and the Humanitarian Reformers*. Boston: Little, Brown, 1955.

Smith, Goldwin. *The Moral Crusader, William Lloyd Garrison: A Biographical Essay*. New York: Funk and Wagnalls, 1892.

Stewart, James B. *William Lloyd Garrison and the Challenge of Emancipation*. Arlington Heights, Ill.: H. Davidson, 1992.

Thomas, John L. *The Liberator, William Lloyd Garrison, a Biography*. Boston: Little, Brown, 1963.

■ Web Sites

Garrison, William Lloyd. "On the Constitution and the Union." Fair Use Repository Web site
   http://fair-use.org/the-liberator/1832/12/29/on-the-constitution-and-the-union">http://fair-use.org/the-liberator/1832/12/29/on-the-constitution-and-the-union.
"The Liberator Files." Boston African American National Historic Site Web site.
   http://www.theliberatorfiles.com/">http://www.theliberatorfiles.com/.

"William Lloyd Garrison, 1805–1879." Public Broadcasting System "Africans in America" Web site.
   http://www.pbs.org/wgbh/aia/part4/4p1561.html">http://www.pbs.org/wgbh/aia/part4/4p1561.html.

"William Lloyd Garrison." NNDB Web site.
   http://www.nndb.com/people/966/000049819/.

—Barry Alfonso

William Lloyd Garrison's First *Liberator* Editorial

◆ TO THE PUBLIC.

In the month of August, I issued proposals for publishing "The Liberator" in Washington City; but the enterprise, though hailed in different sections of the country, was palsied by public indifference. Since that time, the removal of the *Genius of Universal Emancipation* to the Seat of Government has rendered less imperious the establishment of a similar periodical in that quarter.

During my recent tour for the purpose of exciting the minds of the people by a series of discourses on the subject of slavery, every place that I visited gave fresh evidence of the fact, that a greater revolution in public sentiment was to be effected in the free States—*and particularly in New-England*—than at the South. I found contempt more bitter, opposition more active, detraction more relentless, prejudice more stubborn, and apathy more frozen, than among slave-owners themselves. Of course, there were individual exceptions to the contrary. This state of things afflicted, but did not dishearten me. I determined, at every hazard, to lift up the standard of emancipation in the eyes of the nation, *within sight of Bunker Hill and in the birthplace of liberty*. That standard is now unfurled; and long may it float, unhurt by the spoliations of time or the missiles of a desperate foe—yea, till every chain be broken, and every bondman set free! Let Southern oppressors tremble—let their secret abettors tremble—let their Northern apologists tremble—let all the enemies of the persecuted blacks tremble.

I deem the publication of my original Prospectus unnecessary, as it has obtained a wide circulation. The principles therein inculcated will be steadily pursued in this paper, excepting that I shall not array myself as the political partisan of any man. In defending the great cause of human rights, I wish to derive the assistance of all religions and of all parties.

Assenting to the "self-evident truth" maintained in the American Declaration of Independence, "that all men are created equal, and endowed by their Creator with certain inalienable rights—among which are life, liberty and the pursuit of happiness," I shall strenuously contend for the immediate enfranchisement of our slave population. In Park-Street Church, on the Fourth of July, 1829, I unreflectingly assented to the popular but pernicious doctrine of *gradual* abolition. I seize this moment to make a full and unequivocal recantation, and thus publicly to ask pardon of my God, of my country, and of my brethren the poor slaves, for having uttered a sentiment so full of timidity, injustice, and absurdity. A similar recantation, from my pen, was published in the *Genius of Universal Emancipation* at Baltimore, in September, 1829. My conscience is now satisfied.

I am aware that many object to the severity of my language; but is there not cause for severity? I *will be* as harsh as truth, and as uncompromising as justice. On this subject, I do not wish to think, or to speak, or write, with moderation. No! no! Tell a man whose house is on fire to give a moderate alarm; tell him to moderately rescue his wife from the hands of the ravisher; tell the mother to gradually extricate her babe from the fire into which it has fallen;—but urge me not to use moderation in a cause like the present. I am in earnest—I will not equivocate—I will not excuse—I will not retreat a single inch—AND I WILL BE HEARD. The apathy of the people is enough to make every statue leap from its pedestal, and to hasten the resurrection of the dead.

It is pretended, that I am retarding the cause of emancipation by the coarseness of my invective and the precipitancy of my measures. *The charge is not true*. On this question of my influence,—humble as it is,—is felt at this moment to a considerable extent, and shall be felt in coming years—not perniciously, but beneficially—not as a curse, but as a blessing; and posterity will bear testimony that I was right. I desire to thank God, that he enables me to disregard "the fear of man which bringeth a snare," and to speak his truth in its simplicity and power. And here I close with this fresh dedication:

Oppression! I have seen thee, face to face,
And met thy cruel eye and cloudy brow,
But thy soul-withering glance I fear not now—
For dread to prouder feelings doth give place
Of deep abhorrence! Scorning the disgrace
Of slavish knees that at thy footstool bow,
I also kneel—but with far other vow
Do hail thee and thy herd of hirelings base:—
I swear, while life-blood warms my throbbing veins,

Document Text

Still to oppose and thwart, with heart and hand,
Thy brutalising sway—till Afric's
    chains
Are burst, and Freedom rules the rescued
    land,—
Trampling Oppression and his iron rod:
    Such is the vow I take—SO HELP ME
    GOD!

[by the Scottish poet Thomas Pringle (1789–1834)]
William Lloyd Garrison.
Boston, January, 1831.

Glossary

abettors	those who incite, sanction, or help, especially in wrongdoing
discourses	communications, especially lectures or writings
hirelings	persons whose loyalty or services are for hire
imperious	urgent, imperative
inculcated	impressed upon the mind by frequent repetition or strong urging
pernicious	causing great injury, destruction, or ruin
prospectus	a document outlining the main features of a new enterprise or project
recantation	an act of withdrawal or renunciation, especially in a public setting

THE CONFESSIONS OF NAT TURNER

1831

"On the appearance of the sign, (the eclipse of the sun last February) I should arise and prepare myself, and slay my enemies with their own weapons."

Overview

In late 1831 Thomas Ruffin Gray published *The Confessions of Nat Turner, the Leader of the Late Insurrection in Southampton, Va.* Gray was the court-appointed attorney who represented Nat Turner, the leader of a bloody slave revolt in the summer of that year, in his subsequent legal defense. The pamphlet was based on Gray's own investigations after the revolt and on the interview he conducted with Turner after his arrest in October 1831, and most of the pamphlet purportedly consists of Turner's own words. Gray's pamphlet is the principal surviving document about the revolt and is a primary source of information about Turner's motivations for and activities in launching the revolt. Gray's contemporary account is not to be confused with the Pulitzer Prize–winning novel of the same (shortened) title, *The Confessions of Nat Turner*, published by William Styron in 1967.

Nat Turner's Rebellion, sometimes called the Southampton Insurrection after the Virginia county in which it took place, was the latest in a series of slave rebellions that struck fear into the hearts of southern slave owners. Turner organized a small group of slaves who, beginning late in the day on August 21, 1831, and into the early-morning hours of August 22, roamed from house to house liberating slaves and killing white people they encountered. By the time they were finished, the band consisted of about seventy slaves and free blacks; they killed about fifty-five to sixty people, including children, before the rebellion was suppressed by the Virginia militia. Most of the participants in the revolt were tried and executed. Turner, who later claimed that he personally killed only one person during the revolt, went into hiding, but he was captured in late October. On November 1 he spoke with Gray, narrating events from his point of view before his execution later that month. Gray was immediately able to find a publisher, and the pamphlet came out just days after Turner's execution.

Context

Nat Turner's Rebellion was the latest in a string of slave revolts in the United States and throughout the Americas

that dated back to the early eighteenth century. In 1712 a slave revolt was suppressed in New York City. In 1733 a revolt took place on Saint John, in the Danish West Indies (now in the U.S. Virgin Islands). One of the largest rebellions, the Stono Rebellion (also called Cato's Rebellion or Cato's Conspiracy), took place in 1739 in South Carolina. The Conspiracy of 1741 (also called the Negro Plot of 1741 or the Slave Insurrection of 1741) was an alleged plot on the part of slaves in New York City to level the city by fire. Tacky's War, named after its leader, was suppressed in Jamaica in 1760. One of the most significant rebellions, led by Toussaint-Louverture, liberated Haiti from slavery under the French during the years 1791 to 1803. Back in the United States, Virginia—with the help of a storm that postponed the attack—forestalled a rebellion planned by Gabriel Prosser in 1800. In 1815 George Boxley, a white former slave owner, tried to foment a rebellion among slaves in Virginia, and in 1822 Denmark Vesey, a free black, planned what could have been the largest slave revolt in history had authorities in South Carolina not learned of the plot and suppressed it before it materialized. The collective sociological impact of these earlier revolts would play a role in the reactions of southerners and southern legislatures to Turner's revolt.

Nat Turner's Rebellion began late in the day on August 21, 1831, as Turner and his accomplices began traveling through the woods from house to house, liberating slaves and killing whites, though Turner and his men spared some poor whites who, in Turner's view, did not hold themselves out as superior to blacks. As the hours went by, Turner's force grew to about seventy men. Turner and his men conducted themselves quietly, for they did not want to raise any alarms; initially their weapons were knives, clubs, and hatchets rather than firearms. Their methods were particularly brutal. At one home, that of the Waller family, the rebels killed Levi Waller and his wife and decapitated ten of their children, piling their bodies at the front of the house.

As word of the rampage spread, Virginia authorities mobilized local contingents of the state militia. Joining the Virginia militia were detachments from U.S. Navy vessels anchored at Norfolk, Virginia, as well as detachments of militias from other Virginia counties and from North Carolina. Less than forty-eight hours after the revolt began, the

1800

■ **October 2**
Nat Turner is born into slavery in Southampton County, Virginia.

1815

■ **March 6**
George Boxley tries to launch a slave rebellion in Virginia.

1822

■ **July**
Denmark Vesey plans a major slave rebellion in South Carolina.

1831

■ **February 12**
Turner interprets a solar eclipse as a sign from God that the time has come for him to take action against his enemies.

■ **April 7**
Virginia passes An Act to Amend the Act concerning Slaves, Free Negroes and Mulattoes to limit slaves' privileges.

■ **August 13**
Turner interprets an atmospheric disturbance as another sign from God that it was time for him to launch a revolt.

■ **August 21**
Turner and his accomplices launch their revolt; it is suppressed less than forty-eight hours later.

■ **October 30**
Turner is captured while hiding on a local farm.

■ **November 1**
Turner meets with his court-appointed attorney, Thomas Ruffin Gray, and narrates the events of the rebellion.

■ **November 5**
Turner is tried and convicted.

■ **November 11**
Turner is executed in Jerusalem, Virginia; days later, Gray publishes *The Confessions of Nat Turner*.

1822

■ **October 16**
The abolitionist John Brown leads a raid on the federal armory at Harpers Ferry, Virginia.

rebels were defeated. In the rebellion's aftermath, extralegal retaliation was widespread, accomplishing the violent deaths of at least a hundred African Americans, though the number was likely much higher. African Americans were openly attacked and killed—and in some instances they were beheaded and their heads were put on poles as a warning. Rumors began to spread that the rebellion was not limited to Southampton County but was in fact part of a more general slave revolt, prompting acts of barbarism against blacks in North Carolina and elsewhere throughout the South. To his credit, General Richard Eppes, who commanded troops in Virginia, ordered all reprisals stopped when he learned of them.

Forty-eight rebels, both men and women, were initially captured and tried on charges of treason, insurrection, and conspiracy; ultimately, fifty-five participants (or alleged participants) in the revolt were executed, while others were banished from the state. A handful of those tried were acquitted. Turner himself eluded capture for over nine weeks, until he was discovered on October 30 hiding on a local farm. He was taken into custody and then tried and convicted in a Southampton County court on November 5. On November 11 he was hanged in Jerusalem (now Courtland), Virginia. Afterward, his body was beheaded and quartered. Shortly thereafter, a firm in Baltimore, Maryland, published Gray's *The Confessions of Nat Turner*.

About the Author

The nominal author of the 1831 pamphlet *The Confessions of Nat Turner* was Thomas Ruffin Gray. Not a great deal is known about Gray's life, particularly after the publication of Turner's confessions. Gray was born in 1800, making him the same age as Turner, but he grew up in dramatically different circumstances. Gray had connections in local and state governments and inherited extensive landholdings and slaves in Southampton County, Virginia. Because of a series of financial reversals, he sold off his land and slaves and moved to Jerusalem, Virginia, where he built a home, married, and practiced law. When the Turner case arose, Gray seized the opportunity to use it to his advantage by publishing a record of the events surrounding the rebellion.

Most of the words in *The Confessions of Nat Turner* are Turner's own, though it is difficult to assess how accurately Gray transcribed them and the extent to which he might have altered Turner's words to suit his purposes. Turner was born on October 2, 1800. At the time, he would have been called simply Nat; it was common practice, however, for slaves to take as a surname that of their masters—in this instance, Samuel Turner. Nat Turner was able to educate himself and could read from an early age. He was deeply religious and spent much of his time in fasting, prayer, and reading the Bible. He came to conduct Baptist services, deliver religious sermons, and instruct his fellow slaves about the Bible—to the extent that they called him "the Prophet." When he was twenty-one years old, he fled from his master, but he returned a

Illustration of the capture of Nat Turner (AP/Wide World Photos)

month later after, as he said, he received a vision ordering him to do so. By the time he was twenty-four, he had a new owner, Thomas Moore, and during this period of his life his religious visions, convincing him that he was destined for some great purpose, increased.

In 1830 Turner was purchased by yet another master, Joseph Travis. Turner never had any particular grievances against Travis and, in fact, confessed that Travis treated him with kindness. Nevertheless, Turner was growing increasingly convinced that his destiny in life was to lead a great slave revolt. He stated that on February 12, 1831, he witnessed a solar eclipse, which he interpreted as a sign from God that it was time for him to take action. In the months that followed he planned an insurrection with the help of four other slaves he had taken into his confi-

dence. Initially the revolt was to take place on July 4, but Turner postponed it to give himself and his collaborators time for further planning. Then, on August 13, a disturbance in the atmosphere cast a bluish-green hue over the sun; it has been speculated that atmospheric dust from an eruption that year of Mount Saint Helens, in Washington State, accounted for this phenomenon. Turner interpreted the event as another sign from God that the time was ripe for him to take action against his enemies. Accordingly, he launched the rebellion on the night of August 21, 1831. After the revolt was suppressed, he went into hiding. He was captured on October 30 and, in jail, narrated his account of events to Thomas Gray on November 1. Turner was tried and convicted on November 5 and executed on November 11, 1831.

"As I was praying one day at my plough, the spirit spoke to me … the Spirit that spoke to the prophets in former days—and I was greatly astonished, and for two years prayed continually, whenever my duty would permit—and then again I had the same revelation, which fully confirmed me in the impression that I was ordained for some great purpose in the hands of the Almighty."

(Paragraph 2)

"And on the appearance of the sign, (the eclipse of the sun last February) I should arise and prepare myself, and slay my enemies with their own weapons. And immediately on the sign appearing in the heavens, the seal was removed from my lips, and I communicated the great work laid out for me to do, to four in whom I had the greatest confidence."

(Paragraph 2)

"I gave up all hope for the present; and on Thursday night after having supplied myself with provisions from Mr. Travis's, I scratched a hole under a pile of fence rails in a field, where I concealed myself for six weeks, never leaving my hiding place but for a few minutes in the dead of night to get water which was very near."

(Paragraph 6)

"I shall not attempt to describe the effect of his narrative, as told and commented on by himself, in the condemned hole of the prison. The calm, deliberate composure with which he spoke of his late deeds and intentions, the expression of his fiend-like face when excited by enthusiasm, still bearing the stains of the blood of helpless innocence about him; clothed with rags and covered with chains; yet daring to raise his manacled hands to heaven."

(Paragraph 7)

Explanation and Analysis of the Document

Gray's *The Confessions of Nat Turner* consists predominantly of Turner's own words, although some of Gray's questions to him are presented, and at the end of the account Gray comments on it. Gray asserts at the opening of the document that he visited Turner in his jail cell on November 1, 1831, and that Turner, without prompting, began to narrate the events as he recalled them.

In the long second paragraph, Turner discusses his early life. He emphasizes an incident in his childhood when he told a story to other children based on events that had taken place before he was born. In Turner's view, this was an early indication that he was destined to be a prophet. He goes on to note that his parents confirmed him in the belief that he was destined for great things, and others noted that his uncommon intelligence and powers of observation would make him unsuitable as a slave. A mark of that intelligence was his ability to read and the "most perfect ease" with which he acquired that ability. He discusses the fertility of his imagination and his efforts to use his intelligence to make such things as paper and gunpowder. He also emphasizes that others placed great confidence in his judgment and his ability to plan, so his peers often took him along when they were planning "roguery."

The paragraph continues with Turner describing the role of religion in his life. He spent much of his time in fasting and prayer and notes the impact that certain verses from the Bible had on him. As he reiterates, he came to believe that he was destined to become a great prophet, like the prophets of the Old Testament. He discusses the "communion of the Spirit" that he felt when he arrived at young adulthood and began to consider how he might fulfill his destiny. Because of religious visions, he withdrew himself from his fellow slaves; he cites the year 1825 as the time when he experienced numerous such visions, including Christ on the Cross, blood on the corn in the field, and inspiration from the Holy Spirit. He discusses how he was able to use his religious convictions to help a white man named Etheldred T. Brantley see his wickedness. A key religious vision occurred on May 12, 1828, when, Turner says, he saw that "Christ had laid down the yoke he had borne for the sins of men, and that I should take it on and fight against the Serpent." At the end of the paragraph, he discusses the solar eclipse in February 1831 and his conviction that it was a sign from God for him to begin his fight. He took four other slaves—Henry, Hark, Nelson, and Sam—into his confidence, and they planned the rebellion for July 4. The rebellion was delayed, in part because Turner became sick, but another sign from the heavens—an atmospheric disturbance that colored the sun bluish-green on August 13—convinced him that the time to strike had come.

From the standpoint of southern slave owners, paragraph 3 of the document offers crucial revelations. Here Turner notes that by this time he was owned by Joseph Travis, and he acknowledges that Travis treated him kindly and with "confidence." For defenders of slavery, this was proof that Turner acted neither out of desire for revenge against a cruel master nor out of any considered opposition to the slave system. Turner then begins to detail the events of the rebellion, which began with a dinner on August 20, when the conspirators agreed to meet and form their plans.

After the two one-line paragraphs giving Gray's brief question and Turner's initial answer, paragraph 6 is yet another extremely long paragraph, consisting entirely of details of the men's activities once the revolt started. Turner offers a record of the murders he and his men committed, beginning with the five members of the Travis family, including an infant who was killed only after one of the men went back to the house for that purpose. The men continued to the home of Mr. Salathul Francis and then to the home of Mrs. Reese, where they murdered her and her son in their beds. Numerous other victims followed: the Turners, the Whiteheads (including a daughter, Margaret Whitehead—the only person Turner himself killed during the rampage), T. Doyle, the Wallers (including ten children), and others. Turner details how the marauders gathered guns and ammunition as well as any money and other property they could collect.

By this time, the authorities had been alerted and were on the hunt for the men. Still in paragraph 6, Turner records an encounter with militia under the command of Captain Alexander Peete. After a brief skirmish, the men encountered another military contingent, prompting an aside from Gray, who refers to the men as "barbarous villains." As a result of these skirmishes several of Turner's men were wounded, so Turner and a party of twenty men pursued a path that would take them by a back way into the town of Jerusalem. The men paused to rest, but the military was in pursuit and discovered the men's whereabouts. By this point the killings had stopped, and the men were in flight. Turner knew that at least some of his confederates had been captured, and he suspected that they would be forced to betray him. Accordingly, he went into hiding in a hole he dug under a pile of fence rails. The paragraph continues with details about the time Turner spent in hiding, particularly how his hiding place was discovered by a dog that smelled some meat he had. Fearing that he would be captured, Turner found another hiding place but was eventually discovered by a Mr. Benjamin Phipps. Phipps was armed, so Turner quietly surrendered and allowed Phipps to take him to the local jail.

In paragraph 7, Gray recalls intervening to ask Turner whether his rebellion was part of a larger slave revolt—"if he knew of any extensive or concerted plan." Turner's response was, "I do not." Gray then questioned Turner about a supposed insurrection in North Carolina, but again Turner denied any knowledge of such an insurrection. Again, these responses were a matter of grave concern to people throughout the South, many of whom believed that Turner's rebellion was part of a more widespread slave revolt. Whether they were reassured by Turner's denial is an open question. Gray points out that he questioned Turner about various details, and his statements were corroborated by the accounts of others involved in the rebellion. Gray comments on Turner's intelligence and ability to read, suggesting that Turner was not motivated by greed or the desire for money: "It is notorious, that he was never known to have a dollar in his life; to swear an oath, or drink a drop of spirits." At this point Gray presents his own assessment of Turner. He refers to Turner as a "complete fanatic" with a "fiend-like face." He concludes the paragraph by saying, "I looked on him and my blood curdled in my veins."

In the final paragraph, Gray provides additional details about the revolt, including stories of those who escaped from Turner's men. Gray refers to the revolt as an "unparalleled and inhuman massacre" and cites the men's "fiend-like barbarity." He concludes by saying, "The hand of retributive justice has overtaken them; and not one that was known to be concerned has escaped."

Audience

Gray's *The Confessions of Nat Turner* was a success, eventually selling some fifty thousand copies, primarily to whites who were curious about the rebellion and wanted to gain insight into Turner's motivations. In all, the pamphlet had several different audiences. One audience was northern abolitionists. William Lloyd Garrison, for example, the prominent abolitionist and publisher of *The Liberator* newspaper, saw the work as a valuable tool in the abolition movement, for it could inspire admiration of Turner and turn him into a hero, leading perhaps to other insurrections. The historian Scot French quotes Garrison as writing that the pamphlet would "only serve to rouse up other black leaders and cause other insurrections, by creating among blacks admiration for the character Nat, and a deep undying sympathy for his cause."

At the same time, the pamphlet attracted considerable attention among southerners. They argued that it offered a "lesson" to northern abolitionists, for it documented what many southerners regarded as the fanaticism of the abolition movement. Further, they used the pamphlet to emphasize that the uprising did not stem from mistreatment on the part of slave owners. Indeed, the pamphlet presented plausible alternative motives for the revolt—Turner's own twisted fanaticism combined with a charisma that enabled him to attract followers. It thus provided the southern slave-owning class with a scapegoat other than the institution of slavery—Nat Turner himself.

Impact

It is possible that without Gray's published account, Nat Turner's Rebellion, though it was sensational at the time, might have been largely forgotten, a footnote to the history of slavery in the early nineteenth century. But Gray, who was heavily involved in the official investigation following the rebellion, stated that he wanted to put aside idle speculation and rumor about the event. To that end, he insisted that the account he published was voluntary on Turner's part and that the confession was almost entirely in Turner's own words, with little or no variation. Gray also maintained that he compared Turner's account with the statements of other participants in the rebellion and found them consistent.

The fear that Turner's rebellion created led to intense curiosity about the pamphlet, and Gray's account in time sold some fifty thousand copies. Newspapers in Virginia promoted the pamphlet, running lengthy excerpts and commenting on its importance. Some newspaper editors, though, questioned the veracity of the account, arguing that its eloquence and extensive vocabulary cast doubt on Gray's claim that he recorded Turner's own words. It was known that Gray's law practice was not very successful, so there was speculation that he seized on the rebellion as a way to get his name before the public and build up his law practice.

Before Turner's rebellion, the Virginia General Assembly had debated the issue of slavery. Following the rebellion and the publicity it received from Gray's account, debate began to focus on the question of whether freed slaves should be deported to Africa. Ultimately, the assembly passed strict laws prohibiting slaves from being educated and curtailing the rights of both free and enslaved blacks. The result was widespread illiteracy among Virginia's black population, which continued until after the Civil War.

Contrary to the hopes of abolitionists like Garrison, Turner's rebellion and the publicity it received from Gray virtually ended the antislavery movement in the South. Opponents of slavery were discouraged from questioning the slave system, for they feared that doing so might inspire similar massacres. In the rebellion's aftermath, some states passed laws banning abolitionist material from the mail. In the Upper South, numerous slaveholders sold their slaves to owners in Deep South states to lessen the risk of another bloody revolt. In the North, however, the revolt galvanized abolitionists. Attacks on the slave system grew more heated, offending many southerners who felt that their way of life was under attack. The result was that southerners began to defend slavery as an institution that provided slaves with the necessities of life and with Christian values. The resulting polarization would intensify and, less than three decades later, would rend the nation in civil war. Meanwhile, Turner's rebellion, along with earlier slave revolts, inspired the white abolitionist John Brown to carry out a raid at Harpers Ferry, Virginia, on October 16, 1859. The raid was unsuccessful, and Brown was convicted and executed, but the raid continued to fuel the abolitionist movement and impelled the nation closer to civil war.

Modern readers have been more likely to know about Turner's rebellion through William Styron's novel *The Confessions of Nat Turner* (1967), which won a Pulitzer Prize in 1968. The book is a fictional re-creation for which the author relied heavily on the facts as known from Turner's confession and from other contemporary accounts. The book was enormously successful and came to be used as a textbook in high-school and college classrooms during the turbulent years of the civil rights movement in the late 1960s and early 1970s. During this period, considerable emphasis was being placed on black culture and history through the creation, for example, of black studies departments at many colleges and universities. In this climate, Styron's book—written by a white southerner whose ancestors had owned slaves—provoked an angry backlash among numerous black intellectuals, although it was defended by such prominent black writers as James Baldwin and Ralph Ellison. Critics accused Styron of racist stereotyping, particularly in his portrayal of a fantasy sequence that depicts Turner as having lust for a white woman.

The controversy ran deeper, however, for the publication of Styron's version prompted a flood of books, scholarly articles, and document collections reexamining the original event—and Gray's account—from a modern perspective. A central question raised concerned who "owns" the history of someone like Nat Turner. Styron's critics at the time argued that because he was white, he had no "ownership," literary or otherwise, of the events—in effect, that he lacked any foundation from which to write about it. By the same line of reasoning, some critics argued that Turner's version of events as recorded by Gray was an instrument in the continued repression of African Americans. According to this view, the notion that Turner and Gray actually collaborated in the production of the original version was absurd, because Gray, like Styron, was a white southerner who was arguably motivated by a desire to preserve the status quo. Accordingly, he manipulated his character to present him as a crazed, bloodthirsty religious zealot who had little interest in the issue of slavery. Put simply, some modern critics yet doubt the veracity of Gray's account, arguing that he distorted Turner's words in a way that confirmed the prejudices of the southern slaveholding class of the early nineteenth century.

See also William Lloyd Garrison's First *Liberator* Editorial (1831).

Further Reading

■ Articles

Fabricant, Daniel S. "Thomas R. Gray and William Styron: Finally, a Critical Look at the 1831 *Confessions of Nat Turner*." *American Journal of Legal History* 37 (July 1993): 332–361.

■ Books

Aptheker, Herbert. *Nat Turner's Slave Rebellion*. New York: Humanities Press, 1966.

———. *American Negro Slave Revolts*. 5th ed. New York: International Publishers, 1983.

Brodhead, Richard H. "Millennium, Prophecy and the Energies of Social Transformation: The Case of Nat Turner." In *Imagining the End: Visions of Apocalypse from the Ancient Middle East to Modern America*, eds. Abbas Amanat and Magnus Bernhardsson. London: I. B. Tauris, 2002.

French, Scot. *The Rebellious Slave: Nat Turner in American Memory*. Boston: Houghton Mifflin, 2004.

Greenberg, Kenneth S., ed. *Nat Turner: A Slave Rebellion in History and Memory*. New York: Oxford University Press, 2003.

Oates, Stephen B. *The Fires of Jubilee: Nat Turner's Fierce Rebellion*. New York: HarperPerennial, 1990.

Tragle, Henry Irving, ed. *The Southampton Slave Revolt of 1831: A Compilation of Source Material*. Amherst: University of Massachusetts Press, 1971.

Questions for Further Study

1. To what extent was Turner's rebellion actually one based on opposition to slavery? Put differently, was Turner perhaps simply an insane murderer who was not cognizant of the implications of his actions in opposition to slavery? Or was he a hero?

2. The document consists almost entirely of Gray's transcription of Turner's words. To what extent do you think it is possible, or perhaps likely, that Gray edited or even distorted Turner's words? What would have been his motive for doing so?

3. Why did the document offer some comfort to southern slave owners? What did they see in the document that convinced them that Turner's rebellion was not directly specifically against slavery as an institution?

4. What was the response of the Virginia legislature to the publication of Turner's confession?

5. What is your position on the question of who "owns" Nat Turner's story?

■ **Web Sites**

Ely, Mike. "The Slave Rebellion of General Nat Turner." Kasama Web site.
    http://kasamaproject.org/interviews/the-slave-rebellion-of-general-nat-turner/.

Garrison, William Lloyd. "The Insurrection." Fair Use Repository Web site.
    http://fair-use.org/the-liberator/1831/09/03/the-insurrection.

Gibson, Christine. "Nat Turner, Lightning Rod." AmericanHeritage.com "American Heritage People" Web site.
    http://www.americanheritage.com/people/articles/web/20051111-nat-turner-slavery-rebellion-virginia-civil-war-thomas-r-gray-abolitionist.shtml.

"Nat Turner's Rebellion." PBS "Africans in America" Web site.
    http://www.pbs.org/wgbh/aia/part3/3p1518.html.

—Michael J. O'Neal

THE CONFESSIONS OF NAT TURNER

Agreeable to his own appointment, on the evening he was committed to prison, with permission of the jailer, I visited NAT on Tuesday the 1st November, when, without being questioned at all, commenced his narrative in the following words:—

Sir,—You have asked me to give a history of the motives which induced me to undertake the late insurrection, as you call it—To do so I must go back to the days of my infancy, and even before I was born. I was thirty-one years of age the 2d of October last, and born the property of Benj. Turner, of this county. In my childhood a circumstance occurred which made an indelible impression on my mind, and laid the ground work of that enthusiasm, which has terminated so fatally to many, both white and black, and for which I am about to atone at the gallows. It is here necessary to relate this circumstance—trifling as it may seem, it was the commencement of that belief which has grown with time, and even now, sir, in this dungeon, helpless and forsaken as I am, I cannot divest myself of. Being at play with other children, when three or four years old, I was telling them something, which my mother overhearing, said it had happened before I was I born—I stuck to my story, however, and related somethings which went, in her opinion, to confirm it—others being called on were greatly astonished, knowing that these things had happened, and caused them to say in my hearing, I surely would be a prophet, as the Lord had shewn me things that had happened before my birth. And my father and mother strengthened me in this my first impression, saying in my presence, I was intended for some great purpose, which they had always thought from certain marks on my head and breast—[a parcel of excrescences which I believe are not at all uncommon, particularly among negroes, as I have seen several with the same. In this case he has either cut them off or they have nearly disappeared]—My grandmother, who was very religious, and to whom I was much attached—my master, who belonged to the church, and other religious persons who visited the house, and whom I often saw at prayers, noticing the singularity of my manners, I suppose, and my uncommon intelligence for a child, remarked I had too much sense to be raised, and if I was, I would never be of any service to any one as a slave—To a mind like mine, restless, inquisitive and observant of every thing that was passing, it is easy to suppose that religion was the subject to which it would be directed, and although this subject principally occupied my thoughts—there was nothing that I saw or heard of to which my attention was not directed—The manner in which I learned to read and write, not only had great influence on my own mind, as I acquired it with the most perfect ease, so much so, that I have no recollection whatever of learning the alphabet—but to the astonishment of the family, one day, when a book was shewn me to keep me from crying, I began spelling the names of different objects—this was a source of wonder to all in the neighborhood, particularly the blacks—and this learning was constantly improved at all opportunities—when I got large enough to go to work, while employed, I was reflecting on many things that would present themselves to my imagination, and whenever an opportunity occurred of looking at a book, when the school children were getting their lessons, I would find many things that the fertility of my own imagination had depicted to me before; all my time, not devoted to my master's service, was spent either in prayer, or in making experiments in casting different things in moulds made of earth, in attempting to make paper, gunpowder, and many other experiments, that although I could not perfect, yet convinced me of its practicability if I had the means. I was not addicted to stealing in my youth, nor have ever been—Yet such was the confidence of the negroes in the neighborhood, even at this early period of my life, in my superior judgment, that they would often carry me with them when they were going on any roguery, to plan for them. Growing up among them, with this confidence in my superior judgment, and when this, in their opinions, was perfected by Divine inspiration, from the circumstances already alluded to in my infancy, and which belief was ever afterwards zealously inculcated by the austerity of my life and manners, which became the subject of remark by white and black. —Having soon discovered to be great, I must appear so, and therefore studiously avoided mixing in society, and wrapped myself in mystery, devoting my time to fasting and prayer—By this time, having arrived to man's estate, and hearing the scriptures commented on at meetings, I was struck with that particular passage which says: "Seek ye the kingdom of Heaven and all things shall be added unto you." I reflected much on this passage, and prayed daily for light on this subject—As I was praying one day at my plough, the spirit spoke to me, saying "Seek ye the kingdom of Heaven and all things shall be added unto you." *Question*—what do you mean by the Spirit. *Ans.* The Spirit that spoke to the prophets in former days—and I was greatly astonished, and for two years prayed continually, whenever my duty would permit—and then again I had the same revelation, which fully confirmed me in the impression that I was ordained for some great purpose in the hands of the Almighty. Several years rolled round, in which many events occurred to strengthen me in this my belief. At this time I reverted in my mind to the remarks made of me in my childhood, and the things that had been shewn me—and as it had been said of me in my childhood by those by whom I had been taught to pray, both white and black, and in whom I had the greatest confidence, that I had too much sense to be raised, and if I was, I would never be of any use to any one as a slave. Now finding I had arrived to man's estate, and was a slave, and these revelations being made known to me, I began to direct my attention to this great object, to fulfil the purpose for which, by this time, I felt assured I was intended. Knowing the influence I had obtained over the minds of my fellow servants, (not by the means of conjuring and such like tricks—for to them I always spoke of such things with contempt) but by the communion of the Spirit whose revelations I often communicated to them, and they believed and said my wisdom came from God. I now began to prepare them for my purpose, by telling them something was about to happen that would terminate in fulfilling the great promise that had been made to me—About this time I was placed under an overseer, from whom I ran away—and after remaining in the woods thirty days, I returned, to the astonishment of the negroes on the plantation, who thought I had made my escape to some other part of the country, as my father had done before. But the reason of my return was, that the Spirit appeared to me and said I had my wishes directed to the things of this world, and not to the kingdom of Heaven, and that I should return to the service of my earthly master—"For he who knoweth his Master's will, and doeth it not, shall be beaten with many stripes, and thus, have I chastened you." And the negroes found fault, and murmured against me, saying that if they had my sense they would not serve any master in the

world. And about this time I had a vision—and I saw white spirits and black spirits engaged in battle, and the sun was darkened—the thunder rolled in the Heavens, and blood flowed in streams—and I heard a voice saying, "Such is your luck, such you are called to see, and let it come rough or smooth, you must surely bare it." I now withdrew myself as much as my situation would permit, from the intercourse of my fellow servants, for the avowed purpose of serving the Spirit more fully—and it appeared to me, and reminded me of the things it had already shown me, and that it would then reveal to me the knowledge of the elements, the revolution of the planets, the operation of tides, and changes of the seasons. After this revelation in the year 1825, and the knowledge of the elements being made known to me, I sought more than ever to obtain true holiness before the great day of judgment should appear, and then I began to receive the true knowledge of faith. And from the first steps of righteousness until the last, was I made perfect; and the Holy Ghost was with me, and said, "Behold me as I stand in the Heavens"—and I looked and saw the forms of men in different attitudes—and there were lights in the sky to which the children of darkness gave other names than what they really were—for they were the lights of the Saviour's hands, stretched forth from east to west, even as they were extended on the cross on Calvary for the redemption of sinners. And I wondered greatly at these miracles, and prayed to be informed of a certainty of the meaning thereof—and shortly afterwards, while laboring in the field, I discovered drops of blood on the corn as though it were dew from heaven—and I communicated it to many, both white and black, in the neighborhood—and I then found on the leaves in the woods hieroglyphic characters, and numbers, with the forms of men in different attitudes, portrayed in blood, and representing the figures I had seen before in the heavens. And now the Holy Ghost had revealed itself to me, and made plain the miracles it had shown me—For as the blood of Christ had been shed on this earth, and had ascended to heaven for the salvation of sinners, and was now returning to earth again in the form of dew—and as the leaves on the trees bore the impression of the figures I had seen in the heavens, it was plain to me that the Saviour was about to lay down the yoke he had borne for the sins of men, and the great day of judgment was at band. About this time I told these things to a white man, (Etheldred T. Brantley) on whom it had a wonderful effect—and he ceased from his wickedness, and was attacked immediately with a cutaneous eruption, and blood oozed from the pores of his skin, and after praying and fasting nine days, he was healed, and the Spirit appeared to me again, and said, as the Saviour had been baptised so should we be also—and when the white people would not let us be baptised by the church, we went down into the water together, in the sight of many who reviled us, and were baptised by the Spirit—After this I rejoiced greatly, and gave thanks to God. And on the 12th of May, 1828, I heard a loud noise in the heavens, and the Spirit instantly appeared to me and said the Serpent was loosened, and Christ had laid down the yoke he had borne for the sins of men, and that I should take it on and fight against the Serpent, for the time was fast approaching when the first should be last and the last should be first.

Ques. Do you not find yourself mistaken now? *Ans.* Was not Christ crucified. And by signs in the heavens that it would make known to me when I should commence the great work—and until the first sign appeared, I should conceal it from the knowledge of men—And on the appearance of the sign, (the eclipse of the sun last February) I should arise and prepare myself, and slay my enemies with their own weapons. And immediately on the sign appearing in the heavens, the seal was removed from my lips, and I communicated the great work laid out for me to do, to four in whom I had the greatest confidence, (Henry, Hark, Nelson, and Sam)—It was intended by us to have begun the work of death on the 4th July last—Many were the plans formed and rejected by us, and it affected my mind to such a degree, that I fell sick, and the time passed without our coming to any determination how to commence— Still forming new schemes and rejecting them, when the sign appeared again, which determined me not to wait longer.

Since the commencement of 1830, I had been living with Mr. Joseph Travis, who was to me a kind master, and placed the greatest confidence in me; in fact, I had no cause to complain of his treatment to me. On Saturday evening, the 20th of August, it was agreed between Henry, Hark and myself, to prepare a dinner the next day for the men we expected, and then to concert a plan, as we had not yet determined on any. Hark, on the following morning, brought a pig, and Henry brandy, and being joined by Sam, Nelson, Will and Jack, they prepared in the woods a dinner, where, about three o'clock, I joined them.

Q. Why were you so backward in joining them.

A. The same reason that had caused me not to mix with them for years before.

I saluted them on coming up, and asked Will how came he there, he answered, his life was worth no more than others, and his liberty as dear to him. I asked him if he thought to obtain it. He said he would, or lose his life. This was enough to put him in full confidence. Jack, I knew, was only a tool in the hands of Hark, it was quickly agreed we should commence at home (Mr. J. Travis') on that night, and until we had armed and equipped ourselves, and gathered sufficient force, neither age nor sex was to be spared, (which was invariably adhered to.) We remained at the feast until about two hours in the night, when we went to the house and found Austin; they all went to the cider press and drank, except myself. On returning to the house, Hark went to the door with an axe, for the purpose of breaking it open, as we knew we were strong enough to murder the family, if they were awaked by the noise; but reflecting that it might create an alarm in the neighborhood, we determined to enter the house secretly, and murder them whilst sleeping. Hark got a ladder and set it against the chimney, on which I ascended, and hoisting a window, entered and came down stairs, unbarred the door, and removed the guns from their places. It was then observed that I must spill the first blood. On which, armed with a hatchet, and accompanied by Will, I entered my master's chamber, it being dark, I could not give a death blow, the hatchet glanced from his head, he sprang from the bed and called his wife, it was his last word, Will laid him dead, with a blow of his axe, and Mrs. Travis shared the same fate, as she lay in bed. The murder of this family, five in number, was the work of a moment, not one of them awoke; there was a little infant sleeping in a cradle, that was forgotten, until we had left the house and gone some distance, when Henry and Will returned and killed it; we got here, four guns that would shoot, and several old muskets, with a pound or two of powder. We remained some time at the barn, where we paraded; I formed them in a line as soldiers, and after carrying them through all the manoeuvres I was master of, marched them off to Mr. Salathul Francis', about six hundred yards distant. Sam and Will went to the door and knocked. Mr. Francis asked who was there, Sam replied, it was him, and he had a letter for him, on which he got up and came to the door, they immediately seized him, and dragging him out a little from the door, he was dispatched by repeated blows on the head; there was no other white person in the family. We started from there for Mrs. Reese's, maintaining the most perfect silence on our march, where finding the door unlocked, we entered, and murdered Mrs. Reese in her bed, while sleeping; her son awoke, but it was only to sleep the sleep of death, he had only time to say who is that, and he was no more. From Mrs. Reese's we went to Mrs. Turner's, a mile distant, which we reached about sunrise, on Monday morning. Henry, Austin, and Sam, went to the still, where, finding Mr. Peebles, Austin shot him, and the rest of us went to the house; as we approached, the family discovered us, and shut the door. Vain hope! Will, with one stroke of his axe, opened it, and we entered and found Mrs. Turner and Mrs. Newsome in the middle of a room, almost frightened to death. Will immediately killed Mrs. Turner, with one blow of his axe. I took Mrs. Newsome by the hand, and with the sword I had when I was apprehended, I struck her several blows over the head, but not being able to kill her, as the sword was dull. Will turning around and discovering it, despatched her also. A general destruction of property and search for money and ammunition always succeeded the murders. By this time my company amounted to fifteen, and nine men mounted, who started for Mrs. Whitehead's, (the other six were to go through a by way to Mr. Bryant's and rejoin us at Mrs. Whitehead's,) as we approached the house we discovered Mr. Richard Whitehead standing in the cotton patch, near the lane fence; we called him over into the lane, and Will, the executioner, was near at hand, with his fatal axe, to send him to an untimely grave. As we pushed on to the house, I discovered some one run round the garden, and thinking it was some of the white family, I pursued them, but finding it was a servant girl belonging to the house, I returned to commence the work of death, but they whom I left, had not been idle; all the family were already murdered, but Mrs. Whitehead and her daughter Margaret. As I came round to the door I saw Will pulling Mrs. Whitehead out of the house, and at the step he nearly severed her head from her body, with his broad axe. Miss Margaret, when I discovered her, had concealed herself in the corner, formed by the projection of the cellar cap from the house; on my approach she fled, but was soon overtaken, and after repeated blows with a sword, I killed her by a blow on the head, with a fence rail. By this time, the six who had gone by Mr. Bryant's, rejoined us, and informed me they had done the work of death assigned them. We again divided, part going to Mr. Richard Porter's, and from thence to Nathaniel Francis', the others to Mr. Howell Harris', and Mr. T. Doyles. On my reaching Mr. Porter's, he had escaped with his family. I understood there, that the alarm

had already spread, and I immediately returned to bring up those sent to Mr. Doyles, and Mr. Howell Harris'; the party I left going on to Mr. Francis', having told them I would join them in that neighborhood. I met these sent to Mr. Doyles' and Mr. Harris' returning, having met Mr. Doyle on the road and killed him; and learning from some who joined them, that Mr. Harris was from home, I immediately pursued the course taken by the party gone on before; but knowing they would complete the work of death and pillage, at Mr. Francis' before I could there, I went to Mr. Peter Edwards', expecting to find them there, but they had been here also. I then went to Mr. John T. Barrow's, they had been here and murdered him. I pursued on their track to Capt. Newit Harris', where I found the greater part mounted, and ready to start; the men now amounting to about forty, shouted and hurrahed as I rode up, some were in the yard, loading their guns, others drinking. They said Captain Harris and his family had escaped, the property in the house they destroyed, robbing him of money and other valuables. I ordered them to mount and march instantly, this was about nine or ten o'clock, Monday morning. I proceeded to Mr. Levi Waller's, two or three miles distant. I took my station in the rear, and as it 'twas my object to carry terror and devastation wherever we went, I placed fifteen or twenty of the best armed and most to be relied on, in front, who generally approached the houses as fast as their horses could run; this was for two purposes, to prevent their escape and strike terror to the inhabitants—on this account I never got to the houses, after leaving Mrs. Whitehead's, until the murders were committed, except in one case. I sometimes got in sight in time to see the work of death completed, viewed the mangled bodies as they lay, in silent satisfaction, and immediately started in quest of other victims—Having murdered Mrs. Waller and ten children, we started for Mr. William Williams'—having killed him and two little boys that were there; while engaged in this, Mrs. Williams fled and got some distance from the house, but she was pursued, overtaken, and compelled to get up behind one of the company, who brought her back, and after showing her the mangled body of her lifeless husband, she was told to get down and lay by his side, where she was shot dead. I then started for Mr. Jacob Williams, where the family were murdered—Here we found a young man named Drury, who had come on business with Mr. Williams—he was pursued, overtaken and shot. Mrs. Vaughan was the next place we visited— and after murdering the family here, I determined on starting for Jerusalem—Our number amounted now to fifty or sixty, all mounted and armed with guns, axes, swords and clubs—On reaching Mr. James W. Parkers' gate, immediately on the road leading to Jerusalem, and about three miles distant, it was proposed to me to call there, but I objected, as I knew he was gone to Jerusalem, and my object was to reach there as soon as possible; but some of the men having relations at Mr. Parker's it was agreed that they might call and get his people. I remained at the gate on the road, with seven or eight; the others going across the field to the house, about half a mile off. After waiting some time for them, I became impatient, and started to the house for them, and on our return we were met by a party of white men, who had pursued our blood-stained track, and who had fired on those at the gate, and dispersed them, which I knew nothing of, not having been at that time rejoined by any of them—Immediately on discovering the whites, I ordered my men to halt and form, as they appeared to be alarmed—The white men, eighteen in number, approached us in about one hundred yards, when one of them fired, (this was against the positive orders of Captain Alexander P. Peete, who commanded, and who had directed the men to reserve their fire until within thirty paces). And I discovered about half of them retreating, I then ordered my men to fire and rush on them; the few remaining stood their ground until we approached within fifty yards, when they fired and retreated. We pursued and overtook some of them who we thought we left dead; (they were not killed) after pursuing them about two hundred yards, and rising a little hill, I discovered they were met by another party, and had halted, and were re-loading their guns, (this was a small party from Jerusalem who knew the negroes were in the field, and had just tied their horses to await their return to the road, knowing that Mr. Parker had family were in Jerusalem, but knew nothing of the party that had gone in with Captain Peete; on hearing the firing they immediately rushed to the spot and arrived just in time to arrest the progress of these barbarous villains, and save the lives of their friends and fellow citizens.) Thinking that those who retreated first, and the party who fired on us at fifty or sixty yards distant, had all only fallen back to meet others with ammunition. As I saw them re-loading their guns, and more coming up than I saw at first, and several of my bravest men being wounded, the others became panic struck and squandered over the field; the white men pursued and fired on us several times. Hark had his horse shot under him, and I caught another for him as it was

running by me; five or six of my men were wounded, but none left on the field; finding myself defeated here I instantly determined to go through a private way, and cross the Nottoway river at the Cypress Bridge, three miles below Jerusalem, and attack that place in the rear, as I expected they would look for me on the other road, and I had a great desire to get there to procure arms and ammunition. After going a short distance in this private way, accompanied by about twenty men, I overtook two or three who told me the others were dispersed in every direction. After trying in vain to collect a sufficient force to proceed to Jerusalem, I determined to return, as I was sure they would make back to their old neighborhood, where they would rejoin me, make new recruits, and come down again. On my way back, I called at Mrs. Thomas's, Mrs. Spencer's, and several other places, the white families having fled, we found no more victims to gratify our thirst for blood, we stopped at Maj. Ridley's quarter for the night, and being joined by four of his men, with the recruits made since my defeat, we mustered now about forty strong. After placing out sentinels, I laid down to sleep, but was quickly roused by a great racket; starting up, I found some mounted, and others in great confusion; one of the sentinels having given the alarm that we were about to be attacked, I ordered some to ride round and reconnoiter, and on their return the others being more alarmed, not knowing who they were, fled in different ways, so that I was reduced to about twenty again; with this I determined to attempt to recruit, and proceed on to rally in the neighborhood, I had left. Dr. Blunt's was the nearest house, which we reached just before day; on riding up the yard, Hark fired a gun. We expected Dr. Blunt and his family were at Maj. Ridley's, as I knew there was a company of men there; the gun was fired to ascertain if any of the family were at home; we were immediately fired upon and retreated, leaving several of my men. I do not know what became of them, as I never saw them afterwards. Pursuing our course back and coming in sight of Captain Harris', where we had been the day before, we discovered a party of white men at the house, on which all deserted me but two, (Jacob and Nat,) we concealed ourselves in the woods until near night, when I sent them in search of Henry, Sam, Nelson, and Hark, and directed them to rally all they could, at the place we had had our dinner the Sunday before, where they would find me, and I accordingly returned there as soon as it was dark and remained until Wednesday evening, when discovering white men riding around the place as though they were looking for some one, and none of my men joining me, I concluded Jacob and Nat had been taken, and compelled to betray me. On this I gave up all hope for the present; and on Thursday night after having supplied myself with provisions from Mr. Travis's, I scratched a hole under a pile of fence rails in a field, where I concealed myself for six weeks, never leaving my hiding place but for a few minutes in the dead of night to get water which was very near; thinking by this time I could venture out, I began to go about in the night and eaves drop the houses in the neighborhood; pursuing this course for about a fortnight and gathering little or no intelligence, afraid of speaking to any human being, and returning every morning to my cave before the dawn of day. I know not how long I might have led this life, if accident had not betrayed me, a dog in the neighborhood passing by my hiding place one night while I was out, was attracted by some meat I had in my cave, and crawled in and stole it, and was coming out just as I returned. A few nights after, two negroes having started to go hunting with the same dog, and passed that way, the dog came again to the place, and having just gone out to walk about, discovered me and barked, on which thinking myself discovered, I spoke to them to beg concealment. On making myself known they fled from me. Knowing then they would betray me, I immediately left my hiding place, and was pursued almost incessantly until I was taken a fortnight afterwards by Mr. Benjamin Phipps, in a little hole I had dug out with my sword, for the purpose of concealment, under the top of a fallen tree. On Mr. Phipps' discovering the place of my concealment, he cocked his gun and aimed at me. I requested him not to shoot and I would give up, upon which he demanded my sword. I delivered it to him, and he brought me to prison. During the time I was pursued, I had many hair breadth escapes, which your time will not permit you to relate. I am here loaded with chains, and willing to suffer the fate that awaits me.

I here proceeded to make some inquiries of him after assuring him of the certain death that awaited him, and that concealment would only bring destruction on the innocent as well as guilty, of his own color, if he knew of any extensive or concerted plan. His answer was, I do not. When I questioned him as to the insurrection in North Carolina happening about the same time, he denied any knowledge of it; and when I looked him in the face as though I would search his inmost thoughts, he replied, "I see sir, you doubt my word; but can you not think the same ideas, and strange appearances about this time in the heaven's might prompt others, as well as myself, to this undertaking." I now had much conversation with and asked him many questions, having forborne to do so previously, except in the cases noted in parenthesis; but during his statement, I had, unnoticed by him, taken notes as to some particular circumstances, and having the advantage of his statement before me in writing, on the evening of the third day that I had been with him, I began a cross examination, and found his statement corroborated by every circumstance coming within my own knowledge or the confessions of others whom had been either killed or executed, and whom he had not seen nor had any knowledge since 22d of August last, he expressed himself fully satisfied as to the impracticability of his attempt. It has been said he was ignorant and cowardly, and that his object was to murder and rob for the purpose of obtaining money to make his escape. It is notorious, that he was never known to have a dollar in his life; to swear an oath, or drink a drop of spirits. As to his ignorance, he certainly never had the advantages of education, but he can read and write, (it was taught him by his parents,) and for natural intelligence and quickness of apprehension, is surpassed by few men I have ever seen. As to his being a coward, his reason as given for not resisting Mr. Phipps, shews the decision of his character. When he saw Mr. Phipps present his gun, he said he knew it was impossible for him to escape as the woods were full of men; he therefore thought it was better to surrender, and trust to fortune for his escape. He is a complete fanatic, or plays his part most admirably. On other subjects he possesses an uncommon share of intelligence, with a mind capable of attaining any thing; but warped and perverted by the influence of early impressions. He is below the ordinary stature, though strong and active, having the true negro face, every feature of which is strongly marked. I shall not attempt to describe the effect of his narrative, as told and commented on by himself, in the condemned hole of the prison. The calm, deliberate composure with which he spoke of his late deeds and intentions, the expression of his fiend-like face when excited by enthusiasm, still bearing the stains of the blood of helpless innocence about him; clothed with rags and covered with chains; yet daring to raise his manacled hands to heaven, with a spirit soaring above the attributes of man; I looked on him and my blood curdled in my veins.

I will not shock the feelings of humanity, nor wound afresh the bosoms of the disconsolate sufferers in this unparalleled and inhuman massacre, by detailing the deeds of their fiend-like barbarity.

There were two or three who were in the power of these wretches, had they known it, and who escaped in the most providential manner. There were two whom they thought they left dead on the field at Mr. Parker's, but who were only stunned by the blows of their guns, as they did not take time to reload when they charged on them. The escape of a little girl who went to school at Mr. Waller's, and where the children were collecting for that purpose. excited general sympathy. As their teacher had not arrived, they were at play in the yard, and seeing the negroes approach, ran up on a dirt chimney (such as are common to log houses,) and remained there unnoticed during the massacre of the eleven that were killed at this place. She remained on her hiding place till just before the arrival of a party, who were in pursuit of the murderers, when she came down and fled to a swamp, where, a mere child as she was, with the horrors of the late scene before her, she lay concealed until the next day, when seeing a party go up to the house, she came up, and on being asked how she escaped, replied with the utmost simplicity, "The Lord helped her." She was taken up behind a gentleman of the party, and returned to the arms of her weeping mother. Miss Whitehead concealed herself between the bed and the mat that supported it, while they murdered her sister in the same room,

without discovering her. She was afterwards carried off, and concealed for protection by a slave of the family, who gave evidence against several of them on their trial. Mrs. Nathaniel Francis, while concealed in a closet heard their blows, and the shrieks of the victims of these ruthless savages; they then entered the closet where she was concealed, and went out without discovering her. While in this hiding place, she heard two of her women in a quarrel about the division of her clothes. Mr. John T. Baron, discovering them approaching his house, told his wife to make her escape, and scorning to fly, fell fighting on his own threshold. After firing his rifle, he discharged his gun at them, and then broke it over the villain who first approached him, but he was overpowered, and slain. His bravery, however, saved from the hands of these monsters, his lovely and amiable wife, who will long lament a husband so deserving of her love. As directed by him, she attempted to escape through the garden, when she was caught and held by one of her servant girls, but another coming to her rescue, she fled to the woods, and concealed herself. Few indeed, were those who escaped their work of death. But fortunate for society, the hand of retributive justice has overtaken them; and not one that was known to be concerned has escaped.

Calvary	the site of Christ's Crucifixion
"For he who knoweth his Master's will ..."	loosely quoted from the biblical book of Luke, Chapter 12, verses 47–48
infancy	childhood, youth
Jerusalem	a nearby town in Virginia
Saviour	Jesus Christ
"Seek ye the kingdom of Heaven ..."	loosely quoted from the biblical books of Matthew (Chapter 6, verse 33) and Luke (Chapter 12, verse 31)
shewn	an antique form of "shown"

Portrait of Joseph Cinqué (Library of Congress)

"Supposing these African negroes not to be slaves, but kidnapped, and free negroes, the treaty with Spain cannot be obligatory upon them."

Overview

Issued on March 9, 1841, the decision of the U.S. Supreme Court in the *Amistad* case was the most significant one issued by the Court on the question of slavery before the *Dred Scott* decision of 1857. The case arose from the seizure of the schooner *La Amistad*, its passengers, and cargo in 1839 by a U.S. naval vessel. Among the passengers were fifty-three Africans, a slave named Antonio owned by the captain, and two Spaniards. The Spaniards claimed that the Africans were their slaves, but the Africans asserted they were free. For the next two years, American abolitionists provided legal counsel to the Africans, hoping to secure their freedom and to record a legal victory in the battle against slavery. Unlike the *Dred Scott* decision, in which Chief Justice Roger Taney would say that blacks "had no rights which the white man was bound to respect," Justice Joseph Story's opinion in *Amistad*, based on "the eternal principles of justice and international law," held that "these negroes ought to be deemed free" because they were entitled to equal justice in America's courts, just like any other foreign subject, no matter his or her color. The abolitionist movement claimed a victory and termed it a triumph of justice. The decision freed the Africans but not Antonio. In other words, the case was limited to its facts. The Africans were entitled to their freedom because they had been kidnapped and illegally sold into slavery, but those held legally to be slaves could not be freed.

Context

In the early days of the Republic many Americans believed that slavery would eventually disappear, and there was some basis for such hope. As early as 1780, Pennsylvania began gradually emancipating all slaves born after that year, and Massachusetts banned slavery. Even Maryland and North Carolina banned the importation of slaves in the 1780s. But after the Revolution, the slave-based economy of the South did not diminish. The invention of the cotton gin and other agricultural advances increased the demand for slave labor. While the northern states had mixed economies based on small farmers and merchants and a growing industrial base, the South's economy had become even more dependent on slave labor. Instead of becoming more united, the regions grew more polarized.

In 1820 the Missouri Compromise formalized the great divide between the regions on the issue of slavery. Under the terms of the Missouri Compromise, the North would consist of free states, but the South would consist of states where slavery remained legal. The growth of slavery also engendered a growth in antislavery sentiment outside the South. By the 1830s the American Anti-Slavery Society had attracted thousands of abolitionists. While abolitionists enjoyed little early political success, they resorted to aggressive propaganda campaigns and vigorous legal attacks to secure freedom for as many blacks as possible.

In the South, there was less antislavery sentiment among whites. The Denmark Vesey Uprising in South Carolina in 1822 and Nat Turner's Rebellion in Virginia in 1831 demonstrated that there was strong desire for freedom among the South's slaves. But this black resistance was met with white resistance. Southern planters drew inward and more strident in their support for slavery. Abolitionist literature was banned in some southern communities, and some states made it illegal to teach slaves to read and write. Throughout the 1830s numerous southern legislatures pleaded with northern states to control the abolitionists.

Slavery was also a troubling issue diplomatically. Even though the U.S. Congress banned the importation of slaves as of January 1, 1808, the slave population in the South grew from about 1 million in 1808 to over 2.4 million in 1840. The increase came primarily through natural population growth, but the illegal Caribbean slave trade provided inexpensive African slaves. Treaties between Spain and other countries prohibited the slave trade, but Cuba, a Spanish colony, became a major source of illegal slaves. With Cuba so close and white Americans so divided, America's slave trade ban was difficult to enforce and often simply ignored.

In this context it is not surprising that the plight of the Africans from *La Amistad* became both a national and an international issue. In the spring of 1839, more than five hundred Africans were kidnapped on the west coast of Af-

1836

- Martin Van Buren is elected president as a proslavery Democrat.

1839

- More than five hundred Africans are enslaved on the ship *Tecora*, an illegal Portuguese slaver, and begin crossing the Atlantic; after two months, only two-thirds of the Africans survive to arrive in Cuba.

- **June**
  José Ruiz and Pedro Montez hire the schooner *La Amistad* to transport the slaves they claim to have purchased.

- **July 2**
  The Africans aboard *La Amistad* mutiny and take over the ship.

- **August 26**
  The *Amistad* is seized by the captain of the USS *Washington* and taken to Connecticut; the Africans are jailed and admiralty actions begin.

- **September**
  Abolitionists form a committee to free the Africans.

1840

- **January 13**
  Judge Andrew T. Judson rules that the Africans are free.

- **September**
  The cases are appealed to the U.S. Supreme Court.

- **November**
  President Martin Van Buren is defeated for reelection by William Henry Harrison.

1841

- **February–March**
  The *Amistad* case is argued before the U.S. Supreme Court.

- **March 9**
  The Supreme Court issues its decision in the *Amistad* case.

- **November**
  The Africans sail for home accompanied by missionaries.

rica and loaded onto the Portuguese slaver *Tecora* for the voyage to Cuba. During the 4,500-mile journey fewer than two-thirds survived. From the survivors, forty-nine adult men and four children were purchased by José Ruiz and Pedro Montez. Montez procured passports that permitted him to transport his "slaves" from Havana to Puerto Príncipe, Cuba, on *La Amistad*. If the "slaves" had been born in Cuba, these passports would have been legal. However, these blacks were native-born Africans and were free under Spanish law. After the Africans were herded onto *La Amistad*, the schooner waited until nightfall to set sail, to avoid British patrols. Once the ship was under way, the Africans, under the leadership of a young man named Joseph Cinqué, overpowered the crew and killed the captain, two crewmen, and the cook. They spared the captain's slave, Antonio, as well as Montez and Ruiz because the two Spaniards promised to sail the Africans back to Africa. But the two men had other plans. At daylight they sailed east, but after dark they reversed course so that the vessel zigzagged west and north for two months. On August 25, 1839, the ship neared the coast of Long Island. When the ship anchored there, Cinqué and three others went ashore to obtain water. There they met two New Yorkers who tried to trick the Africans into bringing the schooner ashore so that the boat and its "cargo" could be claimed as salvage. But a U.S. naval officer spotted the schooner and intervened. The crew of the cutter USS *Washington* boarded *La Amistad* and discovered that it was a slave ship. Lieutenant Thomas Gedney ordered the seizure of *La Amistad*, its passengers, and its cargo and transported the ship to Connecticut. So began the complex legal case that ensued.

U.S. district court judge Andrew T. Judson conducted an inquiry. Montez and Ruiz asserted their claim using the Cuban passports and by informing the court that the Africans were slaves who had mutinied and murdered the captain and crew. Judson ordered that the Africans be held over for grand jury proceedings in September and said that the property claims could be decided then. Formal legal proceedings soon intensified. Numerous claims to salvage rights on the vessel and its cargo were filed on behalf of the crew of the USS *Washington*. A petition for a writ of habeas corpus was begun on behalf of the Africans. Federal criminal charges were filed against the Africans, and four civil actions in the courts of New York were filed by the Africans against the two Spaniards. Fortunately for the Africans, the seizure drew the interest of American abolitionists, who provided legal counsel and translators. Consequently, the subsequent legal proceedings pitted the Africans against an array of whites. Under admiralty law, the naval officers and the two New Yorkers theoretically had a claim for rescuing the distressed ship and claiming the ship as well as its cargo as salvage. However, if the Africans were not slaves, the claims would be greatly diminished in value. So even at the earliest stages of the case, the fight was over whether the Africans were free or slaves. If they were slaves, they could be seized and sold. If not, the Africans were free.

U.S. Supreme Court justice Smith Thompson, sitting as a circuit court judge, ruled that the alleged offenses had occurred on the high seas beyond the jurisdiction of American courts. However, Thompson refused to release the Africans and referred the matter to the U.S. district court to decide whether the Africans were slaves under Spanish law. Then Judson heard the salvage cases, which were drawn out, contentious, and dramatic. The parties to the cases included the U.S. government headed by President Martin Van Buren, the queen of Spain, the vice-consul of Spain, four Spanish civilians, more than forty Africans, two naval officers, and two white civilians from New York. Each had varying interests. Van Buren was up for reelection in 1840 and needed proslavery, southern votes. Under a treaty with Spain, the administration asserted that the U.S. government was obligated to seize the Africans and return them to Spain. The queen of Spain claimed that the ship and the Africans were property under Spanish law. The two Spaniards claimed the Africans as their property. Three other Spanish residents of Cuba also filed claims to certain goods. The vice-consul of Spain claimed Antonio as a slave on behalf of the deceased captain's heirs. The naval officers and the two New Yorkers claimed *La Amistad*, its cargo, and the Africans as salvage.

While the courts had to decide who had rights to the vessel and its nonhuman cargo, the real battle was between the Africans, represented by lawyers recruited by abolitionists, and the Spanish Crown, as represented by the U.S. government. Based on that evidence, the lawyers for the Africans argued that the passports presented by Montez and Ruiz were fraudulent. Sensing that public sentiment seemed to favor the Africans, the Van Buren administration tried to end the case. In an attempt to have the blacks turned over to the administration as quickly as possible, U.S. District Attorney William S. Holabird contended that the Africans were "free men" whom the government must send back to Africa. That concession did not end the matter, because Ruiz and Montez still contended that the Africans were their property. Also, the Africans and their lawyers knew that allowing the Van Buren administration to take custody of them might result in their persecution by the Spanish for murder and piracy. Based on the evidence and the government's concession, the lower courts determined that the Africans had been born free in Sierra Leone and therefore had been illegally kidnapped into slavery.

By the time the case came to the U.S. Supreme Court, most of the admiralty claims had been resolved. The only parties left were Spain, represented by the government of the United States; Gedney, represented by private counsel; and the Africans, represented by Roger Baldwin and John Quincy Adams. By this time the administration had reversed course and argued that the Africans were slaves and thus that the administration was obligated to return them to Spain. Baldwin argued that international law guaranteed equal rights to all free men. He pointed out that the Africans had never resided in Cuba and never were subject to Spanish law. Baldwin continued to request that the case against the Africans be dismissed and that they be freed from jail. He urged the Supreme Court to reverse the lower court ruling that the Africans should be turned over to the president for return to Africa.

Replica of the schooner **Amistad** (AP/Wide World Photos)

About the Author

When the *Amistad* case was argued beginning in February 1841, the U.S. Supreme Court was composed of Chief Justice Roger Taney of Maryland, Smith Thompson of New York, John McLean of Ohio, Henry Baldwin of Pennsylvania, James Wayne of Georgia, Philip Barbour of Virginia, John Catron of Tennessee, John McKinley of Alabama, and Joseph Story of Massachusetts. Taney, Barbour, Catron, McKinley, and Wayne had all owned slaves. Moreover, McLean, Wayne, Baldwin, Taney, and McKinley had been appointed to the Court by Democratic presidents Andrew Jackson and Martin Van Buren. Generally Democrats supported the institution of slavery, and Van Buren's administration was adamantly opposed to freeing the *Amistad* blacks. But there were two members of the Court who were not only less friendly to slavery but were not friendly to Van Buren. Justice Smith Thompson was the circuit justice for Connecticut and as such had heard the petition and the appeals that had confirmed that the blacks were free. The other justice was Joseph Story, author of the opinion in the case. When the case was argued in February and March

"We may lament the dreadful acts, by which they asserted their liberty, and took possession of the Amistad, and endeavoured to regain their native country; but they cannot be deemed pirates or robbers in the sense of the law of nations, or the treaty with Spain, or the laws of Spain itself."

(Paragraph 14)

"Supposing these African negroes not to be slaves, but kidnapped, and free negroes, the treaty with Spain cannot be obligatory upon them; and the United States are bound to respect their rights as much as those of Spanish subjects. The conflict of rights between the parties under such circumstances, becomes positive and inevitable, and must be decided upon the eternal principles of justice and international law."

(Paragraph 16)

"Upon the whole, our opinion is, that ... the said negroes be declared to be free, and be dismissed from the custody of the Court, and go without delay."

(Paragraph 20)

1841, Justice McKinley was ill, and during the course of the multiday arguments Justice Barbour died. So when the decision was announced, six justices joined in the opinion of Justice Story, and only one justice, Henry Baldwin, dissented.

Joseph Story, born on September 18, 1779, in Marblehead, Massachusetts, was appointed by President James Madison in 1811 at age thirty-two, the youngest person to ever serve on the Court. Despite his inexperience, he became one of the most distinguished justices in the history of the Court. By the time of the *Amistad* decision, he was the senior member. He was also a professor at Harvard Law School and the author of numerous legal treatises. Story had been an ally of Chief Justice John Marshall, and the two laid the cornerstones of the federal government and the judiciary. At the time of the *Amistad* case, Story's views on slavery were well known. He had spoken out publicly in a Salem, Massachusetts, town meeting against slavery and the Missouri Compromise. His judicial record clearly exhibited his distaste for the illegal slave trade. However, there were limits to Story's judicial philosophy. In 1842 he authored the lead opinion in *Prigg v. Pennsylvania*, which held that the Fugitive Slave Act of 1793 preempted all state law to the contrary. Story did attempt to limit his ruling by

stating that states were not required to enforce the federal statute, only that states could not enact statutes that tried to subvert the federal act. However, Story's opinion earned him no credit with abolitionists. Despite his personal opinion of slavery, Story's opinions demonstrated his strict adherence to the law and facts. Story died on September 10, 1845.

Explanation and Analysis of the Document

Story's opinion begins by summarizing the facts of the case in paragraph 1. Then, in paragraphs 2 through 7, Story summarizes the convoluted legal proceedings that resulted in the case's being heard before the U.S. Supreme Court. To review briefly: At issue in the case was who was entitled to the ship and its cargo and what was to be the fate of the Africans on the ship. Were the Africans, in fact, slaves to be returned to the owner who claimed them, or were they free men who had been kidnapped from Africa illegally and hence to be freed to return to Africa?

The key paragraph in Story's summary of the legal proceedings to date is paragraph 6, which notes that on January 23, 1840, a district court had ruled on the various matters before it. In addition to the salvage claims, the court "decreed that they [that is, the "negroes"] should be delivered to the President of the United States, to be transported to Africa, pursuant to the act of 3d March, 1819." The act in question was the Act of March 3, 1819, Relative to the Slave Trade, which was crucial to the case and which read in part:

> Be it enacted by the Senate and House of Representatives of the United States of America, in Congress assembled, That the President of the United States be, and he is hereby, authorized, whenever he shall deem it expedient, to cause any of the armed vessels of the United States, to be employed to cruise on any of the coasts of the United States, or territories thereof, or of the coast of Africa, or elsewhere, where he may judge attempts may be made to carry on the slave trade by citizens or residents of the United States, in contravention of the acts of Congress prohibiting the same.

Paragraph 7 then notes that the district court ruling was appealed and that the appellate court simply affirmed the rulings of the district court. Accordingly, the case was appealed to the U.S. Supreme Court.

Story's analysis of the case and his ruling begin with paragraph 8, where he lays out what he perceives to be the two central issues in the case: whether, under the terms of the 1795 treaty with Spain (often called Pinckney's Treaty or, more formally, the Treaty of San Lorenzo or the Treaty of Madrid), sufficient proof was given as the to the ownership of the ship, its cargo, and the Africans; and whether the U.S. government has a right to intervene in the case. It should be noted that at this point in the proceedings, the United States, as one of the parties to the case, was simply attempting to defend the rights of Spain under the treaty; the U.S. government was not, for example, asserting any ownership rights over the ship, cargo, and Africans, nor was it interested in prosecuting the Africans for their mutiny aboard the ship. A second party to the case, Lieutenant Thomas Gedney, was still trying to assert his right to the ship and cargo as salvage; in connection with this claim, the term "libel" is used, but in this context, the word refers simply to an admiralty lawsuit, or a lawsuit brought under the laws of the sea. Finally, the third party to the case consists of the Africans led by Cinqué, who were asserting that they were not slaves and should be granted their freedom.

From the standpoint of African American history and the history of the abolition of the slave trade, the core of Story's opinion begins with paragraph 12. In this paragraph, Story examines the U.S. treaty with Spain and searches for the clause in the treaty that would apply in this case. The treaty was designed to establish rights when, for example, a ship flying under one country's flag was pursued by pirates and had to put into a port of the other country. An alternative case would be a ship of one country that had to be rescued by a ship from the other because it was, for example, sinking. The purpose of the treaty was simply to agree that one country's property should be returned by the other. The

facts in the *Amistad* case, though, did not conform precisely to any of the clauses in the treaty with Spain. Accordingly, it was up to the Supreme Court to determine what the property rights were. With regard to the ship and its cargo, the issue was relatively simple. The more complicated issue involved the Africans and whether they were "merchandise" under the terms of the treaty.

In paragraph 13, Story takes up this issue. He uses some Latin legal language, including the phrase *onus probandi*, which means "burden of proof." Additionally, he uses the phrase *casus foederis*, which literally means "case of the alliance" and refers to a situation in which the terms of an alliance between nations come into play. He concludes in this paragraph that "these negroes never were the lawful slaves of Ruiz or Montez, or of any other Spanish subjects." He goes on to say that "they are natives of Africa, and were kidnapped there, and were unlawfully transported to Cuba, in violation of the laws and treaties of Spain, and the most solemn edicts and declarations of that government." But then the question arises as to whether the Africans, because of their mutiny, were "pirates or robbers." In paragraph 14, Story concludes: "If, then, these negroes are not slaves, but are kidnapped Africans, who, by the laws of Spain itself, are entitled to their freedom, and were kidnapped and illegally" then "they cannot be deemed pirates or robbers in the sense of the law of nations, or the treaty with Spain, or the laws of Spain itself."

Paragraph 15 takes up the issue of the evidence that the Africans were the property of the Spaniards who claimed them. Story acknowledges that, in general, the U.S. government is obligated to accept any proof of ownership asserted by the citizens of another country and is not obligated to "look behind" any documents the presumed owner provides. Story concedes that the Spaniards' documents would normally be taken as "prima facie" evidence that they, in fact, owned the Africans. But Story goes on to reject the notion that the documents have to be accepted at face value. Such documents can be "impugned for fraud," and if they are found to be fraudulent, they do not have to be accepted as proof. Put simply, Story asserts that the ownership documents of the Spaniards are fraudulent, and therefore the U.S. government is under no obligation to accept them. In paragraph 16, then, Story concludes that if the Africans are not slaves but "free negroes," then the U.S. treaty with Spain is inoperative and "the United States are bound to respect their rights as much as those of Spanish subjects." He states that "the treaty with Spain never could have intended to take away the equal rights of all foreigners" and, on the basis of "the eternal principles of justice and international law," he concludes that "these negroes ought to be deemed free; and that the Spanish treaty interposes no obstacle to the just assertion of their rights."

Paragraph 17 takes up the question of what is to be done with the Africans. The problem Story faced was this: If Africans were brought into the country illegally in contravention of laws prohibiting the slave trade, then the United States, in the person of the president, was obligated to return them to Africa. The problem here was the circumstances under which the Africans had set foot on U.S. soil. They were not brought by slave traders. They, in essence, brought themselves by seizing the ship, and when they arrived in the United States, they had no intention of becoming slaves. Accordingly, Story rules that the United States is under no obligation to return them to Africa.

Paragraph 19 briefly affirms the right of Lieutenant Gedney to salvage. That is, the Court ruled that because of his actions, he was entitled to claim the ship and its cargo under the maritime version of "finders keepers." Of course, Gedney did not want the actual physical property; what he wanted was the value of the property in money. Story affirms his right to salvage.

Audience

When the Supreme Court decided a case, the decision was announced by the reading of the opinion by the justice who authored it. Justice Story's opinion was delivered to a mostly empty courtroom. However, the parties, and the entire country and much of Europe, were interested. The case was of particular interest to abolitionists, who heralded it as a great victory for the cause of abolition, although they were distressed that Antonio, who was in fact a slave, was not freed. The *Amistad* committee took the Africans to Farmington, Connecticut, where abolitionists taught them English, instructed them in Christianity, and raised funds to pay for their return to Africa. Meanwhile, newspapers reporting on the case reflected regional biases. Northern newspapers tended to report on the case from an antislavery perspective, while southern newspapers tended to regard northern reporting as slanted and designed to foment abolitionist sentiment.

Impact

Some historians believe that the *Amistad* case may have helped defeat Martin Van Buren in his quest to be reelected president in 1840. When the case came to his attention, he backed the initial U.S. position as formed by Secretary of State John Forsyth, which favored the claims of Spain and urged that the Africans be returned to Cuba as pirates, murderers, and escaped slaves. Both Van Buren, a Democrat, and his opponent, William Henry Harrison, courted the southern vote, and neither wanted to be perceived as soft on the issue of slavery. Although the *Amistad* case did not figure directly in the election campaign, it formed part of the backdrop of American regional politics in the pre–Civil War decades.

The outcome of the case galvanized the abolition movement, but it angered much of the South. As a legal precedent, the case has been cited only once in a subsequent U.S. Supreme Court decision. The reality was that the case had limited direct impact. It had freed the Africans, but not the slave Antonio. The evidence presented at the initial admiralty trial proved that the Africans were free and not slaves. Moreover, the U.S. attorney had admitted that they were not slaves but free. This admission foreclosed any further argument by the Van Buren administration on behalf of the Spanish. Consequently the case has to be seen as one decided strictly upon its facts. However, Story did use the international law on the slave trade to make clear that a free black man had rights in American courts—an important holding in the ultimate collapse of the slave system.

See also *Dred Scott v. Sandford* (1857).

Questions for Further Study

1. In what sense was the *Amistad* case a victory for abolitionists?

2. The *Amistad* case was a highly complex one. Summarize the facts of the case and the legal issues it presented.

3. What were the international implications of the *Amistad* case? What role did issues involving the transportation of slaves and maritime law play in the outcome of the case?

4. What role did domestic politics play in attitudes toward the case and the U.S. government's position on it?

5. Why were Joseph Cinqué and the other Africans aboard the vessel not put on trial for murder and mutiny?

Further Reading

■ Articles

Jackson, Donald Dale. "Mutiny on the *Amistad*." *Smithsonian* 28 (December 1997): 114–124.

Jones, Howard. "Cinqué of the *Amistad* a Slave Trader? Perpetuating a Myth." *Journal of American History* 87, no. 3 (2000): 923–939.

■ Books

Finkelman, Paul, ed. *Slavery, Race, and the American Legal System 1700–1872.* New York: Garland, 1988.

Jones, Howard. *Mutiny on the Amistad: The Saga of a Slave Revolt and Its Impact on American Abolition, Law, and Diplomacy.* New York: Oxford University Press, 1987.

Osagie, Iyunolu Folayan. *The Amistad Revolt: Memory, Slavery, and the Politics of Identity in the United States and Sierra Leone.* Athens: University of Georgia Press, 2000.

■ Web Sites

"Act of March 3, 1819, Relative to the Slave Trade." Schomburg Center for Research in Black Culture "The Abolition of the Slave Trade" Web site.
http://abolition.nypl.org/content/docs/text/Act_of_1819.pdf.

"Amistad Trials 1839–1840." Famous American Trials Web site.
http://www.law.umkc.edu/faculty/projects/ftrials/amistad/Amistd.htm.

"Argument of John Quincy Adams before the Supreme Court of the United States in the case of the United States, Appellants vs. Cinque, and others, Africans, captured in the schooner Amistad, by Lieut. Gedney." HistoryCentral.com Web site.
http://www.historycentral.com/amistad/amistad.html.

—W. Lewis Burke

UNITED STATES v. AMISTAD

Mr. Justice Story delivered the opinion of the Court.

This is the case of an appeal from the decree of the Circuit Court of the District of Connecticut, sitting in admiralty. The leading facts, as they appear upon the transcript of the proceedings, are as follows: On the 27th of June, 1839, the schooner L'Amistad, being the property of Spanish subjects, cleared out from the port of Havana, in the island of Cuba, for Puerto Principe, in the same island. On board of the schooner were the captain, Ransom Ferrer, and Jose Ruiz, and Pedro Montez, all Spanish subjects. The former had with him a negro boy, named Antonio, claimed to be his slave. Jose Ruiz had with him forty-nine negroes, claimed by him as his slaves, and stated to be his property, in a certain pass or document, signed by the Governor General of Cuba. Pedro Montez had with him four other negroes, also claimed by him as his slaves, and stated to be his property, in a similar pass or document, also signed by the Governor General of Cuba. On the voyage, and before the arrival of the vessel at her port of destination, the negroes rose, killed the captain, and took possession of her. On the 26th of August, the vessel was discovered by Lieutenant Gedney, of the United States brig Washington, at anchor on the high seas, at the distance of half a mile from the shore of Long Island. A part of the negroes were then on shore at Culloden Point, Long Island; who were seized by Lieutenant Gedney, and brought on board. The vessel, with the negroes and other persons on board, was brought by Lieutenant Gedney into the district of Connecticut, and there libelled for salvage in the District Court of the United States. A libel for salvage was also filed by Henry Green and Pelatiah Fordham, of Sag Harbour, Long Island. On the 18th of September, Ruiz and Montez filed claims and libels, in which they asserted their ownership of the negroes as their slaves, and of certain parts of the cargo, and prayed that the same might be "delivered to them, or to the representatives of her Catholic majesty, as might be most proper." On the 19th of September, the Attorney of the United States, for the district of Connecticut, filed an information or libel, setting forth, that the Spanish minister had officially presented to the proper department of the government of the United States, a claim for the restoration of the vessel, cargo, and slaves, as the property

of Spanish subjects, which had arrived within the jurisdictional limits of the United States, and were taken possession of by the said public armed brig of the United States; under such circumstances as made it the duty of the United States to cause the same to be restored to the true proprietors, pursuant to the treaty between the United States and Spain: and praying the Court, on its being made legally to appear that the claim of the Spanish minister was well founded, to make such order for the disposal of the vessel, cargo, and slaves, as would best enable the United States to comply with their treaty stipulations. But if it should appear, that the negroes were persons transported from Africa, in violation of the laws of the United States, and brought within the United States contrary to the same laws; he then prayed the Court to make such order for their removal to the coast of Africa, pursuant to the laws of the United States, as it should deem fit.

On the 19th of November, the Attorney of the United States filed a second information or libel, similar to the first, with the exception of the second prayer above set forth in his former one. On the same day, Antonio G. Vega, the vice-consul of Spain, for the state of Connecticut, filed his libel, alleging that Antonio was a slave, the property of the representatives of Ramon Ferrer, and praying the Court to cause him to be delivered to the said vice-consul, that he might be returned by him to his lawful owner in the island of Cuba.

On the 7th of January, 1840, the negroes, Cinque and others, with the exception of Antonio, by their counsel, filed an answer, denying that they were slaves, or the property of Ruiz and Montez, or that the Court could, under the Constitution or laws of the United States, or under any treaty, exercise any jurisdiction over their persons, by reason of the premises; and praying that they might be dismissed. They specially set forth and insist in this answer, that they were native born Africans; born free, and still of right ought to be free and not slaves; that they were, on or about the 15th of April, 1839, unlawfully kidnapped, and forcibly and wrongfully carried on board a certain vessel on the coast of Africa, which was unlawfully engaged in the slave trade, and were unlawfully transported in the same vessel to the island of

Cuba, for the purpose of being there unlawfully sold as slaves; that Ruiz and Montez, well knowing the premises, made a pretended purchase of them: that afterwards, on or about the 28th of June, 1839, Ruiz and Montez, confederating with Ferrer, (captain of the Amistad,) caused them, without law or right, to be placed on board of the Amistad, to be transported to some place unknown to them, and there to be enslaved for life; that, on the voyage, they rose on the master, and took possession of the vessel, intending to return therewith to their native country, or to seek an asylum in some free state; and the vessel arrived, about the 26th of August, 1839, off Montauk Point, near Long Island; a part of them were sent onshore, and were seized by Lieutenant Gedney, and carried on board; and all of them were afterwards brought by him into the district of Connecticut.

On the 7th of January, 1840, Jose Antonio Tellincas, and Messrs. Aspe and Laca, all Spanish subjects, residing in Cuba, filed their claims, as owners to certain portions of the goods found on board of the schooner L'Amistad.

On the same day, all the libellants and claimants, by their counsel, except Jose Ruiz and Pedro Montez, (whose libels and claims, as stated of record, respectively, were pursued by the Spanish minister, the same being merged in his claims,) appeared, and the negroes also appeared by their counsel; and the case was heard on the libels, claims, answers, and testimony of witnesses.

On the 23d day of January, 1840, the District Court made a decree. By that decree, the Court rejected the claim of Green and Fordham for salvage, but allowed salvage to Lieutenant Gedney and others, on the vessel and cargo, of one-third of the value thereof, but not on the negroes, Cinque and others; it allowed the claim of Tellincas, and Aspe and Laca with the exception of the above-mentioned salvage; it dismissed the libels and claims of Ruiz and Montez, with costs, as being included under the claim of the Spanish minister; it allowed the claim of the Spanish vice-consul for Antonio, on behalf of Ferrer's representatives; it rejected the claims of Ruiz and Montez for the delivery of the negroes, but admitted them for the cargo, with the exception of the above-mentioned salvage; it rejected the claim made by the Attorney of the United States on behalf of the Spanish minister, for the restoration of the negroes under the treaty; but it decreed that they should be delivered to the President of the United States, to be transported to Africa, pursuant to the act of 3d March, 1819.

From this decree the District Attorney, on behalf of the United States, appealed to the Circuit Court, except so far as related to the restoration of the slave Antonio. The claimants, Tellincas, and Aspe and Laca, also appealed from that part of the decree which awarded salvage on the property respectively claimed by them. No appeal was interposed by Ruiz or Montez, or on behalf of the representatives of the owners of the Amistad. The Circuit Court, by a mere pro forma decree, affirmed the decree of the District Court, reserving the question of salvage upon the claims of Tellincas, and Aspe and Laca. And from that decree the present appeal has been brought to this Court.

The cause has been very elaborately argued, as well upon the merits, as upon a motion on behalf of the appellees to dismiss the appeal. On the part of the United States, it has been contended, 1. That due and sufficient proof concerning the property has been made to authorize the restitution of the vessel, cargo, and negroes to the Spanish subjects on whose behalf they are claimed pursuant to the treaty with Spain, of the 27th of October, 1795. 2. That the United States had a right to intervene in the manner in which they have done, to obtain a decree for the restitution of the property, upon the application of the Spanish minister. These propositions have been strenuously denied on the other side. Other collateral and incidental points have been stated, upon which it is not necessary at this moment to dwell.

Before entering upon the discussion of the main points involved in this interesting and important controversy, it may be necessary to say a few words as to the actual posture of the case as it now stands before us. In the first place, then, the only parties now before the Court on one side, are the United States, intervening for the sole purpose of procuring restitution of the property as Spanish property, pursuant to the treaty, upon the grounds stated by the other parties claiming the property in their respective libels. The United States do not assert any property in themselves, or any violation of their own rights, or sovereignty, or laws, by the acts complained of. They do not insist that these negroes have been imported into the United States, in contravention of our own slave trade acts. They do not seek to have these negroes delivered up for the purpose of being transported to Cuba as pirates or robbers, or as fugitive criminals found within our territories, who have been guilty of offences against the laws of Spain. They do not assert that the seizure, and bringing the vessel, and cargo, and negroes into port, by Lieutenant Gedney, for the purpose of adjudication, is a tortious act. They simply confine themselves to the right of the Spanish claimants to the restitution of their property, upon the facts asserted in their respective allegations.

In the next place, the parties before the Court on the other side as appellees, are Lieutenant Gedney, on his libel for salvage, and the negroes, (Cinque, and others,) asserting themselves, in their answer, not to be slaves, but free native Africans, kidnapped in their own country, and illegally transported by force from that country; and now entitled to maintain their freedom.

No question has been here made, as to the proprietary interests in the vessel, and cargo. It is admitted that they belong to Spanish subjects, and that they ought to be restored. The only point on this head is, whether the restitution ought to be upon the payment of salvage or not? The main controversy is, whether these negroes are the property of Ruiz and Montez, and ought to be delivered up; and to this, accordingly, we shall first direct our attention.

It has been argued on behalf of the United States, that the Court are bound to deliver them up, according to the treaty of 1795, with Spain, which has in this particular been continued in full force, by the treaty of 1819, ratified in 1821. The sixth article of that treaty, seems to have had, principally, in view cases where the property of the subjects of either state had been taken possession of within the territorial jurisdiction of the other, during war. The eighth article provides for cases where the shipping of the inhabitants of either state are forced, through stress of weather, pursuit of pirates, or enemies, or any other urgent necessity, to seek shelter in the ports of the other. There may well be some doubt entertained, whether the present case, in its actual circumstances, falls within the purview of this article. But it does not seem necessary, for reasons hereafter stated, absolutely to decide it. The ninth article provides, "that all ships and merchandise, of what nature soever, which shall be rescued out of the hands of any pirates or robbers, on the high seas, shall be brought into some port of either state, and shall be delivered to the custody of the officers of that port, in order to be taken care of and restored entire to the true proprietor, as soon as due and sufficient proof shall be made concerning the, property thereof." This is the article on which the main reliance is placed on behalf of the United States, for the restitution of these negroes. To bring the case within the article, it is essential to establish, First, That these negroes,

under all the circumstances, fall within the description of merchandise, in the sense of the treaty. Secondly, That there has been a rescue of them on the high seas, out of the hands of the pirates and robbers; which, in the present case, can only be, by showing that they themselves are pirates and robbers; and, Thirdly, That Ruiz and Montez, the asserted proprietors, are the true proprietors, and have established their title by competent proof.

If these negroes were, at the time, lawfully held as slaves under the laws of Spain, and recognised by those laws as property capable of being lawfully bought and sold; we see no reason why they may not justly be deemed within the intent of the treaty, to be included under the denomination of merchandise, and, as such, ought to be restored to the claimants: for, upon that point, the laws of Spain would seem to furnish the proper rule of interpretation. But, admitting this, it is clear, in our opinion, that neither of the other essential facts and requisites has been established in proof; and the onus probandi of both lies upon the claimants to give rise to the casus foederis. It is plain beyond controversy, if we examine the evidence, that these negroes never were the lawful slaves of Ruiz or Montez, or of any other Spanish subjects. They are natives of Africa, and were kidnapped there, and were unlawfully transported to Cuba, in violation of the laws and treaties of Spain, and the most solemn edicts and declarations of that government. By those laws, and treaties, and edicts, the African slave trade is utterly abolished; the dealing in that trade is deemed a heinous crime; and the negroes thereby introduced into the dominions of Spain, are declared to be free. Ruiz and Montez are proved to have made the pretended purchase of these negroes, with a full knowledge of all the circumstances. And so cogent and irresistible is the evidence in this respect, that the District Attorney has admitted in open Court, upon the record, that these negroes were native Africans, and recently imported into Cuba, as alleged in their answers to the libels in the case. The supposed proprietary interest of Ruiz and Montez, is completely displaced, if we are at liberty to look at the evidence or the admissions of the District Attorney.

If, then, these negroes are not slaves, but are kidnapped Africans, who, by the laws of Spain itself, are entitled to their freedom, and were kidnapped and illegally carried to Cuba, and illegally detained and restrained on board of the Amistad; there is no pretence to say, that they are pirates or robbers. We may lament the dreadful acts, by which they asserted their liberty, and took possession of the Amistad, and endeavoured to regain their native country; but they cannot be deemed pirates or robbers in the sense of the law of nations, or the treaty with Spain, or the laws of Spain itself; at least so far as those laws have been brought to our knowledge. Nor do the libels of Ruiz or Montez assert them to be such.

This posture of the facts would seem, of itself, to put an end to the whole inquiry upon the merits. But it is argued, on behalf of the United States, that the ship, and cargo, and negroes were duly documented as belonging to Spanish subjects, and this Court have no right to look behind these documents; that full faith and credit is to be given to them; and that they are to be held conclusive evidence in this cause, even although it should be established by the most satisfactory proofs, that they have been obtained by the grossest frauds and impositions upon the constituted authorities of Spain. To this argument we can, in no wise, assent. There is nothing in the treaty which justifies or sustains the argument. We do not here meddle with the point, whether there has been any connivance in this illegal traffic, on the part of any of the colonial authorities or subordinate officers of Cuba; because, in our view, such an examination is unnecessary, and ought not to be pursued, unless it were indispensable to public justice, although it has been strongly pressed at the bar. What we proceed upon is this, that although public documents of the government, accompanying property found on board of the private ships of a foreign nation, certainly are to be deemed prima facie evidence of the facts which they purport to state, yet they are always open to be impugned for fraud; and whether that fraud be in the original obtaining of these documents, or in the subsequent fraudulent and illegal use of them, when once it is satisfactorily established, it overthrows all their sanctity, and destroys them as proof. Fraud will vitiate any, even the most solemn transactions; and an asserted title to property, founded upon it, is utterly void. The very language of the ninth article of the treaty of 1795 requires the proprietor to make due and sufficient proof of his property. And how can that proof be deemed either due or sufficient, which is but a connected and stained tissue of fraud? This is not a mere rule of municipal jurisprudence. Nothing is more clear in the law of nations, as an established rule to regulate their rights, and duties, and Intercourse, than the doctrine, that the ship's papers are but prima facie evidence, and that, if they are shown to be fraudulent, they are not to be held proof of any valid title. This rule is familiarly applied, and, indeed,

is of every-days occurrence in cases of prize, in the contests between belligerents and neutrals, as is apparent from numerous cases to be found in the Reports of this Court; and it is just as applicable to the transactions of civil intercourse between nations in times of peace. If a private ship, clothed with Spanish papers, should enter the ports of the United States, claiming the privileges, and immunities, and rights belonging to bona fide subjects of Spain, under our treaties or laws, and she should, in reality, belong to the subjects of another nation, which was not entitled to any such privileges, immunities, or rights, and the proprietors were seeking, by fraud, to cover their own illegal acts, under the flag of Spain; there can be no doubt, that it would be the duty of our Courts to strip off the disguise, and to look at the case according to its naked realities. In the solemn treaties between nations, it can never be presumed that either state intends to provide the means of perpetrating or protecting frauds; but all the provisions are to be construed as intended to be applied to bona fide transactions. The seventeenth article of the treaty with Spain, which provides for certain passports and certificates, as evidence of property on board of the ships of both states, is, in its terms, applicable only to cases where either of the parties is engaged in a war. This article required a certain form of passport to be agreed upon by the parties, and annexed to the treaty. It never was annexed; and, therefore, in the case of the Amiable Isabella, 6 Wheaton, 1, it was held inoperative.

It is also a most important consideration in the present case, which ought not to be lost sight of, that, supposing these African negroes not to be slaves, but kidnapped, and free negroes, the treaty with Spain cannot be obligatory upon them; and the United States are bound to respect their rights as much as those of Spanish subjects. The conflict of rights between the parties under such circumstances, becomes positive and inevitable, and must be decided upon the eternal principles of justice and international law. If the contest were about any goods on board of this ship, to which American citizens asserted a title, which was denied by the Spanish claimants, there could be no doubt of the right of such American citizens to litigate their claims before any competent American tribunal, notwithstanding the treaty with Spain. A fortiori, the doctrine must apply where human life and human liberty are in issue; and constitute the very essence of the controversy. The treaty with Spain never could have intended to take away the equal rights of all foreigners, who should contest their claims before any of our Courts, to equal justice; or to deprive such foreigners of the protection given them by other treaties, or by the general law of nations. Upon the merits of the case, then, there does not seem to us to be any ground for doubt, that these negroes ought to be deemed free; and that the Spanish treaty interposes no obstacle to the just assertion of their rights.

There is another consideration growing out of this part of the case, which necessarily rises in judgment. It is observable, that the United States, in their original claim, filed it in the alternative, to have the negroes, if slaves and Spanish property, restored to the proprietors; or, if not slaves, but negroes who had been transported from Africa, in violation of the laws of the United States, and brought into the United States contrary to the same laws, then the Court to pass an order to enable the United States to remove such persons to the coast of Africa, to be delivered there to such agent as may be authorized to receive and provide for them. At a subsequent period, this last alternative claim was not insisted on, and another claim was interposed, omitting it; from which the conclusion naturally arises that it was abandoned. The decree of the District Court, however, contained an order for the delivery of the negroes to the United States; to be transported to the coast of Africa, un-

der the act of the 3d of March, 1819, ch. 224. The United States do not now insist upon any affirmance of this part of the decree; and, in our judgment, upon the admitted facts, there is no ground to assert that the case comes within the purview of the act of 1819, or of any other of our prohibitory slave trade acts. These negroes were never taken from Africa, or brought to the United States in contravention of those acts. When the Amistad arrived she was in possession of the negroes, asserting their freedom; and in no sense could they possibly intend to import themselves here, as slaves, or for sale as slaves. In this view of the matter, that part of the decree of the District Court is unmaintainable, and must be reversed.

The view which has been thus taken of this case, upon the merits, under the first point, renders it wholly unnecessary for us to give any opinion upon the other point, as to the right of the United States to intervene in this case in the manner already stated. We dismiss this, therefore, as well as several minor points made at the argument.

As to the claim of Lieutenant Gedney for the salvage service, it is understood that the United States do not now desire to interpose any obstacle to the allowance of it, if it is deemed reasonable by the Court. It was a highly meritorious and useful service to the

Glossary

a fortiori	a Latin phrase meaning roughly "with stronger or greater reason"
act of the 3d of March, 1819	Act of March 3, 1819, Relative to the Slave Trade, giving the president the power to block illegal transportation of slaves
casus foederis	Latin for "case of the alliance," referring to a situation in which the terms of an alliance between nations come into play
clothed	in law, refers to a pretense or fraud
information	in law, a lawsuit
libel	in maritime law, a lawsuit
onus probandi	Latin for "burden of proof"
prima facie	Latin for "at first sight," referring to a legal matter not needing proof unless contrary evidence is shown
sitting in admiralty	functioning as an admiralty court, or one that hears cases involving maritime law
tortious act	an act that subjects the doer to liability, or fault, in tort law
treaty between the United States and Spain	Pinckney's Treaty or, more formally, the Treaty of San Lorenzo or the Treaty of Madrid, signed in 1795

proprietors of the ship and cargo; and such as, by the general principles of maritime law, is always deemed a just foundation for salvage. The rate allowed by the Court, does not seem to us to have been beyond the exercise of a sound discretion, under the very peculiar and embarrassing circumstances of the case.

Upon the whole, our opinion is, that the decree of the Circuit Court, affirming that of the District Court, ought to be affirmed, except so far as it directs the negroes to be delivered to the President, to be transported to Africa, in pursuance of the act of the 3d of March, 1819; and, as to this, it ought to be reversed: and that the said negroes be declared to be free, and be dismissed from the custody of the Court, and go without delay.

Mr. Justice Baldwin dissented.

This cause came on to be heard on the transcript of the record from the Circuit Court of the United States, for the District of Connecticut, and was argued by counsel. On consideration whereof, it is the opinion of this Court, that there is error in that part of the decree of the Circuit Court, affirming the decree of the District Court, which ordered the said negroes to be delivered to the President of the United States, to be transported to Africa, in pursuance of the act of Congress, of the 3d of March, 1819; and that, as to that part, it ought to be reversed: and, in all other respects, that the said decree of the Circuit Court ought to be affirmed. It is therefore ordered adjudged, and decreed by this Court, that the decree of the said Circuit Court be, and the same is hereby, affirmed, except as to the part aforesaid, and as to that part, that it be reversed; and that the cause be remanded to the Circuit Court, with directions to enter, in lieu of that part, a decree, that the said negroes be, and are hereby, declared to be free, and that they be dismissed from the custody of the Court, and be discharged from the suit, and go thereof quit without delay.

Joseph Story (Library of Congress)

PRIGG V. PENNSYLVANIA

"The States ... possesses full jurisdiction to arrest and restrain runaway slaves, and remove them from their borders."

Overview

Prigg v. Pennsylvania was the first decision of the U.S. Supreme Court to interpret the fugitive slave clause of the U.S. Constitution and also the first decision to consider the constitutionality of the Fugitive Slave Act of 1793. In his "opinion of the Court," Justice Joseph Story of Massachusetts reached six major conclusions: that the federal Fugitive Slave Act of 1793 was constitutional in all its provisions; that no state could pass any law that added requirements to the federal law or impeded the return of fugitive slaves, such as requiring that a state judge hear the case; that masters or their agents had a constitutional right of self-help (the technical term was "recaption") to seize any fugitive slave anywhere and to bring that slave back to the South and that this could be done without complying with the provisions of the Fugitive Slave Act or even bringing the alleged fugitive before a judge; that if a captured fugitive slave was brought before a judge, he or she was entitled to only a summary proceeding to determine whether he or she was the person described in the papers provided by the master; that a judge was not to decide whether the person before him was a slave or free but only whether he or she was the person described in the papers; and that state officials should enforce but could not be required to enforce the Fugitive Slave Act.

With the exception of *Dred Scott v. Sandford* (1857), this was the Supreme Court's most important decision concerning slavery and race before the Civil War. Justice Story wrote an overwhelmingly proslavery opinion for the court, with the dissent of only one justice, John McLean of Ohio. However, most of the majority justices could not agree with each other on all the details. Thus, there were five separate opinions agreeing with the outcome but not necessarily agreeing with all of Justice Story's points. Chief Justice Roger B. Taney agreed with the result but so emphatically disagreed with some of Story's points that his opinion is sometimes mistakenly called a dissent. Only two justices in the majority failed to write an opinion.

Context

Prigg v. Pennsylvania came to the U.S. Supreme Court as an appeal from a decision in Pennsylvania, where Edward Prigg, a citizen of Maryland, had been convicted of kidnapping a black woman named Margaret Morgan and her children. Prigg claimed that Morgan and her children were slaves in Maryland, owned by Margaret Ashmore, who was the mother-in-law of one of the other original defendants, Nathan Bemis. In 1837, Prigg, Bemis, and two other men traveled to Pennsylvania and seized Morgan and her children. They brought the group before Pennsylvania justice of the peace Thomas Henderson and asked for a certificate that would allow them to take the fugitive slaves back to Maryland. This was the proper procedure under an 1826 Pennsylvania personal liberty law designed to prevent the kidnapping of free blacks. Henderson refused to issue the certificate because he did not believe that Morgan was a slave. At this point Prigg and Bemis released Morgan and her children and then offered to take them home. Instead, Prigg and his companions took them all to Maryland, where they were eventually sold as slaves. A Pennsylvania grand jury indicted all four Maryland men for kidnapping. After two years of negotiations, Maryland agreed to return just one of them, Prigg, for trial. He was quickly convicted, and the Pennsylvania Supreme Court upheld this result. Prigg then appealed to the U.S. Supreme Court.

The facts of the case were complicated. Margaret Morgan was, in fact, the child of a slave woman, and under Maryland law that made her a slave as well. But shortly after the War of 1812, when she was just a child, her owner, John Ashmore, told Margaret's parents that they were free. From that point on, Margaret always considered herself a free person. In the 1820s she married Jerry Morgan, who was born free in Pennsylvania. In the 1830 census Margaret, her children, and her husband were listed as "free persons of color" living in Harford County, Maryland. In 1832 the Morgans all moved to York, Pennsylvania, where they lived until 1837, when Prigg and Bemis claimed them as slaves. In Pennsylvania, Margaret gave birth to at least one child and perhaps two. Under Pennsylvania law they were free, *even* if Margaret was a fugitive slave.

Time Line

1780

■ Pennsylvania's gradual abolition act provides for the return of fugitive slaves who escape into Pennsylvania or who escape from masters who are visiting Pennsylvania.

1787

■ **July**
Meeting in New York under the Articles of Confederation, Congress passes the Northwest Ordinance, which prohibits slavery in the territories north of the Ohio River. The slavery clause also allows for the return of fugitive slaves who escape into the territory.

■ **August**
The Constitutional Convention, meeting in Philadelphia, adds the fugitive slave clause to what would become Article IV of the Constitution. The clause follows a similar clause—the criminal extradition clause—providing for the return of fugitives from justice.

1791

■ The governor of Pennsylvania requests that Virginia extradite three white men accused of kidnapping a free black. The request is rejected. The governor of Pennsylvania appeals to President George Washington, who hands it off to the attorney general. Eventually it is given to Congress and leads to the passage of the Fugitive Slave Act of 1793.

1793

■ **February**
Congress passes and President George Washington signs the Fugitive Slave Act of 1793.

1826

■ Pennsylvania passes a personal liberty law, requiring that all fugitive slaves be brought before a state magistrate before being removed from the state.

1830

■ Margaret Morgan; her husband, Jerry Morgan; and their children are listed in the U.S. census as free blacks living in Harford County, Maryland.

The circumstances of this case illustrate the complexity of returning fugitive slaves. Most people imagine fugitive slaves to have been literally on the run, captured by hard-charging slave hunters in hot pursuit of African Americans seeking their freedom. Certainly there were cases like that. But often those claimed as fugitive slaves had lived in the North for months or years and had established themselves within a community. Even if Margaret Morgan was technically a fugitive slave, by 1837 she was also the wife of a free black citizen of Pennsylvania and the mother of one or two Pennsylvania-born free African American children. Returning her to bondage would affect more than just her life—it would directly affect her family and, indirectly, a whole community.

The return of fugitive slaves presented enormous legal, political, moral, and emotional controversies for the United States. By 1812 the nation had become truly divided into two sections. All of the northern states had either ended slavery or were doing so through gradual abolition acts. The small antislavery movements in the South that sprang up during the Revolution had all but disappeared. The nation had become, as Abraham Lincoln characterized it in his "House Divided" speech (1858), "half slave and half free."

While slavery was dying out in the North, the free black population was growing. Many white northerners were uncomfortable with the presence of free blacks, and discrimination was significant. Still, almost all northerners disliked slavery, and most were appalled at the idea of holding people in bondage. Furthermore, the overwhelming majority of northerners were opposed to seeing their free black neighbors kidnapped and sold as slaves. Many northerners felt the same way about fugitive slaves who were brave, lucky, and enterprising enough to escape from bondage and become free.

The federal Fugitive Slave Act of 1793 provided that masters or their agents could bring an alleged slave before any state or federal judge and obtain a certificate of removal on the basis of an affidavit from the state where the person was allegedly a slave. There was no hearing into the status of the alleged slave, no jury trial, and no real opportunity for the person claimed to prove that he or she was actually free or that the wrong person had been seized. The law contemplated a summary process. In addition, the federal law provided no punishment for people who seized blacks and did not bring them before a judge or magistrate.

Starting in the 1790s there were persistent complaints from northern blacks and their white allies that southerners were roaming the streets of cities like Philadelphia and New York or scouring rural areas near Virginia and Maryland, kidnapping free blacks and hurrying them off to the South. There were also complaints that southerners were falsely claiming free people as fugitive slaves. Some of these people were free-born citizens of the northern states. Others were fugitive slaves who had recently escaped to the North. Some were like Margaret Morgan and her children, whose status was uncertain and murky. In response to kidnappings, starting in the 1820s the legislatures in a number of free states, including New Jersey, Pennsylvania, and New York, passed personal liberty laws to protect free blacks.

These laws made it a crime to remove a black from the state without a judicial hearing by a state official. Thus Prigg was prosecuted under the Pennsylvania law after he removed Morgan and her children from the state without obtaining the proper papers from a state magistrate.

By the time Prigg's case reached the U.S. Supreme Court, state judges in New York and New Jersey had held that the Fugitive Slave Act of 1793 was unconstitutional. The New York courts believed that Congress had no power to pass the law and that the return of fugitive slaves was a matter left entirely to the states. In the case at hand, *Jack v. Martin* (1835), the New York court returned the slave Jack to his owner but did so under state law. In other words, New York accepted its constitutional obligation to return runaway slaves, but the state did not accept the idea that this should be done under federal law. In New Jersey the highly respected Chief Justice Joseph Hornblower questioned the constitutionality of the Fugitive Slave Act of 1793 in an unpublished opinion, complaining that it provided for a "summary and dangerous proceeding" and afforded "but little protection of security to the free colored man, who may be falsely claimed as a fugitive from labor." Hornblower believed that even if the Congress had the power to pass the law, it was unconstitutional because it denied alleged fugitives due process and a jury trial.

Southerners complained that these laws made it impossible for them to recover their runaway slaves. They also argued that since Congress had passed a law on this subject, it was unfair to make them also comply with the rules set out by the different states. This argument was complicated by the fact that Prigg and Bemis had only partially followed the procedures set out under the 1793 law. They did bring Morgan before a judge, as the federal law required, but when he gave them a ruling they did not like, they took the law into their own hands and simply forced Morgan and her children to go to Maryland without any legal documents or the authorization of any court.

By 1841 slavery had become one of the most important and divisive issues in American politics. A small but growing abolitionist movement in the North was noisily calling for an end to slavery everywhere in the nation. The House of Representatives refused to even read antislavery petitions sent by abolitionists. More ominously for the South, northern politicians, such as New York's Governor William H. Seward, Congressmen Joshua Giddings of Ohio, and Congressman (and former president) John Quincy Adams of Massachusetts, were increasingly openly hostile to slavery. Southerners believed that they could never recover fugitive slaves, even though in the late 1830s there were famous cases in Maine and New York where masters did recover runaway slaves. It was in this context that Prigg's case went to the Supreme Court.

About the Author

There are three authors of the opinions reprinted here: Joseph Story, Roger B. Taney, and John McLean. Joseph Story was born in 1779 and raised in a solidly middle-class

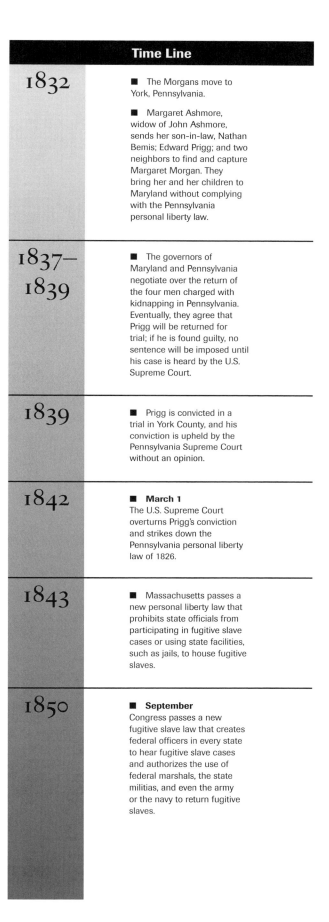

Time Line

1832
- The Morgans move to York, Pennsylvania.
- Margaret Ashmore, widow of John Ashmore, sends her son-in-law, Nathan Bemis; Edward Prigg; and two neighbors to find and capture Margaret Morgan. They bring her and her children to Maryland without complying with the Pennsylvania personal liberty law.

1837–1839
- The governors of Maryland and Pennsylvania negotiate over the return of the four men charged with kidnapping in Pennsylvania. Eventually, they agree that Prigg will be returned for trial; if he is found guilty, no sentence will be imposed until his case is heard by the U.S. Supreme Court.

1839
- Prigg is convicted in a trial in York County, and his conviction is upheld by the Pennsylvania Supreme Court without an opinion.

1842
- **March 1**
  The U.S. Supreme Court overturns Prigg's conviction and strikes down the Pennsylvania personal liberty law of 1826.

1843
- Massachusetts passes a new personal liberty law that prohibits state officials from participating in fugitive slave cases or using state facilities, such as jails, to house fugitive slaves.

1850
- **September**
  Congress passes a new fugitive slave law that creates federal officers in every state to hear fugitive slave cases and authorizes the use of federal marshals, the state militias, and even the army or the navy to return fugitive slaves.

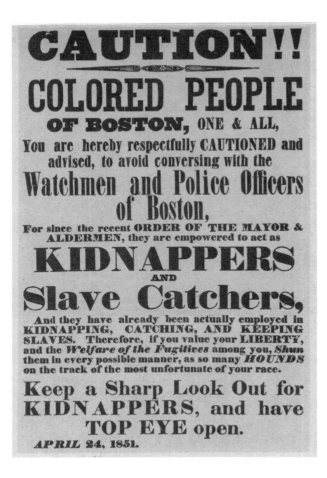

A poster warning "Colored People" in Boston, Massachusetts, of the dangers of kidnappers and slave catchers
(AP/Wide World Photos)

family in Marblehead, Massachusetts (outside Boston). A hard-working and brilliant student, he graduated second in his class from Harvard University in 1798, at the age of nineteen. He then became a lawyer, held local offices, and served in Congress in 1808–1809. On November 15, 1811, President James Madison nominated him to the Supreme Court. He remained on the Court until his death on September 10, 1845.

Story was learned, scholarly, and a firm believer in a strong Supreme Court. He was Chief Justice John Marshall's closest ally on the Court. A northerner, Story personally opposed slavery and, in his early years, issued a number of opinions and charges to grand juries that supported a strict suppression of the illegal African slave trade. In 1820 he made a speech opposing the spread of slavery into the western territories. In addition to his Supreme Court duties, Story was a professor at Harvard Law School and the author of more than a dozen books and treatises on law. His most important was *Commentaries on the Constitution of the United States* (1833), a three-volume treatise that argued for a highly nationalist interpretation of the Constitution and rejected notions of states' rights. His decision in *Prigg* was consistent with these values because it national-

ized the return of fugitive slaves and rejected the idea that the states could regulate this issue. It was totally at odds, however, with his opposition to slavery and deeply inconsistent with the values of most New Englanders, the section of the nation he represented on the Court.

Chief Justice Roger B. Taney was born in 1777 into a wealthy slaveholding planter family in Maryland. He graduated from Dickinson College in 1795 at age eighteen, practiced law, and served in the state legislature. He was initially a Federalist, but in the 1820s he became an avid supporter of Andrew Jackson. He served as Jackson's attorney general and secretary of the Treasury before becoming chief justice of the United States in 1836. As a young man, Taney had freed most of his own slaves and once defended a minister accused of giving antislavery sermons. However, while serving as Jackson's attorney general, he argued that free blacks were not entitled to passports because they could never be considered citizens of the United States. By the early 1840s he was committed to supporting slavery, even if he did not own slaves. In 1857 he would write the opinion of the Court in *Dred Scott v. Sandford*, holding that free blacks had no rights under the Constitution and could never be considered citizens of the nation. Taney was far more sympathetic to states' rights than Story and less supportive of a strong national government. His opinion in *Prigg* was inconsistent with these legal principles, since he rejected the idea that states should be able to protect their free black citizens in fugitive slave cases. However, his opinion in *Prigg* was consistent with his strong support for slavery. He died in 1864.

John McLean was born in 1785 in New Jersey but grew up on a small farm on the Ohio frontier. He had no formal education until age sixteen and never attended college. He edited a newspaper, practiced law, and then held a series of political offices, serving in Congress, on the Ohio Supreme Court, as commissioner of the General Land Office, and then as postmaster general under three successive presidents: James Monroe, John Quincy Adams, and Andrew Jackson. Even his opponents believed that McLean was the most competent and honest postmaster of his age. Shortly after he took office, President Jackson appointed McLean to the Supreme Court, where he served for thirty-two years, making him the twelfth-longest-serving justice in the first two and a quarter centuries of the Court's history. He died in 1861.

McLean was always antislavery and, as Ohio justice, wrote a strong opinion holding that any slave voluntarily brought into the state was free. Later in life he became related through marriage to Salmon P. Chase, the most important antislavery lawyer in the nation, who was nicknamed "the Attorney General for Fugitive Slaves." At the time McLean was on the Court, justices were required to "ride circuit," where they presided over federal court trials in the states of the circuit to which they were assigned. McLean, riding circuit in Ohio, Indiana, Illinois, and Michigan, heard more fugitive slave cases than any other justice. He took seriously his obligation to enforce the fugitive slave clause of the Constitution and the 1793 Fugitive Slave Act. However, he also believed in protecting the rights of free blacks and preventing the enslavement of anyone unless there was an absolutely clear legal right to send that person into bondage. His opinion in *Prigg* is consistent with these views and with his vast experience with fugitive slave cases, which far exceeded the combined experience of Taney and Story.

Explanation and Analysis of the Document

As noted, seven of the nine justices wrote opinions in this case. Eight of the nine justices believed that Prigg's conviction should be overturned. The main point of disagreement was between Story and Taney, on whether state officials could be required to participate in the return of fugitive slaves. McLean's dissent argued that the Pennsylvania law was constitutional and thus it was permissible to prosecute Prigg for kidnapping.

In his opinion Story reached six major conclusions: that the federal Fugitive Slave Act of 1793 was constitutional; that no state could pass any law that added requirements to the federal law or impeded the return of fugitive slaves; that people claiming fugitive slaves (masters or their agents) had a constitutionally protected common law right of recaption, or "self-help," which allowed a claimant to seize any fugitive slave anywhere and bring that slave back to the South without complying with the provisions of the Fugitive Slave Act; that a captured fugitive slave was entitled to only a summary proceeding to determine whether he or she was indeed the person described in the papers provided by the claimant; that a judge was not to decide whether the person before him was a slave or free but only whether he or she was the person described in the papers; and that state officials should, but could not be required to, enforce the Fugitive Slave Act.

When combined, these conclusions created an overwhelming proslavery result. Story's notion of self-help was the most important for slave owners and the most dangerous for free blacks. Story claimed that the fugitive slave clause created "a positive, unqualified right on the part of the owner of the slave which no state law or regulation can in any way qualify, regulate, control, or restrain." In Story's view, under the Constitution,

> the owner of a slave is clothed with entire authority, in every State in the Union, to seize and recapture his slave whenever he can do it without any breach of the peace or any illegal violence. In this sense and to this extent, this clause of the Constitution may properly be said to execute itself, and to require no aid from legislation, state or national.

Under this extraordinary conclusion any southerner could seize any black and remove that person to the South without any state interference, as long no "breach of the peace" occurred.

One might presume that a "breach of the peace" would always occur when a black, especially a free one, was seized by a slave catcher or kidnapper, but this was hardly the case. In his dissent, Justice McLean pointed out the logical problems of limiting Story's right of self-help to instances in which there was no breach of the peace:

> But it is said, the master may seize his slave wherever he finds him, if by doing so he does not violate the public peace; that the relation of master and slave is not affected by the laws of the State to which the slave may have fled, and where he is found. If the master has a right to seize and remove the slave without claim, he can commit no breach of the peace by using all the force necessary to accomplish his object.

In other words, the logic of Story's opinion was that no amount of violence against an alleged slave would be illegal. Slavery was based on force, and thus it would never be a breach of the peace for a master to take his slave by brutal force.

Violent seizures at night or in isolated areas could be accomplished without anyone's observing a breach of the peace. This happened with Margaret Morgan and her children. One moment they were in a wagon on their way home after Justice Henderson had released them. The next moment, in the middle of the night on a rural road with no one to help them, they were overpowered by four men and taken to Maryland. Once a black was shackled, intimidated, and perhaps beaten into submission, travel from the North to the South could be accomplished without any obvious breach of the peace. If state officials could not stop whites from transporting a black in chains, then kidnapping of any black could always be accomplished. Under such a rule anyone, especially children, might be kidnapped and enslaved. Kidnappings of this sort had led to the enactment of Pennsylvania's 1826 personal liberty law.

In his majority opinion, Justice Story ignored the fact that one or more of Morgan's children was born free in Pennsylvania. Instead, he held that the fugitive slave clause gave masters an absolute right to claim their runaway slaves without any interference from state laws or state officials. Thus, Pennsylvania's 1826 personal liberty law was unconstitutional. Story held that only Congress could regulate the return of fugitive slaves, as it had in the 1793 law. That law required a master to bring a slave before any magistrate or judge, federal or state, to obtain a certificate of removal to take the slave with him. Even though Story found this law to be constitutional—and all state laws supplementing it to be unconstitutional—he also held that a master did not have to follow the procedure set out in the 1793 law. Instead, Story asserted that under the Constitution itself masters had a right of "self-help." Thus, if a master found it convenient to return a fugitive slave without going before a judge, he could do so, as long as it was accomplished without a "breach of the peace." For free blacks and their white allies this seemed like an invitation for kidnapping.

Story left the states powerless to prevent this type of kidnapping. His opinion effectively made the law of the South the law of the nation. In the South, race was a presumption of slave status; by giving masters and slave hunters a common law right of "recaption," Story nationalized this presumption. As a result, slave catchers could operate in the North without having to prove the seized person's slave status. The consequences for the nearly one hundred and seventy-five thousand free blacks in the North could have been dire. In his dissenting opinion, Justice McLean protested the result, but his complaints fell on deaf ears.

Story also ruled that northern states should help enforce the federal law, but they could not be forced to do so. This was a logical outcome of his reading of the Constitution. It was also consistent with nineteenth-century notions of states' rights: that the national government could not compel the states to act in a certain way. Story emphatically declared that the northern states *should* enforce the law, but from his perspective whatever they did would be a useful outcome. If the northern states enforced the law, it would prove to the South that it had nothing to fear from a stronger union and a more powerful national government. If, on the other hand, the northern states did not enforce the law, the national government would have to create an enforcement system, and this would have the dual value of strengthening the national government—a lifetime goal of Story's—and emphatically tying the South to support a nationalization of law.

In his concurring opinion, Chief Justice Taney misstated Story's position. He claimed that Story would not allow the states to capture fugitive slaves. As the very end of Story's opinion shows, this is not true. Story wanted the states to help with the return of fugitive slaves. He just did not believe they could be forced to do so.

Audience

Most Supreme Court opinions are directed at lawyers and judges. This one was not. All authors of opinions in this case clearly had a political audience in mind. Justice Story had two audiences: First, he wanted to reach southern leaders and politicians to reassure them that strengthening federal law to empower the national government would not harm slavery or threaten the South. On the contrary, the burden of his opinion was to show that the South would be protected by a strong national government. His second audience was the moderates in the North. He believed that they supported his goals of a stronger national government and stronger national Union. Thus, he wanted them to see that they should voluntarily cooperate with the return of fugitives. His plea to them was that the return of fugitive slaves was an essential bargain for the health of the nation and the success of the Constitution. In the end, he accepted (but not did explicitly state) that the loss of freedom for people like Margaret Morgan and her children was a small price to pay for a stronger Union and sectional harmony.

Chief Justice Taney was speaking to both the South and the North. His position was, of course, different from Story's. He wanted to assure the South that he would fight for their needs to secure slavery at all costs and was, in effect, warning the North that it had to cooperate in the return of fugitive slaves. On the other side, Justice McLean was speaking for the North to the nation, reminding the Court and politicians that northerners were unwilling to allow the unsupervised seizure of their neighbors. The warning was ignored, which helped lead to the fugitive slave crisis of the 1850s, when significant and sometimes violent opposition to the return of fugitive slaves emerged.

Impact

The impact of *Prigg* was mixed. Southerners were generally pleased with the outcome but complained that Justice Story's opinion undermined enforcement of the 1793 Fugitive Slave Act, because Story said that northern judges could not be required to enforce the law. Most northerners, especially abolitionists, other opponents of slavery, and free blacks, were appalled by the decision. Northern opponents of slavery attacked the opinion for protecting slavery and failing to protect the liberties of free blacks. In Story's home state of Massachusetts many of his colleagues were horrified by the opinion. John Quincy Adams spent a whole day reading all the opinions, saddened by the case and the fact the opinion had been written by someone from his own state. Abolitionists, predictably, denounced Story and the decision.

After Justice Story died, his son, who was himself antislavery, claimed that his father believed that the opinion was a "triumph of freedom" because it allowed northern states to refuse to participate in the return of fugitive slaves. However, there is no evidence to support this claim. In fact, it would have been utterly inconsistent for Story to have purposely undermined his opinion in that way. Moreover, there is other evidence to suggest that Story fully backed his opinion. Shortly after the case was decided, he wrote to Senator John M. Berrien of Georgia, urging that he introduce legislation that would allow the federal courts to appoint commissioners to enforce any federal law that a state judge could enforce. Thus, if the state judges refused to hear cases under the 1793 law, the federal court commissioners could do so. Story naively believed such a law could be passed without even mentioning fugitive slaves.

Many northern judges and legislatures acted on Story's single line suggesting that the states *should* enforce the federal law but could not be required to do so. Starting in 1843, a number of free states prohibited law enforcement and judicial officers from hearing fugitive slave cases and closed their jails to slave catchers. This led to increasing demands from the South for a new fugitive slave law, which was finally passed in 1850. That law adopted Story's suggestion to authorize the appointment of federal commissioners in every state to enforce the law.

Justice McLean, who dissented from Story's opinion, may also have been harmed by the case. In 1844 he was proposed as a presidential candidate by the Whig Party. However, southern Whigs blocked any consideration of him

"The [Fugitive Slave] clause manifestly contemplates the existence of a positive, unqualified right on the part of the owner of the slave which no state law or regulation can in any way qualify, regulate, control, or restrain. The slave is not to be discharged from service or labor in consequence of any state law or regulation."

(Justice Story's Opinion)

"It is proper to state that we are by no means to be understood ... to doubt or to interfere with the police power belonging to the States in virtue of their general sovereignty. That police power extends over all subjects within territorial limits of the States, and has never been conceded to the United States.... The States ... possesses full jurisdiction to arrest and restrain runaway slaves, and remove them from their borders."

(Justice Story's Opinion)

"According to the opinion just delivered, the state authorities are prohibited from interfering for the purpose of protecting the right of the master and aiding him in the recovery of his property. I think the States are not prohibited, and that, on the contrary, it is enjoined upon them as a duty to protect and support the owner when he is endeavoring to obtain possession of his property found within their respective territories."

(Chief Justice Taney's Opinion)

"The slave is found in a State where every man, black or white, is presumed to be free, and this State, to preserve the peace of its citizens, and its soil and jurisdiction from acts of violence, has prohibited the forcible abduction of persons of color. Does this law conflict with the Constitution? It clearly does not, in its terms."

(Justice McLean's Dissent)

because, they argued, he was hostile to slavery. McLean very much wanted to be president, and his fidelity to liberty may have cost him dearly.

In the end, this case was a disaster for African Americans. It left all free blacks in the North vulnerable to kidnapping, with no chance that their state or local governments could interfere to protect them. It dramatically threatened the growing population of fugitive slaves in the North, who could now be seized without any warrant or legal procedure. It further allowed for cases of mistaken identity, because even if blacks were brought before a court, alleged fugitives could not get a trial to prove their freedom. The case underscored that the proslavery clauses of the Constitution of 1787 were in full flower in the 1840s.

The greatest cost of the decision was born by the free blacks of the North. They were now subject to capture and enslavement without any hope that local governments could protect them. Like Margaret Morgan and her children, they could be swept up by slave catchers, dragged to the South, and sold into lifetime bondage. When the dust from the case finally settled, Edward Prigg remained a free man, while Margaret Morgan and her children, including those born in the free state of Pennsylvania, remained slaves, sold into the Deep South, where they would toil away in anonymity, far from their family and friends.

See also Pennsylvania: An Act for the Gradual Abolition of Slavery (1780); Slavery Clauses in the U.S. Constitution (1787); Fugitive Slave Act of 1793; Fugitive Slave Act of 1850; *Dred Scott v. Sandford* (1857).

Further Reading

■ Articles

Finkelman, Paul. "Sorting Out *Prigg v. Pennsylvania*." *Rutgers Law Journal* 24 (Spring 1993): 605–665.

■ Books

Finkelman, Paul. *An Imperfect Union: Slavery, Federalism, and Comity.* Chapel Hill: University of North Carolina Press, 1981.

———. "Story Telling on the Supreme Court: *Prigg v. Pennsylvania* and Justice Joseph Story's Judicial Nationalism." In *Supreme Court*

Review, 1994, ed. Dennis J. Hutchinson et al. Chicago: University of Chicago Press, 1995.

Hyman, Harold M., and William M. Wiecek. *Equal Justice under Law: Constitutional Development, 1835–1875.* New York: Harper and Row, 1982.

Morris, Thomas D. *Free Men All: The Personal Liberty Laws of the North, 1780–1861.* Baltimore: Johns Hopkins University Press, 1974.

Newmyer, R. Kent. *Supreme Court Justice Joseph Story: Statesman of the Old Republic.* Chapel Hill: University of North Carolina Press, 1985.

■ Web Sites

"Notes on the Debates in the Federal Convention." Avalon Project Web site.
  http://avalon.law.yale.edu/subject_menus/debcont.asp.

—Paul Finkelman

Questions for Further Study

1. Compare the portion of this opinion written by Justice Joseph Story with his opinion just a year earlier in *United States v. Amistad.* What inferences can you draw about Story's attitude toward slavery from the two cases?

2. Similarly, read the portion of this opinion written by Justice Roger Taney with his opinion in the landmark *Dred Scott v. Sandford.* What consistencies do you see in the two opinions? Are there any significant differences?

3. Read this document in connection with the Fugitive Slave Act of 1793 and the Fugitive Slave Act of 1850. What impact might Story's decision have had, directly or indirectly, on the later law?

4. It is often quipped that if one party to a legal dispute is entirely happy with the outcome, the court has probably not done its job properly. To what extent were both sides—North and South, supporters and opponents of slavery—unhappy with the decision in this case?

5. In what way way, if any, did the Court's decision in *Prigg v. Pennsylvania* contribute to the divisions that led to the U.S. Civil War?

PRIGG V. PENNSYLVANIA

Mr. Justice Story delivered the opinion of the court

This is a writ of error to the Supreme Court of Pennsylvania, brought under the 25th section of the Judiciary Act of 1789, ch. 20, for the purpose of revising the judgment of that court, in a case involving the construction of the Constitution and laws of the United States. The facts are briefly these:

The plaintiff in error was indicted in the Court of Oyer and Terminer for York County, for having, with force and violence, taken and carried away from that county, to the State of Maryland, a certain negro woman, named Margaret Morgan, with a design and intention of selling and disposing of, and keeping her, as a slave or servant for life, contrary to a statute of Pennsylvania, passed on the 26th of March, 1826. That statute, in the first section, in substance provides that, if any person or persons shall, from and after the passing of the act, by force and violence, take and carry away, or cause to be taken and carried away, and shall, by fraud or false pretense, seduce, or cause to be seduced, or shall attempt to take, carry away or seduce, any negro or mulatto from any part of that Commonwealth, with a design and intention of selling and disposing of, or causing to be sold, or of keeping and detaining, or of causing to be kept and detained, such negro or mulatto, as a slave or servant for life, or for any term whatsoever, every such person or persons, his or their aiders or abettors, shall, on conviction thereof, be deemed guilty of felony, and shall forfeit and pay a sum not less than five hundred, nor more than one thousand dollars, and moreover shall be sentenced to undergo servitude for any term or terms of years, not less than seven years nor exceeding twenty-one years, and shall be confined and kept to hard labor, &c....

The plaintiff in error pleaded not guilty to the indictment, and, at the trial, the jury found a special verdict which in substance states that the negro woman, Margaret Morgan, was a slave for life, and held to labor and service under and according to the laws of Maryland, to a certain Margaret Ashmore, a citizen of Maryland; that the slave escaped and fled from Maryland into Pennsylvania in 1832; that the plaintiff in error, being legally constituted the agent and attorney of the said Margaret Ashmore, in 1837 caused the said negro woman to be taken and apprehended as a fugitive from labor by a state constable under a warrant from a Pennsylvania magistrate; that the said negro woman was thereupon brought before the said magistrate, who refused to take further cognizance of the case; and thereupon the plaintiff in error did remove, take and carry away the said negro woman and her children out of Pennsylvania into Maryland, and did deliver the said negro woman and her children into the custody and possession of the said Margaret Ashmore. The special verdict further finds that one of the children was born in Pennsylvania more than a year after the said negro woman had fled and escaped from Maryland....

Before proceeding to discuss the very important and interesting questions involved in this record, it is fit to say that the cause has been conduced in the court below, and has been brought here by the cooperation and sanction, both of the State of Maryland and the State of Pennsylvania in the most friendly and courteous spirit, with a view to have those questions finally disposed of by the adjudication of this Court so that the agitations on this subject in both States, which have had a tendency to interrupt the harmony between them, may subside, and the conflict of opinion be put at rest. It should also be added that the statute of Pennsylvania of 1826 was (as has been suggested at the bar) passed with a view of meeting the supposed wishes of Maryland on the subject of fugitive slaves, and that, although it has failed to produce the good effects intended in its practical construction, the result was unforeseen and undesigned.

1. The question arising in the case as to the constitutionality of the statute of Pennsylvania, has been most elaborately argued at the bar.... Few questions which have ever come before this Court involve more delicate and important considerations, and few upon which the public at large may be presumed to feel a more profound and pervading interest. We have accordingly given them our most deliberate examination, and it has become my duty to state the result to which we have arrived, and the reasoning by which it is supported....

There are two clauses in the Constitution upon the subject of fugitives, which stands in juxtaposition with each other and have been thought mutually to illustrate each other. They are both contained in the second section of the fourth Article, and are in the following words:

"A person charged in any State with treason, felony, or other crime who shall flee from justice and be found in another State shall, on demand of the executive authority of the State from which he fled, be delivered up, to be removed to the State having jurisdiction of the crime."

"No person held to service or labor in one State, under the laws thereof, escaping into another, shall, in consequence of any law or regulation therein, be discharged from such service or labor, but shall be delivered up on claim of the party to whom such service or labor may be due."

The last clause is that the true interpretation whereof is directly in judgment before us. Historically, it is well known that the object of this clause was to secure to the citizens of the slave-holding States the complete right and title of ownership in their slaves, as property, in every State in the Union into which they might escape from the State where they were held in servitude. The full recognition of this right and title was indispensable to the security of this species of property in all the slave-holding States, and indeed was so vital to the preservation of their domestic interests and institutions that it cannot be doubted that it constituted a fundamental article without the adoption of which the Union could not have been formed. Its true design was to guard against the doctrines and principles prevalent in the non-slaveholding States, by preventing them from intermeddling with, or obstructing, or abolishing the rights of the owners of slaves.

By the general law of nations, no nation is bound to recognize the state of slavery as to foreign slaves found within its territorial dominions, when it is in opposition to its own policy and institutions, in favor of the subjects of other nations where slavery is recognized. If it does it, it is as a matter of comity, and not as a matter of international right. The state of slavery is deemed to be a mere municipal regulation, founded upon and limited to the range of the territorial laws. This was fully recognized in *Somerset's Case* [Great Britain, 1771], ... which decided before the American revolution. It is manifest from this consideration that, if the Constitution had not contained this clause, every non-slaveholding State in the Union would have been at liberty to have declared free all runaway slaves coming within its limits, and to have given them entire immunity and protection against the claims of their masters—a course

which would have created the most bitter animosities and engendered perpetual strife between the different States. The clause was therefore of the last importance to the safety and security of the southern States, and could not have been surrendered by them, without endangering their whole property in slaves. The clause was accordingly adopted into the Constitution by the unanimous consent of the framers of it—a proof at once of its intrinsic and practical necessity.

How then are we to interpret the language of the clause? The true answer is in such a manner as, consistently with the words, shall fully and completely effectuate the whole objects of it. If, by one mode of interpretation, the right must become shadowy and unsubstantial, and without any remedial power adequate to the end, and, by another mode, it will attain its just end and secure its manifest purpose, it would seem, upon principles of reasoning, absolutely irresistible, that the latter ought to prevail. No court of justice can be authorized so to construe any clause of the Constitution as to defeat its obvious ends when another construction, equally accordant with the words and sense thereof, will enforce and protect them.

The clause manifestly contemplates the existence of a positive, unqualified right on the part of the owner of the slave which no state law or regulation can in any way qualify, regulate, control, or restrain. The slave is not to be discharged from service or labor in consequence of any state law or regulation. Now certainly, without indulging in any nicety of criticism upon words, it may fairly and reasonably be said that any state law or state regulation which interrupts, limits, delays, or postpones the right of the owner to the immediate possession of the slave and the immediate command of his service and labor operates *pro tanto* a discharge of the slave therefrom. The question can never be how much the slave is discharged from, but whether he is discharged from any, by the natural or necessary operation of state laws or state regulations. The question is not one of quantity or degree, but of withholding or controlling the incidents of a positive and absolute right.

We have said that the clause contains a positive and unqualified recognition of the right of the owner in the slave, unaffected by any state law or legislation whatsoever, because there is no qualification or restriction of it to be found therein, and we have no right to insert any which is not expressed and cannot be fairly implied. Especially are we estopped from so doing when the clause puts the right to the service or labor upon the same ground, and to the same extent, in every other State as in the State from which the slave escaped and in which he was held to the service or labor. If this be so, then all the incidents to that right attach also. The owner must, therefore, have the right to seize and repossess the slave, which the local laws of his own State confer upon him, as property, and we all know that this right of seizure and recaption is universally acknowledged in all the slave-holding States. Indeed, this is no more than a mere affirmance of the principles of the common law applicable to this very subject. [Blackstone's Commentaries] … lays it down as unquestionable doctrine.

"Recaption or reprisal [says he] is another species of remedy by the mere act of the party injured. This happens when anyone hath deprived another of his property in goods or chattels personal, or wrongfully detains one's wife, child or servant, in which case the owner of the goods, and the husband, parent or master, may lawfully claim and retake them wherever he happens to find them, so it be not in a riotous manner or attended with a breach of the peace."

Upon this ground, we have not the slightest hesitation in holding that, under and in virtue of the Constitution, the owner of a slave is clothed with entire authority, in every State in the Union, to seize and recapture his slave whenever he can do it without any breach of the peace or any illegal violence. In this sense and to this extent, this clause of the Constitution may properly be said to execute itself, and to require no aid from legislation, state or national.

But the clause of the Constitution does not stop here, nor, indeed, consistently with its professed objects, could it do so. Many cases must arise in which, if the remedy of the owner were confined to the mere right of seizure and recaption, he would be utterly without any adequate redress. He may not be able to lay his hands upon the slave. He may not be able to enforce his rights against persons who either secrete or conceal or withhold the slave. He may be restricted by local legislation as to the mode of proofs of his ownership, as to the courts in which he shall sue, and as to the actions which he may bring or the process he may use to compel the delivery of the slave. Nay, the local legislation may be utterly inadequate to furnish the appropriate redress, by authorizing no process *in rem*, or no specific mode of repossessing the slave, leaving the owner, at best, not that right which the Constitution designed to secure, a specific delivery and repossession of the slave, but a mere remedy in damages, and that, perhaps, against persons utterly insolvent or worthless. The state legislation may be entirely silent on the whole subject, and its ordinary remedial process framed with different views and objects, and this may be innocently, as well as designedly, done, since every State is perfectly competent, and has the exclusive right, to prescribe the remedies in its own judicial tribunals, to limit the time as well as the mode of redress, and to deny jurisdiction over cases which its own policy and its own institutions either prohibit or discountenance.

If, therefore, the clause of the Constitution had stopped at the mere recognition of the right, without providing or contemplating any means by which it might be established and enforced, in cases where it did not execute itself, it is plain that it would have been, in a great variety of cases, a delusive and empty annunciation. If it did not contemplate any action, either through state or national legislation, as auxiliaries to its more perfect enforcement in the form of remedy, or of protection, then, as there would be no duty on either to aid the right, it would be left to the mere comity of the States to act as they should please, and would depend for its security upon the changing course of public opinion, the mutations of public policy, and the general adaptations of remedies for purposes strictly according to the *lex fori*.

And this leads us to the consideration of the other part of the clause, which implies at once a guarantee and duty. It says, "but he [the slave] shall be delivered up on claim of the party to whom such service or labor may be due." Now we think it exceedingly difficult, if not impracticable, to read this language and not to feel that it contemplated some further remedial redress than that which might be administered at the hands of the owner himself. A claim is to be made! What is a claim? It is, in a just juridical sense, a demand of some matter, as of right, made by one person upon another, to do or to forbear to do some act or thing as a matter of duty. A more limited but, at the same time, an equally expressive, definition was given by Lord Dyer, as cited in *Stowel v. Zouch*, … and it is equally applicable to the present case: that "a claim is a challenge by a man of the propriety or ownership of a thing which he has not in possession, but which is wrongfully detained from him."

The slave is to be delivered up on the claim. By whom to be delivered up? In what mode to be delivered up? How, if a refusal takes place, is the right of delivery to be enforced? Upon what proofs? What shall be the evidence of a rightful recaption or delivery? When and under what circumstances shall the possession of the owner, after it is obtained, be conclusive of his right, so as to preclude any further inquiry or examination into it by local tribunals or otherwise, while the slave, in possession of the owner, is *in transitu* to the State from which he fled?

These and many other questions will readily occur upon the slightest attention to the clause; and it is obvious that they can receive but one satisfactory answer. They require the aid of legislation to protect the right, to enforce the delivery, and to secure the subsequent possession of the slave. If, indeed, the Constitution guaranties the right, and if it requires the delivery upon the claim of the owner (as cannot well be doubted), the natural inference certainly is that the National Government is clothed with the appropriate authority and functions to enforce it. The fundamental principle, applicable to all cases of this sort, would seem to be that, where the end is required, the means are given; and where the duty is enjoined, the ability to perform it is contemplated to exist on the part of the functionaries to whom it is entrusted. The clause is found in the National Constitution, and not in that of any State. It does not point out any state functionaries, or any state action, to carry its provisions into effect. The States cannot, therefore, be compelled to enforce them, and it might well be deemed an unconstitutional exercise of the power of interpretation to insist that the States are bound to provide means to carry into effect the duties of the National Government, nowhere delegated or entrusted to them by the Constitution. On the contrary, the natural, if not the necessary, conclusion is, that the National Government, in the absence of all positive provisions to the contrary, is bound, through its own proper departments, legislative, judicial or executive, as the case may require, to carry into effect all the rights and duties imposed upon it by the Constitution. The remark of Mr. Madison, in the Federalist (No. 43), would seem in such cases to apply with peculiar force. "A right [says he] implies a remedy, and where else would the remedy be deposited than where it is deposited by the Constitution?"—meaning, as the context shows, in the Government of the United States.

It is plain, then, that where a claim is made by the owner, out of possession, for the delivery of a slave, it must be made, if at all, against some other person; and, inasmuch as the right is a right of property, capable of being recognized and asserted by proceedings before a court of justice, between parties adverse to each other, it constitutes, in the strictest sense, a controversy between the parties, and a case "arising under the Constitution" of the United States within the express delegation of judicial power given by that instrument. Congress, then, may call that power into

activity for the very purpose of giving effect to that right; and, if so, then it may prescribe the mode and extent in which it shall be applied, and how and under what circumstances the proceedings shall afford a complete protection and guarantee to the right.

Congress has taken this very view of the power and duty of the National Government.... The result of their deliberations was the passage of the act of the 12th of February 1793, ch. 51, which, after having, in the first and second sections, provided by the case of fugitives from justice, by a demand to be made of the delivery, through the executive authority of the State where they are found, proceeds, in the third section, to provide that, when a person held to labor or service in any of the United States, shall escape into any other of the States or territories, the person to whom such labor or service may be due, his agent or attorney, is hereby empowered to seize or arrest such fugitive from labor, and take him or her before any judge of the circuit or district courts of the United States, residing or being within the State, or before any magistrate of a county, city or town corporate, wherein such seizure or arrest shall be made; and, upon proof to the satisfaction of such judge or magistrate, either by oral evidence or affidavit, &c., that the person so seized or arrested, doth, under the laws of the State or territory from which he or she fled, owe service or labor to the person claiming him or her, it shall be the duty of such judge or magistrate to give a certificate thereof to such claimant, his agent or attorney which shall be sufficient warrant for removing the said fugitive from labor to the State or territory from which he or she fled. The fourth section provides a penalty against any person who shall knowingly and willingly obstruct or hinder such claimant, his agent, or attorney in so seizing or arresting such fugitive from labor, or rescue such fugitive from the claimant, or his agent or attorney when so arrested, or who shall harbor or conceal such fugitive after notice that he is such; and it also saves to the person claiming such labor or service his right of action for or on account of such injuries.

In a general sense, this act may be truly said to cover the whole ground of the Constitution, both as to fugitives from justice and fugitive slaves—that is, it covers both the subjects in its enactments, not because it exhausts the remedies which may be applied by Congress to enforce the rights if the provisions of the act shall in practice be found not to attain the object of the Constitution; but because it points out fully all the modes of attaining those objects which Congress, in their discretion, have as yet deemed expedient or proper to meet the exigencies of the Constitution. If this be so, then it would seem, upon just principles of construction, that the legislation of Congress, if constitutional, must supersede all state legislation upon the same subject and, by necessary implication, prohibit it. For, if Congress have a constitutional power to regulate a particular subject, and they do actually regulate it in a given manner, and in a certain form, it cannot be that the state legislatures have a right to interfere and, as it were, by way of complement to the legislation of Congress, to prescribe additional regulations and what they may deem auxiliary provisions for the same purpose. In such a case, the legislation of Congress, in what it does prescribe, manifestly indicates that it does not intend that there shall be any further legislation to act upon the subject matter. Its silence as to what it does not do is as expressive of what its intention is as the direct provisions made by it.... [Thus,] it is not competent for state legislation to add to the provisions of Congress upon that subject, for that the will of Congress upon the whole subject is as clearly established by what it has not declared as by what it has expressed.

But it has been argued that the act of Congress is unconstitutional because it does not fall within the scope of any of the enumerated powers of legislation confided to that body, and therefore it is void. Stripped of its artificial and technical structure, the argument comes to this—that although rights are exclusively secured by, or duties are exclusively imposed upon, the National Government, yet, unless the power to enforce these rights or to execute these duties can be found among the express powers of legislation enumerated in the Constitution, they remain without any means of giving them effect by any act of Congress, and they must operate solely *proprio vigore*, however defective may be their operation—nay! even although, in a practical sense, they may become a nullity from the want of a proper remedy to enforce them or to provide against their violation. If this be the true interpretation of the Constitution, it must in a great measure fail to attain many of its avowed and positive objects as a security of rights and a recognition of duties. Such a limited construction of the Constitution has never yet been adopted as correct either in theory or practice. No one has ever supposed that Congress could constitutionally, by its legislation, exercise powers or enact laws beyond the powers delegated to it by the Constitution. But it has on various occasions exercised powers which were necessary and proper as means to carry into effect rights expressly given and duties expressly enjoined thereby. The end being required, it

has been deemed a just and necessary implication that the means to accomplish it are given also, or, in other words, that the power flows as a necessary means to accomplish the end....

In respect to fugitives from justice, the Constitution, although it expressly provides that the demand shall be made by the executive authority of the State from which the fugitive has fled, is silent as to the party upon whom the demand is to be made and as to the mode in which it shall be made. This very silence occasioned embarrassments in enforcing the right and duty at an early period after the adoption of the Constitution; and produced a hesitation on the part of the executive authority of Virginia to deliver up a fugitive from justice upon the demand of the executive of Pennsylvania in the year 1791; and, as we historically know from the message of President Washington and the public documents of that period, it was the immediate cause of the passing of the Act of 1793, which designated the person (the state executive) upon whom the demand should be made, and the mode and proofs upon and in which it should be made. From that time down to the present hour, not a doubt has been breathed upon the constitutionality of this part of the act, and every executive in the Union has constantly acted upon and admitted its validity....

The same uniformity of acquiescence in the validity of the Act of 1793 upon the other part of the subject matter that of fugitive slaves has prevailed throughout the whole Union until a comparatively recent period. Nay, being from its nature and character more readily susceptible of being brought into controversy in courts of justice than the former, and of enlisting in opposition to it the feelings, and it may be, the prejudices, of some portions of the non-slaveholding States, it has naturally been brought under adjudication in several States in the Union, and particularly in Massachusetts, New York, and Pennsylvania, and, on all these occasions, its validity has been affirmed.... Under such circumstances, if the question were one of doubtful construction, such long acquiescence in it, such contemporaneous expositions of it, and such extensive and uniform recognition of its validity would, in our judgment, entitle the question to be considered at rest unless, indeed, the interpretation of the Constitution is to be delivered over to interminable doubt throughout the whole progress of legislation and of national operations. Congress, the executive, and the judiciary have, upon various occasions, acted upon this as a sound and reasonable doctrine....The remaining question is whether the power of legislation upon this subject is exclusive in the National Government or concurrent in the States until it is exercised by Congress. In our opinion, it is exclusive....

In the first place, it is material to state (what has been already incidentally hinted at) that the right to seize and retake fugitive slaves and the duty to deliver them up, in whatever State of the Union they may be found, and, of course, the corresponding power in Congress to use the appropriate means to enforce the right and duty, derive their whole validity and obligation exclusively from the Constitution of the United States, and are there, for the first time, recognized and established in that peculiar character.

Before the adoption of the Constitution, no State had any power whatsoever over the subject except within its own territorial limits, and could not bind the sovereignty or the legislation of other States.... It is, therefore, in a just sense, a new and positive right ... [and the] natural inference deductible from this consideration certainly is, in the absence of any positive delegation of power to the state legislatures that it belongs to the Legislative Department of the National Government, to which it owes its origin and establishment. It would be a strange anomaly and forced construction to suppose that the National Government meant to rely for the due fulfillment of its own proper duties, and the rights it intended to secure, upon state legislation, and not upon that of the Union. *A fortiori*, it would be more objectionable to suppose that a power which was to be the same throughout the Union should be confided to state sovereignty, which could not rightfully act beyond its own territorial limits....

[If] the States have a right, in the absence of legislation by Congress, to act upon the subject, each State is at liberty to prescribe just such regulations as suit its own policy, local convenience, and local feelings. The legislation of one State may not only be different from, but utterly repugnant to and incompatible with, that of another. The time and mode and limitation of the remedy, the proofs of the title, and all other incidents applicable thereto may be prescribed in one State which are rejected or disclaimed in another. One State may require the owner to sue in one mode, another in a different mode. One State may make a statute of limitations as to the remedy, in its own tribunals, short and summary; another may prolong the period and yet restrict the proofs. Nay, some States may utterly refuse to act upon the subject of all, and others may refuse to open its courts to any remedies *in rem* because they would interfere with their own domestic policy, institutions, or habits. The right, therefore, would never, in a practical

sense, be the same in all the States. It would have no unity of purpose or uniformity of operation. The duty might be enforced in some States, retarded or limited in others, and denied as compulsory in many, if not in all. Consequences like these must have been foreseen as very likely to occur in the non-slaveholding States where legislation, if not silent on the subject and purely voluntary, could scarcely be presumed to be favorable to the exercise of the rights of the owner.

It is scarcely conceivable that the slaveholding States would have been satisfied with leaving to the legislation of the non-slaveholding States a power of regulation, in the absence of that of Congress, which would or might practically amount to a power to destroy the rights of the owner. If the argument, therefore, of a concurrent power in the States to act upon the subject matter, in the absence of legislation by Congress, be well founded, then, if Congress had never acted at all, or if the act of Congress should be repealed without providing a substitute, there would be a resulting authority in each of the States to regulate the whole subject at its pleasure, and to dole out its own remedial justice or withhold it at its pleasure and according to its own views of policy and expediency. Surely such a state of things never could have been intended under such a solemn guarantee of right and duty. On the other hand, construe the right of legislation as exclusive in Congress, and every evil and every danger vanishes. The right and the duty are then coextensive and uniform in remedy and operation throughout the whole Union. The owner has the same security, and the same remedial justice, and the same exemption from state regulation and control through however many States he may pass with his fugitive slave in his possession *in transitu* to his own domicile. But, upon the other supposition, the moment he passes the state line, he becomes amenable to the laws of another sovereignty whose regulations may greatly embarrass or delay the exercise of his rights, and even be repugnant to those of the State where he first arrested the fugitive. Consequences like these show that the nature and objects of the provisions imperiously require that, to make it effectual, it should be construed to be exclusive of state authority....

And we know no case in which the confusion and public inconvenience and mischiefs thereof could be more completely exemplified than the present.

These are some of the reasons, but by no means all, upon which we hold the power of legislation on this subject to be exclusive in Congress. To guard, however, against any possible misconstruction of our views, it is proper to state that we are by no means to be understood in any manner whatsoever to doubt or to interfere with the police power belonging to the States in virtue of their general sovereignty. That police power extends over all subjects within territorial limits of the States, and has never been conceded to the United States. It is wholly distinguishable from the right and duty secured by the provision now under consideration, which is exclusively derived from and secured by the Constitution of the United States and owes its whole efficacy thereto. We entertain no doubt whatsoever that the States, in virtue of their general police power, possesses full jurisdiction to arrest and restrain runaway slaves, and remove them from their borders, and otherwise to secure themselves against their depredations and evil example, as they certainly may do in cases of idlers, vagabonds and paupers. The rights of the owners of fugitive slaves are in no just sense interfered with or regulated by such a course, and, in many cases, the operations of this police power, although designed generally for other purposes—for protection, safety and peace of the State—may essentially promote and aid the interests of the owners. But such regulations can never be permitted to interfere with or to obstruct the just rights of the owner to reclaim his slave, derived from the Constitution of the United States, or with the remedies prescribed by Congress to aid and enforce the same.

Upon these grounds, we are of opinion that the act of Pennsylvania upon which this indictment is founded is unconstitutional and void. It purports to punish as a public offense against that State the very act of seizing and removing a slave by his master which the Constitution of the United States was designed to justify and uphold. The special verdict finds this fact, and the state courts have rendered judgment against the plaintiff in error upon that verdict. That judgment must, therefore, be reversed, and the cause remanded to the Supreme Court of Pennsylvania with directions to carry into effect the judgment of this Court rendered upon the special verdict, in favor of the plaintiff in error.

Mr. Chief Justice Taney

I concur in the opinion pronounced by the Court that the law of Pennsylvania, under which the plaintiff in error was indicted, is unconstitutional and void, and that the judgment against him must be reversed. But, as the questions before us arise upon the construction of the Constitution of the United

States, and as I do not assent to all the principles contained in the opinion just delivered, it is proper to state the points on which I differ....

The act of February 12th, 1793, is a constitutional exercise of this power, and every state law which requires the master, against his consent, to go before any state tribunal or officer before he can take possession of his property, or which authorizes a state officer to interfere with him when he is peaceably removing it from the State, is unconstitutional and void.

But, as I understand the opinion of the Court, it goes further, and decides that the power to provide a remedy for this right is vested exclusively in Congress, and that all laws upon the subject passed by a State since the adoption of the Constitution of the United States are null and void, even although they were intended in good faith to protect the owner in the exercise of his rights of property, and do not conflict in any degree with the act of Congress.

I do not consider this question as necessarily involved in the case before us, for the law of Pennsylvania under which the plaintiff in error was prosecuted is clearly in conflict with the Constitution of the United States, as well as with the law of 1793. But, as the question is discussed in the opinion of the Court, and as I do not assent either to the doctrine or the reasoning by which it is maintained, I proceed to state very briefly my objections.

The opinion of the Court maintains that the power over this subject is so exclusively vested in Congress that no State, since the adoption of the Constitution, can pass any law in relation to it. In other words, according to the opinion just delivered, the state authorities are prohibited from interfering for the purpose of protecting the right of the master and aiding him in the recovery of his property. I think the States are not prohibited, and that, on the contrary, it is enjoined upon them as a duty to protect and support the owner when he is endeavoring to obtain possession of his property found within their respective territories.

The language used in the Constitution does not, in my judgment, justify this construction given to it by the court. It contains no words prohibiting the several States from passing laws to enforce this right. They are, in express terms, forbidden to make any regulation that shall impair it, but there the prohibition stops....

And why may not a State protect a right of property acknowledged by its own paramount law? Besides, the laws of the different States in all other cases constantly protect the citizens of other States in their rights of property when it is found within their respective territories, and no one doubts their power to do so. And, in the absence of any express prohibition, I perceive no reason for establishing by implication a different rule in this instance where, by the national compact, this right of property is recognized as an existing right in every State of the Union.

I do not speak of slaves whom their masters voluntarily take into a non-slaveholding State. That case is not before us. I speak of the case provided for in the Constitution—that is to say, the case of a fugitive who has escaped from the service of his owner and who has taken refuge and is found in another State....

I cannot understand the rule of construction by which a positive and express stipulation for the security of certain individual rights of property in the several States is held to imply a prohibition to the States to pass any laws to guard and protect them....

Indeed, if the state authorities are absolved from all obligation to protect this right, and may stand by and see it violated without an effort to defend it, the act of Congress of 1793 scarcely deserves the name of a remedy. The state officers mentioned in the law are not bound to execute the duties imposed upon them by Congress unless they choose to do so or are required to do so by a law of the State, and the state legislature has the power, if it thinks proper, to prohibit them. The Act of 1793, therefore, must depend altogether for its execution upon the officers of the United States named in it. And the master must take the fugitive, after he has seized him, before a judge of the district or circuit court, residing in the State, and exhibit his proofs, and procure from the judge his certificate of ownership, in order to obtain the protection in removing his property which this act of Congress profess to give.

Now, in many of the States, there is but one district judge, and there are only nine States which have judges of the Supreme Court residing within them. The fugitive will frequently be found by his owner in a place very distant from the residence of either of these judges, and would certainly be removed beyond his reach before a warrant could be procured from the judge to arrest him, even if the act of Congress authorized such a warrant. But it does not authorize the judge to issue a warrant to arrest the fugitive, but evidently relied on the state authorities to protect the owner in making the seizure. And it is only when the fugitive is arrested and brought before the judge that he is directed to take the proof and give the certificate of ownership. It is only necessary to state the provisions of this law in order to show how ineffectual and delusive is the remedy provided by Congress if state authority is forbidden to come to its aid....

Fugitives from the more southern States, when endeavoring to escape into Canada, very frequently pass through [other slave states]..... But if the States are forbidden to legislate on this subject, and the power is exclusively in Congress, then these state laws are unconstitutional and void, and the fugitive can only be arrested according to the provisions of the act of Congress. By that law, the power to seize is given to no one but the owner, his agent, or attorney. And if the officers of the State are not justified in acting under the state laws, and cannot arrest the fugitive and detain him in prison without having first received an authority from the owner, the territory of the State must soon become an open pathway for the fugitives escaping from other states. For they are often in the act of passing through it by the time that the owner first discovers that they have absconded, and, in almost every instance, they would be beyond its borders (if they were allowed to pass through without interruption) before the master would be able to learn the road they had taken....

It is true that Maryland, as well as every other slaveholding State, has a deep interest in the faithful execution of the clause in question. But the obligation of the compact is not confined to them; it is equally binding upon the faith of every State in the Union, and has heretofore, in my judgment, been justly regarded as obligatory upon all.

I dissent, therefore, upon these grounds, from that part of the opinion of the Court which denies the obligation and the right of the state authorities to protect the master when he is endeavoring to seize a fugitive from his service in pursuance of the right given to him by the Constitution of the United States, provided the state law is not in conflict with the remedy provided by Congress.

Mr. Justice McLean

As this case involves questions deeply interesting, if not vital, to the permanency of the Union of these States, and as I differ on one point from the opinion of the court, I deem it proper to state my own views on the subject....

The plaintiff, being a citizen of Maryland, with others, took Margaret Morgan, a colored woman and a slave, by force and violence, without the certificate required by the act of Congress, from the State of Pennsylvania, and brought her to the State of Maryland. By an amicable arrangement between the two States, judgment was entered against the defendant in the court where the indictment was found, and, on the cause's being removed to the Supreme Court of the State, that judgment, *pro forma*, was affirmed. And the case is now here for our examination and decision.

The last clause of the second section of the Fourth Article of the Constitution of the United States declares that

"No person held to service or labor in one State, under the laws thereof, escaping into another, shall, in consequence of any law or regulation therein, be discharged from such service or labor, but shall be delivered up, on claim of the party to whom such service or labor may be due."

This clause of the Constitution is now for the first time brought before this Court for consideration....

Does the provision in regard to the reclamation of fugitive slaves vest the power exclusively in the Federal Government?

This must be determined from the language of the Constitution and the nature of the power.

The language of the provision is general; it covers the whole ground, not in detail, but in principle. The States are inhibited from passing "any law or regulation which shall discharge a fugitive slave from the service of his master," and a positive duty is enjoined on them to deliver him up, "on claim of the party to whom his service may be due."

The nature of the power shows that it must be exclusive.

It was designed to protect the rights of the master, and against whom? Not against the State, nor the people of the State in which he resides, but against the people and the legislative action of other States where the fugitive from labor might be found. Under the Confederation, the master had no legal means of enforcing his rights in a State opposed to slavery. A disregard of rights thus asserted was deeply felt in the South; it produced great excitement, and would have led to results destructive of the Union. To avoid this, the constitutional guarantee was essential.

The necessity for this provision was found in the views and feelings of the people of the States opposed to slavery, and who, under such an influence, could not be expected favorably to regard the rights of the master. Now, by whom is this paramount law to be executed? ...

I come now to a most delicate and important inquiry in this case, and that is whether the claimant of a fugitive from labor may seize and remove him by force out of the State in which he may be found, in defiance of its laws. I refer not to laws which are in conflict with the Constitution, or the Act of 1793. Such state laws, I have already said, are void. But I have reference to those laws which regulate the police of the State, maintain the peace of its citizens, and preserve its territory and jurisdiction from acts of violence....

Both the Constitution and the Act of 1793 require the fugitive from labor to be delivered up on claim being made by the party or his agent to whom the service is due. Not that a suit should be regularly instituted; the proceeding authorized by the law is summary and informal. The fugitive is seized by the claimant, and taken before a judge or magistrate within the State, and on proof, parol or written that he owes labor to the claimant, it is made the duty of the judge or magistrate to give the certificate which authorizes the removal of the fugitive to the State from whence he absconded.

The counsel inquire of whom the claim shall be made. And they represent that the fugitive, being at large in the State, is in the custody of no one, nor under the protection of the State, so that the claim cannot be made, and consequently that the claimant may seize the fugitive and remove him out of the State.

A perusal of the act of Congress obviates this difficulty and the consequence which is represented as growing out of it.

The act is framed to meet the supposed case. The fugitive is presumed to be at large, for the claimant is authorized to seize him; after seizure, he is in custody; before it, he was not; and the claimant is required to take him before a judicial officer of the State; and it is before such officer his claim is to be made.

To suppose that the claim is not to be made, and indeed, cannot be, unless the fugitive be in the custody or possession of some public officer or individual is to disregard the letter and spirit of the Act of 1793. There is no act in the statute book more precise in its language and, as it would seem, less liable to misconstruction. In my judgment, there is not the least foundation in the act for the right asserted in the argument, to take the fugitive by force and remove him out of the State.

Such a proceeding can receive no sanction under the act, for it is in express violation of it. The claimant, having seized the fugitive, is required by the act to take him before a federal judge within the State, or a state magistrate within the county, city or town corporate, within which the seizure was made. Nor can there be any pretence that, after the seizure under the statute, the claimant may disregard the other express provision of it by taking the fugitive, without claim, out of the State. But it is said, the master may seize his slave wherever he finds him, if by doing so he does not violate the public peace; that the relation of master and slave is not affected by the laws of the State to which the slave may have fled and where he is found.

If the master has a right to seize and remove the slave without claim, he can commit no breach of the peace by using all the force necessary to accomplish his object.

It is admitted that the rights of the master, so far as regards the services of the slave, are not impaired by this change, but the mode of asserting them, in my opinion, is essentially modified. In the State where the service is due, the master needs no other law than the law of force to control the action of the slave. But can this law be applied by the master in a State which makes the act unlawful?

Can the master seize his slave and remove him out of the State, in disregard of its laws, as he might take his horse which is running at large? This ground is taken in the argument. Is there no difference in principle in these cases?

The slave, as a sensible and human being, is subject to the local authority into whatsoever jurisdiction he may go; he is answerable under the laws for his acts, and he may claim their protection; the State may protect him against all the world except the claim of his master. Should anyone commit lawless violence on the slave, the offender may unquestionably be punished; and should the slave commit murder, he may be detained and punished for it by the State in disregard of the claim of the master. Being within the jurisdiction of a State, a slave bears a very different relation to it from that of mere property.

In a State where slavery is allowed, every colored person is presumed to be a slave, and, on the same principle, in a non-slaveholding State, every person is presumed to be free, without regard to color. On this principle, the States, both slaveholding and non-slaveholding, legislate. The latter may prohibit, as Pennsylvania has done, under a certain penalty, the forcible removal of a colored person out of the State. Is such law in conflict with the Act of 1793?

The Act of 1793 authorizes a forcible seizure of the slave by the master not to take him out of the State, but to take him before some judicial officer within it. The law of Pennsylvania punishes a forcible removal of a colored person out of the State. Now here is no conflict between the law of the State and the law of Congress; the execution of neither law can, by any just interpretation, in my opinion, interfere with the execution of the other; the laws in this respect stand in harmony with each other.

It is very clear that no power to seize and forcibly remove the slave, without claim, is given by the act of Congress. Can it be exercised under the Constitution? Congress have legislated on the constitutional power, and have directed the mode in which it shall be executed. The act, it is admitted, covers the whole ground, and that it is constitutional there seems to be no reason to doubt. Now, under such circumstances, can the provisions of the act be disregarded, and an assumed power set up under the Constitution? This is believed to be wholly inadmissible by any known rule of construction.

The terms of the Constitution are general, and, like many other powers in that instrument, require legislation. In the language of this Court in *Martin v. Hunter's Lessee*, …

"the powers of the Constitution are expressed in general terms, leaving to the legislature, from time to time, to adopt its own means to effectuate legitimate objects, and to mould and model the exercise of its powers as its own wisdom and the public interests should require."

This Congress have done by the Act of 1793. It gives a summary and effectual mode of redress to the master, and is he not bound to pursue it? It is the legislative construction of the Constitution, and is it not a most authoritative construction? I was not prepared to hear the counsel contend that, notwithstanding this exposition of the Constitution, and ample remedy provided in the act, the master might disregard the act and set up his right under the Constitution. And, having taken this step, it was easy to take another and say that this right may be asserted by a forcible seizure and removal of the fugitive.

This would be a most singular constitutional provision. It would extend the remedy by recaption into another sovereignty, which is sanctioned neither by the common law nor the law of nations. If the master may lawfully seize and remove the fugitive out of the State where he may be found, without an exhibition of his claim, he may lawfully resist any force, physical or legal, which the State, or the citizens of the State, may interpose.

To hold that he must exhibit his claim in case of resistance is to abandon the ground assumed. He is engaged, it is said, in the lawful prosecution of a constitutional right; all resistance, then, by whomsoever made or in whatsoever form, must be illegal. Under such circumstances, the master needs no proof of his claim, though he might stand in need of additional physical power; having appealed to his power, he has only to collect a sufficient force to put down all resistance and attain his object; having done this, he not only stands acquitted and justified, but he has recourse for any injury he may have received in overcoming the resistance.

If this be a constitutional remedy, it may not always be a peaceful one. But if it be a rightful remedy that it may be carried to this extent no one can deny. And if it may be exercised without claim of right, why may it not be resorted to after the unfavorable decision of the judge or magistrate? This would limit the necessity of the exhibition of proof by the master to the single case where the slave was in the actual custody of some public officer. How can this be the true construction of the Constitution? That such a procedure is not sanctioned by the Act of 1793 has been shown. That act was passed expressly to guard against acts of force and violence.

I cannot perceive how anyone can doubt that the remedy given in the Constitution, if, indeed, it give any remedy, without legislation, was designed to be a peaceful one; a remedy sanctioned by judicial authority; a remedy guarded by the forms of law. But the inquiry is reiterated, is not the master entitled to his property? I answer that he is. His right is guarantied by the Constitution, and the most summary means for its enforcement is found in the act of Congress, and neither the State nor its citizens can obstruct the prosecution of this right.

The slave is found in a State where every man, black or white, is presumed to be free, and this State, to preserve the peace of its citizens, and its soil and jurisdiction from acts of violence, has prohibited the forcible abduction of persons of color. Does this law conflict with the Constitution? It clearly does not, in its terms.

The conflict is supposed to arise out of the prohibition against the forcible removal of persons of color generally, which may include fugitive slaves. *Prima facie* it does not include slaves, as every man within the State is presumed to be free, and there is no provision in the act which embraces slaves. Its language clearly shows that it was designed to protect free persons of color within the State. But it is admitted there is no exception as to the forcible removal of slaves, and here the important and most delicate question arises between the power of the State and the assumed but not sanctioned power of the Federal Government.

No conflict can arise between the act of Congress and this State law; the conflict can only arise between the forcible acts of the master and the law of the State. The master exhibits no proof of right to the services of the slave, but seizes him and is about to remove him by force. I speak only of the force exerted on the slave. The law of the State presumes him to be free and prohibits his removal. Now, which shall give way, the master or the State? The law of the State does in no case discharge, in the language of the Constitution, the slave from the service of his master.

It is a most important police regulation. And if the master violate it, is he not amenable? The offense consists in the abduction of a person of color, and this is attempted to be justified upon the simple ground that the slave is property. That a slave is property must be admitted. The state law is not violated by the seizure of the slave by the master, for this is authorized by the act of Congress, but by removing him out of the State by force and without proof of right, which the act does not authorize. Now, is not this an act which a State may prohibit? The presumption, in a non-slaveholding State, is against the right of the master, and in favor of the freedom of the person he claims. This presumption may be rebutted, but until it is rebutted by the proof required in the Act of 1793, and also, in my judgment, by the Constitution, must not the law of the State be respected and obeyed?

The seizure which the master has a right to make under the act of Congress, is for the purpose of taking the slave before an officer. His possession the subject for which it was made.

The certificate of right to the service the subject for which it was made. The certificate of right to the service of the slave is undoubtedly for the protection of the master, but it authorizes the removal of the slave out of the State where he was found to the State from whence he fled, and, under the Constitution, this authority is valid in all the States.

The important point is shall the presumption of right set up by the master, unsustained by any proof or the presumption which arises from the laws and institutions of the State, prevail; this is the true issue. The sovereignty of the State is on one side, and the asserted interest of the master on the other; that interest is protected by the paramount law, and a special, a summary, and an effectual, mode of redress is given. But this mode is not pursued, and the remedy is taken into his own hands by the master.

The presumption of the State that the colored person is free may be erroneous in fact, and, if so, there can be no difficulty in proving it. But may not the assertion of the master be erroneous also, and, if so, how is his act of force to be remedied? The colored person is taken and forcibly conveyed beyond the jurisdiction of the State. This force, not being authorized by the act of Congress nor by the Constitution, may be prohibited by the State. As the act covers the whole power in the Constitution and carries out, by special enactments, its provisions, we are, in my judgment, bound by the act. We can no more, under such circumstances, administer a remedy under the Constitution in disregard of the act than we can exercise a commercial or other power in disregard of an act of Congress on the same subject.

This view respects the rights of the master and the rights of the State; it neither jeopards nor retards the reclamation of the slave; it removes all state action prejudicial to the rights of the master; and recognizes in the State a power to guard and protect its own jurisdiction and the peace of its citizen.

It appears in the case under consideration that the state magistrate before whom the fugitive was brought refused to act. In my judgment, he was bound to perform the duty required of him by a law paramount to any act, on the same subject, in his own State. But this refusal does not justify the subsequent action of the claimant; he should have taken the fugitive before a judge of the United States, two of whom resided within the State.

It may be doubted, whether the first section of the act of Pennsylvania under which the defendant was indicted, by a fair construction, applies to the case under consideration. The decision of the Supreme Court of that State was *pro forma*, and, of course, without examination. Indeed, I suppose, the case has been made up merely to bring the question before this Court. My opinion, therefore, does not rest so much upon the particular law of Pennsylvania as upon the inherent and sovereign power of a State to protect its jurisdiction and the peace of its citizens in any and every mode which its discretion shall dictate, which shall not conflict with a defined power of the Federal Government.

This cause came on to be heard on the transcript of the record from the Supreme Court of Pennsylvania, and was argued by counsel, on consideration whereof it is the opinion of this Court that the act of the Commonwealth of Pennsylvania upon which the indictment in this case is founded is repugnant to the Constitution and laws of the United States, and therefore, void, and that the judgment of the Supreme Court of Pennsylvania upon the special verdict found in the case ought to have been that the said Edward Prigg was not guilty. It is, therefore, ordered and adjudged by this Court that the judgment of the said Supreme Court of Pennsylvania be, and the same is hereby, reversed.

And this Court proceeding to render such judgment in the premises as the said Supreme Court of Pennsylvania ought to have rendered, do hereby

a fortiori	Latin for "with even stronger reason"
act of the 12th of February 1793	the Fugitive Slave Act of 1793
Blackstone	Sir William Blackstone, a preeminent jurist in eighteenth-century England and the author of *Commentaries on the Laws of England*
comity	legal reciprocity, or the principle that a jurisdiction will recognize the validity and effect of another jurisdiction's executive, legislative, and judicial acts
Confederation	the United States under the Articles of Confederation
Court of Oyer and Terminer	in the United States, the name given to courts of criminal jurisdiction in some states
estopped	legally prevented
in rem	Latin for "in a thing" and referring to a legal action in connection with a specific piece of property
in transitu	Latin for "in transit"

order and adjudge that judgment upon the special verdict aforesaid be here entered that the said Edward Prigg is not guilty in manner and form as is charged against him in the said indictment, and that he go thereof quit, without day; and that this cause be remanded to the Supreme Court of Pennsylvania with directions accordingly, so that such other proceeding may be had therein as to law and justice shall appertain.

Glossary

lex fori	Latin for "law of the forum," referring to the law of the jurisdiction where a case is pending
Lord Dyer	Sir James Dyer, a preeminent jurist in sixteenth-century England
Madison	James Madison, one of the authors of the Federalist Papers and the fourth U.S. president
prima facie	Latin for "at first sight," describing a fact that is presumed to be true unless disproved by contrary evidence
pro forma	Latin for "as a matter of form"
pro tanto	Latin for "only to that extent"; partially
proprio vigore	Latin for "by its own force or vigor"
recaption	self-help in seizing a fugitive slave
take further cognizance	hear, consider
writ of error	a judicial writ from an appellate court ordering the court of record to produce the records of trial; an appeal

Toussaint-Louverture (Library of Congress)

"No oppressed people have ever secured their liberty without resistance."

Overview

Henry Highland Garnet's "Address to the Slaves of the United States of America" was delivered at the National Convention of Colored Citizens in Buffalo, New York, on August 16, 1843. A former slave, Garnet was pastor of the African American Liberty Street Presbyterian Church in Troy, New York, and editor of *The Clarion*, a weekly newspaper that published abolitionist and church-related articles. At age twenty-eight, he was a rising figure among young African American abolitionists, who were increasingly at odds with William Lloyd Garrison and the American Anti-Slavery Society. Garrison and his followers (both white and African American) had essentially abandoned politics in favor of nonviolent moral suasion in their fight against slavery. Garnet first signaled his disaffection with Garrison's position in 1840 as one of the founding members of the American and Foreign Anti-Slavery Society, which advocated political action as the primary way to achieve emancipation. His subsequent newspaper articles and sermons had carried him well beyond mere dissatisfaction, and because he was a gifted speaker with a reputation as a firebrand, most of the seventy delegates from a dozen states came to Buffalo anticipating a stirring address.

Context

The abolition movement to eliminate slavery in the United States had its infancy in seventeenth-century Pennsylvania when the Germantown Friends declared that slaveholding violated the tenets of Christianity. The Commonwealth of Massachusetts outlawed slavery in its constitution of 1780, and in the early 1800s legislatures in Pennsylvania, Connecticut, Rhode Island, New York, and New Jersey followed suit. The Northwest Ordinance of 1787 barred slavery in territories north of the Ohio River, and the Constitution of the United States ended the international slave trade in 1807. (Slavery, however, was constitutionally protected in a number of ways, notably in the infamous three-fifths compromise, and Congress enacted the Fugi-

tive Slave Act in 1793, which required all states to return runaway slaves to their owners.)

In December 1816 the American Colonization Society was founded in Washington, D.C., by Robert Finley with the support of such men as James Madison, James Monroe, and Henry Clay, who believed that free blacks were incapable of assimilating into white society and would be happier if they emigrated to Africa. The society enjoyed an early success, but its membership was soon riven by ideological differences when a minority of members, thinking the society also supported the abolition of slavery, found that the majority (many of them slaveholders) wanted only to reduce the number of free blacks in the country; slavery itself would be untouched. By 1830, despite the decline in membership, the society had established the West African colony of Liberia (later an independent state) and by 1860 had relocated some fifteen thousand free blacks to its shores.

On January 1, 1831, William Lloyd Garrison revived abolitionism with the first issue of *The Liberator*. In his famous opening statement, "To the Public," he demanded the immediate emancipation of all slaves and refused even to moderate his language in seeking slavery's destruction. Vowing to be "as harsh as truth, and as uncompromising as justice," he declared, "I am in earnest—I will not equivocate—I will not excuse—I will not retreat a single inch—And I Will Be Heard." Through many of the thirty-five years he published his paper—1,820 consecutive editions—he was vilified, threatened, and on occasion physically attacked by angry mobs. North Carolina indicted him in absentia, and the state of Georgia offered a reward for his arrest.

Garrison formed the Massachusetts Anti-Slavery Society in 1832 and the American Anti-Slavery Society in 1833, which in seven years numbered two thousand chapters outside the South, each of which sought to educate the public through lectures by former slaves like William Wells Brown, petitions, and pamphleteering. The society was based on the conviction that black people are in all respects equal to whites, that blacks could readily assimilate into white society, and that gradualism (allowing slavery to wither away through its inherent economic and social weaknesses) would take too long. In summary, immediate emancipation

1815

■ **December 23**
Henry Highland Garnet is born a slave in New Market, Maryland.

1816

■ **December 21**
The American Colonization Society organizes in Washington, D.C.

1822

■ **June 23**
Denmark Vesey, accused of conspiring to lead a slave insurrection, is found guilty and later hanged in Charleston, South Carolina.

1829

■ **September**
David Walker's Appeal, In Four Articles: Together With A Preamble To The Coloured Citizens Of The World, But In Particular, And Very Expressly, To Those Of The United States Of America is published.

1830

■ **September 15**
The ten-day National Negro Convention begins in Philadelphia to consider purchasing land in Canada where African Americans could live in freedom.

1831

■ **January 1**
William Lloyd Garrison begins publishing *The Liberator*, for the next thirty-five years the single most important abolitionist publication.

■ **August 22**
Nat Turner's Rebellion in Southampton County, Virginia, takes the lives of at least fifty-five white men, women, and children.

1833

■ **December**
William Lloyd Garrison and others organize the American Anti-Slavery Society in Philadelphia, Pennsylvania.

1837

■ **May 9**
The first Anti-Slavery Convention of American Women is held in New York City to consider such topics as abolition, women's rights, and women's suffrage.

without repatriation or reparations was a moral imperative that must be achieved through "moral suasion," that is, by nonviolent and nonpolitical means.

Garrison served as president of the American Anti-Slavery Society until 1865 and was its dominant voice. He was adamantly opposed to linking the society to any political party, he denounced the U.S. Constitution as a proslavery document and the churches for their support of slavery, and he admitted women to the society. By 1840 a number of its members had had enough of Garrison's radical leadership. A major rift led to the formation of the Liberty Party, dedicated to legislating abolition and the American and Foreign Anti-Slavery Society opposed to women's participation.

Free black abolitionism took several forms. The best known was the Underground Railroad, a loosely organized (and often spontaneously formed) network in which blacks and whites aided runaway slaves to reach Canada or safe havens in the North. Henry Highland Garnet and his family were given such help when they escaped from slavery in Maryland to safety in Pennsylvania in 1824. The family was again protected when slave catchers, operating under the Fugitive Slave Act, found them in New York City. The family scattered to safety, helped by the New York Vigilance Society, one of several aid societies run by African Americans in nearly every city where runaway slaves were in hiding.

Beginning in 1830 and intermittently to the 1850s black abolitionists (many of them clergymen and teachers) met in National Negro Conventions to discuss matters of mutual interest. Black abolitionist lecturers and writers like Frederick Douglass and Sojourner Truth were in high demand after 1840. In their books and lectures they emphasized the evils of slavery within conventional Christian morality and advocated moral suasion and nonviolent resistance. All that changed when the Mexican-American War, the Compromise of 1850, and the new Fugitive Slave Act of 1850 transformed the nation's moral and political landscapes.

The Buffalo meeting was itself a reason for excitement because, after a lapse of seven years, its convening renewed a convention movement that had begun thirteen years earlier with the National Convention of Colored Citizens in Philadelphia in 1830. Five annual gatherings followed the first, but the 1836 convention divided over doctrinal matters, and no further national meetings were held until the Buffalo convention was called to order on August 15, 1843. The chairman, Samuel H. Davis, a minister and the principal of the local elementary school for black children, struck the gavel. All delegates were aware that groups in Buffalo had fiercely opposed their meeting. Some openly threatened them and their meeting place, the Vine Street American Methodist Episcopal Church, but the proceedings over the next five days took place without any outside interference. Davis, a graduate of Oberlin College, set the tone with his keynote address, "We Must Assert Our Rightful Claims and Plead Our Own Cause." He reminded the delegates that the work of white abolitionists had thus far failed to win the slaves' emancipation or full civil liberties for free blacks. Those goals could be reached, he said, only if African Americans themselves "make known our wrongs to the world and to our oppressors." To leave the goals to others to achieve was a commitment to failure, Davis warned. When his turn came to speak, Henry Highland Garnet carried that message to a far more radical conclusion.

About the Author

A Presbyterian minister, leading abolitionist, and diplomat, Henry Highland Garnet was born into slavery on a plantation near Chestertown in Kent County, Maryland, on December 23, 1815, to George and Henrietta (Henny) Trusty. In 1824, following the death of their owner, the Trustys, aided by the Underground Railroad, made their way to the North, where they adopted Garnet as their new name. In 1827 they settled in New York City, and Garnet's father worked as a shoemaker. Henry attended the African Free School until he went to sea in 1828, first as a cabin boy and then as a cook on a coastal schooner. He later worked as an indentured field hand on Long Island, where in his second year he severely injured a knee, which healed poorly, leaving him in pain and on crutches for the rest of his life. In 1840 the leg was amputated at the hip.

In 1831 Garnet returned to a high school for blacks in New York and in July 1835 entered Noyes Academy in Canaan, New Hampshire, a school founded by abolitionists to serve both black and white students. Local townspeople, unhappy with the school's racial mix, destroyed the building in August and attacked the house where the black students were living. Garnet fired a shotgun from his bedroom window, and the mob dispersed, but Garnet and two friends returned to New York via the Hudson River on the open foredeck of a steamboat because blacks were not permitted to mingle with the white passengers. Early in 1836 Garnet was admitted to the Oneida Institute in Whitesboro, New York, from which he graduated with honors in 1840.

Not ordained until 1842, Garnet was named minister of the African American Liberty Street Presbyterian Church in Troy, New York, in 1840. He married Julia Ward Williams, a teacher, in 1841. The couple had three children. Garnet became active in abolitionist affairs; edited *The Clarion*, a weekly abolitionist newspaper; and taught school. An organizer of the convention movement in New York State, he campaigned briefly for the Liberty Party.

Following his speech in Buffalo, Garnet returned to his pulpit in Troy. In 1850, he lectured on antislavery in Great Britain and Germany and in 1852 was sent by the United Presbyterian Church of Scotland to Jamaica, where he stayed for two years as a missionary. In 1854 he returned to England and then, in 1855, to New York City as pastor of the Shiloh Presbyterian Church. During the Civil War, he was pastor of the Fifteenth Street Presbyterian Church in Washington, D.C. On February 12, 1865, he became the first African American to deliver a sermon to the U.S. House of Representatives. In 1881 President James Garfield appointed Garnet the U.S. minister resident and consul general to Liberia. He died two months after taking up his post in Monrovia, on February 13, 1882.

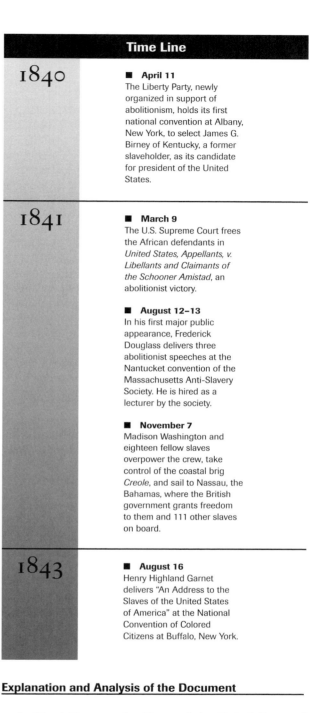

Time Line

1840

■ **April 11**
The Liberty Party, newly organized in support of abolitionism, holds its first national convention at Albany, New York, to select James G. Birney of Kentucky, a former slaveholder, as its candidate for president of the United States.

1841

■ **March 9**
The U.S. Supreme Court frees the African defendants in *United States, Appellants, v. Libellants and Claimants of the Schooner Amistad*, an abolitionist victory.

■ **August 12–13**
In his first major public appearance, Frederick Douglass delivers three abolitionist speeches at the Nantucket convention of the Massachusetts Anti-Slavery Society. He is hired as a lecturer by the society.

■ **November 7**
Madison Washington and eighteen fellow slaves overpower the crew, take control of the coastal brig *Creole*, and sail to Nassau, the Bahamas, where the British government grants freedom to them and 111 other slaves on board.

1843

■ **August 16**
Henry Highland Garnet delivers "An Address to the Slaves of the United States of America" at the National Convention of Colored Citizens at Buffalo, New York.

Explanation and Analysis of the Document

In "An Address to the Slaves of the United States of America," Henry Highland Garnet presents his audience with a series of carefully connected themes, woven together in forceful images and powerful language. He begins with a direct appeal to those in bondage to recognize their close ties to those who are free, their common memory of past and present injustices, and their mutual connection to past generations of slaves. He points to heroic rebels as examples of what the slaves themselves must do to secure their freedom, and he urges them to see the strengths that lie in their numbers and their shared consciousness of their condition. He highlights their masters' dependency on slavery and the slave owners' deep-seated fear of a slave insurrection. He tells them in ringing terms that violence is their only recourse if they wish to be free.

◆ Paragraphs 1–6

The opening three paragraphs set the tone for the rest of the speech. Garnet uses the word *brethren* dualistically, directing it to both the immediate audience and the absent slaves, who are his real audience. As he notes in the second sentence, this direct address is a departure from past practice, which produced passivity in the speaker and the convention delegates. In the second paragraph Garnet spells out the connection between free person and slave and, in the third, how the institution of slavery has kept them apart. Paragraph 4 provides a brief but powerful indictment of the slavers and slave owners. The last sentence, in particular, is a haunting statement about the perpetual horrors of slavery reaching from generation to generation.

Although Garnet was an ordained Presbyterian minister and the abolitionist ranks were filled with clergymen, only the Quakers, he asserts, have consistently taken public stands against slavery since the seventeenth century. Because institutional Christianity has remained silent, Garnet takes the churches to task in paragraph 5. In paragraph 6, the highly educated Garnet laments both the laws in the South that make it a crime to teach slaves to read and write and public opinion in the North, which often denies education to blacks, almost three million of whom have been left in intellectual darkness. (The 1840 census gives the number of slaves as 2.5 million.) As a minister he is particularly angry that slaves are denied the right to read the "Book of Life," meaning the Bible.

◆ Paragraphs 7–11

In paragraph 7, Garnet celebrates the American Revolution and the Declaration of Independence, but he laments the missed opportunity to abolish slavery and the inclusion of protections for slaveholders in the Constitution. He praises the colonists for risking death to win their freedom and suggests that blacks should be prepared to do the same. In paragraphs 8 and 9 Garnet invokes the human need for freedom and equates the slave's failure to openly oppose slavery, even at the risk of death, as a violation of the Ten Commandments. What follows is the most theologically charged language of his address, as he introduces the theme that the slaves must themselves bring an end to slavery. In paragraph 10 he says explicitly that resistance in the name of freedom is right and just and will be blessed by God.

The "old and true saying" Garnet paraphrases in paragraph 11 is from the 1812 poem *Childe Harold's Pilgrimage* (canto 2, stanza 76) by George Gordon, Lord Byron: "Hereditary bondsmen! know ye not, / Who would be free, themselves must strike the blow?" Garnet uses it to encourage African American slaves to plead their own case for freedom, because they are in a better position to know what must be done. He notes that freedom from slavery has been granted elsewhere in the world by European states.

Britain abolished the slave trade in 1807, with the Abolition of the Slave Trade Act (which came into force in 1808). Holland followed suit in 1814, France in 1818, and Spain in 1820. England, however, did not abolish slavery in its Caribbean colonies until the Slavery Emancipation Act, enacted in 1833 and taking effect in 1834. Although the United States ended the African trade in 1807, as required by the Constitution, domestic slave trading continued in the American South, including the nation's capital, even as Garnet delivered his address.

The New York Evangelist, which Garnet quotes in passing, was an abolitionist newspaper. The quotation introduces a graphic litany of daily abuses that Garnet connects to a theme of slave resistance that he will return to twice more, in paragraphs 13 and 21, urging slaves to rebel to save their families, especially their women, from the unpunished physical abuse of the slave owners. Here in paragraph 11 Garnet reminds the slaves that they are native-born American citizens. He instructs them to remind their owners that their birthright is freedom, even at the cost of whippings or death. There is no other way, he tells them. They cannot be like the children of Israel, who were freed from bondage in Egypt when God visited ten plagues on the Pharaoh and his people, the first of which was turning water into blood. They cannot move en masse to Canada, the destination of many on the Underground Railroad, or to Mexico, because American settlers have carried slavery ("the black flag") into Texas and Mexican lands in the Southwest. The Reverend Robert Hall, who is quoted, was a Baptist minister in Bristol, England, whose sermons were popular reading in Britain and the United States.

◆ Paragraphs 12–16

Garnet turns in paragraphs 12 and 13 to the strengths that the slaves possess. He compares them to the American rebels in the Revolution, who endured hardship, and reminds them that hardship is what they have known. Given the abuses to their loved ones, there is no longer a debate over what they must do. To encourage them further, Garnet offers them as exemplars of resistance, in paragraphs 14 through 18, thirteen "noble men" who chose to fight for liberty at the risk of or price of death. All of them were likely to be known to the slaves across the South, having heard of them from travelers, or through interplantation contacts or possibly at Sunday gatherings after church.

Garnet begins his list of heroes in paragraph 14 with a former slave from West Africa, Denmark "Veazie" (Vesey) of South Carolina. In 1800 Vesey won a lottery prize of $1,500 and used it to purchase his freedom after more than twenty years as a slave. A skilled carpenter, he acquired money and property and became a leader among African Americans in and around Charleston. Driven by a deep hatred of slavery and slave owners, Vesey allegedly recruited over nine thousand slaves and free blacks for an insurrection scheduled for July 14, 1822, in which all whites would be killed and slaves set free. Unknown blacks betrayed Vesey in early June; despite the lack of solid evidence, Vesey and thirty-four others were charged with conspiracy and hanged on June 23, 1822, bringing to an end what would have been the largest slave uprising in the American South. For weeks afterward, tales of the failed insurrection spread fear throughout the South.

Garnet connects Vesey to eight historic heroes, beginning with Moses, who led the Israelites out of bondage in Egypt to the fertile land of Canaan, the promised land of freedom. The Old Testament story of the deliverance of "the children of Israel" was among the best known and most-often-repeated biblical lessons in black Christian churches and in many abolitionist orations. It was often linked to the story of Joshua, Moses's successor, who led the violent and bloody invasion of Canaan. Vesey, for example, frequently quoted God's instructions to Joshua to kill every non-Israelite in Canaan as justification for his own plan to kill as many whites as possible in an effort to destroy slavery.

Each of the remaining seven men identified by Garnet in paragraph 13 is identified as a fighter for freedom through violence: John Hampden, a leading opponent of King Charles I, died of wounds sustained in 1643 in the second year of the English Civil War. William Tell, the legendary marksman, was a leader of the rebellion against the Habsburg rulers in the fourteenth century that produced the Swiss Confederation. Robert the Bruce and William Wallace fought for Scotland against the English, also in the fourteenth century. Toussaint-Louverture successfully freed Haiti from French rule in the 1790s, outlawed slavery, and established native government, only to be betrayed by Napoléon, who sentenced him to death in a French prison. The Marquis de Lafayette is famous for his military role in two eighteenth-century revolutions, the American and the French. George Washington, of course, led the Continental army to victory and America to independence in 1783.

Garnet introduces Nat Turner (as Nathaniel, a name unknown to Nat) in paragraph 15, calling him a patriot and noting that while his name was made infamous by his captors, future generations will understand and praise him for what he did. Nat Turner's rebellion in Southampton County, Virginia, in August 1831—just eleven years before Garnet spoke—was the most successful of all slave revolts. A deeply religious man, Turner interpreted a number of apocalyptic visions and an eclipse of the sun as God's commands for him to kill as many slaveholding whites as he could find. At 2 AM on August 22, Nat and six trusted accomplices entered his master's house and killed the entire family, sparing only an infant. The seven, joined through the night by some seventy other slaves, moved from farm to farm, murdering some fifty-five white men, women, and children as they went. Within hours, the state's mounted militia intercepted Turner's roving band, but Turner himself escaped capture. He remained in hiding for nearly two months, during which time the militia and white mobs killed at least two hundred blacks, many of whom had nothing to do with the rebellion. Eventually discovered and brought to trial, Turner was found guilty. He was hanged on November 11, 1831.

In paragraph 16, Garnet praises Joseph Cinqué, a captive African, who on July 2, 1839, led fifty-two fellow Africans in gaining control of *La Amistad*, a Cuban-owned vessel transporting them from Havana to another port on Cuba's coast. Having freed themselves from their chains in the ship's main hold, they went on deck armed with sugarcane knives and took over the ship, killing the captain and the cook. Cinqué demanded they be taken to their African homeland, but the crew instead sailed the *Amistad* north along the North American coast to the eastern end of Long Island, New York, where the USS *Washington* intercepted the ship. Federal officers then took the Africans to New London, Connecticut, to be sold, in clear violation of the Constitution's ban on importing slaves. Abolitionists quickly came to the blacks' aid. In a dramatic appearance before the Supreme Court, the former president John Quincy Adams argued the abolitionists' position that the Africans had been illegally enslaved, that they were justified in using force to gain their freedom, and that the court should return them to their homeland. On March 9, 1841, the court ruled in favor of the abolitionists in *United States, Appellants, v. Libellants and Claimants of the Schooner Amistad*, and the Africans, including Cinqué, were set free.

♦ **Paragraphs 17–21**

The heroism of Madison Washington, whom Garnet introduces in paragraph 17, followed close on the Court's decision in that case. On the night of November 7, 1841, Washington led a slave revolt on board the *Creole*, a coastal slave ship, carrying him and 134 other slaves from Virginia to New Orleans, where they were to be sold. (The constitutional prohibition on the importation of slaves did not apply to the domestic slave trade.) Washington and eighteen of his fellow slaves overpowered the ship's crew and forced the captain to take them to Nassau in the Bahamas, a British colony. Great Britain had abolished slavery in her overseas possessions in 1834, and despite protests from the American government, the British declared the slaves to be free persons. Washington and his rebel partners were briefly imprisoned as mutineers, but in the end they, too, were granted their freedom.

Paragraph 18 is a transitional passage in which Garnet eloquently reminds his audience that what all these men have done is not forgotten, that collective memory gives each of the heroes a form of immortality, in itself a fitting reward for the sacrifices they made. What Garnet has said to this point is preparation for the rousing finish to his address in paragraphs 19 through 22: his call for a slave rebellion that, through violence, would destroy the evils of slavery and bring freedom to African Americans at long last. "Brethren, arise, arise!" Garnet says in paragraph 19, reminding the nation's slaves that they number four million (the number in 1848 was closer to 3.2 million) and that if they join together, they can wipe out a dying institution. They have, he adds, nothing to lose but the restrictions that already were limiting their lives and making their wives and children subject to every cruelty; they cannot be made to suffer more than they already have.

Paragraph 20 is a forceful reminder that the slaves have within their hands the power to awaken the fear that overtook southern whites during the Vesey conspiracy and Nat

> "Brethren, the time has come when you must act for yourselves. It is an old and true saying that, 'if hereditary bondmen would be free, they must themselves strike the blow.'"
>
> (Paragraph 11)

> "Brethren, arise, arise! Strike for your lives and liberties. Now is the day and the hour. Let every slave throughout the land do this, and the days of slavery are numbered."
>
> (Paragraph 19)

> "Let your motto be resistance! resistance! resistance! No oppressed people have ever secured their liberty without resistance."
>
> (Paragraph 21)

Turner's Rebellion. In an Old Testament reference well known to his audience, Garnet invokes the ten plagues (which ranged from water turned to blood to the death of the first-born child in Egyptian families) that Moses promised that God would inflict on Egypt unless the pharaoh freed the Israelites from bondage (as described in the book of Exodus). What holds slavery together, Garnet says, is the passivity of the slaves, their patience and inaction in the face of daily cruelty and humiliation. It is time for them to awaken. Paragraph 21, the conclusion of the address, needs no explication. Its stirring words brought many of Garnet's listeners to tears and others to rage. For some it was a justified call to revolution. For others, it was a call too radical.

Audience

The Buffalo convention audience numbered seventy delegates from twelve states. Among the many African American abolitionists in attendance were such younger leaders such as Frederick Douglass, a former slave and already a celebrated orator; William Wells Brown, a runaway slave who would carry his message to Great Britain and the Continent in the 1850s; Charles B. Ray, a Congregational minister and "conductor" on the Underground Railroad, who in 1843 joined the New York Vigilance Committee to protect runaway slaves from slave catchers in the city; Charles L. Redmond, an abolitionist speaker, born in Massachusetts, who accompanied William Lloyd Garrison to London in 1838 and then traveled extensively on his own in England,

Scotland, and Ireland; and James McCune Smith, an experienced abolitionist speaker and the nation's first African American medical doctor. Four of these five came to the convention as Garrisonians supporting moral suasion as the means of achieving emancipation and were opposed to the use of violence. Only Smith spoke in favor of Garnet's radical position.

Impact

"An Address to the Slaves of the United States of America" was like a thunderclap to the assembled delegates at the Buffalo convention. The first major abolitionist speech directed to the nation's slaves since David Walker's "Appeal to the Coloured Citizens of the World," its call for armed resistance shocked both the convention audience and the nation at large. Contemporary reports tell of some delegates being reduced to tears, of others given to outrage and clenched fists. During the discussion that followed, Frederick Douglass, in an hour-long speech (now lost), denounced the address as dangerous in the extreme and argued forcefully for the Garrisonian position of moral suasion and passive, not violent, resistance. Given a chance to respond, Garnet offered a rebuttal lasting an hour and a half (also lost) that Smith said was more powerful than the original address and perhaps the greatest of Garnet's speeches or sermons up to that time.

Since the address was intended as a resolution reflecting the consensus of the convention, a committee undertook to soften its language, but their effort was in vain. The edited address was defeated by a margin of one vote, and the convention adjourned on April 19 without producing a consensus statement. In 1848, Garnet published *Walker's Appeal, with a Brief Sketch of His Life. By Henry Highland Garnet. And also Garnet's Address to the Slaves of the United States of America*. In the printed version of the speech, Garnet noted two reasons for its defeat by the convention: First, "the document was warlike and encouraged insurrection." Second, had the convention adopted it, delegates from the border states (the immediate neighbors of the slave states) "would not dare return to their homes." He refused to withdraw or apologize for his radical proposal and in the next decade was gratified to see—especially after the passage of the Fugitive Slave Act of 1850—many of those who had earlier rebuffed him, including Douglass, Brown, Redmond, and Ray, embrace the idea that abolition could not be achieved without violence.

See also Pennsylvania: An Act for the Gradual Abolition of Slavery (1780); Slavery Clauses in the U.S. Constitution (1787); Fugitive Slave Act of 1793; David Walker's *Appeal to the Coloured Citizens of the World* (1829); William Lloyd Garrison's First *Liberator* Editorial (1831); *The Confessions of Nat Turner* (1831); *United States v. Amistad*(1841); Fugitive Slave Act of 1850.

Further Reading

■ Articles

Stuckey, Sterling. "A Last Stern Struggle: Henry Highland Garnet and Liberation Theory." In *Black Leaders of the Nineteenth Century*, eds. Leon Litwack and August Meier. Chicago: University of Illinois Press, 1988.

"'To the Public.' January 1, 1831." In *William Lloyd Garrison and the Fight against Slavery: Selections from the* Liberator, ed. William E. Cain. New York: Bedford/St. Martins, 1997.

■ Books

Hutchinson, Earl Ofari. *Let Your Motto Be Resistance: The Life and Thought of Henry Highland Garnet*. Boston: Beacon Press, 1972.

Quarles, Benjamin. *Black Abolitionists*. New York: Da Capo Press, 1991.

Schor, Joel. *Henry Highland Garnet: A Voice of Black Radicalism in the Nineteenth Century*. Westport, Conn.: Greenwood Publishing, 1977.

—Allan L. Damon

Questions for Further Study

1. What was the basis of the dispute between Garnet and the abolitionist William Lloyd Garrison?

2. In the early nineteenth century, there were two camps in the movement against slavery. One group wanted its immediate abolition. Others favored a more gradual approach. On what basis did each of the two camps make its arguments?

3. In what ways did the Mexican-American War, the Compromise of 1850, and the new Fugitive Slave Act of 1850 transform "the nation's moral and political landscapes"?

4. Garnet's audience expected to hear a forceful, "fiery" address. To what extent did Garnet meet their expectations? Put differently, what characteristics of Garnet's address, such as its language and tone, strike a defiant note? Be specific.

5. Garnet published his speech in a volume that also contained David Walker's *Appeal to the Coloured Citizens of the World*. Compare the two documents. Do they make similar arguments? Are they different in any fundamental ways?

HENRY HIGHLAND GARNET: "AN ADDRESS TO THE SLAVES OF THE UNITED STATES OF AMERICA"

Brethren and Fellow-Citizens: —Your brethren of the North, East, and West have been accustomed to meet together in National Conventions, to sympathize with each other, and to weep over your unhappy condition. In these meetings we have addressed all classes of the free, but we have never, until this time, sent a word of consolation and advice to you. We have been contented in sitting still and mourning over your sorrows, earnestly hoping that before this day your sacred liberties would have been restored. But, we have hoped in vain. Years have rolled on, and tens of thousands have been borne on streams of blood and tears, to the shores of eternity. While you have been oppressed, we have also been partakers with you; nor can we be free while you are enslaved. We, therefore, write to you as being bound with you.

Many of you are bound to us, not only by the ties of a common humanity, but we are connected by the more tender relations of parents, wives, husbands, children, brothers, and sisters, and friends. As such we most affectionately address you.

Slavery has fixed a deep gulf between you and us, and while it shuts out from you the relief and consolation which your friends would willingly render, it afflicts and persecutes you with a fierceness which we might not expect to see in the fiends of hell. But still the Almighty Father of mercies has left to us a glimmering ray of hope, which shines out like a lone star in a cloudy sky. Mankind are becoming wiser, and better—the oppressor's power is fading, and you, every day, are becoming better informed, and more numerous. Your grievances, brethren, are many. We shall not attempt, in this short address, to present to the world all the dark catalogue of this nation's sins, which have been committed upon an innocent people. Nor is it indeed necessary, for you feel them from day to day, and all the civilized world look upon them with amazement.

Two hundred and twenty-seven years ago, the first of our injured race were brought to the shores of America. They came not with glad spirits to select their homes in the New World. They came not with their own consent, to find an unmolested enjoyment of the blessings of this fruitful soil. The first dealings they had with men calling themselves Christians, exhibited to them the worst features of corrupt and sordid hearts: and convinced them that no cruelty is too great, no villainy and no robbery too abhorrent for even enlightened men to perform, when influenced by avarice and lust. Neither did they come flying upon the wings of Liberty, to a land of freedom. But they came with broken hearts, from their beloved native land, and were doomed to unrequited toil and deep degradation. Nor did the evil of their bondage end at their emancipation by death. Succeeding generations inherited their chains, and millions have come from eternity into time, and have returned again to the world of spirits, cursed and ruined by American slavery.

The propagators of the system, or their immediate ancestors, very soon discovered its growing evil, and its tremendous wickedness, and secret promises were made to destroy it. The gross inconsistency of a people holding slaves, who had themselves "ferried o'er the wave" for freedom's sake, was too apparent to be entirely overlooked. The voice of Freedom cried, "Emancipate your slaves." Humanity supplicated with tears for the deliverance of the children of Africa. Wisdom urged her solemn plea. The bleeding captive pleaded his innocence, and pointed to Christianity who stood weeping at the cross. Jehovah frowned upon the nefarious institution, and thunderbolts, red with vengeance, struggled to leap forth to blast the guilty wretches who maintained it. But all was vain. Slavery had stretched its dark wings of death over the land, the Church stood silently by—the priests prophesied falsely, and the people loved to have it so. Its throne is established, and now it reigns triumphant.

Nearly three millions of your fellow-citizens are prohibited by law and public opinion (which in this country is stronger than law) from reading the Book of Life. Your intellect has been destroyed as much as possible, and every ray of light they have attempted to shut out from your minds. The oppressors themselves have become involved in the ruin. They have become weak, sensual, and rapacious—they have cursed you—they have cursed themselves—they have cursed the earth which they have trod

The colonists threw the blame upon England. They said that the mother country entailed the evil upon them, and that they would rid themselves of it if they could. The world thought they were sincere, and the philanthropic pitied them. But time soon tested their sincerity. In a few years the colonists grew strong, and severed themselves from the British Government. Their independence was declared, and they took their station among the sovereign powers of the earth. The declaration was a glorious document. Sages admired it, and the patriotic of every nation reverenced the God-like sentiments which it contained. When the power of Government returned to their hands, did they emancipate the slaves? No; they rather added new links to our chains. Were they ignorant of the principles of Liberty? Certainly they were not. The sentiments of their revolutionary orators fell in burning eloquence upon their hearts, and with one voice they cried, *Liberty or Death*. Oh what a sentence was that! It ran from soul to soul like electric fire, and nerved the arm of thousands to fight in the holy cause of Freedom. Among the diversity of opinions that are entertained in regard to physical resistance, there are but a few found to gainsay that stern declaration. We are among those who do not.

Slavery! How much misery is comprehended in that single word. What mind is there that does not shrink from its direful effects? Unless the image of God be obliterated from the soul, all men cherish the love of Liberty. The nice discerning political economist does not regard the sacred right more than the untutored African who roams in the wilds of Congo. Nor has the one more right to the full enjoyment of his freedom than the other. In every man's mind the good seeds of liberty are planted, and he who brings his fellow down so low, as to make him contented with a condition of slavery, commits the highest crime against God and man. Brethren, your oppressors aim to do this. They endeavor to make you as much like brutes as possible. When they have blinded the eyes of your mind— when they have embittered the sweet waters of life—when they have shut out the light which shines from the word of God—then, and not till then, has American slavery done its perfect work.

To such Degradation it is sinful in the Extreme for you to make voluntary Submission. The divine commandments you are in duty bound to reverence and obey. If you do not obey them, you will surely meet with the displeasure of the Almighty. He requires you to love him supremely, and your neighbor as yourself—to keep the Sabbath day holy—to search the Scriptures—and bring up your children with respect for his laws, and to worship no other God but him. But slavery sets all these at nought, and hurls defi-

ance in the face of Jehovah. The forlorn condition in which you are placed, does not destroy your moral obligation to God. You are not certain of heaven, because you suffer yourselves to remain in a state of slavery, where you cannot obey the commandments of the Sovereign of the universe. If the ignorance of slavery is a passport to heaven, then it is a blessing, and no curse, and you should rather desire its perpetuity than its abolition. God will not receive slavery, nor ignorance, nor any other state of mind, for love and obedience to him. Your condition does not absolve you from your moral obligation. The diabolical injustice by which your liberties are cloven down, *neither God; nor angels, or just men, command you to suffer for a single moment. Therefore it is your solemn and imperative duty to use every means, both moral, intellectual and physical that promises success.* If a band of heathen men should attempt to enslave a race of Christians, and to place their children under the influence of some false religion, surely, Heaven would frown upon the men who would not resist such aggression, even to death. If, on the other hand, a band of Christians should attempt to enslave a race of heathen men, and to entail slavery upon them, and to keep them in heathenism in the midst of Christianity, the God of heaven would smile upon every effort which the injured might make to disenthral themselves.

Brethren, it is as wrong for your lordly oppressors to keep you in slavery, as it was for the man thief to steal our ancestors from the coast of Africa. You should therefore now use the same manner of resistance, as would have been just in our ancestors, when the bloody footprints of the first remorseless soul-thief was placed upon the shores of our fatherland. The humblest peasant is as free in the sight of God as the proudest monarch that ever swayed a sceptre. Liberty is a spirit sent out from God, and like its great Author, is no respecter of persons.

Brethren, the time has come when you must act for yourselves. It is an old and true saying that, "if hereditary bondmen would be free, they must themselves strike the blow." You can plead your own cause, and do the work of emancipation better than any others. The nations of the old world are moving in the great cause of universal freedom, and some of them at least will, ere long, do you justice. The combined powers of Europe have placed their broad seal of disapprobation upon the African slave-trade. But in the slaveholding parts of the United States, the trade is as brisk as ever. They buy and sell you as though you were brute beasts. The North has done much— her opinion of slavery in the abstract is known. But in regard to the South, we adopt the opinion of the New York Evangelist—"We have advanced so far, that the cause apparently waits for a more effectual door to be thrown open than has been yet." We are about to point you to that more effectual door. Look around you, and behold the bosoms of your loving wives heaving with untold agonies! Hear the cries of your poor children! Remember the stripes your fathers bore. Think of the torture and disgrace of your noble mothers. Think of your wretched sisters, loving virtue and purity, as they are driven into concubinage and are exposed to the unbridled lusts of incarnate devils. Think of the undying glory that hangs around the ancient name of Africa:—and forget not that you are native-born American citizens, and as such, you are justly entitled to all the rights that are granted to the freest. Think how many tears you have poured out upon the soil which you have cultivated with unrequited toil and enriched with your blood; and then go to your lordly enslavers and tell them plainly, that you *are determined to be free.* Appeal to their sense of justice, and tell them that they have no more right to oppress you, than you have to enslave them. Entreat them to remove the grievous burdens which they have imposed upon you, and to remunerate you for your labor. Promise them renewed diligence in the cultivation of the soil, if they will render to you an equivalent for your services. Point them to the increase of happiness and prosperity in the British West Indies since the Act of Emancipation. Tell them in language which they cannot misunderstand, of the exceeding sinfulness of slavery, and of a future judgment, and of the righteous retributions of an indignant God. Inform them that all you desire is *freedom*, and that nothing else will suffice. Do this, and for ever after cease to toil for the heartless tyrants, who give you no other reward but stripes and abuse. If they then commence the work of death, they, and not you, will be responsible for the consequences. You had far better all die—*die immediately*, than live slaves, and entail your wretchedness upon your posterity. If you would be free in this generation, here is your only hope. However much you and all of us may desire it, there is not much hope of redemption without the shedding of blood. If you must bleed, let it all come at once—rather *die freemen, than live to be the slaves.* It is impossible, like the children of Israel, to make a grand exodus from the land of bondage. The Pharaohs are on both sides of the blood-red waters! You cannot move *en masse*, to the dominions of the British Queen—nor can you pass through Florida and overrun Texas, and at last find

peace in Mexico. The propagators of American slavery are spending their blood and treasure, that they may plant the black flag in the heart of Mexico and riot in the halls of the Montezumas. In the language of the Rev. Robert Hall, when addressing the volunteers of Bristol, who were rushing forth to repel the invasion of Napoleon, who threatened to lay waste the fair homes of England, "Religion is too much interested in your behalf, not to shed over you her most gracious influences."

You will not be compelled to spend much time in order to become inured to hardships. From the first moment that you breathed the air of heaven, you have been accustomed to nothing else but hardships. The heroes of the American Revolution were never put upon harder fare than a peck of corn and a few herrings per week. You have not become enervated by the luxuries of life. Your sternest energies have been beaten out upon the anvil of severe trial. Slavery has done this to make you subservient to its own purposes; but it has done more than this, it has prepared you for any emergency. If you receive good treatment, it is what you could hardly expect; if you meet with pain, sorrow, and even death, these are the common lot of the slaves.

Fellow-men! patient sufferers! Behold your dearest rights crushed to the earth! See your sons murdered, and your wives, mothers and sisters doomed to prostitution. In the name of the merciful God, and by all that life is worth, let it no longer be a debatable question whether it is better to choose *Liberty or death.*

In 1822, Denmark Veazie, of South Carolina, formed a plan for the liberation of his fellow-men. In the whole history of human efforts to overthrow slavery, a more complicated and tremendous plan was never formed. He was betrayed by the treachery of his own people, and died a martyr to freedom. Many a brave hero fell, but history, faithful to her high trust, will transcribe his name on the same monument with Moses, Hampden, Tell, Bruce and Wallace, Toussaint L'Ouverture, Lafayette and Washington. That tremendous movement shook the whole empire of slavery. The guilty soul thieves were overwhelmed with fear. It is a matter of fact, that at that time, and in consequence of the threatened revolution, the slave States talked strongly of emancipation. But they blew but one blast of the trumpet of freedom, and then laid it aside. As these men became quiet, the slaveholders ceased to talk about emancipation: and now behold your condition today! Angels sigh over it, and humanity has long since exhausted her tears in weeping on your account!

The patriotic Nathaniel Turner followed Denmark Veazie. He was goaded to desperation by wrong and injustice. By despotism, his name has been recorded on the list of infamy; and future generations will remember him among the noble and brave.

Next arose the immortal Joseph Cinque, the hero of the *Amistad*. He was a native African, and by the help of God he emancipated a whole ship-load of his fellow-men on the high seas. And he now sings of liberty on the sunny hills of Africa and beneath his native palm-trees, where he hears the lion roar and feels himself as free as that king of the forest.

Next arose Madison Washington, that bright star of freedom, and took his station in the constellation of true heroism. He was a slave on board the brig *Creole* of Richmond, bound to New Orleans, that great slave mart, with a hundred and four others. Nineteen struck for liberty or death. But one life was taken, and the whole were emancipated, and the vessel was carried into Nassau, New Providence.

Noble men! Those who have fallen in freedom's conflict, their memories will be cherished by the true-hearted and the God-fearing in all future generations; those who are living, their names are surrounded by a halo of glory.

Brethren, arise, arise! Strike for your lives and liberties. Now is the day and the hour. Let every slave throughout the land do this, and the days of slavery are numbered. You cannot be more oppressed than you have been—you cannot suffer greater cruelties

Glossary

Book of Life	the Bible
British West Indies since the Act of Emancipation	a reference to Great Britain's 1833 Slavery Abolition Act
Children of Israel … Pharaohs	reference to the Old Testament Israelites and their bondage under ancient Egypt
concubinage	the condition of being forced to submit to sexual relations
Denmark Veazie	usually spelled "Vesey"; the leader of a planned slave rebellion in South Carolina in 1822
"ferried o'er the wave"	a quotation from William Cowper's 1785 poem "The Task"
Florida … Mexico	a reference to the disputes that arose over slavery as the nation expanded
Hampton … Washington	John Hampden, a leading opponent of King Charles I, who died of wounds sustained in 1643 in the second year of the English Civil War; William Tell, the legendary marksman, leader of a rebellion against the Hapsburg rulers in the fourteenth century; Robert the Bruce and William Wallace, who fought for Scotland against the English in the fourteenth century; Toussaint-Louverture, who successfully freed Haiti from French rule in the 1790s, outlawed slavery, and established native government; the Marquis de Lafayette, famous for his military role in the American and the French revolutions; George Washington, who led the Continental army to victory and America to independence in 1783
Jehovah	God, a name commonly used in the biblical Old Testament
Liberty or Death	an allusion to Patrick Henry's revolutionary statement, "Give me liberty, or give me death"
Montezumas	Aztec emperors in Mexico
Nathaniel Turner	Nat Turner, the leader of a slave rebellion in Virginia in 1831
Robert Hall	a British Baptist minister of the late eighteenth and early nineteenth centuries

than you have already. *Rather die freemen than live to be slaves.* Remember that you are *four millions*!

It is in your power so to torment the God-cursed slaveholders, that they will be glad to let you go free. If the scale was turned, and black men were the masters and white men the slaves, every destructive agent and element would be employed to lay the oppressor low. Danger and death would hang over their heads day and night. Yes, the tyrants would meet with plagues more terrible than those of Pharaoh. But you are a patient people. You act as though you were made for the special use of these devils. You act as though your daughters were born to pamper the lusts of your masters and overseers. And worse than all, you tamely submit while your lords tear your wives from your embraces and defile them before your eyes. In the name of God, we ask, are you men? Where is the blood of your fathers? Has it all run out of your veins? Awake, awake; millions of voices are calling you! Your dead fathers speak to you from their graves. Heaven, as with a voice of thunder, calls on you to arise from the dust.

Let your motto be resistance! *resistance! resistance!* No oppressed people have ever secured their liberty without resistance. What kind of resistance you had better make, you must decide by the circumstances that surround you, and according to the suggestion of expediency. Brethren, adieu! Trust in the living God. Labor for the peace of the human race, and remember that you are *four millions*.

IN THE COTTON FIELD.

Nineteenth-century lithograph showing African Americans picking cotton (Library of Congress)

WILLIAM WELLS BROWN'S "SLAVERY AS IT IS"

1847

"There is no liberty for the American Slave; and yet we hear a great deal about liberty!"

Overview

"Slavery As It Is" was an address presented before the Female Anti-Slavery Society of Salem, Massachusetts, in November 1847. This speech by the African American author and abolitionist William Wells Brown offers an eloquent condemnation of slavery in the antebellum United States. After spending the first two decades of his life in slavery, Brown was particularly qualified to testify to the evils of slavery. The lecture was delivered shortly after the publication of his autobiography, *Narrative of William W. Brown, a Fugitive Slave, Written by Himself,* so the lecture was also part of a promotion for his book. Many of the ideas and some of the passages in the address also appear in his *Narrative.*

Context

The movement for the immediate abolition of slavery in the United States began in the 1830s and gained significant support among the emerging northern middle class, especially in New England and New York. The inception of the immediatism movement is often traced to the publication of William Lloyd Garrison's weekly antislavery newspaper, *The Liberator,* beginning January 1, 1831. The abolition movement was racially integrated and often included female activists. Abolitionists organized reform societies at the national, state, and local levels. Women abolitionists often formed their own auxiliary societies that raised funds for abolition activities and helped fund antislavery newspapers, and the Salem Female Anti-Slavery Society, formed in 1832, was probably among the earliest of these female antislavery groups.

Abolitionists, especially the followers of Garrison, aimed for a peaceful end to slavery. Their main tactic was moral suasion, meaning that they believed that slaveholders could be persuaded to free their slaves once they came to understand that slavery was morally wrong. Other means in the movement included lecturing on the evils of slavery, publishing newspapers and pamphlets, and petitioning the legislature to end slavery in Washington, D.C., which was controlled by Congress. Radical followers of Garrison also

rejected political participation, because they saw the U.S. Constitution as a proslavery document. They objected to the established Protestant denominations' failure to condemn slavery, and so they urged followers to avoid attending church services. More so than other factions of the antislavery movement, Garrisonians supported an active role for women and men together in their organizations. This approach put them in a minority position even among abolitionists, but their tactics gained much attention, and sometimes they came under verbal or even physical attack for their outspoken beliefs.

William Wells Brown belonged to various antislavery societies in New York and New England and acted as a lecturing agent for the Garrisonian American Anti-Slavery Society at midcentury. Once he moved to Boston with his children, he became actively tied to the Garrisonians. As an African American and former slave, Brown held a special place in the abolitionist movement. Like the more famous Frederick Douglass, he was able to offer a firsthand account of life in slavery. His lectures frequently drew a large crowd of abolitionists and those curious to see a fugitive slave firsthand. In 1847 he published his autobiography, *Narrative of William W. Brown, a Fugitive Slave, Written by Himself,* in which can be found many of the ideas put forth in the lecture he delivered that year to the Female Anti-Slavery Society of Salem, Massachusetts.

About the Author

The African American reformer and author William Wells Brown was born enslaved on a plantation near Lexington, Kentucky, in March 1815. His mother was a slave, and his father was George Harris, a white man believed to have been the half brother of his slave master, John Young. During his youth, Brown's master moved to the area near Saint Louis, Missouri, where the young slave was often hired out as a servant or a waiter on steamships, spending a year in the employ of a New Orleans slave trader. In 1833 Brown made his first attempt to escape slavery, crossing into Illinois with his mother, but the pair were caught after only ten days of freedom. His mother was subsequently sold to a steamship owner. Brown passed through several owners and eventually became the property

1815

■ **March**
William, later known as William Wells Brown, is born on a plantation near Lexington, Kentucky.

1833

■ William and his mother attempt to escape slavery but are caught ten days after leaving the plantation.

1834

■ **January 1**
William escapes from a steamship, after which he blends into the black community of Cincinnati, Ohio, and changes his name to William Wells Brown.

1847

■ Brown's autobiography, *Narrative of William W. Brown, a Fugitive Slave, Written by Himself* is published in Boston.

■ **November 14**
Brown addresses the Salem Female Anti-Slavery Society in Salem, Massachusetts, in a lecture titled "Slavery As It Is."

1848

■ Brown's last slave master, Enoch Price, offers Wells his freedom in exchange for $325, but Brown refuses to pay.

1849

■ Traveling to Europe to avoid returning to slavery, Brown serves as a delegate to the International Peace Conference held in Paris and then remains in Europe for the next five years.

1854

■ Brown publishes *Clotel; or, The President's Daughter*, the first novel by an African American.

1855

■ A year after European associates help Brown purchase his freedom, he returns to the United States as a free man.

1884

■ **November 6**
Brown dies at his home, after three decades of freedom in which he published numerous plays, travel narratives, and works of history.

of a man named Enoch Price. He made a second, successful escape on January 1, 1834, when he walked off a steamship in Cincinnati, Ohio. He added "Wells Brown" to his given name in honor of the Quaker man who aided his escape.

Brown settled in Cleveland, Ohio, where he obtained employment as a steward on a Lake Erie–based steamship. He married Elizabeth Schooner in 1834 and moved to Buffalo, New York, two years later. There Brown was active in aiding fugitives on the Underground Railroad and became a leader in the local temperance reform movement, helping to form the Union Total Abstinence Society. He joined the Western New York Anti-Slavery Society and began lecturing against slavery and in support of black civil rights. His commitment to William Lloyd Garrison's brand of radical abolitionism grew stronger when Brown moved to Boston with his daughters, apparently having become estranged from his wife. He acted as a lecturing agent, speaking often before groups such as the Salem Female Anti-Slavery Society. In 1847 he published his autobiography, *Narrative of William W. Brown, a Fugitive Slave, Written by Himself*, to positive critical response. The following year a collection of antislavery songs, *The Anti-Slavery Harp: A Collection of Songs for Anti-Slavery Meetings*, appeared. Thereafter, Brown's reputation as an author became firmly established.

In 1848, following his successfully distributed autobiography, Brown's last slave master offered Brown his freedom in exchange for $325. After widely publicizing the offer in his lectures, Brown refused to pay. Instead, to maintain his freedom, Brown accepted an offer to join an antislavery and reform lecture tour of Europe and embarked to Great Britain in 1849. He spent several years abroad, where he lectured on American slavery and contributed frequent letters to the British press. During his time abroad, Brown continued to write, in 1853 publishing *Three Years in Europe*, the first travel memoir by an African American, and in 1854 the first novel by a black American, *Clotel; or, The President's Daughter*. The novel offered a daring fictional account of the relationship between Thomas Jefferson and his slave Sally Hemings. In the same year that the novel appeared, friends in the reform community purchased his freedom, and Brown returned to the United States a free man in 1855.

In subsequent years Brown continued to write, publishing plays and updating both his autobiography and his travel narrative. He studied medicine on his own and began a limited medical practice in the 1860s. Brown also published several volumes of history, including *The Black Man, His Antecedents, His Genius, and His Achievements* (1863) and *The Negro in the America Rebellion* (1867). He died in Boston on November 6, 1884.

Explanation and Analysis of the Document

Brown's address was delivered before an audience of women and men gathered at the Salem, Massachusetts, Lyceum Hall. The audience was made up primarily of abolitionists and antislavery sympathizers.

Receipt for $250 as payment for Negro man, January 20, 1840 (Library of Congress)

♦ "My Subject for This Evening Is Slavery as It Is"

Brown's address begins with an apology, pointing to the obvious educational disparity between himself and the audience. Most abolitionists were drawn from the emerging middle class and had benefit of formal education, possibly including college. Brown explains that his speech could be lacking in polish and grammatical style because he had no real education before age twenty-one, having spent the first two decades of his life in slavery. He tells the audience in his opening that he is offering the address because he owes a duty to the three million African Americans who remain in slavery. (His estimate of the number of slaves in 1847 was fairly accurate. When the 1850 census was calculated, enumerators counted 3,204,313 slaves in the United States.) Brown's intent is to offer the audience a narrative of slavery as it existed in the southern states, based on his personal experience.

Brown follows with an explanation of the legal position of slaves as chattel: "He is a piece of property in the hands of a master, as much as is the horse that belongs to the individual that may ride him through your streets tomorrow." Throughout the southern states, enslaved men, women, and children were considered personal property that could be bought and sold. Deeds conferring ownership were recorded in property record books alongside the sales

of real estate. Slaves also appeared in wills and estate property listings, categorized along with farm animals, horses, and furniture.

Brown had experienced slavery firsthand, and he tells the audience that it is a dehumanizing institution that tears apart families. As cotton cultivation became more important after 1800, slavery had shifted southward and westward in an interstate slave trade that separated husbands from wives and mothers from children. States in the Upper South, such as Virginia and Brown's native Kentucky, made the transition from labor-intensive crops such as tobacco to less-demanding grains, resulting in a surplus of enslaved workers. The historian Robert William Fogel has estimated that between 1790 and 1860 approximately 835,000 slaves were moved into the expanding cotton states. Many Upper South slave owners sold their slaves to plantation owners in the expanding Deep South states, such as Mississippi, Alabama, and Texas. Although some slave owners were careful to keep families together, many others had few qualms about splitting up families and communities so long as they earned a profit.

If slaves' being sold away from family and friends were not enough to horrify Brown's audience, he continues by outlining the punitive nature of slavery. He describes the methods slave society uses to keep control: "its blood-hounds,

"The system of Slavery, that I, in part, represent here this evening, is a system that strikes at the foundation of society, that strikes at the foundation of civil and political institutions. It is a system that takes man down from that lofty position which his God designed that he should occupy; that drags him down, places him upon a level with the beasts of the field, and there keeps him, that it may rob him of his liberty."

("My Subject for This Evening Is Slavery as It Is")

"There is no liberty here for me; there is no liberty for those with whom I am associated; there is no liberty for the American Slave; and yet we hear a great deal about liberty!"

("What is Democracy?")

"In conclusion let me say, that the character of the American people and the influence of Slavery upon that character have been blighting and withering the efforts of all those that favor liberty, reform, and progression."

("What Is Democracy?")

"Recollect that you have come here to-night to hear a Slave, and not a man, according to the laws of the land; and if the Slave has failed to interest you, charge it not to the race, charge it not to the colored people, but charge it to the blighting influences of Slavery."

("The Tree of Liberty")

its chains, its negrowhips, its dungeons, and almost every instrument of cruelty that the human eye can look at." To prevent resistance on the part of slaves, which could take the form of running away, passively refusing to work, or fighting back, southern states had enacted a series of slave codes, laws that restricted slaves' movements and authorized slave patrols to monitor their behavior. The oppressive system was largely effective in keeping slaves in bondage.

Brown next compares American acceptance of slavery with the experience of the German youth Kaspar Hauser (spelled "Caspar" in the document). In 1828, Hauser had appeared in a German city claiming he had been imprisoned in a dark cell for his entire life. His sensational and mysterious story gained international attention and outrage over his prolonged captivity, and it prompted a German law that made "murder of the soul" a crime. Brown and other abolitionists often invoked Hauser's experience and the German reaction to that singular event to declare U.S. slaveholders as murderers of the souls of the millions enslaved. He notes that some twenty thousand escaped slaves, he himself among them, are helping to raise awareness but that collectively they had failed to make an impact equivalent to Hauser's on American public opinion.

Brown's temper flares as he references the general apathy of Americans toward the evils of slavery. In his autobiography, Brown had described numerous examples of the cruelty slaves faced on a daily basis. Among his recollections was witnessing a plantation overseer, Grove Cook, beat his mother severely for being fifteen minutes late for work in the field. Following a failed escape attempt in 1833, Brown's mother, Elizabeth, was jailed and then sold to the New Orleans slave market. She fell victim along with numerous slaves who were separated from family and friends as slavery shifted to the Deep South and West.

♦ "The Influence of Slavery upon the Morals of the People"

Speaking before a sympathetic antislavery audience, Brown declares that slaves received no physical protection from bodily harm or murder by whites under southern law. While he was generally correct that the imbalance of power left slaves vulnerable under the law, most southern states had enacted statutes criminalizing the murder of enslaved persons. Across the South, slaveholders theoretically could be held responsible for the death of a slave, and in 1851 the Virginia Supreme Court upheld one conviction of a slaveholder for murdering a slave. Sexual predation by slave masters of enslaved women, however, was rarely if ever punished under the law, and the rape of African American women was common. Brown compares the inability of black men to protect their daughters with the example of the Roman Virginius. In the seventeenth-century play *Appius and Virginia*, by John Webster, Virginius kills his daughter Virginia to protect her virtue from the Roman politician Appius Claudius. Brown mourns the fact that slaves are unable similarly to protect their women from violation. Like Virginius, slaves' lack of protection could lead them to desperate strategies.

Brown next turns to the effect of slavery on moral and social institutions in the United States. He argues that "so far as the people of the North are connected with Slaveholding, they necessarily become contaminated by the evils that follow in the train of Slavery." Likely this reference is to the business connections between northerners and slavery. The growing textile industry of New England was fed by the cotton plantations of the South, and most of the merchants who shipped crops grown by slave labor to Europe and beyond were northerners. He points out the moral flaw that exists in the failure of the South to legally recognize slave marriages, and he deplores the connection of slavery and churches, including slave ownership by the clergy.

Brown then offers his audience evidence of the evils of slavery and its demoralizing influence on southern society by demonstrating advertisements and articles in the southern press that promote such violent pastimes as cockfighting, bullbaiting, and dogfighting. These activities are evidence of the moral contamination of the southern population, says Brown. Other advertisements offer slaves for sale to benefit churches, missionary activities, and a theological seminary.

This discussion of the advertisements leads Brown toward a more general conversation on the link between slavery and established Protestant denominations. He notes that in the early years of the United States, the Methodists, Presbyterians, and other denominations condemned slavery, but after 1830 this attitude changed, until most churches in the South openly supported the institution. Southern clergy and most major denominations came to embrace the proslavery argument that slavery had a positive value and that enslavement was the rightful place for African Americans. Slaveholders and slaves often attended the same churches; likewise, slaveholders sometimes paid white ministers to preach to their slaves. The growing complicity with slaveholders in the South of Protestant denominations such as the Methodists, Presbyterians, and Baptists resulted in a schism between North and South, as northern ministers removed their support for proslavery elements within their denominations. Because he was a Garrisonian abolitionist, Brown found the connection between the churches and slavery to be particularly important and offensive. Followers of William Lloyd Garrison rejected organized religion because the major Protestant denominations had a presence in the South and because some ministers there openly supported slavery. They also felt that northern churches failed to take a strong stand against the evils of slavery and urged men and women to leave those churches.

Brown next considers the influences of slavery on those living in the North. In the 1840s northerners formed numerous benevolent associations and reform societies, many of which were connected with Christian churches, but here Brown condemns northern institutions and societies for their failure to fight openly against slavery. He attacks the American Bible Society, founded in 1816 to distribute Bibles to underprovided populations around the world, for ignoring enslaved southerners. Other organizations aimed at distributing Bibles also failed to send them to the South. Brown fails to mention, however, that in most southern states it was illegal to teach slaves to read, which likely figured in the organizations' decisions to exclude the enslaved population from Bible distribution. Another important reform organization with which Brown takes issue is the American Tract Society, formed in 1825 to deliver Christian-oriented reform and especially temperance pamphlets to Americans. Like other moral-reform organizations, the American Tract Society did not extend its distribution to the southern states, and never, says Brown, had it "published a single line against the sin of slaveholding."

Brown continues his condemnation of the complicity of northerners and the government in the continuance of slavery by describing newspaper and other accounts of slaves sold in the South for the direct financial benefit of northern merchants. He holds special disdain for a slave auction scheduled on December 22, a date (says Brown) that coincides with the anniversary of the Pilgrims' landing in the New World. (This statement is actually in error. Although the religious separatists known familiarly as Pilgrims did move to Plymouth at some time in December 1620, historical accounts vary on the exact date; in any case, the Pilgrims landed first at Cape Cod, Massachusetts, in November 1620.)

♦ "What Is Democracy?"

If northerners benefit financially from southern slavery, Brown finds even more blame in the federal government's willingness to allow the institution. He contrasts the values behind the American Revolution, fought "for the purpose of instituting a democratic, republican government" and the aim of gaining liberty from Great Britain, with the new nation's acceptance of slavery. He asks his audience to consider the meaning of democracy and invokes the example

of the Athenian statesman Solon, who fought for democratic reform on behalf of the individual citizen injured by
a corrupt political system. Brown juxtaposes Solon's virtue
with the assertion by South Carolina's governor Stephen D.
Miller that slavery is crucial because of its national benefit.
Brown argues that democracy requires liberty and freedom
for every individual in the United States and that without
an end to slavery the nation cannot be fully democratic.
Brown also suggests that there is an inherent contradiction
in the ubiquitous annual orations and celebrations on the
Fourth of July while slavery continues to exist and receive
government sanction—a theme that was also taken up in
1852 by Frederick Douglass in his speech "What to the
Slave Is the Fourth of July?"

Other nations in the world must view the U.S. sanction
of slavery with disdain, Brown declares; the nation cannot criticize other nations for mistreatment of their citizens while slavery exists within U.S. borders. He gives as
an example the hypocrisy of American criticism of Russian
serfdom under Czar Nicholas I, arguing that the United
States cannot credibly disparage the plight and treatment
of the serfs while enslaving millions of African Americans.
After passage of the Fugitive Slave Act of 1793, which required northerners to return runaway slaves to their owners, slaves had no hope anywhere in the United States, and
Brown reminds his audience that those who escape slavery
could only run north to Canada, where slavery did not exist.
To achieve freedom, they are forced to leave families and
homes forever. Brown scorns the common symbols called
"liberty-poles" (tall posts set in the ground and sometimes
bearing a flag, which had been a symbol of freedom and liberty since the Revolutionary era) as being meaningless, in
light of the nation's constitutional endorsement of slavery.

"I ask you to look at the efforts of other countries" that
have ended slavery, says Brown, noting again that in order
to experience real freedom and enjoy civil rights, African
Americans have to leave the United States. He singles out
England for praise: Great Britain had abolished slavery
in its West Indies colonies in 1834. Under pressure from
Great Britain, the bey of Tunis emancipated that state's
slaves in 1846, declaring that all slaves who reached its
shores would be considered forever free. Brown proclaims
that the American people are therefore behind the nations
of the Old World, including "those who are ... almost living in the dark ages." He quotes a stanza from the poem
"Expostulation" by the American abolitionist John Greenleaf Whittier, expressing a similar sentiment about the
backward position of the United States on freedom and
liberty, and he follows his commentary on the Whittier
poem with more poetry, offering lines from the Scottish
reformer and poet Thomas Campbell, whose "Epigram to
the United States of North America" points out the stark
contradiction between slavery and democracy.

♦ **"The Tree of Liberty"**

As he moves into the closing portion of his speech,
Brown praises the antislavery movement for having adopted
principles that he believes are capable of redeeming the na-

tion's character. He singles out William Lloyd Garrison as
the catalyst of the movement demanding the immediate,
complete, and uncompensated end to slavery. Garrison has
"planted the tree of Liberty," says Brown, referring to the
publication of Garrison's weekly newspaper, *The Liberator*,
begun in 1831. At the time of Brown's address, Garrison
and his movement for immediate emancipation had been
active for fifteen years. Continuing the metaphor about the
tree of liberty, Brown quotes a verse from a popular antislavery political song, "The Liberty Party."

Brown then returns to his condemnation of the government sanction of slavery in America. At the time of this address, the United States was engaged in a war with Mexico
(1846–1848), a war that abolitionists believed was rooted
in the desire to add additional territory, and especially slave
states, to the nation. The popular conception of Manifest
Destiny, that the United States was ordained by God to
stretch to the Pacific Ocean, partly fueled the expansion
drive. Brown maintains that slavery's expansion undermines
respect for the democratic institutions of the United States
in the eyes of the nation and Europe. He describes the in-
congruous existence of slavery and open slave auctions in the
capital of an ostensibly democratic nation. (Abolishing slavery in Washington, D.C., which was controlled by Congress,
had long been a goal of immediate abolitionists.) With its location near the Upper South states of Virginia and Maryland,
Washington was on the route of many slave traders, and so,
says Brown, in addition to open auctions, "you can scarcely
stand an hour but you will see caufles of Slaves driven past
the Capitol"—that is, groups of slaves bound together with
chains, moving through the city on their way to plantations
in the Deep South. Foreign visitors to the capital would be
confronted by the embarrassing reality of U.S. slavery.

Brown's conclusion returns to his personal experiences
in slavery. His description of slave auctions pulls at the sympathy of his audience, as he describes an auction in which
a young woman fetches a high price once the bidder was
assured of her piety. He notes that the United States has a
million women in bondage and says that "as long as a single
woman is in Slavery, every woman in the community should
raise her voice against that sin," aiming this remark directly
at the members of the Salem Female Anti-Slavery Society
in the audience. Brown again makes the humble disclaimer
that his poor grammar is the result of his lack of education
and his condition as a slave. However, his eloquent intellectual address must have left his audience realizing they
were in the presence of a singular man of letters, his lack of
formal education notwithstanding.

Audience

Brown delivered this address in Massachusetts to the Salem Female Anti-Slavery Society, an organization of women
abolitionists drawn from Salem's black elite. The men and
women in attendance there on the evening of November
14, 1847, were the first to hear the speech, but the primary
audience for Brown's oration was the northern abolition-

ist community: The speech was subsequently published in pamphlet form by the Massachusetts Anti-Slavery Society and widely distributed in abolitionist circles. These pamphlets, and likely Brown's speaking tour, were also meant to attract readers and sales for his autobiography, *Narrative of William W. Brown, a Fugitive Slave, Written by Himself*, which was also published in 1847 by the American Anti-Slavery Society's Boston printing office.

Impact

Brown's speech was delivered before a small audience, but as a fine example of antislavery propaganda the speech was reported extensively in newspapers throughout New England and in the antislavery press of western New York and Ohio. In pamphlet form, the text was widely distributed throughout abolitionist communities, so that his words ultimately had a far-reaching influence across the North. The address, along with his autobiography, helped Brown gain credibility in the U.S. abolitionist community and among reformers in Europe. The address was a first step toward promoting his autobiography and increasing readership for that volume and Brown's publications that followed, which established his literary reputation. Moreover, the Salem women's group was associated with William Lloyd Garrison and his circle of reformers in the Boston area: Garrison's abolitionist newspaper, *The Liberator*, was the beneficiary of funds raised in Salem by society-sponsored talks such as Brown's.

See also Fugitive Slave Act of 1793; William Lloyd Garrison's First *Liberator* Editorial (1831); Frederick Douglass's "What to the Slave Is the Fourth of July?" (1852).

Further Reading

■ Books

Brown, William Wells. *Narrative of William W. Brown, a Fugitive Slave, Written by Himself*. Boston: Anti-Slavery Office, 1847.

Ellison, Curtis, W., and E. W. Metcalf. *William Wells Brown and Martin R. Delany: A Reference Guide*. Boston: G. K. Hall, 1978.

Ernest, John. *Liberation Historiography: African American Writers and the Challenge of History, 1794–1861*. Chapel Hill: University of North Carolina Press, 2004.

Farrison, William Edward. *William Wells Brown: Author and Reformer*. Chicago: University of Chicago Press, 1969.

Fogel, Robert William. *Without Consent or Contract: The Rise and Fall of American Slavery*. New York: W. W. Norton, 1989.

Genovese, Eugene D. *Roll, Jordan, Roll: The World the Slaves Made*. New York: Vintage, 1976.

■ Web Sites

"William Wells Brown, 1814?–1884." Documenting the American South Web site.
　　http://docsouth.unc.edu/fpn/brownw/bio.html.

—L. Diane Barnes

Questions for Further Study

1. Describe the role that women played in the abolitionist movement.

2. Compare this document with other documents opposing slavery, such as Frederick Douglass's "What to the Slave Is the Fourth of July?" (1852). How are the documents similar and different in tone and in the nature of the arguments the writers use?

3. One of the links between North and South in the antebellum years was cotton. How did the cotton industry contribute to tacit approval of southern slavery in the North?

4. At the beginning and end of his speech, Brown apologizes to his audience for his comparative lack of education. Do you believe that this was just a rhetorical ploy to gain the sympathy of his audience? What evidence from the speech suggests that Brown was more educated that he suggests?

5. This speech was printed as a pamphlet and distributed in abolitionist circles. To what extent do you believe that a document like this was a case of "preaching to the choir"—that is, to people who already agree with the writer? How much of an impact do you believe a document such as this would have had on those who were not abolitionists?

WILLIAM WELLS BROWN'S "SLAVERY AS IT IS"

Mr. Chairman, and Ladies and Gentlemen:— In coming before you this evening to speak upon this all important, this great and commanding subject of freedom, I do not appear without considerable embarrassment; nor am I embarrassed without a cause. I find myself standing before an audience whose opportunities for education may well be said to be without limit. I can scarcely walk through a street in your city, or through a city or a town in New England, but I see your common schools, your high schools, and your colleges. And when I recollect that but a few years since, I was upon a Southern plantation, that I was a Slave, a chattel, a thing, a piece of property,—when I recollect that at the age of twenty-one years I was entirely without education, this, every one will agree, is enough to embarrass me. But I do not come here for the purpose of making a grammatical speech, nor for the purpose of making a speech that shall receive the applause of my hearers. I did not accept the invitation to lecture before this association, with the expectation or the hope that I should be able to present anything new. I accepted the invitation because I felt that I owed a duty to the cause of humanity; I felt that I owed a duty to three millions of my brethren and sisters, with some of whom I am identified by the dearest ties of nature, and with most of whom I am identified by the scars which I carry upon my back. This, and this alone, induced me to accept the invitation to lecture here.

My subject for this evening is Slavery as it is, and its influence upon the morals and character of the American people.

I may try to represent to you Slavery as it is; another may follow me and try to represent the condition of the Slave; we may all represent it as we think it is; and yet we shall all fail to represent the real condition of the Slave. Your fastidiousness would not allow me to do it; and if it would, I, for one, should not be willing to do it;—at least to an audience. Were I about to tell you the evils of Slavery, to represent to you the Slave in his lowest degradation, I should wish to take you, one at a time, and whisper it to you.

Slavery has never been represented; Slavery never can be represented. What is a Slave? A Slave is one that is in the power of an owner. He is a chattel; he is a thing; he is a piece of property. A master can dis-

pose of him, can dispose of his labor, can dispose of his wife, can dispose of his offspring, can dispose of everything that belongs to the Slave, and the Slave shall have no right to speak; he shall have nothing to say. The Slave cannot speak for himself; he cannot speak for his wife, or his children. He is a thing. He is a piece of property in the hands of a master, as much as is the horse that belongs to the individual that may ride him through your streets to-morrow. Where we find one man holding an unlimited power over another, I ask, what can we expect to find his condition? Give one man power *ad infinitum* over another, and he will abuse that power; no matter if there be no law; no matter if there be public sentiment in favor of the oppressed.

The system of Slavery, that I, in part, represent here this evening, is a system that strikes at the foundation of society, that strikes at the foundation of civil and political institutions. It is a system that takes man down from that lofty position which his God designed that he should occupy; that drags him down, places him upon a level with the beasts of the field, and there keeps him, that it may rob him of his liberty. Slavery is a system that tears the husband from the wife, and the wife from the husband; that tears the child from the mother, and the sister from the brother; that tears asunder the tenderest ties of nature. Slavery is a system that has its blood-hounds, its chains, its negrowhips, its dungeons, and almost every instrument of cruelty that the human eye can look at; and all this for the purpose of keeping the Slave in subjection; all this for the purpose of obliterating the mind, of crushing the intellect, and of annihilating the soul.

I have read somewhere of an individual named Caspar Hauser, who made his appearance in Germany some time since, and represented that he had made his escape from certain persons who had been trying to obliterate his mind, and to annihilate his intellect. The representation of that single individual raised such an excitement in Germany, that lawmakers took it in hand, examined it, and made a law covering that particular case and all cases that should occur of that kind; and they denominated it the "murder of the soul." Now, I ask, what is Slavery doing in one half of the States of this Union, at the present time? The souls of three millions of American citizens are being murdered every day, under the blighting influence of American Slavery. Twenty thousand have made their escape from the prison-house; some have taken refuge in the Canadas, and others are lurking behind the stumps in the Slave-States. They are telling their tales, and representing that Slavery is not only trying to murder their souls, but the souls of three million of their countrymen at the present day; and the excitement that one individual raised in monarchical Germany, three millions have failed to raise in democratic, Christian, republican America!

I ask, is not this a system that we should examine? Ought we not to look at it? Ought we not to see what the cause is that keeps the people asleep upon the great subject of American Slavery? When I get to talking about Slavery as it is,—when I think of the three millions that are in chains at the present time, I am carried back to the days when I was a Slave upon a Southern plantation; I am carried back to the time when I saw dear relatives, with whom I am identified by the tenderest ties of nature, abused and ill-treated. I am carried back to the time when I saw hundreds of Slaves driven from the Slave-growing to the Slave-consuming States. When I begin to talk of Slavery, the sighs and the groans of three millions of my countrymen come to me upon the wings of every wind; and it causes me to feel sad, even when I think I am making a successful effort in representing the condition of the Slave.

What is the protection from the masters which Slaves receive? Some say, law; others, public sentiment. But, I ask, Where is the law; where is the public sentiment? If it is there, it is not effectual; it will not protect the Slave. Has the case ever occurred where the Slaveholder has been sent to the State's Prison, or anything of the kind, for ill-treating, or for murdering a Slave? No such case is upon record; and it is because the Slave receives no protection and can expect no protection from the hands of the master. What has the brother not done, upon the Slave-plantation, for the purpose of protecting the chastity of a dearly beloved sister? What has the father not done to protect the chastity of his daughter? What has the husband not done to protect his wife from the hands of the tyrant? They have committed murders. The mother has taken the life of her child, to preserve that child from the hands of the Slave-trader. The brother has taken the life of his sister, to protect her chastity. As the noble Virginius seized the dagger, and thrust it to the heart of the gentle Virginia, to save her from the hands of Appius Claudius of Rome, so has the father seized the deadly knife, and taken the life of his daughter, to save her from the hands of the master or the Negro-driver. And yet we are told that the Slave is protected; that there is law and public sentiment! It is all a dead letter to the Slave.

But why stand here and try to represent the condition of the Slave? My whole subject must necessarily represent his condition, and I will therefore pass to the second part,—the influence of Slavery upon the morals of the people; not only upon the morals of the Slave-holding South, or of the Slave, but upon the morals of the people of the United States of America. I am not willing to draw a line between the people of the North and the people of South. So far as the people of the North are connected with Slaveholding, they necessarily become contaminated by the evils that follow in the train of Slavery.

Let me look at the influence which Slavery has over the morals of the people of the South. Three millions of Slaves unprotected! A million females that have no right to marriage! Among the three millions of Slaves upon the Southern plantations, not a single lawful marriage can be found! They are out of the pale of the law. They are herded together, so far as the law is concerned, as so many beasts of burden are in the free States.

Talk about the influence of Slavery upon the morals of the people, when the Slave is sold in the Slave-holding States for the benefit of the church? when he is sold for the purpose of building churches? when he is sold for the benefit of the minister?

I have before me a few advertisements, taken from public journals and papers, published in the Slave-holding States of this Union. I have one or two that I will read to the audience for I am satisfied that no evidence is so effectual for the purpose of convincing the people of the North of the great evils of Slavery as is the evidence of Slaveholders themselves. I do not present to you the assertion of the North; I do not bring before you the advertisement of the Abolitionists, or my own assertion; but I bring before you the testimony of the Slaveholders themselves,—and by their own testimony must they stand or fall.

The first is an advertisement from the columns of the New Orleans Picayune, one of the most reputable papers published in the State of Louisiana, and I may say one of the most reputable papers published South of Mason and Dixon's line. If you take up the Boston Courier, or any other reputable paper, you will probably find in it an extract from the New Orleans Picayune, whose editor is at the present time in Mexico, where our people are cutting the throats of their neighbors.

"Cock-Pit.—*Benefit of Fire Company No. 1, Layfayette.*—A cock-fight will take place on Sunday, the 17th inst., at the well-known house of the subscriber. As the entire proceeds are for the benefit of the Fire Company, a full attendance is respectfully solicited. ADAM ISRANG.

Corner of Josephine and Tchoupitolas Streets, Lafayette." [N. O. Pic. of Sunday, Dec. 17.]

"Turkey Shooting.—This day, Dec. 17, from 10 o'clock, A.M., until 6 o'clock, P.M., and the following Sundays, at M'Donoughville, opposite the Second Municipality Ferry." [From the same paper.]

The next is an advertisement from the New Orleans Bee, an equally popular paper.

"A Bull Fight, between a ferocious bull and a number of dogs, will take place on Sunday next, at 4¼ o'clock, P.M., on the other side of the river, at Algiers, opposite Canal Street. After the bull fight, a fight will take place between a bear and some dogs. The whole to conclude by a combat between an ass and several dogs.

Amateurs bringing dogs to participate in the fight will be admitted gratis. Admittance-Boxes, 50 cts.; Pit, 30 cts. The spectacle will be repeated every Sunday, weather permitting. PEPE LLULLA."

Now these are not strange advertisements to be found in a Southern journal. They only show what Slavery has been doing there to contaminate the morals of the people. Such advertisements can be found in numbers of the public journals that are published in the Slave-holding States of this Union. You would not find such an advertisement in a Boston or a Salem paper. Scarcely a paper in New England would admit such an advertisement; and why? Because you are not so closely connected with Slavery; you are not so much under its blighting influences as are the Slave-owners in the Slave-holding States of the Union.

I have another advertisement, taken from a Charleston paper, advertising the property of a deceased Doctor of Divinity, probably one of the most popular men of his denomination that ever resided in the United States of America. In that advertisement it says, that among the property are "twenty-seven Negroes, two mules, one horse, and an old wagon." That is the property of a Slave-holding Doctor of Divinity! [Dr. Furman, of South Carolina]

I have another advertisement before me, taken from an Alabama paper, in which eight Slaves are advertised to be sold for the benefit of an Old School Theological Seminary for the purpose of making ministers. I have another, where ten Slaves are advertised to be sold for the benefit of Christ Church Parish. I have another, where four slaves are advertised to be sold for the benefit of the Missionary cause,—a very benevolent cause indeed. I might go on and present to you advertisement after advertisement representing the system of American Slavery, and its contaminating influence upon the morals of the people. I have an account, very recent, that a Slave-trader,—one of the meanest and most degrading positions in which a man can be found upon the God's footstool,—buying and selling the bodies and souls of his fellow-countrymen, has joined the church, and was, probably, hopefully converted. It is only an evidence that when Wickedness, with a purse of gold, knocks at the door of Church, she seldom, if ever, is refused admission.

This is not the case here; for, some forty years since, the Church was found repudiating Slavery; she was found condemning Slavery as man-stealing; and a sin of the deepest dye. The Methodists, Presbyterians, and other denominations, and some of the first men in the country, bore their testimony against it. But Slavery has gone into all the ramifications of society; it has taken root in almost every part of society, and now Slavery is popular. Slavery has become popular, because it has power.

Speak of the blighting influence of Slavery upon the morals of the people? Go into the Slaveholding States, and there you can see the master going into the church, on the Sabbath, with his Slave following him into the church, and waiting upon him,—both belonging to the same church. And the day following, the master puts his Slave upon the auction-stand, and sells him to the highest bidder. The Church does not condemn him; the law does not condemn him; public sentiment does not condemn him; but the Slaveholder walks through the community as much respected after he has sold a brother belonging to the same church with himself, as if he had not committed an offense against God.

Go into the Slaveholding States, and to-morrow you may see families of Slaves driven to the auction-stand, to be sold to the highest bidder; the husband to be sold in presence of the wife, the wife in presence of the husband, and the children in presence of them both. All this is done under the sanction of law and order; all is done under the sanction of public sentiment, whether that public sentiment be found in Church or in State.

Leaving the Slaveholding States, let me ask what is the influence that Slavery has over the minds of the Northern people? What is its contaminating influence over the great mass of the people of the North?

It must have an influence, either good or bad. People of the North, being connected with the Slaveholding States, must necessarily become contaminated. Look all around, and you see benevolent associations formed for the purpose of carrying out the principles of Christianity; but what have they been doing for Humanity? What have they ever done for the Slave?

First, we see the great American Bible Society. It is sending bibles all over the world for the purpose of converting the heathen. Its agents are to be found in almost every country and climate. Yet three millions of Slaves have never received a single bible from the American Bible Society. A few years since, the American Anti-Slavery Society offered to the American Bible Society a donation of $5,000 if they would send bibles to the Slaves, or make an effort to do it, and the American Bible Society refused even to *attempt* to send the bible to the Slaves!

A Bible Society, auxiliary to the American Bible Society, held a meeting a short time since, at Cincinnati, in the State of Ohio. One of its members brought forward a resolution that the Society should do its best to put the bible into the hands of every poor person in the country. As soon as that was disposed of, another member brought forward a resolution that the Society should do its best to put the bible into the hands of every Slave in the country. That subject was discussed for two days, and at the end of that time they threw the resolution under the table, virtually resolving that they would not make an attempt to send bibles to the Slaves.

Leaving the American Bible Society, the next is the American Tract Society. What have you to say against the American Tract Society? you may ask. I have nothing to say against any association that is formed for a benevolent purpose, if it will only carry out the purpose for which it was formed. Has the American Tract Society ever published a single line against the sin of slaveholding? You have all, probably, read tracts treating against licentiousness, against intemperance, against gambling, against Sabbath-breaking, against dancing, against almost every sin that you can think of; but not a single syllable has ever been published by the American Tract Society against the sin of Slaveholding. Only a short time since they offered a reward of $500 for the best treatise against the sin of dancing. A gentleman wrote the treatise, they awarded him the $500, and the tract is now in the course of publication, if it is not already published. Go into a nice room, with fine music, and good company, and they will publish a tract against your dancing; while three millions are dancing every day at the end of the master's cowhide, and they cannot notice it! Oh, no; it is too small fry for them! They cannot touch that, but they can spend their money in publishing tracts against your dancing here at the North, while the Slave at the South may dance until he dances into his grave, and they care nothing about him.

A friend of mine, residing at Amsterdam, N.Y., who had been accustomed every year to make a donation to the American Tract Society and Bible Societies, some two years since said to the Agent when he was called upon, "I will not give you anything now, but tell the Board at New York that if they will publish a tract against the sin of Slaveholding, they may draw on me for $50."

The individual's name is Ellis Clisby, a member of the Presbyterian church, and a more reputable individual than he cannot be found. The next year when the Agent called upon him, he asked where was the tract. Said the Agent, "I laid it before the Committee and they said they dared not publish it. If they published it their Southern contributions would be cut off." So they were willing to sacrifice the right, the interest, and the welfare of the Slave for the "almighty dollar." They were ready to sacrifice humanity for the sake of receiving funds from the South. Has not Slavery an influence over the morals of the North?

I have before me an advertisement where some Slaves are advertised to be sold at the South for the benefit of merchants in the city of New York, and I will read it to you. It is taken from the Alabama Beacon.

"Public Sale of Negroes.—By virtue of a deed of trust made to me by Charles Whelan, for the benefit of J.W. & R. Leavitt, and of Lewis B. Brown, all of the city of New York, which deed is on record in Greene County, I shall sell at public auction, for cash, on Main Street, in the town of Greensborough, on Saturday, the 22d day of December next, a Negro Woman, about 30 years old, and her child, eleven months old; a Negro Girl about 10 years old, and a Negro Girl about 8 years old. Wm. Trapp, *Trustee*."

Now if I know anything about the history of this country, the 22d day of December is the anniversary of the landing of the Pilgrims; the anniversary of the day when those ambassadors, those leaders in religion, came to the American shore; when they landed within the encircling arms of Cape Cod and Cape Ann, fleeing from political and religious tyranny, seeking political and religious freedom in the New World. The anniversary of that day is selected for selling an American mother and her four children for the benefit of New York merchants.

I happen to know something of one of the parties. He is a member of Dr. Spring's church, and it is said that he gives more money to support that church than any other individual. And I should not wonder, when the bones, and muscles, and sinews, and hearts of human beings are put upon the auction-stand and sold for his benefit, if he could give a little to the church. I should not wonder if he could give a little to some institution that might throw a cloak over him, whitewash him, and make him appear reputable in the community. Has not Slavery an influence over the morals of the North, and the whole community?

Now let us leave the morals of the American people and look at their character. When I speak of the character of the American people, I look at the nation. I place all together, and draw no mark between the people, and the government. The government is the people, and the people are the government. You who are here, all who are to be found in New England, and throughout the United States of America, are the persons that make up the great American confederacy; and I ask, what is the influence that Slavery had had upon the character of the American People? But for the blighting influence of Slavery, the United States of America would have a character, would have a reputation, that would outshine the reputation of any other government that is to be found upon God's green earth.

Look at the struggle of the fathers of this country for liberty. What did they struggle for? What did they go upon the battle-field for, in 1776? They went there, it is said, for the purpose of obtaining liberty; for the purpose of instituting a democratic, republican government. What is Democracy? Solon, upon one occasion, while speaking to the Athenians said, "A democratic government is a government where an injury done to the least of its citizens is regarded as an insult and an injury to the whole commonwealth." That was the opinion of an old law-maker and statesman upon the subject of Democracy. But what says an American statesman? A South Carolina governor says that Slavery is the corner-stone of our Republic. Another eminent American statesman says that two hundred years have sanctioned and sanctified American Slavery, and that is property which the law declares to be property. Which shall we believe? One that is reared in republican America, or one that is brought up in the lap of aristocracy? Every one must admit that democracy is nothing more or less than genuine freedom and liberty, protecting every individual in the community.

I might carry the audience back to the time when your fathers were struggling for liberty in 1776. When they went forth upon the battle-field and laid down their bones, and moistened the soil with their blood, that their children might enjoy liberty. What was it for? Because a three-penny tax upon tea, a tax upon paper, or something else had been imposed upon them. We are not talking against such taxes upon the Slave. The Slave has no tea; he has no paper; he has not even himself; he has nothing at all.

When we examine the influence of Slavery upon the character of the American people, we are led to believe that if the American Government ever had a character, she has lost it. I know that upon the 4th of July, our 4th of July orators talk of Liberty, Democracy, and Republicanism. They talk of liberty, while three millions of their own countrymen are groaning in abject Slavery. This is called the "land of the free, and the home of the brave;" it is called the "Asylum of the oppressed;" and some have been foolish enough to call it the "Cradle of Liberty." If it is the "cradle of liberty," they have rocked the child to death. It is dead long since, and yet we talk about democracy and republicanism, while one-sixth of our countrymen are clanking their chains upon the very soil which our fathers moistened with their blood. They have such scenes even upon the holy Sabbath, and the American people are perfectly dead upon the subject. The cries, and shrieks, and groans of the Slave do not wake them.

It is deplorable to look at the character of the American people, the character that has been given to them by the institution of Slavery. The profession of the American people is far above the profession of the people of any other country. Here the people profess to carry out the principles of Christianity. The American people are a sympathising people. They not only profess, but appear to be a sympathizing people to the inhabitants of the whole world. They sympathise with everything else but the American Slave. When the Greeks were struggling for liberty, meetings were held to express sympathy. Now they are sympathising with the poor down-trodden serfs of Ireland, and are sending their sympathy across the ocean to them.

But what will the people of the Old World think? Will they not look upon the American people as hypocrites? Do they not look upon your professed sympathy as nothing more than hypocrisy? You may hold your meetings and send your words across the ocean; you may ask Nicholas of Russia to take the chains from his poor down-trodden serfs, but they look upon it all as nothing but hypocrisy. Look at our twenty thousand fugitive Slaves, running from under the stars and stripes, and taking refuge in the Canadas; *twenty thousand*, some leaving their wives, some their husbands, some leaving their children, some their brothers, and some their sisters,—fleeing to take refuge in the Canadas. Wherever the stars and stripes are seen flying in the United States of America, they point him out as a Slave.

If I wish to stand up and say, "I am a man," I must leave the land that gave me birth. If I wish to ask protection as a man, I must leave the American stars and stripes. Wherever the stars and stripes are seen flying upon American soil, I can receive no protection; I am a Slave, a chattel, a thing. I see your liberty-poles around in your cities. If to-morrow morning you are hoisting the stars and stripes upon one of your liberty-poles, and I should see the man following me who claims my body and soul as his property, I might climb to the very top of your liberty-pole, I might cut the cord that held your stars and stripes and bind myself with it as closely as I could to your liberty-pole, I might talk of law and the Constitution, but nothing could save me unless there be public sentiment enough in Salem. I could not appeal to law or the Constitution; I could only appeal to public sentiment; and if public sentiment would not protect me, I must be carried back to the plantations of the South, there to be lacerated, there to drag the chains that I left upon the Southern soil a few years since.

This is deplorable; and yet the American Slave *can* find a spot where he may be a man;—but it is not under the American flag. Fellow citizens, I am the last to eulogise any country, where they oppress the poor. I have nothing to say in behalf of England or any other country, any further than as they extend protection to mankind. I say that I honor England for protecting the black man. I honor every country that shall receive the American Slave, that shall protect him, and that shall recognise him as a man.

I know that the United States will not do it; but I ask you to look at the efforts of other countries. Even the Bey of Tunis, a few years since, has decreed that there shall not be a Slave in his dominions; and we see that the subject of liberty is being discussed throughout the world. People are looking at it; they are examining it; and it seems as though every country, and every people, and every government were doing something, excepting the United States. But Christian, democratic, republican America is doing nothing at all. It seems as though she would be the last. It seems as though she was determined to be the

last to knock the chain from the limbs of the Slave. Shall the American people be behind the people of the Old World? Shall they be behind those who are represented as almost living in the dark ages?

"Shall every flap of England's flag
Proclaim that all around are free,
From farthest Ind to each blue crag
That beetles o'er the western sea?
And shall we scoff at Europe's kings,
When Freedom's fire is dimmed with us;
And round our country's altar clings
The damning shade of Slavery's curse?"

Shall we, I ask, the American people be the last? I am here, not for the purpose of condemning the character of the American people, but for the purpose of trying to protect or vindicate their character. I would to God that there was some feature that I could vindicate. There is no liberty here for me; there is no liberty for those with whom I am associated; there is no liberty for the American Slave; and yet we hear a great deal about liberty! How do the people of the Old World regard the American people? Only a short time since, an American gentleman, in travelling through Germany, passed the window of a bookstore where he saw a number of pictures. One of them was a cut representing an American Slave on his knees, with chains upon his limbs. Over him stood a white man, with a long whip; and underneath was written, "the latest specimen of American democracy." I ask my audience, who placed that in the hands of those that drew it? It was the people of the United States. Slavery, as it is to be found in this country, has given the serfs of the Old World an opportunity of branding the American people as the most tyrannical people upon God's footstool.

Only a short time since an American man-of-war was anchored in the bay opposite Liverpool. The English came down by hundreds and thousands. The stars and stripes were flying; and there stood those poor persons that had never seen an American man-of-war, but had heard a great deal of American democracy. Some were eulogising the American people; some were calling it the "land of the free and the home of the brave." And while they stood there, one of their number rose up, and pointing his fingers to the American flag, said:

"United States, your banner wears
Two emblems,—one of fame;
Alas, the other that it bears,

Reminds us of your shame.
The white man's liberty entyped,
Stands blazoned by your stars;
But what's the meaning of your stripes?
They mean your Negro-scars."

What put that in the mouth of that individual? It was the system of American Slavery; it was the action of the American people; the inconsistency of the American people; their profession of liberty, and their practice in opposition to their profession.

I find that the time admonishes me that I am going on too far; but when I got upon this subject, and find myself surrounded by those who are willing to listen, and who seem to sympathise with my downtrodden countrymen, I feel that I have a great duty to discharge. No matter what the people may say upon this subject; no matter what they may say against the great Anti-Slavery movement of this country; I believe it is the Anti-Slavery movement that is calculated to redeem the character of the American people. Much as I have said against the character of the American people this evening, I believe that it is the Anti-Slavery movement of this country that is to redeem its character. Nothing can redeem it but the principles that are advocated by the friends of the Slave in this country.

I look upon this as one of the highest and noblest movements of the age. William Lloyd Garrison, a few years since, planted the tree of Liberty, and that tree has taken root in all branches of Government. That tree was not planted for a day, a week, a month, or a year; but to stand still till the last chain should fall from the limbs of the last Slave in the United States of America, and in the world. It is a tree that will stand. Yes, it was planned of the very best plant that could be found among the great plants in the world.

"Our plant is of the cedar,
That knoweth, not decay;
Its growth shall bless the mountains.
Till mountains pass away;
Its top shall greet the sunshine,
Its leaves shall drink the rain,
While on its lower branches
The Slave shall hang his chain."

Yes, it is a plant that will stand. The living tree shall grow up and shall not only liberate the Slave in this country, but shall redeem the character of the American people.

The efforts of the American people not only to keep the Slaves in Slavery, but to add new territory, and to spread the institution of Slavery all over Christendom,—their high professions and their inconsistency, have done more to sadden the hearts of the reformers in the Old World than anything else that could have been thought of. The reformers and lovers of liberty in the Old World look to the American Government, look to the lovers of liberty in America, to aid them in knocking the chains from their own limbs in Europe, to aid them in elevating themselves; but instead of their receiving cooperation from the Government of the United States, instead of their being cheered on by the people of the United States, the people and the Government have done all that they could to oppose liberty, to oppose democracy, and to oppose reform.

Go to the capital of our country, the city of Washington; the capital of the freest government upon the face of the world. Only a few days since, an American mother and her daughter were sold upon the auction-block in that city, and the money was put into the Treasury of the United States of America. Go there and you can scarcely stand an hour but you will see caufles of Slaves driven past the Capitol, and likely as not you will see the foremost one with the stars and stripes in his hand; and yet the American Legislators, the people of the North and of the South, the "assembled wisdom" of the nation, look on and see such things and hold their peace; they say not a single word against such oppression, or in favor of liberty.

In conclusion let me say, that the character of the American people and the influence of Slavery upon that character have been blighting and withering the efforts of all those that favor liberty, reform, and progression. But it has not quite accomplished it. There are those who are willing to stand by the Slave. I look upon the great Anti-Slavery platform as one upon which those who stand, occupy the same position,—I would say, a higher position, than those who put forth their Declaration in 1776, in behalf of American liberty. Yes, the American Abolitionists now occupy a higher and holier position than those who carried on the American Revolution. They do not want that the husband should be any longer sold from his wife. They want that the husband should have a right to protect his wife; that the brother should have a right to protect his sister.

They are tired and sick at heart in seeing human beings placed upon the auction-block and sold to the highest bidder. They want that man should be protected. They want that a stop should be put to this system of iniquity and bloodshed; and they are laboring for its overthrow.

I would that every one here could go into the Slave-States, could go where I have been, and see the workings of Slavery upon the Slave. When I get to talking upon this subject I am carried back to the day when I saw a dear mother chained and carried off in a Southern steamboat to supply the cotton, sugar, or rice plantations of the South. I am carried back to the day when a dear sister was sold and carried off in my presence. I stood and looked at her. I could not protect her. I could not offer to protect her. I was a Slave, and the only testimony that I could give her that I sympathised with her, was to allow the tears to flow freely down my cheeks; and the tears flowing freely down her cheeks told me that my affection was reciprocated. I am carried back to the day when I saw three dear brothers sold, and carried off.

When I speak of Slavery I am carried back to the time when I saw, day after day, my own fellow-countrymen placed upon the auction-stand; when I saw the bodies, and sinews, and hearts, and the souls of men sold to the highest bidder. I have with me an account of a Slave recently sold upon the auction-stand. The auctioneer could only get a bid of $400, but as he was about to knock her off, the owner of the Slave made his way through those that surrounded him and whispered to the auctioneer. As soon as the owner left, the auctioneer said, "I have failed to tell you all the good qualities of this Slave. I have told you that she was strong, healthy, and hearty, and now I have the pleasure to announce to you that she

Glossary

ad infinitum	Latin for "without end or limit"
Bey of Tunis	the ruler of an Islamic country, Tunisia, on the north coast of Africa
Canadas	the various provinces that would later form the nation of Canada
Cape Cod and Cape Ann	peninsulas off the coast of Massachusetts that provided harbor
caufles	droves, or herds of animals such as cattle
Ind	India
inst.	short for "instant," meaning "in the present month"
liberty-pole	a tall wooden pole often used as a flagstaff
N.O. Pic.	the New Orleans *Picayune* newspaper
Nicholas of Russia	Czar Nicholas I, who ruled from 1825 to 1855
"Our plant is of the cedar…"	from a contemporary song called "The Liberty Party"
"Shall every flap of England's flag…"	an excerpt from "Our Countrymen in Chains!", a poem by John Greenleaf Whittier published in 1837
Solon	a lawgiver and legal reformer in ancient Athens
"United States, your banner wears…"	from a poem by Thomas Campbell, a Scottish poet
Virginius	a centurion in the ancient Roman Republic who killed his daughter Virginia to protect her from slavery and from the lust of Appius Claudius Crassus, a Roman ruler
William Lloyd Garrison	noted abolitionist and publisher of *The Liberator*, an abolitionist newspaper

is very pious. She has got religion." And although, before that, he could only get $400, as soon as they found she had got religion they commenced bidding upon her, and the bidding went up to $700. The writer says that her body and mind were sold $400, and her religion was sold for $300. My friends, I am aware that there are people at the North who would sell their religion for a $5 bill, and make money on it; and that those who purchased it would get very much cheated in the end. But the piety of the Slave differs from the piety of the people in the nominally free States. The piety of the Slave is to be a good servant.

This is a subject in which I ask your cooperation. I hope that every individual here will take hold and help carry on the Anti-Slavery movement. We are not those who would ask the men to help us and leave the women at home. We want all to help us. A million of women are in Slavery, and as long as a single woman is in Slavery, every woman in the community should raise her voice against that sin, that crying evil that is degrading her sex. I look to the rising generation. I expect that the rising generation will liberate the Slave. I do not look to the older ones. I have sometimes thought that the sooner we got rid of the older ones the better it would be. The older ones have got their old prejudices, and their old associations, and they cling to them, and seem not to look at the Slave or to care anything about him.

Now, fellow-citizens, when you shall return home, and be scattered around your several firesides, and when you have an opportunity to make a remark about what I have said here this evening, all I ask of you is to give the cause, justice; to give what I have said, justice. Give it a fair investigation. If you have not liked my grammar, recollect that I was born and brought up under an institution, where, if I an individual was found teaching me, he would have been sent to the State's Prison. Recollect that I was brought up where I had not the privilege of education. Recollect that you have come here to-night to hear a Slave, and not a man, according to the laws of the land; and if the Slave has failed to interest you, charge it not the race, charge it not to the colored people, but charge it to the blighting influences of Slavery,—that institution that has made me property, and that is making property of three millions of my countrymen at the present day. Charge it upon that institution that is annihilating the minds of three millions of my countrymen. Charge it upon that institution, whether found in the political arena or in the American churches. Charge it upon that institution, cherished by the American people, and looked upon as the essence of Democracy,—upon American Slavery.

Illustration of Frederick Douglass speaking in England on his experiences as a slave (AP/Wide World Photos)

First Editorial of the *North Star*

"It is evident we must be our own representatives and advocates."

Overview

Frederick Douglass, well-known abolitionist and civil rights activist, edited three newspapers between 1847 and 1863. The first was the *North Star*, an antislavery paper in which he and other African American reformers (along with some whites) expressed their views; it began publishing as a weekly on December 3, 1847, at Rochester, New York. In 1841, Douglass, an escaped slave, had begun acting as a lecturer for white-dominated antislavery societies. William Lloyd Garrison, the most prominent abolitionist in America, brought Douglass into his circle of reformers, where he proved to be a quick study. Garrison was also the most radical of the abolitionists, demanding an immediate, complete, and uncompensated end to slavery. Garrison and his followers rejected the U.S. Constitution as a proslavery document and urged all to avoid organized religion because most denominations had ties to southern churches that openly supported slavery. Although Douglass initially adopted all the arguments of the Garrisonians, his travels and intellectual development led him to question the effectiveness of their positions. Initiating his own newspaper and physically moving away from New England allowed Douglass to develop independent views on many reform issues.

Context

Nineteenth-century reformers relied extensively on print media to spread their message that slavery was morally wrong. Many national and regional antislavery organizations had their own weekly newspapers that incorporated editorials, fiction, poetry, and letters to the editor describing the abolitionist campaign. The most successful were edited by white abolitionists in northeastern cities such as Boston and New York. In 1842 Douglass acted as a correspondent for several newspapers, including Garrison's *Liberator* and the *National Anti-Slavery Standard*, the official organ of the American Anti-Slavery Society, based in New York City. During the years Douglass lectured (1841–1847), his letters to the editor informed readers of abolitionist activities and sentiments across the northern states. He gained considerable skill as a writer, along with a desire to publish his own newspaper, which would allow for the expression of the black reform perspective.

In Douglass's evolving view, black elevation was intimately tied to the abolition movement. He sought to expand his involvement with his race peers. In the 1830s, African American abolitionists and civil rights activists began gathering in a series of so-called National Negro Conventions aimed at directing action toward issues that would uplift or elevate their position in society. In addition to the abolition of slavery, attention was given to ending racial discrimination and gaining the right to vote in states where black suffrage rights were denied or restricted. Douglass became a strong leader of this movement in the late 1840s, especially after traveling abroad and experiencing a distinct lack of prejudice in Europe.

Following the publication of his 1845 autobiography, *Narrative of the Life of Frederick Douglass, an American Slave, Written by Himself*, Douglass left the United States for an extended speaking tour of Great Britain and Ireland. During his time abroad he acquired an international reputation as an orator and leader in the movement to end American slavery. While he was overseas, British reformers raised funds to purchase Douglass's freedom from his slave master, Hugh Auld. Upon receiving a deed of emancipation, Douglass returned to the United States a free man. He also returned with a substantial sum of money donated to help him start an independent newspaper.

Douglass arrived back in the United States in April 1847 and, along with William Lloyd Garrison, soon began a lengthy lecture tour of western states, including Ohio. Douglass continued on the lecture circuit alone when Garrison fell ill at Cleveland, never mentioning to his close friend and mentor that he planned to move to Rochester, New York, to begin publishing the *North Star*. Garrison was less than supportive when he learned of Douglass's plans, for two reasons. Douglass's relocation to Rochester and engagement in editing a weekly newspaper would necessarily reduce the time he could be expected to lecture on behalf of Garrison's American Anti-Slavery Society. More ominously, Garrison feared that the *North Star* would be potential competition for his own weekly abolitionist news-

Time Line

1818
- **February**
  Frederick Douglass is born a slave on a farm in Talbot County, Maryland.

1838
- **September 3**
  Douglass boards a train in Baltimore, Maryland, and escapes from slavery.

1841
- **August**
  Douglass is invited to address an antislavery meeting in Nantucket, Massachusetts. Afterward he is hired as a field lecturer for the Massachusetts Anti-Slavery Society.

1845
- **May**
  Douglass's first autobiography, *Narrative of the Life of Frederick Douglass, an American Slave, Written by Himself*, is published.

1845–1847
- Douglass travels to Great Britain and Ireland as an abolitionist lecturer and raises money to start his own newspaper.

1846–1848
- The Mexican-American War adds approximately five hundred thousand square miles of territory to the United States and sparks debate over the extension of slavery.

1847
- **December 3**
  The first issue of the weekly *North Star* is published from Douglass's base of Rochester, New York.

1850
- **September**
  Congress passes the Compromise of 1850, which includes a new and stricter fugitive slave law.

paper. Beginning publication in January 1831, Garrison's weekly, *The Liberator* was soon the most widely circulated reform paper in the northern states. Despite the reaction of Garrison and others in Boston, abolitionists and reformers in Rochester offered considerable encouragement and support for Douglass's venture.

A number of factors influenced Douglass's choice of cities from which to publish the paper. The region of western New York in which Rochester is located was an important center of reform activity, often referred to as the "Burned-over District" because of the intense religious fervor during the Second Great Awakening of the 1820s and 1830s. This Protestant religious reawakening inspired many to get involved in reform movements, including that for the abolition of slavery. Rochester was also known as the last stop for fugitive slaves traveling the Underground Railroad to Canada. Douglass had passed through the region during a lecture tour in 1842 and befriended a number of families in Rochester's reform community. Rochester was also far removed from the circle of abolitionists in New England, and especially Boston, which had influenced his early career as an abolitionist. The city appealed to Douglass as he sought a place to express his independent voice and brand of reform, which incorporated a push for black civil rights as well as the abolition of slavery.

The somewhat unenthusiastic response of Garrison and his followers for Douglass's newspaper venture made support from the African American community crucial to achieving his goal. Douglass's autonomy and the potential for his newspaper's successful launch grew more certain after he encountered Martin R. Delany, a Pittsburgh physician and editor of the *Mystery*, the most widely circulated reform paper edited by an African American west of the Allegheny Mountains. The two met during Douglass's western tour in the summer of 1847. Unlike most of Douglass's Garrisonian colleagues, Delany was first and foremost a black reformer, who as early as the 1830s flirted with the notion that blacks could succeed only if they left the United States. Although Delany and Douglass would famously argue over African colonization by blacks from the United States and over Harriet Beecher Stowe's novel *Uncle Tom's Cabin* in the 1850s, in 1847 they were two black activists of like mind. Douglass's newspaper would be an opportunity for Douglass to explore his own views on moral reform and incorporate self-improvement and black uplift, serving as an expression of his newfound independence. Delany was the perfect partner to lend a hand in this transition. An experienced editor, Delany agreed to help launch the *North Star*, and his name would appear on the masthead as coeditor until June 1849.

Two months before initiating the *North Star*, Douglass attended a black convention held at Troy, New York. The convention raised Douglass's awareness of the most pressing issues of debate among black intellectuals, including the establishment of independent colleges for blacks, fostering business and commerce, black suffrage, and a prominent presence for the black press. In a report submitted by a committee headed by the African American physician

James McCune Smith, the convention called for a national press that would promote the interests of African Americans in the North as well as advocate for the abolition of slavery. Considering Douglass was in the midst of plans for the *North Star*, he must have been pleased with this discussion. He entertained thoughts that his paper would become the national organ Smith called for at the convention. In the first issue of his paper, Douglass expressed a similar desire for the African American reform voice to be heard.

About the Author

Frederick Augustus Washington Bailey was born in a slave cabin at the Holme Hill Farm in Talbot County, Maryland, in February 1818. Later changing his name to Frederick Douglass, he became renowned as a civil rights activist and eternal opponent of slavery. He spent twenty years in slavery, first on Maryland's Eastern Shore and then in the shipbuilding city of Baltimore. During his years in bondage, he was the property of two men, first Aaron Anthony, who may have been his father, and then Thomas Auld, who inherited Douglass in the distribution of Anthony's estate. He learned to read and write with the assistance of one of his owners and from white youths with whom he traded food for lessons. His favorite lesson book was *The Columbian Orator*, a collection of famous speeches, which helped him develop his skill as a public speaker. When he was twenty, Douglass borrowed identity papers from a free black sailor and, on September 3, 1838, boarded a train to freedom in the North.

Douglass was assisted in his escape by Anna Murray, a free black woman from Baltimore. He was reunited with her when he reached New York City, and on September 15, 1838, the two were married. They settled in New Bedford, Massachusetts, where he hoped to find employment as a caulker. However, racial segregation was more evident in the shipyards of New Bedford than in Baltimore, where whites and blacks often worked side by side. Douglass worked for three years in the only job he could find, as a stevedore loading and unloading cargo from the harbor's ships. He also began to read antislavery newspapers and interact with the abolitionist community. In August 1841 he was invited to address an abolitionist meeting on Nantucket Island in Massachusetts, where he detailed his personal experience in slavery. Soon after, he was hired as an antislavery lecturer by the Massachusetts Anti-Slavery Society and toured New England and the western states with other abolitionists. Among his new associates was William Lloyd Garrison, publisher of the antislavery weekly, *The Liberator*, and the most prominent white abolitionist in the North.

Douglass became an accomplished lecturer and the most recognized black abolitionist of the pre–Civil War era. In 1845 he published his first autobiography, *Narrative of the Life of Frederick Douglass, an American Slave, Written by Himself*. To dispel the criticism of those who did not believe that he had ever been enslaved, Douglass departed from the common practice of slave narrative authors of hiding

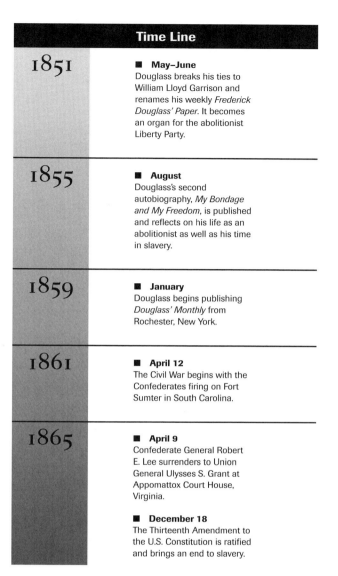

Time Line

1851
■ **May–June**
Douglass breaks his ties to William Lloyd Garrison and renames his weekly *Frederick Douglass' Paper*. It becomes an organ for the abolitionist Liberty Party.

1855
■ **August**
Douglass's second autobiography, *My Bondage and My Freedom*, is published and reflects on his life as an abolitionist as well as his time in slavery.

1859
■ **January**
Douglass begins publishing *Douglass' Monthly* from Rochester, New York.

1861
■ **April 12**
The Civil War begins with the Confederates firing on Fort Sumter in South Carolina.

1865
■ **April 9**
Confederate General Robert E. Lee surrenders to Union General Ulysses S. Grant at Appomattox Court House, Virginia.

■ **December 18**
The Thirteenth Amendment to the U.S. Constitution is ratified and brings an end to slavery.

their own identity and disguising names and locations. His autobiography named his slave owner and described events, including his torture and that of other slaves, and locations and individuals with whom he had interacted as a slave in Maryland. Because he was still legally a fugitive slave at the time of the *Narrative*'s publication, and thus subject to capture and return to Maryland, Douglass was advised to put himself out of harm's way abroad. He embarked on a lengthy tour of Great Britain and Ireland, traveling in the company of other American and British reformers and gaining an international reputation as America's most famous fugitive slave. He experienced significantly less discrimination and had the opportunity to meet activists involved in a variety of causes in addition to the abolition of slavery.

British reformers raised funds to purchase Douglass's freedom and permit his return to the United States. Following the publication of Douglass's autobiography, Thomas Auld transferred ownership of Douglass to his brother Hugh Auld for the sum of $100. The reformers Anna and Henry Richardson negotiated the purchase of Douglass's

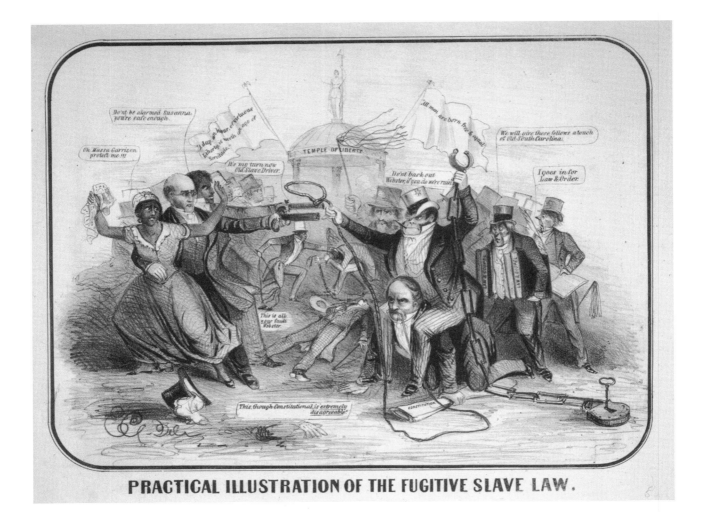

PRACTICAL ILLUSTRATION OF THE FUGITIVE SLAVE LAW.

A satire on the antagonism between northern abolitionists and supporters of enforcement of the Fugitive Slave Act of 1850 (Library of Congress)

freedom for the sum of £150 sterling, or approximately $711.66 in U.S. currency. A combination of British and American abolitionists coordinated the purchase, and Hugh Auld filed Douglass's manumission papers in Baltimore County, Maryland, on December 5, 1846. On that date, more than eight years after leaving slavery, Douglass legally became a free man.

Douglass's reform colleagues in Britain were also eager to aid in his aspirations to begin his own antislavery paper. Fund-raising in England raised $2,175. When this money was combined with the money contributed by reformers in other areas of Britain and Ireland, Douglass left for home with almost $4,000 to begin operation of his weekly antislavery newspaper the *North Star*. Returning to the United States in the spring of 1847, Douglass moved his family to Rochester, New York, and began publication on December 3. He continued to lecture on the evils of slavery but broke away from his association with Garrison in 1851 to pursue a brand of antislavery activism that embraced politics. He renamed the weekly *Frederick Douglass' Paper* and made it

an organ for the antislavery Liberty Party. In contrast to the Garrisonians, who rejected politics and condemned the Constitution as a proslavery document, Douglass came to associate with politically active abolitionists first in the Liberty Party and then in the Free Soil and Republican Parties.

Douglass continued to advocate for civil rights and the abolition of slavery. During the Civil War, he acted as an army recruiter and saw two of his sons enlist in the famed Fifty-Fourth Massachusetts Infantry unit. He was twice invited to the White House to advise President Abraham Lincoln on the participation of African Americans in the Union war effort. In 1872, Douglass moved his family to Washington, D.C., where he served briefly as president of the Freedman's Savings Bank in 1874. He subsequently held minor political appointments as a U.S. marshal and as recorder of deeds for the District of Columbia. In 1889, President Benjamin Harrison appointed him as resident minister and consul general (ambassador) to Haiti. Douglass died at Cedar Hill, his home in Washington, D.C., on February 20, 1895.

"It has long been our anxious wish to see, in this slave-holding, slave-trading, and negro-hating land, a printing-press and paper, permanently established, under the complete control and direction of the immediate victims of slavery and oppression."

(Paragraph 1)

"It is evident we must be our own representatives and advocates, not exclusively, but peculiarly—not distinct from, but in connection with our white friends."

(Paragraph 4)

"Nine years ago, as most of our readers are aware, we were held as a slave, shrouded in the midnight ignorance of that infernal system—sunken in the depths of servility and degradation—registered with four footed beasts and creeping things—regarded as property.... By a singular combination of circumstances we finally succeeded in escaping from the grasp of the man who claimed us as his property."

(Paragraph 6)

Explanation and Analysis of the Document

In his inaugural editorial, Douglass outlines his reasons for starting his own newspaper. In the first paragraph he notes that he has long desired to see a newspaper edited from the perspective of the former slave. Although there had been a number of African American newspapers, beginning with *Freedom's Journal* in 1827, most had been short-lived, and all had been headed by men who were born free. Douglass believed that as a former slave he could offer a unique position on both the antislavery movement and the civil rights issues that concerned black Americans.

The second paragraph establishes that the *North Star* was operating out of offices in the central business district of Rochester. Douglass was not trained as a printer, so he planned to rely on local skilled artisans to assist with the actual printing of his weekly. In fact, it turned out that the printing equipment Douglass purchased was inadequate, and the *North Star* contracted with a local printing firm to produce its weekly paper. Douglass expresses optimism

that the newspaper would be well received, noting that a steady number of subscriptions had come in and that he had engaged many individuals to contribute letters and editorials. It was common for abolitionists to act as reporting agents, writing letters of their experiences on the lecture circuit. These abolitionists also acted as field agents, gathering subscriptions for the newspapers. The first issue of Douglass's paper counted agents in nine states, from New York to Michigan.

Douglass next turns to circumstances surrounding the tension between white and black abolitionists. Douglass states that his desire to start his own antislavery newspaper stems from his ability as a black reformer to address the particular concerns of African Americans in American society. In paragraph 4, he argues that as a former slave, he is the best qualified to advocate for the abolition of the institution. Although Douglass was a strong advocate of an integrated society and of blacks and whites working together for the abolition of slavery, he began to seek a way to make his unique voice heard. When Douglass took up antislavery lecturing for Garrisonian organizations in 1841, those groups were dominated by white reformers, especially, of course, by William Lloyd Garrison. Since Douglass was one of the few lecturers who could attest to the evils of slavery based on personal experience, antislavery societies wanted him to focus and limit his orations to telling his personal story. However, within a few years of gaining his freedom, Douglass had expanded his knowledge and wanted to express his thoughts and opinions on a wider variety of issues related to abolition and society at large. He came to resent that he was used essentially as an exhibit to show northern audiences that slavery was real and required their attention.

One reason that Douglass wrote his first autobiography in 1845 at the age of twenty-seven was to refute the common accusation that a man with such poise and eloquence could not possibly have been a slave. As he traveled the lecture circuit and read widely in literature and history, Douglass longed to engage with men and women outside the circle of Garrisonian abolitionists who had been his almost constant companions. This editorial expresses his ambivalence about angering the white abolitionists with whom he had worked so closely for more than six years. Although he became more engaged with black reformers and a civil rights agenda, Douglass always valued integrated reform activity.

Since many white abolitionists did not have a personal stake in seeing an end to racial discrimination, they were also not as committed to black civil rights as were black reformers. For this reason, even though most black abolitionists still affiliated with integrated organizations such as the American Anti-Slavery Society, they formed other associations to focus on specific economic concerns, to increase educational opportunities, and to gain full and equal suffrage. While Douglass rarely wavered in his belief that slavery could be overcome only through the actions of an integrated force of reformers, his involvement in the National Negro Convention movement increasingly influenced his belief that African Americans needed to be more than token examples of the wrongness of slavery. In paragraph 4 he argues that the struggle to end slavery requires strong black orators, editors, and authors. Since he filled all of those roles, Douglass saw himself and his newspaper as the appropriate extension and example of racial activism.

African American newspapers had little success before the *North Star*. Most were very short-lived, and none was profitable. The editorial addresses this issue in the fifth paragraph. By the time Douglass began publishing his weekly, there had been at least nine newspapers edited by African Americans. The first of these, *Freedom's Journal*, was published in New York from 1827 to 1829 by John Russwurm and Samuel Cornish. New York City was the location for five additional black publications in the early nineteenth century, all of which eventually failed. After Cornish's first newspaper failed when his partnership dissolved, he issued the *Rights of All* in 1829. He partnered with Phillip Bell and Charles B. Ray in the short-lived *Weekly Advocate* (1837) and in the *Colored American* (1837–1841). David Ruggles tried his hand with the *Mirror of Liberty* (1838–1840) and starting in 1843 Thomas Van Rensselaer edited the *Ram's Horn*, which failed in 1848. In Philadelphia, the *National Reformer* was edited by William Whipper, and the *Northern Star and Freedmen's Advocate* was briefly edited at Albany, New York, by Stephen Myers. Douglass's partner, Martin R. Delany, edited the *Mystery* from Pittsburgh beginning in 1843. Both the *Mystery* and the *Ram's Horn* were in publication at the time Douglass began the *North Star*. William Lloyd Garrison, himself the longtime editor of *The Liberator*, and others had warned Douglass of the uncertainty of success in a newspaper venture. Although Douglass edited a newspaper continuously from 1847 until 1863, he always struggled financially to keep his business solvent and often relied on donations from wealthy abolitionists for business expenses. Despite the risks, Douglass's editorial makes clear that the *North Star* aimed to demonstrate that a black newspaper could be successful. He noted that the venture was risky but that he was resolved to move forward.

In the final paragraph, Douglass shares part of his life history, demonstrating how fortunate he was to escape from slavery and to be in a position to edit a newspaper. A mere nine years earlier he had been a slave, "shrouded in the midnight ignorance of that infernal system" and with a "spirit crushed and broken." Settling in New Bedford, Massachusetts, he worked for three years as a "daily laborer" until he was hired as a full-time antislavery lecturer. He speaks of having embarked for England, under "the apprehension of being re-taken into bondage." Douglass then describes the aid provided by his friends in England for both gaining his freedom and starting his newspaper. Now, "urged on in our enterprise by a sense of duty to God and man," he believes "that our effort will be crowned with entire success."

Audience

The first editorial and edition of the *North Star* was aimed at those who knew Douglass well and readers newly acquainted with his reform activities. The readers of Douglass's *North Star* were generally drawn from the abolitionist and reform community. Douglass intended that the newspaper would be an organ for black abolitionists and especially for the expression of his own evolving brand of reform, which incorporated both activities on behalf of ending slavery and bringing an end to the racial discrimination African Americans faced in northern states. Subscribers to the *North Star*, which was distributed through the U.S. mail, lived across the northern states, but most were concentrated in New York and the New England states. A few subscribers lived in the United Kingdom and Ireland.

Impact

The success of Frederick Douglass's newspaper proved to be long-lasting. The *North Star* reached a wider audience than earlier black-edited newspapers for several reasons. At the time of its inception in 1847, Douglass had gained a reputation as America's most famous former slave, both in the United States and abroad. His *Narrative of the Life of Frederick Douglass* was published in several editions including editions in England and Ireland. His name attracted many subscribers in both the white and the African American reform community. Between 1846 and 1850, the nation's attention was drawn into a debate over the extension of slavery. The Mexican-American War (1846–1848) added an additional five hundred thousand square miles to the United States, and many southerners favored the expansion of slavery into the new territories. Abolitionists hotly opposed any new slave states. The *North Star* began in the midst of this war and was poised to offer a unique black perspective on the Wilmot Proviso, which opposed the extension of slavery in territories obtained from the war. The growing interest in slavery among northerners during the controversy surrounding the Fugitive Slave Act and other parts of the Compromise of 1850 also served to keep readers interested in reading antislavery papers. The Fugitive Slave Act focused the attention of many northerners on slavery for the first time, as the law required more active participation among northerners in the return of fugitive slaves. Douglass benefited from starting his weekly on the cusp of this controversy.

As this first *North Star* editorial demonstrates, the weekly created a special place for African American abolitionists and civil rights activists to express their own methods and solutions to the problems that faced the black race.

Douglass's increasing involvement in the movement for black elevation was reflected in the pages of the *North Star*. His editorials calling for suffrage, opposing colonization, and supporting equal rights established Douglass as a leader among African Americans. Quoting his favorite line from Lord Byron's *Childe Harold's Pilgrimage*, "Hereditary bondsmen? know ye not, / Who would be free, themselves must strike the blow?" Douglass urged African Americans to work actively on behalf of their race. Although Douglass has sometimes been criticized for his commitment to assimilation and integration, his editorials began warning against relying on white reformers to advance the cause of African Americans.

Douglass's editing career started with the *North Star*'s first issue on December 3, 1847, and stretched longer than that of other African American editors. He continuously edited a newspaper from 1847 until 1863, and during that time his stature grew in the African American community. As slavery moved into the mainstream national debate in the 1850s, Douglass was almost universally recognized as both America's most famous former slave and its most prominent black abolitionist. Douglass published the *North Star* until 1851, when his changing political views led him to rename his weekly *Frederick Douglass' Paper*. Until 1860, Douglass's newspaper filled an important role as an organ for the Liberty Party and was a strong advocate for the Free Soil movement and those who sought political means to

Questions for Further Study

1. Why do you believe Douglass came to question the views of the abolitionist William Lloyd Garrison and move away to more independent positions? To what extent did this fissure represent a broader fissure between white and black abolitionists?

2. Many, if not virtually all, abolitionist tracts and newspapers were published in the northern states (such as New York and Massachusetts), where slavery was no longer practiced. This was particularly the case in Rochester, New York, where abolitionist sentiment was already strong. How effective would these publications have been in the South, where opinions about slavery had to be changed?

3. Frederick Douglass is arguably the most famous abolitionist from this era, one whose name is still widely recognized. Why do you believe he was able to attain this stature?

4. In the modern era, Douglass is regarded as important not only as an abolitionist but also as a man of letters. His writings are regarded as an important part of American literature from the nineteenth century, alongside the more literary works of Edgar Allan Poe, Herman Melville, Nathaniel Hawthorne, and others. Why do you think his writings are held in such regard?

5. What impact did the Mexican-American War and the Wilmot Proviso have on Douglass and on the abolition movement? Why?

end slavery. Beginning in January 1859, Douglass began a new monthly publication, *Douglass' Monthly*, which freed him from weekly editing tasks but still offered readers his own brand of reform journalism. He continued this publication until the middle of the Civil War in 1863, when he began actively recruiting African American troops to fight for the Union cause. Douglass rejoiced in December 1865 when ratification of the Thirteenth Amendment to the Constitution formally ended slavery in the United States.

See also Slavery Clauses in the U.S. Constitution (1787); William Lloyd Garrison's First *Liberator* Editorial (1831); Frederick Douglass's "What to the Slave Is the Fourth of July?" (1852); Thirteenth Amendment to the U.S. Constitution (1865)

Further Reading

■ Books

Blassingame, John, et al., eds. *The Frederick Douglass Papers*, Series 2: *Autobiographical Writings*, Volume 2: *My Bondage and My Freedom*. New Haven, Conn.: Yale University Press, 2003.

Douglass, Frederick. *Narrative of the Life of Frederick Douglass, an American Slave*, ed. John W. Blassingame et al. New Haven, Conn.: Yale University Press, 2001.

Hutton, Frankie. *The Early Black Press in America, 1827 to 1860*. Westport, Conn.: Greenwood Press, 1993.

McFeely, William S. *Frederick Douglass*. New York: W. W. Norton, 1995.

Pride, Armistead Scott, and Clint C. Wilson. *A History of the Black Press*. Washington, D.C.: Howard University Press, 1997.

■ Web Sites

"The Frederick Douglass Papers" Library of Congress "American Memory" Web site.
    http://memory.loc.gov/ammem/doughtml/doughome.html.

—Diane Barnes

FIRST EDITORIAL OF THE *NORTH STAR*

Our Paper and Its Prospects

We are now about to assume the management of the editorial department of a newspaper, devoted to the cause of Liberty, Humanity and Progress. The position is one which, with the purest motives, we have long desired to occupy. It has long been our anxious wish to see, in this slave-holding, slave-trading, and negro-hating land, a printing-press and paper, permanently established, under the complete control and direction of the immediate victims of slavery and oppression.

Animated by this intense desire, we have pursued our object, till on the threshold of obtaining it. Our press and printing materials are bought, and paid for. Our office secured, and is well situated, in the centre of business, in this enterprising city. Our office Agent, an industrious and amiable young man, thoroughly devoted to the interests of humanity, has already entered upon his duties. Printers well recommended have offered their services, and are ready to work as soon as we are prepared for the regular publication of our paper. Kind friends are rallying round us, with words and deeds of encouragement. Subscribers are steadily, if not rapidly coming in, and some of the best minds in the country are generously offering to lend us the powerful aid of their pens. The sincere wish of our heart, so long and so devoutly cherished seems now upon the eve of complete realization.

It is scarcely necessary for us to say that our desire to occupy our present position at the head of an Anti-Slavery Journal, has resulted from no unworthy distrust or ungrateful want of appreciation of the zeal, integrity, or ability of the noble band of white laborers, in this department of our cause; but, from a sincere and settled conviction that such a Journal, if conducted with only moderate skill and ability, would do a most important and indispensable work, which would be wholly impossible for our white friends to do for us.

It is neither a reflection on the fidelity, nor a disparagement of the ability of our friends and fellow-laborers, to assert what "common sense affirms and only folly denies," that the man who has suffered the wrong is the man to demand redress,—that the man STRUCK is the man to CRY OUT—and that he who has endured the cruel pangs of Slavery is the man to advocate Liberty. It is evident we must be our own representatives and advocates, not exclusively, but peculiarly—not distinct from, but in connection with our white friends. In the grand struggle for liberty and equality now waging, it is meet, right and essential that there should arise in our ranks authors and editors, as well as orators, for it is in these capacities that the most permanent good can be rendered to our cause.

Hitherto the immediate victims of slavery and prejudice, owing to various causes, have had little share in this department of effort: they have frequently undertaken, and almost as frequently failed. This latter fact has often been urged by our friends against our engaging in the present enterprise; but, so far from convincing us of the impolicy of our course, it serves to confirm us in the necessity, if not the wisdom of our undertaking. That others have failed, is a reason for our earnestly endeavoring to succeed. Our race must be vindicated from the embarrassing imputations resulting from former non-success. We believe that what ought to be done, can be done. We say this, in no self-confident or boastful spirit, but with a full sense of our weakness and unworthiness, relying upon the Most High for wisdom and strength to support us in our righteous undertaking. We are not wholly unaware of the duties, hardships and responsibilities of our position. We have easily imagined some, and friends have not hesitated to inform us of others. Many doubtless are yet to be revealed by that infallible teacher, experience. A view of them solemnize, but do not appal us. We have counted the cost. Our mind is made up, and we are resolved to go forward.

In aspiring to our present position, the aid of circumstances has been so strikingly apparent as to almost stamp our humble aspirations with the solemn sanctions of a Divine Providence. Nine years ago, as most of our readers are aware, we were held as a slave, shrouded in the midnight ignorance of that infernal system—sunken in the depths of servility and degradation—registered with four footed beasts and creeping things—regarded as property—compelled to toil without wages—with a heart swollen with bitter anguish—and a spirit crushed and broken. By a singular combination of circumstances we finally succeeded in escaping from the grasp of the man who claimed us as his property, and succeeded in safely reaching New Bedford, Mass. In this town we worked three years as a daily laborer on the wharves. Six years ago we became a Lecturer on Slavery. Under the apprehension of being re-taken into bondage, two years ago we embarked for England. During our stay in that country, kind friends, anxious for our safety, ransomed us from slavery, by the payment of a large sum. The same friends, as unexpectedly as generously, placed in our hands the necessary means of purchasing a printing press and printing materials. Finding ourself now in a favorable position for aiming an important blow at slavery and prejudice, we feel urged on in our enterprise by a sense of duty to God and man, firmly believing that our effort will be crowned with entire success.

ROBERTS V. CITY OF BOSTON

"The plaintiff had access to a school, set apart for colored children."

Overview

The case of *Sarah C. Roberts v. The City of Boston* brought the first challenge to segregated schools in the United States. The case was argued before the Massachusetts Supreme Court in December 1849, and the court handed down its decision in April 1850. The case established the principle of "separate but equal" that was used to codify racial segregation in education and other aspects of public life for more than a century. *Roberts v. Boston* began with a movement to end the practice of separating white and black students in Boston's primary schools. Although the local body governing public education, the Boston School Committee, designated separate primary schools for African American students, Massachusetts state law did not prohibit integrated schools. In fact, in a number of Massachusetts cities and towns, black and white children attended the same schools.

The first African American school was opened as a private institution by members of Boston's black community in 1798, but it was assumed by the city's public school system in 1815. Housed for decades first in a private home and later in a church basement, this all-black segregated school was relaunched in its own building in 1835. By the 1840s, however, Boston's African Americans had petitioned the school committee several times to end the practice of segregating black students in separate schools. Changing attitudes led many African Americans to believe that integration was important and necessary for their children to succeed. Poor maintenance and substandard conditions at the segregated schools also led many in the black community to condemn the policy. As ground for abolishing segregation, the petitioners cited school committee regulations designating that students attend the school nearest their residence; many black children had to pass several whites-only schools before reaching the segregated schools to which they were assigned. The legal challenge brought in *Roberts v. Boston* was a carefully planned attack aimed at reversing the school committee's policy of segregation, part of a larger strategy to desegregate Boston schools.

Context

The struggle to provide quality education for their children was a longtime concern for Boston's African American community. At the turn of the nineteenth century many blacks believed that separate schools were necessary to ensure that their children were properly educated and not subjected to the sort of mistreatment likely to result in an integrated setting. The city's blacks actually initiated school segregation in 1798 with the creation of the independent, privately funded African School, which began operating in the private home of a local black leader. It moved to the basement of the African Baptist Church on Belknap Street in 1806 and became known as the Smith School after the white philanthropist Abiel Smith left the school a substantial endowment. By 1815 the school had come under the control of the Boston School Committee, making it eligible for partial but meager public funding. A portion of the Smith endowment was later used to construct a new facility for students, the Abiel Smith School on Joy Street in Boston, which opened its doors in 1835.

Deteriorating physical conditions in the African American school coincided with a shift in thought among members of the black community about segregated schooling. Blacks began calling for an end to segregation in other aspects of life, including the abolishment of separate Jim Crow cars on Massachusetts railroads. In 1846 Boston blacks debated the issue of segregated schools and subsequently submitted a petition demanding that the school committee close the Smith School and move toward full integration of the city's educational facilities. Not all members of the black community supported the integration movement, and a substantial number petitioned separately to have Thomas Paul, an African American, appointed as master of the Smith School. His appointment was confirmed by the school committee in September 1849—shortly before the Roberts case was argued before the Massachusetts Supreme Court—and over the next few years some integrationists established short-lived private protest schools, withdrawing their children from the Smith School. The Abiel Smith School was officially closed in 1855 and is now a National Trust Historic Site.

Time Line

1798
- Boston African Americans establish the first independent African School, later named the Smith School after the white philanthropist Abiel Smith.

1806
- The Smith School moves to the basement of the African Meeting House, also home to the African Baptist Church, on Belknap Street in Boston.

1815
- The Boston School Committee assumes control of the Smith School.

1835
- **March 3**
The newly constructed Abiel Smith School opens on Joy Street in Boston.

1845
- Massachusetts law provides that children unlawfully excluded from public school instruction may recover damages from the city or town supporting the public instruction.

1846
- African Americans petition the Boston School Committee demanding the abolition of segregated schools.

1847
- **April**
Five-year-old Sarah C. Roberts is denied a ticket of admission to the primary school nearest her home because of her color.

1848
- **February 15**
Sarah Roberts attempts to enter the all-white primary school nearest to her home and is "ejected from the school by the teacher." She must walk past five schools for whites before reaching the all-black Smith School on Belknap Street.

- Benjamin F. Roberts, Sarah's father, files suit, demanding that his daughter be admitted to the white school nearest her home.

Amid these divisions in the black community over the question of integration came the case of *Sarah C. Roberts v. The City of Boston*. The case stemmed from an all-white school's refusal to allow a black girl, Sarah Roberts, to officially enroll in and attend classes in its building. Her father, Benjamin Franklin Roberts, was the son of the active abolitionists Robert and Sarah Easton Roberts. He had been raised in the Boston free black community among strong advocates for racial equality and apprenticed as a shoemaker but found his career path in journalism. Roberts's writings appeared in William Lloyd Garrison's *Liberator* in the 1830s, and by April 1838 he began publishing his own weekly, the *Anti-Slavery Herald*. The paper's emphasis on African American economic concerns angered white abolitionists, who rescinded their initial support. The paper failed within six months of its inception. In 1843 Roberts opened a printing establishment in Boston, where he focused on printing pamphlets and books promoting black elevation and history. In the late 1840s Roberts began a legal campaign to enroll his daughter in a whites-only school. The Boston public school system generally mandated that students attend the school nearest their residence. The closest primary school to the Roberts home was approximately nine hundred feet away, yet Sarah was required to travel about a fifth of a mile farther and to pass five whites-only schools before reaching the segregated Abiel Smith School. Clearly, the backdrop of integrationist ideology in the 1840s figured prominently in Roberts's decision to file the discrimination case on behalf of his daughter.

About the Author

While they are not considered authors of the opinion, the attorneys Robert Morris and Charles Sumner represented Roberts in the case and so were responsible for crafting the arguments addressed by the Massachusetts court. Morris (1823–1882) was one of the first African Americans admitted to practice law in the United States, passing the Massachusetts bar exam in 1847. His first cases dealt with issues of civil rights, and it is not surprising that he was the legal counsel Benjamin Roberts and other Boston activists sought to initiate the case against the school committee. Although he deferred major argument to the more prominent Sumner, Morris's appearance in the case marked the first time an African American attorney appeared before the highest court of any state. Morris continued to advance his law career and worked as a member of the Boston vigilance committee to protect African Americans from prosecution under the Fugitive Slave Act of 1850. Later that decade he became a justice of the peace, and he continued to practice law in Massachusetts until his death in 1882.

Charles Sumner (1811–1874) served as the dominant voice in the Roberts case. A committed abolitionist and prominent Republican politician, Sumner hailed from a family of middle-class reformers in the Boston area. Having studied law with the Supreme Court justice Joseph Story, Sumner was elected to the U.S. Senate from Massachusetts in 1851, where he served continuously until his death in 1874. Sumner's outspoken opposition to the Kansas-Nebraska Act and the resulting tensions that erupted in the region in the mid-1850s prompted Congressman Preston Brooks of South Carolina to severely beat the senator with a cane on the floor of the Senate in May 1856. During his three-year absence following the attack, Sumner was hailed as a martyr in opposition to slavery. He returned to the Senate on the eve of the Civil War, where he pushed the Radical Republican agenda during the war and Reconstruction. Sumner remained one of the strongest advocates for the full civil rights of African Americans throughout his career.

Morris and Sumner prepared the argument for the Roberts case, but the decision of the Massachusetts Supreme Court was authored by Chief Justice Lemuel Shaw (1781–1861). An attorney and jurist from a prominent Massachusetts family, Shaw was educated at Harvard before reading law under David Everett. Admitted to the bar in both New Hampshire and Massachusetts in 1804, he practiced law in Boston before entering politics. Shaw was elected to the Massachusetts house (1811–1815, 1820–1821, and 1829), served as state senator (1821–1822), and wrote the first city charter for Boston in 1822. He became the commonwealth's chief justice on August 30, 1830, holding the position until his retirement in August 1860.

The politically conservative Shaw dominated the state supreme court during his tenure as chief. His decisions, widely cited throughout the nation, influenced the direction of railroad development, industrialization, and labor and race relations. His rulings on cases involving issues of race were varied. In *Commonwealth v. Aves* (1836)—citing British precedent, the Massachusetts constitution, and even the Declaration of Independence—he determined that a slave girl brought into Massachusetts was free. In subsequent years, he was less likely to offer fugitive slaves protection; after the passage of the Fugitive Slave Law of 1850, he twice refused to intervene in cases involving fugitives.

Shaw's decision to uphold the practice of segregating schools in the city of Boston fell in line with his record of conservative rulings. He argued that segregated schools neither caused nor encouraged racial prejudice. Although the Massachusetts legislature prohibited segregated schools within the state in 1855, Shaw's decision in *Roberts v. Boston* was far-reaching, establishing the concept of "separate but equal," which was used to justify segregation until the middle 1950s. Shaw resigned from the state supreme court in August 1860 and died seven months later.

Explanation and Analysis of the Document

The text of the opinion in the case of *Sarah C. Roberts v. The City of Boston* outlines the legal position of the Boston School Committee and the argument made on the plaintiff's behalf by her attorney Charles Sumner. Initially, the case was argued before the Suffolk County Court of Common Pleas; it was later brought before the Massachusetts Supreme Court on appeal.

Time Line

1849

■ **December 4**
Attorneys Robert Morris and Charles Sumner argue the case of *Sarah C. Roberts v. The City of Boston* before the Supreme Court of Massachusetts.

1850

■ **April 8**
Massachusetts supreme court justice Lemuel Shaw denies Roberts's petition and upholds the practice of school segregation in Boston's public schools.

1855

■ The Massachusetts legislature bans school segregation and the Abiel Smith School closes.

◆ **Statement of Facts from the Court of Common Pleas**

The beginning of the document recaps the initial court case concerning Sarah Roberts, beginning with the line: "The case was submitted to the court of common pleas, from whence it came to this court by appeal, upon the following statement of facts." The next several paragraphs offer an overview of the case and outline the policies and regulations of the primary school committee charged with overseeing the education of Boston youths from four to seven years of age. Sarah Roberts's father, Benjamin F. Roberts, brought suit against the city of Boston, alleging his daughter was excluded from attending the public school nearest her home because she was black. The text notes that Boston's public school system was divided into twenty-one districts, but these districts were not necessarily created on the basis of geography. An exception to the rule that students attend the school closest to their residence was made for students attending Latin and English high schools. Thereby, the city established that it was not entirely unusual for students to go to a school other than the one nearest their residence, including schools designated for special populations, among them, African Americans.

The court heard evidence detailing Roberts's attempts to enroll in the whites-only primary schools nearest her home. Boston school regulations required that an enrolling student obtain an admissions ticket from a member of the school committee. Sarah Roberts's request was denied first by an individual committee member and also by the wider primary school committee. Both denials were made on the basis of her race. Despite the fact that she had no ticket, Sarah Roberts attempted to attend the school nearest her home on February 15, 1848, but was turned away by the teacher. The evidence presented established that the nearest primary school was located nine hundred feet from the Roberts residence, while the segregated Smith School on Belknap Street was 2,100 feet away, or about a fifth of a mile farther.

Charles Sumner (Library of Congress)

◆ The Plaintiff's Case Argued by Charles Sumner

The next section of the document, which begins with the line "Mr. Sumner argued as follows," details the seven-point argument put forth by Charles Sumner, who along with Robert Morris, represented Sarah Roberts in the case. Sumner, the more prominent attorney, presented the plaintiff's oral argument, making the case that Massachusetts law and the commonwealth's constitution recognized the equality of all citizens regardless of race. He argues that the state constitution proclaimed all men "equal before the law" and quotes legislation establishing public schools, demonstrating that this legislation did not specify special treatment for any class, color, or race of students. The single exception in Massachusetts school law was the small amount of funds designated for Indian schools. Sumner argues that there was no law establishing separate Indian schools and nothing to indicate that Indians would be excluded from attending the existing schools in their neighborhoods.

Sumner next turns his attack to the moral nature of the issue. Segregated schools violated the principles of equality outlined in the Massachusetts constitution and in prior court rulings that generally upheld the equal rights of all in the commonwealth. He claims that excluding African American children from the schools nearest their homes violated equality because it forced the children and their parents to endure an inconvenience not demanded of whites. Similarly, separating children based on race created a caste system that violated equality principles.

The scope of authority school committees held also draws fire in Sumner's argument. Citing the statutes conferring power on the committees, the plaintiff's attorney claims that the committees had no power to discriminate against any class of students attending Boston public schools. School committees were charged with operating public schools and determining the number and qualifications of pupils. Sumner argues that although school committees could classify students based on age, sex, and moral and intellectual ability, race was not among the attributes that could be considered a qualification. Nor, in the case of African American students, could it be used to disqualify students from attending the school nearest their homes. He argues that an entire race of people could not be considered to have the same certain moral or intellectual qualities and therefore could not be placed in a separate class. Continuing his attack on the school committee's actions, Sumner concludes that African American children had an equal right along with white children to attend the city's nonsegregated public schools.

The plaintiff's case concludes with Sumner's plea for the court to find the school committee's policy unconstitutional and illegal. He cites two important decisions, including one delivered earlier by Chief Justice Shaw as evidence to support such a ruling. The first involved a fugitive slave girl named Med. In *Commonwealth v. Aves* (1836), Shaw's ruling to free Med established the principle that slavery was local and liberty universal. The second ruling, *Boston v. Shaw* (1840), voided a city bylaw determined to be unequal and unreasonable. Sumner then quotes the French philosopher Jean-Jacques Rousseau, who declared that law should protect the fragile nature of equality. Despite his reasoned and impassioned argument, Sumner lost the case.

◆ Chief Justice Lemuel Shaw's Opinion

Following the seven points outlined by Mr. Sumner in the document text, Chief Justice Lemuel Shaw's ruling appears under the line "The opinion was delivered at the March term, 1850." This unanimous opinion represented the Massachusetts Supreme Court's denial of the plaintiff's petition to attend nonsegregated public schools. Shaw's opinion begins with a statement reflecting the charges in the action. The father of the five-year-old plaintiff brought the charge against the city of Boston for violating an 1845 statute allowing a child lawfully excluded from public schools to recover damages from the city or town supporting the school. Shaw notes that the city of Boston supported 160 primary schools, two of which were designated exclusively for African American children.

Justice Shaw lays the foundation for his denial of the case in the first third of his ruling. His decision ignores the moral issue Sumner presented and instead focuses on the narrower question of whether segregated schools violated the plaintiff's right to enjoy political, social, and civil equality. Shaw notes that while Benjamin Roberts had followed the correct procedure for enrolling his daughter Sarah in the primary school nearest his home, the school committee's policies did not make such an admission possible. Although the Smith School was approximately one-fifth of a

"The continuance of the separate schools for colored children, and the regular attendance of all such children upon the schools, is not only legal and just, but is best adapted to promote the education of that class of our population."

(Statement of Facts from the Court of Common Pleas)

"The plaintiff had access to a school, set apart for colored children, as well conducted in all respects, and as well fitted, in point of capacity and qualifications of the, instructors, to advance the education of children under seven years old, as the other primary schools."

(Chief Justice Lemuel Shaw's Opinion)

"It is urged, that this maintenance of separate schools tends to deepen and perpetuate the odious distinction of caste, founded in a deep-rooted prejudice in public opinion. This prejudice, if it exists, is not created by law, and probably cannot be changed by law."

(Chief Justice Lemuel Shaw's Opinion)

mile farther from the Roberts's home, the segregated school was, according to Shaw, equally appointed and staffed. This is the first reference to the important principle of "separate but equal" established by this ruling. Shaw upholds the authority of the Boston School Committee to continue its policy of maintaining separate schools for African American children. He notes that according to the school committee's policy such segregation of the races offered the best educational opportunities and instruction for African American students. The opinion also notes that the important matter in the case was whether the Boston School Committee had the legal authority to designate segregated schools.

Toward the middle of his opinion, Shaw makes reference to the argument of the plaintiff's attorney Charles Sumner that the Massachusetts constitution (Part the First and Articles I and VI) upheld the equality of all citizens of the commonwealth without regard to race, gender, or other factors. Shaw agrees with the general principle; however, his ruling states that the rights accorded to various populations, including women and children, can be qualified based on laws specifically affecting their place in society and other special conditions. He concedes that African Americans were entitled to equal rights, and therefore the court had to decide if the school committee's segregation policy violated those rights.

The ruling goes on to outline Massachusetts law and procedures for establishing public schools. Building on the assumption that the main question to be answered related to the authority of the school committee, this section explores the structure of the commonwealth's public school system. The ruling establishes the authority of school committees to adapt educational opportunities based on local needs. Public schools in Boston were to be operated under the direction of local school committees, elected by voters, across a district. These committees held full responsibility for organizing schools, making rules of governance, and regulating operations. Under this authority, school committees were empowered to classify and distribute enrollment in arrangements thought to be best suited to their pupils. Although most schools operated under open enrollment, special schools were occasionally designated, such as for poor or neglected children. Such children could be organized into a separate school for special training "adapted to their condition." The authority to designate a special school rested with the local school committee. A segregated school for African American children could be designated as fitting these criteria at the insistence of a local school committee.

The last third of the opinion addresses the complaint that Sarah Roberts had to pass five schools before reaching the segregated Smith School. Shaw's ruling notes that the population and housing arrangements of different towns made it inexpedient for the commonwealth's legislature to outline a single law governing school operation and management. He observes that in towns with a large territory and small population it would be difficult to provide different schools for special populations of pupils. However, the small geographic area encompassing Boston's large population reduced such inconvenience. Shaw reasons that in those circumstances, a system of distribution and classification was more practical, would not adversely affect students, and would actually improve the quality of education provided. Since the commonwealth did not have special legislation in the area of school distribution and classification, the court believed that power and authority for such decisions was vested in the school committee.

In the final three paragraphs, Shaw upholds the power of the Boston School Committee to maintain segregated schools for African American students. The ruling supported the judgment of the committee that such racial separation offered the best learning environment for the students of Boston public primary schools. Refusing to sustain the plaintiff's charge that segregated schools exacerbated racial prejudice, the ruling maintained that such prejudice was not created by the law and could not be changed by the law. This assertion that prejudice was a phenomenon outside the law's control foreshadowed reasoning often cited in future cases involving segregationist law. The unanimous opinion of the court found that the proper authority to determine the harm or benefit of segregated education rested with the Boston School Committee. Finally, the ruling denied the plaintiff's claim to attend the primary school nearest the Roberts residence. Shaw here declares that the increased distance between her home and the Smith School was not so far as to be unreasonable.

Audience

The immediate audience for this ruling of the Massachusetts Supreme Court was the Boston School Committee and the family of Sarah Roberts. The court clearly communicated its unwillingness to challenge the status quo that granted authority to local education boards. The ruling also sent an important message to Boston's African American community, telling blacks that since the legal system did not create racial prejudice, the law could not erase it. Among others interested in this decision were school committees across the commonwealth of Massachusetts and advocates of school segregation throughout the United States. In the coming years, as other states in both the North and the South wrestled with issues of civil rights and segregation, *Roberts v. Boston* became the standard used by proponents of segregation to promote the concept of "separate but equal."

Impact

Although the Massachusetts Supreme Court denied Roberts's petition, the controversy over separating students on the basis of race made many of the state's citizens aware of the inequity of segregated schools. In April 1855 the Massachusetts legislature passed a law forbidding racially separated schools and entitling all children excluded from a public school because of their race to damages in the amount of $1,000. Thus, Justice Shaw's ruling was rendered moot for Massachusetts. As for the plaintiffs, following the segregation case, Benjamin Roberts traveled with the famous escaped slave Henry "Box" Brown, acting as narrator for Brown's drama about his flight from slavery in a wooden box. Roberts tried his hand at newspaper editing again in 1853, but his antislavery *Self-Elevator* failed. He died of complications from epilepsy in 1881. The life of his daughter Sarah is lost to the historical record after her appearance as plaintiff in this important case.

Ironically, a clear trajectory shows *Roberts v. Boston* to be the root of twentieth-century prosegregation law. Despite being negated by the state legislature within a mere half decade, the decision of the Massachusetts Supreme Court to uphold Boston's policy of separating black and white students influenced numerous court decisions across the United States through the later nineteenth century. This segregationist trend culminated in the 1896 *Plessy v. Ferguson* decision concerning public transportation, which firmly established the "separate but equal" principle. *Plessy* guided segregationist rulings until it was overturned by the historic *Brown v. Board of Education of Topeka* ruling in 1954 that deemed racially separate facilities "inherently unequal."

As race relations became more unsettled in post–Civil War America, *Roberts v. Boston* was cited in a number of school segregation rulings. The first came in 1872 from the Nevada Supreme Court in the case of *Stoutmeyer v. Duffy*, in which the majority used the Roberts case to find that school boards held the right to determine classifications and make school assignment policies. The Massachusetts court ruling became even more influential when coupled with the 1873 U.S. Supreme Court ruling in the Slaughter-House Cases. These cases concerned the business rights of New Orleans butchers and led to a major reinterpretation of the Fourteenth Amendment to the U.S. Constitution. The majority opinion held that the first clause of the Fourteenth Amendment designated a dual citizenship—of state and of country—for Americans and that the Constitution protected only federal rights. The ruling empowered states to make broad claims in terms of citizenship rights. Courts quickly came to rule that the definition and regulation of public education fell under the authority of state constitutions.

Thereafter, state-level decisions involving cases of school segregation often cited both *Roberts v. Boston* and the Slaughter-House Cases. The argument that "separate but equal" was acceptable spread through state rulings across the country. In *Ward v. Flood* (1874), for instance, the California State Supreme Court denied the claim of a San Francisco plaintiff who argued that segregated schools in that city violated the equal protection and due process clause of the Fourteenth Amendment. When the plaintiff argued that segregation created an unequal caste system, the justices quoted *Roberts v. Boston* at length in their denial. The New York Supreme Court made a similar ruling in the 1883 case of *People ex. rel. King v. Gallagher*. In this case the plaintiff Gallagher demanded that his daughter be admitted to a whites-only school. Again, the court cited *Roberts v. Boston* to argue that the long-standing state policy of segregated schooling provided the best educational environment for African American children.

A series of cases in the 1880s and 1890s continued to use the ruling in the Boston school segregation case to build support for legalized segregation in state and regional school systems, making segregation a fundamental concept in America law. The influence of the "separate but equal" concept as first outlined in *Roberts v. Boston* stretched across more than forty years of legal rulings, culminating in the U.S. Supreme Court ruling in the 1896 case of *Plessy v. Ferguson*. In this case, an African American man named Homer Plessy challenged Louisiana laws that required him to ride in a separate railroad car from whites. After intentionally violating the law by refusing to move to a nonwhite car, he was arrested and tried for violating the segregation ordinance. When the case reached the Louisiana State Supreme Court, the majority ruling cited fifteen opinions upholding segregation and quoted at length from *Roberts v. Boston* to demonstrate the long reach of segregation rulings across the second half of the nineteenth century. The case was brought before the U.S. Supreme Court, which, in its landmark ruling, upheld Plessy's conviction and declared segregation to be constitutional. *Roberts v. Boston* was the leading case cited in the decision. What began as a movement of Boston African Americans to secure equal educational access for their children led to sanctioned seg-regation in all facets of American life, supported by the nation's highest court. In the decades that followed, African Americans, especially in southern states, faced widespread segregation in public accommodations as well as in educational settings.

See also *Plessy v. Ferguson* (1896).

Further Reading

■ Articles

Flicker, Douglas J. "From Roberts to Plessy: Educational Segregation and the 'Separate but Equal' Doctrine." *Journal of Negro History* 84 (Autumn 1999): 301–314.

Horton, James Oliver, and Michele Gates Moresi. "Roberts, Plessy, and Brown: The Long, Hard Struggle against Segregation." *OAH Magazine of History* 15 (Winter 2001): 14–16.

Levy, Leonard W., and Harlan B. Philips. "The Roberts Case: Source of the 'Separate but Equal' Doctrine." *American Historical Review* 56 (April 1951): 510–518.

Price, George R., and James Brewer Stewart. "The Roberts Case, the Easton Family, and the Dynamics of the Abolitionist Movement in Massachusetts, 1776–1870." *Massachusetts Historical Review* 4 (2002): 89–115.

White, Arthur O. "School Reform in Boston: Integrationists and Segregationists." *Phylon* 34 (1973): 203–217.

Questions for Further Study

1. In what ways did *Roberts v. City of Boston* anticipate the U.S. Supreme Court case *Brown v. Board of Education* just over a century later?

2. Compare this case with the cases discussed in connection with Charles Hamilton Houston's "Educational Inequalities Must Go!" in 1935 and with the Supreme Court case *Sweatt v. Painter* in 1950. In what ways did the *Roberts* case begin to lay the foundation for twentieth-century efforts to integrate education?

3. Why were African Americans in Boston divided over the issue of segregated versus integrated schools? To what extent does the issue continue to be debated in modern life, if at all?

4. What was the impact in the legal community of the *Roberts* case? How was the ruling in the case used in the post–Civil War period leading to the landmark case *Plessy v. Ferguson* in 1896?

5. In the early decades of the nineteenth century, a considerable amount of activity involving the rights and condition of African Americans, including abolitionist activity, centered in Boston and Massachusetts generally. Why do you think Boston became a hub of such activity?

■ Books

Cushing, Luther S. *Reports of Cases Argued and Determined in the Supreme Judicial Court of Massachusetts*. Vol. 5. Boston: Little, Brown, 1883.

Kendrick, Stephen, and Paul Kendrick. *Sarah's Long Walk: The Free Blacks of Boston and How Their Struggle for Equality Changed America*. Boston: Beacon Press, 2004.

   —L. Diane Barnes

ROBERTS v. CITY OF BOSTON

The general school committee of the city of Boston have power, under the constitution and laws of this commonwealth, to make provision for the instruction of colored children, in separate schools established exclusively for them, and to prohibit their attendance upon the other schools.

This was an action on the case, brought by Sarah C. Roberts, an infant, who sued by Benjamin F. Roberts, her father and next friend, against the city of Boston, under the statute of 1845, *c.* 214, which provides that any child, unlawfully excluded from public school instruction in this commonwealth, shall recover damages therefor against the city or town by which such public instruction is supported.

The case was submitted to the court of common pleas, from whence it came to this court by appeal, upon the following statement of facts:—

"Under the system of public schools established in the city of Boston, primary schools are supported by the city, for the instruction of all children residing therein between the ages of four and seven years. For this purpose, the city is divided for convenience, but not by geographical lines, into twenty-one districts, in each of which are several primary schools making the whole number of primary schools in the city of Boston one hundred and sixty-one. These schools are under the immediate management and superintendence of the primary school committee, so far as that committee has authority, by virtue of the powers conferred by votes of the general school committee.

"At a meeting of the general school committee, held on the 12th of January, 1848, the following vote was passed:—

"*Resolved*, that the primary school committee be, and they hereby are, authorized to organize their body and regulate their proceedings as they may deem most convenient; and to fill all vacancies occurring in the same, and to remove any of their members at their discretion during the ensuing year; and that this board will cheerfully receive from said committee such communications as they may have occasion to make."

"The city of Boston is not divided into territorial school districts; and the general school committee, by the city charter, have the care and superintendence of the public schools. In the various grammar and primary schools, white children do not always or necessarily go to the schools nearest their residences; and in the case of the Latin and English high schools (one of each of which is established in the city) most of the children are obliged to go beyond the schoolhouses nearest their residences.

"The regulations of the primary school committee contain the following provisions:—

"ADMISSIONS. No pupil shall be admitted into a primary school, without a ticket of admission from a member of the district committee.

"ADMISSIONS OF APPLICANT. Every member of the committee shall admit to his school, all applicants, of suitable age and qualifications, residing nearest to the school under his charge, (excepting those for whom special provision has been made,) provided the number in his school will warrant the admission.

"SCHOLARS TO GO TO SCHOOLS NEAREST THEIR RESIDENCES. Applicants for admission to the schools, (with the exception and provision referred to in the preceding rule,) are especially entitled to enter the schools nearest to their places of residence."

"At the time of the plaintiff's application, as hereinafter mentioned, for admission to the primary school, the city of Boston had established, for the exclusive use of colored children, two primary schools, one in Belknap street, in the eighth school district, and one in Sun Court street, in the second school district.

"The colored population of Boston constitute less than one sixty-second part of the entire population of the city. For half a century, separate schools have been kept in Boston for colored children, and the primary school for colored children in Belknap street was established in 1820, and has been kept there ever since. The teachers of this school have the same compensation and qualifications as in other like schools in the city. Schools for colored children were originally established at the request of colored citizens, whose children could not attend the public schools, on account of the prejudice then existing against them.

"The plaintiff is a colored child, of five years of age, a resident of Boston, and living with her father, since the month of March, 1847, in Andover street, in the sixth primary school district. In the month of April, 1847, she being of suitable age and qualifications, (unless her color was a disqualification,) applied to a member of the district primary school committee, having under his charge the primary school nearest to her place of residence, for a ticket of admission to that school, the number of scholars therein warranting her admission, and no special provision having been made for her, unless the establishment of the two schools for colored children exclusively, is to be so considered.

"The member of the school committee, to whom the plaintiff applied, refused her application on the ground of her being a colored person, and of the, special provision made as aforesaid. The plaintiff thereupon applied to the primary school committee of the district, for admission to one of their schools, and was in like manner refused admission, on the ground of her color and the provision aforesaid. She thereupon petitioned the general primary school committee, for leave to enter one of the schools nearest her residence. That committee referred the subject to the committee of the district, with full powers, and the committee of the district thereupon again refused the plaintiff's application, on the sole ground of color and the special provision aforesaid, and the plaintiff has not since attended any school in Boston. Afterwards, on the 15th of February, 1848, the plaintiff went into the primary school nearest her residence, but without any ticket of admission or other leave granted, and was on that day ejected from the school by the teacher.

"The school established in Belknap street is twenty-one hundred feet, distant from, the residence of the plaintiff, measuring through the streets; and in passing from the plaintiff's residence to the Belknap street school, the direct route passes the ends of two streets in which there are five primary schools.

The distance to the school in Sun Court street is much greater. The distance from the plaintiff's residence to the nearest primary school is nine hundred feet. The plaintiff might have attended the school in Belknap street, at any time, and her father was so informed, but he refused to have her attend there.

"In 1846, George Putnam and other colored citizens of Boston petitioned the primary school committee, that exclusive schools for colored children might be abolished, and the committee, on the 22d of June, 1846, adopted the report of a sub-committee, and a resolution appended thereto, which was in the following words:—

"*Resolved*, that in the opinion of this board, the continuance of the separate schools for colored children, and the regular attendance of all such children upon the schools, is not only legal and just, but is best adapted to promote the education of that class of our population."

The court were to draw such inferences from the foregoing facts as a jury would be authorized to draw; and the parties agreed that if the plaintiff was entitled to recover, the case should be sent to a jury to assess damages; otherwise the plaintiff was to become nonsuit.

C. Sumner and R. Morris, Jr., for the plaintiff

Mr. Sumner argued as follows:

1. According to the spirit of American institutions, and especially of the constitution of Massachusetts, (Part First, Articles I. and VI.) all men, without distinction of color or race, are equal before the law.

2. The legislation of Massachusetts has made no discrimination of color or race in the establishment of the public schools. The laws establishing public schools, speak of "schools for the instruction of children," generally, and "for the benefit of all the inhabitants of the town," not specifying any particular class, color, or race. Rev. Sts. *c.* 23; Colony law of 1647, (Anc. Ch. *c.*186.) The provisions of Rev. Sts. *c.* 23, §68, and St. 1838, *c.* 154, appropriating small sums out of the school fund for the support of common schools among the Indians, do not interfere with this system. They partake of the anomalous character of all our legislation with regard to the Indians. And it does not appear, that any separate schools are established by law among the Indians, or that they are in any way excluded from the public schools in their neighborhood.

3. The courts of Massachusetts have never admitted any discrimination, founded on color or race, in the administration of the common schools, but have recognized the equal rights of all the inhabitants. *Commonwealth v. Dedham*, 16 Mass. 141, 146; *Withington v. Eveleth*, 7 Pick. 106; *Perry v. Dover*, 12 Pick. 206, 213.

4. The exclusion of colored children from the public schools, which are open to white children, is a source of practical inconvenience to them and their parents, to which white persons are not exposed, and is, therefore, a violation of equality.

5. The separation of children in the public schools of Boston, on account of color or race, is in the nature of caste, and is a violation of equality.

6. The school committee have no power, under the constitution and laws of Massachusetts, to make any discrimination on account of color or race, among

children in the public schools. The only clauses in the statutes, conferring powers on the school committee, are the tenth section of Rev. Sts. c.23, declaring that they "shall have the general charge and superintendence of all the public schools in the town," and the fifteenth section of the same chapter, providing that they "shall determine the number and qualifications of the scholars, to be admitted into the school kept for the use of the whole town." The power to determine the "qualifications" of the scholars must be restrained to the qualifications of, age, sex, and moral and intellectual fitness. The fact, that a child is black, or that he is white, cannot of itself be considered a qualification, or a disqualification.

The regulations and by-laws of municipal corporations must be reasonable, or they are inoperative and void. *Commonweath v. Worcester*, 3 Pick. 462; *Vandine's Case*, 6 Pick. 187; *Shaw v. Boston*, 1 Met. 130. So, the regulations and by-laws of the school committee must be reasonable; and their discretion must be exercised in a reasonable manner. The discrimination made by the school committee of Boston, on account of color, is not legally reasonable. A colored person may occupy any office connected with the public schools, from that of governor, or secretary of the board of education, to that of member of a school committee, or teacher in any public school, and as a voter he may vote for members of the school committee. It is clear, that the committee may classify scholars, according to age and sex, for these distinctions are inoffensive, and recognized as legal (Rev. Sts. c. 23, §63); or according to their moral and intellectual qualifications, because such a power is necessary to the government of schools. But the committee cannot assume, without individual examination, that an entire race possess certain moral or intellectual qualities, which render it proper to place them all in a class by themselves.

But it is said, that the committee, in thus classifying the children, have not violated any principle of equality, inasmuch as they have provided a school with competent instructors for the colored children, where they enjoy equal advantages of instruction with those enjoyed by the white children. To this there are several answers: 1st, The separate school for colored children is not one of the schools established by the law relating to public schools, (Rev. Sts. c. 23,) and having no legal existence, cannot be a legal equivalent. 2d. It is not in fact an equivalent. It is the occasion of inconveniences to the colored :children, to which they would not be exposed if they had

access to the nearest public schools; it inflicts upon them the stigma of caste; and although the matters taught in the two schools may be precisely the same, a school exclusively devoted to one class must differ essentially, in its spirit and character, from that public school known to the law, where all classes meet together in equality. 3d. Admitting that it is an equivalent, still the colored children cannot be compelled to take it. They have an equal right with the white children to the general public schools.

7. The court will declare the by-law of the school committee, making a discrimination of color among children, entitled to the benefit of the public schools, to be unconstitutional and illegal, although there are no express words of prohibition in the constitution and laws. Slavery was abolished in Massachusetts, by virtue of the declaration of rights in our constitution, without any specific words of abolition in that instrument, or in any subsequent legislation.*Commonwealth v. Aves*, 18 Pick. 193, 210. The same words, which are potent to destroy slavery, must be equally potent against any institution founded on caste. And see *Shaw v. Boston*, 1 Met. 130, where a by-law of the city was set aside as unequal and unreasonable, and therefore void. If there should be any doubt in this case, the court should incline in favor of equality; as every interpretation is always made in favor of life and liberty. Rousseau says that "it is precisely because the force of things tends always to destroy equality, that the force of legislation ought always to tend to maintain it." In a similar spirit the court should tend to maintain it.

The fact, that the separation of the schools was originally made at the request of the colored parents, cannot affect the rights of the colored people, or the powers of the school committee. The separation of the schools, so far from being for the benefit of both races, is an injury to both. It tends to create a feeling of degradation in the blacks, and of prejudice and uncharitableness in the whites.

P. W. Chandler, city solicitor, for the defendants

The opinion was delivered at the March term, 1850

Shaw, C. J. The plaintiff, a colored child of five years of age, has commenced this action, by her father and next friend, against the city of Boston, upon the statute of 1845, c. 214, which provides, that any child unlawfully excluded from public school instruction, in this commonwealth, shall recover damages therefor, in an action against the city or town, by which such public school instruction is supported. The question therefore is, whether, upon the facts agreed, the plaintiff has been unlawfully excluded from such instruction.

By the agreed statement of facts, it appears, that the defendants support a class of schools called primary schools, to the number of about one, hundred and sixty, designed for the instruction of children of both sexes, who are between the ages of four and seven years. Two of these schools are appropriated by the primary school committee, having charge of that class of schools, to the exclusive instruction of colored children, and the residue to the exclusive instruction of white children.

The plaintiff, by her father, took proper measures to obtain admission into one of these schools appropriated to white children, but pursuant to the regulations of the committee, and in conformity therewith, she was not admitted. Either of the schools appropriated to colored children was open to her; the nearest of which was about a fifth of a mile, or seventy rods more distant from her father's house than the nearest primary school. It further appears, by the facts agreed, that the committee having charge of that class of schools had, a short time previously to the plaintiff's application, adopted a resolution, upon a report of a committee, that in the opinion of that board, the continuance of the separate schools for colored children, and the regular attendance of all such children upon the schools, is not only legal and just, but is best adapted to promote the instruction of that class of the population.

The present case does not involve any question in regard to the legality of the Smith school, which is a school of another class, designed for colored children more advanced in age and proficiency; though much of the argument, affecting the legality of the separate primary schools, affects in like manner that school. But the question here is confined to the primary schools alone. The plaintiff had access to a school, set apart for colored children, as well conducted in all respects, and as well fitted, in point of capacity and qualification of the, instructors, to advance the education of children under seven years old, as the other primary schools; the objection is, that the schools thus open to the plaintiff are exclusively appropriated to colored children, and are at a greater distance from her home. Under these circumstances, has the plaintiff been unlawfully excluded from public school instruction? Upon the best consideration we, have been able to give the subject, the court are all of opinion that she has not.

It will be considered, that this is a question of power, or of the legal authority of the committee intrusted by the city with this department of public instruction; because, if they have the legal authority, the expediency of exercising it in any particular way is exclusively with them.

The great principle, advanced by the learned and eloquent advocate of the plaintiff, is, that by the constitution and laws of Massachusetts, all persons without distinction of age or sex, birth or color, origin or condition, are equal before the law. This, as a broad general principle, such as ought to appear in a declaration of rights, is perfectly sound; it is not only, expressed in terms, but pervades and animates the whole spirit of our constitution of free government. But, when this great principle comes to be applied to the actual and various conditions of persons in society, it will not warrant the assertion, that men and women are legally clothed with the same civil and political powers, and that children and adults are legally to have the same functions and be subject to the same treatment; but only that the rights of all, as they are settled and regulated by law, are equally entitled to the paternal consideration and protection of the law, for their maintenance and security. What those rights are, to which individuals, in the infinite variety of circumstances by which they are surrounded in society, are entitled, must depend on laws adapted to their respective relations and conditions.

Conceding, therefore, in the fullest manner, that colored persons, the descendants of Africans, are entitled by law, in this commonwealth, to equal rights, constitutional and political, civil and social, the question then arises, whether the regulation in question, which provides separate schools for colored children, is a violation of any of these rights.

Legal rights must, after all, depend upon the provisions of law; certainly all those rights of individuals which can be asserted and maintained in any judicial tribunal. The proper province of a declaration of rights and constitution of government, after directing its form, regulating its organization and the distribution of its powers, is to declare great principles and fundamental truths; to influence and direct the judgment and conscience of legislators in making laws, rather than to limit and control them, by directing what precise laws they shall make. The provision, that it shall be the duty of legislatures and magistrates to cherish the interests of literature and the sciences, especially the university at Cambridge, public schools, and grammar schools, in the towns, is precisely of this character. Had the legislature failed to comply with this injunction, and neglected to provide public schools in the towns, or should they so far fail in their duty as to repeal all laws on the subject, and leave all education to depend on private means, strong and explicit as the direction of the constitution is, it would afford no remedy or redress to the thousands of the rising generation, who now depend on these schools to afford them a most valuable education, and an introduction to useful life.

We must then resort to the law, to ascertain what are the rights of individuals, in regard to the schools. By the Rev. Sts. *c.* 23, the general system is provided for. This chapter directs what money shall be raised in different towns, according to their population; provides for a power of dividing towns into school districts, leaving, it however at the option of the inhabitants to divide the towns into districts, or to administer the system and provide schools, without such division. The latter course has, it is believed, been constantly adopted in Boston, without forming the territory into districts.

The statute, after directing what length of time schools shall be kept in towns of different numbers of inhabitants and families, provides (§10) that the inhabitants shall annually choose, by ballot, a school committee, who shall have the general charge and superintendence of all the public schools in such towns. There being no specific direction how schools shall be organized; how, many schools shall be kept; what shall be the qualifications for admission to the schools; the age at which children may enter; the age to which they may continue; these must all be regulated by the committee, under their power of general superintendence.

There is indeed, a provision (§§5 and 6,) that towns may and in some cases must provide a high school and classical school, for the benefit of all the inhabitants. It is obvious how this clause was introduced; it was to distinguish such classical and high schools, in towns districted, from the district schools. These schools being of a higher character, and designed for pupils of more advanced age and greater proficiency, were intended for the benefit of the whole of the town, and not of particular districts. Still it depends upon the committee, to prescribe the qualifications, and make all the reasonable rules, for organizing such schools and regulating and conducting them.

The power of general superintendence vests a plenary authority in the committee to arrange, classify, and distribute pupils, in such a manner as they think best adapted to their general proficiency and welfare.

If it is thought expedient to provide for very young children, it may be, that such schools may be kept exclusively by female teachers, quite adequate to their instruction, and yet whose services maybe obtained at a cost much lower than that of more highly qualified male instructors. So if they should judge it expedient to have a grade of schools for children from seven to ten, and another for those from ten to fourteen, it would seem to be within their authority to establish such schools. So to separate male and female pupils into different schools. It has been found necessary, that is to say, highly expedient, at times, to establish special schools for poor and neglected children, who have passed the age of seven, and have become too old to attend the primary school, and yet have not acquired the rudiments of learning, to enable them to enter the ordinary schools. If a class of youth, of one or both sexes, is found in that condition, and it is, expedient to organize them into a separate school, to receive the special training, adapted to their condition, it seems to be within the power of the superintending committee, to provide for the organization of such special school.

A somewhat more specific rule, perhaps, on these subjects, might be beneficially provided by the legislature; but yet, it would probably be quite impracticable to make full and precise laws for this purpose, on account of the different condition of society in different towns. In towns of a large territory, over which the inhabitants are thinly settled, an arrangement or classification going far into detail, providing different schools for pupils of different ages, of each sex, and the like, would require the pupils to go such long distances from their homes to the schools, that it would be quite unreasonable. But in Boston, where more than one hundred thousand inhabitants live within a space, so small, that it would be scarcely an inconvenience to require a boy of good health to traverse daily the whole extent of it, a system of distribution and classification may be adopted and carried into effect, which may be useful and beneficial in its influence on the character of the schools, and in its adaptation to the improvement and advancement of the great purpose of education, and at the same time practicable and reasonable in its operation.

In the absence of, special legislation on this subject, the law, has vested the power in the committee to regulate the system of distribution and classification; and when this power is reasonably exercised, without being abused or perverted by colorable pretences, the decision of the committee must be deemed conclusive. The committee, apparently upon great deliberation, have come to the conclusion, that the good of both classes of schools will be best promoted, by maintaining the separate primary schools for colored and for white children and we can perceive no ground to doubt, that this is the honest result of their experience and judgment.

It is urged, that this maintenance of separate schools tends to deepen and perpetuate the odious distinction of caste, founded in a deep-rooted prejudice in public opinion. This prejudice, if it exists, is not created by law, and probably cannot be changed by law. Whether this distinction and prejudice, existing in the opinion and feelings of the community, would not be as effectually fostered by compelling colored and white children, to associate together in the same schools, may well be doubted; at all events, it is a fair and proper question for the committee to consider and decide upon, having in view, the best interests of both classes, of children placed under their superintendence, and we cannot say, that their decision upon it is not founded on just grounds of reason and experience, and in the results of a discriminating and honest judgment.

The increased distance, to which the plaintiff was obliged to go to school from her father's house, is not such, in our opinion, as to render the regulation in question unreasonable, still less illegal.

On the whole the court are of opinion, that upon the facts stated, the action cannot be maintained.

Plaintiff nonsuit.

colorable	seemingly valid, but intending to deceive
infant	minor child
Latin … high schools	college preparatory schools that typically provide instruction in the classical languages
nonsuit	a judgment against a plaintiff
rod	a unit of measurement equal to 16.5 feet
Rousseau	Jean-Jacque Rousseau, eighteenth-century French philosopher; the quotation is from Book II, Chapter 11 of *Of the Social Contract.*
university at Cambridge	Harvard University

James Murray Mason (Library of Congress)

FUGITIVE SLAVE ACT OF 1850

"In no trial or hearing under this act shall the testimony of such alleged fugitive be admitted in evidence."

Overview

The Fugitive Slave Act of 1850 represented an effort by white southerners to use federal power to protect slavery by providing for the recovery of fugitive slaves who crossed state boundaries in their efforts to escape. Meant to improve upon previous legislation to enforce the Constitution's provision for the return of fugitives "held to service or labor," the new law became the most controversial measure passed as part of what became known as the Compromise of 1850, an omnibus package of five bills. Many northerners who were at best vaguely antislavery still found the new measure objectionable, with its denial of any rights for the accused, an inherent unfairness in the compensation due commissioners depending on the verdict, and provisions that might draw northerners into enforcing the measure.

Throughout the nineteenth century many northerners, black and white, had been assisting slaves escaping to freedom. Several states had passed laws offering some protection for those accused fugitives, who might well have been free blacks wrongly taken into custody. Southern whites, for all their talk of states' rights, protested the efforts of northern states to defend their rights against the federal government; in turn, they had no objection to invoking the federal government on behalf of slavery even as they protested any measures at the federal level that impaired their own rights as slaveholders or challenged the peculiar institution's expansion economically or territorially. Although the Fugitive Slave Act proved to be quite controversial, by itself it represented but a single step in the process that led to secession and civil war, and it was not until war broke out that the federal government took steps to rid itself of the shadow cast by the 1850 act.

Context

Article IV, Section 2, of the U.S. Constitution included the following clause:

No Person held to Service or Labour in one State, under the Laws thereof, escaping into another, shall, in Consequence of any Law or Regulation therein, be discharged from such Service or Labour, But shall be delivered up on Claim of the Party to whom such Service or Labour may be due.

By itself, the clause did not call for the federal government to assume the responsibility of recovering fugitives, and it did not employ the terms *slave* or *slavery*. Recognizing this, Congress in 1793 passed legislation providing for enforcement of this pledge by the federal judiciary as well as by local and state officials. The resulting act came to be known as the Fugitive Slave Act.

For decades to come slave catchers were employed by masters seeking the recovery of runaway slaves who had crossed state lines. Fugitive slaves could be recaptured at any time: There was no statute of limitations as to their status. At times slave catchers apprehended free blacks and sold them into slavery, the most famous case being that of Solomon Northup, a freeborn New Yorker who was enslaved for twelve years and later wrote about his captivity. In the case of Frederick Douglass, it was not until years after his escape that he had his freedom secured under law when a group of British benefactors bought his freedom.

The arbitrary nature of the recovery process—there was no provision about identifying the accused or definitions of standards of proof—led several northern states to pass legislation that offered some degree of legal protection for those apprehended under the statute. Such personal liberty laws, sometimes known as antikidnap laws, had existed in several states prior to the ratification of the Constitution, but more states adopted them in the decades after the passage of the Fugitive Slave Act of 1793. Although the specific provisions varied from state to state, such legislation came to embody prohibitions against certain state officials from enforcing the act (sometimes under penalty of a fine), jury trials for the accused, the need to present evidence to prove the fact of identity and ownership, the necessity of a warrant, and other measures designed to protect free blacks from being captured and brought south. These measures multiplied in the 1830s and early 1840s as the nature of both the proslavery and abolition

Time Line

1793

- **February 12**
  The Fugitive Slave Act is passed, covering both fugitives from justice and escaped slaves.

1842

- **March 1**
  In *Prigg v. Pennsylvania* the Supreme Court strikes down provisions of a Pennsylvania personal liberty law.

1850

- **September 18**
  Congress passes the Fugitive Slave Act, with stronger provisions.

1854

- **May**
  In Boston, the trial of Anthony Burns, convicted of being an escaped slave, excites riots and an effort to liberate Burns from federal confinement.

1859

- **March 7**
  The Supreme Court, in *Ableman v. Booth*, strikes down the ruling of a Wisconsin court that had declared the Fugitive Slave Act unconstitutional.

1861

- **August 6**
  Congress passes the First Confiscation Act, authorizing the seizure as contraband of all slaves who had been employed in active support of the Confederate war effort.

1862

- **March 13**
  Congress forbids military personnel to return fugitive slaves to their owners.

- **July 17**
  Congress passes the Second Confiscation Act, declaring free those slaves owned by supporters of secession.

1863

- **January 1**
  Lincoln issues the Emancipation Proclamation, freeing slaves in areas he specified as being under Confederate control.

1864

- **June 28**
  Congress repeals the Fugitive Slave Act.

movements changed and debates over slavery became a more divisive aspect of American politics.

In 1842 the Supreme Court had a chance to rule on the constitutionality of personal liberty laws as a result of a case in which Pennsylvania and Maryland authorities cooperated to test Pennsylvania's legislation federally. Edward Prigg of Maryland, who had been involved in an attempt to capture Margaret Morgan, a slave who had escaped from Maryland into Pennsylvania in violation of Pennsylvania law, was convicted of violating the law, with an eye toward bringing the dispute before the Supreme Court for final adjudication. Speaking for a majority of the Court, Associate Justice Joseph Story ruled that the Fugitive Slave Act of 1793 was constitutional, that the Pennsylvania personal liberty law was unconstitutional, and that the recovery of runaway slaves across state boundaries was a federal responsibility. He did, however, also rule that states need not enlist their officials to assist in the recapture and return of fugitive slaves from other states.

Prigg v. Pennsylvania thus opened the way for a new approach to the question of how to implement the Constitution's fugitive slave recovery clause. Some northern states, led by Massachusetts, passed new personal liberty laws, as did Pennsylvania in 1847; northern states as a whole withdrew state assistance from enforcing the federal legislation. In 1848 South Carolina senator Andrew P. Butler introduced a bill to improve existing legislation on the recovery of fugitive slaves, but his ideas did not get far prior to 1850.

The 1850 fugitive slave legislation was introduced by Virginia senator James Murray Mason on January 4, 1850, several weeks before Senator Henry Clay of Kentucky incorporated it into his proposal designed to settle all outstanding issues related to slavery. He based the bill in part on Butler's 1848 proposal. Several southern senators were enraged when New York senator William H. Seward sought to amend the bill to provide for trial by jury for accused fugitives. Such opposition caused Mason to modify his proposal in order to strengthen it against such critics, including a provision authorizing the formation of a *posse comitatus*—that is, a temporary local police force—to execute warrants, a measure that could transform northern bystanders into slave catchers.

The debate over Mason's measure proved divisive. Some southerners cited northern resistance to the recovery of fugitive slaves as a reason to convene in Nashville that summer so that southerners could consider their options, including possibly secession: Clay himself conceded the justice of southern complaints on that score, as did Massachusetts senator Daniel Webster. That Mason was unbending in his support of southern measures became apparent when he rose to deliver what proved to be the last Senate speech of John C. Calhoun, who was too ill to deliver it himself. That some antislavery northerners could not tolerate his proposal became evident when Seward denounced it in a lengthy speech in which he argued that there was a higher law than the Constitution.

Although Mason favored new legislation concerning the recapture of fugitive slaves, he opposed other compro-

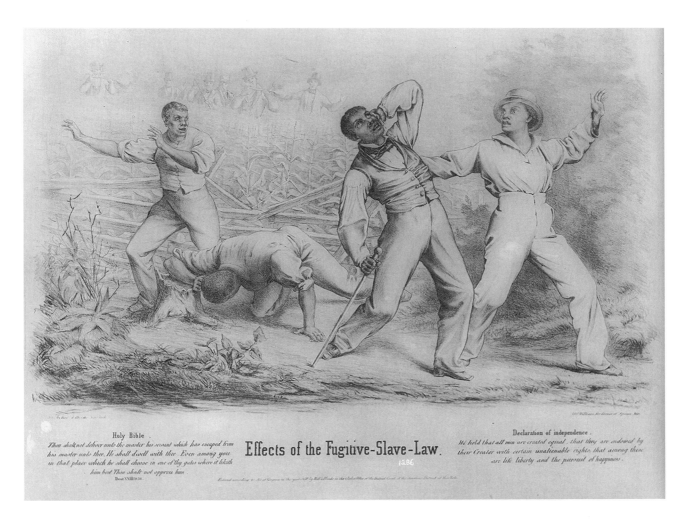

Holy Bible.

Thou shalt not deliver unto the master his servant which has escaped from his master unto thee. He shall dwell with thee. Even among you in that place which he shall choose in one of thy gates where it liketh him best Thou shalt not oppress him.

Deut. XXIII.15,16.

Effects of the Fugitive-Slave-Law.

1286

Declaration of independence.

We hold that all men are created equal, that they are endowed by their Creator with certain unalienable rights, that among these are life, liberty and the pursuit of happiness.

A group of four black men—possibly freedmen—are ambushed by a posse of six armed whites in this illustration of the effects of the Fugitive Slave Act of 1850. (Library of Congress)

mise proposals, and he was not unhappy when Clay's omnibus effort failed in July. Within weeks, however, due in large part to the legislative skill of Illinois senator Stephen A. Douglas, the bill passed as part of a decision to present each proposal separately under the assumption that each had a majority in support but that taken together not enough people would engage in the give-and-take of compromise needed to pass all the proposals as part of a larger bill. Mason aided this effort by once more proposing changes to his original measure while successfully resisting attempts to incorporate jury trials for the accused. This time his efforts were rewarded: The Fugitive Slave Act passed on September 18, 1850.

About the Author

Senator James M. Mason of Virginia, grandson of Founding Father George Mason, framed the original bill that eventually passed into law as the Fugitive Slave Act of 1850. Born on November 3, 1798, in the District of Columbia on an island in the Potomac now known as Theodore Roosevelt Island, Mason pursued a career in law and became active in Virginia politics, serving as a delegate to Virginia's constitutional convention in 1829 and in the state legislature. He was elected to the House of Representatives in 1836 for one term and then to the U.S. Senate in 1847. In later life he would head the congressional committee that investigated the abolitionist John Brown's raid on Harpers Ferry before siding with the Confederacy and serving as a diplomatic representative to France and Great Britain. When a U.S. vessel boarded the British mail packet *Trent* in 1861 and captured Mason and his fellow Confederate diplomat John Slidell, the resulting international incident threatened to bring Great Britain and the United States to war. He was released in 1862, represented the Confederacy in Great Britain until the end of the Civil War, and died on April 28, 1871, in Virginia.

"It shall be the duty of all marshals and deputy marshals to obey and execute all warrants and precepts issued under the provisions of this act, when to them directed; and should any marshal or deputy marshal refuse to receive such warrant, or other process, when tendered, or to use all proper means diligently to execute the same, he shall, on conviction thereof, be fined."

(Section 5)

"And the better to enable the said commissioners, when thus appointed, to execute their duties faithfully and efficiently, in conformity with the requirements of the Constitution of the United States and of this act, they are hereby authorized and empowered ... to appoint ... any one or more suitable persons, from time to time, to execute all such warrants and other process as may be issued by them in the lawful performance of their respective duties."

(Section 5)

"When a person held to service or labor in any State or Territory of the United States, has heretofore or shall hereafter escape into another State or Territory of the United States, the person or persons to whom such service or labor may be due ... may pursue and reclaim such fugitive person."

(Section 6)

"In no trial or hearing under this act shall the testimony of such alleged fugitive be admitted in evidence."

(Section 6)

Explanation and Analysis of the Document

The Fugitive Slave Act of 1850 is best understood first as a document that sought to close the loopholes that allowed northerners and northern state governments to evade the intent of the Constitution's clause calling for the recovery of fugitives from labor who crossed state lines. The Fugitive Slave Act of 1793 had proved insufficient as a way to secure the recovery of fugitives, in large part because of the efforts of several northern states to block its effective implementa-

tion through the passage of "personal liberty laws." Further, the Fugitive Slave Act of 1793 specified federal judges as the only federal officials who could determine the status of an accused fugitive, but the new law extended this authority to federal commissioners and allowed federal courts to appoint more such commissioners.

◆ Sections 1–3

The first section of the law identifies commissioners who have been appointed by any act of Congress or by the circuit courts and who have the same authority as a justice of the peace or local magistrate to arrest, imprison, or grant bail to offenders of the law. The section then states that these commissioners were to have the authority to exercise the powers granted to them under the present act. The second section essentially extends these same powers to commissioners in the Territories, that is, to those regions that were under the control of the U.S. government but had not yet been admitted to the Union as states. Commissioners in the Territories were to be appointed by the circuit court that had jurisdiction in them. The third section simply authorizes the circuit courts to expand the number of commissioners needed to "reclaim fugitives from labor." In essence, the first three sections of the act established a class of legal authorities outside the courts that would have the power to enforce the provisions of the Fugitive Slave Act.

◆ Sections 4 and 5

With Section 4, the act turns to the specific powers and duties of this body of commissioners. Section 4 specifies that commissioners were to have "concurrent jurisdiction" with the circuit courts and superior courts. Concurrent jurisdiction refers to a situation in which two (or more) courts at different levels—a state court and federal court, for example—have jurisdiction over a case. By granting the commissioners concurrent jurisdiction, the act in essence removed the legalities of capturing fugitive slaves from the courts and placed it in the hands of commissioners. These commissioners were then granted the authority to capture runaway slaves and return them to their states.

Section 5 introduces some of the more draconian provisions of the act. It begins by stating that "it shall be the duty of all marshals and deputy marshals to obey and execute all warrants and precepts issued under the provisions of this act." The section goes on to specify that if a marshal failed to execute a claim by a slave owner (a "claimant"), he could be fined. Making matters worse for the marshal, it is decreed that if a slave held in the marshal's custody escaped, whether through the collusion of the marshal or not, the marshal could be held liable by the claimant for the full value of the slave. To help the marshal avoid these legal difficulties in carrying out his duties, he had the authority to appoint persons to assist him in capturing runaway slaves. Further, marshals had the authority to "summon and call to their aid ... bystanders," that is, to invoke the principle of *posse comitatus*. This is a Latin term used in the law; its literal meaning is "power of the county," and it refers to the authority of a marshal to appoint a temporary police force. Compare the posse of Western movies and television shows, where groups of townsmen, with the sanction of the marshal, temporarily gather to hunt down criminals. Making matters worse for ordinary citizens was that the law specifies that "all good citizens are hereby commanded to aid and assist in the prompt and efficient execution of this law." In effect, everyone became a potential slave catcher.

◆ Sections 6 and 7

Section 6 continues with the somewhat tortuous legislative language of the preceding sections, but buried within the language is a key component of the law: Accused fugitive slaves are stripped of their civil rights. The section first states that a presumed slave owner may "pursue and reclaim" a "person held to service or labor." He could do so either by procuring a warrant or by "seizing and arresting such fugitive, where the same can be done without process" (that is, without court proceedings). The seized person could then be taken to court, where the issue was to be decided in a "summary" manner. All the claimant had to do was assert by affidavit the identity of the fugitive and claim that the fugitive was in fact a slave; no other legal proof was required. The claimant, or his agent, was authorized to "use such reasonable force and restraint as may be necessary," giving slave catchers a free hand in hunting down and subduing a runaway. Further, the act states that "in no trial or hearing under this act shall the testimony of such alleged fugitive be admitted in evidence." In effect, the accused was rendered unable to defend him or herself. Of course, this provision would have struck fear into the hearts of free blacks: All a claimant had to do was seize a black and claim runaway status, and the authorities had to support the claim.

Section 7 made it illegal to aid a runaway slave, stating that any person who obstructed, hindered, or prevented a claimant from arresting a fugitive, rescued a fugitive, helped a fugitive escape from the claimant, or harbored or concealed a fugitive could be fined or imprisoned, or both. Additionally, such a person could be required to pay restitution to the claimant.

◆ Sections 8–10

Section 8 created an interesting conflict of interest. In the wake of *Prigg v. Pennsylvania* there was a vast increase in the number of government officials involved in the process of capture, determination of status, and return of fugitives. These commissioners were to be paid by fees resulting from the cases over which they presided. If a commissioner ruled that the accused was not the slave in question, he would be paid five dollars. But if the commissioner determined that the accused was in fact the slave in question and issued a certificate authorizing removal of the slave, he would receive ten dollars, supposedly because of the increased administrative costs of such a decision. Thus, the law provided a financial incentive for commissioners to side with claimants rather than with the accused, who might very well have been free blacks not allowed to prove their status. Section 8 also provided for payment to any individuals who assisted a marshal in capturing and holding a runaway slave. Again, this provision of the law had the effect of turning a class of persons into bounty hunters with a potential incentive to seize any black person, claim runaway status, and collect a fee.

Section 9 turned to the issue of transporting a runaway back to another state. This provision states that if the possibility existed that the claimant would meet with any interference (that is, that rescue attempts would be made), the marshal was obligated to provide protection until he had passed over the state's border; indeed, it was the marshal's duty to return the slave to his or her home state. The Fugitive Slave Act concludes with Section 10, which established procedures for a claimant to appeal to a court in his home state when a slave escaped. The court was then required to create a record that the claimant could use in another state to enforce his claim to the slave. Section 10, though, states that such a record was not required, so that a claimant who did not have a record from his home state was still entitled to enforce his claim in another state.

Audience

As one might expect, white southerners and slaveholders celebrated the new legislation. Nothing was heard as to whether the act, with its expansion of federal power, constituted a violation of states' rights or federalism, which were otherwise cornerstones of southern political philosophy when it came to the defense of slavery. The act itself appeared to be a vindication of southern rights, specifically slaveholder rights, and a rebuke against northern efforts to resist the recapture of fugitive slaves by various means.

Northern critics of the legislation noted that it denied basic civil rights to the accused, gave greater compensation to a commissioner who ruled in favor of the slave catcher and against the accused, and compelled uninvolved bystanders to become involved in an effort to recapture fugitives and bring them to court. Northern blacks were alarmed that the legislation represented a renewed threat to their freedom, as indeed it did. Other white northerners who had supported the compromise measures or who deplored the disruptive impact of the slavery issue on American politics were far more supportive of the new legislation as a suitable implementation of the Constitution's pledge concerning the recovery of fugitive slaves.

Impact

Few measures fueled as much sectional controversy as the Fugitive Slave Act of 1850. It was not long before some northerners actively resisted the enforcement of the new act, and white southerners called upon federal authorities, including President Millard Fillmore, to use military force to subdue such obstruction. Several cases attracted national attention. In October 1850 a slave catcher was foiled in his efforts to capture William and Ellen Craft, whose 1848 escape from Georgia had gained much attention, with Ellen posing as a male slaveholder and William as his valet. Rather than risk another recapture effort, the Crafts sailed for England by year's end. Boston's black community, aided by white allies, thwarted several more efforts to recover runaway slaves. However, on February 15, 1851, federal marshals apprehended Shadrach Minkins, who had fled Virginia the previous year, prior to the passage of the

Fugitive Slave Act. Members of Boston's Vigilance Committee sprang into action, crowding the courtroom in which a hearing would be held to determine Minkins's status. Antislavery lawyers prepared to defend him, despite the terms of the 1850 legislation that simply called for a determination of the accused's identity and status. In a scuffle that followed, Minkins was freed and whisked off to Canada.

Eight months later another confrontation occurred in Syracuse, New York, where an effort to recapture William Henry (known as "Jerry") and return him to his Missouri master resulted in a mob's taking affairs into its own hands and freeing Henry. Secretary of State Daniel Webster fumed that such behavior constituted treason: Four men faced trial for their role in the rescue, but only the lone black defendant was convicted for violating the Fugitive Slave Act of 1793 (not the 1850 law). Syracuse abolitionists celebrated "Jerry Rescue Day" for years to come.

In 1854 Boston witnessed yet another confrontation over the enforcement of the Fugitive Slave Act of 1850. Anthony Burns, a preacher, escaped from Richmond, Virginia, in 1853, and made his way to Boston. A year later Burns was arrested: Determined to avoid a repeat of what had happened in the Minkins case, President Franklin Pierce sent soldiers to Boston to enforce the law. On May 26 a mob stormed the courthouse intending to free Burns, but Burns was returned to his master in Virginia, who sold him after rejecting offers from abolitionists who sought to buy Burns's freedom. Burns's new owner had no such compunctions about selling Burns, who returned to Boston a free man.

These sensational events provided only part of the story, however. Although slaveholders and their agents prevailed in 80 percent of the cases brought before commissioners, the number of alleged fugitives brought before the commissioners was but a small percentage of the slaves who had escaped from captivity. If personal liberty laws presented no real obstacle to the recovery of fugitives, their continued presence still stood as a mark of defiance against the federal government's efforts to support slavery. If, in the end, only twenty-three slaves escaped federal custody, the presence of northern antislavery mobs, litigious antislavery lawyers, and operators of the Underground Railroad in facilitating the escape of slaves northward complicated the task of federal authorities. Many northern whites simply wanted nothing to do with the recapture of runaway slaves.

White southerners pointed to northern resistance as highlighting the necessity for greater safeguards for their constitutional property rights. They were joined in this sentiment by several prominent northerners, including presidents Millard Fillmore, Franklin Pierce, and James Buchanan, as well as Daniel Webster. When several northern states fashioned new measures to protect the rights of accused runaways, the federal government did what it could to set those measures aside, most notably in the Supreme Court's 1859 decision in *Ableman v. Booth*, which overturned a decision by Wisconsin's supreme court that had declared the Fugitive Slave Act of 1850 unconstitutional.

By itself, although the Fugitive Slave Act of 1850 aroused controversy, it did little to shift the balance in national politics. Democratic candidate Franklin Pierce swept to victory in the 1852 presidential contest in the wake of the act's passage. It would not be until 1854, with the Kansas-Nebraska Act, that the politics of sectional controversy truly ignited. Antislavery northerners pointed to the act as part of an effort by proslavery southerners to subvert civil rights, and the act's embrace of federal power challenged the notion that proslavery southerners were consistent advocates of states' rights and restrictions on federal power. In turn, white southerners pointed to resistance in the North as evidence of bad faith at best and treason at worst, and proponents of secession highlighted the northern response to the Fugitive Slave Act as evidence that slavery was not safe within the Union.

As distasteful as many white northerners found the business of recapturing slaves and involving northerners in the preservation of slavery, they conceded that the U.S. Constitution provided for the recovery of runaway slaves. They criticized the law as a poor and unfair implementation of that promise. Among such critics was Abraham Lincoln, who repeatedly claimed that he would honor the constitutional promise while objecting to the way the Fugitive Slave Act of 1850 proposed to keep that promise. In the late 1850s Lincoln favored a revision of fugitive slave legislation consistent with other principles, although he never offered a specific proposal. Lincoln hoped to calm southern concerns about the violations of the constitutional provisions, and he reiterated his position as president-elect in an effort to counter secessionists' use of northern resistance to the Fugitive Slave Act as justification for secession. He repeated his pledge in his first inaugural address.

The Civil War provided a Republican-controlled Congress with a means to destroy the Fugitive Slave Act through a series of acts. In August 1861 Congress authorized the seizure of any slave who was being used to support the Confederate war effort as contraband of war. That law simply turned slaveholders' insistence that slaves were property on its head by saying that such property was subject to seizure under the laws of war. As Union forces penetrated the Confederacy, more slaves sought refuge within Union lines. Lacking an overall policy, Union military personnel devised a number of responses to slave owners' requests for protection. Some units closed their lines to fugitives; others returned them to owners on a case-by-case basis, sometimes offering refuge to the runaways. Congress remedied this confusion in March 1862, when it forbade military authorities to return slaves who entered their lines, although this mandate was not always observed. The following July, Congress passed a second confiscation act, declaring free all slaves who belonged to Confederate supporters and sympathizers. Five days later President Abraham Lincoln broached to his cabinet the idea of issuing a proclamation of emancipation. The proposal was shelved until September, when Lincoln issued a preliminary emancipation proclamation, giving the Confederate states one hundred days in which to return to the Union or face the loss of their slaves. The offer was ignored, whereupon Lincoln issued the Emancipation Proclamation on January 1, 1863, declaring free those slaves in enumerated areas deemed to be under Confederate control.

In less than two years, the U.S. government had gone from enforcing a legal obligation to capture and return fugitive slaves to harboring fugitives and granting them their freedom. However, the Fugitive Slave Act remained on the books, and it still applied in areas under Union control when loyal masters sought the return of fugitives not un-

Questions for Further Study

1. The Fugitive Slave Act of 1850 is written in arcane, repetitive, complex legal language; section 6, for example, contains a 451-word sentence. Why do you think laws at this time were written in such language?

2. In what important respects did the Fugitive Slave Act of 1850 alter the Fugitive Slave Act of 1793? What change in circumstances motivated Congress to change the existing law? What role did the Supreme Court case *Prigg v. Pennsylvania* (1842) play?

3. The 1850s were a decade of crisis for the United States, one that would culminate in the Civil War. How did the Fugitive Slave Act contribute to this atmosphere of crisis?

4. In what specific ways did some people defy the Fugitive Slave Act of 1850?

5. Putting aside the obvious injustice of slavery, what specific provisions of the Fugitive Slave Act of 1850 were regarded as particularly unjust by slavery's opponents? What do you think your reaction to the law would have been if you had lived in a northern city or in a southern community?

der military control. This situation did not last long, for on June 28, 1864, Congress repealed the Fugitive Slave Acts of 1793 and 1850.

See also Slavery Clauses in the U.S. Constitution (1787); Fugitive Slave Act of 1793; *Prigg v. Pennsylvania* (1842); *Twelve Years a Slave: Narrative of Solomon Northup* (1853); Emancipation Proclamation (1863).

Further Reading

■ Books

Campbell, Stanley W. *The Slave Catchers: Enforcement of the Fugitive Slave Law*. Chapel Hill: University of North Carolina Press, 1970.

Collison, Gary. *Shadrach Minkins: From Fugitive Slave to Citizen*. Cambridge, Mass.: Harvard University Press, 1997.

Cover, Robert. *Justice Accused: Antislavery and the Judicial Process*. New Haven, Conn.: Yale University Press, 1975.

Gara, Larry. *The Liberty Line: The Legend of the Underground Railroad*. Lexington: University of Kentucky Press, 1961.

Hamilton, Holman. *Prologue to Conflict: The Crisis and Compromise of 1850*. Lexington: University of Kentucky Press, 1964.

Morris, Thomas D. *Free Men All: The Personal Liberty Laws of the North, 1780–1861*. Baltimore, Md.: Johns Hopkins University Press, 1974.

Von Frank, Albert J. *The Trials of Anthony Burns: Freedom and Slavery in Emerson's Boston*. Cambridge, Mass.: Harvard University Press, 1998.

■ Web Sites

Hummel, Jeffrey Rogers, and Barry R. Weingast. "The Fugitive Slave Act of 1850: Symbolic Gesture or Rational Guarantee?" http://politicalscience.stanford.edu/faculty/documents/weingast-the%20fugitive%20slave%20act.pdf.

—Brooks D. Simpson

FUGITIVE SLAVE ACT OF 1850

Be it enacted by the Senate and House of Representatives of the United States of America in Congress assembled, That the persons who have been, or may hereafter be, appointed commissioners, in virtue of any act of Congress, by the Circuit Courts of the United States, and Who, in consequence of such appointment, are authorized to exercise the powers that any justice of the peace, or other magistrate of any of the United States, may exercise in respect to offenders for any crime or offense against the United States, by arresting, imprisoning, or bailing the same under and by the virtue of the thirty-third section of the act of the twenty-fourth of September seventeen hundred and eighty-nine, entitled "An Act to establish the judicial courts of the United States" shall be, and are hereby, authorized and required to exercise and discharge all the powers and duties conferred by this act.

§2. And be it further enacted, That the Superior Court of each organized Territory of the United States shall have the same power to appoint commissioners to take acknowledgments of bail and affidavits, and to take depositions of witnesses in civil causes, which is now possessed by the Circuit Court of the United States; and all commissioners who shall hereafter be appointed for such purposes by the Superior Court of any organized Territory of the United States, shall possess all the powers, and exercise all the duties, conferred by law upon the commissioners appointed by the Circuit Courts of the United States for similar purposes, and shall moreover exercise and discharge all the powers and duties conferred by this act.

§3. And be it further enacted, That the Circuit Courts of the United States shall from time to time enlarge the number of the commissioners, with a view to afford reasonable facilities to reclaim fugitives from labor, and to the prompt discharge of the duties imposed by this act.

§4. And be it further enacted, That the commissioners above named shall have concurrent jurisdiction with the judges of the Circuit and District Courts of the United States, in their respective circuits and districts within the several States, and the judges of the Superior Courts of the Territories, severally and collectively, in term-time and vacation; shall grant certificates to such claimants, upon satisfactory proof being made, with authority to take and remove such fugitives from service or labor, under the restrictions herein contained, to the State or Territory from which such persons may have escaped or fled.

§5. And be it further enacted, That it shall be the duty of all marshals and deputy marshals to obey and execute all warrants and precepts issued under the provisions of this act, when to them directed; and should any marshal or deputy marshal refuse to receive such warrant, or other process, when tendered, or to use all proper means diligently to execute the same, he shall, on conviction thereof, be fined in the sum of one thousand dollars, to the use of such claimant, on the motion of such claimant, by the Circuit or District Court for the district of such marshal; and after arrest of such fugitive, by such marshal or his deputy, or whilst at any time in his custody under the provisions of this act, should such fugitive escape, whether with or without the assent of such marshal or his deputy, such marshal shall be liable, on his official bond, to be prosecuted for the benefit of such claimant, for the full value of the service or labor of said fugitive in the State, Territory, or District whence he escaped: and the better to enable the said commissioners, when thus appointed, to execute their duties faithfully and efficiently, in conformity with the requirements of the Constitution of the United States and of this act, they are hereby authorized and empowered, within their counties respectively, to appoint, in writing under their hands, any one or more suitable persons, from time to time, to execute all such warrants and other process as may be issued by them in the lawful performance of their respective duties; with authority to such commissioners, or the persons to be appointed by them, to execute process as aforesaid, to summon and call to their aid the bystanders, or posse comitatus of the proper county, when necessary to ensure a faithful observance of the clause of the Constitution referred to, in conformity with the provisions of this act; and all good citizens are hereby commanded to aid and assist in the prompt and efficient execution of this law, whenever their services may be required, as aforesaid, for that purpose; and said warrants shall run, and be executed by said officers, anywhere in the State within which they are issued.

§6. And be it further enacted, That when a person held to service or labor in any State or Territory of the United States, has heretofore or shall hereafter escape into another State or Territory of the United States, the person or persons to whom such service or labor may be due, or his, her, or their agent or attorney, duly authorized, by power of attorney, in writing, acknowledged and certified under the seal of some legal officer or court of the State or Territory in which the same may be executed, may pursue and reclaim such fugitive person, either by procuring a warrant from some one of the courts, judges, or commissioners aforesaid, of the proper circuit, district, or county, for the apprehension of such fugitive from service or labor, or by seizing and arresting such fugitive, where the same can be done without process, and by taking, or causing such person to be taken, forthwith before such court, judge, or commissioner, whose duty it shall be to hear and determine the case of such claimant in a summary manner; and upon satisfactory proof being made, by deposition or affidavit, in writing, to be taken and certified by such court, judge, or commissioner, or by other satisfactory testimony, duly taken and certified by some court, magistrate, justice of the peace, or other legal officer authorized to administer an oath and take depositions under the laws of the State or Territory from which such person owing service or labor may have escaped, with a certificate of such magistracy or other authority, as aforesaid, with the seal of the proper court or officer thereto attached, which seal shall be sufficient to establish the competency of the proof, and with proof, also by affidavit, of the identity of the person whose service or labor is claimed to be due as aforesaid, that the person so arrested does in fact owe service or labor to the person or persons claiming him or her, in the State or Territory from which such fugitive may have escaped as aforesaid, and that said person escaped, to make out and deliver to such claimant, his or her agent or attorney, a certificate setting forth the substantial facts as to the service or labor due from such fugitive to the claimant, and of his or her escape from the State or Territory in which he or she was arrested, with authority to such claimant, or his or her agent or attorney, to use such reasonable force and restraint as may be necessary, under the circumstances of the case, to take and remove such fugitive person back to the State or Territory whence he or she may have escaped as aforesaid. In no trial or hearing under this act shall the testimony of such alleged fugitive be admitted in evidence; and the certificates in this and the first [fourth] sec-

tion mentioned, shall be conclusive of the right of the person or persons in whose favor granted, to remove such fugitive to the State or Territory from which he escaped, and shall prevent all molestation of such person or persons by any process issued by any court, judge, magistrate, or other person whomsoever.

§7. And be it further enacted, That any person who shall knowingly and willingly obstruct, hinder, or prevent such claimant, his agent or attorney, or any person or persons lawfully assisting him, her, or them, from arresting such a fugitive from service or labor, either with or without process as aforesaid, or shall rescue, or attempt to rescue, such fugitive from service or labor, from the custody of such claimant, his or her agent or attorney, or other person or persons lawfully assisting as aforesaid, when so arrested, pursuant to the authority herein given and declared; or shall aid, abet, or assist such person so owing service or labor as aforesaid, directly or indirectly, to escape from such claimant, his agent or attorney, or other person or persons legally authorized as aforesaid; or shall harbor or conceal such fugitive, so as to prevent the discovery and arrest of such person, after notice or knowledge of the fact that such person was a fugitive from service or labor as aforesaid, shall, for either of said offences, be subject to a fine not exceeding one thousand dollars, and imprisonment not exceeding six months, by indictment and conviction before the District Court of the United States for the district in which such offence may have been committed, or before the proper court of criminal jurisdiction, if committed within any one of the organized Territories of the United States; and shall moreover forfeit and pay, by way of civil damages to the party injured by such illegal conduct, the sum of one thousand dollars for each fugitive so lost as aforesaid, to be recovered by action of debt, in any of the District or Territorial Courts aforesaid, within whose jurisdiction the said offence may have been committed.

§8. And be it further enacted, That the marshals, their deputies, and the clerks of the said District and Territorial Courts, shall be paid, for their services, the like fees as may be allowed for similar services in other cases; and where such services are rendered exclusively in the arrest, custody, and delivery of the fugitive to the claimant, his or her agent or attorney, or where such supposed fugitive may be discharged out of custody for the want of sufficient proof as aforesaid, then such fees are to be paid in whole by such claimant, his or her agent or attorney; and in all cases where the proceedings are before a commissioner, he shall be entitled to a fee of ten dollars in full for his services in each case, upon the delivery of the said certificate to the claimant, his agent or attorney; or a fee of five dollars in cases where the proof shall not, in the opinion of such commissioner, warrant such certificate and delivery, inclusive of all services incident to such arrest and examination, to be paid, in either case, by the claimant, his or her agent or attorney. The person or persons authorized to execute the process to be issued by such commissioner for the arrest and detention of fugitives from service or labor as aforesaid, shall also be entitled to a fee of five dollars each for each person he or they may arrest, and take before any commissioner as aforesaid, at the instance and request of such claimant, with such other fees as may be deemed reasonable by such commissioner for such other additional services as may be necessarily performed by him or them; such as attending at the examination, keeping the fugitive in custody, and providing him with food and lodging during his detention, and until the final determination of such commissioners; and, in general, for performing such other duties as may be required by such claimant, his or her attorney or agent, or commissioner in the premises, such fees to be made up in conformity with the fees usually charged by the officers of the courts of justice within the proper district or county, as near as may be practicable, and paid by such claimants, their agents or attorneys, whether such supposed fugitives from service or labor be ordered to be delivered to such claimant by the final determination of such commissioner or not.

§9. And be it further enacted, That, upon affidavit made by the claimant of such fugitive, his agent or attorney, after such certificate has been issued, that he has reason to apprehend that such fugitive will he rescued by force from his or their possession before he can be taken beyond the limits of the State in which the arrest is made, it shall be the duty of the officer making the arrest to retain such fugitive in his custody, and to remove him to the State whence he fled, and there to deliver him to said claimant, his agent, or attorney. And to this end, the officer aforesaid is hereby authorized and required to employ so many persons as he may deem necessary to overcome such force, and to retain them in his service so long as circumstances may require. The said officer and his assistants, while so employed, to receive the same compensation, and to be allowed the same expenses, as are now allowed by law for transportation of criminals, to be certified by the judge of the district within which the arrest is made, and paid out of the treasury of the United States.

§10. And be it further enacted, That when any person held to service or labor in any State or Territory, or in the District of Columbia, shall escape therefrom, the party to whom such service or labor shall be due, his, her, or their agent or attorney, may apply to any court of record therein, or judge thereof in vacation, and make satisfactory proof to such court, or judge in vacation, of the escape aforesaid, and that the person escaping owed service or labor to such party. Whereupon the court shall cause a record to be made of the matters so proved, and also a general description of the person so escaping, with such convenient certainty as may be; and a transcript of such record, authenticated by the attestation of the clerk and of the seal of the said court, being produced in any other State, Territory, or district in which the person so escaping may be found, and being exhibited to any judge, commissioner, or other office, authorized by the law of the United States to cause persons escaping from service or labor to be delivered up, shall be held and taken to be full and conclusive evidence of the fact of escape, and that the service or labor of

Circuit Court	a court that sits at more than one location in the district it serves
concurrent jurisdiction	the concept that courts at different levels (for example, a state court and a federal court) both have jurisdiction over a case
District Court	a federal trial court, first established by Congress in the Judiciary Act of 1789
person held to service or labor	a slave
posse comitatus	Latin for "power of the county" and referring to the power to create a temporary police force from the citizenry
Territory	any of the western regions that were organized under the federal government but had not yet been admitted to the Union as states

the person escaping is due to the party in such record mentioned. And upon the production by the said party of other and further evidence if necessary, either oral or by affidavit, in addition to what is contained in the said record of the identity of the person escaping, he or she shall be delivered up to the claimant, And the said court, commissioner, judge, or other person authorized by this act to grant certificates to claimants or fugitives, shall, upon the production of the record and other evidences aforesaid, grant to such claimant a certificate of his right to take any such person identified and proved to be owing service or labor as aforesaid, which certificate shall authorize such claimant to seize or arrest and transport such person to the State or Territory from which he escaped: Provided, That nothing herein contained shall be construed as requiring the production of a transcript of such record as evidence as aforesaid. But in its absence the claim shall be heard and determined upon other satisfactory proofs, competent in law.

NARRATIVE OF THE LIFE OF HENRY BOX BROWN, WRITTEN BY HIMSELF

"I felt a cold sweat coming over me which seemed to be a warning that death was about to terminate my earthly miseries."

Overview

Narrative of the Life of Henry Box Brown, Written by Himself is one of many autobiographies composed by former slaves documenting their lives in bondage and their escape to freedom. Henry "Box" Brown was born a slave in Virginia in 1815; he escaped slavery in 1849 after being crated in a box (hence his nickname) in Richmond, Virginia, and shipped to Philadelphia, Pennsylvania. His story, especially the clever method he devised to flee slavery, made him a popular figure in abolitionist circles. Brown and a white abolitionist named Charles Stearns published the first version of Brown's autobiography, *Narrative of Henry Box Brown, Who Escaped from Slavery Enclosed in a Box 3 Feet Long and 2 Wide, Written from a Statement of Facts Made by Himself; With Remarks upon the Remedy for Slavery by Charles Stearns*, in 1849 in Boston. Brown revised and reprinted it two years later as *Narrative of the Life of Henry Box Brown, Written by Himself*, after he had fled to England, fearing reenslavement. The passage of the 1850 Fugitive Slave Act—a federal mandate requiring the return of runaway slaves to their owners—had prompted a mass migration of African Americans to Canada and the United Kingdom. Brown himself spent twenty-five years abroad before returning to the United States in 1875.

Brown's narrative was a useful tool in promoting abolition among men and women who were undecided on the issue of slavery. While there were other such narratives by former slaves in print, Brown's story drew more attention because of his remarkable means of escape. For those who might not have the opportunity to hear him lecture, the *Narrative* proved an effective means of persuading Americans to abolish the nation's "peculiar institution." First-person narratives such as Brown's are important historical records because they provide a view of slavery from someone who experienced it firsthand. These stories are not filtered through the eyes of the white owners but rather come straight from the slaves' perspective. Slave narratives, whether in the form of autobiographies such as Henry "Box" Brown's or a more modern version, such as the online oral histories gleaned from the Works Progress Administration slave narrative project of the 1930s, present true eyewitness accounts of the lives of enslaved African Americans.

Context

Wherever there has been oppression, there has been resistance to it in the form of individual acts of rebellion as well as organized efforts by groups of people united in a single cause. Such is the story of the Underground Road, later dubbed the Underground Railroad after the invention of steam railroad transportation in the nineteenth century. From the first instance of Europeans' bringing enslaved Africans to Virginia in 1619 to the time slavery was outlawed by the Thirteenth Amendment to the U.S. Constitution, slaves always attempted to flee captivity and assert their freedom. Escape was a means of protest, but the consequences, which varied from recapture and punishment to the mistreatment and separation of family members or even death, made slaves think hard before pursuing this avenue. Several options presented themselves to desperate, disconsolate slaves, and some managed to flee north, often to Canada (especially after passage of the Fugitive Slave Act of 1850) or south into Mexico, where land was available and, after 1830, slavery was prohibited. Although some runaways fled randomly, the most successful ones deliberately plotted their departure. Methods of escape varied widely among runaways, and personal accounts verify the challenges slaves faced to gain freedom.

The origin of the term *Underground Railroad* is hard to pin down, but historians generally credit one of several different sources. Eber M. Petitt, an Underground Railroad operator in western New York, claimed that the name was coined in Washington, D.C., where it appeared in an 1839 newspaper. A runaway slave is said to have told his captors that he journeyed north by "an underground road." Another story revolves around Tice Davids, a fugitive slave who swam to freedom from Kentucky and sought shelter and protection with an Ohio minister named John Rankin. Davids's owner wondered whether his slave had "disappeared through an underground road." According to a similar story

Time Line

1815
- Henry Brown is born in Louisa County, Virginia.

1830
- Brown's owner, John Barret, dies; his son, William, inherits Brown and takes him to Richmond, Virginia, to work in his tobacco factory.

1836
- Brown marries his first wife, Nancy, who is also a slave.

1848
- Brown's wife and three children are sold away from Richmond, which provides the impetus for Henry "Box" Brown's escape from slavery.

1849
- **March 29**
  Brown makes his escape from Richmond in a small wooden crate.

- **March 30**
  After a twenty-seven-hour journey, Brown—now a fugitive slave—arrives in Philadelphia, Pennsylvania.

- **September**
  Brown, with the help of the abolitionist Charles Stearns, publishes the first edition of his story, *Narrative of Henry Box Brown, Who Escaped from Slavery Enclosed in a Box 3 Feet Long and 2 Wide, Written from a Statement of Facts Made by Himself; With Remarks upon the Remedy for Slavery by Charles Stearns.*

1850
- **September 18**
  The Fugitive Slave Act is passed as a part of the Compromise of 1850.

- **October**
  Brown flees the United States for Great Britain and begins a lecture tour there.

1851
- **May**
  The revised version of Brown's autobiography is published as *Narrative of the Life of Henry Box Brown, Written by Himself.*

told by the abolitionist Levi Coffin, a Pennsylvania slave owner speculated that his slave had "gone off on an underground road." Whatever the origin of the term, participants began using railroad terminology around 1840 to help describe and hide their illegal activities.

Collaborators in the Underground Railroad could be sentenced to long prison terms, from five to twenty years, if caught and convicted of helping fugitive slaves escape their owners. The Underground Railroad aided hundreds of slaves and fueled discontent, anger, and hostility between northerners and southerners, ultimately leading to war. Aid to fugitive slaves came in various forms, which might include supplying food, clothing, protection from slave hunters, a place to sleep or hide, money, or guidance to the next "station" on the journey to freedom. Such assistance came from individuals, mutual aid societies, free African Americans, and benevolent societies. Rapid growth and expansion of African American communities in northern cities helped escalate the involvement of black churches and fraternal organizations, which provided safety and basic necessities to runaway slaves from the South. Free blacks in the North established vigilance committees and mutual aid societies in an effort to help escaping slaves. These all-black, or nearly all-black, groups aided fugitives by providing them with a safe place to stay, a good meal, medical attention, clothing, modest amounts of money, information on their legal rights, and protection from kidnappers in the area, along with forged identity papers indicating that the runaways were free persons.

It is impossible to accurately assess the success of the Underground Railroad. Census records and antislavery advocates and opponents never agreed on the number of slaves who reached freedom; the North as well as the South always expanded the number of slave losses for propaganda purposes—the North because it exemplified how much the slaves wanted freedom and the South in order to point out how the Yankees were interfering with their cherished way of life. Runaways relied largely on their own resources, with free African Americans and sympathetic whites contributing significant amounts toward aiding and protecting fleeing slaves. Generally, runaway slaves traveled the most hazardous part of their journey with little or no assistance. In certain areas or neighborhoods, houses or "stations" on the Underground Railroad could be spaced twelve to fifteen miles apart, the approximate distance a runaway could walk in a night. Typically, the lines in rural areas were places for fugitives to hide, seek nourishment, and change clothing. Some stops on the northward Underground Railroad were thirty miles apart, and escaping slaves rode concealed in wagons that could cover the distance in a night's journey.

Although the Underground Railroad did have some semblance of organization and operated successfully in its aid of runaway slaves to freedom, many people mistakenly believe that it was a fully operational system, widely linked from locations in the South directly through the North. Such was not the case. Because Underground Railroad employees engaged in activities that were illegal, opposed by most southerners, and a violation of federal and state laws, secrecy and spontaneity were the keys to its ultimate success. Much of the romanticism of the Underground Railroad and the various myths and legends that have become entrenched in Americana over time can be traced, initially, to the white abolitionist Harriet Beecher Stowe's famous novel *Uncle Tom's Cabin*. There is no doubt that the Underground Railroad did operate in various forms; nonetheless, most slaves had little knowledge of its existence. Southern slave owners took special care to keep such information away from their slaves, lest they attempt to flee. Although daring runaway attempts often ended in recapture and severe punishment, thousands of bound blacks—usually acting solo until they could find a safe house—continued to plan and carry out dangerous escapes to freedom. One slave who found a unique way to free himself was Henry "Box" Brown.

About the Author

Henry "Box" Brown was born into slavery in 1815 on Hermitage Plantation, located in Louisa County, Virginia. Both of his parents were also slaves; he was separated at the age of fifteen from his family (which included both parents and three brothers and four sisters). Following the death of his owner, John Barret, the property of Hermitage was divided among Barret's four sons. In 1830 Brown and his mother and sister Jane were given to one of the Barret sons, William, who owned a tobacco factory in Richmond. William Barret took Henry to Richmond but left Brown's parents on the plantation. Over the course of nearly two decades in Richmond, Brown had a total of four different overseers—some considerate and some abusive. Brown describes his last overseer, John F. Allen, as a "thorough-going villain." Despite having knowledge of Allen's mistreatment of the slaves, William Barret did not intervene on their behalf. As Brown notes, it really did not matter how kind the master was; denying anyone freedom was evil and wrong.

In 1836 Brown married a woman named Nancy who belonged to another slaveholder in Richmond. He and Nancy had three children. When her master sold her and the children away from Richmond in 1848, Brown decided that he had had enough, especially after Barret reneged on his offer to help reunite his family. At this point, Henry Brown began to plan his flight from slavery. From his work in the tobacco factory, he had been able to earn a little bit of money on the side, which he used to finance his escape. With the help of several friends, including a freedman, James Smith, and a sympathetic white storekeeper, Samuel Smith, Brown had himself crated into a box three feet, one inch long by two feet, six inches high and two feet wide. Brown paid Samuel Smith $86 (of his total savings of $166) for assistance in his getaway. On the morning of March 29, 1849, Brown began his journey in the box (as a shipment of "dry goods") toward freedom in Philadelphia, where the "package" was delivered to the Pennsylvania Anti-Slavery Society. The entire journey took twenty-seven hours, some of which Brown spent upside down.

Upon his arrival in the North, Brown began his lecture tour of New England. The following year, with assistance

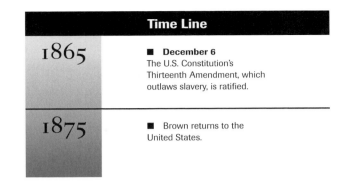

Time Line

1865

■ **December 6**
The U.S. Constitution's Thirteenth Amendment, which outlaws slavery, is ratified.

1875

■ Brown returns to the United States.

from a white abolitionist and writer named Charles Stearns, he published the first version of his autobiography, *Narrative of Henry Box Brown, Who Escaped from Slavery Enclosed in a Box 3 Feet Long and 2 Wide, Written from a Statement of Facts Made by Himself; With Remarks upon the Remedy for Slavery by Charles Stearns*. Accompanying his lectures was a set of images that were scrolled on screens, graphically depicting his harrowing flight from slavery and serving as a critical appraisal of capitalism and its reliance on slave labor. Following the passage of the Fugitive Slave Act in 1850, several attempts were made to capture him and return him to William Barret in Richmond. Consequently, Brown fled to England, where he went on another round of lecture tours, much as the former slaves and longtime freedom fighters Frederick Douglass and Ellen Craft had. In 1851 he published a revised version of his story without any help from Stearns. He called it *Narrative of the Life of Henry Box Brown, Written by Himself*. Brown later remarried and had one daughter, Annie. He continued touring, performing as a magician and mesmerist. Brown returned to the United States in 1875, but the cause and date of his death remain unknown.

Explanation and Analysis of the Document

Narrative of the Life of Henry Box Brown, Written by Himself, published in England in 1851, tells of Brown's journey from slavery to freedom. This version of Brown's story is a revision of his first memoir, *Narrative of Henry Box Brown, Who Escaped from Slavery Enclosed in a Box 3 Feet Long and 2 Wide, Written from a Statement of Facts Made by Himself; With Remarks upon the Remedy for Slavery by Charles Stearns*, which was published in Boston two years earlier. There are substantive differences between the two versions. The 1849 edition contains a different preface as well as lengthy remarks by the white abolitionist Charles Stearns on how to end slavery. The latter version drops the Stearns piece but includes letters from such abolitionists as the Unitarian minister Samuel J. May and an activist in the Pennsylvania Anti-Slavery Society named James Miller McKim, attesting to the importance of Brown's history. The styles of the two versions are also dissimilar; it is widely believed that Stearns ghostwrote the 1849 publication, which may account for the difference. While many of the details

Illustration of the escape of Henry "Box" Brown (Library of Congress)

of Brown's life as a slave are similar in both versions, the earlier edition is more of a diatribe on the evils of slavery in general from Stearns's perspective than a recounting of what it was like for Brown himself to live in bondage. Indeed, the Encyclopedia Virginia Web site lists Stearns as the author of the 1849 volume and refers to the 1851 edition as Brown's autobiography.

The excerpt presented here is chapter VII of the 1851 edition, which details Brown's escape. In this version, the story of his flight to freedom is much longer than in the previous edition. While Brown's account of his life as a slave is compelling, it was his unique method of escaping bondage that really gripped those who heard him speak or who read his *Narrative*. Brown's decision to flee was sparked by the sale of his wife and children to a new owner in North Carolina. Brown asked William Barret for help in pleading with the new owner to remain in Richmond; after initially agreeing to intervene, Barret ultimately refused.

◆ Introduction

Brown opens chapter VII by revealing the path toward his decision to escape from slavery. Brown was a religious

man, faithfully attending his church and even singing in the choir. His owner, William Barret, was a Christian, as was his wife's owner, Samuel Cottrell. Brown became disgusted with these so-called religious people who perpetuated the institution of slavery. After his wife and children were sold, Brown stopped attending church services because of his antipathy toward those who owned other human beings, yet he professed to continue worshiping the Lord in his own way. However, he did return to church on Christmas Day in 1848 at the behest of his friend, the freedman Dr. James Smith, who wanted him to sing with the choir. Dr. Smith, who was a conductor on the Underground Railroad, was overcome with grief during the choir's performance and vowed from that point on to sever ties with a congregation of slaveholders. Smith eventually went to New England and worked to end slavery. Brown, who was moved by the music (two verses of two songs are included here) decided at that point to engineer his own escape from slavery.

◆ Planning the Escape

Brown tells of his meeting with a white storekeeper (a person he does not name but who we know is Sam-

> "I prayed fervently that he who seeth in secret and knew the inmost desires of my heart, would lend me his aid in bursting my fetters asunder, and in restoring me to the possession of those rights, of which men had robbed me; when the idea suddenly flashed across my mind of shutting myself up in a box, and getting myself conveyed as dry goods to a free state."

> "The box which I had procured was three feet one inch wide, two feet six inches high, and two feet wide: and on the morning of the 29th day of March, 1849, I went into the box—having previously bored three gimlet holes opposite my face, for air, and provided myself with a bladder of water, both for the purpose of quenching my thirst and for wetting my face, should I feel getting faint."

> I felt a cold sweat coming over me which seemed to be a warning that death was about to terminate my earthly miseries, but as I feared even that, less than slavery, I resolved to submit to the will of God, and under the influence of that impression, I lifted up my soul in prayer to God, who alone, was able to deliver me."

> "A number of persons soon collected round the box after it was taken in to the house, but as I did not know what was going on I kept myself quiet. I heard a man say, 'let us rap upon the box and see if he is alive'; and immediately a rap ensued and a voice said, tremblingly, 'Is all right within?'; to which I replied—'all right.'"

uel Smith) and relating the story about the sale of his wife and children away from Richmond. Brown indicated he would pay the storekeeper $86, a little over half of what he had saved, if the storekeeper would help him escape. The shopkeeper discussed several possible plans with Brown, who also consulted with Dr. Smith about the best means of escape. Then, as Brown prayed to God to help him, the idea came to him of crating himself up in box and being shipped to the North. Brown told Dr. Smith of his plan, as well as Samuel Smith; the latter was willing to help but was

doubtful that anyone could survive in a box for the lengthy northward journey.

Brown then procured his box with the help of a carpenter. To keep his overseer, the unsympathetic Mr. Allen, from becoming suspicious, Brown deliberately poured oil of vitriol (sulfuric acid) on one of his own fingers; Brown's intent was to request time off while the supposedly accidental wound healed, but he had inadvertently used too much of the chemical and it burned his skin through to his bone. He showed his injured finger to Allen, who gave him time off to recover. In the meantime, Smith heard from his acquaintance in Philadelphia, who promised to make sure that Brown was delivered to the Philadelphia chapter of the Pennsylvania Anti-Slavery Society. At 4:00 AM on March 29, 1849, Brown was crated into his box; three holes had been bored opposite his face to allow for airflow. He also had a small container of water and a gimlet (a small hand tool) in case he needed to bore more holes for air. His friends took the crate, labeled "dry goods," to the Express Office for shipping.

♦ The Journey North

Brown's box was placed on a wagon, which carried him to the freight depot. He spent that part of the trip upside down. Once in the baggage car, he landed on his right side. At Potomac Creek, Brown's box was removed from the train and loaded onto a steamer—again upside down. Despite the terrible discomfort, Brown prayed to God to give him strength. Miraculously, two men who were on-board the steamer decided they needed to sit down, so they righted Brown's box and sat on it, much to the slave's relief. The steamer arrived in Washington, where Brown was placed on a wagon. The workers handled the box roughly, and Brown could hear his neck crack and was knocked out. When he awoke, he overheard a conversation about how there was not enough room for his box on the train; because it was stamped "express," however, it had to be shipped on at once. Brown was briefly upside down, but then his box was righted again, and he spent the remainder of his journey right side up. He finally arrived in Philadelphia after a twenty-seven hour journey covering 350 miles.

♦ Freedom

Once in Philadelphia, Brown's box was placed on a wagon and taken to the Anti-Slavery Society, as his friend in Richmond had arranged. A number of people gathered around the box once it was delivered. One person suggested they rap on the box to make sure Brown was still alive; they did and then asked if everything was all right. Brown responded that everything was fine. The box was opened and Brown tried to stand up, but he was too weak from his long confinement in the small space and ended up fainting. When he recovered, Brown was so overjoyed that he sang a hymn of thanksgiving, which he included in his *Narrative*. This momentous event was commemorated in a famous lithograph, "The Resurrection of Henry Box Brown," which was sold to fund the moving panorama that accompanied his lectures. The former slave was welcomed by a number of people, including James Miller McKim of the Anti-Slavery Society. It was decided that Brown could not stay in Philadelphia, so he set out for Boston. Once there, he went to an antislavery meeting, where he told the story of his escape. After Boston, he toured Maine, New Hampshire, Vermont, Connecticut, Rhode Island, parts of Pennsylvania, and New York, relating his experiences on the road to freedom. Brown ends the chapter with a song commemorating his journey in a box.

Audience

Henry "Box" Brown's *Narrative* was used by abolitionists to rouse opposition to the institution of slavery. Many antislavery advocates believed that the stories told by former slaves of their lives in bondage were far more effective in bringing home the horrors of the "peculiar institution" than were all the speeches and writings of free white men and women. It was hoped that such true stories would sway those who were uncertain about the issue to understand why slavery had to be abolished. More than abolitionist propaganda, slave narratives like Brown's also demonstrated the basic humanity of all people, regardless of the color of their skin. The narratives helped to humanize slaves, giving whites a face to go with each story of bondage. The depictions of slavery penned by bound African Americans were widely read in the antebellum North. Brown's *Narrative* resonates even in the contemporary world; it sheds light on the world of the slave and reveals the lengths that someone like Brown would go to in the quest for a free life.

Impact

Slave narratives in general had a great impact on those who read them. Many were published throughout the antebellum period and were widely read, including Henry "Box" Brown's *Narrative*. These thought-provoking stories sparked dialog on various issues besides slavery, among them the importance of basic human rights and dignity as well as the enduring thirst for freedom. The questions raised by slave narratives resonated in their own time and continue to do so today. Historians regard primary sources such as Brown's *Narrative* as vital to understanding the "peculiar institution" from the viewpoint of the enslaved. The perspective of slaveholders and proslavery advocates has been well documented; the slave narratives provide the underside of the story, delineating the multifaceted relationships between owners and slaves within a slave society while documenting the everyday lives and thoughts of those in bondage. The published slave narratives of the nineteenth century provide firsthand, eyewitness accounts of American slavery. These recollections have been augmented by the Works Progress Administration slave narratives collected during the New Deal in the 1930s. The administration employed historians and writers to interview and record the recollections of former slaves. This invaluable resource, along with earlier slave narratives, has helped historians better interpret the past while reminding future generations to cherish freedom and respect the essential human dignity of all people.

Brown's *Narrative* provided fuel for the cause of American abolitionists. The emotionalism aroused by the true stories of former slaves was invaluable to the movement. Brown's *Narrative* is similar in spirit to other famous works by escaped slaves, such as Henry Bibb's *Narrative of the Life and Adventures of Henry Bibb, an American Slave, Written by Himself* and William Wells Brown's *Narrative of William W. Brown, an American Slave. Written by Himself*. Although Frederick Douglass, whose own autobiography was popular, chastised Brown for revealing his unique method of flight because he felt that it would prevent other slaves from attempting the same thing, Brown nonetheless became a popular figure on the antislavery circuit both in the United States and in England.

See also Fugitive Slave Act of 1850; Thirteenth Amendment to the U.S. Constitution (1865).

Further Reading

■ Articles

Spencer, Suzette. "International Fugitive: Henry Box Brown, Anti-Imperialism, Resistance, and Slavery." *Social Identities: Journal for the Study of Race, Nation, and Culture* 12, no. 2 (2006): 227–248.

Wolff, Cynthia Griffin. "Passing beyond the Middle Passage: Henry 'Box' Brown's Translations of Slavery." *Massachusetts Review* 37, no. 1 (1996): 23–44.

■ Books

Blassingame, John W. *Slave Testimony: Two Centuries of Letters, Speeches, Interviews, and Autobiographies.* Baton Rouge: Louisiana State Press, 1978.

Franklin, John Hope, and Alfred A. Moss. *From Slavery to Freedom: A History of African Americans.* New York: McGraw-Hill, 1997.

Franklin, John Hope, and Loren Schweninger. *Runaway Slaves: Rebels on the Plantation.* New York: Oxford University Press, 1999.

Gara, Larry. *The Liberty Line: The Legend of the Underground Railroad.* Lexington: University of Kentucky Press, 1967.

Quarles, Benjamin. *Black Abolitionists.* New York: W. W. Norton, 1973.

Ripley, C. Peter, et al., eds. *Witness for Freedom: African American Voices on Race, Slavery, and Emancipation.* Chapel Hill: University of North Carolina Press, 1993.

Ruggles, Jeffrey. *The Unboxing of Henry Brown.* Richmond: Library of Virginia, 2003.

◆ Web Sites

"American Slave Narratives: An Online Anthology." American Studies at the University of Virginia Web site.
   http://xroads.virginia.edu/~hyper/wpa/wpahome.html.

"Born in Slavery: Slave Narratives from the Federal Writers' Project, 1936–1938." Library of Congress "American Memory" Web site.
   http://memory.loc.gov/ammem/snhtml/.

"Henry 'Box' Brown." Encyclopedia Virginia Web site.
   http://www.encyclopediavirginia.org/.

"North American Slave Narratives." Documenting the American South Web site.
   http://docsouth.unc.edu/neh/intro.html.

—Donna M. DeBlasio

Questions for Further Study

1. Compare Brown's narrative with William Wells Brown's "Slavery As It Is" (1847). What experiences did the two writers have in common? How, taken together, did the two narratives give readers a picture of slavery in the early nineteenth century?

2. Consult the entry titled Fugitive Slave Act of 1850. What impact did the passage of this act have on African Americans?

3. What role did the Underground Railroad play in the abolition movement? Why were so many people willing to run afoul of the law to participate in the Underground Railroad?

4. So-called slave narratives became highly popular in the decades before the Civil War. Why do you believe these narratives were so popular?

5. Many members of religious communities were staunch abolitionists, but many were not. What is Brown's attitude toward the religious leaders he encountered? Why do you think so many mainstream religious leaders defended, or at least tolerated, slavery?

NARRATIVE OF THE LIFE OF HENRY BOX BROWN, WRITTEN BY HIMSELF

Chapter VII.

I had for a long while been a member of the choir in the Affeviar church in Richmond, but after the severe family affliction to which I have just alluded in the last chapter and the knowledge that these cruelties were perpetrated by ministers and church members, I began strongly to suspect the christianity of the slave-holding church members and hesitated much about maintaining my connection with them. The suspicion of these slave-dealing christians was the means of keeping me absent from all their churches from the time that my wife and children were torn from me, until Christmas day in the year 1848; and I would not have gone then but being a leading member of the choir, I yielded to the entreaties of my associates to assist at a concert of sacred music which was to be got up for the benefit of the church. My friend Dr. Smith, who was the conductor of the under-ground railway, was also a member of the choir, and when I had consented to attend he assisted me in selecting twenty four pieces to be sung on the occasion.

On the day appointed for our concert I went along with Dr. Smith, and the singing commenced at half-past three o'clock, p.m. When we had sung about ten pieces and were engaged in singing the following verse—

Again the day returns of holy rest,
Which, when he made the world, Jehovah blest;
When, like his own, he bade our labours cease,
And all be piety, and all be peace,

The members were rather astonished at Dr. Smith, who stood on my right hand, suddenly closing his book, and sinking down upon his seat his eyes being at the same time filled with tears. Several of them began to inquire what was the matter with him, but he did not tell them. I guessed what it was and afterwards found out that I had judged of the circumstances correctly. Dr. Smith's feelings were overcome with a sense of doing wrongly in singing for the purpose of obtaining money to assist those who were buying and selling their fellow-men. He thought at that moment he felt reproved by Almighty God for lending his aid to the cause of slave-holding religion; and it was under this impression he closed his book and formed the resolution which he still acts upon, of never singing again or taking part in the services of a pro-slavery church. He is now in New England publicly advocating the cause of emancipation.

After we had sung several other pieces we commenced the anthem, which run thus—

Vital spark of heavenly flame,
Quit, O! quit the mortal frame,—

These words awakened in me feelings in which the sting of former sufferings was still sticking fast, and stimulated by the example of Dr. Smith, whose feelings I read so correctly, I too made up my mind that I would be no longer guilty of assisting those bloody dealers in the bodies and souls of men; and ever since that time I have steadfastly kept my resolution.

I now began to get weary of my bonds; and earnestly panted after liberty. I felt convinced that I should be acting in accordance with the will of God, if I could snap in sunder those bonds by which I was held body and soul as the property of a fellow man. I looked forward to the good time which every day I more and more firmly believed would yet come, when I should walk the face of the earth in full possession of all that freedom which the finger of God had so clearly written on the constitutions of man, and which was common to the human race; but of which, by the cruel hand of tyranny, I, and millions of my fellow-men, had been robbed.

I was well acquainted with a store-keeper in the city of Richmond, from whom I used to purchase my provisions; and having formed a favourable opinion of his integrity, one day in the course of a little conversation with him, I said to him if I were free I would be able to do business such as he was doing; he then told me that my occupation (a tobacconist) was a money-making one, and if I were free I had no need to change for another. I then told him my circumstances in regard to my master, having to pay him 25 dollars per month, and yet that he refused to assist me in saving my wife from being sold and taken away to the South, where I should never see her again; and even refused to allow me to go and see her until my hours of labour were over. I told him this took place about five months ago, and I had been meditating my escape from slavery since, and asked him, as no person was near us, if he could give me any information about how I should proceed. I told him I had a little money and if he would assist me I would pay him for so doing. The man asked me if I was not afraid to speak that way to him; I said no, for I imagined he believed that every man had a right to liberty. He said I was quite right, and asked me how much money I would give him if he would assist me to get away. I told him that I had 166 dollars and that I would give him the half; so we ultimately agreed that I should have his service in the attempt for $86. Now I only wanted to fix upon a plan. He told me of several plans by which others had managed to effect their escape, but none of them exactly suited my taste. I then left him to think over what would be best to be done, and, in the mean time, went to consult my friend Dr. Smith, on the subject. I mentioned the plans which the storekeeper had suggested, and as he did not approve either of them very much, I still looked for some plan which would be more certain and more safe, but I was determined that come what may, I should have my freedom or die in the attempt.

One day, while I was at work, and my thoughts were eagerly feasting upon the idea of freedom, I felt my soul called out to heaven to breathe a prayer to Almighty God. I prayed fervently that he who seeth in secret and knew the inmost desires of my heart, would lend me his aid in bursting my fetters asunder, and in restoring me to the possession of those rights, of which men had robbed me; when the idea suddenly flashed across my mind of shutting myself *up in a box*, and getting myself conveyed as dry goods to a free state.

Being now satisfied that this was the plan for me, I went to my friend Dr. Smith and, having acquainted him with it, we agreed to have it put at once into execution not however without calculating the chances of danger with which it was attended; but buoyed up by the prospect of freedom and increased hatred to slavery I was willing to dare even death itself rather than endure any longer the clanking of those galling chains. It being still necessary to have the assistance of the store-keeper, to see that the box was kept in its right position on its passage, I then went to let him know my intention, but he said although he was willing to serve me in any way he could, he did not think I could live in a box for so long a time as would be necessary to convey me to Philadelphia, but as I had already made up my mind, he consented to accompany me and keep the box right all the way.

My next object was to procure a box, and with the assistance of a carpenter that was very soon accomplished, and taken to the place where the packing was to be performed. In the mean time the store-keeper had written to a friend in Philadelphia, but as no answer had arrived, we resolved to carry out our purpose as best we could. It was deemed necessary that I should get permission to be absent from my work for a few days, in order to keep down suspicion until I had once fairly started on the road to liberty; and as I had then a gathered finger I thought that would form a very good excuse for obtaining leave of absence; but when I showed it to one overseer, Mr. Allen, he told me it was not so bad as to prevent me from working, so with a view of making it bad enough, I got Dr. Smith to procure for me some oil of vitriol in order to drop a little of this on it, but in my hurry I dropped rather much and made it worse than there was any occasion for, in fact it was very soon eaten in to the bone, and on presenting it again to Mr. Allen I obtained the permission required, with the advice that I should go home and get a poultice of flax-meal to it, and keep it well poulticed until it got better. I took him instantly at his word and went off directly to the store-keeper who had by this time received an answer from his friend in Philadelphia, and had obtained permission to address the box to him, this friend in that city, arranging to call for it as soon as it should arrive. There being no time to be lost, the store-keeper, Dr. Smith, and myself, agreed to meet next morning at four o'clock, in order to get the box ready for the express train. The box which I had procured was three feet one inch wide, two feet six inches high, and two feet wide: and on the morning of the 29th day of March, 1849, I went into the box—having previously bored three gimlet holes opposite my face, for air, and provided myself with a bladder of water, both for the purpose of quenching my thirst and for wetting my face, should I feel getting faint. I took the gimlet also with me, in order that I might bore more holes if I found I had not sufficient air. Being thus equipped for the battle of liberty, my friends nailed down the lid and had me conveyed to the Express Office, which was about a mile distant from the place where I was packed. I had no sooner arrived at the office than I was turned heels up, while some person nailed something on the end of the box. I was then put upon a waggon and driven off to the depot with my head down, and I had no sooner arrived at the depot, than the man who drove the waggon tumbled me roughly into the baggage car, where, however, I happened to fall on my right side.

The next place we arrived at was Potomac Creek, where the baggage had to be removed from the cars, to be put on board the steamer; where I was again placed with my head down, and in this dreadful position had to remain nearly an hour and a half, which, from the sufferings I had thus to endure, seemed like an age to me, but I was forgetting the battle of liberty, and I was resolved to conquer or die. I felt my eyes swelling as if they would burst from their sockets; and the veins on my temples were dreadfully distended with pressure of blood upon my head. In this position I attempted to lift my hand to my face but I had no power to move it; I felt a cold sweat coming over me which seemed to be a warning that death was about to terminate my earthly miseries, but as I feared even that, less than slavery, I resolved to submit to the will of God, and under the influence of that impression, I lifted up my soul in prayer to God, who alone, was able to deliver me. My cry was soon heard, for I could hear a man saying to another, that he had travelled a long way and had been standing there two hours, and he would like to get somewhat to sit down; so perceiving my box, standing on end, he threw it down and then two sat upon it. I was thus relieved from a state of agony which may be more easily imagined than described. I could now listen to the men talking, and heard one of them asking the other what he supposed *the box contained*; his companion replied he guessed it was "The Mail." I too thought it was a mail but not such a mail as he supposed it to be.

The next place at which we arrived was the city of Washington, where I was taken from the steamboat, and again placed upon a waggon and carried to the depot right side up with care; but when the driver arrived at the depot I heard him call for some person to help to take the box off the waggon, and some one answered him to the effect that he might throw it off; but, says the driver, it is marked "this side up with care;" so if I throw it off I might break something, the other answered him that it did not matter if he broke all that was in it, the railway company were able enough to pay for it. No sooner were these words spoken than I began to tumble from the waggon, and falling on the end where my head was, I could hear my neck give a crack, as if it had been snapped asunder and I was knocked completely insensible. The first thing I heard after that, was some person saying, "there is no room for the box, it will have to remain and be sent through to-morrow with the luggage train"; but the Lord had not quite forsaken me, for in answer to my earnest prayer He so ordered affairs that I should not be left behind; and I

now heard a man say that the box had come with the express, and it must be sent on. I was then tumbled into the car with my head downwards again, but the car had not proceeded far before, more luggage having to be taken in, my box got shifted about and so happened to turn upon its right side; and in this position I remained till I got to Philadelphia, of our arrival in which place I was informed by hearing some person say, "We are in port and at Philadelphia". My heart then leaped for joy, and I wondered if any person knew that such a box was there.

Here it may be proper to observe that the man who had promised to accompany my box failed to do what he promised; but, to prevent it remaining long at the station after its arrival, he sent a telegraphic message to his friend, and I was only twenty seven hours in the box, though travelling a distance of three hundred and fifty miles.

I was now placed in the depot amongst the other luggage, where I lay till seven o'clock, P.M., at which time a waggon drove up, and I heard a person inquire for such a box as that in which I was. I was then placed on a waggon and conveyed to the house where my friend in Richmond had arranged I should be received. A number of persons soon collected round the box after it was taken in to the house, but as I did not know what was going on I kept myself quiet. I heard a man say, "let us rap upon the box and see if he is alive;" and immediately a rap ensued and a voice said, tremblingly, "Is all right within?" to which I replied—"all right." The joy of the friends was very great; when they heard that I was alive they soon managed to break open the box, and then came my resurrection from the grave of slavery. I rose a freeman, but I was too weak, by reason of long confinement in that box, to be able to stand, so I immediately swooned away. After my recovery from the swoon the first thing, which arrested my attention, was the presence of a number of friends, every one seeming more anxious than another, to have an opportunity of rendering me their assistance, and of bidding me a hearty welcome to the possession of my natural rights, I had risen as it were from the dead; I felt much more than I could readily express; but as the kindness of Almighty God had been so conspicuously shown in my deliverance, I burst forth into the following hymn of thanksgiving,

I waited patiently, I waited patiently for the Lord, for the Lord;
And he inclined unto me, and heard my calling:
I waited patiently, I waited patiently for the Lord,

And he inclined unto me, and heard my calling:
And he hath put a new song in my mouth,
Even a thanksgiving, even a thanksgiving, even a
    thanksgiving unto our God.
Blessed, Blessed, Blessed, Blessed is the man,
    Blessed is the man,
Blessed is the man that hath set his hope, his hope
    in the Lord;
O Lord my God, Great, Great, Great,
Great are the wondrous works which thou hast done.
Great are the wondrous works which thou hast done,
    which thou hast done:
If I should declare them and speak of them, they
    would be more, more, more than I am able to express.
I have not kept back thy loving kindness and truth
    from the great congregation.
I have not kept back thy loving kindness and truth
    from the great congregation.
Withdraw not thou thy mercy from me,
Withdraw not thou thy mercy from me, O Lord;
Let thy loving kindness and thy truth always preserve me,
Let all those that seek thee be joyful and glad,
    Let all those that seek thee be joyful and glad, be
    joyful, and glad, be joyful and glad, be joyful, be
    joyful, be joyful, be joyful, be joyful and glad--be
    glad in thee.
And let such as love thy salvation,
And let such as love thy salvation, say, always,
The Lord be praised,
The Lord be praised.
Let all those that seek thee be joyful and glad,
And let such as love thy salvation, say always,
The Lord be praised,
The Lord be praised,
The Lord be praised.

    I was then taken by the hand and welcomed to the houses of the following friends:—Mr. J. Miller, Mr. M'Kim, Mr. and Mrs. Motte, Mr. and Mrs. Davis, and many others, by all of whom I was treated in the kindest manner possible. But it was thought proper that I should not remain long in Philadelphia, so arrangements were made for me to proceed to Massachusetts, where, by the assistance of a few Anti-slavery friends, I was enabled shortly after to arrive. I went to New York, where I became acquainted with Mr. H. Long, and Mr. Eli Smith, who were very kind to me the whole time I remained there. My next journey was to New Bedford, where I remained some weeks under the care of Mr. H. Ricketson, my finger being still bad from the effects of the oil of vitriol with which I dressed it before I left Richmond. While I was here I heard of a great Anti-slavery meeting which was to take place in Boston, and being anxious to identify myself with that public movement, I proceeded there and had the pleasure of meeting the hearty sympathy of thousands to whom I related the story of my escape. I have since attended large meetings in different towns in the states of Maine, New Hampshire, Vermont, Connecticut, Rhode Island, Pennsylvania, and New York, in all of which places I have found many friends and have endeavoured, according to the best of my abilities, to advocate the cause of the emancipation of the slave; with what success I will not pretend to say—but with a daily increasing confidence in the humanity and justice of my cause, and in the assurance of the approbation of Almighty God.

    I have composed the following song in commemoration of my fete in the box:—
    Air:—"Uncle Ned."

I.
Here you see a man by the name of Henry Brown,
Ran away from the South to the North;
Which he would not have done but they stole all his
    rights,
But they'll never do the like again.

Chorus—
Brown laid down the shovel and the hoe
Down in the box he did go;
No more Slave work for Henry Box Brown,
In the box by Express he did go.

II.
Then the orders they were given, and the cars did
    start away;
Roll along—roll along—roll along,
Down to the landing, where the steamboat lay,
To bear the baggage off to the north.

Chorus—

III.
When they packed the baggage on, they turned him
    on his head,
There poor Brown liked to have died;
There were passengers on board who wished to sit
    down,
And they turned the box down on its side.

Chorus—

IV.
When they got to the cars they threw the box off,
And down upon his head he did fall,
Then he heard his neck crack, and he thought it was
    broke,
But they never threw him off any more.

Chorus—

V.
When they got to Philadelphia they said he was in
    port,
And Brown then began to feel glad,

He was taken on the waggon to his final destination,
And left, "this side up with care."

Chorus—

VI.
The friends gathered round and asked if all was right,
As down on the box they did rap,
Brown answered them, saying; "yes all is right!"
He was then set free from his pain.

Chorus—

Glossary

"Again the day returns of holy rest …"	a Protestant hymn written by William Mason in 1796, slightly misquoted by Brown
gimlet	a tool for boring holes
"I waited patiently, I waited patiently for the Lord …"	a hymn based on Psalm 40, verse 1, of the biblical book of Psalms
oil of vitriol	concentrated sulfuric acid
25 dollars	roughly the equivalent of $5,000 wages for an unskilled worker today
"Vital spark of heavenly flame …"	a Protestant hymn based on a poem by the eighteenth-century British poet Alexander Pope titled "The Dying Christian to His Soul"

Sojourner Truth (Library of Congress)

SOJOURNER TRUTH'S "AIN'T I A WOMAN?"

1851

"If the first woman God ever made was strong enough to turn the world upside down all alone, these women together ought to be able to ... get it right side up again!"

Overview

On May 29, 1851, a former slave named Sojourner Truth stood before a crowd at a Women's Rights Convention in Akron, Ohio, and spoke about human rights and gender equity. Her comments on the strength, intelligence, and character of women captured the audience's attention and struck a particularly deep chord with the nineteenth-century lecturer and coordinator of the convention, Frances Dana Gage. Truth's speech is commonly referred to as the "Ain't I a Woman?" speech.

After her history-making address before the Women's Rights Convention, Truth added to her already growing reputation as a forceful reformer, a gifted itinerant preacher and singer, and a compelling public speaker. Her gripping discourse reflected the pain she had experienced as an African American woman in and out of bondage. Because she could not read or write, Truth never penned a memoir; however, an activist named Olive Gilbert crafted Truth's reminiscences into a book titled *Narrative of Sojourner Truth*. The book was first published in 1850, just one year before Truth delivered her "Ain't I a Woman?" speech.

Because Sojourner Truth was illiterate, she never wrote down her speeches. Accordingly, no "authorized" version of the speech exists. Four contemporaneous versions of the speech were produced by those in attendance at the convention. One of those was the work of Marius Robinson and appeared on June 21, 1851, in the *Anti-Slavery Bugle*, a newspaper published in Salem, Ohio. Twelve years after Truth delivered the speech, in 1863, Gage published her own recollections of and commentary on the now-famous oration. This version then appeared in the 1875 edition of *Narrative of Sojourner Truth* and in 1881 in *History of Woman Suffrage*, a volume edited by Elizabeth Cady Stanton, Susan B. Anthony, and Matilda Joslyn Gage. Both Robinson and Frances Gage were relying on their own recollections, so historians continue to dispute the issue of which version of the speech is closest to the speech as Sojourner Truth actually delivered it. Most agree that Gage's version probably incorporates many of her own words, including the refrain, "Ain't I a woman?", but it is often considered

the "standard" version of the speech in part because of its republication and in part because it is more poetic than the more sober version published by Robinson. Gage's original version of the speech reproduced many features of stereotypical southern plantation dialect, which Truth probably did not employ, for she spoke Dutch until she was ten years old. Both versions are reproduced here, with the dialect removed from the Gage version.

Context

The image of slavery in early U.S. history has an undeniably southern face; however, slavery also existed in the American North until the early nineteenth century. New York State, where Sojourner Truth was enslaved, did not emancipate its adult slaves until July 4, 1827. Although the institution of slavery was practiced on a much smaller scale in places such as Upstate New York, there was a time when slavery was a given and was accepted in many of the northern states.

Nevertheless, once emancipation was achieved in some states, Pennsylvania, Massachusetts, and New Hampshire being among the first (with Vermont never tolerating slavery at all), the idea—and practice—of abolition spread throughout the North. Antislavery societies began to spring up in the northern states; although they were composed of only a small number of people, this core began to have a much wider impact all over the North. Many abolitionists were not only campaigning for southern states to emancipate their slaves, they were also working to achieve some semblance of equality for African Americans outside the South. While northerners were by and large antislavery advocates, at least in a philosophical sense, some whites in the region were reluctant to support the complete integration of African Americans into mainstream white society. There were harsh Black Codes in many states, and whites often discriminated against blacks on issues such as equal access to education, employment, housing, and an array of other social matters.

As the idea of abolitionism began to take a more coherent shape in the 1830s and 1840s, women emerged as key leaders, speakers, and workers in the movement. Their newfound roles as agents of change were questioned by both men and other women as they began to assume more

1797
- Isabella Baumfree (later, Sojourner Truth) is born in Ulster County, New York, a slave of Johannes Hardenbergh.

1799
- New York State adopts a policy allowing for the gradual abolition of slavery.

1810
- Isabella is purchased by John Dumont.

1815
- Isabella marries a fellow slave, Tom, with whom she has five children.

1826
- **Fall**
  In a bold move, Isabella "walks away" from Dumont's farm with her infant daughter, Sophia, and is taken in by the Van Wagenen family.

1827
- **July 4**
  All adult slaves in New York State are legally freed.

1828
- Isabella succeeds in bringing her son, Peter, back from Alabama, where he was taken illegally.

1829
- Isabella moves with Peter to New York City.

1843
- **June 1**
  Isabella leaves New York City to become an itinerant preacher under the name "Sojourner."

1848
- The first convention on women's rights is held in Seneca Falls, New York, where the Declaration of Sentiments, modeled on the Declaration of Independence, is signed by sixty-eight women and thirty-two men.

and more power and visibility. In time, another, larger question arose: Might all women be viewed as a type of slave in nineteenth-century American society? At the time, women's rights to vote, own property, speak in public, travel freely, obtain an education, choose a career, and make basic decisions about the course of their own lives and the lives of their children were not guaranteed. Some women felt their own fetters when considering the abolitionist movement, and these women began to speak out on their own behalf.

The acknowledged formal beginning of the feminist movement took place in the summer of 1848 at a gathering of women's rights advocates in Seneca Falls, New York. It was at this convention that the Declaration of Sentiments, written by the activists Elizabeth Cady Stanton and Lucretia Mott, was first presented. The motivation behind the writing of the document, which is modeled on the Declaration of Independence, was Mott's being refused permission to speak at the world antislavery convention in London, England, despite the fact that she was an official delegate to the convention. Sixty-eight women and thirty-two men signed the document, which stated that women, as human beings with the same "unalienable rights" as men and as citizens of the United States of America, should have those rights recognized and respected.

After this conference came others, and support—from men and women, both black and white—began to grow. Although some women wanted their movement to be recognized on its own, entirely separate from that of abolition, the majority of women's rights supporters viewed both movements as equally important calls for reform.

Sojourner Truth, as both a woman and a former slave, turned her efforts to the twin causes of women's rights and abolition, serving as a living symbol of both. As slavery in the 1840s and 1850s had firmly acquired that southern face, Truth was often characterized in articles and reports as speaking with a southern dialect; she objected to this stereotypical depiction, as her experience was not of southern slavery but of *American* slavery, and her accent reflected her Dutch heritage. Because she had been a slave of the North, Truth felt it was her duty to agitate for abolition across the whole United States. Her memorable speech before the Women's Rights Convention in 1851 demonstrates her commitment to equality in all areas and marries her outrage over black oppression with her anger over the second-class status of American women in the mid-nineteenth century.

About the Author

Isabella Baumfree, who later renamed herself Sojourner Truth, is believed to have been born in 1797 in Ulster County, New York. Her parents, both Dutch-speaking slaves, were named James and Betsey. When their owner, Johannes Hardenbergh, died approximately two years later, James and Betsey, along with Isabella and her brother, went to live with Hardenbergh's son Charles. For the next seven years Isabella and her family lived with the rest of Hardenbergh's slaves in the damp cellar of his hotel and residence.

During this time Isabella learned the Lord's Prayer from her mother and heard the heartbreaking stories of her older siblings being sold away from their parents.

When Charles Hardenbergh died, Isabella's parents, too old to work anymore, were freed, but Isabella and her brother were sold at auction to separate masters. Over the next two years Isabella lived in two different Ulster County households, one of which treated her severely, since she spoke only Dutch and could not understand their English commands. She eventually learned English but acquired many permanent scars from her owner's whippings.

In 1810 a farmer and businessman named John Dumont bought Isabella. She spent the next fifteen years as his slave. Dumont apparently treated her well, but his wife did not. While in the Dumont family's employ, Isabella married an older slave named Tom and between 1815 and 1826 had five children, one of whom died in infancy.

New York emancipated all adult slaves on July 4, 1827, but Dumont had promised Isabella and Tom that they would be freed in July of 1826. He reneged on his promise, though, on the ground that Isabella still owed him several months' work to make up for the time she had been incapacitated the previous year with a hand injury. Isabella worked into the fall of 1826, until she felt that she had paid her debt to a master she looked up to; then she walked away with her infant daughter, leaving two of her children and her husband at the Dumont house. Her marriage had not been a particularly happy one, and technically her children would be slaves until they were in their twenties under New York's emancipation laws. Traveling by foot with the baby, Isabella reached the home of Isaac and Maria Van Wagenens, who agreed to take them in. When Dumont came looking for Isabella, the Van Wagenens purchased her and her infant, but they treated them as if they were already free.

After the 1827 emancipation date, Isabella worked over the next year to recover her young son, Peter, who had been illegally taken from the state of New York into Alabama. With help from the Van Wagenens, she eventually brought her son back from the Deep South. Around this time she also joined the Methodist Church. After leaving the Van Wagenens, Isabella lived with Peter in New York City from 1829 to 1842, when Peter was lost on a whaling ship. Prior to losing her son for the second time, she worked as a domestic; however, in 1843 the grieving Isabella decided to become a wandering preacher. Calling herself "Sojourner" (meaning one who stays only temporarily in one place), she later added a second name, "Truth." Sojourner Truth said she changed her name in order to put behind her all vestiges of her life in New York City.

In 1844 Truth purchased her own home in Northampton, Massachusetts—no small feat for an illiterate freedwoman. She began preaching across the Northeast, and—with the help of the writer Olive Gilbert and William Lloyd Garrison, the American abolitionist and editor of *The Liberator*—her *Narrative of Sojourner Truth* was published in 1850. Although there was always a religious element to her speeches, Truth soon became more of a reformer than a preacher, speaking out against slavery and for women's

Time Line

1850

■ **April 15**
Sojourner Truth buys a house in Northampton, Massachusetts.

■ Truth's *Narrative* is published.

1851

■ **May 29**
Truth delivers her "Ain't I a Woman?" speech at the Women's Rights Convention in Akron, Ohio.

■ **June 21**
Marius Robinson prints his recollected version of Truth's speech in the *Anti-Slavery Bugle*, a newspaper published in Salem, Ohio.

1861

■ **April 12**
Confederates fire on Fort Sumter, South Carolina, signaling the start of the Civil War.

1863

■ **April**
Harriet Beecher Stowe publishes an article about Truth in the *Atlantic Monthly*.

■ **May 2**
Frances Dana Gage publishes her version of Truth's speech.

1864

■ Sojourner Truth meets President Abraham Lincoln at the White House in Washington, D.C.

1865

■ **January 31**
The Thirteenth Amendment to the U.S. Constitution is passed by Congress, outlawing slavery in the United States; however, it is not ratified by all the states until December 6.

■ **April 9**
The Civil War ends with Confederate general Robert E. Lee's surrender to General Ulysses S. Grant at Appomattox Court House in Virginia.

1883

■ **November 26**
Truth dies at her home in Battle Creek, Michigan.

2009

■ **April 28**
American first lady Michelle Obama unveils a bronze statue of Sojourner Truth that will remain on permanent display in the visitor's center of the nation's capitol.

rights. This led her to attend the women's rights conventions in Worcester, Massachusetts, in 1850, and in Akron, Ohio, in 1851, the latter being where she delivered her famous "Ain't I a Woman?" speech.

Truth is said to have had a keen knack for sizing up her audiences. According to most historians, she spoke extemporaneously, tailoring each address to the particular group of listeners present at a given event. In addition, because she never learned to read or write, she was unable to prepare notes for her lectures. Nevertheless, her deep voice, her Dutch accent, her turns of phrase, and her distinctive oratory manner stuck with people, making her speeches very memorable. At one particular speaking engagement in Indiana in 1858, some members of the audience thought she was a man disguised as a woman because of her height of almost six feet, her low voice, and her gutsy intelligence; in response, she is said to have opened her shirt to expose her breasts.

Truth moved to Battle Creek, Michigan, in the late 1850s. She continued to speak, and, during and after the Civil War, she worked to help freed slaves adjust to life after emancipation. In 1863 the white abolitionist and author of *Uncle Tom's Cabin*, Harriet Beecher Stowe, published an article in the April issue of *Atlantic Monthly* about a visit she had received from Truth. The following month, Frances Dana Gage, the chairperson of the 1851 women's rights meeting in Akron, published her own version of the speech Truth had made there a dozen years earlier. Despite Truth's Dutch accent, Gage for some reason endowed the speaker with a decidedly southern drawl in her account. Thereafter the speech was widely referred to as "Ain't I a Woman?"

By 1870 Truth's lecture topics had expanded beyond the subject of equal rights to encompass issues such as temperance and a ban on capital punishment. The expanded version of her *Narrative*, including Gage's version of her "Ain't I a Woman?" speech, was published in 1875. During the rest of her years Truth campaigned for the fair treatment of former slaves, equal rights for women, and other causes she deemed important. She spoke for and unsuccessfully attempted to vote for President Ulysses S. Grant when he campaigned for his second term in office, and she rode on the streetcars of the nation's capital, working to desegregate them. On November 26, 1883, she died at her home in Battle Creek, Michigan.

Explanation and Analysis of the Document

No written transcript of Sojourner Truth's speech at the 1851 Women's Rights Convention held in Akron, Ohio, has ever been found. The words commonly attributed to Truth in her "Ain't I a Woman?" address come from secondary sources, so their authenticity remains in question. Several journalists had covered the convention for area newspapers, and their accounts differ from Gage's on certain key points. Marius Robinson published the best known of these alternative pieces on Truth's speech in the June 21, 1851, edition of the *Anti-Slavery Bugle*. Critics point out that this version of the speech appeared only three weeks after Truth delivered it, making it a far more contemporary and probably more accurate rendering than Gage's account, which is actually a recollection published twelve years after the convention. A lecturer and writer, Gage presided over the 1851 women's rights meeting in Akron. In 1863 she decided to publish a report of Truth's landmark speech as a sort of companion to Harriet Beecher Stowe's piece about a visit from Truth, which appeared in the April issue of *Atlantic Monthly*.

For years critics have speculated on the dependability of Gage's retelling. Truth never wrote down any of her own speeches. Gage herself admits that she is giving "but a faint sketch" of Truth's address at the convention. Still, accounts by Gage and Robinson do share certain elements, including references to Truth's ability to work just as hard as a man, with just as much muscle. In paragraph 2, Gage quotes Truth as saying,

> Look at me! Look at my arm! I have ploughed and planted, and gathered into barns, and no man could head me! And ain't I a woman? I could work as much and eat as much as a man—when I could get it—and bear the lash as well!

Robinson, in contrast, has it that she said "I have as much muscle as any man, and can do as much work as any man. I have plowed and reaped and husked and chopped and mowed, and can any man do more than that?" Other elements common to both accounts include Truth's reasoning that if men could hold a quart of intellect and women a pint, it made no sense for men to object to giving women the right to their full pint. According to Gage in paragraph 3, Truth asks, "Wouldn't you be mean not to let me have my little half measure full?" Robinson, in contrast, says, "As for intellect, all I can say is, if a woman have a pint, and a man a quart—why can't she have her little pint full?"

Truth's commentary on biblical arguments against women's rights is included in both versions as well. Truth takes on the argument for men's entitlement in Gage's paragraph 4: "Then that little man in black there, he says women can't have as much rights as men, 'cause Christ wasn't a woman! Where did your Christ come from?" According to Gage, Truth answers this rhetorical question with the statement, "Man had nothing to do with Him." In her commentary on the speech (not reproduced here), Gage adds, "Oh, what a rebuke that was to the little man." Robinson, in contrast,

Yᵉ MAY SESSION OF Yᵉ WOMAN'S RIGHTS CONVENTION—Yᵉ ORATOR OF Yᵉ DAY DENOUNCING Yᵉ LORDS OF CREATION.

Illustration from Harper's Weekly *of a women's rights convention in the 1850s* (Library of Congress)

says, "And how came Jesus into the world? Through God who created him and the woman who bore him. Man, where was your part?" In paragraph 5 of Gage's version, Truth refutes the notion that women are unworthy of equal rights because the actions of the first woman, Eve, plunged the entire world into sin. She tells the audience that if one woman could turn the world upside down all by herself, a whole group of women could surely "get it right side up again! And now they is asking to do it, the men better let them." Robinson's recollection was "I have heard the Bible and have learned that Eve caused man to sin. Well, if woman upset the world, do give her a chance to set it right side up again." This statement in both versions was apparently directed toward white men who wanted women to be silent, subservient helpers in social and moral reform, including abolitionism.

However, Gage inserts into her reminiscence several ideas that are not found in any of the other accounts of Truth's oration. Some historians have seized upon the key phrase "Ain't I a Woman?" in particular, noting that had these words been used repeatedly by Truth as Gage suggests, at least one contemporary report would have remarked on it. Furthermore, Truth did not usually use poetic repetition to make her points in her speeches, but Gage did. The phrase "Ain't I a Woman?", then, was likely coined by Gage.

Other inconsistencies in Gage's version include Truth's supposed statement about having given birth to thirteen children, most of whom were sold away to various slave-holders. In reality, Truth had only five children, one of whom died; only one of the surviving four was sold (illegally) into slavery, and Truth secured his return from Alabama in a landmark court case in 1828. Some scholars speculate that Gage's memory from twelve years earlier may have been hazy; others hold that she felt justified in her use of poetic license because it added a legitimate sense of urgency to the important causes of abolition and women's rights.

It is not known whether Truth heard Gage's account prior to its publication or if she objected to any of the inconsistencies between Gage's version and her own memories of the speech. The fact that it was added to the 1875 edition of Truth's *Narrative* strengthens the case for Gage's claims, but it is also possible that Truth was unaware of its inclusion in the updated edition of her book. It may be that Truth decided that Gage's version spoke to the issues prominent during the Civil War years, such as compassionate, if not equal, treatment of black Americans and especially of black women. This could explain Gage's inclusion of the phrase "Ain't I a Woman?"—particularly when it is paired with the following lines from paragraph 2: "That man over there says that women need

"And ain't I a woman? Look at me! Look at my arm! I have ploughed and planted, and gathered into barns, and no man could head me! And ain't I a woman? I could work as much and eat as much as a man—when I could get it—and bear the lash as well! And ain't I a woman?"

(Gage, Paragraph 2)

"Then that little man in black there, he says women can't have as much rights as men, 'cause Christ wasn't a woman! Where did your Christ come from? Where did your Christ come from? From God and a woman! Man had nothing to do with Him."

(Gage, Paragraph 4)

"If the first woman God ever made was strong enough to turn the world upside down all alone, these women together ought to be able to turn it back, and get it right side up again! And now they is asking to do it, the men better let them."

(Gage, Paragraph 5)

"I am a woman's rights. I have as much muscle as any man, and can do as much work as any man."

(Robinson, Paragraph 1)

"But man is in a tight place, the poor slave is on him, woman is coming on him, and he is surely between a hawk and a buzzard."

(Robinson, Paragraph 5)

to be helped into carriages, and lifted over ditches, and to have the best place everywhere. Nobody ever helps me into carriages, or over mud-puddles, or gives me any best place!" This observation points out the stark difference in the treatment of black and white women, and it shows that African American women were not seen first as women but as black. If Truth, as an abolitionist and a women's rights activist, agreed with Gage's basic sentiments, then in spirit, if not in letter, her ideas still shine through in Gage's "Ain't I a Woman?" as well as in Robinson's more prosaic version.

Audience

Sojourner Truth delivered her speech, most likely impromptu, at the 1851 Women's Rights Convention held in Akron, Ohio. Most people in the crowd were white women, although some men, black and white, were present. Gage makes reference to the "Methodist, Baptist, Episcopal, Presbyterian, and Universalist ministers [who] came in to hear and discuss the resolutions presented." Although many members of the audience shared the conviction that women in the United States were being denied basic rights, a few of the men in the crowd felt the need to assert their belief that men were superior to women. Truth's speech was no doubt prompted by these assertions.

Impact

The impact of Truth's speech was nothing short of magical. According to Gage, Sojourner Truth "had taken us up in her strong arms and carried us safely over the slough of difficulty, turning the whole tide in our favor." She had "subdued the mobbish spirit of the day, and turned the sneers and jeers of an excited crowd into notes of respect and admiration." But this description conflicts with the contemporary reports, even her own, of both the "spirit of the day" and Truth's impact on the crowd before and after her speech. Indeed, Gage's 1863 recollection seems to project the attitudes toward women's rights groups in later years onto the crowd at the Akron meeting in 1851. None of the other known reports on the convention mention the huge change in the crowd that Gage's version describes. Surely if Truth had exhibited some transforming power over the "spirit of the day," it would have been noted in at least one, if not all, of the four contemporary sources.

Nevertheless, Marius Robinson did comment on Truth's presence at the convention, writing: "It is impossible to transfer to it to paper…. Those only can appreciate it who saw her powerful form, her whole-souled, earnest gesture, and listened to her strong and truthful tones." Robinson was clearly impressed by Truth, but neither he nor the other journalists who covered the story in 1851 allude to her conversion of a hostile audience to a docile one.

This particular speech of Truth's also made an important impact in the 1970s and 1980s, when attention was focused on both women's and black rights. Especially as described by Gage, the speech seemed to highlight both concerns and gave both movements a strong heroine to whom they could look as a role model. Sojourner Truth and her speech continue to inspire, which can be seen, for example, by the erection of a permanent statue of her unveiled in April of 2009, in the visitor's center of the U.S. Capitol.

See also Emancipation Proclamation (1863); Thirteenth Amendment to the U.S. Constitution (1865).

Further Reading

■ Books

Mabee, Carleton, and Susan Mabee Newhouse. *Sojourner Truth: Slave, Prophet, Legend*. New York: New York University Press, 1993.

Painter, Nell Irvin. *Sojourner Truth: A Life, A Symbol*. New York: W. W. Norton, 1996.

Truth, Sojourner, and Olive Gilbert. *Narrative of Sojourner Truth*. New York: Arno Press, 1968.

Questions for Further Study

1. Why do you believe Truth's speech, delivered extemporaneously by a woman who could neither read nor write, continues to attract attention as an important document in African American history as well as in the history of women's struggle for equal rights?

2. Describe the role of women in the abolition movement. Why do you think so many abolitionists at the time were women?

3. What was the relationship between the abolition movement and the women's rights movement at the middle of the nineteenth century?

4. If you had been present at the Akron convention, what do you think your reaction to Truth's speech would have been? Explain why, trying to imagine yourself as living at that time and in that place.

5. What biblical arguments does Truth make? Why do you think she relied on biblical events and concepts in a speech such as this?

■ Web Sites

"Ain't I a Woman? Reminiscences of Sojourner Truth Speaking." History Matters Web site.
   http://historymatters.gmu.edu/d/5740/.

Truth, Sojourner. "Ain't I a Woman?" Sojourner Truth Institute of Battle Creek Web site.
   http://www.sojournertruth.org/Library/Speeches/AintIAWoman.htm.

"A Woman's World: Speaking Out for Women's Equality." American Experience Online,
   http://www.pbs.org/wgbh/amex/lincolns/filmmore/ps_rights.html.

   —Angela M. Alexander

Sojourner Truth's "Ain't I a Woman?"

[Frances Dana Gage version]

Well, children, where there is so much racket there must be something out of kilter. I think that 'twixt the negroes of the South and the women at the North, all talking about rights, the white men will be in a fix pretty soon. But what's all this here talking about?

That man over there says that women need to be helped into carriages, and lifted over ditches, and to have the best place everywhere. Nobody ever helps me into carriages, or over mud-puddles, or gives me any best place! And ain't I a woman? Look at me! Look at my arm! I have ploughed and planted, and gathered into barns, and no man could head me! And ain't I a woman? I could work as much and eat as much as a man—when I could get it—and bear the lash as well! And ain't I a woman? I have borne thirteen children, and seen most all sold off to slavery, and when I cried out with my mother's grief, none but Jesus heard me! And ain't I a woman?

Then they talk about this thing in the head; what's this they call it? ("Intellect," whispered someone near.) That's it, honey. What's that got to do with women's rights or negroes' rights? If my cup won't hold but a pint, and yours holds a quart, wouldn't you be mean not to let me have my little half measure full?

Then that little man in black there, he says women can't have as much rights as men, 'cause Christ wasn't a woman! Where did your Christ come from? Where did your Christ come from? From God and a woman! Man had nothing to do with Him...."

If the first woman God ever made was strong enough to turn the world upside down all alone, these women together ought to be able to turn it back, and get it right side up again! And now they is asking to do it, the men better let them.

Obliged to you for hearing me, and now old Sojourner ain't got nothing more to say.

[Marius Robinson version]

I want to say a few words about this matter. I am a woman's rights. I have as much muscle as any man, and can do as much work as any man. I have plowed and reaped and husked and chopped and mowed, and can any man do more than that? I have heard much about the sexes being equal. I can carry as much as any man, and can eat as much too, if I can get it. I am as strong as any man that is now.

As for intellect, all I can say is, if a woman have a pint, and a man a quart—why can't she have her little pint full? You need not be afraid to give us our rights for fear we will take too much,—for we can't take more than our pint'll hold.

The poor men seems to be all in confusion, and don't know what to do. Why children, if you have woman's rights, give it to her and you will feel better. You will have your own rights, and they won't be so much trouble.

I can't read, but I can hear. I have heard the Bible and have learned that Eve caused man to sin. Well, if woman upset the world, do give her a chance to set it right side up again. The lady has spoken about Jesus, how he never spurned woman from him, and she was right. When Lazarus died, Mary and Martha came to him with faith and love and besought him to raise their brother. And Jesus wept—and Lazarus came forth. And how came Jesus into the world? Through God who created him and the woman who bore him. Man, where was your part?

But the women are coming up blessed be God and a few of the men are coming up with them. But man is in a tight place, the poor slave is on him, woman is coming on him, and he is surely between a hawk and a buzzard.

Frederick Douglass (Library of Congress)

FREDERICK DOUGLASS'S "WHAT TO THE SLAVE IS THE FOURTH OF JULY?"

"What, to the American slave, is your 4th of July? I answer: a day that reveals to him ... the gross injustice and cruelty to which he is the constant victim."

Overview

Frederick Douglass's "What to the Slave Is the Fourth of July" is the most famous speech delivered by the abolitionist and civil rights advocate Frederick Douglass. In the nineteenth century, many American communities and cities celebrated Independence Day with a ceremonial reading of the Declaration of Independence, which was usually followed by an oral address or speech dedicated to the celebration of independence and the heritage of the American Revolution and the Founding Fathers. On July 5, 1852, the Ladies' Anti-Slavery Society of Rochester, New York, invited Douglass to be the keynote speaker for their Independence Day celebration.

The "Fourth of July" speech, scheduled for Rochester's Corinthian Hall, attracted a crowd of between five hundred and six hundred, each of whom paid twelve and a half cents for admission. The meeting opened with a prayer offered by the Reverend S. Ottman of Rush, New York, followed by a reading of the Declaration of Independence by the Reverend Robert R. Raymond of Syracuse, New York. Douglass then delivered his address, which the local press reported to be eloquent and admirable and which drew much applause. Upon the conclusion of the address, the crowd thanked Douglass and called for the speech to be published in pamphlet form. Douglass complied, publishing a widely distributed pamphlet of the address. He also reprinted a text of the speech in his newspaper *Frederick Douglass' Paper* on July 9, 1852.

Context

The 1850s were a time of rising sectional tensions as slavery became the single most divisive issue in the United States. The United States' war with Mexico (1846–1848) resulted in the acquisition of a continental United States that stretched from the Atlantic to Pacific oceans. Even before the war concluded, Americans began debating whether slavery should be allowed in California and the New Mexico territories. The matter was settled with the Compromise of 1850, which admitted California as a free state but left the matter of slavery open in the territory that would become the states of Utah, New Mexico, and Arizona. In exchange for agreeing to the compromise, southerners in Congress demanded more protection for slavery where it existed, which resulted in the Fugitive Slave Act of 1850. The new law, passed in September 1850, superseded the Fugitive Slave Act of 1793 and required northerners to assist in returning escaped slaves. It also provided an unfair fee structure for fugitive slave commissioners, failed to provide jury trials, and did not permit an alleged fugitive to testify in his or her own defense. The Fugitive Slave Act led a number of northern states to pass personal liberty laws that aimed to skirt the act by routing fugitive slave cases through state courts.

The Fugitive Slave Act of 1850 also led many formerly pacifist antislavery activists to take a more militant stance against slavery. On numerous occasions in the 1850s, abolitionists planned and executed the escape of fugitive slaves held in custody or liable for capture. In September 1851 antislavery activists killed the Maryland slaveholder Edward Gorsuch near Christiana, Pennsylvania, as he attempted to capture some fugitives. The following month abolitionists in Syracuse, New York, successfully rescued a slave by the name of Jerry Henry from fugitive slave commissioners in that city. Although Douglass did not participate in that rescue, many of his closest friends did, and he often spoke at annual "Jerry Rescue" celebrations.

If the Fugitive Slave Act served to heighten awareness and prompt physical action against slavery among abolitionists, the March 1852 publication of Harriet Beecher Stowe's *Uncle Tom's Cabin* succeeded in bringing the evils of slavery to the attention of the citizens of the northern states. This novel, which provided a vivid depiction of the lives of slaves, sold an amazing three hundred thousand copies in 1852, but many in Douglass's audience had already read the novel, as it had been published in forty installments beginning in June 1851 in the abolitionist weekly newspaper the *National Era*. Arriving on the heels of the highly publicized injustices of the Fugitive Slave Act, the novel had a profound effect on American attitudes toward slavery.

1845

■ The *Narrative of the Life of Frederick Douglass* is published in Boston.

1846–1848

■ The United States' war with Mexico results in the acquisition of California and New Mexico territories and escalates the debate over the extension of slavery into the new territories.

1850

■ The Compromise of 1850 is negotiated, including the Fugitive Slave Act of 1850, which requires northerners to assist in the return of escaped slaves.

1852

■ Harriet Beecher Stowe's antislavery novel *Uncle Tom's Cabin* is published and widely read.

■ **July 5**
Frederick Douglass delivers his "Fourth of July" speech at Corinthian Hall in Rochester, New York.

1854

■ **May 30**
The Kansas-Nebraska Act is passed, allowing new territories to enter as slave or free states on the basis of popular sovereignty.

1857

■ **March 6**
The Supreme Court rules in *Dred Scott v. Sandford* that African Americans have "no rights whites are bound to obey."

1859

■ **October 16–18**
John Brown, an abolitionist, leads a failed raid on the federal arsenal at Harpers Ferry, Virginia, in an attempt to overthrow slavery; he is convicted of treason and hanged on December 2.

1860

■ **November 6**
Abraham Lincoln is elected as the president of the United States; the southern states begin to secede from the Union.

Douglass's "Fourth of July" speech came in the early years of the turbulent 1850s, which began with the Fugitive Slave Act of 1850. Advocates and opponents of slavery clashed again in 1854 when the Kansas-Nebraska Act opened up those territories to slavery if the residents so desired. In 1857 the U.S. Supreme Court stepped into the debate with Chief Justice Roger Taney's ruling in *Dred Scott v. Sandford*, which proclaimed that African Americans, enslaved or not, were not citizens of the United States and that Congress had no authority to prohibit slavery in the territories. Two years later, in October 1859, the abolitionist John Brown led a failed slave uprising and raid on the federal arsenal at Harpers Ferry, Virginia. Brown, a friend of Douglass's, was hanged for treason in December 1859. The 1850s ended with a nation more divided than ever before on the issue of slavery and teetering on the edge of civil war.

About the Author

Frederick Douglass, abolitionist and civil rights activist, was born into slavery on a Maryland plantation in February 1818—the exact date of his birth cannot be determined. He was known in his youth as Frederick Washington Augustus Bailey, and he spent twenty years in bondage—first on Wye Plantation near St. Michaels in Talbot County, Maryland, and then in the shipbuilding city of Baltimore. His mother, Harriet Bailey, was a fieldworker, and his father was most likely his first owner, Aaron Anthony.

During his enslavement, Douglass gained literacy, learning the basics of reading from his mistress, Sophia Auld, and improving his reading and writing on his own after Auld's husband chastised her for illegally teaching a slave to read. While living and working in Baltimore, Douglass obtained a copy of *The Columbian Orator*, a collection of famous speeches published in a single, portable volume by the bookseller Caleb Bingham. Douglass pored over the speeches, improving his reading skills and beginning to develop the oratory style for which he would become famous. In September 1838 Douglass borrowed the free papers of a friend and boarded a train for the North. This rather uneventful escape from the bonds of slavery marked the beginning of his life as a crusader against the evils of slavery and in favor of civil rights for African Americans and women.

By 1841 Douglass had been hired as a field lecturer for the Massachusetts Anti-Slavery Society, and he was well on his way to becoming one of the most powerful orators of the nineteenth century. In 1845 the publication of his first autobiography, *Narrative of the Life of Frederick Douglass*, afforded him an international reputation as America's most famous fugitive slave. In 1847 he moved his family to Rochester, New York, where he began publishing an antislavery newspaper called the *North Star*, later renamed *Frederick Douglass' Paper*. In 1852 the Rochester Ladies' Anti-Slavery Society invited Douglass to offer the annual Fourth of July address at their July 5 event.

During and after the Civil War, Douglass was a strong advocate for civil rights. During the war, he recruited African American troops and advised President Abraham Lincoln on the best plan to incorporate blacks into the Union war effort. In 1872 Douglass moved his family to Washington, D.C., where he accepted a post as president of the Freedman's Savings Bank in 1874. In 1877 President Rutherford B. Hayes appointed him U.S. marshal for the District of Columbia, and in 1881 he became recorder of deeds for the District of Columbia. His highest federal post came as U.S. resident minister and consul general (ambassador) to Haiti. He died at Cedar Hill, his home in Washington, D.C., on February 20, 1895.

Explanation and Analysis of the Document

In the opening three paragraphs of the introductory section of his "Fourth of July" speech, Douglass establishes a tone of humility, expressing his gratitude to the event's organizers for deeming him worthy of addressing American independence. Here he juxtaposes himself as a former slave with those in the audience whom he deems the true beneficiaries of the Declaration of Independence. He notes the considerable distance between "this platform and the slave plantation, from which I escaped." He further reveals humility by discounting the amount of preparation put into the address. In reality, the oration was carefully crafted to offer the utmost contrast between the celebration of Independence Day and the continuance of racial slavery in the United States. Douglass would write to his friend and fellow abolitionist Gerrit Smith on July 7, 1852, that writing the oration took "much of my extra time for the last two or three weeks."

Although traditional Fourth of July addresses tended to emphasize the achievements of the American Revolution and its legacy, Douglass's address intended to bring focus to the present. To this end, in the introductory section he carefully distances himself from the historical events of the Revolution, preparing the way to contrast the rights white Americans enjoy and the oppression of slavery. He describes the day as one celebrating "your National Independence" and "your political freedom."

Once he establishes that he is not a beneficiary of the freedom and benefits of the Revolution, Douglass compares the abolitionist reformers of the 1850s with the independence seekers of the founding generation. Douglass tells the assembled crowd that "your fathers" spoke out and acted in opposition to the unjust government of the British Crown. They petitioned, complained, and eventually declared their independence from tyranny and slavery. Although it seemed that achieving the goal of independence was insurmountable owing to a lack of organization, a widely scattered population, insufficient resources, and other factors, the founding generation prevailed, and independence was achieved.

The paragraphs near the end of this section provide a transition into the heart of the address. Douglass heaps

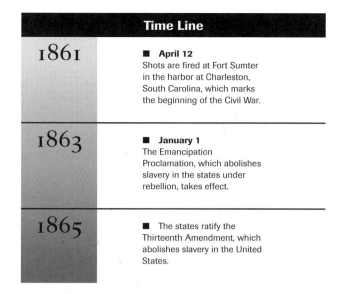

Time Line

1861

■ **April 12**
Shots are fired at Fort Sumter in the harbor at Charleston, South Carolina, which marks the beginning of the Civil War.

1863

■ **January 1**
The Emancipation Proclamation, which abolishes slavery in the states under rebellion, takes effect.

1865

■ The states ratify the Thirteenth Amendment, which abolishes slavery in the United States.

praise on the Revolutionary generation and assures the audience that "I am not wanting in respect for the fathers of this republic." He clearly states that he is transitioning into matters affecting the present state of the nation, noting that he intends to leave "the great deeds of your fathers to other gentlemen," most notably to those who were not born into slavery as he was.

♦ **"The Present"**

Douglass's tone changes to a critical assessment of the way that Americans reap the benefits of the founding generation's achievements in this section as he turns toward the influence of those achievements in the present. He quotes a stanza from Henry Wadsworth Longfellow's poem "A Psalm of Life" at the start of the section, which emphasizes the importance of acting in the present instead of dwelling on the future or past. The problem of the present that most concerns Douglass is the existence of slavery in the United States and the inherent contradiction between celebrating American independence while many suffer under the bonds of slavery. His allusion to Sydney Smith (1771–1845) refers to an Anglican minister who wrote satirically in criticism of the British Crown and who was a strong activist for Catholic emancipation in that country. Douglass also alludes to the biblical passage Luke 3:8: "Bring forth therefore fruits worthy of repentance, and begin not to say within yourselves, We have Abraham to *our* father: for I say unto you, That God is able of these stones to raise up children to Abraham." He points out that George Washington, the most revered of the Founders, freed his slaves in his will. Douglass argues that many of those celebrating American independence and the legacy of the Revolutionary generation are hypocrites who hold slaves and engage in slave trafficking. The quote that follows, noting that men's evil deeds often follow them to the grave, originates from William Shakespeare's *Julius Caesar* (act 3, scene 2).

After outlining a series of rhetorical questions about the application of the principles of freedom and justice to all,

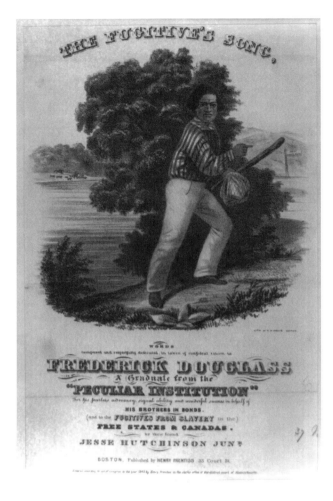

A sheet music cover portraying the black abolitionist Frederick Douglass as a runaway slave (Library of Congress)

Douglass powerfully asks the crowd if it was their intention to mock him by inviting him to speak on the Fourth of July. He notes in the seventh paragraph, "The rich inheritance of justice, liberty, prosperity and independence, bequeathed by your fathers, is shared by you, not by me." Douglass quotes Psalms 135:1–6 in the eighth paragraph of this section, comparing the experiences of American slaves to the unjust biblical enslavement of the Jews. In the following passages, Douglass transitions from the celebration of the Fourth of July to a more familiar topic, American slavery. Many in the audience were abolitionist-minded, and most would have anticipated the shift in topic. He argues that the character and conduct of the nation "never looked blacker." Following the passage of the federal Fugitive Slave Act of 1850, northern states were required to take a more active role in returning fugitive slaves to the South, greatly angering abolitionists and others who viewed the new law as a demonstration of the federal government's support for slavery. Douglass condemns the use of religion and the U.S. Constitution to support slavery and vows to actively oppose slavery in every way he can, taking the quote "I will not equivocate; I will not excuse" from the first issue of

William Lloyd Garrison's antislavery newspaper, the *Liberator*, which appeared January 1, 1831.

Douglass next examines a series of issues commonly found in abolitionists' denunciations of slavery, including the humanity of the enslaved, their entitlement to liberty, and biblical justifications for the institution. The tone of these passages is full of irony, as Douglass argues that each of these issues has already been settled and really requires no additional comment. He turns first to the question of the humanity of slaves. An early justification for slavery argued that men and women of African descent were descended from a species different from whites. Their full humanity was sometimes considered questionable. Douglass argues persuasively in the tenth and eleventh paragraphs that the question of the humanity of slaves has been put to rest and that even in the South, the slave is considered a man. He cites a series of seventy-two crimes for which a black man might be given the death penalty in Virginia as partial evidence that southerners recognize the humanity of slaves. Douglass likely pulled this information from the writings of the abolitionist Theodore Dwight Weld, whose 1839 book *American Slavery As It Is* included a careful exploration of slave laws and punishments. At the close of this section, Douglass turns to the argument that slaves as men are entitled to liberty. He proclaims that this issue is also widely settled; in fact, he remarks, "There is not a man beneath the canopy of heaven, that does not know that slavery is wrong *for him*." Likewise, he touches on the fact that slavery is neither divinely sanctioned nor created by God. Such common arguments, Douglass contends, have run their course, and now a new course of action must be undertaken. He announces to the crowd, "We need the storm, the whirlwind, and the earthquake." The speech changes course again as Douglass begins a scathing condemnation of the country with the famous title line "What, to the American slave, is your 4th of July?"

Douglass argues that, for enslaved Americans, the Fourth of July is the one day of the year that most represents the "gross injustice and cruelty to which he is the constant victim." He finds that the celebration of liberty and equality is hypocritical while slavery continues to exist in the United States. In the final paragraph of the section, he claims that the hypocrisy of the United States is deeper than the abuses of European and other world monarchies and that even the cruelties of South American slavery do not match the cruelty brought about by the contradiction between slavery and freedom in America. This was an especially harsh criticism, because it is widely known that South American slavery was particularly callous.

♦ **"The Internal Slave Trade"**

In the next section of the speech, Douglass's critical eye turns to the slave trade within the United States. Although the importation of slaves from Africa or the Caribbean was outlawed after 1808, the boom in cotton production after the War of 1812 increased the need for labor in the developing southwestern cotton states. The labor gap was filled by moving large numbers of enslaved men and women from the Upper South states, such as Virginia and Maryland, to the Lower South. It is estimated that between 1820 and 1860 about nine hundred thousand slaves were sold or moved into the developing cotton fields in such states as Alabama, Mississippi, Louisiana, and Texas. The practice often separated family members and is considered one of the cruelest elements of U.S. slavery. Douglass references the former senator Thomas Hart Benton (1782–1858), who served as a U.S. senator from Missouri from 1821 to 1851 and as one of that state's congressmen from 1853 to 1855.

In the first paragraph of this section, Douglass points out that some important ministers have spoken out against the slave trade and slavery but that many of them support a movement to colonize free blacks in Africa. This movement began in earnest with the creation of the American Colonization Society in 1816, which established the colony of Liberia on the west coast of Africa. Although a number of freed blacks did emigrate to Liberia and other places, the movement was largely unsuccessful. Douglass adamantly opposes colonization and other expatriation schemes.

Douglass follows this with a condemnation of the internal slave trade. These passages offer some details about the ways that the slave trade functioned and of how it affected and dehumanized those who were subjected to sale and movement. Douglass describes men, women, and children being bound in chains, screams, whippings, and the separation of mothers and children. In the second paragraph he asks his audience to tell him "WHERE, under the sun, you can witness a spectacle more fiendish and shocking." The following passages detail Douglass's own experiences as he recalls the Baltimore slave market controlled by a man he remembers as Austin Woldfolk. This notorious man's name was actually Austin Woolfolk of Augusta, Georgia. He came to Baltimore around 1819 and was the most prominent slave trader in the area during the 1820s and 1830s, exporting between 230 and 460 slaves to New Orleans each year. This discussion concludes with a slight alteration of the first four lines of the poem "Stanzas for the Times" by the abolitionist poet John Greenleaf Whittier.

In the final two paragraphs of this section, Douglass heartily condemns the Fugitive Slave Act, which was passed as a part of the Compromise of 1850 and was negotiated to settle matters of territorial and slavery expansion following the United States' war with Mexico (1846–1848). The Fugitive Slave Act angered abolitionists and led many who had previously been neutral on the issue of slavery to speak out against the measure. The law required northern states to aid in returning fugitive slaves. It established commissioners and special hearings to handle the cases of alleged fugitives. As Douglass describes in the tenth paragraph, the commissioner received a fee of $10 if an individual was determined to be a fugitive but only $5 if he or she was determined to be free. Although the law did not specify the number of witnesses needed to establish one as a fugitive, it did specify that evidence or testimony from the alleged fugitive was inadmissible. The injustice inherent in this law led many formerly pacifist abolitionists to take more active roles in helping fugitives

to escape, sometimes physically rescuing them from jails and courthouses across the North.

♦ **"Religious Liberty"**

In a section comprising two paragraphs, Douglass places blame on the established churches and denominations of the United States for their failure to condemn the Fugitive Slave Act as "one of the grossest infringements of Christian Liberty." He makes his case for the churches' culpability in this section. Douglass argues that if the matter involved financial benefit or harm to the church, clergy would call for the law's repeal. The following passage refers to the struggle against Mary Stuart's (Mary, Queen of Scots) attempt to halt the Protestant Reformation and bring Scotland back into the fold of the Roman Catholic Church. John Knox was the most outspoken minister fighting to push the Protestant Reformation forward in Scotland. Douglass believed that American ministers should fight to repeal the Fugitive Slave Act in the same way that Knox fought against Catholicism. The other person mentioned in this brief section is President Millard Fillmore, who presided over the Senate as vice president during the negotiation of the Compromise of 1850. He became president in July 1850, following the death of President John Tyler. The "mint, anise, and cumin" allusion at the end of the section is drawn from Matthew 23:23: "Woe unto you, scribes and Pharisees, hypocrites! For ye pay tithe of mint, anise and cumin, and have omitted the weightier matters of the law, judgment, mercy and faith; these ought ye to have done, and not to leave the other undone."

♦ **"The Church Responsible"**

In this section of the address, Douglass condemns the established churches in the United States, claiming that they have taken the side of slaveholders in the debate over slavery. He refers to three famous supporters of deism from the eighteenth and nineteenth centuries: Thomas Paine (1737–1809), an American Revolutionary and author of *Common Sense*; François-Marie Arouet de Voltaire (1694–1778), a French playwright and author; and Henry St. John, Viscount Bolingbroke, an English statesman and author. In the second paragraph of the section, Douglass quotes biblical passages from James 1:27, "Pure religion and undefiled ... is this," and James 3:17, "But the wisdom that is from above is first pure, then peaceable, gentle, and easy to be intreated, full of mercy and good fruits, without partiality and without hypocrisy." The second series of quotes originates from Isaiah 1:13–17. The fourth paragraph refers to the radical New Light Presbyterian minister Albert Barnes (1798–1870), who opposed slavery and made a similar condemnation of the complicity of the American church in maintaining slavery. In the sixth paragraph of this section, Douglass names several well-known American ministers as individuals particularly supportive of slaveholding and teaching "that we ought to obey man's laws before the law of God," including John Chase Lord, Gardiner Spring, Leonard Elijah Lathrop, Samuel Hanson Cox, Ichabod Smith Spencer, Ezra Stiles Gannett, Daniel

"This Fourth [of] July is yours, not mine. You may rejoice, I must mourn."

("The Present," paragraph 7)

"What, to the American slave, is your 4th of July? I answer: a day that reveals to him, more than all other days in the year, the gross injustice and cruelty to which he is the constant victim."

("The Present," paragraph 16)

Sharp, and Orville Dewey. Douglass concludes this section by reminding the audience that although his words apply to the majority of American ministers, notable exceptions include the Reverend Robert R. Raymond, who also spoke at the Corinthian Hall event.

♦ **"Religion in England and Religion in America"**

To draw a clear contrast between the antislavery activism of the British and those in the United States, Douglass includes this segment juxtaposing prominent antislavery British activists including Granville Sharp, Thomas Clarkson, William Wilberforce, Thomas Fowell Buxton, Thomas Burchell, and William Knibb. Douglass had traveled for a year and a half in Great Britain and Ireland in 1845 to 1847, during which time he met and worked with a number of British reformers. Unlike the U.S. antislavery movement, when Great Britain ended slavery under the Act for the Abolition of Slavery of 1833, the established Anglican Church supported the abolition of slavery in the British West Indies. In the second paragraph of the section, Douglass contrasts the failure of American clergy to oppose slavery with their sympathy for such foreign causes as the movement of Hungarians to shake off an invasion by Russian and Austrian troops in 1849. Near the end of this lengthy paragraph, Douglass paraphrases Acts 17:26, "And [God] hath made of one blood all the nations of men for to dwell upon the earth," and quotes the Declaration of Independence. Douglass attributes the quote to a letter written on June 26, 1786, by Thomas Jefferson to the French author and politician Jean-Nicolas Démeunier.

♦ **"The Constitution"**

The final section of the speech turns to the constitutionality of slavery. Although Douglass once held the view that the U.S. Constitution was a proslavery document, by 1852 he was committed to using political means to end slavery. In the opening paragraph he paraphrases Shakespeare's *Macbeth* to emphasize the fallacy of those who believe that the Constitution sanctions slavery. He mentions

several prominent northerners committed to antislavery politics, each of whom had published works arguing that the Constitution does not support slavery. Beginning with the third paragraph, Douglass outlines the evidence for his argument, pointing especially to the fact that the words *slave* and *slavery* do not appear anywhere in the document. Although some historians argue that slavery was implicitly protected in several articles of the Constitution, Douglass does not see a single proslavery clause. In support of his position, he points to prominent politicians outside the antislavery circle, including George Mifflin Dallas, who served as vice president under James Polk; the Georgia senator John MacPherson Berrien; the Illinois Democrat Sidney Breese; and Lewis Cass, Michigan senator and Democratic candidate for president in 1848.

Douglass turns more hopeful for the speech's conclusion. He believes that slavery will one day be abolished, paraphrasing Isaiah 59:1 in the sixth paragraph of the section: "Behold, the Lord's hand is not shortened, that it cannot save, neither His ear heavy, that it cannot hear." He takes inspiration that the Declaration of Independence will one day apply to all. In the final paragraph, he proclaims that slavery will end when the light of freedom reaches the United States, alluding to Psalms 68:31: "Princes shall come out of Egypt; Ethiopia shall soon stretch out her hands unto God." The essay concludes with the poem "The Triumph of Freedom" authored by the famous abolitionist William Lloyd Garrison.

Audience

Douglass's speech was delivered before a crowd of reform-minded citizens of Rochester, New York. Many in the audience probably shared his belief that slavery was a moral sin and should be immediately ended. With publication of the speech in pamphlet form, Douglass was able to increase the number of Americans who heard his words. At least seven hundred copies of the speech were printed and distributed for a nominal fee that covered printing. Douglass aimed his message at the American public and hoped his words might persuade many to join the antislavery cause.

Impact

Douglass's "Fourth of July" speech made an immediate impact on the northern American reading public. It was published in pamphlet form in the weeks following the address and read by hundreds who had not attended the Rochester event. The speech endures as one of the most articulate expressions of what it means to be excluded from the republican experiment that resulted in the democracy of the United States. Yet beyond a condemnation of slavery, the speech endures because Douglass adopted a hopeful tone, believing that the United States would be more complete once slavery ended. Today scholars and students of American history still widely read Douglass's "Fourth of July" speech.

See also Fugitive Slave Act of 1850; *Dred Scott v. Sandford* (1857); Frederick Douglass: "Men of Color to Arms!" (1863).

Further Reading

■ Books

Blassingame, John W., et al., eds. *The Frederick Douglass Papers*, Series One: *Speeches, Debates, and Interviews*, Vol. 2: 1847–54. New Haven, Conn.: Yale University Press, 1982.

Colaiaco, James A. *Frederick Douglass and the Fourth of July*. New York: Palgrave Macmillan, 2006.

Douglass, Frederick. *Narrative of the Life of Frederick Douglass, An American Slave*. Boston, 1845.

—L. Diane Barnes

Questions for Further Study

1. How does Douglass align himself with the audience while still expressing a point of view that differs from theirs?

2. Douglass was a renowned orator who drew large audiences to hear him speak on many topics. What rhetorical and persuasive devices does he employ in this address?

3. For Douglass, freedom is clearly tied to the idea of the progress of the American empire. What portions of the speech best reflect this assertion?

Frederick Douglass's "What to the Slave Is the Fourth of July?"

July 5, 1852

Mr. President, Friends and Fellow Citizens:

He who could address this audience without a quailing sensation, has stronger nerves than I have. I do not remember ever to have appeared as a speaker before any assembly more shrinkingly, nor with greater distrust of my ability, than I do this day. A feeling has crept over me, quite unfavorable to the exercise of my limited powers of speech. The task before me is one which requires much previous thought and study for its proper performance. I know that apologies of this sort are generally considered flat and unmeaning. I trust, however, that mine will not be so considered. Should I seem at ease, my appearance would much misrepresent me. The little experience I have had in addressing public meetings, in country school houses, avails me nothing on the present occasion.

The papers and placards say, that I am to deliver a 4th July oration. This certainly, sounds large, and out of the common way, for me. It is true that I have often had the privilege to speak in this beautiful Hall, and to address many who now honor me with their presence. But neither their familiar faces, nor the perfect gage I think I have of Corinthian Hall, seems to free me from embarrassment.

The fact is, ladies and gentlemen, the distance between this platform and the slave plantation, from which I escaped, is considerable—and the difficulties to be overcome in getting from the latter to the former, are by no means slight. That I am here to-day, is, to me, a matter of astonishment as well as of gratitude. You will not, therefore, be surprised, if in what I have to say, I evince no elaborate preparation, nor grace my speech with any high sounding exordium. With little experience and with less learning, I have been able to throw my thoughts hastily and imperfectly together; and trusting to your patient and generous indulgence, I will proceed to lay them before you.

This, for the purpose of this celebration, is the 4th of July. It is the birthday of your National Independence, and of your political freedom. This, to you, is what the Passover was to the emancipated people of God. It carries your minds back to the clay, and to the act of your great deliverance; and to the signs, and to the wonders, associated with that act that day.

This celebration also marks the beginning of another year of your national life; and reminds you that the Republic of America is now 76 years old. I am glad, fellow-citizens, that your nation is so young. Seventy-six years, though a good old age for a man, is but a mere speck in the life of a nation. Three score years and ten is the allotted time for individual men; but nations number their years by thousands. According to this fact, you are, even now only in the beginning of your national career, still lingering in the period of childhood. I repeat, I am glad this is so. There is hope in the thought, and hope is much needed, under the dark clouds which lower above the horizon. The eye of the reformer is met with angry flashes, portending disastrous times; but his heart may well beat lighter at the thought that America is young, and that she is still in the impressible stage of her existence. May he not hope that high lessons of wisdom, of justice and of truth, will yet give direction to her destiny? Were the nation older, the patriot's heart might be sadder, and the reformer's brow heavier. Its future might be shrouded in gloom, and the hope of its prophets go out in sorrow. There is consolation in the thought, that America is young. Great streams are not easily turned from channels, worn deep in the course of ages. They may sometimes rise in quiet and stately majesty, and inundate the land, refreshing and fertilizing the earth with their mysterious properties. They may also rise in wrath and fury, and bear away, on their angry waves, the accumulated wealth of years of toil and hardship. They, however, gradually flow back to the same old channel, and flow on as serenely as ever. But, while the river may not be turned aside, it may dry up, and leave nothing behind but the withered branch, and the unsightly rock, to howl in the abyss-sweeping wind, the sad tale of departed glory. As with rivers so with nations.

Fellow-citizens, I shall not presume to dwell at length on the associations that cluster about this day. The simple story of it is, that, 76 years ago, the people of this country were British subjects. The style and title of your "sovereign people" (in which you now glory) was not then born. You were under the British Crown. Your fathers esteemed the English Government as the home government and England as the fatherland. This home government, you know, although a considerable distance from your home, did, in the exercise of its parental prerogatives, impose upon its colonial children, such restraints, burdens and limitations, as, in its mature judgment, it deemed wise, right and proper.

But, your fathers, who had not adopted the fashionable idea of this day, of the infallibility of government, and the absolute character of its acts, presumed to differ from the home government in respect to the wisdom and the justice of some of those burdens and restraints. They went so far in their excitement as to pronounce the measures of government unjust, unreasonable, and oppressive, and altogether such as ought not to be quietly submitted to. I scarcely need say, fellow-citizens, that my opinion of those measures fully accords with that of your fathers. Such a declaration of agreement on my part, would not be worth much to anybody. It would, certainly, prove nothing, as to what part I might have taken, had I lived during the great controversy of 1776. To say now that America was right, and England wrong, is exceedingly easy. Everybody can say it; the dastard, not less than the noble brave, can flippantly discant on the tyranny of England towards the American Colonies. It is fashionable to do so; but there was a time when, to pronounce against England, and in favor of the cause of the colonies, tried men' souls. They who did so were accounted in their day, plotters of mischief, agitators and rebels, dangerous men. To side with the right, against the wrong, with the weak against the strong, and with the oppressed against the oppressor! here lies the merit, and the one which, of all others, seems un fashionable in our day. The cause of liberty may be stabbed by the men who glory in the deeds of your fathers. But, to proceed.

Feeling themselves harshly and unjustly treated, by the home government, your fathers, like men of honesty, and men of spirit, earnestly sought redress. They petitioned and remonstrated; they did so in a decorous, respectful, and loyal manner. Their conduct was wholly unexceptionable. This, however, did not answer the purpose. They saw themselves treated with sovereign indifference, coldness and scorn. Yet they persevered. They were not the men to look back.

As the sheet anchor takes a firmer hold, when the ship is tossed by the storm, so did the cause of your fathers grow stronger, as it breasted the chilling blasts of kingly displeasure. The greatest and best of British statesmen admitted its justice, and the loftiest eloquence of the British Senate came to its support.

But, with that blindness which seems to be the unvarying characteristic of tyrants, since Pharaoh and his hosts were drowned in the Red sea, the British Government persisted in the exactions complained of.

The madness of this course, we believe, is admitted now, even by England; but, we fear the lesson is wholly lost on our present rulers.

Oppression makes a wise man mad. Your fathers were wise men, and if they did not go mad, they became restive under this treatment. They felt themselves the victims of grievous wrongs, wholly incurable in their colonial capacity. With brave men there is always a remedy for oppression. Just here, the idea of a total separation of the colonies from the crown was born! It was a startling idea, much more so, than we, at this distance of time, regard it. The timid and the prudent (as has been intimated) of that day, were, of course, shocked and alarmed by it.

Such people lived then, had lived before, and will, probably, ever have a place on this planet; and their course, in respect to any great change, (no matter how great the good to be attained, or the wrong to be redressed by it,) may be calculated with as much precision as can be the course of the stars. They hate all changes, but silver, gold and copper change! Of this sort of change they are always strongly in favor.

These people were called tories in the days of your fathers; and the appellation, probably, conveyed the same idea that is meant by a more modern, though a somewhat less euphonious term, which we often find in our papers, applied to some of our old politicians.

Their opposition to the then dangerous thought was earnest and powerful; but, amid all their terror and affrighted vociferations against it, the alarming and revolutionary idea moved on, and the country with it.

On the 2d of July, 1776, the old Continental Congress, to the dismay of the lovers of ease, and the worshippers of property, clothed that dreadful idea with all the authority of national sanction. They did so in the form of a resolution; and as we seldom hit upon resolutions, drawn up in our day, whose transparency is at all equal to this, it may refresh your minds and help my story if I read it.

Resolved, That these united colonies are, and of right, ought to be free and Independent States; that they are absolved from all allegiance to the British Crown; and that all political connection between them and the State of Great Britain is, and ought to be, dissolved.

Citizens, your fathers Made good that resolution. They succeeded; and today you reap the fruits of their success. The freedom gained is yours; and you, therefore, may properly celebrate this anniversary. The 4th of July is the first great fact in your nation's history—the very ring-bolt in the chain of your yet undeveloped destiny.

Pride and patriotism, not less than gratitude, prompt you to celebrate and to hold it in perpetual remembrance. I have said that the Declaration of Independence is the RINGBOLT to the chain of your nation's destiny; so, indeed, I regard it. The principles contained in that instrument are saving principles. Stand by those principles, be true to them on all occasions, in all places, against all foes, and at whatever cost.

From the round top of your ship of state, dark and threatening clouds may be seen. Heavy billows, like mountains in the distance, disclose to the leeward huge forms of flinty rocks! That bolt drawn, that chain, broken, and all is lost. Cling to this day—cling to it, and to its principles, with the grasp of a storm-tossed mariner to a spar at midnight.

The coining into being of a nation, in any circumstances, is an interesting event. But, besides general considerations, there were peculiar circumstances which make the advent of this republic an event of special attractiveness.

The whole scene, as I look back to it, was simple, dignified and sublime.

The population of the country, at the time, stood at the insignificant number of three millions. The country was poor in the munitions of war. The population was weak and scattered, and the country a wilderness unsubdued. There were then no means of concert and combination, such as exist now. Neither steam nor lightning had then been reduced to order and discipline. From the Potomac to the Delaware was a journey of many days. Under these, and innumerable other disadvantages, your fathers declared for liberty and independence and triumphed.

Fellow Citizens, I am not wanting in respect for the fathers of this republic. The signers of the Declaration of Independence were brave men. They were great men too—great enough to give fame to a great age. It does not often happen to a nation to raise, at one time, such a number of truly great men. The point from which I am compelled to view them is not, certainly the most favorable; and yet I cannot contemplate their great deeds with less than admiration. They were statesmen, patriots and heroes, and for the good they did, and the principles they contended for, I will unite with you to honor their memory.

They loved their country better than their own private interests; and, though this is not the highest form of human excellence, all will concede that it is a rare virtue, and that when it is exhibited, it ought to command respect. He who will, intelligently, lay down his life for his country, is a man whom it is not in human nature to despise. Your fathers staked their lives, their fortunes, and their sacred honor, on the cause of their country. In their admiration of liberty, they lost sight of all other interests.

They were peace men; but they preferred revolution to peaceful submission to bondage. They were quiet men; but they did not shrink from agitating against oppression. They showed forbearance; but that they knew its limits. They believed in order; but not in the order of tyranny. With them, nothing was "settled" that was not right. With them, justice, liberty and humanity were "final;" not slavery and oppression. You may well cherish the memory of such men. They were great in their day and generation. Their solid manhood stands out the more as we contrast it with these degenerate times.

How circumspect, exact and proportionate were all their movements! How unlike the politicians of an hour! Their statesmanship looked beyond the passing moment, and stretched away in strength into the distant future. They seized upon eternal principles, and set a glorious example in their defence. Mark them!

Fully appreciating the hardships to be encountered, firmly believing in the right of their cause, honorably inviting the scrutiny of an on-looking world, reverently appealing to heaven to attest their sincerity, soundly comprehending the solemn responsibility they were about to assume, wisely measuring the terrible odds against them, your fathers, the fathers of this republic, did, most deliberately, under the inspiration of a glorious patriotism, and with a sublime faith in the great principles of justice and freedom, lay deep, the corner-stone of the national superstructure, which has risen and still rises in grandeur around you.

Of this fundamental work, this day is the anniversary. Our eyes are met with demonstrations of joyous enthusiasm. Banners and pennants wave exultingly on the breeze. The din of business, too, is hushed. Even mammon seems to have quitted his grasp on this day. The ear-piercing fife and the stirring drum unite their accents with the ascending peal of a thousand church bells. Prayers are made, hymns are sung, and sermons are preached in honor of this day; while the quick martial tramp of a great and multitudinous nation, echoed back by all the hills, valleys and mountains of a vast continent, bespeak the occasion one of thrilling and universal interest—a nation's jubilee.

Friends and citizens, I need not enter further into the causes which led to this anniversary. Many of you understand them better than I do. You could instruct me in regard to them. That is a branch of knowledge in which you feel, perhaps, a much deeper interest than your speaker. The causes which led to the separation of the colonies from the British crown have never lacked for a tongue. They have all been taught in your common schools, narrated at your firesides, unfolded from your pulpits, and thundered from your legislative halls, and are as familiar to you as household words. They form the staple of your national poetry and eloquence.

I remember, also, that, as a people, Americans are remarkably familiar with all facts which make in in their own favor. This is esteemed by some as a national trait—perhaps a national weakness. It is a fact, that whatever makes for the wealth or for the reputation of Americans, and can be had cheap! will be found by Americans. I shall not be charged with slandering Americans, if I say I think the American side of any question may be safely left in American hands.

I leave, therefore, the great deeds of your fathers to other gentlemen whose claim to have been regularly descended will be less likely to be disputed than mine!

♦ **The Present**

My business, if I have any here today, is with the present. The accepted time with God and his cause is the ever-living now.

"Trust no future, however pleasant, Let the dead past bury its dead; Act, act in the living present, Heart within, and God overhead."

We have to do with the past only as we can make it useful to the present and to the future. To all inspiring motives, to noble deeds which can be gained from the past, we are welcome. But now is the time, the important time. Your fathers have lived, died, and have done their work, and have done much of it well. You live and must die, and you must do your work. You have no right to enjoy a child's share in the labor of your fathers, unless your children are to be blest by your labors. You have no right to wear out and waste the hard-earned fame of your fathers to cover your indolence. Sydney Smith tells us that men seldom eulogize the wisdom and virtues of their fathers, but to excuse some folly or wickedness of their own. This truth is not a doubtful one. There are illustrations of it near and remote, ancient and modern. It was fashionable, hundreds of years ago, for the children of Jacob to boast, we have "Abraham to our father," when they had long lost Abraham's faith and spirit. That people contented themselves under the shadow of Abraham's great name, while they repudiated the deeds which made his name great. Need I remind you that a similar thing is being done all over this country today? Need I tell you that the Jews are not the only people who built the tombs of the prophets, and garnished the sepulchres of the righteous? Washington could not die till he had broken the chains of his slaves. Yet his monument is built up by the price of human blood, and the traders in the bodies and souls of men, shout, "We have Washington to 'our father.'" Alas! that it should be so; yet so it is.

"The evil that men do, lives after them, The good is oft interred with their bones."

Fellow-citizens, pardon me, allow me to ask, why am I called upon to speak here today? What have I, or those I represent, to do with your national independence? Are the great principles of political freedom and of natural justice, embodied in that Declaration of Independence, extended to us? and am I, therefore, called upon to bring our humble offering to the national altar, and to confess the benefits and express devout gratitude for the blessings resulting from your independence to us?

Would to God, both for your sakes and ours, that an affirmative answer could be truthfully returned to these questions! Then would my task be light, and my burden easy and delightful. For who is there so cold, that a nation's sympathy could not warm him? Who so obdurate and dead to the claims of gratitude, that would not thankfully acknowledge such priceless benefits? Who so stolid and selfish, that would not give his voice to swell the hallelujahs of a nation's jubilee, when the chains of servitude had been torn from his limbs? I am not that man. In a case like that, the dumb might eloquently speak, and the "lame man leap as an hart."

But, such is not the state of the case. I say it with a sad sense of the disparity between us. I am not included within the pale of this glorious anniversary! Your high independence only reveals the immeasurable distance between us. The blessings in which you, this day, rejoice, are not enjoyed in common. The rich inheritance of justice, liberty, prosperity and independence, bequeathed by your fathers, is shared by you, not by me. The sunlight that brought life and healing to you, has brought stripes and death to me. This Fourth [of] July is yours, not mine. You may rejoice, I must mourn. To drag a man in fetters into the grand illuminated temple of liberty, and call upon him to join you in joyous anthems, were inhuman mockery and sacrilegious irony. Do you mean, citizens, to mock me, by asking me to speak today? If so, there is a parallel to your conduct. And let me warn you that it is dangerous to copy the example of a nation whose crimes, towering up to heaven, were thrown down by the breath of the Almighty, burying that nation in irrecoverable ruin! I can today take up the plaintive lament of a peeled and woe-smitten people!

"By the rivers of Babylon, there we sat down. Yea! we wept when we remembered Zion. We hanged our harps upon the willows in the midst thereof. For there, they that carried us away captive, required of us a song; and they who wasted us required of us mirth, saying, Sing us one of the songs of Zion. How can we sing the Lord's song in a strange land? If I forget thee, O Jerusalem, let my right hand forget her cunning. If I do not remember thee, let my tongue cleave to the roof of my mouth."

Fellow citizens; above your national, tumultuous joy, I hear the mournful wail of millions! whose chains, heavy and grievous yesterday, are, today, rendered more intolerable by the jubilee shouts that reach them. If I do forget, if I do not faithfully remember those bleeding children of sorrow this day, "may my right hand forget her cunning, and may my tongue cleave to the roof of my mouth!" To forget them, to pass lightly over their wrongs, and to chime in with the popular theme, would be treason most scandalous and shocking, and would make me a reproach before God and the world. My subject, then, fellow-citizens, is AMERICAN SLAVERY. I shall see, this day, and its popular characteristics, from the slave's point of view. Standing, there, identified with the American bondman, making his wrongs mine, I do not hesitate to declare, with all my soul, that the character and conduct of this nation never looked blacker to me than on this 4th of July! Whether we turn to the declarations of the past, or to the professions of the present, the conduct of the nation seems equally hideous and revolting. America is false to the past, false to the present, and solemnly binds herself to be false to the future. Standing with God and the crushed and bleeding slave on this occasion, I will, in the name of humanity which is outraged, in the name of liberty which is fettered, in the name of the constitution and the Bible, which are disregarded and trampled upon, dare to call in question and to denounce, with all the emphasis I can command, everything that serves to perpetuate slavery—the great sin and shame of America! "I will not equivocate; I will not excuse;" I will use the severest language I can command; and yet not one word shall escape me that any man, whose judgment is not blinded by prejudice, or who is not at heart a slaveholder, shall not confess to be right and just.

But I fancy I hear some one of my audience say, it is just in this circumstance that you and your brother abolitionists fail to make a favorable impression on the public mind. Would you argue more, and denounce less, would you persuade more, and rebuke less, your cause would be much more likely to succeed. But, I submit, where all is plain there is nothing to be argued. What point in the anti-slavery creed would you have me argue? On what branch of the subject do the people of this country need light? Must I undertake to prove that the slave is a man? That point is conceded already. Nobody doubts it. The slave-holders themselves acknowledge it in the enactment of laws for their government. They acknowledge it when they punish disobedience on the part of the slave. There are seventy-two crimes in the State of Virginia, which, if committed by a black man (no matter how ignorant he be), subject him to the punishment of death; while only two of the same crimes will subject a white man to the like punishment. What is this but the acknowledgement that the slave is a moral, intellectual and responsible being. The manhood of the slave is conceded. It is admitted in the fact that Southern statute books are covered with enactments forbidding, under severe fines and penalties, the teaching of the slave to read or to write. When you can point to any such laws, in reference to the beasts of the field, then I may consent to argue the manhood of the slave. When the dogs in your streets, when the fowls of the air, when the cattle on your hills, when the fish of the sea, and the reptiles that crawl, shall be unable to distinguish the slave from a brute, then will I argue with you that the slave is a man.

For the present, it is enough to affirm the equal manhood of the negro race. Is it not astonishing that, while we are ploughing, planting and reaping, using all kinds of mechanical tools, erecting houses, constructing bridges, building ships, working in metals of brass, iron, copper, silver and gold; that, while we are reading, writing and cyphering, acting as clerks, merchants and secretaries, having among us lawyers, doctors, ministers, poets, authors, editors, orators and teachers; that, while we are engaged in all manner of enterprises common to other men, digging gold in California, capturing the whale in the Pacific, feeding sheep and cattle on the hillside, living, moving, acting, thinking, planning, living in families as husbands, wives and children, and, above all, confessing and worshipping the Christian's God, and looking hopefully for life and immortality beyond the grave, we are called upon to prove that we are men!

Would you have me argue that man is entitled to liberty? that he is the rightful owner of his own body? You have already declared it. Must I argue the wrongfulness of slavery? Is that a question for Republicans? Is it to be settled by the rules of logic and argumentation, as a matter beset with great difficulty, involving a doubtful application of the principle of justice, hard to be understood? How should I look today, in the presence of Americans, dividing, and subdividing a discourse, to show that men have a natural right to freedom? speaking of it relatively, and positively, negatively, and affirmatively. To do so, would be to make myself ridiculous, and to offer an insult to your understanding. There is not a man beneath the canopy of heaven, that does not know that slavery is wrong for him.

What, am I to argue that it is wrong to make men brutes, to rob them of their liberty, to work them without wages, to keep them ignorant of their relations to their fellow men, to beat them with sticks, to flay their flesh with the lash, to load their limbs with irons, to hunt them with dogs, to sell them at auction, to sunder their families, to knock out their teeth, to burn their flesh, to starve them into obedience and submission to their masters? Must I argue that a system thus marked with blood, and stained with pollution, is wrong? No I will not. I have better employment for my time and strength, than such arguments would imply.

What, then, remains to be argued? Is it that slavery is not divine; that God did not establish it; that our doctors of divinity are mistaken? There is blasphemy in the thought. That which is inhuman, cannot be divine! Who can reason on such a proposition? They that can, may; I cannot. The time for such argument is past.

At a time like this, scorching irony, not convincing argument, is needed. O! had I the ability, and could I reach the nation' ear, I would, to day, pour out a fiery stream of biting ridicule, blasting reproach, withering sarcasm, and stern rebuke. For it is not light that is needed, but fire; it is not the gentle shower, but thunder. We need the storm, the whirlwind, and the earthquake. The feeling of the nation must be quickened; the conscience of the nation must be roused; the propriety of the nation must be startled; the hypocrisy of the nation must be exposed; and its crimes against God and man must be proclaimed and denounced.

What, to the American slave, is your 4th of July? I answer: a day that reveals to him, more than all other days in the year, the gross injustice and cruelty to which he is the constant victim. To him, your celebration is a sham; your boasted liberty, an unholy license; your national greatness, swelling vanity; your sounds of rejoicing are empty and heartless; your denunciations of tyrants, brass fronted impudence; your shouts of liberty and equality, hollow mockery; your prayers and hymns, your sermons and thanksgivings, with all your religious parade, and solemnity, are, to him, mere bombast, fraud, deception, impiety, and hypocrisy—a thin veil to cover up crimes which would disgrace a nation of savages. There is not a nation on the earth guilty of practices, more shocking and bloody, than are the people of these United States, at this very hour.

Go where you may, search where you will, roam through all the monarchies and despotisms of the old world, travel through South America, search out every abuse, and when you have found the last, lay your facts by the side of the every day practices of this nation, and you will say with me, that, for revolting barbarity and shameless hypocrisy, America reigns without a rival.

◆ The Internal Slave Trade

Take the American slave-trade, which we are told by the papers, is especially prosperous just now. Ex-Senator Benton tells us that the price of men was never higher than now. He mentions the fact to show that slavery is in no danger. This trade is one of the peculiarities of American institutions. It is carried on in all the large towns and cities in one half of this confederacy; and millions are pocketed every year, by dealers in this horrid traffic. In several states, this trade is a chief source of wealth. It is called (in contradistinction to the foreign slave-trade) "the internal slave-trade." It is, probably, called so, too, in order to divert from it the horror with which the foreign slave-trade is contemplated. That trade has long since been denounced by this government, as piracy. It has been denounced with burning words, from the high places of the nation, as an execrable traffic. To arrest it, to put an end to it, this nation keeps a squadron, at immense cost, on the coast of Africa. Everywhere, in this country, it is safe to speak of this foreign slave-trade, as a most inhuman traffic, opposed alike to the laws of God and of man. The duty to extirpate and destroy it, is admitted even by our DOCTORS OF DIVINITY. In order to put an end to it, some of these last have consented that their colored brethren (nominally free) should leave this country, and establish themselves on the western coast of Africa! It is, however, a notable fact, that, while so much execration is poured out by Americans, upon those engaged in the foreign slave-trade, the men engaged in the slave-trade between the states pass without condemnation, and their business is deemed honorable.

Behold the practical operation of this internal slave-trade, the American slave-trade, sustained by American politics and American religion. Here you will see men and women, reared like swine, for the market. You know what is a swine-drover? I will show you a man-drover. They inhabit all our Southern States. They perambulate the country, and crowd the highways of the nation, with droves of human stock. You will see one of these human flesh jobbers, armed with pistol, whip and bowie-knife, driving a company of a hundred men, women, and children, from the Potomac to the slave market at New Orleans. These wretched people are to be sold singly, or in lots, to suit purchasers. They are food for the cotton-field, and the deadly sugar-mill. Mark the sad procession, as it moves wearily along, and the inhuman wretch who drives them. Hear his savage yells and his blood-chilling oaths, as he hurries on his affrighted captives! There, see the old man, with locks thinned and gray. Cast one glance, if you please, upon that young mother, whose shoulders are bare to the scorching sun, her briny tears falling on the brow of the babe in her arms. See, too, that girl of thirteen, weeping, yes! weeping, as she thinks of the mother from whom she has been torn! The drove moves tardily. Heat and sorrow have nearly consumed their strength; suddenly you hear a quick snap, like the discharge of a rifle; the fetters clank, and the chain rattles simultaneously; your ears are saluted with a scream, that seems to have torn its way to the centre of your soul! The crack you heard, was the sound of the slave-whip; the scream you heard, was from the woman you saw with the babe. Her speed had faltered under the weight of her child and her chains! that gash on her shoulder tells her to move on. Follow this drove to New Orleans. Attend the auction; see men examined like horses; see the forms of women rudely and brutally exposed to the shocking gaze of American slave-buyers. See this drove sold and separated for ever; and never forget the deep, sad sobs that arose from

that scattered multitude. Tell me citizens, WHERE, under the sun, you can witness a spectacle more fiendish and shocking. Yet this is but a glance at the American slave-trade, as it exists, at this moment, in the ruling part of the United States.

I was born amid such sights and scenes. To me the American slave-trade is a terrible reality. When a child, my soul was often pierced with a sense of its horrors. I lived on Philpot Street, Fell's Point, Baltimore, and have watched from the wharves, the slave ships in the Basin, anchored from the shore, with their cargoes of human flesh, waiting for favorable winds to waft them down the Chesapeake. There was, at that time, a grand slave mart kept at the head of Pratt Street, by Austin Woldfolk. His agents were sent into every town and county in Maryland, announcing their arrival, through the papers, and on flaming "hand-bills," headed CASH FOR NEGROES. These men were generally well dressed men, and very captivating in their manners. Ever ready to drink, to treat, and to gamble. The fate of many a slave has depended upon the turn of a single card; and many a child has been snatched from the arms of its mother, by bargains arranged in a state of brutal drunkenness.

The flesh-mongers gather up their victims by dozens, and drive them, chained, to the general depot at Baltimore. When a sufficient number have been collected here, a ship is chartered, for the purpose of conveying the forlorn crew to Mobile, or to New Orleans. From the slave prison to the ship, they are usually driven in the darkness of night; for since the anti-slavery agitation, a certain caution is observed.

In the deep still darkness of midnight, I have been often aroused by the dead heavy footsteps, and the piteous cries of the chained gangs that passed our door. The anguish of my boyish heart was intense; and I was often consoled, when speaking to my mistress in the morning, to hear her say that the custom was very wicked; that she hated to hear the rattle of the chains, and the heart-rending cries. I was glad to find one who sympathized with me in my horror.

Fellow-citizens, this murderous traffic is, to-day, in active operation in this boasted republic. In the solitude of my spirit, I see clouds of dust raised on the highways of the South; I see the bleeding footsteps; I hear the doleful wail of fettered humanity, on the way to the slave-markets, where the victims are to be sold like horses, sheep, and swine, knocked off to the highest bidder. There I see the tenderest ties ruthlessly broken, to gratify the lust, caprice and rapacity of the buyers and sellers of men. My soul sickens at the sight.

"Is this the land your Fathers loved, The freedom which they toiled to win? Is this the earth whereon they moved? Are these the graves they slumber in?"

But a still more inhuman, disgraceful, and scandalous state of things remains to be presented.

By an act of the American Congress, not yet two years old, slavery has been nationalized in its most horrible and revolting form. By that act, Mason & Dixon's line has been obliterated; New York has become as Virginia; and the power to hold, hunt, and sell men, women and children, as slaves, remains no longer a mere state institution, but is now an institution of the whole United States. The power is co-extensive with the star-spangled banner, and American Christianity. Where these go, may also go the merciless slave-hunter. Where these are, man is not sacred. He is a bird for the sportsman's gun. By that most foul and fiendish of all human decrees, the liberty and person of every man are put in peril. Your broad republican domain is hunting ground for men. Not for thieves and robbers, enemies of society, merely, but for men guilty of no crime. Your lawmakers have commanded all good citizens to engage in this hellish sport. Your President, your Secretary of State, your lords, nobles, and ecclesiastics, enforce, as a duty you owe to your free and glorious country, and to your God, that you do this accursed thing. Not fewer than forty Americans, have, within the past two years, been hunted down, and, without a moment's warning, hurried away in chains, and consigned to slavery, and excruciating torture. Some of these have had wives and children, dependent on them for bread; but of this, no account was made. The right of the hunter to his prey, stands superior to the right of marriage, and to all rights in this republic, the rights of God included! For black men there are neither law, justice, humanity, nor religion.

The Fugitive Slave Law makes MERCY TO THEM, A CRIME; and bribes the judge who tries them. An American JUDGE GETS TEN DOLLARS FOR EVERY VICTIM HE CONSIGNS to slavery, and five, when he fails to do so. The oath of any two villains is sufficient, under this hell-black enactment, to send the most pious and exemplary black man into the remorseless jaws of slavery! His own testimony is nothing. He can bring no witnesses for himself. The minister of American justice is bound by the law to hear but one side; and that side, is the side of the oppressor. Let this damning fact be perpetually told. Let it be thundered around the world, that, in tyrant-killing, king-hating, people-loving, democratic, Christian America, the seats of justice are filled with judges, who hold their offices under an open and palpable bribes, and are bound, in deciding in the case of a man's liberty, to hear only his accusers!

In glaring violation of justice, in shameless disregard of the forms of administering law, in cunning arrangement to entrap the defenceless, and in diabolical intent, this Fugitive Slave Law stands alone in the annals of tyrannical legislation. I doubt if there be another nation on the globe, having the brass and the baseness to put such a law on the statute-book. If any man in this assembly thinks differently from me in this matter, and feels able to disprove my statements, I will gladly confront him at any suitable time and place he may select.

♦ **Religious Liberty**

I take this law to be one of the grossest infringements of Christian Liberty, and, if the churches and ministers of our country were not stupidly blind, or most wickedly indifferent, they, too, would so regard it.

At the very moment that they are thanking God for the enjoyment of civil and religious liberty, and for the right to worship God according to the dictates of their own consciences, they are utterly silent in respect to a law which robs religion of its chief significance, and makes it utterly worthless to a world lying in wickedness. Did this law concern the "mint, anise and cumin," abridge the right to sing psalms, to partake of the sacrament, or to engage in any of the ceremonies of religion, it would be smitten by the thunder of a thousand pulpits. A general shout would go up from the church, demanding repeal, repeal, instant repeal! And it would go hard with that politician who presumed to solicit the votes of the people without inscribing this motto on his banner. Further, if this demand were not complied with, another Scotland would be added to the history of religious liberty, and the stern old covenanters would be thrown into the shade. A John Knox would be seen at every church door, and heard from every pulpit, and Fillmore would have no more quarter than was shown by Knox, to the beautiful, but treacherous Queen Mary of Scotland. The fact that the church of our country, (with fractional exceptions,) does not esteem "the Fugitive Slave Law" as a declaration of war against religious liberty, implies that that church regards religion simply as a form of worship, an empty ceremony, and not a vital principle, requiring active benevolence, justice, love and good will towards man. It esteems sacrifice above mercy; psalm-singing above right doing; solemn meetings above practical righteousness. A worship that can be conducted by persons who refuse to give shelter to the houseless, to give bread to the hungry, clothing to the naked, and who enjoin obedience to a law forbidding these acts of mercy, is a curse, not a blessing to mankind. The Bible addresses all such persons as "scribes, pharisees, hypocrites, who pay tithe of mint, anise, and cumin, and have omitted the weightier matters of the law, judgment, mercy and faith."

♦ **The Church Responsible**

But the church of this country is not only indifferent to the wrongs of the slave, it actually takes sides with the oppressors. It has made itself the bulwark of American slavery, and the shield of American slave-hunters. Many of its most eloquent Divines, who stand as the very lights of the church, have shamelessly given the sanction of religion, and the bible, to the whole slave system. They have taught that man may, properly, be a slave; that the relation of master and slave is ordained of God; that to send back an escaped bondman to his master is clearly the duty of all the followers of the Lord Jesus Christ; and this horrible blasphemy is palmed off upon the world for Christianity.

For my part, I would say, welcome infidelity! welcome atheism! welcome anything! in preference to the gospel, as preached by those Divines! They convert the very name of religion into an engine of tyranny, and barbarous cruelty, and serve to confirm more infidels, in this age, than all the infidel writings of Thomas Paine, Voltaire, and Bolingbroke, put together, have done! These ministers make religion a cold and flinty-hearted thing, having neither principles of right action, nor bowels of compassion. They strip the love of God of its beauty, and leave the throne of religion a huge, horrible, repulsive form. It is a religion for oppressors, tyrants, man-stealers, and thugs. It is not that "pure and undefiled religion" which is from above, and which is "first pure, then peaceable, easy to be entreated, full of mercy and good fruits, without partiality, and without hypocrisy." But a religion which favors the rich against the poor; which exalts the proud above the humble; which divides mankind into two classes, tyrants and slaves; which says to the man in chains, stay there; and to the oppressor, oppress on; it is a religion which may be professed and enjoyed by all the robbers and enslavers of mankind; it makes God a respecter of persons, denies his fatherhood of the race, and tramples in the dust the great truth of the brotherhood of man. All this we affirm to be true of the popular church, and the popular worship of our land and nation—a religion, a church

and a worship which, on the authority of inspired wisdom, we pronounce to be an abomination in the sight of God. In the language of Isaiah, the American church might be well addressed, "Bring no more vain oblations; incense is an abomination unto me: the new moons and Sabbaths, the calling of assemblies, I cannot away with; it is iniquity, even the solemn meeting. Your new moons, and your appointed feasts my soul hateth. They are a trouble to me; I am weary to bear them; and when ye spread forth your hands I will hide mine eyes from you. Yea! when ye make many prayers, I will not hear. YOUR HANDS ARE FULL OF BLOOD; cease to do evil, learn to do well; seek judgment; relieve the oppressed; judge for the fatherless; plead for the widow."

The American church is guilty, when viewed in connection with what it is doing to uphold slavery; but it is superlatively guilty when viewed in connection with its ability to abolish slavery.

The sin of which it is guilty is one of omission as well as of commission. Albert Barnes but uttered what the common sense of every man at all observant of the actual state of the case will receive as truth, when he declared that "There is no power out of the church that could sustain slavery an hour, if it were not sustained in it."

Let the religious press, the pulpit, the Sunday school, the conference meeting, the great ecclesiastical, missionary, bible and tract associations of the land array their immense powers against slavery, and slave-holding; and the whole system of crime and blood would be scattered to the winds, and that they do not do this involves them in the most awful responsibility of which the mind can conceive.

In prosecuting the anti-slavery enterprise, we have been asked to spare the church, to spare the ministry; but how, we ask, could such a thing be done? We are met on the threshold of our efforts for the redemption of the slave, by the church and ministry of the country, in battle arrayed against us; and we are compelled to fight or flee. From what quarter, I beg to know, has proceeded a fire so deadly upon our ranks, during the last two years, as from the Northern pulpit? As the champions of oppressors, the chosen men of American theology have appeared—men, honored for their so called piety, and their real learning. The LORDS of Buffalo, the SPRINGS of New York, the LATHROPS of Auburn, the COXES and SPENCERS of Brooklyn, the GANNETS and SHARPS of Boston, the DEWEYS of Washington, and other great religious lights of the land, have, in utter denial of the authority of Him, by whom they professed to be called to the ministry, deliberately taught us, against the example of the Hebrews, and against the remonstrance of the Apostles, they teach that we ought to obey man' law before the law of God.

My spirit wearies of such blasphemy; and how such men can be supported, as the "standing types and representatives of Jesus Christ," is a mystery which I leave others to penetrate. In speaking of the American church, however, let it be distinctly understood that I mean the great mass of the religious organizations of our land. There are exceptions, and I thank God that there are. Noble men may be found, scattered all over these Northern States, of whom Henry Ward Beecher, of Brooklyn, Samuel J. May, of Syracuse, and my esteemed friend on the platform, are shining examples; and let me say further, that, upon these men lies the duty to inspire our ranks with high religious faith and zeal, and to cheer us on in the great mission of the slave's redemption from his chains.

♦ Religion in England and Religion in America

One is struck with the difference between the attitude of the American church towards the anti-slavery movement, and that occupied by the churches in England towards a similar movement in that country. There, the church, true to its mission of ameliorating, elevating, and improving the condition of mankind, came forward promptly, bound up the wounds of the West Indian slave, and restored him to his liberty. There, the question of emancipation was a high religious question. It was demanded, in the name of humanity, and according to the law of the living God. The Sharps, the Clarksons, the Wilberforces, the Buxtons, the Burchells and the Knibbs, were alike famous for their piety, and for their philanthropy. The anti-slavery movement there, was not an anti-church movement, for the reason that the church took its full share in prosecuting that movement: and the anti-slavery movement in this country will cease to be an anti-church movement, when the church of this country shall assume a favorable, instead of a hostile position towards that movement.

Americans! your republican politics, not less than your republican religion, are flagrantly inconsistent. You boast of your love of liberty, your superior civilization, and your pure Christianity, while the whole political power of the nation, (as embodied in the two great political parties), is solemnly pledged to support and perpetuate the enslavement of three millions of your countrymen. You hurl your anathemas at the crowned headed tyrants of Russia and Austria, and pride yourselves on your Democratic institutions, while you yourselves consent to be the mere tools and body-guards of the tyrants of Virginia and Carolina. You invite to your shores fugitives of oppression from abroad, honor them with banquets, greet them with ovations, cheer them, toast them, salute them, protect them, and pour out your money to them like water; but the fugitives from your own land, you advertise, hunt, arrest, shoot and kill. You glory in your refinement, and your universal education; yet you maintain a system as barbarous and dreadful, as ever stained the character of a nation—a system begun in avarice, supported in pride, and perpetuated in cruelty. You shed tears over fallen Hungary, and make the sad story of her wrongs the theme of your poets, statesmen and orators, till your gallant sons are ready to fly to arms to vindicate her cause against her oppressors; but, in regard to the ten thousand wrongs of the American slave, you would enforce the strictest silence, and would hail him as an enemy of the nation who dares to make those wrongs the subject of public discourse! You are all on fire at the mention of liberty for France or for Ireland; but are as cold as an iceberg at the thought of liberty for the enslaved of America. You discourse eloquently on the dignity of labor; yet, you sustain a system which, in its very essence, casts a stigma upon labor. You can bare your bosom to the storm of British artillery, to throw off a three-penny tax on tea; and yet wring the last hard earned farthing from the grasp of the black laborers of your country. You profess to believe "that, of one blood, God made all nations of men to dwell on the face of all the earth," and hath commanded all men, everywhere to love one another; yet you notoriously hate, (and glory in your hatred,) all men whose skins are not colored like your own. You declare, before the world, and are understood by the world to declare, that you "hold these truths to be self evident, that all men are created equal; and are endowed by their Creator with certain inalienable rights; and that, among these are, life, liberty, and the pursuit of happiness"; and yet, you hold securely, in a bondage, which according to your own Thomas Jefferson, "is worse than ages of that which your fathers rose in rebellion to oppose," a seventh part of the inhabitants of your country.

Fellow-citizens! I will not enlarge further on your national inconsistencies. The existence of slavery in this country brands your republicanism as a sham, your humanity as a base pretence, and your Christianity as a lie. It destroys your moral power abroad it corrupts your politicians at home. It saps the foundation of religion; it makes your name a hissing, and a bye-word to a mocking earth. It is the antagonistic force in your government, the only thing that seriously disturbs and endangers your Union. It fetters your progress; it is the enemy of improvement, the deadly foe of education; it fosters pride; it breeds insolence; it promotes vice; it shelters crime; it is a curse to the earth that supports it; and yet, you cling to it, as if it were the sheet anchor of all your hopes. Oh! be warned! be warned! a horrible reptile is coiled up in your nation's bosom; the venomous creature is nursing at the tender breast of your youthful republic; for the love of God, tear away, and fling from you the hideous monster, and let the weight of twenty millions, crush and destroy it forever!

◆ The Constitution

But it is answered in reply to all this, that precisely what I have now denounced is, in fact, guaranteed and sanctioned by the Constitution of the United States; that, the right to hold, and to hunt slaves is a part of that Constitution framed by the illustrious Fathers of this Republic. Then, I dare to affirm, notwithstanding all I have said before, your fathers stooped, basely stooped. "To palter with us in a double sense: And keep the word of promise to the ear, But break it to the heart."

And instead of being the honest men I have before declared them to be, they were the veriest imposters that ever practiced on mankind. This is the inevitable conclusion, and from it there is no escape; but I differ from those who charge this baseness on the framers of the Constitution of the United States. It is a slander upon their memory, at least, so I believe. There is not time now to argue the constitutional question at length; nor have I the ability to discuss it as it ought to be discussed. The subject has been handled with masterly power by Lysander Spooner, Esq., by William Goodell, by Samuel E. Sewall, Esq., and last, though not least, by Gerritt Smith, Esq. These gentlemen have, as I think, fully and clearly vindicated the Constitution from any design to support slavery for an hour.

Fellow-citizens! there is no matter in respect to which, the people of the North have allowed themselves to be so ruinously imposed upon, as that of the pro-slavery character of the Constitution. In that instrument I hold there is neither warrant, license, nor sanction of the hateful thing; but interpreted, as it ought to be interpreted, the Constitution is a GLORIOUS LIBERTY DOCUMENT. Read its preamble, consider its purposes. Is slavery among them? Is it at the gateway? or is it in the temple? It is neither. While I do not intend to argue this question on the present oc-

casion, let me ask, if it be not somewhat singular that, if the Constitution were intended to be, by its framers and adopters, a slave-holding instrument, why neither slavery, slaveholding, nor slave can anywhere be found in it. What would be thought of an instrument, drawn up, legally drawn up, for the purpose of entitling the city of Rochester to a track of land, in which no mention of land was made? Now, there are certain rules of interpretation, for the proper understanding of all legal instruments. These rules are well established. They are plain, common-sense rules, such as you and I, and all of us, can understand and apply, without having passed years in the study of law. I scout the idea that the question of the constitutionality, or unconstitutionality of slavery, is not a question for the people. I hold that every American citizen has a right to form an opinion of the constitution, and to propagate that opinion, and to use all honorable means to make his opinion the prevailing one. Without this right, the liberty of an American citizen would be as insecure as that of a Frenchman. Ex-Vice-President Dallas tells us that the constitution is an object to which no American mind can be too attentive, and no American heart too devoted. He further says, the constitution, in its words, is plain and intelligible, and is meant for the home-bred, unsophisticated understandings of our fellow-citizens. Senator Berrien tells us that the Constitution is the fundamental law, that which controls all others. The charter of our liberties, which every citizen has a personal interest in understanding thoroughly. The testimony of Senator Breese, Lewis Cass, and many others that might be named, who are everywhere esteemed as sound lawyers, so regard the constitution. I take it, therefore, that it is not presumption in a private citizen to form an opinion of that instrument.

Now, take the constitution according to its plain reading, and I defy the presentation of a single pro-slavery clause in it. On the other hand it will be found to contain principles and purposes, entirely hostile to the existence of slavery.

I have detained my audience entirely too long already. At some future period I will gladly avail myself of an opportunity to give this subject a full and fair discussion.

Allow me to say, in conclusion, notwithstanding the dark picture I have this day presented, of the state of the nation, I do not despair of this country. There are forces in operation, which must inevitably, work the downfall of slavery. "The arm of the Lord is not shortened," and the doom of slavery is certain.

I, therefore, leave off where I began, with hope. While drawing encouragement from "the Declaration of Independence," the great principles it contains, and the genius of American Institutions, my spirit is also cheered by the obvious tendencies of the age. Nations do not now stand in the same relation to each other that they did ages ago. No nation can now shut itself up, from the surrounding world, and trot round in the same old path of its fathers without interference. The time was when such could be done. Long established customs of hurtful character could formerly fence themselves in, and do their evil work with social impunity. Knowledge was then confined and enjoyed by the privileged few, and the multitude walked on in mental darkness. But a change has now come over the affairs of mankind. Walled cities and empires have become unfashionable. The arm of commerce has borne away the gates of the strong city. Intelligence is penetrating the darkest corners of the globe. It makes its pathway over and under the sea, as well as on the earth. Wind, steam, and lightning are its chartered agents. Oceans no longer divide, but link nations together. From Boston to London is now a holiday excursion. Space is comparatively annihilated. Thoughts expressed on one side of the Atlantic, are distinctly heard on the other.

The far off and almost fabulous Pacific rolls in grandeur at our feet. The Celestial Empire, the mystery of ages, is being solved. The fiat of the Almighty, "Let there be Light," has not yet spent its force. No abuse, no outrage whether in taste, sport or avarice, can now hide itself from the all-pervading light. The iron shoe, and crippled foot of China must be seen, in contrast with nature. Africa must rise and put on her yet unwoven garment. "Ethiopia shall stretch out her hand unto God." In the fervent aspirations of William Lloyd Garrison, I say, and let every heart join in saying it:

God speed the year of jubilee
The wide world o'er!
When from their galling chains set free, Th'
    oppress'd shall vilely bend the knee, And
    wear the yoke of tyranny
    Like brutes no more.
That year will come, and freedom's reign, To man his
    plundered rights again Restore.
God speed the day when human blood
Shall cease to flow!
In every clime be understood,
The claims of human brotherhood,
And each return for evil, good, Not blow for blow;
That day will come all feuds to end,
And change into a faithful friend
Each foe.
God speed the hour, the glorious hour, When none
    on earth
Shall exercise a lordly power,
Nor in a tyrant's presence cower; But all to manhood's stature tower, By equal birth!
THAT HOUR WILL COME, to each, to all,
And from his prison-house, the thrall Go forth.
Until that year, day, hour, arrive,
With head, and heart, and hand I'll strive, To
    break the rod, and rend the gyve, The spoiler of
    his prey deprive
So witness Heaven!
And never from my chosen post,
Whate'er the peril or the cost,
Be driven.

Glossary

despotisms	absolute rules
ecclesiastics	priests and ministers
euphonious	agreeable sounding, pleasing to the ear
exordium	introduction, especially in a classic or rhetorical text
mammon	riches
perambulate	walk around

Martin Delany: The Condition, Elevation, Emigration, and Destiny of the Colored People of the United States

1852

"Our elevation must be the result of self-efforts, and work of our own hands."

Overview

Martin Robison Delany's famous 1852 work *The Condition, Elevation, Emigration, and Destiny of the Colored People of the United States, Politically Considered* is an early black nationalist manifesto. Delany was a significant early founder of the philosophy of black nationalism, and over the course of his life he contributed in a variety of ways to the black freedom struggle. He developed a number of practical strategies, including education, to promote black independence, self-determination, and self-sufficiency. To this end, he also strongly supported African emigration. Delany stands at the head of a succession of black leaders known for their staunch advocacy of black nationalism, including Henry McNeal Turner, Marcus Garvey, Malcolm X, and Louis Farrakhan. In his influential work, Delany offers a close examination of the merits of black emigration as a means of elevation to freedom and equality.

Context

The African and Native American Quaker Paul Cuffe, the African Methodist Episcopal bishop Daniel Coker, and other black nationalists of the late eighteenth and early nineteenth centuries, such as Alexander Crummell and Henry Highland Garnet, first advanced the Back to Africa movement because of their belief that African Americans could never achieve equality in the United States under the existing oppressive conditions promoted by whites. In 1811, Cuffe addressed Congress regarding the establishment of African American Christian colonies on the African continent. In 1815 he enacted such a plan himself, taking thirty-four African Americans to settle in the British colony of Sierra Leone. At about this time, between eight thousand and thirteen thousand African Americans immigrated to Haiti, though, despite early idealism, their experience proved less than optimal. About one-third of these emigrants returned to the United States.

With the notion of mass emigration in mind, the Society for the Colonization of Free People of Color of America was officially formed in 1816 at a meeting in Washington, D.C. Although it was nominally an antislavery organization, the American Colonization Society (ACS), as the society was known, was primarily concerned with eliminating the threat of the class of free African Americans deemed dangerous to the maintenance of slavery. Early presidents of the society included Bushrod Washington, George Washington's nephew, and the Kentucky senator Henry Clay. The ACS emphasized two main aims: First, it supported the gradual abolition of slavery, with an added measure of compensation to slave owners for their losses, and, second, it advocated the resettlement of free blacks in colonies outside the United States, arguing that slave owners would eventually be more open to emancipation if they were not fearful of increases in the American free black population. In 1821 the ACS established Liberia as a colony for the resettlement of free African Americans.

Initially, black abolitionists such as Cuffe supported the work of the ACS. Most black abolitionists, however, including David Walker, viewed the ACS as a proslavery plan to drive African Americans from the United States, diluting abolitionist efforts to end slavery. Thus arose a debate about the sociocultural fit of Africa as a place of settlement for those who had been exposed to slavery in the United States. Put simply, the debate was between the holders of two competing positions. The "integrationists" argued that the United States was their home and sought ways to become more fully integrated into American society. The "nationalists" believed that blacks could achieve freedom and equality only in their own nation.

One of the key figures in that debate was the abolitionist Frederick Douglass. Delany was a contemporary of Douglass and worked for some time on Douglass's newspaper, the *North Star*. However, the two came to differ on the direction and destiny of the black freedom struggle. Douglass supported the integrationist philosophy, which concentrated energies on working within the American system to improve the condition of African Americans. Delany, on the other hand, adopted a more culture-centered and independent approach, one that concentrated on his unique form of black nationalism. In 1852, he wrote the small, yet significant book *The Condition, Elevation, Emigration, and Destiny of the Colored People of the United States, Politi-*

1811	■ Paul Cuffe addresses Congress regarding the establishment of African American Christian colonies in Africa.
1812	■ **May 6** Martin Robison Delany is born in what is now known as Charles Town, West Virginia.
1815	■ Paul Cuffe takes thirty-four African Americans to settle in the British colony of Sierra Leone.
1816	■ **December 21** The Society for the Colonization of Free People of Color of America, also called the American Colonization Society (ACS), is officially formed in Washington, D.C.
1820	■ The black educator and diplomat Prince Saunders launches plans to transport African Americans to Haiti; the plans collapse after a military coup in Haiti.
1822	■ The ACS establishes the nation of Liberia in Africa.
1833	■ The American Anti-Slavery Society, one of the nation's most significant abolitionist groups, is established; Delany joins the Pittsburgh Anti-Slavery Society.
1841	■ **August** Delany organizes the Convention of the Colored Freemen of Pennsylvania in Pittsburgh.
1843	■ Delany founds a newspaper, *The Mystery,* one of the earliest African American newspapers.
1847	■ **July 26** Americo-Liberian settlers declare the independence of the Republic of Liberia.

cally Considered. In this work, Delany advanced a serious and thoughtful plan of action for the emigration of African Americans. He advocated Central and South America as prime destinations for the race, also supporting the continent of Africa in the book's appendix.

About the Author

Martin Robison Delany was born on May 6, 1812, in what is now known as Charles Town, West Virginia, although at the time the territory was located in Virginia. Delany was born to the enslaved Samuel Delany and Pati Peace Delany, a free woman of color. Delany's grandparents were native Africans, who were brought to the United States as slaves. In fact, his paternal grandfather was known to be a Mandingo prince, while his maternal grandfather was believed to be a Gullah village chieftain. Delany and his siblings were taught to read by a northern peddler, and, as a result, a white neighbor threatened to imprison Delany's mother. In response to this threat, Pati Delany uprooted her children and took them to Chambersburg, Pennsylvania, just across the Mason-Dixon Line. In 1822, Delany's father bought his freedom and was reunited with his family.

Delany received an elementary education in Chambersburg, where he remained until he was nineteen. He then traveled to Pittsburgh on foot, via the Allegheny Mountains. In Pittsburgh, he attended a night school held in the basement of one of the local African Methodist Episcopal churches, gaining instruction from a young divinity student. Thereafter he began studying medicine with a local white doctor, gaining enough expertise to practice "as a cupper, leecher, and bleeder." Delany soon became a local leader in the fast-developing black community in Pittsburgh. While working as an officer with the Pittsburgh Anti-Slavery Society, he served as an ardent activist on the Underground Railroad. In these capacities he aided in the organization and development of temperance, literary, and reform groups. In 1836, he served as a delegate to one National Negro Convention in Philadelphia and another in New York.

The 1840s were a busy time for Delany. In 1843 he married Catherine Richards, whose grandfather Benjamin Richards was reportedly the richest black man in the city, and the couple had eleven children. Shortly after his marriage, Delany launched the newspaper *The Mystery*, the first black newspaper west of the Allegheny Mountains, which he edited until the paper went out of business in 1847. That year he joined Frederick Douglass's *North Star* newspaper in Rochester, New York. At the same time, he maintained a vigorous speaking schedule, making antislavery addresses in many areas of the antebellum public sphere, including churches, schools, and farmhouses. He maintained a regular schedule of three meetings a day, traveling by horseback from one event to the next. In a rural Ohio town, Delany barely escaped with his life when he faced the very real threat of lynching.

In 1849 he was accepted as a student by Harvard Medical School, though he and three other black students were dismissed after complaints from the student body about the admission of African Americans. In 1854 he led the National Emigration Convention of Colored People in Cleveland, Ohio. During the 1850s he worked on a novel, *Blake; or, The Huts of America*, which was published in two parts in 1859 and 1862. During the Civil War he recruited African American troops and achieved distinction himself by being promoted to major, the first African American line field officer in U.S. military history. By 1864, Delany had moved with his family to Wilberforce, Ohio. In a tragic set of circumstances, on April 14, 1865—the evening of President Abraham Lincoln's assassination, just days following the end of the Civil War—Delany's personal papers and memorabilia, stored at Wilberforce University, were destroyed in a fire.

Delany ran an unsuccessful bid for the position of lieutenant governor of the state of South Carolina in 1874. After the attempt, Delany lectured and found support in the areas of medicine and anthropology, selling copies of his 1879 *Principia of Ethnology: The Origin of Races and Color, with an Archeological Compendium of Ethiopian and Egyptian Civilization, from Years of Careful Examination and Enquiry* to attending crowds. During the latter part of 1884, Delany returned to Wilberforce, where he died on January 24, 1885.

Explanation and Analysis of the Document

Overall, *The Condition, Elevation, Emigration, and Destiny of the Colored People of the United States* has three significant aspects: It provides a unique report on the successes and achievements of black men and women in the United States, a severe indictment of abolitionists for what Delany believed to be a serious lack of consistent effort in fighting for the rights of blacks and gaining for them full integration into American society, and advocacy of emigration as a solution to racial discrimination. Of paramount importance in this book is one of the most compelling concepts to capture the essence of black nationalist philosophy, as coined by Delany—the idea of a nation within a nation. With this key idea, Delany instituted a conceptualization of African America that stands to this very day, having been adopted in various contexts by a number of scholars and race leaders, including E. Franklin Frazier, W. E. B. Du Bois, Albert B. Cleage, Jr., and Darlene Clark Hine.

◆ "V. Means of Elevation"

In "Means of Elevation," Delany opens by questioning the manner in which what he calls "moral theories" have been advanced as a means of racial empowerment for black people in America. Delany asserts that, instead of the continued dispersal of moral pronouncements as a solution to the race problem, another approach needs to be adopted. Using experience as his source, he argues for not just the development of moral principles but also "the *practical* application of principles adduced."

In the second paragraph, Delany bemoans the incongruence of equality and politics in the current world system,

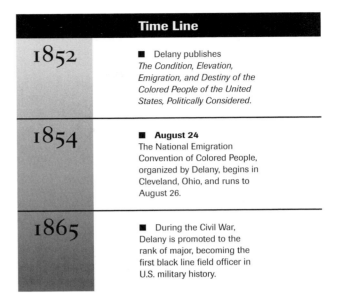

Time Line

1852
■ Delany publishes *The Condition, Elevation, Emigration, and Destiny of the Colored People of the United States, Politically Considered.*

1854
■ **August 24**
The National Emigration Convention of Colored People, organized by Delany, begins in Cleveland, Ohio, and runs to August 26.

1865
■ During the Civil War, Delany is promoted to the rank of major, becoming the first black line field officer in U.S. military history.

but he recognizes that certain policies are needed in the regulation of "well-organized institutions and corporate bodies." Here he concentrates his attention on business and social policies. Using the infamous euphemism "the white man," he launches into a discussion about how blacks have become dependent upon the skill of whites. Drawing attention to the vast array of industry, infrastructure, and architecture produced by white Americans, Delany seems baffled that blacks, in their present condition, can claim any measure of equality. He notes the social circumstance whereby free blacks often function primarily in service-oriented capacities toward whites, such that the latter benefit exclusively and the former remain dependent. To illustrate his point, he mentions black men serving as coachmen, cooks, and "waiting-men" of whites, whereas black women function as "nurse-women," "scrubwomen," maids, and washerwomen. Delany ends the fourth paragraph with the declaration that in watching African Americans, the world harbors "feelings of commiseration, sorrow, and contempt." He notes his belief that African Americans do not deserve any form of sympathy as long as they refuse to take advice concerning their present dismal condition.

In the fifth paragraph, Delany begins by offering a powerful commentary stating that "white men are producers" and blacks "are consumers." He further contrasts blacks as renters and whites as owners of homes; whites as manufacturers of clothing and blacks as wearers of clothing; whites as developing "coaches, vessels, cars, hotels, saloons, and other vehicles and places of accommodation" while blacks complain about their rights to enter institutions not designed for them. Last, Delany characterizes whites as contributors to science, religion, law, medicine, and other subjects, whereas blacks function "with no reference to ancient times," speaking only "of modern things."

Delany then appeals to religious rhetoric, denoting the aforementioned approaches to life practiced by whites as being the God-given means of success; in doing so, he

Henry Clay, an early president of the American Coloni-
zation Society (Library of Congress)

ironically associates whites' success with wickedness and
black subjugation with an overly religious posture, yield-
ing no real, tangible results insofar as equality goes. Delany
explains that he is providing this hard-hitting, clear critique
of the black condition in America so as to make the truth
of black people's lives as visible as possible. His wake-up
call to black America includes a serious indictment of the
seeming complacency exhibited by the race. He forcefully
argues that unless blacks demonstrate their determination
to change their condition, they should hang their heads in
shame. It is not enough for black people to be aware of the
conditions of their race but only talk about the problems
and never do anything to confront or change the conditions
themselves. He goes so far as to state that he and many
others are weary of this strictly discursive approach. He
squarely argues that what is needed is the ushering in of a
remedy, which he pointedly ties to "*self-efforts, and work of
our own hands."* He asserts that nothing else can bring the
kind of change African Americans desire, assuring blacks
that if they would just decide to act, they would accomplish
what they set out to do. Delany challenges each and every
African American to get involved in a spirited contest of
collective self-determination.

Delany ends this section with a resounding appeal to
embolden the black self, stating that the approach he is
outlining represents the only sure means of elevating the
race, be it in the United States or in any other country

where blacks would settle. He poses a series of questions to
gauge the mettle in African Americans' desire for freedom.
As a stark example, he contrasts blacks' possibly remaining
noncommittal at this juncture with the determination of
those of his parents' generation who moved north to acquire a greater measure of equality than they had in the
South. But he then discusses their dismay at realizing that
conditions for blacks in the North were not in a real sense
much better than in the South, despite their vision of the
North as the domain of the free states. Considering that
black labor is typically restricted to the domestic sphere
anyway, especially in the positions of maid, servant, cook,
waiter, and general menial, Delany asserts that there really is no difference, north or south, regarding the nature
of black labor and the race's constrained economic condition in the United States. In this contrast, he draws out
the falsity of the northern black notion of superiority over
southern blacks. Delany essentially concludes that African
Americans, regardless of where they reside or any small measures of difference in their conditions, share the same experience as an oppressed cultural group in the United States.

♦ **"VI. The United States Our Country"**

In chapter VI, Delany begins by stating the obvious point
that the United States functions as the common country
of every African American. This relates to matters of birth,
education, and familial and community relations as well
as death and burial, all of which contribute to a common
experience familiar to most African Americans. Delany affirms the American birthright of African Americans, relating their rights of citizenship as natural rights that though
repeatedly denied "never can be annulled."

♦ **"XXIII. Things as They Are"**

In the twenty-third chapter of his work, Delany states
his single overarching purpose: "to inform the minds of
the colored people at large, upon many things pertaining
to their elevation, that but few among us are acquainted
with." He cites the inability of African Americans to think
for themselves as a collective, without a supposed spokesperson speaking for them and telling them what to think.
He notes that black inferiority is assumed by many, such
that the expertise of African Americans, regardless of their
level of intelligence or qualifications, goes unappreciated,
dismissed, or ignored, whereas any ordinary white American gains instant credibility, even reverence, for no other
reason than whiteness and its associated privileges and perceived superiority, among blacks as well as whites.

Delany condemns prior advice that things could improve
for American blacks if they would simply follow the path
to equality proposed by friends of the race. He cites the
current 1850s climate as one of "hate and jealousy" toward
blacks that has diminished any sort of hope among blacks
for equality on the horizon. With respect to voting, Delany
distinguishes between the ideal of having the right to vote
as well as to run for office, in which case blacks could vote
for those of their own race, and the present circumstance
in which some African Americans have the "elective fran-

Theatrical poster with scenes from Uncle Tom's Cabin (Library of Congress)

chise" but cannot run for office, such that they can vote only for whites who will "help to make laws to degrade us."

Delany cites the spheres of religion and politics in furthering his argument. He mentions again that, in these areas and others, African Americans are discouraged from thinking for themselves and are constantly told what to think and believe. Even those taking part in the antislavery movement are considered suspect, as he indicts white abolitionists for dominating the debate. Regarding the possibility of emigration, he conveys that there are African Americans who automatically adopt the positions of "white brethren" who happen to be representing the interests of slave owners, such as with the establishment of Liberia as a settlement for free slaves—an option Delany rejects outright, labeling that nation as being under "a government of American slaveholders."

In contrast to the constrained and limited opportunities available to blacks in America and even Liberia, Delany offers alternatives for African Americans in places like Mexico, Central America, the West Indies, and South America. He places a high premium on the education and training African American men and women need in order to take advantage of these opportunities. While acknowledging the importance of a classical or "finished education," Delany bluntly states, in a manner that prefigures the debate between Booker T. Washington—an advocate of practical industrial education and assimilation—and W. E. B. Du Bois—who wrote for the more militant "thinking class of American Negroes"—that "a good business practical Education" is what is most needed for the race.

Delany indeed advocates that young black women receive an education. The type of education he advances for women is one that will provide them with information that is useful and has practical applications. He argues against what he calls "light superficial acquirements" that masquerade as "accomplishments." Here Delany seems to offer a more far-reaching educational philosophy for women than was generally supported during his era in many quarters of the United States.

♦ "XXIV. A Glance at Ourselves—Conclusion"

In chapter XXIV, as a final plea and closing argument, Delany returns to the reasons for his black nationalist position. He appeals to race loyalty and love of race as reasons for his insistent urging of emigration for African Americans. Here Delany offers what has been interpreted by some scholars as evidence of his "Africana womanist" views, as he articulates convincingly that the black race cannot rise any higher than the position and condition of black women. He argues that with black women being subjected persistently to degrading and menial jobs, the entire black race is disgraced across the globe.

"Until we are determined to change the condition of things, and raise ourselves above the position in which we are now prostrated, we must hang our heads in sorrow, and hide our faces in shame."

("V. Means of Elevation")

"What we desire to learn now is, how to effect a remedy; this we have endeavored to point out. Our elevation must be the result of self-efforts, and work of our own hands. No other human power can accomplish it. If we but determine it shall be so, it will be so."

("V. Means of Elevation")

"Unfortunately for us, as a body, we have been taught to believe, that we must have some person to think for us, instead of thinking for ourselves. So accustomed are we to submission and this kind of training, that it is with difficulty, even among the most intelligent of the colored people, an audience may be elicited for any purpose whatever, if the expounder is to be a colored person."

("XXIII. Things as They Are")

"Let us have an education, that shall practically develop our thinking faculties and manhood; and then, and not until then, shall we be able to vie with our oppressors, go where we may."

("XXIII. Things as They Are")

"No people are ever elevated above the condition of their females; hence, the condition of the mother determines the condition of the child. To know the position of a people, it is only necessary to know the condition of their females; and despite themselves, they cannot rise above their level."

("XXIV. A Glance at Ourselves")

"To compete now with the mighty odds of wealth, social and religious preferences, and political influences of this country, at this advanced stage of its national existence, we never may expect. A new country, and a new beginning, is the only true, rational, politic remedy for our disadvantageous position."

("XXIV. A Glance at Ourselves")

Delany positions himself not as a man of great prestige but as a humble person who has worked hard to obtain what he has in life. He presents this aside in an accessible manner, stating that other young men can achieve similar levels of success in their own lifetimes if they apply themselves. He also addresses the matter of the socioeconomic condition of the race. He cites "consummate poverty" as "one of our great temporal curses." He characterizes contemporary African Americans as the poorest class of people in the civilized world, with one result being that they are unable to adequately assist one another. This was indeed a stark and sobering reality that has had implications well beyond Delany's mid-nineteenth-century context. Considering the odds against African Americans in a wide variety of spheres, as demonstrated by their lagging significantly behind white Americans in terms of social, religious, economic, and political indicators and circumstances, Delany suggests that the best option for many—perhaps even for the entire class of free blacks—would be to start fresh in a new country.

Delany concludes by addressing certain concerns and objections to the project of emigration. Among them he cites blacks' attachment to whites as objects of love and admiration along with reluctance to leave loved ones behind. Dismissing those claims and others, Delany argues that free African Americans have a duty to elevate themselves, as the freedom of those enslaved is tied to those who are free and make the most of their freedom.

Audience

Delany's words were addressed to all African Americans in the United States, although many other Americans read and reacted to them, including politicians and abolitionists. Delany was mainly attempting to persuade everyday African Americans that the benefits of emigration made such a prospect a preferable alternative to the race conundrum in the United States. Within the black community, reactions to his proposals differed widely in accord with the variety of political stances adopted by black intellectuals.

Impact

Delany's text was published in Philadelphia and represented the very first book-length distillation of black nationalism as a political philosophy. The book thus met with a great deal of criticism as well as staunch support. Many figures of national black leadership at the time, including Frederick Douglass, made the decision to ignore the work. Members of the antislavery press condemned Delany's overall strategy and position in the work. Other members of black communities, on the other hand, strongly supported Delany's proposed plan. For example, his urgings were powerful enough to persuade one hundred men and women to meet at his National Emigration Convention of Colored People, held August 24–26, 1854, in Cleveland, Ohio. The Delany biographer Victor Ullman asserts that the Cleveland emigration convention represented the societal birth of modern black nationalism. There, conferees designated Delany as head of a board of commissioners tasked with locating a potential black homeland in Central or South America. Having his marching orders, Delany proceeded to investigate Hawaii and Central America while also sending a representative to Haiti.

During the Cleveland convention, Delany delivered a report titled "The Political Destiny of the Colored Race." In this report, Delany admonished the group on the need to develop an independent black nation, predating the black nationalist pleas later issued by groups such as the Nation of Islam and the Shrine of the Black Madonna. Anticipating Du Bois's notion of the color line by almost a half century, Delany also emphasized that "the great issue" facing the world would involve "the question of black and white." Delany also stated that every individual person would have to make a decision as to which identity or side he or she would assume.

Delany's plans for a mass emigration of blacks to Liberia never materialized as he had hoped. In 1859 he traveled to Liberia and spent nine months in the region. In the Abeokuta region of Liberia he signed an agreement with a number of chiefs that would allow American blacks to settle on unused land in exchange for a promise that they would work for the good of the community. He published the results of his explorations in an 1861 book, *Official Report of the Niger Valley Exploring Party*, providing information about conditions in the region. The agreement, though, was never exercised. After he returned to the United States in 1860, he began to gather funding and prospective settlers for the Abeokuta project. But the plans collapsed in part because of warfare in the region, in part because the plan was opposed by white missionaries, and in part by the beginning of the U.S. Civil War and Delany's decision to remain in the United States and work for emancipation. In the late nineteenth century, Liberia remained an isolated nation. In effect, it was two nations in one—the community of native Africans with an overlay of black American settlers with a government modeled on that of the United States. The two components of the nation were never able to merge, with native Africans looking on the settlers with distrust and the settlers, perhaps reflecting their own exposure to the caste system of the American South, regarding the natives as backward.

Despite the partial failure of his plans, Delany became a critical figure in African American history and, in particular, in the black nationalist movement. His views would influence those of contemporary and later black nationalists such as Henry Highland Garnet, Henry McNeal Turner, Marcus Garvey (founder of the Universal Negro Improvement Association), Elijah Muhammad (the leader of the Nation of Islam), and numerous others. Throughout its history, different strands of black nationalism emerged. For some, the only solution to discrimination was the actual establishment of a separate black nation. While Africa remained central to this line of thinking for some and spawned the Back to Africa movement, for others the notion of mass migration of American blacks to Africa was impractical, so

Africa to them would remain a symbol, not a destination. At the extreme, these black nationalists called for the establishment of a black nation in the Western Hemisphere. More mainstream black nationalists placed less emphasis on geography and more on the structure and goals of the black community. Rejecting anything approaching assimilation, they called on American blacks to ameliorate their own condition by focusing their attention on black institutions, including culture, art, and religion. Further, the call was for blacks to achieve a greater measure of self-determination in the economic arena by pooling resources and supporting black-owned enterprises. Put simply, black nationalists came to call not for a black country but for self-governing black communities and black enterprise.

In recent years, the black nationalist movement has remained alive in various forms. One was the Black Power movement, which gained momentum in the 1960s and 1970s in such organizations as the Black Panther Party. In 1980 the Uhuru Movement was founded in Saint Petersburg, Florida. The movement, whose name is the Swahili word for "freedom," comprises a number of affiliated organizations, including the African People's Socialist Party, the African Socialist International, the Black Is Back Coalition, and similar groups.

See also David Walker's *Appeal to the Coloured Citizens of the World* (1829); Henry Highland Garnet: "An Address to the Slaves of the United States of America" (1843); First Editorial of the *North Star* (1847); Henry McNeal Turner's Speech on His Expulsion from the Georgia Legislature (1868); Booker T. Washington's Atlanta Exposition Address (1895); W. E. B. Du Bois: *The Souls of Black Folk* (1903); Marcus Garvey: "The Principles of the Universal Negro Improvement Association" (1922); Stokely Carmichael's "Black Power" (1966).

Further Reading

■ Articles

Adeleke, Tunde. "Martin R. Delany's Philosophy of Education: A Neglected Aspect of African American Liberation Thought." *Journal of Negro Education* 63, no. 2 (Spring 1994): 221–236.

Ogunleye, Tolagbe. "Dr. Martin Robison Delany, 19th-Century Africana Womanist: Reflections on His Avant-Garde Politics concerning Gender, Colorism, and Nation Building." *Journal of Black Studies* 28, no. 5 (May 1998): 628–649.

Shelby, Tommie. "Two Conceptions of Black Nationalism: Martin Delany on the Meaning of Black Political Solidarity." *Political Theory* 31, no. 5 (October 2003): 664–692.

■ Books

Adeleke, Tunde. *Without Regard to Race: The Other Martin Robison Delany.* Jackson: University Press of Mississippi, 2003.

Franklin, John Hope, and Evelyn Brooks Higginbotham. *From Slavery to Freedom: A History of African Americans.* 9th ed. New York: McGraw-Hill, forthcoming.

Questions for Further Study

1. Given the condition of most African Americans before the Civil War, why do you think so few immigrated to Liberia, Haiti, and other places?

2. On what basis did some people at the time view the American Colonization Society as proslavery? Do you believe they were correct? Explain.

3. In what ways did Delany anticipate the views of Booker T. Washington, as outlined in his Atlanta Exposition Address?

4. Delany wrote that "the redemption of the bondman depends entirely upon the elevation of the freeman; therefore, to elevate the free colored people of America, anywhere upon this continent; forebodes the speedy redemption of the slaves." What did he mean by this? Would you have agreed with this statement?

5. Comment on whether African Americans in general and particularly those still living under slavery in the South would have learned of Delany and his views—as well as the views of other African American writers at the time. What problems would Delany have faced in reaching his intended audience?

Griffith, Cyril E. *The African Dream: Martin R. Delany and the Emergence of Pan-African Thought*. University Park: Pennsylvania State University Press, 1975.

Hine, Darlene Clark, et al. *African Americans: A Concise History*. 2nd ed. Upper Saddle River, N.J.: Pearson Prentice Hall, 2006.

Levine, Robert S., ed. *Martin R. Delany: A Documentary Reader*. Chapel Hill: University of North Carolina Press, 2003.

Logan, Rayford W., and Michael R. Winston, eds. *Dictionary of American Negro Biography*. New York: W. W. Norton, 1982.

Sterling, Dorothy. *The Making of an Afro-American: Martin Robison Delany, 1812–1885*. New York: Da Capo Press, 1996.

Ullman, Victor. *Martin R. Delany: The Beginnings of Black Nationalism*. Boston: Beacon Press, 1971.

■ Web Sites

"To Be More Than Equal: The Many Lives of Martin R. Delany, 1812–1885." Martin Delany Web site. http://www.libraries.wvu.edu/delany/home.htm.

—Zachery Williams

MARTIN DELANY: *THE CONDITION, ELEVATION, EMIGRATION, AND DESTINY OF THE COLORED PEOPLE OF THE UNITED STATES*

V. Means of Elevation

Moral theories have long been resorted to by us, as a means of effecting the redemption of our brethren in bonds, and the elevation of the free colored people in this country. Experience has taught us, that speculations are not enough; that the *practical* application of principles adduced, the thing carried out, is the only true and proper course to pursue.

We have speculated and moralised much about equality—claiming to be as good as our neighbors, and everybody else—all of which, may do very well in ethics—but not in politics. We live in society among men, conducted by men, governed by rules and regulations. However arbitrary, there are certain policies that regulate all well-organized institutions and corporate bodies. We do not intend here to speak of the legal political relations of society, for those are treated on elsewhere. The business and social, or voluntary and mutual policies, are those that now claim our attention. Society regulates itself—being governed by mind, which like water, finds its own level. "Like seeks like," is a principle in the laws of matter, as well as of mind. There is such a thing as inferiority of things, and positions; at least society has made them so; and while we continue to live among men, we must agree to all *just* measures—all those we mean, that do not necessarily infringe on the rights of others. By the regulations of society, there is no equality of persons, where there is not an equality of attainments. By this, we do not wish to be understood as advocating the actual equal attainments of every individual; but we mean to say, that if these attainments be necessary for the elevation of the white man, they are necessary for the elevation of the colored man. That some colored men and women, in a like proportion to the whites, should be qualified in all the attainments possessed by them. It is one of the regulations of society the world over, and we shall have to conform to it, or be discarded as unworthy of the associations of our fellows.

Cast our eyes about us and reflect for a moment, and what do we behold! Every thing that presents to view gives evidence of the skill of the white man. Should we purchase a pound of groceries, a yard of linen, a vessel of crockeryware, a piece of furniture, the very provisions that we eat,—all, all are the products of the white man, purchased by us from the white man, consequently, our earnings and means, are all given to the white man.

Pass along the avenues of any city or town, in which you live—behold the trading shops—the manufactories—see the operations of the various machinery—see the stage-coaches coming in, bringing the mails of intelligence—look at the railroads interlining every section, bearing upon them their mighty trains, flying with the velocity of the swallow, ushering in the hundreds of industrious, enterprising travelers. Cast again your eyes widespread over the ocean—see the vessels in every direction with their white sheets spread to the winds of heaven, freighted with the commerce, merchandise and wealth of many nations. Look as you pass along through the cities, at the great and massive buildings—the beautiful and extensive structures of architecture—behold the ten thousand cupolas, with their spires all reared up towards heaven, intersecting the territory of the clouds—all standing as mighty living monuments, of the industry, enterprise, and intelligence of the white man. And yet, with all these living truths, rebuking us with scorn, we strut about, place our hands akimbo, straighten up ourselves to our greatest height, and talk loudly about being "as good as any body." How do we compare with them? Our fathers are their coachmen, our brothers their cookmen, and ourselves their waiting-men. Our mothers their nurse-women, our sisters their scrubwomen, our daughters their maid-women, and our wives their washer-women. Until colored men, attain to a position above permitting their mothers, sisters, wives, and daughters, to do the drudgery and "menial" offices of other men's wives and daughters; it is useless, it is nonsense, it is pitiable mockery, to talk about equality and elevation in society. The world is looking upon us, with feelings of commiseration, sorrow, and contempt. We scarcely deserve sympathy, if we peremptorily refuse advice, bearing upon our elevation....

White men are producers—we are consumers. They build houses, and we rent them. They raise produce, and we consume it. They manufacture clothes and wares, and we garnish ourselves with them. They build coaches, vessels, cars, hotels, saloons, and other vehicles and places of accommodation, and we deliberately wait until they have got them in readiness, then walk in, and contend with as much assurance for a "right," as though the whole thing was bought by, paid for, and belonged to us. By their literary attainments, they are the contributors to, authors and teachers of, literature, science, religion, law, medicine, and all other useful attainments that the world now makes use of. We have no reference to ancient times—we speak of modern things.

These are the means by which God intended man to succeed; and this discloses the secret of the white man's success with all of his wickedness, over the head of the colored man, with all of his religion. We have been pointed and plain, on this part of the subject, because we desire our readers to see persons and things in their true position. Until we are determined to change the condition of things, and raise ourselves above the position in which we are now prostrated, we must hang our heads in sorrow, and hide our faces in shame. It is enough to know that these things are so; the causes we care little about. Those we have been examining, complaining about, and moralising over, all our life time. This we are weary of. What we desire to learn now is, how to effect a *remedy*; this we have endeavored to point out. Our elevation must be the result of *self-efforts*, and work of our *own hands*. No other human power can accomplish it. If we but determine it shall be so, it will be so. Let each one make the case his own, and endeavor to rival his neighbor, in honorable competition.

These are the proper and only means of elevating ourselves and attaining equality in this country or any other, and it is useless, utterly futile, to think about going any where, except we are determined to use these as the necessary means of developing our manhood. The means are at hand, within our reach. Are we willing to try them? Are we willing to raise ourselves superior to the condition of slaves, or continue the meanest underlings, subject to the beck and call of every creature bearing a pale complexion? If we are, we had as well remained in the South, as to have come to the North in search of more freedom. What was the object of our parents in leaving the South, if it were not for the purpose of attaining equality in common with others of their fellow citizens, by giving their children access to all the advantages enjoyed by others? Surely this was their object. They heard of liberty and equality here, and they hastened on to enjoy it, and no people are more astonished and disappointed than they, who for the first time, on beholding the position we occupy here in the free North—what is called, and what they expect to find, the free States. They at once tell us, that they have as much liberty in the South as we have in the North—that there as free people, they are protected in their rights—that we have nothing more—that in other respects they have the same opportunity, indeed the preferred opportunity, of being their maids, servants, cooks, waiters, and menials in general, there, as we have here—that had they known for a moment, before leaving, that such was to be the only position they occupied here, they would have remained where they were, and never left. Indeed, such is the disappointment in many cases, that they immediately return back again, completely insulted at the idea, of having us here at the north, assume ourselves to be their superiors. Indeed, if our superior advantages of the free States, do not induce and stimulate us to the higher attainments in life, what in the name of degraded humanity will do it?

VI. The United States Our Country

Our common country is the United States. Here were we born, here raised and educated; here are the scenes of childhood; the pleasant associations of our school going days; the loved enjoyments of our domestic and fireside relations, and the sacred graves of our departed fathers and mothers, and from here will we not be driven by any policy that may be schemed against us.

We are Americans, having a birthright citizenship—natural claims upon the country—claims common to all others of our fellow citizens—natural rights, which may, by virtue of unjust laws, be obstructed, but never can be annulled. Upon these do we place ourselves, as immovably fixed as the decrees of the living God. But according to the economy that regulates the policy of nations, upon which rests the basis of justifiable claims to all freemen's rights, it may be necessary to take another view of, and enquire into the political claims of colored men....

XXIII. Things as They Are

"And if thou boast Truth to utter, Speak, and leave the rest to God."

In presenting this work, we have but a single object in view, and that is, to inform the minds of the colored people at large, upon many things pertaining to their elevation, that but few among us are acquainted with. Unfortunately for us, as a body, we have been taught to believe, that we must have some person to think for us, instead of thinking for ourselves. So accustomed are we to submission and this kind of training, that it is with difficulty, even among the most intelligent of the colored people, an audience may be elicited for any purpose whatever, if the expounder is to be a colored person; and the introduction of any subject is treated with indifference, if not contempt, when the originator is a colored person. Indeed, the most ordinary white person, is almost revered, while the most qualified colored person is totally neglected. Nothing from them is appreciated.

We have been standing comparatively still for years, following in the footsteps of our friends, believing that what they promise us can be accomplished, just because they say so, although our own knowledge should long since, have satisfied us to the contrary. Because even were it possible, with the present hate and jealousy that the whites have towards us in this country, for us to gain equality of rights with them; we never could have an equality of the exercise and enjoyment of those rights—because, the great odds of numbers are against us. We might indeed, as some at present, have the right of the elective franchise—nay, it is not the elective franchise, because the *elective franchise* makes the enfranchised, *eligible* to any position attainable; but we may exercise the right of *voting* only, which to us, is but poor satisfaction; and we by no means care to cherish the privilege of voting somebody into office, to help to make laws to degrade us.

In religion—because they are both *translators* and *commentators*, we must believe nothing, however absurd, but what our oppressors tell us. In Politics, nothing but such as they promulge; in Anti-Slavery, nothing but what our white brethren and friends say we must; in the mode and manner of our elevation, we must do nothing, but that which may be laid down to be done by our white brethren from some quarter or other; and now, even in the subject of emigration, there are some colored people to be found, so lost to their own interest and self-respect, as to be gulled by slave owners and colonizationists, who are led to believe there is no other place in which they can become elevated, but Liberia, a government of American slaveholders, as we have shown—simply, because white men have told them so.

Upon the possibility, means, mode and manner, of our Elevation in the United States—Our Original Rights and Claims as Citizens—Our Determination not to be Driven from our Native Country—the Difficulties in the Way of our Elevation—Our Position in Relation to our Anti-Slavery Brethren—the Wicked Design and Injurious Tendency of the American Colonization Society—Objections to Liberia—Objections to Canada—Preferences to South America, &c., &c., all of which we have treated without reserve; expressing our mind freely, and with candor, as we are determined that as far as we can at present do so, the minds of our readers shall be enlightened. The custom of concealing information upon vital and important subjects, in which the interest of the people is involved, we do not agree with, nor favor in the least; we have therefore, laid this cursory treatise before our readers, with the hope that it may prove instrumental in directing the attention of our people in the right way, that leads to their Elevation. Go or stay—of course each is free to do as he pleases—one thing is certain; our Elevation is the work of our own hands. And Mexico, Central America, the West Indies, and South America, all present now, opportunities for the individual enterprise of our young men, who prefer to remain in the United States, in preference to going where they can enjoy real freedom, and equality of rights. Freedom of Religion, as well as of politics, being tolerated in all of these places.

Let our young men and women, prepare themselves for usefulness and business; that the men may enter into merchandise, trading, and other things of importance; the young women may become teachers of various kinds, and otherwise fill places of usefulness. Parents must turn their attention more to the education of their children. We mean, to educate them for useful practical business purposes. Educate them for the Store and the Counting House—to do every-day practical business. Consult the children's propensities, and direct their education according to their inclinations. It may be, that there is too great a desire on the part of parents to give their children a professional education, before the body of the people are ready for it. A people must be a business people, and have more to depend upon than mere help in people's houses and Hotels, before they are either able to support, or capable of properly appreciating the services of professional men among them. This has been one of our great mistakes—we have gone in advance of ourselves. We have commenced at the superstructure of the building, instead of the foundation—at the top instead of the bottom. We should first be mechanics and common tradesmen, and professions as a matter of course would grow out of the wealth made thereby. Young men and women, must now prepare for usefulness—the day of our Elevation is at hand—all the world now gazes at us—and

Central and South America, and the West Indies, bid us come and be men and women, protected, secure, beloved and Free.

The branches of Education most desirable for the preparation of youth, for practical useful every-day life, are Arithmetic and good Penmanship, in order to be Accountants; and a good rudimental knowledge of Geography—which has ever been neglected, and underestimated—and of Political Economy; which without the knowledge of the first, no people can ever become adventurous—nor of the second, never will be an enterprising people. Geography, teaches a knowledge of the world, and Political Economy, a knowledge of the wealth of nations; or how to make money. These are not abstruse sciences, or learning not easily acquired or understood; but simply, common School Primer learning, that every body may get. And, although it is the very Key to prosperity and success in common life, but few know anything about it. Unfortunately for our people, so soon as their children learn to read a Chapter in the New Testament, and scribble a miserable hand, they are pronounced to have "Learning enough"; and taken away from School, no use to themselves, nor community. This is apparent in our Public Meetings, and Official Church Meetings; of the great number of men present, there are but few capable of filling a Secretaryship. Some of the large cities may be an exception to this. Of the multitudes of Merchants, and Business men throughout this country, Europe, and the world, few are qualified, beyond the branches here laid down by us as necessary for business. What did John Jacob Astor, Stephen Girard, or do the millionaires and the greater part of the merchant princes, and mariners, know about Latin and Greek, and the Classics? Precious few of them know any thing. In proof of this, in 1841, during the Administration of President Tyler, when the mutiny was detected on board of the American Man of War Brig Somers. the names of the Mutineers, were recorded by young S—a Midshipman in Greek. Captain Alexander Slidell McKenzie, Commanding, was unable to read them; and in his despatches to the Government, in justification of his policy in executing the criminals, said that he "discovered some curious characters which he was unable to read," &c.; showing thereby, that that high functionary, did not understand even the Greek Alphabet, which was only necessary, to have been able to read proper names written in Greek.

What we most need then, is a good business practical Education; because, the Classical and Professional education of so many of our young men, before their parents are able to support them, and community ready to patronize them, only serves to lull their energy, and cripple the otherwise, praiseworthy efforts they would make in life. A Classical education, is only suited to the wealthy, or those who have a prospect of gaining a livelihood by it. The writer does not wish to be understood, as underrating a Classical and Professional education; this is not his intention; he fully appreciates them, having had some such advantages himself; but he desires to give a proper guide, and put a check to the extravagant idea that is fast obtaining, among our people especially, that a Classical, or as it is named, a "finished education," is necessary to prepare one for usefulness in life. Let us have an education, that shall practically develop our thinking faculties and manhood; and then, and not until then, shall we be able to vie with our oppressors, go where we may. We as heretofore, have been on the extreme; either no qualification at all, or a Collegiate education. We jumped too far; taking a leap from the deepest abyss to the highest summit; rising from the ridiculous to the sublime; without medium or intermission.

Let our young women have an education; let their minds be well informed; well stored with useful information and practical proficiency, rather than the light superficial acquirements, popularly and fashionably called accomplishments. We desire accomplishments, but they must be useful.

Our females must be qualified, because they are to be the mothers of our children. As mothers are the first nurses and instructors of children; from them children consequently, get their first impressions, which being always the most lasting, should be the most correct. Raise the mothers above the level of degradation, and the offspring is elevated with them. In a word, instead of our young men, transcribing in their blank books, recipes for *Cooking*; we desire to see them making the transfer of *Invoices of Merchandise*. Come to our aid then; the *morning* of our *Redemption* from degradation, adorns the horizon.

In our selection of individuals, it will be observed, that we have confined ourself entirely to those who occupy or have occupied positions among the whites, consequently having a more general bearing as useful contributors to society at large. While we do not pretend to give all such worthy cases, we gave such as we possessed information of, and desire it to be understood, that a large number of our most intelligent and worthy men and women, have not been named, because from their more private position in community, it was foreign to the object and design of this work. If we have said aught to offend, "take the will for the deed," and be assured, that it was given with the purest of motives, and best intention, from a true-hearted man and brother; deeply lamenting the sad fate of his race in this country, and sincerely desiring the elevation of man, and submitted to the serious consideration of all, who favor the promotion of the cause of God and humanity.

XXIV. A Glance at Ourselves—Conclusion

With broken hopes—sad devastation; a race *resigned* to degradation! …

If we did not love our race superior to others, we would not concern ourself about their degradation; for the greatest desire of our heart is, to see them stand on a level with the most elevated of mankind. No people are ever elevated above the condition of their *females;* hence, the condition of the mother determines the condition of the child. To know the position of a people, it is only necessary to know the *condition* of their females; and despite themselves, they cannot rise above their level. Then what is our condition? Our *best ladies* being washerwomen, chambermaids, children's traveling nurses, and common house servants, and menials, we are all a degraded, miserable people, inferior to any other people as a whole, on the face of the globe.

These great truths, however unpleasant, must be brought before the minds of our people in its true and proper light, as we have been too delicate about them, and too long concealed them for fear of giving offence. It would have been infinitely better for our race, if these facts had been presented before us half a century ago—we would have been now proportionably benefitted by it.

As an evidence of the degradation to which we have been reduced, we dare premise, that this chapter will give offence to many, very many, and why? Because they may say, "He dared to say that the occupation of a *servant* is a degradation." It is not necessarily degrading; it would not be, to one or a few people of a land; but a *whole race of servants* are a degradation to that people.

Efforts made by men of qualifications for the toiling and degraded millions among the whites, neither gives offence to that class, nor is it taken unkindly by them; but received with manifestations of gratitude; to know that they are thought to be, equally worthy of, and entitled to stand on a level with the elevated classes; and they have only got to be informed of the

way to raise themselves, to make the effort and do so as far as they can. But how different with us. Speak of our position in society, and it at once gives insult. Though we are servants; among ourselves we claim to be *ladies* and *gentlemen*, equal in standing, and as the popular expression goes, "Just as good as any body"— and so believing, we make no efforts to raise above the common level of menials; because the *best* being in that capacity, all are content with the position. We cannot at the same time, be domestic and lady; servant and gentleman. We must be the one or the other. Sad, sad indeed, is the thought, that hangs drooping in our mind, when contemplating the picture drawn before us. Young men and women, "we write these things unto you, because ye are strong," because the writer, a few years ago, gave unpardonable offence to many of the young people of Philadelphia and other places, because he dared tell them, that he thought too much of them, to be content with seeing them the servants of other people. Surely, she that could be the mistress, would not be the maid; neither would he that could be the master, be content with being the servant; then why be offended, when we point out to you, the way that leads from the menial to the mistress or the master. All this we seem to reject with fixed determination, repelling with anger, every effort on the part of our intelligent men and women to elevate us, with true Israelitish degradation, in reply to any suggestion or proposition that may be offered, "Who made thee a ruler and judge?"

The writer is no "Public Man," in the sense in which this is understood among our people, but simply an humble individual, endeavoring to seek a livelihood by a profession obtained entirely by his own efforts, without relatives and friends able to assist him; except such friends as he gained by the merit of his course and conduct, which he here gratefully acknowledges; and whatever he has accomplished, other young men may, by making corresponding efforts, also accomplish.

In our own country, the United States, there are *three million five hundred thousand slaves;* and we, the nominally free colored people, are *six hundred thousand* in number; estimating one-sixth to be men, we have *one hundred thousand* able bodied freemen, which will make a powerful auxiliary in any country to which we may become adopted—an ally not to be despised by any power on earth. We love our country, dearly love her, but she doesn't love us—she despises us, and bids us begone, driving us from her embraces; but we shall not go where she desires us; but when we do go, whatever love we have for her, we shall love the country none the less that receives us as her adopted children.

For the want of business habits and training, our energies have become paralyzed; our young men never think of business, any more than if they were so many bondmen, without the right to pursue any calling they may think most advisable. With our people in this country, dress and good appearances have been made the only test of gentleman and ladyship, and that vocation which offers the best opportunity to dress and appear well, has generally been preferred, however menial and degrading, by our young people, without even, in the majority of cases, an effort to do better; indeed, in many instances, refusing situations equally lucrative, and superior in position; but which would not allow as much display of dress and personal appearance. This, if we ever expect to rise, must be discarded from among us, and a high and respectable position assumed.

One of our great temporal curses is our consummate poverty. We are the poorest people, as a class, in the world of civilized mankind—abjectly, miserably poor, no one scarcely being able to assist the other. To this, of course, there are noble exceptions; but that which is common to, and the very process by which white men exist, and succeed in life, is unknown to colored men in general. In any and every considerable community may be found, some one of our white fellow-citizens, who is worth more than all the colored people in that community put together. We consequently have little or no efficiency. We must have means to be practically efficient in all the undertakings of life; and to obtain them, it is necessary that we should be engaged in lucrative pursuits, trades, and general business transactions. In order to be thus engaged, it is necessary that we should occupy positions that afford the facilities for such pursuits. To compete now with the mighty odds of wealth, social and religious preferences, and political influences of this country, at this advanced stage of its national existence, we never may expect. A new country, and new beginning, is the only true, rational, politic remedy for our disadvantageous position; and that country we have already pointed out, with triple golden advantages, all things considered, to that of any country to which it has been the province of man to embark.

Every other than we, have at various periods of necessity, been a migratory people; and all when oppressed, shown a greater abhorrence of oppression, if not a greater love of liberty, than we. We cling to our oppressors as the objects of our love. It is true that our enslaved brethren are here, and we have been

led to believe that it is necessary for us to remain, on that account. Is it true, that all should remain in degradation, because a part are degraded? We believe no such thing. We believe it to be the duty of the Free, to elevate themselves in the most speedy and effective manner possible; as the redemption of the bondman depends entirely upon the elevation of the freeman; therefore, to elevate the free colored people of America, anywhere upon this continent; forebodes the speedy redemption of the slaves. We shall hope to hear no more of so fallacious a doctrine—the necessity of the free remaining in degradation, for the sake of the oppressed. Let us apply, first, the lever to ourselves; and the force that elevates us to the position of manhoods considerations and honors, will cleft the manacle of every slave in the land.

When such great worth and talents—for want of a better sphere—of men like Rev. Jonathan Robinson, Robert Douglass, Frederick A. Hinton, and a hundred others that might be named, were permitted to expire in a barber-shop; and such living men as may be found in Boston, New York, Philadelphia, Baltimore, Richmond, Washington City, Charleston (S.C.), New Orleans, Cincinnati, Louisville, St, Louis, Pittsburg, Buffalo, Rochester, Albany, Utica, Cleveland, Detroit, Milwaukee, Chicago, Columbus, Zanesville, Wheeling, and a hundred other places, confining themselves to barber-shops and waiterships in Hotels; certainly the necessity of such a course as we have pointed out, must be cordially acknowledged; appreciated by every brother and sister of oppression; and not rejected as heretofore, as though they preferred inferiority to equality. These minds must become "unfettered," and have "space to rise." This cannot be in their present positions. A continuance in any position, becomes what is termed "Second Nature"; it begets an *adaptation*, and *reconciliation* of *mind* to such condition. It changes the whole physiological condition of the system, and adapts man and woman to a higher or lower sphere in the pursuits of life. The offsprings of slaves and peasantry, have the general characteristics of their parents; and nothing but a different course of training and education, will change the character.

The slave may become a lover of his master, and learn to forgive him for continual deeds of maltreatment and abuse; just as the Spaniel would couch and fondle at the feet that kick him; because he has been taught to reverence them, and consequently, becomes adapted in body and mind to his condition. Even the shrubbery-loving Canary, and lofty-soaring Eagle, may be tamed to the cage, and learn to love it from habit of confinement. It has been so with us in our position among our oppressors; we have been so prone to such positions, that we have learned to love them. When reflecting upon this all important, and to us, all absorbing subject; we feel in the agony and anxiety of the moment, as though we could cry out in the langauge of a Prophet of old: "Oh that my head were waters, and mine eyes a fountain of tears, that I might weep day and night for the" degradation "of my people! Oh that I had in the wilderness a lodging place of wayfaring men; that I might leave my people, and go from them!"

The Irishman and German in the United States, are very different persons to what they were when in Ireland and Germany, the countries of their nativity. There their spirits were depressed and downcast; but the instant they set their foot upon unrestricted soil; free to act and untrammelled to move; their physical condition undergoes a change, which in time becomes physiological, which is transmitted to the offspring, who when born under such circumstances, is a decidedly different being to

what it would have been, had it been born under different circumstances.

A child born under oppression, has all the elements of servility in its constitution; who when bom under favorable circumstances, has to the contrary, all the elements of freedom and independence of feeling. Our children then, may not be expected, to maintain that position and manly bearing; born under the unfavorable circumstances with which we are surrounded in this country; that we so much desire. To use the language of the talented Mr. Whipper, "they cannot be raised in this country, without being stoop shouldered." Heaven's pathway stands unobstructed, which will lead us into a Paradise of bliss. Let us go on and possess the land, and the God of Israel will be our God.

The lessons of every school book, the pages of every history, and columns of every newspaper, are so replete with stimuli to nerve us on to manly aspirations, that those of our young people, who will now refuse to enter upon this great theatre of Polynesian adventure, and take their position on the stage of

Glossary

akimbo	hands at the waist, with elbows out to the side
And if thou boast Truth to utter ...	quotation from William D. Gallagher's poem "Truth and Freedom"
elective franchise	the right to vote
Frederick A. Hinton	the African American proprietor of the Gentleman's Dressing Room in Philadelphia
Israelitish	referring to the people of ancient Israel; Hebrew; Jewish
John Jacob Astor	the nation's first multimillionaire businessman
Jonathan Robinson	a black abolitionist about whom little is known
Mr. Whipper	William Whipper of Pennsylvania, one of the wealthiest African Americans at the time and the leader of the American Moral Reform Society
mutiny	a reference to the "*Somers*' affair," an alleged mutiny aboard the naval ship in 1842, the only shipboard mutiny in American naval history that led to executions of the perpetrators
President Tyler	John Tyler, the tenth U.S. president
Prophet of old	the prophet Jeremiah in the Christian Old Testament; the quotation is from the book of Jeremiah, chapter 9, verse 1, which concludes with the words "slain of the daughter of my people"
Robert Douglass	a well-to-do African American barber in Philadelphia
Stephen Girard	a French-born American banker and among the wealthiest Americans at the time
West Indies	the island nations of the Caribbean Sea

Central and South America, where a brilliant engagement, of certain and most triumphant success, in the drama of human equality awaits them; then, with the blood of *slaves*, write upon the lintel of every door in sterling Capitals, to be gazed and hissed at by every passer by—

Doomed by the Creator
To servility and degradation;
The SERVANT of the *white man*,
And despised of every nation!